Government and Politics
in Latin America

Edited by

HAROLD EUGENE DAVIS

PROFESSOR OF LATIN AMERICAN
HISTORY AND GOVERNMENT
THE AMERICAN UNIVERSITY

Contributors

Robert J. Alexander   Harold E. Davis
George I. Blanksten   Beryl Frank
Frank R. Brandenburg   Laurin L. Henry
Asher N. Christensen   Carlos Mouchet
Helen L. Clagett   Virgil Salera
Robert E. Scott

THE RONALD PRESS COMPANY ⋅ NEW YORK

Library of Congress Catalog Card Number: 58–5649

PRINTED IN THE UNITED STATES OF AMERICA

Preface

This book has been written as a college text for courses in Latin American government and politics. The authors have tried to present government and politics as part of the living, growing, dynamic reality of Latin American society. Seeing the most essential expression of contemporary Latin American politics in its sense of urgent need to accomplish certain social objectives rapidly, they have hoped to portray this dynamic aspect of the area's political life and to convey to English-speaking students something of its sense of urgency. Not overlooking the individual characteristics of each of the twenty nations whose political experience is being examined, the authors have tried to point out the common characteristics of political processes and institutions, common problems, and common trends in political life. While their purpose has been to analyze politics and institutions objectively, they have also tried to take particular account of how the intelligent Latin American views his politics and to portray political behavior within its cultural context. It is their hope that the student will also adopt this point of view.

The seven chapters of Part I, dealing with the dynamics of politics, present the rapidly changing, frequently violent political and social life of a society in which emergent political forces are taking shape in movements of reform and new power structures. These changes amount to a social revolution in many nations. In Part II, the institutions of government are analyzed in relation to power structures and in terms of their functions, against the background of the more than a century and a quarter of Latin American experience—of successes and failures in making constitutional government and the rule of law, rather than of men, the political way of life. Part III, Expansion of Government, embraces the discussion of the social and economic problems which challenge the attention of government today, the policies adopted to deal with them, and the governmental and administrative machinery employed. The book concludes with an analysis and evaluation of democratic trends and prospects as revealed in the preceding chapters.

The present work originated in informal discussions among several Latin American scholars during the course of a postdoctoral seminar at the American University. This seminar was exploratory—concerned with finding some better way to introduce the student to a comparative survey of the political institutions of Latin America, their structure, their operation, their strength and weaknesses. Later the project engaged the interest of the group of political scientists, economists, and historians who have contributed to this book. Despite their divergent backgrounds and specializations, the authors are in agreement on most major points covered; where they disagree, the editor has sought to clarify their differing views and indicate to the student what the issues are, allowing him to form his own conclusions.

A special debt is gratefully acknowledged to the late Dr. Miron Burgin, one of the original participants in the plans for this book, who was unable because of failing health to contribute the chapters planned, but nevertheless gave invaluable counsel.

HAROLD E. DAVIS

Chevy Chase, Maryland
February, 1958

Contents

PART III

EXPANSION OF GOVERNMENT

I

THE DYNAMICS OF POLITICS AND POWER

Chapter 1

The Political Experience
of Latin America

The Problem of Democratic Government

The basic political question of the age may well be this: Can the modern behemoth which we call the state effectively meet the needs of social and economic development and yet be kept responsible to the general popular will? It is generally agreed that modern society requires larger and more complicated social, economic, and political institutions in order to conduct its ever more complex activities. Nor is this need now limited to the Western world where it originated. Today, Asia and Africa, with half the population of the world, are actively seeking economic and social progress through self-government. The way they meet this need will have far-reaching implications for the rest of the world as well, and their answer must be given within the decades just ahead. The scope and nature of this problem of retaining democratic government in the bureaucratic welfare state will be better understood through studies such as the one undertaken in this book. For the richly varied experience in democratic government of the twenty republics of Latin America,[1] extending over nearly a century and a half, is one of the largest bodies of such experience in modern times. Analysis of this experience will not only throw light upon the problems of the region, but also aid in understand-

[1] The term *Latin America* emphasizes the common background of the twenty nations south of the Rio Grande. The term *Hispanic America* or *Ibero-America* embraces the areas of Spanish or Portuguese origin, but not Haiti, although some scholars have used it to refer to the whole region. *Spanish America* and *Portuguese* or *Luso-America* mean, respectively, the nations of Spanish origin and Brazil.

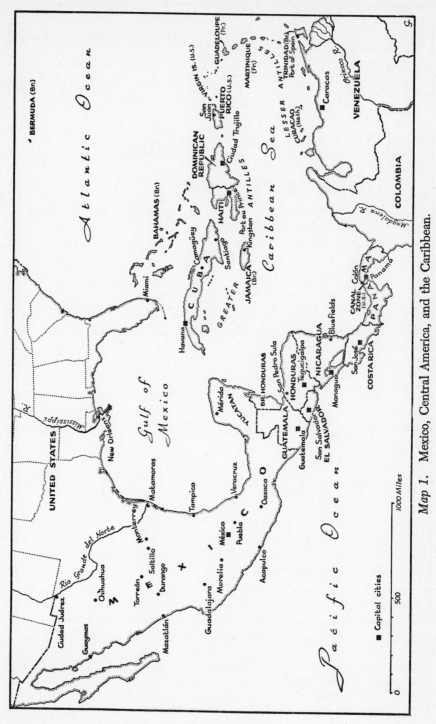

Map 1. Mexico, Central America, and the Caribbean.

Map 2. South America. This map and Map 1, although drawn to different scales, show how much the nations vary in size. The four largest are Brazil, Argentina, Mexico, and Venezuela, but Colombia, Peru, Bolivia, and Chile also have large areas.

5

ing contemporary political problems and trends in the world at large.

Understanding Political Life in Another Culture

THE CULTURAL APPROACH. First, a word of caution is called for. The student of comparative government must rid himself of the preconceptions, prejudices, and values of his own cultural setting, learning to examine the political institutions and practices of another people from the point of view of its own cultural background. He must see political structure in its cultural setting and view the political process as living, changing reality within the larger cultural processes. He must also come to understand how another people explains its own political life, problems, and tendencies, seeking this explanation in their social and political thought and in the meaning they discover in their history, its significance and direction. Value factors which attach to various aspects of culture are fundamentally important for this kind of study and differ, of course, from culture to culture. Sometimes they assume rational and systematic form in systems of ethics, aesthetics, metaphysics, and theology. But more often the value factors most characteristic of a culture are unrationalized. Sometimes they are irrational in their very essence and can be perceived only through the most penetrating study of the culture.

Moreover, while men act and think differently in different cultures, their behavior has many common denominators. Cultural differences must be related to this constant human equation in order to achieve a balanced understanding. A recent study of the political attitudes of university students of various national backgrounds revealed significant differences in the attitudes toward ways and values of living held by the various cultural groups. But the range of difference among individuals of any group, even at the relatively rational and sophisticated level of university students, was much greater than the range of difference between the various nationality-culture groups on any single item.[2] Similarly, in many respects Latin American government and culture are the same as government and culture everywhere, simply because human nature is much the same everywhere.

THE DYNAMIC FACTOR. To understand government in a rapidly changing society, such as that of Latin America in the twentieth century, it is also essential to understand its dynamic character. This dynamism is often expressed in political violence, but this

[2] Report of Charles Morris to Washington Seminar, January 15–16, 1953.

violence may have different meanings. Violence in some aspect of its life is likely to characterize any society undergoing basic changes in its culture pattern. It sometimes happens, moreover, that the part of the culture with which violence is most closely associated is not that which is changing most rapidly. That is to say, political violence is not necessarily an indication of rapid political change, but may, rather, reflect the dynamism of change in other aspects of culture. A comparative study of two Indian communities in Mexico, for example, shows an abnormally high incidence of homicide in that town where economic conditions are changing most rapidly, where the pattern of alcoholism is changing, and the practice of witchcraft declining in significance.[3] But violence may also indicate resistance to change.

The student who looks for these dynamic factors in their cultural setting is less likely to make the mistake which many students of Latin American politics have made in the past, that of assuming that the violence of the political life is "pathological" in any but the most general sense of a society disturbed.[4] Nor will he be misled by the other fallacy, that political violence is simply a product of cultural determinism, an idea which results from overlooking the effects of voluntarism in social action and social change. The history of Latin American politics furnishes too many examples of the heroic defense of lost causes as well as of the successful meeting of force with force for us to accept so simple a theory. In fact, one possible theory of this political violence is that today politics has become the sector of culture in which acts of free choice are permitted to play a larger part than in other cultural sectors.

Assessment of Experience

Most of the Latin American republics have been independent since 1825, but our knowledge of their experience in self-government is meager and superficial. The United States has been closely connected with their history, their trials, and their successes throughout these years, so that we should have an intimate knowledge of their political life. Indeed, scores of books describing their revolutions have been written in English. Too often, however, they have been amusing rather than informative. Nor have Latin American writers helped us greatly, for their political literature has usually been either polemical or highly legalistic. Latin Americans

[3] Carmen Viqueira and Ángel Palerm, "Alcoholismo, brujería, y homicidio en dos comunidades rurales de México," *América Indígena* (Mexico), XIV (Jan. 1954), 7–36.
[4] See "Pathology of Democracy in Latin America," *American Political Science Review*, XLIV (March 1950), 100–149.

actually understand their political life much better than this legalistic and polemical writing would seem to indicate, for there is no lack of leaders who are politicians to their very finger tips. But none of them has yet formulated the kind of synthesis or comprehensive theory of their political phenomena which makes it possible to present a comprehensive and balanced evaluation and analysis.

APPRAISALS OF FOREIGN OBSERVERS. Two foreign appraisals have special importance for the student. In the early years of this century the British statesman Lord Bryce set down the reflections derived from his years of observation as a diplomat.[5] For all its brevity, and despite the limitations implicit in the author's outlook and that of his times, Bryce's appraisal remains one of the best balanced discussions of Latin American political experience. His work has certain shortcomings, particularly those of his own intellectual background, Victorian liberalism. This background kept him from making his analysis in terms of Latin American cultural elements and Latin American political psychology as we understand them today. The second of these appraisals appears in a symposium presented to the American Political Science Association in 1949. The papers of this symposium, prepared by a group of competent students, are fundamental for any serious study of this subject.[6] The reader should be cautious, however, in adopting their too easy conclusion that Latin American democracy is in a pathological state. Violence in political life, as we have seen, does not necessarily reflect a diseased society. It is somewhat more likely, in this case, that it reflects a dynamic changing culture.[7]

ALBERDI'S THEORY. One of the most discerning observations of the Argentine statesman Juan B. Alberdi is that the violence of the nineteenth-century political life of the Spanish American republics reflected the difficulty of transforming an absolute monarchy into a republic.[8] The tensions and changes in the cultural context within which this transformation has taken place, and the difficulties arising out of Latin America's lack of previous experience

[5] James Bryce, *South America* (rev. ed.; New York: The Macmillan Co., 1916).

[6] "Pathology of Democracy in Latin America," *op. cit.*

[7] For a clear Latin American challenge to the concept of Latin American democracy as pathological, see the work of Augusto Mijares of Venezuela, *La interpretación pesimista de la sociología hispano-americana* (2d ed.; Madrid: Afrodisio Aguado, 1952). For an unorthodox but challenging discussion of violence in Latin American political life, with much of which the author of this chapter finds it necessary to disagree, see William S. Stokes, "Violence as a Power Factor in Latin American Politics," *Western Political Quarterly* (September 1952), 445–468.

[8] Juan B. Alberdi, *Bases y puntos de partido para la organización política de la república argentina* (5th ed.; Buenos Aires: L. J. Rosso, 1933).

with representative legislative bodies and elected executives, have often been pointed out. If the former English colonies and Brazil seem to have been more fortunate in this evolution, it was perhaps because they experienced a more gradual evolution under constitutional monarchy. Lord Macaulay observed of the continental revolutions of the eighteenth and nineteenth centuries that they took place in countries in which the limited monarchy of the Middle Ages had long been effaced. Hence, he wrote, it was not surprising that the people turned with disgust from national precedents, seeking principles of government in theorists, and "that confusion should speedily have engendered despotism sterner than that from which it sprung." Had the English been in the same situation in 1689, he added, "a sharp discipline of half a century would hardly have sufficed to educate them into a capacity of enjoying true freedom."[9] If to this lack of an evolutionary development in Spanish America one adds the weakness and frustration resulting from the fractioning of the Spanish empire in America and from the complexity of its ethnic and social problems, the sometimes tragic experiences in its adventures in democratic government become easier to understand.

THE BALANCE SHEET. Indeed, to the casual observer the principles and ideals of political democracy seem to have been honored more in the breach than in the observance. In point of fact, much of Latin American democracy has often consisted of little more than verbalisms, legalism, or "constitutionalism." But the student might easily be deceived by this apparent tendency to substitute verbalisms for democratic reality and to cover arbitrary actions with the appearance of constitutional forms. For the consistency with which political leaders and public opinion have adhered to the principles expressed in these "verbalisms" is in itself a political fact not to be overlooked, showing, as a discerning Venezuelan has pointed out,[10] an "indestructible social aspiration." A realistic balance sheet of democratic government in the area must go further than noting the failures, numerous as they have been. It must weigh notable successes against notable failures with proper attention to the differences in various countries and in certain epochs.

Often the failures have produced a psychology of frustration and defeatism, and many a Spanish American has studied this agonizing experience, with pessimism or with hope, according to his temperament, his social philosophy, or the spirit and conditions of the time, and produced candid works of self-appraisal. Spanish

[9] *History of England* (New York: Harper & Brothers, 1879), II, 603–604.
[10] Augusto Mijares, *op. cit.*, p. 16.

America has produced the most notable books of this character, probably because she has had the most trying experiences. Domingo F. Sarmiento's *Facundo* of the past century set the style which many others have followed. Portuguese Brazil, having been much more stable politically, has not experienced this frustration to the same degree. Why Haiti, whose political experience equals or exceeds that of Spanish America in agony, has not given literary expression to her political tragedies is perhaps sufficiently explained by the scantiness of her literary development, at least until recent years.

Political Heritage

COLONIAL GOVERNMENT. Any adequate view of Latin American political experience must take into account the colonial experience. According to a persistent "black legend," all the traditions of Spanish and Portuguese political life ran counter to constitutional government. Modern historical scholarship has shown, however, that the Hispanic peoples in the new world have been somewhat unjustly condemned for three centuries. The much maligned *cabildo* of colonial days was in many respects a strong institution of government, the influence of which may be seen in the present municipal councils or their equivalents throughout Latin America.

Other inherited political institutions have also been adapted to new needs. It is surprising, in fact, to find the extent to which constitutional government, where most successful in Latin America, has built upon institutions which may be found in the Spanish Laws of the Indies. To be sure, neither Spain nor Portugal developed institutions of representative government in America, except in the municipalities, and this gap in the Latin American tradition has proved to be a source of real weakness. But both Spain and Portugal contributed a well-developed tradition of government which had virtues to balance its shortcomings. It was one of the most successful extensions of old world government to the new. It is less surprising that the monarchism of this colonial political heritage should have been as persistent as it proved to be in the nineteenth century when it is noted how persistent other aspects of Spanish culture have been in the new world. The Spanish constitutions of 1812 and 1820 (and the Portuguese equivalents) were also part of the heritage, and early nineteenth-century Liberal party leadership in Latin America drew heavily upon Iberian political elements associated with the search for constitutional government, thus projecting peninsular constitutional issues into the New World.

THE LEGAL TRADITION. The Spanish legal tradition was a closely integrated part of the colonial heritage. No other European colonizing power developed a body of colonial legislation comparable to the great Spanish Laws of the Indies. Most modern legal codes in Spanish America owe it a great debt, as will be seen in a later chapter, and contemporary court systems have developed out of the same tradition. The discerning student will see in traditional elements in this legal system something basic which distinguishes Latin American political institutions, political behavior, and political thought from those elsewhere. He will at the same time see in it a source of some of the legalism and verbalism of political life. But this should not blind him to one of the strongest elements in a durable tradition.

FAILURE TO ACHIEVE UNION. One basic element in the Spanish American experience is the political frustration growing out of failure to achieve union. The old Spanish empire in America broke up into eighteen nations, and the idea of achieving at least the kind of league of states envisioned by Bolívar lingered on merely as a dream which would not die. This centrifugal tendency within Spanish America was so strong that it brought failure to achieve even the less ambitious federal unions of the states constituting the old colonial vice-royalties and captaincies-general. Thus the union of Mexico and Central America was short-lived, the Central American federation broke up within fifteen years, Bolívar's Great Colombia split up into three nations, and the sprawling, sparsely populated vice-royalty of La Plata (today Argentina, Uruguay, Paraguay, and Bolivia) failed to achieve the union sought by Buenos Aires leaders. Weakness of the spirit of nationalism of these new states during the first half-century of independence was partly the result of these failures to achieve the kind of union essential to political strength. But even after the industrial revolution and other social and economic changes stimulated a feeling of nationality among the middle and lower classes of society, the dream of union remained strong enough to provide the basis for the inter-American movement. This persistent aspiration for some larger form of union gives an ambivalent character to the Spanish American nations, making them both nationalist and internationalist (Hispanic) at the same time.[11]

[11] This idea, which has long been urged by Augusto Mijares of Venezuela, finds an interesting confirmation in the history of international law in Spanish America. See H. B. Jacobini, A Study of the Philosophy of International Law as Seen in Works of Latin American Writers (The Hague: Martinus Nijhoff, 1954).

ADHERENCE TO REPUBLIC. A second important element in the political experience of the Latin American nations is their continued adherence to the form of the republic, despite many failures. This fact alone makes Latin America one of the world's greatest modern laboratories of democratic government. In Mexico, Argentina, and particularly in Haiti, a great argument was carried on and bloody civil wars were fought between the defenders of monarchy and the advocates of republicanism during the first decades of independence. The most notable exception was Brazil, which was successfully governed as a constitutional monarchy from 1822 to 1839, but republicanism ultimately triumphed everywhere in Latin America.

THE STRONG PRESIDENCY. Another striking product of Latin American political experience is the strong executive, generally a popularly elected president. In its external aspects the presidency has been copied in large measure from the United States, but its roots also strike deep into Spanish tradition and into Latin America's own political experience. Spanish antecedents of the executive include the colonial viceroys and captains general, as well as the king under the liberal Spanish constitutions of 1812 and 1820. The presidency has its indigenous aspects, derived from the influence of the special conditions and problems of the area, and especially of the agonizing struggle to achieve stable political life within an unstable, rapidly changing society and culture. Thus, for example, the personalist dictatorships of the nineteenth century, which still appear occasionally in some nations in the twentieth century, were a confession of weakness and defeat on the part of the creole governing class which had brought about independence—of its inability to organize and direct societies changing rapidly at their very base without resorting to arbitrary exercise of power. As a result of this early experience with dictatorships, a highly personal concept of the presidential office evolved in many of the countries. It became a tradition that the office should be held by a vigorous, dominating personality, a "strong man," who controlled the other branches of government through his control of the army, and who either perpetuated himself in office or dictated the choice of his successor, in either case managing elections to effect his purpose.

ARMY POLITICAL TRADITION. In our preoccupation with technical aspects of government we sometimes overlook the fact that every state must be able to depend upon the loyalty of the army and organized police. The Latin American experience has demonstrated this truism in rudimentary and often dramatic form. During the early years of independence, which were frequently years of civil strife as well, the armed forces played a dominant political role, partly because of the personal loyalty of the troops which had been organized by the various *caudillos* during the wars for independence. The growth of professional armies in later years has tended to subordinate this element of personal loyalty in the armed forces. Yet some of it remains, and in most Spanish American nations today one of the president's basic tasks is to ensure the loyalty of the armed forces. Should a serious crisis arise, the nation expects that the army will step in to ensure the functioning of the mechanism of the state. In such civilian-dominated nations as Uruguay, Chile, and Costa Rica the role of the army differs from that in nations like Nicaragua and the Dominican Republic, where the army operates much nearer the surface of political life. But its importance in practically every state should not be minimized.

Lord Bryce believed that the strength of the executive in Latin America was due largely to the presidents' habit of exercising arbitrary authority based upon control of the army. This political custom came about, he said, as the result of "racial and social conditions"[12] which seemed to find expression in the lack of an extensive, well-informed public opinion. If Bryce's phrase, "racial and social conditions," is given meaning more in accord with present-day understanding of ethnic factors than is his somewhat limited "racial" view, his statement is not far from the truth. But it leaves out of account other important factors, one of which we shall now examine —the lack of genuinely popular political parties.

WEAK POLITICAL PARTIES. Nineteenth-century political parties were amorphous factional groups within the small ruling class which emerged from the colonial conquest. This seems to have been true even when parties made genuine popular appeals, as in the case of Juárez' Liberal party in Mexico, or that of Barrios in Guatemala. The political parties of Brazil played a more important role in national life, both under the Empire and under the Republic, either because of the regional and state basis of Brazilian politics or because of the stability of political life arising from other factors. But Brazilian parties, too, lacked a broad popular basis and continuous organization. Only with the rise of such twentieth-century institutionalized army–labor–bureaucratic parties as the Mexican PRI, or Institutional Revolutionary Party (Partido Revolucionario Institucional), was it possible to base political life upon a continuing, cohesive, nonmilitary political force, adequate to provide support to government through times of grave crises, to effect workable compromises between warring factions and interests, and thus to

[12] *Modern Democracies* (New York: The Macmillan Co., 1931), II, 469–470.

furnish a working substitute for the army or national police force as the foundation structure of the state.[13]   When President Lorenzo Latorre of Uruguay resigned his office late in the nineteenth century, saying that his nation was ungovernable, what he probably meant was that he had nothing to govern with except the army and that the army had gone back on him.   Today the structure of political parties in Uruguay, as in a number of other countries, has reversed that situation.   But in many countries the weakness of party structure is still a common cause of political instability, and the army is looked upon as the chief source of stable government.

EXPERIENCE IN MUNICIPAL GOVERNMENT.   The experience with municipal government reveals a number of contradictions.   Under the Spanish colonial system, the American municipality was molded into a form less autonomous than the medieval Spanish city but was retained as a fundamental instrument of colonial development.   As a consequence, colonial municipalities provided wealthy creole landowners and merchants with an instrument of resistance to absolutist measures and policies.   Municipalities also played an important, but mixed role in the achievement of independence.   At times they served as focal points for movements for independence, while at other times they became centers of opposition to the new national regimes.   In the political anarchy of the early nineteenth century municipal government lost some of its colonial importance.   Throughout these trying and uncertain times, however, a strong tradition of municipal government persisted, even under the most adverse conditions.   The influence of this tradition is reflected in the anomalies of the present situation.   In some countries municipalities are merely the local administrative units of national or provincial government, while in others they are autonomous.   The present tendency is toward more local autonomy, and municipal government is beginning to acquire new vigor, freedom, and efficiency as it faces the problems posed by rapid urbanization and by the other dramatic changes which Latin American society and culture have been undergoing.

PARLIAMENTARY TENDENCY.   Latin American political experience has also, from time to time, revealed a tendency toward parliamentary or congressional supremacy in government.   Except in Chile, such arrangements have been unrealistic, since strong presidents have generallly been able to disregard the constitutional provisions upon which the parliamentary structure rests.   Yet the persistent reappearance of provisions intended to subject the execu-

[13] The nature and role of political parties will be discussed in Chapter 7.

tive to legislative control is an important fact to be noted. Some scholars consider such provisions largely a reaction to the exaggerated presidentialism, but a more adequate explanation will include other aspects of Latin American experience as well. In part the constitutional efforts to increase legislative control over the executive are merely an expression of the normal struggle for power under a system of divided or balanced powers. In part, also, they reflect the ideas of the Spanish constitutions of 1812 and 1820 as to the form in which the political responsibility of the crown ministers should be established—an Iberian concept as distinct from the Anglo-French notion of parliamentary government. But to some extent they also reflect new forces arising from basic changes in the structure of Latin American society and the realignment of economic interests or power groups. From these changes the strong presidency emerged as an expression of new and popular forces in political life; yet the legislatures appeared to be more representative of the vested interests of the established power "oligarchies" and to reflect the conflicts of interest within them. Thus in the Latin American socio-political process the presidency has often represented social and economic change, while constitutional congressionalism has frequently stood for conservative opposition to social change.

Twentieth-Century Experience

The influence of social and cultural changes upon the dynamics of political life is the subject of Chapter 3, and it will be noted here only as it is essential to an understanding of the general significance of Latin American political experience in the present century. The population of Latin America has been increasing since the turn of the century at a high rate—one of the highest in the world today. This demographic phenomenon presents all the problems of social and economic adjustment inherent in a population in which youth predominates, a population which tends to exceed the food supply and the production of other consumer goods. The absorbing of large Indian and Negro populations and their cultures into the dominant population and culture of European derivation constitutes an even more profound demographic change. The resulting mestizo populations, because of their mixed ethnic character and their lack of a firm cultural tradition, contribute to a general instability in the society.

The rapid urban development in the present century, with its attendant problems, is another major aspect of recent Latin American political experience. Recent European immigrants rub elbows with less sophisticated country-folk in the burgeoning cities whose populations sometimes have doubled in a decade. Both groups are developing distinct patterns of interest and attitudes toward family life, recreation, religion, employment, and politics, which increase the already sharp cultural differences between the cities and the rural areas where the dominant culture is still Church-centered and based on the patriarchal family. The class distinctions of the older culture have also tended to break down in the cities, giving way to new and more dynamic social hierarchies based more upon wealth and political position.

Sharpening of the differences between city and countryside obviously increases the political difficulties involved in achieving truly national programs of action. But, at the same time, an increase in national consciousness gives some evidence of the growth of social ties which transcend this almost classical division between city and countryside in Latin American society. This evidence appears especially in the developing bonds between urban and rural workers. Moreover, while a middle class in the traditional European sense is not strongly developed, the number of city dwellers who stand midway between the extremes of wealth and poverty is growing. City people are exerting an increasing influence upon every aspect of national life in these countries, and they are in the majority where urban growth has been rapid.

Important contemporary religious changes also enter into recent political experience. In the nineteenth century the state exhausted much of its energy in a conflict with the Church which grew out of the independence movements and the Liberal party's insistence upon secularizing society. In the course of this struggle, the Church was pushed into alliance with the most reactionary elements in society. One of the results was an increase in the number of noncommunicants as the Church failed to expand at the rate of population growth. Urbanization further contributed to religious apathy. By the middle decades of the twentieth cenury the old church–state controversy of the preceding century had become largely a memory, making possible a fresh approach to religious matters. A socially conscious religious revival is under way today, a revival based on the precepts of the papal encyclicals *Rerum Novarum,* of Leo XIII, and *Quadragesimo Anno,* of Pius XI. Clerical and lay leaders have now united, for example, in an aggressive effort to restore Christian influence in the labor movement. The Church is also regaining lost ground among the urban middle classes and capturing the allegiance of political leaders previously committed to anticlericalism.

As will be seen in the chapters which follow, recent political experience vividly reflects these social and cultural changes. For the first time in Latin American political history mass movements have brought changes in national power structures, producing new types of popular, sometimes demagogic, political leaders. These leaders express ideologies ranging from the extreme right to the extreme left, as elsewhere in the world, but often, as we shall see, with certain characteristics derived from New World influence. Reflecting these mass movements, political parties have tended to take on a more popular character. Even the army, traditionally the fundamental instrument of political stability, has not escaped the change. Army groups, in a manner inconceivable in earlier decades, have made political alliances with worker movements.

The most obvious aspect of Latin America's political experience in this century has been the growth of big, bureaucratic government. This change obviously involves modifications in fundamental political beliefs and attitudes, but its full significance remains to be seen, particularly in relation to the traditional personalism of politics. Will the impersonalism of big government eventually eliminate the colorful personalist *caudillo?* Or will it, rather, enhance his opportunities for the daring political deed? Certain aspects of recent experience, as we shall see, support each of these views. The final answer depends, to some extent, upon which of several interpretations is given to Latin American experience with democratic government.

Balance Sheet of Democratic Achievement

THEORIES OF LATIN AMERICAN POLITICS. Perhaps it is indicative of the dynamism of political life that Latin American politics lacks an adequate theory or rationale drawn from experience. Yet there is no lack of theoretical argument. One North American student has been satisfied to note that "changing concepts [as to *what* democracy was to be introduced] have . . . been the subject of widespread and often violent disagreement among professed democrats."[14] Other North American scholars lean toward a Machiavellian theory which explains Latin American political experience as essentially a search for power.[15] Some Latin Americans depict

[14] Arthur Whitaker, "Historian's Point of View," in "Pathology of Democracy in Latin America," *op. cit.*, pp. 101–108.

[15] William S. Stokes, in "Violence as a Power Factor in Latin American Politics," (see footnote 7, above) seems to have accepted such a theory. Richard M. Morse, in "Toward a Theory of Spanish American Government," *Journal of the History of Ideas,* XV (January 1954), 81–93, has skillfully put his finger upon Spanish America's lack of a meaningful, integrating theory of its political experience, but his attempt to correlate this experience with the political philosophy of Machiavelli seems less successful.

the conflict, perhaps too simply, as one between conservative and radical concepts of democracy.[16] Still others speak of discovering the need for "a new and more humane philosophy of perpetual change."[17] Augusto Mijares of Venezuela, perhaps because he has made a less absolute break with nineteenth-century evolutionary and deterministic thought than have some of his contemporaries, explains the dilemma of Spanish American political theory as a conflict of older deterministic and pessimistic views with the newer philosophies of idealism. He insists that the commonly accepted pessimistic interpretation of the history of the republics as one of anarchy, in which *caudillismo* or *caciquismo* is the only positive principle of order, is only partially true, since *caciquismo* has always been opposed by the strong civil tradition in municipal government. Although it has often consisted more of verbalisms than of political reality, this tradition should not be dismissed lightly, he says, for it is the expression of a republican ideal emerging from the American experience.[18] The Spanish literary generation of '98 initiated on both sides of the Atlantic an intellectual renaissance which brought new scholarly appraisals of Spanish and Spanish American political experience. Historians such as the Mexican Silvio Zavala and the Spaniard José Maria Ots Capdequi, who are products of this movement, also stress this civil tradition in their "institutional" studies of the colonial and independence eras.[19]

Further discussion of trends in social and political thought, and the movements with which they are connected, is reserved for a later chapter. For the present it is sufficient to note that any meaningful explanation of the Latin American political experience must take into account the way Latin Americans have interpreted this experience in their social and political thought. It must also consider the distinctive changes which culture and society have undergone in the past and are today undergoing in the various areas. Finally, it must examine the larger movements of which Latin American political experience since independence is a part, particularly the overseas expansion of Europe, a fundamental historical

[16] See José Luis Romero, *Las ideas políticas en Argentina* (Mexico: Fondo de Cultura Económica, 1946).

[17] As, for example, Leopoldo Zea in *Apogeo y decadencia del positivismo en México* (Mexico: Fondo de Cultura Económica, 1944), p. 260.

[18] *Op. cit.*

[19] Silvio Zavala's concept may be found especially in his chapter in Edgar McInnis, *et al., Ensayos sobre la historia del Nuevo Mundo* (Mexico: Pan American Institute of Geography and History, 1951). J. M. Ots Capdequi has written one of the best studies of political institutions in colonial Spanish America, *El estado español en las Indias* (2d ed.; Mexico: Fondo de Cultura Económica, 1946).

movement which has affected Latin America just as it has affected the United States.

DIFFERENT CONCEPTS OF DEMOCRACY. The significance of the lack of an adequate theory becomes apparent at once when dealing with the radically different concepts encountered as to what democracy in Latin America is and should be. The authors of this work assume that Latin Americans differ little, if at all, from other people in their capacity for democratic government and for democracy in other aspects of social life. Their democratic aspirations may be expressed in different political and social institutions and in patterns of behavior which result from a different history, culture, and environment. Democratic achievement may be greater or less; it may also be measured according to a different scheme of values. Some Latin Americans, for example, would say that they are more democratic because they are less class-conscious than Anglo-Americans. This assumption may well have been made on the basis of unpleasant contacts with Anglo-Americans in Latin America or along the Mexican border.

Few Latin Americans expressing such views seem to be aware, however, that class lines are much stronger in Latin America than in the United States. Brazilians, Haitians, and Cubans have decried the undemocratic character of racial segregation and race prejudice in the United States, failing to do justice to the fundamentally democratic spirit of the United States or to note the persistence of class stratification in their own countries where race prejudice is weak. But our understanding of the democratic spirit and the capacity for democracy of Latin Americans has frequently been just as weak. Part of the difficulty lies in the lack of agreement as to what democracy is, and in the fact that democracy differs so much in different cultures. These considerations have led one Mexican to write of the impossibility of agreement on how to strengthen democracy through the Organization of American States because of the impossibility of agreeing on what democracy is.[20]

THE FALLACY OF JUDGMENTS BASED ON ANGLO-AMERICAN MODELS. Nowhere does the need become clearer for the student to rid himself of prejudices and value judgments derived from his own cultural background than in the attempt to pass judgment on this question of democratic achievement. He must remember that the concepts of democracy and democratic institutions in the United States, although they form part of the general stream of modern democracy and nationalism, and like those of Latin America owe a special debt

[20] Luis Quintanilla, *Democracy and Pan Americanism* (Boston: Boston University Press, 1952). A Spanish edition appeared in Mexico the same year.

to France, are also derived in many respects from British constitutional and political traditions as well as from the history of an expanding frontier of western settlement during the nineteenth century. Thus, to North Americans democracy usually has meant a way of social and political life carried on within a constitutional political structure, and processes which include orderly elections, the peaceful transition from one administration to another, the guarantee of universal suffrage and the secret ballot, the federal system for protecting local autonomy against the power of central government, and certain sanctions for the protection of freedom of press, speech, and religion, and for the protection of private property and individual economic enterprise. These are part of the Anglo-American social philosophy. Yet thoughtful students of our national life have usually realized that these political institutions and practices are part of a cultural pattern from which they derive their strength.

Because of the influence of the American and French revolutions and the success of the United States and France as republics, the pattern of political behavior in Latin America has often centered around concepts and institutions derived from this Anglo-American and French democracy. Thus the successes and failures of efforts to achieve universal suffrage, orderly elections, religious freedom, and a free press have been as much a part of the history of democracy there as elsewhere. All of the southern republics, at one time or another, have consciously tried to make over their government after the Anglo-American or French pattern, frequently without enough regard to the peculiar needs of their own conditions and the peculiar values in their inherited political institutions. Sometimes they achieved a measure of success, but often there were failures, traceable to this disregard of their own experience. Many nations tried to develop federal systems modeled on that of the United States. These efforts were usually unrealistic and hence doomed to failure, or at best destined to develop in quite different forms, since the autonomy in governmental units necessary to constitute the federal system had too little existence in fact. Yet four of these federal republics—Brazil, Argentina, Mexico, and Venezuela —still survive as monuments to the strength of the ideal.

In retrospect, it is possible to see that some of the Latin American failures to make the machinery of democratic constitutional government work were simply the result of trying to assimilate alien institutions, practices, and ideals too rapidly. Success has been more likely, on the whole, when reforms have been based upon inherited institutions and traditions, such as the tradition of self-government at the municipal level, which remained alive in some places even when democratic institutions seemed to dissolve into anarchy or dictatorship at the national level. But acceptance of this principle of socio-political structure has been as difficult for Latin Americans as understanding it has been for North Americans.

Latin America's tradition also includes a highly developed sense of individual freedom, equality, independence, and human dignity, as well as devotion to the search for the good society. Her leaders and her people have shown great persistence in that search, even when the difficulties have seemed insuperable. These democratic elements have found expression in a steady tendency to broaden the basis of the Latin American state and society and to break down the class and race distinctions which originated in the European conquest. Political power is still all too frequently exercised by an oligarchy of the owners of wealth in alliance with the military. Yet even within this narrow oligarchical system a degree of free political activity may often be seen, as in the recent political history of Ecuador. Moreover, when the student of government recalls the significant role played by ruling classes of the past in the development of the modern democratic nation-state, he may well see in these elite groups of Latin America a potential source of some broader structure of political power, provided that they act with proper social responsibility. In this connection, the political behavior of the dominating oligarchies in such countries as Ecuador, Peru, and Bolivia, as they have confronted popular revolutionary movements since World War II, deserves careful study.

LATIN AMERICAN DEMOCRATIC REALITIES. Democracy is more, of course, than its political instruments. The latter are means to a larger end, which consists essentially of social aspirations. Political democracy, thus, is not an absolute, but can exist in many different forms and degrees. It is a fact of history, not a dogma, although it has important roots in the Christian ethic and in the Judaic-Christian concepts of the Kingdom of God and the equality of all souls. It is a pattern of political behavior, infused with strong spiritual elements and firm belief in the possibility of attaining a better order of society and a better life for all human beings through fuller and freer participation of the masses of men and women in its making. Democracy in all of the Americas is a complex of social strivings, intimately associated with powerful dynamic elements arising from the conquest of a new continent and from the industrial and technological revolutions of the past century and a half. In the United States, as economic changes opened up more abundant economic and cultural opportunities to the increasing masses of people, democracy called for a broader basis in the structure of political power and in the process by which that structure is established and altered. A similar trend may be seen within the violence of recent Latin American political experience.

AUTHORITARIANISM. Misunderstanding of Latin American politics might be lessened if the term "dictator" were never used, for it is a stereotype embracing situations and types of administrations which differ widely in many fundamental respects. Yet dictatorship, despite all of its contradictory meanings, is so much a part of Latin American political experience that it is virtually impossible to avoid use of the term. Perhaps the most useful thing, therefore, is to distinguish some of the various types of regimes which have been so categorized.

Dictatorships have been of many types. Some of the classic examples of the nineteenth century—for instance, that of President Mariano Melgarejo of Bolivia—were little more than organized violence, that is, a structure of naked power resting narrowly upon control of the army and representing no principle or program. Others rested upon a broader popular basis and fulfilled some real social need expressed in a genuine political movement. In early nineteenth-century Argentina, for example, Juan Manuel de Rosas was an expression of the need for national unification. In general, he rallied the forces of reaction against the liberal reforms of the Buenos Aires creoles who had dominated the nation in its early years. His power was based chiefly upon the support of *estancieros,* the clergy, and conservative provincials. But it also had a more popular basis in the support of the gauchos, or cowboys of the *pampas,* and their popular leaders.

Other dictatorships have grown more directly out of popular reform movements. The popular basis of the mid-nineteenth-century regime of President Ramón Castilla of Peru appears in his emancipation of the Negro slaves. Some of the presidents of Mexico immediately following the Revolution of 1910 were called dictators by their enemies and certainly exercised arbitrary power at times. Yet their power came from their leadership of a social revolution and their ability to control the ever present danger of an uprising of the masses.

Since the majority of these so-called dictatorial regimes have been careful to preserve the forms and the appearance of constitutional government and to talk the language of democracy, it is not always easy to distinguish them from genuinely free regimes. Some of the most eloquent defenses of democracy in recent years, for example, have come out of the dictator-dominated Dominican

Republic. During the nineteenth century many Latin Americans insisted that political improvement could come only by building on the institution of the *caudillo,* or local strong man, which they identified as the principal political reality, a product of the American environment.[21]   Dictatorships which could establish social stability by forging a political order out of these unruly elements, they argued, were a necessary initial step toward a democratic order.

On the whole, these authoritarian regimes have more frequently been symptomatic of the weakness of the state than of its strength. Sometimes they seem to have been a poor substitute for the liberal monarchy envisioned by the Spanish constitution of 1812. *Peronismo* in Argentina and the *estado novo* of Vargas in Brazil may have represented something new in authoritarianism. But even such relatively recent systems seem to have stemmed, at least in part, from the same kinds of governmental weakness and the same defects in the system of political parties as those displayed in the nineteenth century when the creole liberals precipitated the struggles between the Church and the state.

Finally, in reading the literature on Latin American revolutions and "dictators," the student of government should distinguish carefully between the revolutionary *coup d'état* which brings no significant change in the structure of political power and the more significant political changes (whatever the degree of violence of their origin, or however authoritarian they may be) which introduce a new social basis in the power structure and are accompanied by significant new social and economic trends. This is not to say that dictatorships may be good or bad merely because of their aims. To one who believes in democratic constitutional government, the arbitrary exercise of power is never justifiable, except in the direst emergencies. Nor is it usually necessary in order to attain ends which are right and properly defined. Yet the fact remains that some twentieth-century regimes relying upon organized force have been genuine expressions of the general will in a social revolution of broad scope, while others have expressed little or nothing beyond the personal ambitions of the leaders. In the Latin American setting, this has often been a more important distinction than that between "dictators" and constitutional presidents.

One of the encouraging facts in the present Latin American situation is the resurgence of responsible political leadership. This leadership is animated by a political and economic philosophy keyed

---

[21] A good example may be found in Francisco García Calderón, *Latin America, Its Rise and Progress* (New York: Charles Scribner's Sons, 1913).

to twentieth-century needs, and hence is different from that of the nineteenth-century liberals. But it is like the old leadership in its fundamental optimism and in its conviction that the good life is an objective within the reach of the present generation—that the nation's social and economic ills can be cured by political action. Much of the leadership has emerged from a movement current among university students since 1930, a movement also reflected in university reform. Its outstanding characteristic is a complete willingness to face squarely such basic difficulties of Latin American life as land distribution, exploitation of the Indians and other labor groups, the rapid growth of urban population, problems of increasing the workers' productivity, as well as the problems of malnutrition, disease, and illiteracy.

Conclusions

What conclusions are to be drawn from this general evaluation of Latin American political experience? In the first place, it reveals numerous contradictions. The first is that *caudillismo* and *civilismo* are both products of forces in the American scene. The second is that the state in its evolution has been animated not only by the concept of nationalism but also by a persistent aspiration for Spanish American union. The aspiration for union, though largely relegated to the subconscious, remains strong in spite of a century-long record of frustration and defeat of efforts toward its realization (except as they may have found expression in the Organization of American States). In the third place, the phenomenon termed "political instability," sometimes even described in bio-medical terms as a pathological state of the body social and politic, really reflects the dynamism of a society in which the cultural base is changing rapidly and fundamentally. Sometimes it is part of the psychological–cultural process of the reinterpretation of older cultural values. Sometimes it represents continuation of the conflicts between older value systems. Violence in political polemics and in elections becomes intelligible as an aspect of this cultural process.

But does this violence reflect the strength of reactionary elements, of groups and interests which find themselves on the defensive and try to curb the trend toward change by resort to force? Or does it rather suggest that politics is a sector of Spanish American culture which is relatively subject to change, and hence the subject of bitter and acrimonious discussion and violent action? Further comparative studies of both successful and unsuccessful political uprisings and rebellions are essential before we can really answer this question. All that can be said at present is that the answer will vary with the circumstances in the various countries at various times.

Similarly, the excessive verbalism and legalism of Spanish American literature on democratic politics cannot be dismissed either as merely covering up Machiavellian opportunism or as an escape from reality. Rather, it must be understood as part of a cultural process, as a valid expression of social and political aspiration. In this connection, the importance attached to the concept of the juridical norm in Spanish American legal thought, and the nature of that concept, deserve the careful attention of students who wish to penetrate the meaning of Latin American politics.[22]

[22] H. B. Jacobini concludes *A Study of the Philosophy of International Law as Seen in Works of Latin American Writers* (p. 142) by noting that the Latin American tendency to recognize the connection "between law and its moral, sociological, and political formulators . . . is a refreshing breath of juristic realism."

Suggestions for Reading

Despite its age, James Bryce's *South America* (rev. ed.; New York: The Macmillan Co., 1916) and various passages in his *Modern Democracies* (New York: The Macmillan Co., 1931) still afford the best general evaluation of Latin American political experience. Duncan Aikman's *All American Front* (New York: Doubleday & Co., Inc., 1940) is a realistic appraisal. Samuel Guy Inman's *Latin America, Its Place in World Life* (Rev. ed.; New York: Houghton Mifflin Co., 1942) is a useful source for social and cultural aspects of life in the area. Frank Tannenbaum, *Whither Latin America* (New York: The Thomas Crowell Co., 1934) offers a provocative commentary. Several books by Luis Quintanilla, among them *A Latin American Speaks* (New York: The Macmillan Co., 1943) and *Democracy and Pan Americanism* (Boston: Boston University Press, 1952), comprise one of the best evaluations of trends and problems by a Latin American in English. Two volumes by Harold E. Davis, *Makers of Democracy in Latin America* (New York: H. W. Wilson Co., 1945) and *Latin American Leaders* (New York: H. W. Wilson Co., 1949), may prove helpful in understanding political leadership. A comprehensive symposium by United States scholars was published in the *American Political Science Review*, XLIV (March 1950), 100–149, under the title "Pathology of Democracy in Latin America." William L. Schurz provides some judicious observations in his study, *Latin America, A Descriptive Survey* (New York: E. P. Dutton & Co., Inc., 1949). The best general bibliographical guide on Latin American government is that of George I. Blanksten, "Bibliography on Latin American Politics and Government," *Inter-American Review of Bibliography*, IV, No. 3 (1954), 191–214.

Chapter 2

Latin America:
The Land and People

Despite the superficial impression, sometimes gained by the tourist, of unchanging, age-old customs, Latin America today is a region of rapid change. New dynamic forces in political life and changing power structures spring from these changes and from the tensions they produce. Rapid population growth is one of the most obvious sources of the increased political energy. But equally important, in some respects, are the results of tensions arising from ethnic conflict and assimilation, movements of population into new areas and activities, modifications in the class structure, agrarian reforms, and trends toward urbanization and industrialization. We shall return to consider these new trends many times in the course of this volume. But first we must gain a broad understanding of the land, the people, and their interrelationship, as well as the basic elements of the social, economic, and political structures.

Differences and Similarities

It is difficult to find a term appropriate to describe an area more than two and one half times the size of the United States, inhabited by some one hundred seventy million persons of widely differing ethnic, cultural, and economic backgrounds, living in twenty highly differentiated republics. The term Spanish America applies appropriately to the eighteen Spanish-speaking nations, but they embrace only about two-thirds of the area and of the population. Brazil, the largest nation both in area and population, is Portuguese-speaking, while Haiti speaks French. The broader term, Hispanic

America, embraces both the Spanish- and Portuguese-speaking peoples, but excludes Haiti, of course. Brazilians dislike this term and the equivalent Ibero-America because they suggest Spanish dominance in some vague way. Even Latin America, the term used in this book, is not adequate to cover the range of differences in the area, because it overemphasizes the common Latin heritage. Furthermore, all of these terms based upon European origins leave out of account the large Negro, Indian, and mestizo ethnic elements which cannot properly be called Spanish, Hispanic, or Latin, even after four centuries of conquest by and cultural contact with Europeans.

REGIONAL AND NATIONAL DIFFERENCES. Latin America extends from the north temperate zone to the fringes of Antarctica, encompassing a variegated complex of geographical, topographical, and climatic components. It includes such extremes as the highest mountain in the Americas, hot, humid coastal swamps, jungles, great rain forests and semi-arid plateaus, one of the world's most arid deserts, not far removed from the headwaters of the Amazon, and the heavy rainfall area of the Amazon basin.

The nations vary in size from huge Brazil, larger than the United States, to tiny El Salvador, about the size of Massachusetts. Eight of the countries are larger than France, but ten are smaller than the United Kingdom. National populations range from Brazil's 58 million to Panama's 886,000. Four nations have more than ten million inhabitants, while two have less than a million.

Ethnic composition varies just as greatly. Ninety-five per cent or more of the people of Costa Rica and Argentina are descended from European immigrants. In Bolivia, Peru, Ecuador, and Guatemala, on the other hand, Indians constitute a major part of the population. The Indians, too, display great diversity in cultural backgrounds, and these differences sometimes have great social and political significance, as in the case of the language barriers which separate different Indian peoples in Mexico. Mexico is largely a mestizo nation, much of its basic population stock being an ethnic mixture of Indian and European elements. Brazil has nearly as many Negroes as the United States, Haiti is more than 90 per cent Negro, and other Caribbean countries have significant Negroid elements. To add to this ethnic kaleidoscope, various blendings of white and Indian, Negro and Indian, Negro and white, and Indian–Negro–white are found in many places.

Economic, social, and cultural differences are also to be noted. Some nations are predominantly agricultural, but this may mean anything from an agriculture based on small farms to a system of large estates, or from subsistence farming to production for export. In Mexico, Brazil, Chile, and Argentina industrialization has made great strides. In certain other countries the proportion of workers employed in industry is very small. The degree of urbanization also varies greatly from country to country. Literacy ranges from around 11 per cent at one extreme to some 97 per cent at the other. Daily newspaper circulation in one country is as low as 3.4 per thousand inhabitants, while in another it reaches 217.8.

COMMON CHARACTERISTICS. Some characteristics are fairly common to all twenty nations. They had their origin in a common American independence movement, and they share a common Christian European cultural heritage. Eighteen of them have a common bond in the Spanish language, despite the survival of Indian languages. Their greatest bond of unity, perhaps, is religion, since with few exceptions Latin Americans embrace the Roman Catholic faith. Moreover, their religion still bears a strong unique imprint from Spain, and to a lesser degree from Portugal.

The national economies also show common traits. Many of them are dominated by the production of agricultural and mineral raw materials for export. About half of the nations have the kind of "monocultural" economy in which one product accounts for the bulk of exports, for example beef and wheat in Argentina, coffee in several countries, copper in Chile, and petroleum in Venezuela. Other common economic factors include a land system of large estates (*latifundio*), a pattern of inequitable distribution of the national income, weakness of the urban middle class, and a policy of encouraging industrialization. Common problems are encountered in this industrialization, such as lack of certain basic raw materials, power, domestic capital, technicians, and skilled labor.

The nations also share common political characteristics, but since some of these are to be the principal concern of this book, they will be merely noted at this point. They include a high degree of centralization of political power, the consequent weakness of municipal and provincial government, concentration of power in the hands of the chief executive, the relative impotence of legislatures, lack of independence in the courts, and, in some countries, almost chronic revolutions.

The Land

The area of Latin America, 7,767,000 square miles, is more than two and one half times that of the United States. This is a large area in relation to the population. Geographical and topographical factors, however, impose limitations upon this seeming plenty.

Thus, if the formidable mountain barriers, deserts, coastal lowlands and swamps are taken into account, the proportion of arable land is below the world average.

MEXICO AND CENTRAL AMERICA.[1]   The seven nations of Mexico, Costa Rica, El Salvador, Guatemala, Honduras, Nicaragua, and Panama embrace about 13 per cent of the total Latin American land area.   Mexico is the third largest of the Latin American nations, El Salvador the smallest.   (See Table I.)   The region well illustrates the limitations imposed by geography upon the amount of land suitable for cultivation.   Costa Rica, which is least affected by these adverse factors, has 2.3 acres of arable land per capita, while Panama has only 0.5 acre.   (In the United States the ratio is about three acres per capita.)

Population concentrations and the pattern of agricultural organization and production are, of course, directly influenced by geography.   Nearly half of the people in Costa Rica live in the central plateau, where most of the country's principal export product, coffee, is grown.   The same pattern is found in El Salvador, though here the eastern lowlands are assuming a greater importance in the production of cotton, and the western lowlands are producing sugar in significant quantities.   In the past, rivers have had little economic importance in either of these countries, but El Salvador is developing the Lempa River for power and navigation purposes.

Two-thirds of Guatemala's area of 42,000 square miles may be classified as mountainous.   Most of the population lives in this area.   The northern coastal tropical lowlands constitute about one-third of the nation's total area but are much less significant in the national agricultural production.   Honduras, the largest of the Central American republics, has a broad coastal plain, from 60 to 75 miles in width, facing the Caribbean to the north along a coastline of slightly over 400 miles.   The bulk of the population is concentrated in the highlands and the intermontane valleys of the western and central sections.   Here one finds the major areas of coffee production, whereas the northern section is the center of the economically important banana plantations.

Mexico constitutes more than two-thirds of the total area of this

[1] Because of their diversity, it is not possible to treat each nation separately here. In order to make the subject more manageable for the reader, therefore, the twenty nations will be discussed in six regional groups: Mexico and Central America (Mexico, Costa Rica, El Salvador, Guatemala, Honduras, Nicaragua, and Panama), the Caribbean States (Cuba, the Dominican Republic, and Haiti), Northern South America (Colombia and Venezuela), Brazil, the River Plate Republics (Argentina, Paraguay, and Uruguay), and Western South America (Bolivia, Chile, Ecuador, and Peru).

TABLE I.   LAND USE

	Total Area		Land per Capita	
	Sq. Mi. (thousands)	Rank	Acres	Rank
Mexico and Central America				
Costa Rica	20	17	15.5	15
El Salvador	8	20	4.0	19
Guatemala	42	15	7.2	16
Honduras	43	14	30.0	9
Mexico	760	3	20.3	12
Nicaragua	57	12	30.6	8
Panama	29	16	24.0	11
Total for region	959			
Caribbean States				
Cuba	44	13	5.5	18
Dominican Republic	19	18	5.5	17
Haiti	11	19	1.9	20
Total for region	74			
Northern South America				
Colombia	440	5	26.1	10
Venezuela	352	7	49.0	3
Total for region	792			
Brazil				
Brazil	3288	1	43.4	4
River Plate Republics				
Argentina	1084	2	42.5	5
Paraguay	157	9	78.8	1
Uruguay	72	11	19.8	13
Total for region	1333			
Western South America				
Bolivia	424	6	67.1	2
Chile	286	8	32.6	7
Ecuador	105	10	19.8	14
Peru	506	4	38.2	6
Total for region	1321			
United States	3022		13.2	

A dash indicates that the data are not available.

SOURCES: "Statistical Abstract of Latin America for 1955," prepared at the University of California at Los Angeles; and John Carrier Weaver and F. E. Lukerman, *World Resource Statistics* (Minneapolis: Burgess Publishing Co., 1953).

IN LATIN AMERICA

Arable Land		Pasture Land		Forest	
Per Cent of Total Area	Acres per Capita	Per Cent of Total Area	Acres per Capita	Per Cent of Total Area	Acres per Capita
7	2.3	12	0.7	78	12.1
25	0.5	33	0.2	34	2.4
14	2.0	5	0.4	64	4.8
7	1.1	17	0.4	42	—
9	1.0	34	10.3	20	6.6
6	1.0	4	0.6	42	9.9
6	0.5	7	—	70	—
17	0.9	34	1.9	11	0.7
14	0.8	12	0.6	70	3.8
17	0.3	—	—	29	—
2	0.5	32	6.0	60	16.6
3	10.8	15	16.1	40	19.7
2	1.0	13	6.7	56	20.1
11	4.6	41	17.5	25	7.4
1	3.0	2	—	52	16.3
11	15.1	69	—	'3	0.6
—	0.2	—	—	43	—
5	2.6	13	3.0	22	7.2
6	0.9	1	1.1	26	9.2
1	0.5	9	4.2	53	21.5
25	3.0	33	4.6	32	4.2

region.   However, despite its 760,000 squares miles, Mexico has but slightly over one acre of arable land per capita.   Two mountain chains, the eastern and western Sierra Madre mountains, extending from the northwest to the southeast, segment the country.   Much of northern Mexico is arid or semi-arid, in contrast to the tropical humid lowlands fronting the Caribbean.   The central plateau is the chief population and agricultural center.   The formidable mountain ranges create a major transportation and communication problem and help to perpetuate Indian ways and patterns of living. The rivers of Mexico, like those of the other republics of this region, are of little importance as avenues of communication.   Reclamation and power projects have, however, made increasing use of this resource for irrigation or hydroelectric power plants.

Nicaragua is divided into two regions by the Central American *cordillera*.   The heart of the nation, both as a population center and in economic activity, is the broad lowland belt paralleling the Pacific, and extending southeastward toward the Caribbean.   While its rivers are of little importance in the life of the nation, its two large lakes, Managua and Nicaragua, have both scenic and economic significance.   The latter lake at one time entered into the planning of a trans-isthmian canal.   Panama is divided into two almost equal parts by the Canal Zone.   As has often been noted, the western half of Panama is Central American in topography and in social organization, and the eastern is South American.

THE CARIBBEAN STATES.   Cuba, the Dominican Republic, and Haiti are island nations.   Their total area of approximately 74,000 square miles is slightly less than 1 per cent of the total area of Latin America.   Each of the three has less than one acre of arable land per capita.   Of Cuba's 44,000 square miles, three-quarters is rolling land, one-quarter is mountainous.   Although its short and turbulent rivers are of little value for internal communications, Cuba is well endowed with fine natural harbors.   The Dominican Republic is divided by four east-to-west mountain ranges, most of its people living in the fertile valleys between these chains.   The Cibao valley is the largest and most important.   Four-fifths of Haiti consists of low mountain ranges and numerous valleys in which a large proportion of the total population works, most of them in agricultural pursuits.   The remaining one-fifth of the land includes four major plains areas.

NORTHERN SOUTH AMERICA.   Colombia and Venezuela are the fifth and seventh largest of the nations, their combined area being slightly over a tenth of the whole Latin American region.   Colombia, which is the only South American state having both an Atlantic

(Caribbean) and a Pacific coastline, falls into three geographical regions: the coastal lowlands facing both the Caribbean and the Pacific, the west-central mountainous region which is crossed from north to south by three parallel ranges of the Andes, and the eastern, or *oriente,* region, the largest of the three.   This last-named area consists of plains, or *llanos,* in the north, and the forest, or *selva,* region of the south.   Most of the people of Colombia live in the highlands of the west-central section of the nation.   Colombia has fourteen navigable rivers.   Most of them are suitable only for small vessels of shallow draft, but the Magdalena–Cauca river system receives larger boats and is navigable for some 900 miles above its mouth.

Venezuela, about as large as Texas and Utah combined, also has well-defined and highly differentiated regions.   A broad and almost unbroken chain of mountains, the northern highlands, fringes the west and the north.   South and east of this area lie the temperate coffee- and cacao-producing central highlands—the social, cultural, and political center of the nation.   The lowland Maracaibo basin, one of the world's great centers of petroleum resources, occupies the northwestern part of the country.   The low grassy plains, or *llanos,* of the Orinoco river valley lie to the east and north of this highland area.   South and east of the Orinoco are the Guiana Highlands, well known in the United States because of the rapidly growing importance of Cerro Bolívar as a source of iron ore for American steel mills.   The Orinoco, which divides the country in two in its course from west to east, is one of the three major river systems of South America, the other two being the Amazon and the Plata.   Though much of the Orinoco is navigable, it is little used as a communication channel above the city of Cerro Bolívar, some 200 miles from the Orinoco delta.   At first glance, Venezuela would seem to be much more fortunate than Colombia in the amount of arable land, the latter's topography reducing the ratio to about a half-acre per capita.   But unfortunately, much of the arable land in Venezuela is found in the relatively inaccessible plains of the Orinoco.

BRAZIL.   The great size of Brazil, its large population of over 58,000,000, and its distinctive ethnic, linguistic, and cultural traits differentiate it from the other countries of Latin America.   The enormity of its area may be grasped by noting that its 3,300,000 square miles constitute almost half the total surface of South America and more than a third of all Latin America.   Its 14,300-mile border touches all of the other South American states except Chile and Ecuador.   Most of Brazil lies within the tropics, and has a tropical climate since elevations are not high. Only 3 per cent of the country has an elevation of over 3,000 feet, and the highest mountains are well under 10,000 feet. Yet plateaus comprise almost three-fifths of the national area, including much of the immense interior. The remaining two-fifths are the plains of the upper Amazon valley, the valley of the lower Paraná, and the coastal lowlands.

Brazil consists of three major geographic areas: the hot, humid Amazon valley of the north, the half-forest and half-desert expanse of uplands in the northeast, and the mountains and plateaus of central and southern Brazil. In spite of its vast area, the proportion of arable land is not high. Geography, climate, and communication obstacles reduce the amount of arable land per capita to about one acre. The nation has one of the most extensive and well-developed river systems in the world, with over 25,000 miles of navigable inland waterways. The Amazon river system provides a drainage network for almost half of South America, and ocean vessels can move up-river to Manaus, some 900 miles from the delta. River vessels of lighter draft go to Iquitos in Peru.

THE RIVER PLATE REPUBLICS. Argentina, Paraguay, and Uruguay comprise about 17 per cent of Latin America. In geography, topography, and climate, this region is quite unlike the others. For the most part it lies within the temperate zone. Except for western Argentina, it lacks the huge mountain masses characterizing the other countries. Moreover, a larger proportion of the land is available for cultivation. Uruguay, for example, has slightly over fifteen acres per capita, Argentina almost five, and Paraguay three.

Argentina, about a third as large as the United States, consists of four principal zones. The northeastern region includes the alluvial Chaco plain and the fertile flood plain and rolling region known as Mesopotamia. The *pampa* is the fertile heartland of the nation and occupies about one-fourth of the entire area. In this flat sea-level plain, most of Argentina's great wealth in beef and cereals is produced. In the west is the mountainous Andean region, crowned by America's highest peak, Mt. Aconcagua. To the south lies the wind-swept plain of Patagonia, with its numerous large sheep ranches. The Uruguay–Paraná–La Plata river system, which drains almost a million square miles, permits ocean shipping to travel almost 1,000 miles inland. The central Córdoba rivers are of importance as a source of hydroelectric power and water for irrigation.

Paraguay, about the size of California, is divided into two principal zones by the Paraguay River as it flows southward through the nation. The eastern section of plains, grasslands, and heavy forests is the more heavily populated. The western, largely uninhabited Chaco zone consists mainly of flat, swampy grasslands, although some of the *quebracho* forests of Paraguay extend into its northern reaches. The Paraguay River has been the nation's principal link with the outside world. The Pilcomayo, which rises in Bolivia, forms the southern border of Paraguay, joining the Paraguay River at a point opposite Asunción.

Uruguay, the third of the River Plate republics and the smallest nation in South America, is about the size of North Dakota. It has no well-marked or definite zones or regions. Topographically, it is a transition from the flat *pampas* of Argentina to the hilly uplands and plateaus of Brazil. The southern two-thirds of its gently rising land is a grassy plain, and the highest elevation in the nation is just under 2,000 feet. Virtually the entire land surface of Uruguay can be cultivated; her arable land ratio of fifteen acres per capita is the highest in Latin America.

WESTERN SOUTH AMERICA. Bolivia, Chile, Ecuador, and Peru have one outstanding feature in common: the massive Andes ranges which occupy a large proportion of their total areas, presenting each of them with peculiar problems of communication, internal development, and cultural separatism. The region as a whole constitutes about 17 per cent of Latin America.

Bolivia is a land-locked country as large as France, Italy, and Spain combined. It is divided into three principal zones or regions: the arid high plateau, or *altiplano;* the fertile *yungas* and *valles* (mountain valleys), an intermediate region on the eastern Andean slopes; and the semi-tropical and tropical *llanos* (plains) of the Amazon–Chaco lowlands. The *altiplano* has an average height of 12,000 feet. Edged by several peaks rising to over 20,000 feet, it is one of the world's highest inhabited regions. Three mountain ranges, the Cordillera Occidental, the Cordillera Real, and the Cordillera Oriental, greatly reduce the ratio of available arable land, which is about 0.2 acre per capita. Lake Titicaca, at an elevation of over 12,000 feet, lies on the Bolivian west-central border.

Chile, considerably larger than France, has a Pacific coastline which extends over 2,500 miles, from 17° to 56° south latitude. At no point is it wider than 250 miles, and at some places its east–west extension is less than 50 miles. This peculiar configuration of Chile, plus the prominent back-bone ridge formed by the Andes throughout the length of the country, tends to divide Chile into both east–west and north–south zones. From east to west there are three zones: the Andes ranges, the economically important central valley, and the low coastal range. From north to south the first natural division is the northern desert, one of the large desert areas of the world. Agriculture is almost impossible in this region, but the area has a great economic importance in national life. Here is found the mineral wealth of Chile, in copper, nitrates, and sulphur. Immediately south of this desert, and extending to 32° south latitude, the land is less arid. Farms are numerous in the transverse valleys, and the Andes ranges have rich deposits of gold, silver, copper, and lead. The third zone, the rich central valley of Chile, extending southward for over 500 miles, is the agricultural center of the nation. South of the central valley, where the mountains come down to the seacoast, the distinctive feature is the southern archipelago, which extends to the southern tip of the continent. Out of these islands come Chile's wool and lumber. A large part of the arable land is in the central valley, the ratio being about two and one half acres per capita.

The name of Ecuador indicates this nation's location on the north–south axis of the Americas. About the size of Colorado, it is divided into three distinct regions. Facing the Pacific are the tropical coastal plains, ranging in width from 50 to 100 miles. Immediately to the east of this zone is the inter-Andean highland section, the *sierra*. Although this area has only about 15 per cent of the total land area of the country, it is the home of almost two-thirds of its population. The large eastern, or *oriente*, zone extends from the foothills of the Andes to the upper Amazon basin. It embraces two-thirds of the national area, but only 5 per cent of the people reside there. Much of the *oriente* could be used for agricultural purposes, but it is little developed. The nation as a whole has slightly less than one acre of arable land per capita. Of the two major river systems, the short and often turbulent western streams flow into the Pacific, whereas the eastern rivers are tributaries of the Amazon.

Peru, with an area slightly over a half-million square miles, is the fourth largest of the Latin American republics. Like its northern neighbor Ecuador, it has three distinct zones. Its coastal zone is much narrower than the similar zone in Ecuador and extends from 25 to 40 miles inland. In contrast to the coastal zone of Ecuador, that of Peru is arid. Agriculture is possible only by means of irrigation in its numerous river valleys. Yet the principal cities of Peru are in this region. The next region to the east is the *sierra*, the zone of the great Andean ranges. This zone reaches an elevation of over 22,000 feet in the peak of Huascarán. Almost one-third

of the nation's area lies in this zone, and most of the mineral
resources of Peru are found here. A large part of the population
of Peru lives in the high plateaus between the ranges. To the east
of the *sierra* lie the vast uncharted hills, forest, and tropical lowlands, the *montaña*. Containing more than 60 per cent of the
nation's area, this region is partially unexplored and largely underdeveloped. Peru's topography and climate, like those of the other
western South American nations, limit the amount of arable land
to about half an acre per capita, make internal development difficult,
and tend to perpetuate old ways of life among the large Indian
population.

THE INFLUENCE OF GEOGRAPHY. The geography of Latin America
thus presents many salient features and striking contrasts. The
area has one of the greatest mountain ranges in the world, the
Andes, which rises to become the highest natural barrier in the
Americas in the course of its 7,000-mile extension. Most of its
mountain passes are above 10,000 feet. The great desert of northern
Chile and Peru extends for almost 2,000 miles, and other vast arid
expanses are found in Mexico, Brazil, and Argentina. Torrid and
humid jungles, some literally impenetrable, defy the development
of civilization, as in the case of the "green hell" of the Chaco.
Latin America has the world's largest river, the highest navigable
lake, and the highest heavily populated plateau. Nature also has
played queer tricks upon the area. The east coast of South America
has many good harbors, but Chile, Peru, and Ecuador have almost
none. The reverse of this situation is found in Central America
and Mexico. Much of the west coast of South America is lacking
in moisture; yet the area just beyond the crest of the Andes has one
of the world's highest rates of rainfall. Some of its rivers are
enormous but sluggish, others are short and rush precipitously to
the sea.

These geographic features, and many others that could be cited,
have greatly influenced the people of Latin America in their social,
economic, and political organization. The plateau and mountain
areas have offered a place of comfortable living to people of European origin who cannot withstand the heat and humidity of the
tropics. Hence the greatest population density is found in the
plateaus of the highland areas. But the resulting unevenness of
population distribution creates many political problems. It is a
common phrase in Latin America that "the head is too large for
the body," a reference to the great concentration of population in
the national capitals, although it is also applicable to the concentration of population in the temperate plateaus. The mountains,

deserts, rivers, and jungles have isolated great sections of many of the republics from their political, economic, and intellectual centers. This has not only tended to perpetuate old, and perhaps long-outmoded, cultural patterns, but it has also encouraged political separatism in many of the nations.

Geographic barriers have made it extremely difficult to develop internal communications in many nations. A railroad in Peru rises from sea level to an elevation of over 15,000 feet in slightly more than 100 miles! Many of the natural resources in Latin America are located in areas which are isolated by mountains or deserts. Such obstacles add greatly to the cost of exploitation of mineral resources, often making it difficult to build essential railroads or highways between population centers and areas of potential agricultural productivity. The rivers of Latin America suitable for producing hydroelectric power are usually far removed from population centers, while rivers near these centers tend to be unsuitable for this power development. This handicap is particularly serious because Latin America in general is woefully short of power and energy resources on which to base the industrialization to which it aspires.

The term *geografía loca,* or mad geography, was originally applied to Chile, but it may equally well characterize much of Latin America. In this geographical madness one finds the partial cause of many Latin American problems.

The Latin Americans

In our thinking about foreign peoples we often indulge in such broad stereotypes as the "typical Englishman" or a "typical Frenchman." But such types are rarely encountered in real life, and a "typical Latin American" is as difficult to find as a "typical" Englishman or Frenchman. Even within some of these nations it is almost as difficult to generalize. The Argentines of the western or Cuyo region are unlike the *porteños* of Buenos Aires. The Peruvian who lives in the Miraflores suburb of Lima is more like an Ecuadorian of Quito than his own countryman in Huancayo, a scant 100 miles from Lima.

Latin Americans constitute some 7 per cent of the world population and occupy over 16 per cent of the total land area of the world. Thus, in general, Latin America is underpopulated in comparison with the rest of the world. Vast mountain areas, deserts, tropical swamps, and jungles account for the sparse population over large areas such as the Amazon valley, Patagonia, the interior of South America in general, and northern Mexico, including Lower California.   On the whole, South America is less densely populated than Mexico, Central America, and the Caribbean, where dense concentrations of population occur, for example in Haiti and El Salvador.   (See Table II.)

GROWTH OF POPULATION.   Latin America's population is growing rapidly.   While that of the United States increases at about 1.5 per cent per year, thirteen of the Latin American nations show a rate of increase of above 2.5 per cent, and four above 3 per cent. The rate of increase may be more rapid than in any other major region of the world.   It is largely due, moreover, to natural increase, for immigration plays a relatively minor role in the expansion.

As a consequence, the Latin Americans are also a youthful people.   About 40 per cent of them are under fifteen years of age, 55 per cent are between fifteen and fifty-nine, and only 5 per cent are over sixty.   In the United States and Canada these figures are respectively: 25 per cent under fifteen, 64 per cent between fifteen and fifty-nine, and 11 per cent sixty and over.   Birth rates in Latin America are much higher than in the United States, but this has also been true of death rates.   As late as 1947 the death rate was twice as high in the fifty largest cities of Latin America as in the fifty largest cities of the United States.   For the region as a whole, life expectancy was forty years, as contrasted with sixty-eight years in the United States.   Since World War II, however, some Latin American countries have achieved phenomenal reductions in death rates, particularly in infant mortality.   Hence the average life expectancy is probably increasing rather rapidly.

URBANIZATION.   Although agriculture is still the primary economic activity in most of the nations, both as an occupation and in terms of the gross national product, Latin America is becoming highly urbanized, the population of its cities growing more rapidly than the total population.   Five of its cities now have more than one million inhabitants, twenty have over 200,000, and forty-five have over 100,000.   The percentage of urban population ranges from 12 per cent in Haiti to 62 per cent in Argentina.   Many causes explain this trend, among them the Spanish "preference" for urban as against rural life, the lack of roads, sanitation, and schools in rural areas, the land tenure system which makes it more difficult for a farmer to become a landowner, and the greater opportunities for employment in the cities.

ETHNIC COMPOSITION.   Three ethnic strains enter into the composition of the people of Latin America: the Indian, the white, and the Negro.   In many of the regions conquered and colonized by Spain and Portugal, the Indian lived in large numbers and in

TABLE II. POPULATION OF

	Population[a]				Distribution[b] (per cent)	
	Total		Per Sq. Mi.			
	Thousands	Rank	No.	Rank	Rural	Urban
Mexico and Central America						
Costa Rica	951	19	47.6	6	67	33
El Salvador	2,193	15	274.1	2	64	36
Guatemala	3,149	12	75.0	5	75	25
Honduras	1,660	16	38.6	7	71	29
Mexico	28,849	2	38.0	8	57	43
Nicaragua	1,202	18	21.1	14	65	35
Panama	886	20	30.6	11	64	36
Total for region	38,890					
Caribbean States						
Cuba	5,807	7	132.0	3	—	—
Dominican Republic	2,404	14	126.5	4	76	24
Haiti	3,506	10	318.7	1	88	12
Total for region	11,717					
Northern South America						
Colombia	12,657	4	28.8	12	64	36
Venezuela	5,774	8	16.4	18	46	54
Total for region	18,431					
Brazil						
Brazil	58,456	1	17.8	16	64	36
River Plate Republics						
Argentina	19,108	3	17.6	17	38	62
Paraguay	1,565	17	10.0	19	65	35
Uruguay	2,525	13	35.1	9	—	—
Total for region	23,198					
Western South America						
Bolivia	3,198	11	7.5	20	66	34
Chile	6,774	6	23.7	13	40	60
Ecuador	3,567	9	34.9	10	72	28
Peru	9,396	5	18.6	15	—	—
Total for region	22,935					
United States	167,000		51.0		36	64

A dash indicates that data are not available.

Sources: "Statistical Abstract of Latin America for 1955," prepared at the University of California at Los Angeles; and Foreign Operations Administration, *Report on the Economic Situation in Latin America* (Washington, 1954).

[a] Data on population are for 1955, except for Ecuador, Guatemala, Haiti, and Mexico (1954), Cuba and Uruguay (1953).

[b] Data on rural–urban distribution are for 1950, except for Honduras (1945), Argentina (1947), Colombia (1951), Chile (1952).

LATIN AMERICA

Population of Largest City[c] (thousands)	Racial Composition (per cent)[d]				Annual Population Growth (per cent)
	White	Mestizo-Mulatto	Indian	Negro	
87	97 (inc. some mestizos)		1	2	3.1
162	11	78	11	—	2.5
284	5	35	60	—	3.1
72	2	86	10	2	2.9
2,234	15	55	29	—	2.9
109	17	69	5	9	2.9
128	11	65	10	13	2.8
783	75 (inc. mestizos)		—	24	2.7
182	15	70	—	15	2.7
134	—	5	—	95	—
648	20	68	7	5	3.4
495	20	65	7	8	4.0
2,303	63	21	2	14	2.4
3,371	97	—	3	—	2.7
207	97 (inc. many mestizos)		3	—	2.1
850	—	—	—	—	1.2
321	13	28	52	—	1.2
1,348	30	65	5	—	1.5
210	15	25	60	—	3.1
926	53 (inc. many mestizos)		46	—	2.1
7,454	90		—	10	1.5

[c] Data on population of largest city are for 1950, except for Bolivia (1940), Uruguay (1948), Colombia (1951), Chile and Peru (1952), Cuba (1953).

[d] Data on racial composition are for 1953, except for Panama (1940), Nicaragua (1943), Bolivia and Brazil (1945), Ecuador, Chile, and Paraguay (1952).

NOTE: Estimates of racial composition are not very reliable and should be used with great caution. The "Statistical Abstract of Latin America for 1955," the source of these figures, offers no explanation of the discrepancies in the totals of the percentages, as in the case of Bolivia.

advanced stages of culture. In several of the nations today he still constitutes the largest segment of the population. The European reached Latin America at the end of the fifteenth century. Shortly after his arrival he began the importation of Negroes to work the plantations, especially, but not exclusively, in the areas surrounding the Caribbean. Since the arrival of Columbus there has been a mingling of the three racial groups. Hence in many of the Latin American states the mestizo (mixed Indian–white) is a major segment of the population. In a few, mulattoes are numerically significant. One state, Haiti, is overwhelmingly Negro, while several others have large Negro populations; and in many areas blendings of Indian, Negro, and white are encountered.

It is virtually impossible to note the proportion of the total population in the area, or in any specific nation, which is white, Indian, Negro, mestizo, or of other racial mixture. This is partly due to the lack of census data, since many nations do not make racial enumerations. In part it is a problem of definition. What is an "Indian"? a "Negro"? a "mestizo"? Is the classification to be based on physical features, on language, or on the way of life? The phrase "when I was an Indian," not infrequently heard in Latin America, obviously refers to a sociological, rather than a racial, classification.

One author estimated in 1949 that 38 per cent of the Latin Americans were mestizo, 33 per cent white, 28 per cent Negro or mulatto, and 1 per cent Asiatic.[2] Another scholar, writing in 1955, concluded that of the twenty republics, four (Bolivia, Ecuador, Guatemala, and Peru) are predominantly Indian, eight (Chile, Colombia, El Salvador, Honduras, Mexico, Nicaragua, Paraguay, and Venezuela) are mestizo, three (Cuba, the Dominican Republic, and Panama) are Negro and mestizo, three (Argentina, Costa Rica, and Uruguay) are white, one (Haiti) Negro, and one (Brazil) is in a class by itself because of its unique mixtures of white, Negro, and Indian–white–Negro.[3] From the middle of the nineteenth century until the close of the First World War over 60 million Europeans migrated to the Americas. Almost 50 million of them settled in the United States or Canada, and 11 to 12 million in the Americas south of the Rio Grande. The largest fraction of these, 11 per cent, went to Argentina, making that nation, like Uruguay, an immigrant people. Slightly over 7 per cent went to Brazil. The

[2] George Wythe, *Industry in Latin America* (rev. ed.; New York: Columbia University Press, 1950).

[3] Hubert Herring, *A History of Latin America from the Beginnings to the Present* (New York: Alfred A. Knopf, Inc., 1955), pp. 17–18.

great majority of these immigrants to Latin America came from Spain, Italy, and Portugal. Smaller, but significant, numbers came from Germany, China, Japan, and elsewhere. Since the 1920's, however, immigration has been unimportant as a source of new population in Latin America, despite the efforts of such nations as Venezuela and Argentina to encourage it.

OTHER CHARACTERISTICS OF THE PEOPLE. Before turning to a brief discussion of the people of the various nations of Latin America, a few other general observations should be made. They will be referred to again in discussing the Latin American economy, but reference to them now will help to understand what kind of person the "typical" Latin American is.

The standard of living of the majority is very low by North American standards. In 1952, when the per capita gross national product was 2,200 dollars in the United States, it was above 600 dollars in only one Latin American nation (Argentina), below 200 dollars in eleven, and only 62 dollars in Haiti. The existence of large numbers of "have-nots" in Latin America is perhaps widely known, but the extent of this poverty is not as commonly realized. A study made in 1945 concluded that two-thirds, if not more, of all Latin Americans are undernourished, to the point of being victims of starvation in some areas. One-half of the population, it was said, suffered from infectious or diet-deficiency diseases; two-thirds worked under semi-feudal conditions of land tenure and land use; the living conditions of the majority were peculiarly unstable, owing to the economy's monocultural character; and the overwhelming majority of the agricultural population was landless, with little hope of obtaining land.[4]

Changes have occurred in the intervening twelve years, but it is still true in 1958 that many "typical" Latin Americans are poorly fed, poorly clothed, poorly housed, lack even a minimum of social security, and have even less real social and cultural equality. These facts color the political life of most of the nations. More than one Latin American writer has observed that the political leader who urges "Follow me, I will lead you to a better way of life" will get some recruits immediately in all countries, and many followers in some of them, because for so many millions any change is at least possibly a change for the better.

MEXICO AND CENTRAL AMERICA. More than one-fifth (22 per cent) of Latin America's population live in Costa Rica, El Salvador,

---

[4] George H. Soule, *et al., Latin America in the Future World* (New York: Rinehart & Co., Inc., 1945).

Guatemala, Honduras, Mexico, Nicaragua, and Panama. Mexico, with just under 29 million people, is the second most populous Latin American nation, while Costa Rica and Panama, each with less than a million inhabitants, are nineteenth and twentieth. In all seven nations the population is predominantly rural, the proportion ranging from 57 to 75 per cent. The rate of population growth per year is above 2.5 per cent in five of the nations and above 3 per cent in two. With the exception of Costa Rica, which is perhaps 95 per cent or more white, the estimated percentage of white population in each of them is small, ranging from 2 per cent to 17 per cent. Mestizos constitute the major population bloc in El Salvador, Honduras, Mexico, and Nicaragua. In Guatemala the Indians are in a majority, and Panama is predominantly mestizo and mulatto. El Salvador is the only republic of this region with a high population density—274.1 per square mile. In Nicaragua this ratio is 21.1.

As has been indicated, geography and climate conspire to cause an unequal distribution of the population in many Latin American countries. This effect may be seen in the nations of this region. Almost one-half of the Costa Ricans live in the highland area. Three of the fourteen Departments in El Salvador contain more than one-third of the national population, while in Honduras one-third of the people live in three of the seventeen Departments. The population in Nicaragua is much more equally distributed throughout the nation, although the Caribbean coastal area is sparsely inhabited. Panama shows a great concentration of people near its large coastal cities. The greatest population density in Mexico is in the central highlands, although since the turn of the century a movement has taken place from the agricultural areas to the seven largest cities and the border areas of the north. Between 1900 and 1956 the population of these latter areas increased from 2.3 million to 7.8 million.

THE CARIBBEAN STATES. About 7 per cent of all Latin Americans live in the three republics of Cuba, the Dominican Republic, and Haiti. In all three the population density is more than double that of the United States, where density is 51.0 per square mile. Haiti has the highest population density of all the nations of Latin America, 318.7 per square mile. Three-quarters or more of the people of these island republics live in rural areas, and the population is well distributed on the land surface, without the abnormal degree of concentration in a few urban areas encountered in some nations. More than nine-tenths of all Haitians are Negroes, and Negroes or mulattoes constitute a majority in the other two coun-

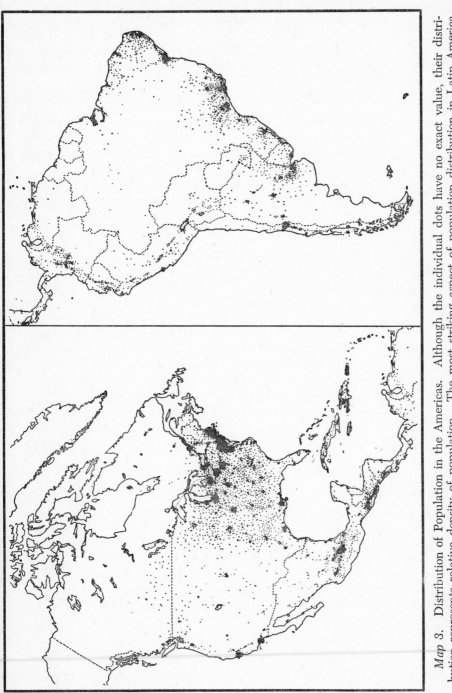

Map 3. Distribution of Population in the Americas. Although the individual dots have no exact value, their distribution represents relative density of population. The most striking aspect of population distribution in Latin America is the concentration along the Atlantic and Caribbean coast lines and in the temperate highland plateaus. The United States and Canada are included for purposes of comparison.

tries. The rate of population growth is about at the average for all of Latin America—just under 3 per cent per year. In the light of the population density in these island republics, however, this population expansion presents troublesome social and economic problems.

NORTHERN SOUTH AMERICA. Colombia and Venezuela contain about 11 per cent of the Latin American population. In point of number of people, Colombia is the fourth largest of the republics and Venezuela is eighth. The rate of population growth per year is higher in this region than in the other five. The number of Colombians is growing at the rate of 3.4 per cent per year, while that of Venezuela increases at the rate of 4 per cent. In no other Latin American country is population growing at this rate. The increase in the United States is only 1.5 per cent per year. Over one-half of all Venezuelans are urban dwellers, but almost two-thirds of the Colombians live in rural surroundings. Racially the people of these two republics are very much alike. About one-fifth are white, about two-thirds mestizo (including mulatto strains in the coastal regions), and roughly 7 per cent are Indian.

Population distribution follows the pattern typical in much of Latin America. The majority of Colombians live in those areas having an elevation of between 4,000 and 9,000 feet. Three of Colombia's ten Departments are in this zone, and they have almost one-third of the nation's total population within their borders. Similarly, in Venezuela, one-third of all its citizens live in three of its twenty states. Venezuela is one of the few Latin American nations in which immigration is an important source of new population. More than 40,000 immigrants have settled there since 1939.

BRAZIL. As was noted earlier, Brazilians constitute about one-third of the population of Latin America. The Brazilian ethnic pattern is unique, and far from homogeneous. Brazilians are a mixture of white, Negro, and Indian, with various blendings of the three strains. The nation shows some distinct ethnic areas within its borders. The Amazon valley is largely Indian, the central coast from Pernambuco to Bahia is about 60 per cent Negroid, the northeast plateau, or *sertão* (backlands), area is mainly mestizo, and about three-quarters of the people in the southern states are white, many of them descendants of recent immigrants.

The rate of population growth is 2.4 per cent per year, largely from natural increase. In the past, however, immigration was an important factor in the rapid expansion of the Brazilian population. Between 1820 and 1945 almost 5 million Europeans migrated to

Brazil, and from the close of World War II until 1949 about 30,000 displaced persons found homes there.

About one-third of all Brazilians are urban dwellers, and two-thirds live in the rural areas of this vast land. Population density is 17.8 per square mile. Brazil shows to a rather marked degree an unequal distribution of population within its borders. Just about one-half of its people live within a few hundred miles of the Atlantic coast, in the four largest states (out of twenty states, the Federal District, and five national territories). One of these states, São Paulo, now has a population of nearly 10 million.

THE RIVER PLATE REPUBLICS. About 13 per cent of Latin America's population lives in Argentina, Paraguay, and Uruguay. Argentina, like Costa Rica, has a predominantly white population. The number of mestizos is small, the colonial mestizo population having been absorbed in the nineteenth- and twentieth-century immigrations. Less than 3 per cent of the Argentines are Indians, who live for the most part in the northern and northwestern areas, with a few in the far south. The annual rate of population growth is 2.7 per cent and in the last two decades has been accounted for mainly by natural increase. Until quite recently, however, immigration had great importance in the accretion of the nation's people. No other Latin American state has received so high a proportion of immigrants. During the decade from 1901 to 1910, 1,764,103 immigrants arrived; 1,204,919 came between 1911 and 1921; and 1,397,415 between 1921 and 1930.

Argentina is the most urbanized of all of the Latin American republics; almost two-thirds of its people live in cities or towns. Several provincial cities exceed 100,000 in population, while the metropolitan region of Buenos Aires (including a large urban area surrounding the capital) is the home of approximately one-fourth of all Argentines. If this same ratio held true in the United States, the metropolitan region of New York would have about 40 million inhabitants.

Racially, Uruguay's people are much like those of Argentina, with perhaps a slightly higher percentage of Indian blood derived from the colonial mestizo population. The rate of annual population growth, 1.2 per cent per year, compares with that of Bolivia, the lowest in the continent. Perhaps no other Latin American country has so large a proportion of its population concentrated in one urban area, over one-third of all Uruguayans living within the metropolitan area of Montevideo.

Paraguay is ethnically unlike the other two River Plate republics.

Over nine-tenths of all Paraguayans are mestizos, between 2 and 3 per cent are Indians, and the remaining less than 10 per cent are white. The rate of population growth, 2.1 per cent per year, is slightly below the average for Latin America. Two-thirds of the people live in rural areas, mainly in eastern Paraguay. Asunción, the capital, is the only large city.

WESTERN SOUTH AMERICA. Bolivia, Chile, Ecuador, and Peru claim 14.5 per cent of Latin America's people. In three of these four nations—Bolivia, Ecuador, and Peru—40 per cent or more of the population is Indian. The proportion of white population ranges from 13 per cent in Bolivia to 30 per cent in Chile. The mestizo proportion is high, possibly as high as 65 per cent in Chile. In Bolivia and Chile, the rate of population growth is below the Latin American average, in Peru it is average, and in Ecuador it is considerably above the average rate for Latin America. In Ecuador, Peru, and Bolivia, the fact that many of the Indians speak only Quechua or Aymara sets them apart from other citizens, making it difficult to incorporate them into national social, economic, and political organization.

THE "TYPICAL" LATIN AMERICAN. What, then, is the "typical Latin American"? In Mexico he is probably a mestizo, in Argentina a sophisticated urban dweller, in Haiti a Negro farmer, an *altiplano* Indian in Bolivia. He is most likely to speak Spanish in Guadalajara, Spanish greatly modified by a *porteño* accent in Buenos Aires, French in the Artibonite valley of Haiti, Portuguese in Recife, and Quechua in Huancayo. He may live in a country which is much more urbanized than is the United States, or in one in which three-quarters or more of all of the people are farmers. His standard of living may be on a level about a third as high as that of the United States, or on one which is one-tenth or even less of that which North Americans enjoy. His country may have been heavily influenced by immigration from Europe, or relatively untouched by peoples from other lands.

His surname may be Martínez, Smith, Figueiredo, LaFond, Antonelli, or even Kubitschek.

He is a "typical Latin American" because he lives in that area of the world which lies between the Rio Grande and the Straits of Magellan.

Suggestions for Reading

A standard reference on Latin American geography is Preston James, *Latin America* (rev. ed.; New York: Odyssey Press, 1950). Several of the chapters in R. H. Whitbeck and F. E. Williams, *Economic Geography of South America* (New York: The

McGraw-Hill Book Co., 1940) deal with the effects of geographical factors on the economy of South America. Part I of William L. Schurz' excellent book, *Latin America* (rev. ed.; New York: E. P. Dutton & Co., 1949) is entirely devoted to the land. Two chapters of Simon G. Hanson, *Economic Development in Latin America* (Washington, D.C.: The Inter-American Affairs Press, 1951), Chapter 3, "The Physical Resources" and Chapter 4, "Organization for Production: The Land," discuss the land in terms of economic problems and development.

No comprehensive study of Latin American population has been published. Part III of William Schurz' *Latin America* gives a good, brief summary of ethnic composition, which is expanded in his *This New World* (New York: E. P. Dutton & Co., 1954). See Chapters II, "The Indian," III, "The Spaniard," V, "The Negro," VI, "The Foreigner," and X, "The Brazilian." Especially noteworthy are the article by Kingsley Davis, "Latin America's Multiplying Peoples," *Foreign Affairs*, XXV (July, 1947), 643–645, reprinted in Asher N. Christensen, *The Evolution of Latin American Government* (New York: Henry Holt & Co., 1951), and the article by T. L. Smith, "Current Population Trends in Latin America," *The American Journal of Sociology*, LXII (January, 1957) 399–406.

The student may also consult the various general works on individual countries, such as those in the series published by the British Royal Institute of International Affairs, which usually include chapters on the land and the people.

Chapter 3

A Changing Society
and Economy

Land and people do not act in a vacuum to shape political institutions and practices. The way of life of the people, their ethical and religious values and views, and the fabric of their social organization also exert a formative influence on their politics. Similarly, the use they make of the land and its resources, their standards of living, and their avenues of productive employment have a direct bearing on the manner in which governments are organized and political activities conducted. To such questions as these, therefore, we must now turn our attention.

The Latin American Way of Life

RELIGION. Many North Americans, and especially the Catholics of the United States, are puzzled by the fact that Latin America, while overwhelmingly Catholic, has had many bitter Church–state conflicts, growing out of strong, sometimes violent, anti-clerical movements. To understand this seeming contradiction it is necessary to look first at the position of the Church during the three centuries of the colonial period.

The Church held a privileged position in colonial society, partly because of the politico-religious institutions of Spain and Portugal, and partly because of certain developments in America. It was closely linked to the state in Spain and Portugal, owing to the fact that the wars against the Moors for the reconquest of the peninsula were in effect religious crusades, and because of the leading role Spain played in the Catholic Counter-Reform. In America the

50

Spanish crown used the Church as an instrument of colonization and generously supported a vigorous missionary movement to Christianize the natives. Ecclesiastical dignitaries were not only the spiritual advisers of governmental officials, but also held important civil positions in Spain and Portugal, as well as in America.

The Church was also powerful economically. It became a large landowner, partly through crown grants, and partly through gifts and bequests of adherents. It has been estimated that by 1800 the total property of the secular and lay clergy in Mexico amounted to not less than half of all the real estate in the colony.

The Church was not blind to the social problems and injustices of the colonial period. From the earliest days of the Conquest, the clergy took an active part in establishing schools. They founded and maintained hospitals and other welfare agencies, worked unceasingly to better the unfortunate lot of the Indian, and sought to alleviate the conditions under which Negro slaves lived and worked. Christian missionaries were largely responsible for the "reform laws" promulgated by the Council of the Indies in the sixteenth century, thus gaining the fealty of the Indians which the Church still enjoys. Such activities also earned many churchmen the hostility of the Spanish and Portuguese settlers.

Because of the particularly close relationship between Church and state in the Spanish empire, many of the clergy supported the Spanish cause during the independence movements. It must be noted, however, that many of them, especially the lower clergy, supported and sometimes led these revolutionary movements. After independence, the Church naturally opposed Liberal party programs which threatened its position in society, including the substitution of public schools for church schools, the secularization of the family, public, as opposed to ecclesiastical, welfare programs, and land reforms.

Thus, throughout the nineteenth and well into the twentieth century in some countries, the Church allied itself with conservative political parties against the anti-clerical Liberals. It has often been said that during this period *caudillos* rose to political power in alliance with landowners, the army, and the Church. Yet these anti-clerical Liberals were usually not hostile to Christianity. In fact, they often thought of themselves as particularly devout Catholics, intent on reforming the position of the Church in society. Benito Juárez of Mexico in the nineteenth and José Batlle y Ordóñez of Uruguay in the twentieth century, both strongly anti-clerical, were devout Catholics from their own point of view.

The position of the Church varies considerably among the twenty republics today. In Peru and Colombia, in spite of its official separation from the state, its position remains "strong" in the older sense. In Chile, Uruguay, Argentina, and Brazil its status is more like that of the Church in Italy or France. In many nations, the Church is still a major educational force, particularly for the education of the middle and upper classes. At the other extreme are such nations as Mexico, where church schools cannot legally exist. Competing religious faiths may freely enter into most Latin American countries and freely conduct missionary activities; their adherents and converts suffer no social, economic, or political discriminations. But in some countries, such as Colombia since World War II, official or quasi-official opposition to other than Catholic religious activities occasionally appears. The number of adherents to other religious groups is small, although Jewish synagogues and Protestant churches of various denominations are found in most cities.

Protestant missionaries entered Latin America in the mid-nineteenth century, reaching the peak of their activity in the first three decades of the twentieth. They brought with them the growing social consciousness of churches in the United States, and their schools and hospitals contributed to movements for social reform and to a strong student movement in the years which followed. Catholic missionaries from the United States appeared somewhat later, bringing something of the social consciousness of the Catholic Church in the United States, which historically has been close to the interests of workers. These influences from the United States may well have helped to stimulate the religious revival and the Catholic Action groups which have gained strength in Latin America since World War II, emphasizing the social Christianity of the encyclicals *Rerum Novarum* and *Quadrigesimo Anno*. Some influence in this direction also stems from Spain and Portugal, and some has come from within Latin America. This change in the Church has been occurring even in Mexico, where it would have seemed impossible in the 1920's, when a particularly violent revival of the old controversy between Church and state took place.

COLONIAL SOCIETY. At the time of the discovery of America, Spain and Portugal were just emerging from a feudal organization of society. Wealth and prestige were in the hands of a small elite of landowning families, which tended to prefer living in the cities, leaving the management of their estates to major-domos. The peasants who worked the land, constituting the bulk of the population, lived in poverty, with little hope of bettering their socio-economic position.   Class stratification was thus a major factor in social life.

The Spanish and Portuguese empires in America developed a somewhat similar social structure.   In accordance with the expanding mercantilism of the sixteenth century, crown policy in both Spain and Portugal sought to minimize the older feudal aspects of the institutions transplanted to America, preferring a society more in line with an economy based upon trade.   But their colonists in America successfully resisted these royal policies to a large degree. They developed instead a highly stratified society having some feudal aspects derived from the homelands, and other characteristics arising from the conquest of the native peoples and from Negro slavery.

These creole landowners, like their home-land cousins, preferred to live in Buenos Aires, Rio de Janeiro, Mexico City, or Bogotá. Their estates were managed by overseers, and the work was done by peasants, sometimes Spanish or creole but more often mestizos, Indians, or Negroes.   The Negroes were slaves, and the Indians worked under conditions little better than those of slavery.   Spanish and Portuguese peasant immigrants, on the other hand, began to think of themselves as belonging to an upper class as soon as they reached America, and most of them soon became landowners.   Thus Indians and Negroes stood at the bottom of the social ladder, separated from the rest of society not only by class lines but by basic ethnic differences as well.

SOCIAL STRUCTURE SINCE INDEPENDENCE.   The wars of independence did little to change this basic social pattern, and it changed little during the nineteenth century.   Even in the mid-twentieth century its remnants are visible in some degree in all the nations. The farm worker, *peón, campesino,* or *cholo,* lives on the ragged edge of security.   His livelihood is dependent on the owner, or *patrón,* who also tends to influence his social and political behavior. Under such circumstances, some Latin Americans have despaired of achieving real political democracy, since even today in some countries most of the people are conditioned to remove their hats and bow humbly when passing the *patrón.*

Even the industrialization and urban growth of the present century have not brought to the industrial worker the same opportunity to better his socio-economic position which industrialization brought to North American workers.   This is in part due to the prevailing attitude toward manual labor.   The culture of the United States accords a high place to the person who has worked his way up from section hand to railroad executive or from office boy to corporation president, but a common Latin American attitude is still expressed by the remark attributed to Cortez, "I did not come to work with my hands like a peasant." Furthermore, the system has fed upon itself. Wealth, prestige, and political power have been concentrated in a small ruling class, which has either opposed basic social and economic changes, or grudgingly assented to them under pressure.

The society places a great emphasis on family connections, family cohesion, and family loyalty. It is not only quite proper for an official to aid his relatives when he holds an important position, but it may even be considered a kind of moral obligation to do so. The prevalence of nepotism in government and the lack of a merit system in the civil service in most of the nations have sometimes been attributed to this family attitude. Quite commonly the roster of employees in any government department includes many branches and even twigs of the family tree of the minister. North Americans have often wondered why Latin Americans are so indifferent to the practice of the *mordida,* or bribe (literally the "bite"), so common among governmental officials, and to the fact that public officials often enrich themselves at the expense of the public treasury. Some sociologists have believed that the importance of the family in Latin American society helps to explain this cynicism toward government and its officials, as well as the general public apathy to political events.

This social system produces great extremes of wealth and poverty, discourages the growth of a stabilizing middle class, and perpetuates rigid class stratification. These latter social factors, in turn, increase the difficulty of the problems faced by political leaders, for it is easier to make workable political compromises in a society which is less rigidly confined within hard and fast class lines. Hence democratic government has made most progress in those nations experiencing rapid growth of labor unions, basic changes in the educational systems, and the growth of social insurance and other public welfare programs. Class structure is breaking down in Latin America today, and social mobility is increasing with these changes. But the old structure persists with enough strength to retard these transformations, and in some countries virtually to prevent them.

SCHOOLS AND EDUCATION. How much and what kind of education does the "typical" Latin American receive? Perhaps the first thing to be noted is the great variation among the several nations in educational programs, in the numbers attending primary and secondary schools, and in literacy levels. Changes in the nature and scope of Latin American education are coming rapidly, but the present picture has many dark spots. Educational statistics are not very dependable in some countries, but the best available figures, as in Table III, show degrees of national literacy ranging from 97 per cent in Argentina to 11 per cent in Haiti. Enrollment in the primary schools varies from 145.1 per 1,000 population in Costa Rica to 53.1 in Haiti, while secondary-school enrollment ranges from 15 per 1,000 population in Uruguay to 0.6 in Honduras.

Despite these wide differences, some generalizations can be made. The school systems of Latin America fall into three patterns at all three levels—primary, secondary, and higher education. In some nations, Church-supported schools are found at one or more of these three levels. Others, such as Peru or Chile, have what might be called a dual system of state or public schools and Church schools. In a few nations, such as Mexico, where sectarian schools are prohibited by law, the educational institutions at all levels are mainly public.

If the "typical" Latin American is an urban dweller, his school opportunities are greater than if he lives in the countryside, because in most countries rural schools were neglected until well into the twentieth century. In Venezuela, for example, whose population was more than 75 per cent rural in 1936, the national budget as late as 1945 allocated only 3 per cent of all educational funds to rural schools. All of the republics have compulsory attendance laws, but these are limited to primary education and vary considerably in the ages to which attendance is required. Many rural areas are so poorly supplied with schools that it is impossible to enforce attendance laws. Finally, the low standards of living force families to take their children out of school at an early age so that they may help support the family. In general, those countries having higher per capita income levels are more successful in enforcing school attendance laws. A vigorous rural education movement was launched in Mexico in the 1920's, and a crusade to eliminate illiteracy has since been undertaken in many other countries. But most Latin American children still look forward to no more than three to six years of schooling, and many receive none at all.

Table III also shows a rapid rate of "dropping out" between primary and secondary school. About 40 pupils per 1,000 population attend secondary schools in the United States. Uruguay, with the best record in all Latin America, has only half as many, while in Honduras less than one pupil per 1,000 population goes on to secondary school. The "drop out" between high school and institutions

TABLE III.   EDUCATION AND

	Population[a]		Primary Schools[b]				
			Enrollment				
	Total (thousands)	Rank	Total (thousands)	Per 1000 Pop.		Teachers per 1000 Pop.	
				No.	Rank	No.	Rank
Mexico and Central America							
Costa Rica	951	19	138	145.1	1	6.03	1
El Salvador	2,193	15	213	97.1	10	2.60	10
Guatemala	3,149	12	199	63.2	18	2.60	11
Honduras	1,660	16	116	69.9	16	2.18	15
Mexico	28,849	2	2,926	101.4	9	2.70	7
Nicaragua	1,202	18	84	69.9	17	2.80	6
Panama	886	20	125	141.1	2	4.29	3
Total for region	38,890		3,801				
Caribbean States							
Cuba	5,807	7	530	91.3	12	3.87	5
Dominican Republic	2,404	14	259	107.7	7	2.08	17
Haiti	3,506	10	186	53.1	19	2.30	14
Total for region	11,717		975				
Northern South America							
Colombia	12,657	4	1,073	84.8	13	1.64	18
Venezuela	5,774	8	609	105.5	8	2.62	9
Total for region	18,431		1,682				
Brazil							
Brazil	58,456	1	4,359	74.6	14	2.17	16
River Plate Republics							
Argentina	19,108	3	2,120	110.9	4	5.53	2
Paraguay	1,565	17	—	—	—	4.26	4
Uruguay	2,525	13	273	108.1	6	—	—
Total for region	23,198		—				
Western South America							
Bolivia	3,198	11	234	73.2	15	2.33	13
Chile	6,774	6	806	119.0	3	—	—
Ecuador	3,567	9	346	97.0	11	2.41	12
Peru	9,396	5	1,023	108.9	5	2.66	8
Total for region	22,935		2,409				
United States	167,000		22,367	133.9		—	

A dash indicates that data are not available.

SOURCES: "Statistical Abstract of Latin America for 1955," prepared at the University of California at Los Angeles; and Foreign Operations Administration, *Report on the Economic Situation in Latin America* (Washington, 1954).

NOTE: Data are for various years. Because of this and other differences in the bases used in gathering census data, care should be exercised in making comparisons.

[a] Data on population are for 1955, except for Ecuador, Guatemala, Haiti, and Mexico (1954), Cuba and Uruguay (1953).

[b] Data on primary schools are for 1953, except for Argentina (1949), Dominican Republic (1950), Cuba (1951), Ecuador, Mexico, and Nicaragua (1952), Costa Rica

LITERACY IN LATIN AMERICA

Secondary Schools —Enrollment[c]			Higher Education —Enrollment[d]			Literacy[e]	
Total (thousands)	Per 1000 Pop.		Total (thousands)	Per 1000 Pop.		Rate (per cent)	Rank
	No.	Rank		No.	Rank		
13	13.7	3	—	—	—	79	3
12	5.5	10	—	—	—	42	14
10	3.2	17	—	—	—	30	18
1	0.6	20	1	0.6	15	35	16
86	3.0	18	55	1.9	5	57	8
5	4.2	12	1	0.8	14	37	15
13	14.7	2	2	2.3	4	72	5
140			—				
21	3.6	16	17	2.9	3	76	4
10	4.2	13	3	1.2	10	43	13
8	2.3	19	1	0.3	16	11	19
39			21				
66	5.2	11	12	0.9	12	63	7
23	4.0	14	5	0.9	13	49	10
89			17				
536	9.2	5	64	1.1	11	49	11
70	3.7	15	79	4.1	2	97	1
11	7.0	8	2	1.3	9	68	6
38	15.0	1	12	4.8	1	—	—
119			93				
24	7.5	7	—	—	—	31	17
87	12.8	4	10	1.5	7	80	2
21	5.9	9	5	1.4	8	56	9
84	8.9	6	16	1.7	6	43	12
216			—				
6,577	39.4		2,533	15.2		97	

and El Salvador (1954). The figures for Bolivia and the Dominican Republic are for public schools only.

[c] Data on secondary schools are for 1953, except for Argentina (1950), Guatemala (1951), Bolivia, Ecuador, Mexico, Nicaragua, and Uruguay (1952), Brazil, Chile, Costa Rica, and El Salvador (1954).

[d] Data on higher education are for 1953, except for Chile (1949), Argentina (1950), Cuba, Mexico, and Uruguay (1951), Ecuador, Nicaragua, and Venezuela (1952), Brazil and the Dominican Republic (1954).

[e] Data are for 1950, except for Argentina (1947) and Chile (1952).

of higher education is even more marked. These "drop out" data reflect the low economic levels in many Latin American countries. Families cannot afford to send their sons and daughters to high school, much less to the university. This limitation of secondary and higher education to the upper income levels tends to give a class character to high schools and to the university.

For over a generation Latin Americans have been criticizing their education for being too academic in its emphasis and unrelated to the needs of the majority of the pupils. An Indian boy from a village in the Peruvian highlands, who will probably live as his ancestors have lived for generations, receives the same kind of schooling in Huancayo as the urban boy of a middle- or upper-class family in Lima. At the high-school level this purely academic emphasis is the more evident, since the secondary school is largely devoted to training those boys and girls whose family position and wealth will enable them to go on to the university. Although a shift toward vocational and agricultural education has appeared in the twentieth century, secondary education in most of Latin America is still largely academic.

One final observation may be made concerning education. In all of the republics, including those organized on a federal basis, the control of educational policy at all levels, and the major part of the financing of public education, is centralized in the national government. The independent local school district so familiar in the United States, and the consequent control over its educational system and program by the local community, are rarely encountered. The national ministry of education largely determines educational programs, decides upon school construction, and regulates school finance. This centralized control has sometimes deterred the building, equipping, and staffing of rural schools, and has made it more difficult to develop programs adapted to the needs of students.

STANDARDS OF LIVING. In these days of technical assistance and financial aid to the economies of underdeveloped countries much is heard about the low standards of living in the less fortunate parts of the world. Despite this wide discussion, however, few North Americans really perceive how low these standards are in some parts of Latin America, for example. The "typical" Latin American has a living standard much lower than that of the "typical" North American, or that of the "typical" western European, at least in Britain, France, or Scandinavia. If he resides in Haiti, Ecuador, or Bolivia, his standard of living is as low as that of some of the nations of Asia or the Middle East. Even if he is a citizen of one of the more prosperous countries, such as Argentina or Venezuela, his standard of living is significantly lower than that of the average North American. The per capita gross national product (in 1952 U.S. dollars) ranged from 688 dollars in Argentina to 62 dollars in Haiti, as compared with 2,200 dollars in the United States (see Table VI). In two of the twenty republics the per capita share was less than 100 dollars, and in one-half of them it was below 200. It was above 400 dollars in only three.

Table IV shows some of the results of this low per capita productive capacity. In 1955 there were 289 automobiles per 1,000 population in the United States. Venezuela, which stood at the top of the list in Latin America, had only 20 per 1,000. There are 316 telephones per 1,000 people in the United States, but only 56 in Argentina. In the United States there are 7.5 radio sets for every ten persons; in Argentina, 1.5. This ratio drops to four radios for every 1,000 persons in Haiti. If the average Latin American wishes to use a telephone, he must use a public one or one at his place of employment. If he wishes to hear a radio program, he goes to one of the numerous public parks or plazas where broadcasts are constantly heard (usually at a high decibel level).

When he travels, and only a few can afford to, he finds transportation facilities inadequate in most of the nations, as well as very expensive. The United States has several times the railway miles of all Latin America (see Table IV). Moreover, one-third of Latin America's miles of railway is in one country—Argentina (see Map 4, p. 63). Good highways are also lacking. It is true that the area is well traversed by airliners that take off from and land at well-planned and magnificently appointed air terminals. But this form of transportation, at least in most of the nations, is far beyond the means of most people. The Latin American who must travel usually goes on foot, by burro, or in crowded buses. The American tourist who is surprised to see so many Mexicans, Guatemalans, or Bolivians walking along the highways ought to understand that these people walk because they are poor, not because it is picturesque, or because it makes a fine "color shot" to show to friends back home.

The lack of adequate communication facilities is only partly to be ascribed to the low economic levels. As noted earlier, geography, topography, and climate have conspired to make the building of railroads and highways difficult and expensive. Yet the raising of the economic levels of the region generally is partly dependent on the expansion and improvement of the transportation network. Moreover, while radios, telephones, and automobiles are not indisputable evidences of a highly developed civilization and culture, the lack

TABLE IV.   THE LEVEL

	Railway Miles		Highway Miles			Automobiles		
	Total (thou-sands)	Rank	Total (thou-sands)	Improved (thou-sands)	Rank	Total (thou-sands)	Per 1000 Pop. No.	Rank
Mexico and Central America								
Costa Rica	0.4	15	—	1.0	13	8	8.4	7
El Salvador	0.4	16	3.9	1.2	12	8	3.6	12
Guatemala	0.6	13	4.0	3.2	8	9	2.9	13
Honduras	0.6	14	0.9	—	—	2	1.2	19
Mexico	14.5	3	44.9	13.2	4	263	9.1	6
Nicaragua	0.3	17	0.7	—	—	3	2.5	15
Panama	0.2	19	1.0	0.7	15	11	12.4	5
Total for region	17.0					304		
Caribbean States								
Cuba	3.7	5	—	2.1	11	107	18.4	3
Dominican Republic	0.9	10	2.0	0.7	14	6	2.5	14
Haiti	0.2	18	2.0	—	—	4	1.1	20
Total for region	4.8					117		
Northern South America								
Colombia	2.1	7	11.0	8.5	5	59	4.7	11
Venezuela	0.6	12	12.0	4.2	7	120	20.8	1
Total for region	2.7					179		
Brazil								
Brazil	22.1	2	173.0	44.7	2	368	6.3	9
River Plate Republics								
Argentina	26.6	1	259.0	46.7	1	314	16.4	4
Paraguay	0.3	20	4.0	0.5	17	3	1.9	16
Uruguay	1.9	8	25.0	3.0	9	49	19.4	2
Total for region	28.8					366		
Western South America								
Bolivia	1.6	9	8.9	0.6	16	6	1.9	17
Chile	6.6	4	32.0	26.8	3	46	6.8	8
Ecuador	0.7	11	8.0	2.9	10	6	1.7	18
Peru	2.8	6	22.0	8.0	6	44	4.7	10
Total for region	11.7					102		
United States	221.7		—	3,366.7		48,324	289.4	

A dash indicates that data are not available.

SOURCES: "Statistical Abstract of Latin America for 1955," prepared at the University of California at Los Angeles; *United Nations Statistical Yearbook, 1955;* and Foreign Operations Administration, *Report on the Economic Situation in Latin America* (Washington, 1954).

NOTE: Data based on statistics for various years during the period 1949–1955.

of COMMUNICATIONS

Buses and Trucks			Telephones			Radios		
Total (thousands)	Per 1000 Pop.		Total (thousands)	Per 1000 Pop.		Total (thousands)	Per 1000 Pop.	
	No.	Rank		No.	Rank		No.	Rank
5	5.3	9	11	11.6	9	23	24.2	13
6	2.7	14	10	4.6	12	21	9.6	19
8	2.5	15	9	2.9	19	36	11.4	18
4	2.4	18	7	4.2	13	26	15.7	15
211	7.3	5	349	12.1	8	1,220	42.3	9
3	2.5	16	4	3.3	18	16	13.3	17
4	4.5	11	18	20.3	5	81	91.4	4
241			408			1,423		
45	7.7	4	142	24.5	3	700	120.5	3
6	2.5	17	9	3.7	15	100	41.6	10
4	1.1	20	4	1.1	20	14	4.0	20
55			155			814		
69	5.5	8	144	11.4	10	500	39.5	11
86	14.9	2	98	17.0	6	200	34.6	12
155			242			700		
352	6.0	7	746	12.8	7	2,500	42.8	8
163	8.5	3	1,080	56.5	1	2,900	151.8	1
3	1.9	19	6	3.8	14	35	22.4	14
43	17.1	1	109	43.2	2	362	143.4	2
209			1,195			3,297		
15	4.7	10	11	3.4	17	150	46.9	7
44	6.5	6	148	21.8	4	550	81.2	5
15	4.2	13	12	3.4	16	50	14.0	16
40	4.3	12	70	7.4	11	500	53.2	6
114			241			1,250		
9,552	57.2		52,800	316.2		124,000		

Continued on next page

TABLE IV. THE LEVEL OF COMMUNICATIONS (*Continued*)

	TV Sets Total (thou- sands)	Newspapers			
		No. of Dailies	Daily Circulation		
			Total (thousands)	Per 1000 Pop. No.	Rank
Mexico and Central America					
Costa Rica	—	5	78	91	5
El Salvador	—	10	70	33	14
Guatemala	—	9	83	27	15
Honduras	—	5	30	19	18
Mexico	100	162	1,300	48	12
Nicaragua	—	11	56	51	10
Panama	—	11	99	111	3
Total for region		213	1,716		
Caribbean States					
Cuba	200	37	588	101	4
Dominican Republic	5	5	54	24	16
Haiti	—	6	12	4	20
Total for region		48	654		
Northern South America					
Colombia	15	37	650	57	8
Venezuela	—	28	400	71	7
Total for region		65	1,050		
Brazil					
Brazil	130	217	2,932	51	9
River Plate Republics					
Argentina	125	341	2,896	155	2
Paraguay	—	3	17	12	19
Uruguay	—	25	550	233	1
Total for region		369	3,463		
Western South America					
Bolivia	—	12	70	23	17
Chile	—	43	465	79	6
Ecuador	—	24	167	50	11
Peru	—	60	350	40	13
Total for region		139	1,052		
United States	36,180	1,765	55,072	339	

A dash indicates that data are not available.

SOURCES: "Statistical Abstract of Latin America for 1955," prepared at the University of California at Los Angeles; *United Nations Statistical Yearbook, 1955*; and Foreign Operations Administration, *Report on the Economic Situation in Latin America* (Washington, 1954).

NOTE: Data based on statistics for various years during the period 1949–1955.

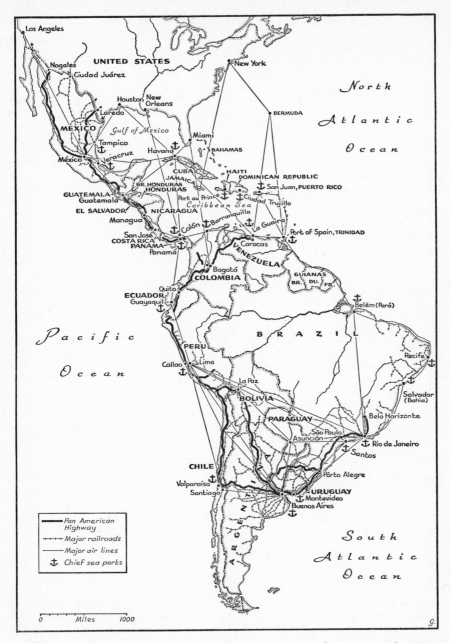

Map 4. Transportation in Latin America. Note the gaps in the Pan American Highway in Costa Rica, Panama, Colombia, Ecuador, and Brazil (highway in the first two areas under construction), and in the railway which will connect São Paulo, Brazil, wth Bolivia. Northern South America, the interior of Brazil, and the Atlantic coastal areas of Central America exhibit the most striking lack of surface transportation development.

63

TABLE V.   THE LEVEL OF

	Gross National Product Per Capita (1952)		Caloric Intake Per Capita	Infant Mortality [a]	
	US $	Rank		Deaths per 1000 Births	Rank
Mexico and Central America					
Costa Rica	203	9	—	101	14
El Salvador	167	14	—	74	7
Guatemala	182	12	—	88	11
Honduras	134	16	2,030	60	2
Mexico	199	10	2,210	81	9
Nicaragua	168	13	—	75	8
Panama	382	5	—	52	1
Total for region					
Caribbean States					
Cuba	454	3	2,730	85	10
Dominican Republic	189	11	—	68	6
Haiti	62	20	—	—	—
Total for region					
Northern South America					
Colombia	231	8	2,400	103	16
Venezuela	457	2	2,200	68	5
Total for region					
Brazil					
Brazil	278	7	2,300	—	—
River Plate Republics					
Argentina	688	1	3,160	62	3
Paraguay	166	15	2,670	62	4
Uruguay	382	4	3,070	99	13
Total for region					
Western South America					
Bolivia	109	18	1,612	102	15
Chile	335	6	2,400	124	18
Ecuador	93	19	—	115	17
Peru	118	17	2,200	98	12
Total for region					
United States	2,200		3,230	27	

A dash indicates that data are not available.

Sources: "Statistical Abstract of Latin America for 1955," prepared at the University of California at Los Angeles; Hubert Herring, *A History of Latin America* (New York: Alfred A. Knopf, Inc., 1955), p. 781; Foreign Operations Administration, *Report on the Economic Situation in Latin America* (Washington, 1954); and *United Nations Monthly Bulletin of Statistics*, October, 1954.

[a] Data on infant mortality are for 1954, except for Uruguay (1930–1934), Ecuador (1949), Paraguay (1950), Bolivia, Panama, and Peru (1953), El Salvador (1955).

HEALTH IN LATIN AMERICA

	Medical Care			Hospital Beds [b]			
	No. of	No. of Persons per Physician				Per 1000 Pop.	
Year	Physicians	Thousands	Rank	Year	Total	No.	Rank
1952	265	2.8	9	1951	4,486	3.0	8
1951	380	6.0	18	—	—	2.1	13
1952	497	5.8	17	1952	6,742	2.4	11
1951–52	232	6.5	19	1948	1,812	1.3	17
1949	12,045	2.4	7	1953	32,005	1.2	18
1950	438	2.2	6	1952	2,131	2.3	12
1950	238	3.3	12	1950	3,244	4.2	3
	14,095						
1948	3,100	1.0	1	1948	17,112	3.3	6
1951	764	5.0	16	1951	5,517	2.8	10
1951	300	10.0	20	1951	2,111	—	—
	4,164				24,740		
1952	4,212	2.8	10	1952	31,351	3.0	9
1953	2,939	1.9	5	1953	19,307	3.6	5
	7,151				50,658		
1949	19,044	3.0	11	1950	162,515	3.1	7
1948	18,301	1.3	3	1946	65,386	4.0	4
1950	507	2.5	8	1946	2,076	1.5	16
1952	2,231	1.1	2	1952	13,567	5.9	1
	21,039				81,029		
1948	633	4.0	14	1945	5,180	1.8	14
1951	3,251	1.8	4	1951	33,738	5.8	2
1946	808	3.7	13	—	—	—	—
1952	1,964	4.5	15	1950	16,515	1.5	15
	6,656						
1950	201,277	0.8		1951	1,521,959	9.9	

[b] Data refer to government hospitals only for Mexico, Paraguay, and Uruguay.

of such fundamental means of communication gives greater meaning to the often-repeated statement that the living standards of Latin America are low. When illiteracy is combined with poverty, millions lack the opportunity to read. A prosperous nation like Uruguay has a daily circulation of 217.8 newspapers for each 1,000 population, while Haiti publishes only 3.4 per 1,000 (see Table IV).

The low living standards also present difficult public health problems in varying degrees in each of the republics. Diet-deficiency diseases have a much higher incidence than in the United States. Poor housing compounds this problem, while the lack of programs of preventive medicine accentuates it even more. A glance at Table V quickly reveals the correlation between per capita income and such health factors as caloric intake, infant mortality, the number of nurses and physicians, and the extent of hospital facilities.

Let us now turn to some of the basic factors of the Latin American economy, for improvement in living standards depends to a large extent upon increasing the efficiency and level of production. Unless this can be achieved, a higher standard of life will be impossible to attain, and without such a rise in the standard of living the way toward political democracy is long and difficult. The standard of living is rising more rapidly in some countries than in others, and more rapidly than population is increasing in much of the area. It can be reasonably expected, therefore, that the Latin American will receive a better education in the future, that he will enjoy better health, that he will be able to purchase more of the necessities for a more comfortable living for his family than he ever has before.

The Economy of Latin America

Almost from the moment of the landing of Columbus on Hispaniola, Latin America was regarded as a land of enormous wealth, richly endowed with natural resources, especially gold and silver. The fact that the early *conquistadores* found great quantities of these precious metals in Mexico and Peru reinforced this belief. *El Dorado* had finally been located!

Because this view still grips the minds and imaginations of men, they are puzzled by the failure of most of the region to reach, in mid-twentieth century, the high economic levels attained by the United States, Canada, and the nations of western Europe. Not understanding the real nature of the Latin American economy and some of the limitations of its resources, they frequently ascribe the failure to achieve a higher standard of living to such factors as the disinclination of the Latin American to engage in hard work (one of the common stereotypes is that he is either at a fiesta or taking a siesta), or to the lack of stable, orderly, and democratic governments. They fail to realize that these political shortcomings may be the result, rather than the cause, of the economic phenomena.

Certainly, part of the explanation of the low living standards in most of the region is to be found in unusual, in some cases unique, features of its economy. The nature of the land, the climate, economic patterns established by the colonizing powers, a shortage of certain natural resources, an inadequate skilled labor supply, a deficiency in technical and managerial skills, and inability to provide proper amounts of investment capital have combined to produce an economic system that has readily observable peculiarities in all its branches—agriculture, mining, and industry.

AGRICULTURE. As can be seen in Table VI, with few national exceptions the economies are essentially agrarian, despite the fact that so much of the area is highly urbanized. About two-thirds of the population are engaged in agricultural pursuits, as compared with the less than 15 per cent of the population of the United States so engaged. The nations differ in this respect, of course. Only one-third of Chile's people work on farms, while two-thirds of those in Colombia do so. In Haiti and Peru the proportion exceeds four-fifths.

In most of the republics, produce from farms constitutes the single most important segment of the total national production, assuming an even greater importance in foreign trade. In seventeen of the twenty nations, some one agricultural product is the largest item in the export list, in nine it furnishes more than one-half of all exports, and in five more than three-quarters.

This product is coffee for seven of the republics, animal products for three, sugar, bananas, or cotton for two, and cacao for one. Thus, the major agricultural effort is dedicated to producing one product for the export market (see Tables VII and IX). If for any reason the ability of the rest of the world to purchase coffee, animal products, sugar, or bananas is seriously curtailed, the result is almost immediate economic distress in the producing nation. This economic distress often leads to political disturbance.

Most of the millions who farm do not own their own land, and many have such small holdings that it is difficult to produce more than a bare subsistence. As a result, much of the agriculture is conducted with obsolete or substandard methods. Draft animals, in some cases human beings, pull the plows and harvest and convey the crops. A tractor inventory of 1948-49 showed that North

TABLE VI.   THE LATIN

| | Population (1955)[a] | | Gross National Product Per Capita (1952) | |
	Total (thousands)	Rank	US Dollars	Rank
Mexico and Central America				
Costa Rica	951	9	203	9
El Salvador	2,193	15	167	14
Guatemala	3,149	12	182	12
Honduras	1,660	16	134	16
Mexico	28,849	2	199	10
Nicaragua	1,202	18	168	13
Panama	886	20	382	5
Total for region	38,890			
Caribbean States				
Cuba	5,807	7	454	3
Dominican Republic	2,404	14	189	11
Haiti	3,506	10	62	20
Total for region	11,717			
Northern South America				
Colombia	12,657	4	231	6
Venezuela	5,774	8	457	9
Total for region	18,431			
Brazil				
Brazil	58,456	1	278	7
River Plate Republics				
Argentina	19,108	3	688	1
Paraguay	1,565	17	166	15
Uruguay	2,525	13	382	4
Total for region	23,198			
Western South America				
Bolivia	3,198	11	109	18
Chile	6,774	6	335	6
Ecuador	3,567	9	93	19
Peru	9,396	5	118	17
Total for region	22,935			
United States	167,000		2,200	

A dash indicates that data are not available.

SOURCES: "Statistical Abstract of Latin America for 1955," prepared at the University of California at Los Angeles; and Foreign Operations Administration, *Report on the Economic Situation in Latin America* (Washington, 1954).

[a] Data on population of Ecuador, Guatemala, and Mexico are for 1954; of Cuba and Uruguay, 1953.

AMERICAN: HIS WORK

Labor Force		Per Cent in Main Occupations				Labor Union Members (1954) (thousands)
Year	Total (thousands)	Agriculture	Industry	Trade, Banking, Insurance	Mining	
—	—	54.7	11.0	—	—	18
1948	1,000	63.6	—	—	—	5
—	—	88.4	—	—	—	294
1949	696	26.6	25.0	—	—	—
1949	7,111	65.5	10.9	9.4	—	1,566
—	—	73	10.0	—	—	2
1947	203	53	7.8	—	—	14
1948	1,136	72	13.0	11.0	—	1,550
—	—	80	—	—	—	68
—	—	—	—	—	—	4
						1,622
1950	2,645	66	9.0	6.0	—	430
1947	1,240	51	14.0	8.0	—	1,531
						1,961
1947	14,014	68	10.0	5.0	—	3,822
1950	6,272	25	29.0	14.0	—	6,043
1944	300	70	—	—	—	65
1949	770	50	11.0	13.0	—	67
						6,175
1949	1,760	85	—	—	4	—
1953	1,704	35	20.0	10.0	5	303
1944	1,701	82	—	—	—	71
1940	2,455	62	16.0	—	—	350
1954	61,238	14.9	28.2	22.2	1.4	17,757

NOTE: The data on labor union membership, based largely on Department of Labor and International Labour Office figures, should be compared with the more conservative estimates by the author of Chapter 7 (see Table XI, p. 170).

TABLE VII.   AGRICULTURE

	Per Cent of Land in Agricultural Production	Live Stock Production (millions)		
		Cattle (1953–54)	Hogs (1955)	Sheep (1953–54)
Mexico and Central America				
Costa Rica	19.0	0.8	—	—
El Salvador	37.0	0.8	0.3	—
Guatemala	18.0	1.2	0.4	0.9
Honduras	18.0	1.2	0.5	—
Mexico	57.0	15.5	7.8	5.0
Nicaragua	6.0	1.2	—	—
Panama	3.0	0.6	0.2	—
Total for region		21.3	—	—
Caribbean States				
Cuba	51.0	4.0	1.4	0.2
Dominican Republic	26.0	0.9	0.9	—
Haiti	16.0	—	—	—
Total for region		—	—	—
Northern South America				
Colombia	36.0	12.0	1.8	1.1
Venezuela	18.0	5.7	1.5	—
Total for region		17.7	3.3	—
Brazil				
Brazil	6.0	57.6	35.6	16.8
River Plate Republics				
Argentina	52.0	45.3	1.5	55.5
Paraguay	4.0	4.2	0.3	0.2
Uruguay	86.0	7.8	0.2	26.8
Total for region		57.3	2.0	82.5
Western South America				
Bolivia	0.3	2.3	0.7	6.5
Chile	26.0	2.4	0.7	6.5
Ecuador	17.0	1.2	—	—
Peru	13.0	3.2	1.3	16.2
Total for region		9.1	—	—
United States	58.0	94.8	50.5	31.2

A dash indicates that data are not available.

SOURCES: "Statistical Abstract of Latin America for 1955," prepared at the University of California at Los Angeles; Hubert Herring, *A History of Latin America* (New York: Alfred A. Knopf, Inc., 1955), pp. 778–779; *Foreign Trade of Latin America Since 1913* (Washington: Pan American Union, 1952); and U.S. Department of Commerce, *Foreign Commerce Yearbook, 1951.*

IN LATIN AMERICA

Crop Production (thousands of metric tons)							Agriculture in Foreign Trade (1951)	
Sugar (1954-55)	Coffee (1954)	Cacao (1955-56)	Corn (1954)	Rice (1954-55)	Wheat (1954)	Ginned Cotton (1954)	Product	Per Cent of Exports
28	33	7	80	32	—	—	coffee	56.4
36	76	—	175	34	—	16	coffee	88.9
62	61	—	369	61	—	7	coffee	76.8
11	18	—	176	9	—	—	bananas	28.7
901	106	11	4,000	172	830	380	cotton	24.5
45	17	—	82	25	—	38	coffee	39.9
16	3	2	76	99	—	—	bananas	37.5
1,099	314	—	4,958	432	—	—		
4,528	38	3	175	170	—	—	sugar	87.7
612	26	39	92	77	—	—	sugar	52.2
56	30	2	—	—		1	coffee	52.4
5,196	94	44	—	—		—		
229	390	16	943	284	146	29	coffee	78.5
84	53	18	326	98	—	4	—	—
313	443	34	1,269	382	—	33		
2,330	1,037	158	6,096	3,853	824	447	coffee	59.8
778	—	—	2,546	183	7,690	111	animal products (1947)	43.3
—	—	—	107	25	2	12		31.5
—	—	—	184	70	832	—		81.2
—			2,747	278	8,524	—		
—	—	—	—	29	—	—	—	—
—	—	—	102	93	1,078	—	—	—
—	24	32	—	136	—	—	cacao	34.0
611	10	5	300	227	169	112	cotton	33.8
—	—	—	—	485	—	—		
2,257			73,305	2,914	26,394	2,970		

America, with about one-fifth of the world's farm lands, had almost three-quarters of the tractors, whereas Latin America with about 7 per cent of the land had just over 1 per cent of the tractors.

The landless condition of the farm workers stems from several causes. One is land shortage, for even though many of these countries are large and have a low-density population, lack of rainfall, difficult topography, or lack of rail and highway communications limits the amount of land available for cultivation. The land tenure system is another cause in many of the nations. Spain and Portugal both encouraged colonization by huge land grants to settlers. During the colonial period and during the nineteenth century these were frequently added to by the seizure of Indian lands. Although the laws relating to primogeniture and entail which maintained these vast estates were changed or abolished in the nineteenth century, the system of large estates remained. As late as 1945, 2,000 individuals or corporations owned one-fifth of all of the land in Argentina, while in the richest of the *pampa* provinces, Buenos Aires, 320 families owned about two-fifths of the land. One study found that 74.5 per cent of all Chilean agricultural properties in 1937, ranging from 0 to 123.5 acres, occupied only 4.7 per cent of all agricultural lands, whereas 1.4 per cent of the holdings, in size from 2,470 to 12,350 acres, occupied 68.2 per cent of the area. A United Nations report gave a similar picture in 1954—that large holdings account for 62.8 per cent of all farm properties in Chile, although they constitute only 1.4 per cent of all farm holdings. In Bolivia, 4.5 per cent of all landowners owned about 70 per cent of the land prior to the agrarian reform. Even in Mexico, which has made considerable progress in land redistribution, less than 1 per cent of the total number of holdings still account for almost 80 per cent of the arable land. (This does not include the acreage of land held under the communal *ejido* system.) The same report notes that *latifundio* (the large estate system) is a major problem in Argentina, Cuba, Ecuador, Peru, and Venezuela.[1]

Many land economists and rural sociologists have commented on the social and economic effects of the *latifundio*. They point out that it forces the estate owner to gear his production to foreign rather than to domestic demands, to emphasize the quick cash crop rather than the needed domestic one, and to rely upon cheap labor rather than to improve the efficiency of production. They also attribute the peonage system of farm labor to the land tenure system.

[1] Statements in this paragraph are drawn from George H. Soule, *et al.*, *Latin America in the Future World* (New York: Rinehart & Co., 1945) and *Progress in Land Reform* (New York: United Nations, 1954).

In spite of these limitations, the agricultural economy produces commodities in amazing quantities, as appears in the following tabulation of the percentage of the world production of certain agricultural products coming from Latin America in 1952 (1951 for henequen and sisal).

Product	Per cent of world production
Henequen	98.1
Coffee	83.3
Cocoa beans	25.1
Cane sugar	25.1
Sisal	24.3
Flaxseed	21.4
Wool	15.0
Cotton	12.5
Cattle	10.1
Hogs	9.8
Corn	9.0

If some of the problems confronting agriculture in Latin America could be surmounted, this great importance in the production of the world supply of foods and fibers might be magnified many times.

MINING. The mineral wealth of Latin America, real or imagined, monopolized the attention of the first European arrivals so much that they often neglected the other potential resources. Argentina, for example, received its name from the supposed treasures in silver to be found there, and the failure to find them resulted in neglect of the colony by Spain. Not until the nineteenth century was it perceived that the topsoil of the *pampas* was as great a resource as the silver mountain of Potosí had been.

The area is a major producer of many of the minerals essential to industry in the contemporary world, yet mining is of scant importance in relation to other occupations. Only two nations, Chile and Bolivia, report a significant proportion of workers in mining in their labor statistics, 5 per cent in the former and 4 in the latter (see Table VI). Nor is Latin American mineral production achieving its potential. This failure can be traced to several causes. Mining is severely handicapped by the lack of adequate transportation. The mineral wealth is often found in remote and mountainous areas, in which few railroads or highways exist and in which it is extremely expensive to build them. A mine which must send its ore to the processing centers, or to the nearest rail line, on the backs of mules or llamas is obviously less efficient than one utilizing giant trucks or railroad hopper cars. It must compensate by finding a cheaper labor supply in order to compete with producers in regions better supplied with transportation.

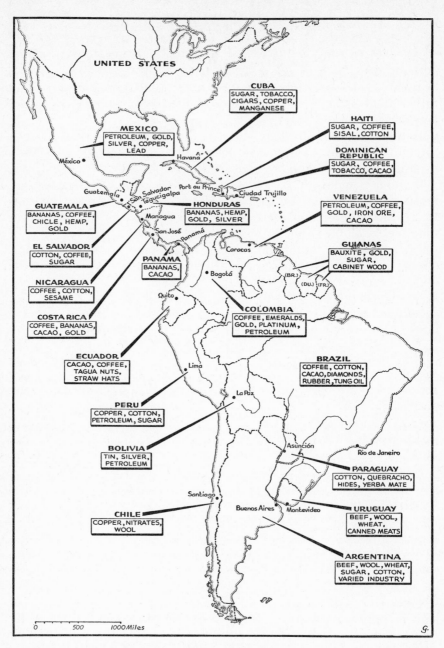

Map 5. Chief Natural Products of Latin America. The map shows only products produced on a large scale for export. Note the widespread production of coffee, cotton, sugar, petroleum, and certain minerals. Many aspects of the economies do not appear, of course. Not shown, for example, are such products as textiles, food crops, and cattle, which are produced in all countries.

74

Most of the mineral production of Latin America, like that of agriculture, is sent to other parts of the world for final processing or refining. In such nations as Chile and Bolivia, a mineral product rather than an agricultural crop is the basis of the monocultural economy. Three-quarters of Bolivia's export trade is in tin, which, with other mineral products, "buys" over 90 per cent of the nation's foreign exchange. Copper accounts for over one-half of Chile's exports, and petroleum for more than 95 per cent of Venezuela's.

Foreign ownership or foreign majority control characterizes most of the mining enterprises. A report of the United Nations Economic Commission for Latin America noted in 1953 that over nine-tenths of the Chilean copper production was in the hands of foreign concerns, that two-thirds of the copper of Peru was produced by foreign enterprises, and that the enormous oil production of Venezuela was largely foreign controlled. This predominance of foreign capital in mining enterprises results partly from natural economic causes. Domestic investment capital accumulates slowly because of the low economic productivity. Moreover, wealthy Latin Americans have been reluctant to depart from the tradition of investment in land and commercial enterprises. Hence, to develop the resources, foreign capital has had to be imported. Foreign investment often causes political trouble, however. The foreign concern may be accused of meddling in the politics of the nation in which it is operating. Moreover, it is almost certain to be attacked for depleting the resources of the country in order to benefit absent and foreign "capitalists." The newly burgeoning nationalist groups will insist that the national defense and the need for conservation require that the nation's resources be controlled by nationals, even though these nationals lack the capital to finance the development. Two examples of this nationalistic tendency occurred in 1957: Brazilian legislation relating to oil exploitation (Petrolbras) and the difficulties encountered by the administration of President Pedro Aramburu in Argentina, with reference to a contract with the Standard Oil Company. The mineral economy is indeed in a dilemma; foreign capital is needed but its use may lead to political situations which cause the foreign investor to be reluctant to invest his capital in that nation.

At the present time some of the Latin American nations occupy a high place in world mineral production. Approximately 15 per cent of all tin deposits are in Bolivia. Brazil and Venezuela have vast iron ore deposits and are rapidly increasing their export of iron ore. Chile is the world's largest producer of natural nitrates and the second largest producer and exporter of copper. Colombia's

TABLE VIII.   LATIN AMERICAN

	Average Monthly Production (thousand metric tons)					
	Petro-leum (1955)	Iron (1955)	Lead (1954)	Copper (1954)	Bauxite (B) & Tin (T) (1954)	Coal (1955)
Mexico and Central America						
Costa Rica		—	—	—	—	—
El Salvador		—	—	—	—	—
Guatemala	—	2	—	—	—	—
Honduras	—	—	—	—	—	—
Mexico	1,066	33	217	55	0.4	112
Nicaragua	—	—	—	—	—	—
Panama	—	—	—	—	—	—
Caribbean States						
Cuba	0.1	0.1	—	16	—	—
Dominican Republic	—	—	—	—	—	—
Haiti	—	—	—	—	—	—
Northern South America						
Colombia	458	—	—	—	—	125
Venezuela	9,618	692	—	—	—	3
Brazil						
Brazil	25	214	—	—	19 (B)	191
River Plate Republics						
Argentina	364	—	21	—	0.1	11
Paraguay	—	—	—	—	—	—
Uruguay	—	—	—	—	—	—
Western South America						
Bolivia	29	—	18.0	4	29 (T)	—
Chile	28	127	5.0	364	—	192
Ecuador	35	—	0.1	—	—	—
Peru	192	147	109.0	38	—	17
United States	27,980	8,888	289	759	2,038 (B)	37,525

A dash indicates that data are not available.

SOURCES: "Statistical Abstract of Latin America for 1955," prepared at the University of California at Los Angeles; Hubert Herring, *A History of Latin America* (New

MINING AND MANUFACTURING

Mine Products in Foreign Trade 1951		Per Cent of Labor Force in Industry	Industrial Establishments				
				Number		Persons Employed	
Product	Per Cent of Exports		Year	Thousands	Rank	Thousands	Rank
—	—	11.0	1950–51	3.2	10	17.1	13
—	—	—	1951	8.3	4	40.7	9
—	—	—	1946	0.7	13	21.6	12
—	—	25.0	1951	0.2	16	10.7	16
lead	9.7	10.9	1935	6.9	7	225.8	3
gold	18.9	10.0	1946	0.08	18	1.7	17
—	—	7.8	1952	0.6	14	—	—
—	—	13.0	1952	1.5	11	35.1	11
—	—	—	1952	3.6	9	61.2	7
—	—	—	—	—	—	—	—
—	—	9.0	1944–45	7.8	6	135.4	6
petroleum	97.0	14.0	1936	8.0	5	47.8	8
—		10.0	1951	11.2	3	725.3	2
—	—	29.0	1948	80.3	1	1142.0	1
—	—	—	—	—	—	—	—
—	—	11.0	1951	24.3	2	180.1	5
tin (1950)	67.4	—	1949	0.9	12	15.9	14
copper	54.7	20.0	1950	4.9	8	184.0	4
—	—	—	1951	0.08	17	15.2	15
—	—	16.0	1951	0.3	15	39.6	10
			1951	262.0		15,613.0	

York: Alfred A. Knopf, Inc., 1955), pp. 778–779; Foreign Operations Administration, *Report on the Economic Situation in Latin America* (Washington, 1954); Foreign Commerce Yearbooks; and United Nations Statistical Yearbooks.

oil production places that nation eighth among the nations of the world and third among those of Latin America. Mexico leads all countries in the production of silver, is second in lead, third in zinc, and seventh in petroleum. Peru is the largest producer of vanadium and bismuth in the world, and the almost fabulous oil reserves of Venezuela make that country the world's second most important producer of oil and the largest exporter of that commodity.

The importance of Latin America in mineral products appears in the following table showing the per cent of the world production of various minerals coming from the area in 1952.

Product	Per cent of world production
Bauxite	46.2
Silver	36.8
Bismuth	34.7
Antimony	34.4
Lead	21.9
Copper	18.9
Petroleum	18.9
Tin	18.9
Zinc	16.0

The industrial machine of the rest of the world would be badly off indeed were it not for the abundant flow of these basic mineral resources from the mines of Latin America.

INDUSTRY. The preceding discussion has shown the dependence of many of the national economies on one agricultural or mineral product and has noted the effects of this monoculturalism on national economy and polity. What are the present trends and the prospects for diversifying these economies, especially through industrialization? To what extent has industrialization taken place in Latin America? Along what lines is this industrial expansion moving? In which of the republics has it developed most fully and why has it proceeded more slowly elsewhere?

For many years Latin American political and economic leaders have urged speeding up the tempo of industrialization. It has been urged as the best way to diversify the economy and thereby escape the hazards of a one-sided economic pattern. Military leaders have advocated industrialization as a necessity for modernizing the armed forces. Political leaders have argued that it is the best way to raise the standard of living. The more utopian assume that industrialization, by itself, is the panacea for all political and economic troubles.

World War II gave renewed impetus to the demand for industrialization. Progress came slowly, however, partly because of the lack of new capital. Twelve years after the war, industry still played a small role in much of Latin America, in terms of providing employment and contributing to the national product. But the movement is under way, and industrial expansion is going on today at a rate unequalled in any other of the world's major regions.

The twenty nations fall into three groups with reference to their industrial economy. Argentina, Brazil, Chile, and Mexico have reached a high level of industrial output (as shown in Table VIII). Of the four, Argentina, perhaps, has made the most marked advance. Its factory output is an important part of the total national product and a high proportion of its citizens earn their living in industrial occupations. Brazil's expansion started later than Argentina's, but has moved rapidly in the past two decades. Much of this growth is in the field of textiles; there are now over 3,000 textile mills in Brazil. Approximately one-fifth of the employed Chileans work in industry, and an equal proportion of the total national output derives from this source. In 1948 Mexico had almost 22,000 industrial establishments employing well over a half-million workers.

In four other nations, Cuba, Colombia, Peru, and Venezuela, industrialization has taken a firm foothold and is expanding with a rapidity equal to the pace of the first four. The number of industrial plants in Colombia expanded from 121 in 1915 to 7,843 in 1945. Between 1940 and 1957 the number of industrial workers in Peru almost doubled.

Bolivia, Costa Rica, Ecuador, Dominican Republic, Guatemala, and Panama are in an earlier stage of industrialization. The importance of industrial activity in the total economy is less than in the two first-named groups, but the speed at which the process is taking place is about the same. The position of Uruguay is unique. For many years she has had an extensive industry of food packing and processing, but only since 1940 has she experienced a great growth of other industrial activities.

El Salvador, Haiti, Honduras, Nicaragua, and Paraguay have been less touched by the march of industry. These nations have had some expansion in food and beverage processing and production, and in lumbering, but are still essentially agrarian in their economies.

When North Americans read of the great expansion of industry taking place in other parts of the world, many of them imagine large-scale steel plants and automobile factories—establishments that employ thousands if not hundreds of thousands of workers. In most of Latin America, however, industry tends to be light industry, producing consumer goods and employing relatively small numbers of workers. Argentina, Chile, Brazil, and Mexico have large steel mills, tire factories, and automobile assembly plants, but these are the exceptions. In Argentina, foods and beverages accounted for 37.3 per cent of the total industrial production in 1943, textiles 19.3 per cent, and basic metals and metal products 14.6 per cent. In Brazil, foods and beverages amounted to 35.8 per cent of total industrial production in 1949, textiles 27.8 per cent, and basic metals 11.3 per cent. In the same year, 40 per cent of Argentina's employed industrial workers worked in food, beverage, or textile plants and only 19.6 per cent in basic metals, while in Brazil the figures were, respectively, 69.4 per cent and 10.7 per cent.

In those nations in which industrialization, though less developed, has made a vigorous initial start, this emphasis on foods, beverages, and textiles is even more marked. In 1945, 69.6 per cent of the total industrial output of Colombia was in these three fields and only 3.4 per cent in basic metals and metal products, while in Venezuela these figures were 58.2 per cent and 1.8 per cent in 1936. Of the labor force employed in Colombia in 1945, 56.4 per cent worked in plants producing foods, beverages, or textiles; only 6.3 per cent worked in basic metals. In Venezuela these figures were 68.0 per cent and 0.1 per cent in 1936.

These data are not presented in order to minimize the importance of Latin American industrialization. They merely indicate where the industrial effort is being made. The fact that Latin America is producing more processed foodstuffs and textiles, rather than automobiles or heavy producer goods, does not indicate a lack of economic progress. Increased production of food and clothing increases the total national output, offers many more employment opportunities, and helps to raise the standard of living. These effects are now seen in many of the nations in the form of rates of increase in national productivity considerably higher than the rapid population increase.

PROBLEMS OF INDUSTRIALIZATION. In considering the industrialization of Latin America, it must be borne in mind that the area suffers from several handicaps that would hinder industrial expansion in any area of the world. Some of these have already been noted, such as difficult topography, unfavorable climate, the lack of a skilled labor force, low living standards which reduce the productivity of the worker, and the lack of technical and managerial skills. To these must be added others more specifically related to industry. The region as a whole is desperately short of energy resources. One author has estimated that Latin America, with about 16 per cent of the world's area, has less than 3 per cent of its energy resources.[2] Latin America uses about 0.1 ton of coal per capita annually, the United States 4.3, and the combined consumption of energy in the twenty republics is probably less than one-tenth that of the United States.

Most of the nations also lack adequate supplies of some mineral resources deemed essential to the development of heavy industry. Most of them have little or no iron ore or coking coal suitable for steel production. The technology of heavy industry may change, of course, but these are serious lacks at the present time. Finally, there is a paucity of investment capital. All the difficulties which have beset foreign capital in the mining economy also arise in respect to its use in industrial development. In spite of these problems and handicaps, the growth of industry in Latin America has been phenomenally successful.

FOREIGN TRADE. The tendency of Latin American foreign trade to depend largely upon one product has already been pointed out. Certain other characteristics may now be noted. First, it is growing rapidly. The value in U.S. dollars almost quadrupled between 1937 and 1952, thus doubling even when allowance is made for the decreased value of the dollar.[3] Table IX shows that the proportion of Latin American trade with United States, which is very large, particularly with certain countries, also increased. Of all the nations, Venezuela sends the smallest portion of her exports to the United States, but even she sent 23 per cent. Panama and El Salvador sent the largest proportion, each shipping 83 per cent of its exports to American buyers. The United States purchased over one-half of the exports of fourteen of the twenty republics, and over three-quarters of five.

The same proportions hold true in respect to imports. The nations south of the Rio Grande bought from 19 per cent to 82 per cent of their foreign purchases from the United States, Argentina being the least dependent on North American producers and Mexico the most. The United States furnished 50 per cent or more of the imports for fifteen of the nations and 75 per cent or more for Honduras and Mexico.

Some indication of where the products of Latin America's expanding industrial output are going appears in the area distri-

[2] Simon G. Hanson, *Economic Development in Latin America* (Washington, D.C.: The Inter-American Affairs Press, 1951).
[3] *Selected Economic Data on the Latin American Republics* (Washington, D.C.: Pan American Union, 1954).

TABLE IX.   THE FOREIGN

	Value of Exports 1952 (thousand US dollars)	Area Distribution of Latin American Exports (per cent)										
		U.S. & Canada		Latin America		Sterling Area		Cont. Europe & Eur. Payments Union		Rest of World	
		1937	1952	1937	1952	1937	1952	1937	1952	1937	1952
Mexico and Central America												
Costa Rica	71,897	44	72	3	8	20	—	29	18	4	—
El Salvador	88,285	64	85	3	3	1	1	28	11	4	—
Guatemala	87,463	65	84	1	2	1	2	30	12	3	—
Honduras	34,466	89	85	1	11	—	—	7	3	3	—
Mexico	592,539	56	83	2	3	13	2	22	5	7	7
Nicaragua	51,300	56	53	4	14	—	13	33	17	7	3
Panama	12,665	93	87	—	10	—	—	3	2	4	1
Caribbean States												
Cuba	675,345	81	63	1	3	11	9	6	15	1	10
Dominican Republic	115,015	35	43	1	—	31	39	29	8	3	10
Haiti	52,925	28	55	—	1	16	—	52	43	4	1
Northern South America												
Colombia	472,158	63	84	1	1	—	1	34	13	2	1
Venezuela	1,450,244	14	35	1	8	4	4	64	51	17	2
Brazil												
Brazil	1,417,936	37	53	7	9	10	4	38	28	8	6
River Plate Republics												
Argentina	701,574	16	26	8	16	30	14	42	34	4	10
Paraguay	33,132	7	25	21	42	10	3	33	27	29	2
Uruguay	208,925	21	25	7	15	26	17	28	39	18	4
Western South America												
Bolivia	142,107	7	68	3	1	60	26	30	5	—	—
Chile	461,756	23	57	4	15	20	5	29	17	24	6
Ecuador	80,012	33	55	7	9	2	7	41	19	17	10
Peru	238,738	29	30	15	31	23	9	27	26	6	4
United States	15,042,300										

A dash indicates that data are not available.

SOURCES: Hubert Herring, *A History of Latin America* (New York: Alfred A. Knopf, Inc., 1955), pp. 778–779; *Selected Economic Data on the Latin American*

bution of exports and imports shown in Table IX.   These figures also show the increasing importance of the United States as both purchaser and seller.   Between 1937 and 1952 sixteen of the Latin American states increased the percentage of their exports to the United States, four of them by over 25 per cent, and one (Bolivia) by 61 per cent.   Of equal significance is the fact that during the same period the proportion of exports to other Latin American countries increased for sixteen of the twenty nations, increases of 21 per cent being registered for Paraguay, 16 per cent for Peru, and 10 per cent each for Honduras and Nicaragua.

The import figures reveal the same general trends.   In the fifteen-year period all twenty countries increased the proportion of their imports from the United States, with increases of from 1 per cent (Argentina) to 26 per cent (Ecuador).   Eleven of the increases were 20 per cent or more.   Similarly, the proportion of imports brought in from other Latin American countries showed increases

TRADE OF LATIN AMERICA

Value of Imports 1952 (thousand US dollars)	Area Distribution of Latin American Imports (per cent)										Monocultural Effect: One Crop or Product as Per Cent of All Exports 1951
	U.S. & Canada		Latin America		Sterling Area		Cont. Europe & Eur. Pay- ments Union		Rest of World		
	1937	1952	1937	1952	1937	1952	1937	1952	1937	1952	
67,874	42	67	6	4	9	6	31	21	12	2	56.4
67,787	40	65	6	11	11	5	38	17	5	2	88.9
75,722	45	66	4	9	8	6	38	17	5	2	76.8
54,589	59	75	4	8	3	3	17	13	17	1	28.7
739,169	63	86	2	1	5	3	26	9	4	1	24.5
39,700	54	73	7	7	7	5	22	15	10	—	39.9
67,873	52	68	2	5	6	7	12	7	28	13	37.5
618,314	69	78	3	3	8	7	14	10	6	2	87.7
96,901	54	71	1	2	9	6	17	17	19	4	52.2
50,695	52	76	—	2	17	5	17	15	14	2	52.4
402,272	49	69	3	4	19	5	26	18	3	4	78.5
722,573	53	73	1	1	9	7	31	13	6	6	97.0
1,985,338	25	44	16	9	14	12	42	35	3	2	59.8
1,177,172	18	19	9	22	26	8	39	37	8	14	43.3
46,413	7	28	44	31	8	11	21	27	19	2	31.5
257,257	23	26	11	25	21	13	34	30	11	6	81.2
92,620	29	54	31	19	8	9	24	17	8	1	67.4
370,966	30	54	16	21	12	10	35	13	7	2	54.6
55,979	39	66	6	6	10	8	36	19	9	1	34.0
287,548	38	63	11	7	13	12	31	17	7	1	33.8

Republics (Washington: Pan American Union, 1954); and Business Information Service, *World Trade Series*, No. 505, December, 1953.

NOTE: The totals of the percentages are not 100 in all cases because figures have been rounded off.

for ten of the twenty buyer nations, no change for four, and a decrease in buying from other Latin American states on the part of Bolivia, Brazil, Costa Rica, Mexico, Paraguay, and Peru.

If the increasingly American (in the continental sense) character of Latin American trade appears striking on the basis of these data, it is even more dramatically apparent in the data shown in Table IX on imports from and exports to the sterling area, continental Europe and the European Payments Union region, and the rest of the world. With few exceptions, the proportion of both exports and imports decreased in these areas between 1937 and 1952.

The nature of Latin American exports was discussed in the sections of this chapter devoted to agriculture and mining. But what products do these nations buy? The answer to this question has been given inferentially in the preceding pages. They buy what they lack in basic resources and what their own industry cannot produce. They also buy capital goods for the development of their economies. Year after year these products appear on the import lists of almost every country: vehicles, tools and machinery, iron and other metal goods, newsprint, chemicals, electrical equipment, coal, oil, gasoline, and other fuels. It may surprise some readers to learn that Latin America imports a large amount of foodstuffs. Half of the twenty nations, most of them primarily agrarian in their economic organization, import large quantities of staple foods.

The previous pages of this chapter have stressed some of the difficulties encountered in Latin America's social and economic life. The dynamic factors generated by the efforts to overcome these difficulties, and their effect upon Latin American society and politics, remain to be discussed.

Trends of Social and Economic Change

Readers familiar with Latin American politics know that it is turbulent and volatile and that bullets rather than ballots often decide who is to govern. They know that in few other regions have so many charters of government been written and abandoned. They also know that political power is usually concentrated in the hands of the president, that most Latin American congresses make few fundamental policy decisions, and that the courts often have little independence; that four of the twenty republics are organized on the federal basis, but have a federal system in which central government very largely controls the states, or provinces. They have probably seen references to the weakness of municipal government in many of the nations and noted that city government is much more dependent on the central political structure, directed much more by central authority, than in the United States.

POLITICAL EFFECTS. Topography and climate, the ethnic and demographic patterns, the "way of life," and the economic organization and levels of that part of America called "Latin" are not necessarily the only factors determining political life, but no one will deny them great importance in fixing political habits and institutions. Changes in these socio-economic factors provide much of the dynamics of politics, giving rise to new movements, new leaders, and new power groups—the dynamics of land, people, and social and economic institutions.

A North American economist wrote in 1950: "Low living standards tend to foster and perpetuate political oligarchy. Deep poverty, and its twin, illiteracy, make it possible to continue a situation in which the political power in a nation is concentrated in the hands of a few."[4] Five years later, a president of Costa Rica stated it this way: "One way of looking at our problem is this: Latin America is unstable, generally speaking, because its level of popular education is low; its deficient education is due to poverty; poverty is the result of many years of insufficient national income . . ."[5]

THE LAND. It has already been noted that geography, topography, and climate conspire to render a large proportion of Latin America submarginal or unusable and complicate the building of an adequate system of rail lines and highways. Almost all of the nations are devoting some effort to overcoming these geographical handicaps, and a few have achieved notable success. The number of irrigation and land reclamation projects has increased rapidly in the past three decades, despite the limitations imposed by national budgets. The leader in this field is Mexico, where water was brought to almost as many parched acres between 1946 and 1952 as in the previous twenty-one years.[6] Only India, Russia, and the United States newly irrigated more acres than Mexico in that six-year period! Peru and Chile, with financial and technical help from the United States, have also engaged in extensive land reclamation projects, as has the republic of Haiti, whose economic underdevelopment is so marked.

The limitations imposed by topography still retard the building of new railroad lines. Other kinds of internal communications, however, are being pushed forward rapidly. Almost all of the twenty republics are increasing their highway mileage, both in improved and unimproved roads. Most of this advance is being accomplished by their own efforts and with their own resources, but some is attributable to the aid received from the United States for the completion of the Pan American Highway. The time is not too far distant when one may drive on an improved highway from Boston to Buenos Aires, or from San Francisco to Santiago, Chile. This highway will further stimulate tourism, which is already a significant part of the area's economy, as well as making it easier for the farmer to send his products to market. Finally, it should be noted that air transportation, through local "feeder" lines

[4] Sanford A. Mosk, "The Pathology of Democracy in Latin America: An Economist's Point of View," The American Political Science Review, XLIV (March 1950), 139.

[5] José Figueres, "The Problems of Democracy in Latin America," Journal of International Affairs, IX, No. 1, (1955) 13.

[6] William P. Tucker, The Mexican Government Today (Minneapolis: University of Minnesota Press, 1957), p. 286.

which increase in number each year, brings formerly remote areas into contact with the urban centers and their markets.

THE PEOPLE.   Three aspects of Latin America's population have been stressed: the existence of diverse ethnic groups which are not incorporated into the total national society, the low density of population in some of the nations, and the unequal distribution of the people in many countries.   Most Latin American writers assign the greatest importance to the first of these three aspects as a factor influencing politics.

The cultural barriers which have separated the Indian, the Negro, and to a lesser extent the mestizo, from the rest of the national community are breaking down everywhere.   In some of the nations this change is coming with great rapidity, in others more slowly.   But everywhere the new highways and airlines bring these culturally isolated peoples into closer and more continuous contact with the rest of the nation.   The expansion of educational programs into rural areas, the increase in public health activities, and even the coverage of social security programs are weaving the Indian more fully into the national social fabric, teaching him to read and write, lowering his death rate, raising his standard of living, and increasing his participation in the political life of the nation.   This cultural assimilation may increase the political tensions of the moment, as it did in Mexico between 1910 and 1930, and more recently in Bolivia, Guatemala, and Peru.   But it is likely that the long-range influence will be toward greater political stability, as it has been in Mexico.   The emergence of a middle class as a result of the diversification of the economy will probably speed this process of assimilation of the Indian, as well as advancing the social, economic, and political position of the mestizo.[7]

It is probable also that much of Latin America will long continue to be an area of low population density.   Immigration from other parts of the world is unlikely to come in as large numbers as during past decades.   On the other hand, Latin Americans are a young people, with a high birth rate, a falling death rate, and an annual rate of increase that is one of the highest in the world.   These factors will tend to fill up the "empty places," particularly if national programs and national policy are directed toward making these places more habitable.

The trend toward urbanization, accelerating in many of the

[7] William L. Schurz, in This New World (New York: E. P. Dutton & Co., 1954), p. 410, notes that the "strength of the middle class, which serves as the major catalytic agent in the process of social evolution, is in proportion to the numbers of the white or light mestizo elements."

nations, accentuates the problem of a "head too large for the body."
Rapid urbanization tends to increase the already one-sided dominance of the urban areas in the political affairs and destiny of the
nation.   It is interesting to note that the "politics" of urbanization
is the reverse of that in the United States, where the large urban
centers are under-represented in legislatures and lack political power
consonant with their numerical size.

THE WAY OF LIFE.   A change is occurring in the role of the
Church in society.   In the past, the Church was little concerned
with many of the basic social and economic problems and was
often allied with political forces and *caudillos* who opposed fundamental socio-economic change.   Today the Church is becoming
increasingly interested in these problems, and is assuming greater
initiative and leadership in their solution.   Many Church leaders
are imbued with the social and political thought of the *Rerum
Novarum*.   Through the Church, the Catholic universities, labor
unions, and even through Christian political parties, they have
become active in social and economic reform movements.

Chile furnishes a good example.   In 1899, eight years after the
announcement of the *Rerum Novarum*, Enrique Concha Suber-
caseaux published a book, *Cuestiones obreras (Worker's Questions)*,
which stimulated the interest of the Church in Chilean social and
economic problems.   In recent years this social concern has extended even to the politically explosive subject of land reform.
Many leading Catholics in Chile support changes in the land
tenure system, and agrarian reform has been urged in a book written by a Catholic priest and published under Vatican imprint,
which noted that 500 families own one-fifth of all the land in Chile!

Catholic Action groups, supporting social reform measures, have
arisen in many of the other nations, and Catholics have displayed
growing interest in the labor union movements in Argentina, Colombia, Costa Rica, and Mexico.   One possible explanation of Perón's
final decision to break with the Church was his concern that the
Church would augment its influence in Argentine labor unions.   In
November of 1956 the Mexican Catholic Episcopate formally and
emphatically denied that it had any intention of entering into that
country's party politics, thus accepting the reform program of the
Mexican Revolution.   Five years earlier, to commemorate the six-
tieth anniversary of the *Rerum Novarum* of Leo XIII, the Mexican
hierarchy had published a letter which said, in part, "The Church
cannot isolate itself in the solitude of its temples and neglect the
mission entrusted to it by Divine Providence to help form a whole
well-rounded man, collaborating in this manner in laying down

the solid foundations of society." The significance of these two statements, for Mexico and for all of Latin America, is the greater when it is recalled that just three decades previously the Church–state conflict was at its bitterest point in that country.

Significant changes are also taking place in the class structure of Latin American society. A middle class, with middle-class mores and middle-class desires for economic opportunity and political stability, is assuming numerical importance in several states, among them Argentina, Chile, Costa Rica, Mexico, and Uruguay. The trend is also apparent in other nations, even though the class is still small.

Class stratification is changing. The rising standard of living and increased urbanization are lessening the rigidity of former class lines, though the tempo of this change varies greatly. In some countries it is well along its way, while in others it is hardly discernible. One evidence of the change, to be seen in many of the nations, is the rise of an urban labor class, a concomitant of the industrial revolution taking place. Politically, the most significant aspect of these labor groups is their potential influence on the power structure, through political parties. In Mexico this political influence of labor has been strong for many years, in Chile for two decades, and in Argentina during, if not after, the Perón regime. A growing labor movement is not necessarily a democratic portent, for powerful labor groups may align themselves with a dictator. But it can be a force for democracy. Labor may take the place of one of the old trilogy in the power base of Latin American politics: army, landowner, and Church. But which of the three will be replaced by labor in each of the countries, or whether labor will simply be added to the other three in some new combination, cannot now be predicted.

Transformations under way in Latin American educational systems will also have profound effects on the society and its political institutions. In all countries public education is being broadened, particularly by expansion into the rural areas. The statistical evidences of this change are seen in the annual increases in the proportion of school-age children attending school, the training of more teachers, the growth of education budgets, and the construction of more schools in rural areas. In most of the countries the number of students attending the universities is also growing apace.

Changes are also to be noted in the school curricula. "Practical" courses, better adapted to the needs of students, are appearing each year in greater number. The movement for vocational and technical schools is well developed in such nations as Argentina, Mexico, and Chile. Even the universities are broadening their curricular offerings, and the number of "faculties" (colleges) of agriculture, mining engineering, journalism, and business administration is increasing each year. The number of illiterates is dropping, in some countries with great rapidity. If it is true, as President José Figueres of Costa Rica wrote, that "Latin America is unstable, generally speaking, because its level of popular education is low,"[8] one element contributing to instability *is* being eliminated.

Progress is being made in meeting public health problems throughout the area. A rise in the standard of living reduces the incidence of disease, especially of those diseases attributable to dietary deficiencies or to poor housing conditions. The percentage of national budget allocations to public health and sanitation programs in all twenty nations is annually increasing. One of the most important factors in this improvement is the series of programs financed and carried on through inter-American and international cooperation. The work of the Pan American Sanitary Bureau, an agency of the Organization of American States, is an excellent example of this kind of effort. Through its activities, malaria and its debilitating effects have been almost wiped out in some of the nations, and its incidence markedly reduced in the others.

THE ECONOMY. The previous section on the economy emphasized the low per capita income level and the low level of productivity. Recent years have seen important changes in these two respects. The annual increase of per capita income between 1945 and 1953 averaged 3.3 per cent, while the total production of all sectors of the economy seems to be increasing at the rate of about 5 per cent each year, a rate which considerably exceeds the annual rate of population growth. If this rate could be maintained for the next two decades, it is estimated that the standard of living would more than double.

Agriculture, as previously noted, presents problems of monoculturalism, *latifundio,* obsolete farming methods, and peonage in farm labor. In the twentieth century, particularly since World War II, trends toward agricultural diversification have appeared. Brazil, which used to import apples from the United States, now has over a half-million apple trees in its own orchards. Mexico is almost self-sufficient now in basic food crops, and is rapidly increasing its production of pineapples, oranges, and grapefruit. Argentina used to import tea, but now almost supplies its domestic needs and

[8] José Figueres, *op. cit.,* p. 13.

expects an exportable surplus by 1959. Cuba has stepped up its campaign to increase the production of edible vegetable oils, all of which are now imported. The year 1953 saw an increase of 9.2 per cent in Latin American agricultural production, a figure about three times as large as the percentage of population increase. A small part of this production was moving in foreign trade; more was destined for domestic use.

Outside of Mexico and Bolivia, little progress can be recorded in the reduction of large land holdings and the spread of land ownership among the millions of landless farm workers. Several other nations have been actively concerned with the problem, however. Some have authorized extensive study and research into various alternative policies which might be followed, and a few have made preliminary and tentative moves. Yet the outlook of the *peón* is not hopeless, even in those nations untouched by agrarian reform. Rising living standards will raise his standards, too. Public health and education programs are already beginning to improve his lot. Even social legislation and social security laws are being extended in Argentina and Chile to include the farm worker.

Mining productivity has risen sharply since the close of World War II. With 1948 as the base (100), the production of Latin American mines stood at 124 for 1952 and 123 for the following year. Mine workers are better protected now by national labor and social security laws than previously.

Industrial production is growing. The rate of annual increase was 7.7 per cent for 1945 to 1951, 2.7 per cent for 1951 to 1953, and 1.3 per cent in 1953. Over the nine-year period from 1945 to 1953 the increase was 6.4 per cent. Much more encouraging was the strong upsurge in capital goods production. Steel production was up 1,500,000 metric tons for the nine-year period. The handicap of an illiterate and underfed labor force is being minimized by rising educational and per capita income rates. That the labor force is growing steadily is indicated by the 4.4 per cent annual rate of growth from 1945 to 1950 and the lower 1.4 per cent rate from 1950 to 1953. Investment capital is accumulating within some of the nations, reducing the need for foreign capital and the political difficulties attending its importation. For an indeterminate period to come, however, Latin America will need outside capital. Nor has much been done to overcome the difficulties deriving from the shortage of energy resources. The development of atomic power for peaceful purposes could have a signal effect upon the output of Latin America's industrial machine.

The diversification of the Latin American agricultural economy and the yearly increasing productivity of its industry have far more than economic effects. As an outstanding student of Latin American industrialization puts it: "Industrialization is never solely a technical and economic development. It is a social and cultural process as well, and in under-developed countries nowadays it is also likely to have profound political repercussions." [9] This writer goes on to state that industry creates a new class of businessmen who see that higher living standards for all of the population are necessary if they are to find markets for the products which flow from their factories. This new class, he thinks, will tend to favor land reform, since the landless peon, in his present condition, cannot buy what they manufacture. They will also tend to support social reforms and social legislation. "Their business interests lead them to favor economic and social changes which establish a better base for democratic institutions."

The growth of inter-Latin American trade, previously commented upon, is increasing the feeling of community among the twenty nations, and may strengthen their domestic as well as their inter-American political institutions. This growing interdependence is evident in the addition of political functions to the Organization of American States and in the growing number of inter-American activities in scientific, economic, social, and cultural spheres. The political importance of Latin America in world affairs and its expanding influence in the councils of the United Nations also tend to increase the sense of political solidarity within the area, thus strengthening the institutions of democratic government.

The Status of Latin American Democracy

In 1956 Professor Russell H. Fitzgibbon published a significant study of the status of Latin American democracy at mid-twentieth century, based on a series of "polls" taken among specialists, academicians, and journalists, in the years 1945, 1950, and 1955. Each of the persons polled (ten in 1945, ten in 1950, and twenty in 1955) was asked to rate democratic developments in the twenty republics on the basis of fifteen criteria. Most of these criteria related to political factors: the absence of foreign domination; freedom of speech, press, radio, and assembly; free elections and honestly counted votes; and an independent judiciary. Six of the criteria,

[9] Sanford A. Mosk, *op. cit.*, p. 142.

however, were social and economic: an educational level sufficient
to give the political process some substance and vitality; a fairly
adequate standard of living; a sense of internal unity; belief by the
people in their individual political dignity; the vitality of social
legislation; and reasonable freedom of political life from the impact
of ecclesiastical controls.[10]

The twenty participants in the 1955 polling regarded these
socio-economic criteria as highly significant in their evaluation of
Latin American democracy.   Freedom from ecclesiastical control
was ranked first, internal unity third, social legislation fourth, political maturity sixth, educational level eighth, and standard of
living ninth.

Uruguay, Costa Rica, and Chile received the three highest
ratings for democracy in all three of the surveys, Uruguay winning
the top position in all three.   Paraguay, the Dominican Republic,
Haiti, and Nicaragua occupied four of the last six positions in the
three surveys, the Dominican Republic and Paraguay being consistently in the nineteenth and twentieth places.   As Professor
Fitzgibbon writes: "We would probably be justified, then, in con-
cluding that a top group of three states and a bottom cluster of
perhaps four can be identified statistically and that the remaining
thirteen are an intermediate class which represents more flux and
at least temporary gain or loss of democracy."[11]

The political stability requisite to political democracy cannot
be the product of a stagnant social order, but must spring from the
dynamic forces generated by social change in search of the good
society.   Clearly Latin America is a land in which society is characterized by social change, as well as varying widely in democratic
achievement.   One of the participants in the 1955 poll summarized
the situation as follows: "These are transitional cultures.   While they
vary in the degree of their evolution, none of them has the air of
completeness or finality that one might expect in Europe or Asia.
They are societies in the making, and at times one has the impression
that the process has begun only lately."[12]   The next chapter will
show how these trends of twentieth-century social change have
produced popular political movements, based on programs of socio-
economic reform and expressed in new and sometimes revolutionary
patterns of social thought.

[10] See *Western Political Quarterly*, IX (September 1956), 607–19.
[11] Russell H. Fitzgibbon, "A Statistical Evaluation of Latin American Democracy,"
The Western Political Quarterly, IX (September 1956), 618.
[12] William L. Schurz, *op. cit.*, p. 414.

Suggestions for Reading

The most comprehensive account of the place of the Church in Latin America is J. Lloyd Mecham, *Church and State in Latin America* (Chapel Hill: University of North Carolina Press, 1934). Part VII of William L. Schurz, *Latin America* (rev. ed.; New York: E. P. Dutton & Co., 1949) has brief, excellent discussions of "Latin American Cultural Characteristics," "Social Organization," "Education," and "Religion." The same author devotes Chapter 7 of his *This New World* (New York: E. P. Dutton & Co., 1954) to "The Church."

There is no good general work in English on the society and social organization of Latin America as a whole, although a number of monographic studies on specific countries are available. See, for example, Carl C. Taylor, *Rural Life in Argentina* (Baton Rouge: Louisiana State University Press, 1948) and T. Lynn Smith, *Brazil: People and Institutions* (Baton Rouge: Louisiana State University Press, 1946).

On education, the work of H. L. Smith and Harold Littell, *Education in Latin America* (New York: The American Book Co., 1934) is out-dated, but still useful. Although limited to one country, George I. Sánchez, *Mexico: A Revolution by Education* (New York: The Viking Press, 1936), well analyzes the relationship of educational programs to social and political reforms. The Pan American Union and the United States Office of Education have published a number of useful studies.

Useful works on the economy of Latin America include: Wendell C. Gordon, *The Economy of Latin America* (New York: Columbia University Press, 1950); Simon G. Hanson, *Economic Development in Latin America* (Washington: Inter-American Affairs Press, 1951); Seymour E. Harris (ed.), *Economic Problems of Latin America* (Englewood Cliffs, N. J.: Prentice-Hall, 1949), and George Wythe, *Industry in Latin America* (rev. ed.; New York: Columbia University Press, 1950). The annual *Economic Survey of Latin America* prepared by the United Nations is a good source for changing trends.

Many other works deal with the economy of a particular country, or with specific aspects of the total economy such as foreign trade, industrialization, and labor organization. The monthly *Américas* of the Pan American Union usually includes a section "On the Economic Front" and frequently contains articles on economic questions.

Chapter 4

Political Movements
and Political Thought

In the preceding chapters we have examined the general character and effects of Latin American political experience and analyzed some of the dynamic factors which influence political life in the twentieth century. These factors, it has been noted, include rapid population growth, increased urbanization, revolutionary agricultural and industrial developments, national crusades against illiteracy, the growth of organized labor, the cultural assimilation of Indian, Negro, and mixed ethnic groups of the population, an increase in the social consciousness of the Church, and expansion in the functions of government. This chapter will be concerned with the political movements emanating from the changes produced by these new forces and with the concepts of political action and of national policy which have accompanied them. These movements of thought and politics are perhaps best understood when seen through the eyes of Latin American writers who have interpreted the basic problems confronted by their nations. Attention will be given, therefore, to trends in political thought and the political movements with which they are associated; in particular, we will examine the theoretical basis which Latin American writers have provided for the social and political movements of their day.

Basic Movements in Thought and Politics

A growing spirit of nationalism and increased reliance upon the state as the instrument for achieving the good society are two of the most obvious characteristics of twentieth-century Latin America. The sources of the growth of this nationalism were noted in the previous chapter, and the expanding role of the state in society will be examined further in Chapters 15 and 16. This chapter will be limited, therefore, to some of the principal national political movements to which these forces have given rise and the changes in thought which have accompanied them.

Since the nations vary widely in population and levels of social and economic development, political movements have differed accordingly. These differences are so great, in fact, that it would at first seem impossible to speak of any general political movement, at least in the sense of a movement supported by identical elements and advocating the same measures throughout the area. But there is a certain unity within this diversity.

GENERAL NATURE OF THE MOVEMENTS. In all these nations, for example, the principal new measures debated or adopted lead in the direction of increased economic and social responsibilities of the nation. In all these nations (though in divergent forms and in varying degrees), new political parties, or groupings within the older parties, represent a broadening political basis of the state which is connected with the breaking down of traditional lines of class stratification. In most, if not all, of these states new combinations of "interests" and new political groupings of labor leaders, army officers, and, sometimes, agrarian leaders either have achieved dominance or threaten to do so, thus bringing new configurations in the power structure and new political parties. Although there is again considerable variation, at least incipient agrarian and labor movements have appeared in all the nations, while in many countries something akin to Christian socialism battles for control of the labor movement. Many of these movements obviously embrace aspects of socialism, but they have been autochthonous in political character to a large degree and have usually rejected the leadership of socialist or other class-conscious labor parties.

FASCISM. Fascist-like movements made considerable headway in some countries during the 1930's. The governments of Getulio Vargas in Brazil (1930–1945), of Luis Sánchez Cerro and of Óscar Benavides in Peru (1930–1939), of Jorge Ubico Castañeda in Guatemala (1930–1944), of Maximiliano Hernández Martínez in El Salvador (1931–1944), and of Juan Perón in Argentina (1943–1955) imitated some of the tactics and followed some of the principles of European fascism. Such political parties as the *integralistas* in Brazil, the *Nacista* party of Gonzalo von Marées in Chile, and the *sinarquistas* in Mexico were also of this type. The Spanish Civil War had deep reverberations throughout Spanish America, and the triumph of Franco strengthened this American fascism after 1937. In Latin America, as in Spain, certain conservative elements within the Church hierarchy were attracted to its support. In general, however, European fascism was too exotic a product to strike deep roots in America. Much of the Latin American fascism, accordingly, was superficial—a new dress for older authoritarian and militarist tendencies. Its importance declined rapidly with the growth of inter-American solidarity after 1938, with the notable exception of *peronismo* in Argentina, and less important ones such as *sinarquismo* in Mexico and the regime of Gualberto Villarroel in Bolivia.

CATHOLIC SOCIAL ACTION. Catholic Social Action, a lay movement based upon the principles of the encyclical *Rerum Novarum* of Pope Leo XIII, has contributed a stream of Christian socialism somewhat at variance with the trend among those more conservative Church elements which leaned toward fascism. Although its roots extend back several decades, during which it has had brilliant exponents among neo-Thomist writers, Catholic Social Action has come into political importance chiefly since the mid-1940's. Leaders animated with the ideals of this Catholic liberalism played an important role in the revolution which drove Perón from Argentina in 1955. Their influence has also been strong in Brazil and Chile. So far, however, the Christian socialist parties, such as the one formed in Argentina after the overthrow of Perón, have not demonstrated the political strength of their European counterparts.

On the other hand, a vigorous development of Catholic social thought, emphasizing principles of free will in social action as against the prevailing sociological concepts of the influence of environment, has accompanied the religious renaissance which has been occurring in most parts of Latin America since around 1940. Its Aristotelian and neo-Thomistic tendencies have found expression in the halls of the universities and in the journals of thought and opinion through such men as Oswaldo Robles of Mexico, Nicolás Derisi of Argentina, Clarence Finlayson of Chile, and Alceu Amoroso Lima of Brazil. In the social realm, this voluntaristic thought finds targets for attack in the Marxist dialectical materialism, in scientific positivism, and in the element of irrationalism characterizing much of contemporary thought, especially those philosophies which assert that the only reality is being or existence.

GENERAL TRENDS IN THOUGHT. The most general trend in the thought animating twentieth-century political movements may be termed idealistic, if that term is given connotation broad enough to embrace both the modern revivals of classical idealism and the more existentialist quest of many contemporary thinkers, who reject universals but still seek an idealistic basis to oppose the materialistic determinism and agnosticism they see in the prevalent social thought. This "existentialist" tendency, based on the assumption that being or existence is reality, reflects the influence of Freudian psychology and of the relativism of modern physics. Sometimes it rejects the Hegelian dialectical pattern, which sees all history as a conflict out of which the absolute truth emerges. But more frequently it attempts a reappraisal or revision of Hegelian thought.

The new trend appears in various forms. The older "scientific" sociological thought continues to dominate university courses in American or national psychology, but it is increasingly penetrated with the neo-idealism. The new idealism has important Germanic sources, although two Spanish philosophers, Miguel Unamuno and José Ortega y Gasset,[1] as well as French, British, North American, and Latin American writers, make important contributions to the stream.

A renaissance of interest in the philosophy of history reflecting ideas of Benedetto Croce, José Ortega y Gasset, R. G. Collingwood, Oswald Spengler, and others is another form assumed by twentieth-century idealistic thought. A new generation of Latin American historians, influenced by this philosophy of history, has sought basic historical significance in the institution as the instrument through which mind has risen above servitude to environment. This "new" historical interest logically extends to the history of law, finding expression, for example, in the Institute of the History of Law directed since 1937 by the historian Ricardo Levene in the University of Buenos Aires.

COMMUNIST THOUGHT. Communism achieved an important vogue among intellectuals in the 1920's, building upon the earlier socialism of intellectual spokesmen of the incipient labor movement. Its most brilliant exponent was the Peruvian Carlos Mariátegui. Since the 1930's, with a few exceptions, Communist thought has followed the lines of Stalinism, displaying little vigor and no originality, and consisting largely of restatements of the shifting party position on immediate issues.

The Mexican Revolution

ORIGINS OF THE REVOLUTION. The initial rumblings against the Díaz dictatorship which ruled Mexico from 1876 to 1910 came from

---

[1] For the influence of these two Spanish philosophers, particularly Unamuno, see Gerhard Masur, "Miguel de Unamuno," *The Americas* (Academy of American Franciscan History), XII (October 1955), 139–156.

labor groups, protesting against the anti-labor policies of the government. One of their most effective spokesmen was Ricardo Flores Magón, who was driven into exile for his revolutionary agitation and died in a penitentiary in the United States in 1922.[2] Although he was a native-born Mexican, his ideas were those of the anarcho-syndicalism which characterized the labor movement in France, Spain, and Italy, and these ideas were prominent in the early stages of the revolutionary movement.

Francisco I. Madero, who led the successful uprising against Díaz and was elected to the presidency in 1911, had political and social ideas inherited from the nineteenth-century liberalism of Benito Juárez and his followers. Madero was a man of intelligence and broad views who approached national problems with a good understanding of the needs of both industrial and landless agricultural workers. But he placed political reform ahead of social revolution, believing that political democracy could be made to work in Mexico and that political freedom would make possible social and economic reforms without resort to violence. His family background influenced him toward this older, orthodox liberalism. But while in Europe he had come under the influence of spiritualism and of Krausism, the mystic idealist philosophy of humanity which had spread widely in Spain and Latin America around the turn of the century. The Krausist doctrines of pacifism, human equality, and the triumph of the spirit over matter contributed a bent toward humanitarianism. All in all, however, these ideas led Madero to think that the political as well as the economic salvation of his country could be achieved within the existing structure of power. Hence he tried to work with the representatives of the old order in the army and in the government. But he paid dearly for this error in judgment when he met death as the victim of one of the most unscrupulous political murders in the history of Mexican politics.[3]

REFORM MOVEMENTS. Much of Madero's failure arose from his reluctance or inability to build his political power around the restless forces of the incipient labor movement and of the agrarian revolt which was personified by Emiliano Zapata. During the years of anarchy and civil war after Madero's overthrow in 1913, these revolutionary forces gained an important place in national life under the leadership of Venustiano Carranza, incorporating

[2] Pedro M. Onaya Ibarra, *Precursores de la Revolución Mexicana* (Mexico: Secretaría de Educación Pública, 1955), pp. 11–51.

[3] For the career of Madero see Stanley R. Ross, *Francisco I. Madero* (New York: Columbia University Press, 1955) and Charles C. Cumberland, *Mexican Revolution: Genesis Under Madero* (Austin, Texas: University of Texas Press, 1952).

their reform programs into the constitutional revision of 1917. The most notable constitutional changes were provisions authorizing a broad program of labor and social legislation (Art. 123) and granting the national government power to modify the system of private land ownership and to nationalize natural resources (Art. 27). Presidents Álvaro Obregón (1920–1924) and Plutarco Elías Calles (1924–1928) encouraged the growth of organized labor. Calles also consolidated the political structure of the revolutionary movement in a well-organized political party, known today as the Institutional Revolutionary party (PRI). This party, based on labor organizations, army officers, and bureaucrats, has dominated the national political scene ever since.

The reform aspects of the Revolution developed slowly on the basis of the decrees of the Carranza administration and a slowly growing body of labor, land, and educational legislation under Obregón and Calles. A vigorous educational and cultural crusade to educate and Europeanize the illiterate Indian masses was launched under the direction of José Vasconcelos, Secretary of Education in the Obregón cabinet. A few large estates were expropriated during these years in order to restore community lands to villages in the form of *ejidos*. Small private holdings were also encouraged. Petroleum-bearing lands were nationalized, giving rise to a bitter conflict with the foreign-owned industry during the Calles administration. Meanwhile, efforts to suppress church schools and to license priests had led to an inconclusive and unnecessarily frustrating struggle with the Church during the 1920's. Social and economic reform tendencies reached their zenith in the presidency of Lázaro Cárdenas (1934–1940) during which land distribution created some two million additional land-owning families. The Cárdenas land reform was a basic social revolution —an agrarian revolution—which transformed Mexico into a nation of farm owners, while at the same time labor and other social and economic legislation raised the standards of living of urban workers and paved the way for industrialization and urbanization on a large scale.

CONSOLIDATION OF GAINS. After 1940, the administrations of Manuel Ávila Camacho (1940–1946), Miguel Alemán (1946–1952), and Adolfo Ruiz Cortines (1952—) followed somewhat more conservative policies, consolidating the revolutionary gains while encouraging agricultural and industrial development. This more conservative trend reflected the fact that a new political generation had appeared on the national scene. The older interests which were targets of the revolutionary movement—large landowners, clergy, foreigners, and Mexicans connected with foreign-owned enterprises—reconciled themselves to the Revolution as a new form of nationalism. The attack on the Church ended under the Cárdenas administration, and the Mexican Church began to regain its social influence, accepting the changes which the Revolution had brought and avoiding any open conflicts with the existing regime. It found increasing support among the growing urban population, among whom its new program of social action, based upon the papal encyclical *Rerum Novarum,* aimed to substitute a Christian basis for the materialist-Marxism of the labor-dominated official party (PRI). The Mexican Constitution specifically prohibits parties with religious titles, but some of this new religious tendency found political expression in various forms in opposition parties.[4]

TRENDS IN SOCIAL THOUGHT. Socialist ideas have been prominent in Mexico's development since 1910, even though international socialism as such has never achieved great popularity. Yet it is not in socialism so much as in Justo Sierra's transition from scientific positivism to the more idealistic thought of the twentieth century that the general ideological setting of the Mexican Revolution is to be found. Sierra barely outlived the advent of Madero on the national scene, however, and no successor arose whose ideas embraced all facets of the revolutionary movement. Although Madero's previously noted "spiritual" Krausism, with its creed of pacifism, human equality, and human welfare, was part of a movement which had gained wide popularity in the Hispanic world, its influence on the Mexican Revolution was superficial and passing. The anarcho-syndicalism of Ricardo Flores Magón, who naturally found a kinship with the IWW in the United States, set the tone of socialist thought in the earliest phase of the Revolution, while Lombardo Toledano, organizer of the Confederation of Mexican Workers (CTM) and the Latin American Confederation of Workers (CTAL) during the Cárdenas days, dominates a later stage of socialist thought which developed certain Communist overtones.

Better than any of the men just mentioned, Andrés Molina Enríquez represents the intellectual current of the Revolution, especially in its early stages. His book, *Los grandes problemas nacionales,* published in 1909, was written within the framework of the turn of the century evolutionary or positivist sociology which had discovered, with Sierra, a new emphasis on action for reform.

[4] Books on modern Mexico are very numerous, but perhaps the best general appraisal of the objectives, problems, and achievements of the Mexican Revolution is to be found in Howard Cline, *Mexico and the United States* (Cambridge, Mass.: Harvard University Press, 1952).

He analyzed the agrarian problem in terms of the ethnic and social relationships of Indians, mestizos, and *criollos* in the social structure, within which he found dynamic forces calling for change. In the field of economic thought, Jesús Silva Herzog reveals a more revolutionary trend. Silva turned from the doctrinaire economics of the socialist movement, however, to develop an economics combining historical analysis with emphasis on more quantitative methods. Still socialist in a certain broad sense, he found the basic objective of economic policy to be that of raising the living level of workers. This objective he would accomplish through nationalizing resources and achieving a balanced economy, including the development of new industries, with the aid of protective measures.[5]

The principal stream of intellectual influences, often representing contradictory tendencies, stems from the Ateneo de Juventud— a group of young intellectuals who, in the years preceding the Revolution, had been attacking the reigning social concepts of positivism as taught in the National University. The intellectual milieu of the Ateneo, in which socialist ideas mingled with those derived from such diverse sources as Bergson, Kirkegaard, Dilthey, Unamuno, and Ortega y Gasset, united a group of divergent personalities in the common quest for a new idealism of social action, often vaguely religious, but also anti-clerical. One member of this group was Diego Rivera, destined to become a popular painter expressing the Communist ideology in art. Another was Antonio Caso, a brilliant young professor of philosophy in the National University, whose thought developed along the lines of personalism and humanism. A third was the pluralistic, anti-Hegelian idealist-empiricist, the enigmatic José Vasconcelos. Two younger men who followed in the footsteps of this older group may also be noted here: Samuel Ramos and Oswaldo Robles. The anti-scientific humanism of Ramos is rooted in a search for historical and philosophical-anthropological bases of social change, perhaps reflecting the continued influence of Caso and Unamuno. Oswaldo Robles, on the other hand, tries to bridge the gap between modern social and natural science and Christian faith with a new philosophical synthesis more closely akin to Aristotelian-Thomistic principles.

A characteristic expression in political theory of this Catholic trend which Robles expresses may be found in a recent work of Francisco Porrúa Pérez.[6] Porrúa defines the state as a complex entity, one aspect of which is "a group of men producing, creating,

[5] See Jesús Silva Herzog, *El pensamiento socialista* (Mexico: Workers University of Mexico, 1937), p. 139.

[6] *Teoría del estado* (Mexico: Porrúa, 1955).

and defining a juridical order." Rejecting any purely sociological theory of the state which denies that law is an essential part of the state, he also avoids the identification of law and state. The social Catholic doctrine, he insists, should lie at its base and should repress the class struggle by means of professional organizations. It should provide psychological, metaphysical, and social (moral) freedom —the latter insofar as it does not interfere with the general welfare which is the predominant objective of the state.

Reform in Uruguay

BATLLISMO. Second in importance only to the Mexican Revolution in the politics of twentieth-century Latin America is the movement of social and political reform which came to a climax during the years 1917–1919 in Uruguay, under the leadership of José Batlle y Ordóñez. As a buffer state between Brazil and Argentina, Uruguay had had an unhappy political history during much of the nineteenth century. After 1875, however, a succession of military dictators had brought order and prosperity. These generals were followed, after 1890, by civilian presidents who governed with normal party support. Meanwhile, an agricultural revolution based upon large-scale production of wool, wheat, and meat for export had brought new prosperity, while extensive immigration of Europeans, Italians and Spaniards, had transformed the predominantly mestizo population. Under the leadership of José Batlle and his followers in the Colorado party, Uruguay rapidly developed into a nation with a predominantly urban society, a moderate socialist economy, and a democratic governmental structure.

Batllismo is the term Uruguayans have applied to the political movement led by Batlle and the constitutional changes of 1919 which revolutionized the nation's social and political structure. The ideals and program of Batlle, who was twice president of his country (1903–1907 and 1911–1915), had two principal aspects. In political structure Batlle advocated a bipartisan collegiate executive or commission to be substituted for the presidency, to which he attributed the turbulence and frequent revolutions of Uruguay's past. In the economic and social realm Batlle supported a broad program of labor and social legislation—laws legalizing labor unions and their activities, limiting hours of work, establishing minimum wages, regulating the labor of women and children, providing public medical services, and offering free education at all levels for the benefit of the working classes. Such basic industries as railroads, electric power, insurance, banking, meat packing, and hotels were to be nationalized. The bipartisan collegiate executive was adopted in limited form only in 1919, was temporarily suppressed in the constitutional revision of 1933–1934, but has since been restored (1951) in full vigor, making Uruguay a unique constitutional experiment among the republics of America. The socio-economic measures which grew out of Batlle's proposals have given Uruguay the further distinction of being a progressive, democratic nation practicing a high degree of state socialism.

As a political movement, *batllismo* absorbed an essentially socialist program into the Colorado party, which traditionally represented mid-nineteenth-century liberalism, thus winning for this party the support of the rapidly growing and predominantly immigrant urban working class. But the *batllista* constitutional changes, which gave the minority party three out of the six seats in the national and provincial executive commissions and provided proportional representation in congress, had a further important influence on the party system itself. Since it provided a share in government for all parties, the change was generally accepted by both major parties (Colorados and Blancos). Moreover, since the electoral laws permitted minority views within each party to find articulate expression without breaking with the parent party, through what are, in effect, legalized sub-parties, the danger of a multi-party system so often connected with a system of proportional representation was minimized, and the two-party system further strengthened.[7]

URUGUAYAN SOCIAL THOUGHT. The social thought implicit in these reforms, especially those leading to state socialism, is largely a mixture of the nationalist, revisionist socialism and the evolutionary positivism of the late nineteenth century. But the earlier nineteenth-century liberalism may also be seen in some of the emphasis upon a secular, democratic society and upon free compulsory education. Anarcho-syndicalist concepts appear to some extent in the support given to the nascent trade unions and of their right to strike, i.e., in support of the idea of regulated industrial warfare. Batlle's own writings, chiefly in his newspaper *El Día*, give the best expression of the ideas behind the reforms, but they do not form a very systematic whole, since he did not generally concern himself with the philosophical bases of ideas. During these years, however, two outstanding though very different Uruguayan writers—Carlos Vaz Ferreira (1873—) and José Rodó (1871–1917) —took up the more fundamental philosophical questions.

[7] On *batllismo* see Simon G. Hanson, *Utopia in Uruguay* (New York: Oxford University Press, 1938); Russell H. Fitzgibbon, *Uruguay* (New Brunswick, N.J.: Rutgers University Press, 1954); and Justino Zavala Múñiz, *Batlle, héroe civil* (Mexico: Fondo de Cultura Económica, 1945).

Although Carlos Vaz Ferreira shows some qualities of originality, his social ideas have strong roots in earlier evolutionary social thought, modified by the new psychology of the twentieth century. Like Unamuno and Ortega he has sought an idealism based upon consciousness and existence (existentialism). His economic ideas, which seem closely akin to the modified individualism of John Stuart Mill, contemplate a field for collective social action and reform sufficiently broad to lead Alfonso Reyes to speak of him as "revolutionary."[8] In rejecting Marxism he signified his general tendency to search for spiritual and ideal elements in the social process. Vaz Ferreira's social philosophy obviously contributed to an intellectual climate favorable to *batllismo*, but he has never been strongly partisan. Perhaps this lack of partisanship may explain his not speaking out in defense of the ideals of *batllismo* when they were temporarily suppressed by forces tinged with fascist-like doctrines in the 1930's—a failure for which some Uruguayans have criticized him.

José Enríque Rodó, one of the most brilliant literary figures of the twentieth-century Spanish-speaking world, remained largely aloof from the struggle over *batllismo*, although the most productive years of his short life roughly parallel those of the *batllista* crusade. The basis of Rodó's thought was an idealist revolt against the growing materialism of his times. He believed that "where democracy does not heighten its spirit by the influence of a strong idealistic preoccupation, which shares its role with that of preoccupation with material interests, it leads fatally to the poverty of mediocrity . . ."[9] Although he too reflected the current European thought, he is essentially the critic of new forces and movements, the voice of an idealism which seeks the basis of society in the Christian sentiments of love, pity, and equality of souls. He wished to unite this Christian element with a sense of hierarchy, reason, and order derived from the classical tradition. Publication of his most famous and influential work, *Ariel* (1900), preceded the struggle over *batllismo*. It made no direct contribution to that movement and may be interpreted in some respects as hostile to it. It was critical of the United States at many points. But it inspired an entire generation of Uruguayan (and other Latin American) youth with its high sense of the role of spirit and ideas in

[8] Cited in Manuel Arturo Claps, "Carlos Vaz Ferreira," *Número* (Montevideo), II (1950) No. 6-7-8, pp. 93–117.

[9] Quoted by Emilio Oribe in *El pensamiento vivo de Rodó* (Buenos Aires: Losada, 1944), p. 41.

democratic leadership. For in spite of his criticism of the materialism and leveling tendency of democracy Rodó did not follow Renan, whom he resembled and greatly admired, in the latter's more general condemnation of democratic equality.   "The spirit of democracy," he wrote, "is . . . for our civilization a principle of life against which it is useless to rebel." His appeal, in essence, is for the acceptance of leadership by a democratic elite.

Peruvian Aprismo

APRA. The American Popular Revolutionary Alliance differs from other Latin American political movements in several respects. While it is an expression of Peruvian national aspirations, it has also sought to be an international, that is, an inter-American, movement with branches in other American republics. It also has an ethnic orientation, seeking the basis of its thought and program in what it terms *Indoamérica*. APRA found much of its original inspiration in the Mexican Revolution, but also nurtured its ideology on Marxism, the Russian Revolution of 1917, the Chinese Kuomintang, and the labor parties of western Europe. It originated during the long dictatorship of Augusto B. Leguía as a movement to unite intellectuals and workers in solving the basic social problem of Peru— the redemption of the suppressed Indian and mestizo masses. Like the Mexican Revolution, it found its principal objectives in agrarian reform, including restoration of the Indian *ayllu* or community as a landowning unit; labor and social legislation, including legalization and encouragement of unions; education to eliminate illiteracy; a national health program; and national economic planning and activity to further industrialization.

As an underground organization it shared in the overthrow of President Augusto B. Leguía in 1930. The following year it unsuccessfully presented Víctor Raúl Haya de la Torre as a candidate for the presidency. The party was suppressed during the decade following the assassination of President Luis Sánchez Cerro in 1933, until it made its peace with President Benavides in 1942. In the elections of 1945 the Aprista party won a majority in the congress and elected the friendly non-Aprista José Luis Bustamante y Rivero to the presidency. After a turbulent four years the party was again outlawed in 1949 after President Bustamante had been driven from office,[10] not returning to participate openly in national politics until the presidential election of 1956.

[10] See Harry Kantor, *The Ideology and Program of the Peruvian Aprista Movement* (Berkeley, California: University of California Press, 1953).

THE IDEAS OF APRA.   The basic ideas of *aprismo* are Marxist, although its greatest leader, Víctor Haya de la Torre, has insisted upon its American character, rejecting not only a political alliance with other socialist and communist parties, but also (in typically American fashion) an exclusively working-class ideology.   In organizing APRA as a national political party, Haya parted company with the other intellectual founder of the movement, Carlos Mariátegui who openly embraced international communism.   Interestingly enough, in spite of this split over party organization, Mariátegui's *Siete ensayos de la realidad peruano*, published in 1928, remains one of the classics of Aprista thought.   Haya's *¿A donde va Indoamérica?* is the best general statement of APRA's ideas and program, and makes an important contribution to a historical theory of Latin American politics.   It would be difficult, indeed, to find another Latin American writer to rival Haya de la Torre in respect to the purely theoretical basis of his work.   Two other literary figures of Peru, Manuel Seoane and Luis Alberto Sánchez, have also given excellent expression to certain aspects of this movement and philosophy of *Indoamérica*.

The Chilean Popular Front

REFORM IN CHILE.   The political movements of Chile during recent decades, more than those of any other Latin American country, have resembled the political movements of western Europe, particularly France and Spain.   Arturo Alessandri, as president from 1920 to 1925, led Chile in the beginning of a modern program of social and labor legislation.   In a later term (1932–1938), however, he relied increasingly on a coalition of conservative parties and failed to take adequate measures to resolve the economic crisis which gripped the nation.   The Radical (Socialist) party, which is somewhat similar to the Radical party of France, at first supported Alessandri.   But by 1934 its leaders had turned to a coalition with the parties of the Left—both right and left wings of the Radical party, Communists, Socialists, the Chilean Confederation of Labor, and the Republican Action.   The coalition was pledged to a broad extension of the labor and social legislation previously enacted in 1925, to agrarian reform, the extension of public education, and industrialization of the economy.   Pedro Aguirre Cerda, the architect of this coalition, was elected to the presidency in 1938 and served three years, until his death in 1941.

Little progress was made in agrarian reform during his brief administration, but the promised social legislation was enacted, and industrialization was encouraged through a Development (*Fomento*)

Corporation.   The Popular Front really came to an end in 1942 when the Communists split off as a result of the election of the Radical party candidate, Antonio Ríos.   But the Radical party succeeded in electing its candidate again in 1946—the vigorous Gabriel González Videla, who made the break with communism definitive by outlawing the Communist party and breaking diplomatic relations with the Soviet Union.   In spite of the shifting political basis of the movement of national economic and social reform and development in Chile, a kind of continuity may be seen since the advent of Arturo Alessandri to the presidential office in 1920.   Not even the election in 1952 of a former dictator, Carlos Ibáñez, with supposed Peronist leanings seems to have interrupted the trend.[11]

CHILEAN SOCIAL THOUGHT.   In view of the generally high level of Chilean intellectual life, and especially of historical and social research, it is somewhat surprising that Chilean social thought has shown little originality in recent years.   Theoretical economic thought tends to fall either into the historical school, thus accepting ideas of state socialism, or into the tradition of classical economics.   The historian-economist, Francisco Encina, is an example of the latter trend.   His work exhibits strong overtones of reform in respect to the pattern of distribution of wealth and in economic development, although the theory remains fundamentally classical. Eduardo Frei M., a journalist and leader of the Falange, has given vigorous and effective expression to the ideas of this party of Catholic social action.   Among sociologists to be noted are Augustín Venturino, who has studied the conflict and amalgamation of races in indigenous and colonial society, and Alejandro Lipschutz, whose attention has been directed to the ethnic basis of the social and political problems of *Indoamérica*.[12]   International communism has found intellectual leadership in Contreras La Barca, secretary of the party, and in Senator Elías Lafferte.   It has also enjoyed the literary prestige attached to the poet Pablo Neruda.

The Vargas Movement in Brazil

THE ESTADO NOVO.   The principal movement in Brazilian politics in recent decades has centered around the personality of Getulio Vargas, who governed the nation as president-dictator from 1930 to 1945 and again as constitutionally elected president from

[11] John Reese Stevenson, *The Chilean Popular Front* (Philadelphia: University of Pennsylvania Press, 1942).

[12] *Indoamericanismo y raza india* (Santiago: Ed. Nascimiento, 1937), and *El indoamericanismo y el problema racial en las Américas* (Santiago: Ed. Nascimiento, 1941).

1950 until his suicide in 1954. The presidential election of 1930 took place in the midst of the severe economic crisis induced by the collapse of the world market for Brazilian sugar, cotton, and coffee. The crisis was most acute in the coffee-producing state of São Paulo, whose influence had led to the adoption of a national "valorization" plan for subsidizing coffee. In order to guarantee continuation of this program, the president, Washington Luiz Pereira de Souza, himself a *paulista*, backed the election of the São Paulo governor, Julio Prestes. This was a violation of the "gentleman's agreement" by which the two traditional parties, liberals and conservatives, had controlled the government, alternating the presidency between the two biggest states, São Paulo and Minas Gerais. Hence the governor of Minas Gerais threw his support to Getulio Vargas of the southern state of Rio Grande do Sul, who was supported by the Liberal Alliance. When Vargas was defeated in the election, he broke political precedent in Brazil by leading a bloodless revolt, with the support of the army. A triumphal march on Rio de Janeiro established him in the presidency for the next fifteen years. He governed as provisional president until a constitutional convention assembled in 1933. This body, after granting to the central government power to legislate on social and economic matters, giving women the right to vote, and forbidding the re-election of presidents, elected Vargas president for a four-year term.

The parallel between the Vargas march on Rio de Janeiro and the march of Mussolini on Rome a decade earlier did not go unnoticed. Vargas relied chiefly upon a group of young army officers and civilians (the "tenentes") rather vaguely animated by purposes of political and economic reform,[13] who made up an essentially personal following. But he also appealed to the forces of popular discontent, which soon gave the Communist party a following of several hundred thousand under the colorful leadership of Luiz Carlos Prestes (not to be confused with the governor of São Paulo), one of the "tenentes" who broke with Vargas. Vargas also had the support of the fascist *integralistas*. When street fighting occurred between the Communists and the green-uniformed *integralistas*, he moved first to outlaw the Communist party and then, a year later, to restrict the activities of the *integralistas*. In the midst of preparations for a presidential election in 1938, he called off the elections, proclaiming a new constitution with many of the characteristics of a corporative state, but providing for a dictatorship

[13] See Robert J. Alexander, "Brazilian Tenentismo," *Hispanic American Historical Review*, XXVI (May 1956), 229–242, and Chapter 7 in this book.

during the "state of grave internal commotion" to be in force until the constitution was submitted to a plebiscite. With the extraordinary powers thus provided, he governed without a congress until forced out of office by an army ultimatum in 1945.

Meanwhile, the President himself virtually ruled the states (Brazil is a federal republic) through interventors and national administrative agencies. Several new federal territories were created, partly to reduce the states' control over public lands and natural resources. Highways and railroads were built under federal authority, while railroads, packing plants, and even two newspapers were brought under direct government control. National development commissions were established to encourage and assist new industries, and an imposing number of social and labor measures, including the establishment of labor courts, were enacted (some of them by the congress under the Constitution of 1934). Municipal, state, and federal appropriations were increased, and education was encouraged.

BASIS OF THE VARGAS MOVEMENT. The resemblance to Italian fascism and the Portuguese corporative state was rather superficial; rather, the *estado novo* (new state) of Vargas is better understood as the product of Brazilian social and political elements. Three aspects of the movement may be noted. First, Vargas' advent to power, his forced resignation in 1945, and the situation which led to his suicide in 1954 all represented more direct intervention by the army in Brazilian politics than had occurred in this generally civilian republic since the revolution of 1889, in which the army overturned the monarchy and established a republic. Second, as the Vargas regime progressed, the President increasingly cultivated a loosely organized "labor" party, into which some, but not all, of his original "tenentes" followed him. It was with the support of this party that he was later (1950) re-elected to the presidency, after an interval in which more conservative forces were in control. Third, the Vargas movement committed the nation to a broad program of social and labor legislation and to measures of economic nationalism which seemed to be required by the industrialization and urbanization of the nation's life. The army supported this program, probably because of the realization that modern warfare required an industrialized nation.[14]

[14] In addition to the article by Alexander previously cited, see Karl Lowenstein, *Brazil Under Vargas* (New York: The Macmillan Co., 1932); T. L. Smith, *Brazil: People and Institutions* (Baton Rouge: Louisiana State University Press, 1946); and Harry Bernstein, *Modern and Contemporary Latin America* (Philadelphia: J. B. Lippincott Co., 1952), Chaps. 22 and 23.

THEORETICAL BASES. Francisco Campos, minister of justice in the Vargas cabinet of 1937, gives the best statement of the ideology of the movement in his *O estado nacional* (1940). He is also the reputed author of much of the ill-omened corporative Constitution of 1937. One of Vargas' original group of personal supporters, Campos had parted company with the *integralistas,* but retained many of their ideas. Society, to Campos, is basically irrational, and "political integration is always the attempt to rationalize the irrational." The rule of a *caudillo* was necessary, he believed, in any society in which the masses achieved political power. He thus advocated a kind of personalism in politics which Brazil had in the main escaped previously. But at the same time he asserted a rational concept of the leader and the state rather than the metaphysical concepts which characterized European fascism. Vargas, a wealthy cattleman, expressed himself lucidly in speeches and interviews but was much less theoretical than Campos, more the practical politician. He believed it was the function of the state "to coordinate and discipline collective interests . . . [and] . . . to take account of our political and economic realities."[15]

OTHER TRENDS IN BRAZILIAN SOCIAL THOUGHT. Within the general trends of social thought in Brazil several other foreign influences may be seen—French, German, and North American. The influence of France has been strong in the University of São Paulo, where a succession of French professors (Roger Bastide since 1937) have carried on studies of primitive societies. North American influence has also been present in São Paulo in the Free School of Sociology and Politics, in the work of Donald Pierson, for example. Emilio Willems, an outstanding Brazilian scholar in socio-anthropological studies, was educated in France and Germany, but has also had close contact with North American scholarship. Gilberto Freyre, whose interests center in regionalism and the influence of tradition, emphasizes (in *Casa grande e senzala* and *Região e tradição*) the importance of the patriarchal tradition derived from the plantation economy and the psychological effect of former slave status in Brazilian Negroes. This concern with ethnic problems has made him in some respects the spokesman of a "Negroism" resembling the Indianism of Spanish America. Alceu Amoroso Lima, professor of philosophy in the Catholic University of Rio de Janeiro, is generally Aristotelian and neo-Thomist in his thought. In his book

[15] *A nova política do Brazil,* III, 30–31, reprinted in Hans Klinghoffer, *La pensée politique du President Getulio Vargas* (Rio de Janeiro: Imprensa Nacional, 1942), p. 10.
[16] (Rio de Janeiro: AGIR, 1947).

on the labor movement (*O problema do trabalho*)[16] and other works on social questions, he is a vigorous advocate for the lay movement of Catholic social action.

Peronismo in Argentina

A proud, stubborn, and powerful political oligarchy grew up throughout the provinces of Argentina after the adoption of the federal constitution of 1853. The strength and leadership of this oligarchy came chiefly from land barons, cattlemen, and wheat farmers who held local and provincial politics in a firm grasp. Only the fortunate presence of vigorous national leaders prevented the personal ambitions of local leaders and the corruption always attendant upon a system of political "bosses" from interrupting the steady flow of constitutional life. As the years went on, large-scale European immigration, substantial investments of British capital, railway construction, and an agricultural revolution brought national prosperity, while increasing the prestige and power of the ruling class by the introduction of new elements based on wealth from these sources. These economic and social changes also brought a disproportionate increase in the wealth and political power of Buenos Aires despite the federalization of the capital city, which was separated from the province of the same name in an effort to check the tension between the metropolis and the provinces.

THE REVOLUTION OF 1930. A new and more popular political party, the Unión Cívica Radical, or Radical party, captured control of the national government from 1916 to 1930. It mustered its chief support among the new immigrants of the province and city of Buenos Aires, but found important leadership also among the professional and business classes of the capital. It was the aging chief of this party, Hipólito Irigoyen, who was president for a second time (1928–1930) when the country faced the severe economic crisis induced by a general breakdown in international trade in 1930. His "do-nothing" policy was partly the result of his age and personal isolation from political life and partly the result of conflict within the Radical party. More specifically, it was the result of the party's failure to evolve a program to meet the social and economic problems posed by industrialization, urbanization, and the workers' movement. Irigoyen's vacillation provided the opportunity for a group of Conservative (Democratic) party leaders, in collaboration with army officers under the leadership of General José Evaristo Uriburu, to force the resignation of the president. The leader of the revolt was installed in his place.

This revolution of 1930 had two far-reaching consequences. It set an example for the direct intervention of the army in the traditionally civilian political process of Argentina and it brought about the formation of the *concordancia*, consisting of Conservatives, anti-Irigoyen Radicals, and a faction of the Socialist party. The political career of Juan B. Perón and his program of *justicialismo* flow directly from these two alterations in Argentine political life. Perón was also a product of an Argentine fascism which increased with the success of the Franco *falangista* movement in Spain.

REVOLT OF 1943. Peronismo began with an army *coup d'état* in 1943 which drove another constitutional executive from office. First from behind the scenes, and after 1946 as president, Perón created a hard-hitting, unscrupulous political machine, based upon a shrewd mixture of militarism, economic planning, and a demagogic appeal to the underprivileged. A long overdue program of labor and social legislation cemented his hold upon the working classes (*descamisados*, or the shirtless), which he organized into political unions. His politics breathed the spirit of unscrupulous opportunism and bred a kind of anarchy in the political life of a nation previously characterized by a high degree of political stability. His greatest single political error may have been the constitutional change providing for presidential re-election, because it forced the opposition Radical party into an uncompromising and eventually successful boycott of the entire political and electoral process.[17]

But *peronismo* was not merely a manifestation of the forces of evil and a conscienceless striving for political power. It also had some of the aspects of the larger social and political movement which has been observed elsewhere in Latin America. In *peronismo*, Argentina belatedly reflected the general Latin American tendency toward economic nationalism and state socialism, with its attendant achievement of modern social and labor legislation. Moreover, in *peronismo*, as in some of the other contemporary movements of Latin America, militarists joined with labor leaders to achieve this social legislation and the industrialization essential to modern warfare.

JUSTICIALISMO. Like other modern fascist-like regimes which have tried to clothe their naked quest for power with the respectable garments of an ideology, *peronismo* used the language of modern philosophical idealism in attacking positivist-scientific

17 On *peronismo* see Robert J. Alexander, *The Perón Era* (New York: Columbia University Press, 1951), and George I. Blanksten, *Perón's Argentina* (Chicago: University of Chicago Press, 1953).

thought as materialist and Marxist. Sometimes, it seemed to be embracing the neo-Thomism of the Argentine philosopher-priest, Nicolás Derisi. More frequently, however, it turned to the more amorphous ideas of Hernán Benítez, whose writings fill many pages of the *Revista de la Universidad de Buenos Aires* during these years.

Perón called his social doctrine *justicialismo,* a title apparently derived from the emphasis on social justice, along with the need for moral reform, idealism, order and discipline, hierarchy, patriotism, and a sense of the heroic.[18] *Justicialismo* is vague and diffuse. Among its chief concepts is the idea that revolutions are changes in social hierarchies, which are defined as moral structures. In spite of its demagogic appeals to the class feeling among the *descamisados,* the official doctrine of *justicialismo* held that class conflict was being overcome in Argentina by social collaboration and by dignifying man.[19]

OTHER TRENDS IN ARGENTINE THOUGHT. The intensity of Argentine nationalism finds a more appropriate expression in the *Eurindia* of Ricardo Rojas. In this plea for an American esthetic and culture, Rojas views culture as "the organization of traditions into a body of political institutions, philosophical doctrines, and emotional symbols which create national self-consciousness."[20] Raúl A. Orgaz, who was perhaps the greatest of the older Argentine sociologists and who was driven from his university post under *peronismo,* developed a scientific sociology which combined much of the best of contemporary thought, especially European. Alfredo Poviña, a younger man who enjoyed great popularity during the years of *peronismo,* was greatly influenced by German thought, especially the "conceptual historicism" of Weber. More generally typical of Argentine thought, as of Latin American thought in general, is the historical institutionalism represented in the numerous works of Ricardo Levene, the dean of Argentine historians. Somewhat similar in social concept is Juan Agustín García's study of the Argentine colonial city, *La ciudad indiana.*[21]

Post-*peronista* trends in social thought include a reassertion of the older tenets of liberal democratic thought, social democracy as expressed in the *Imago Mundi* edited by José Luis Romero, and the Christian socialism of Catholic Social Action.

[18] *Este pueblo necesita* (Buenos Aires, 1934).

[19] *Actas del Primer Congreso Nacional de Filosofía* (Mendoza, Argentine: Universidad Nacional, 1949), I, 143, 150.

[20] *Eurindia* (Buenos Aires: Juan Roldán, 1924), p. 333.

[21] (Buenos Aires: A. Estrada, 1900. New ed.; Ed. Claridad, 1933). On Argentine political thought in general see José Luis Romero, *Las ideas políticas en Argentina* (Mexico: Fondo de Cultura Económica, 1946).

Venezuelan Regeneration

The story of the remarkable regeneration of Venezuela in the few years since the death of Juan Vicente Gómez in 1935 deserves more extensive notice than the brief mention possible in this chapter. To summarize, a group of army officers of the Gómez regime led the nation in an immediate return to orderly constitutional government. Progressive, if moderate, measures of reform were introduced, especially in the field of popular education. Soon, however, a younger and more radical party, Democratic Action, arose under the leadership of Rómulo Betancourt to oppose the older leaders. The revolutionary ideas of this group, which took over the government in 1945 but was driven from power by the army in 1948, resembled those of the Mexican Revolution and Peruvian *aprismo*. More typical of the thought of the group of older leaders who have led the nation through its regeneration since 1935 is Augusto Mijares. His *La interpretación pesimista de la sociología hispano-americana*[22] retains much of older positivist liberalism while tending toward the more idealistic social voluntarism which has come to characterize Latin American social thought in the twentieth century.

Other National Movements

BOLIVIA. Similar movements of thought and politics, of greater or lesser intensity, may be seen in most of the other countries. The present-day Movimiento Nacional Revolucionario (MNR) of Bolivia, which came to power by a revolutionary uprising headed by Víctor Paz Estenssoro in 1952, resembles Argentine *peronismo* in some respects and the Mexican Revolution in others.[23] Its principal strength lies in the organized miners, although peasant support also seems to have been gained through a program of land reform.

COLOMBIA. In Colombia the rise of a radical left wing within the Liberal party resulted in a temporary union of right-wing Liberals with the minority Conservative party. The new party grouping enabled Conservative leaders to postpone the program of labor and agrarian reform toward which the nation was heading under the Liberal party, though not without resorting to arbitrary exercise of power, which led, in turn, to replacement by a series of military regimes.

[22] (Caracas: Artes Gráficus, 1938, and Madrid: Afrodisio Aguado, 1952.)
[23] For social thought in Bolivia see Guillermo Francovich, *El pensamiento boliviano en el siglo XX* (Mexico: Fondo de Cultura Económica, 1956).

CENTRAL AMERICA. During the 1940's the nations of Central America began to reflect in their political behavior the tardy arrival of the influence of the Mexican Revolutionary reforms. Only in Nicaragua, where order was firmly maintained under the regime of President Anastasio Somoza, was the movement for agrarian–labor reform completely checked. President Somoza was assassinated in 1956, but the same group remained in power under the direction of his sons, and Nicaragua's future course still remains uncertain. In Honduras the reform movement has been weak in general, although a land reform has been adopted. In Costa Rica (1949) and in Guatemala (1954) reform regimes which had come too largely under the influence of a small but aggressive Communist leadership were overthrown. In Costa Rica, however, the more conservative regime of President Ulate, who came to power in 1949, soon gave way to the bustling and socially conscious government to which the philosophically inclined José Figueres has given an almost mystic attachment to the ideals of the welfare state.

In Guatemala the conservatively oriented regime of Carlos Castillo Armas (who was assassinated in 1957) slowed down the movement toward state socialism in 1954. But it did not abolish the substantial labor and agrarian reforms initiated after the revolution of 1945, which brought the scholar-reformer Juan José Arévalo from exile in Argentina to head the government. Arévalo has given clear expression in his writing to the social and philosophical concepts animating the contemporary socio-political movement in the Americas.[24]

SOME OTHER MOVEMENTS. In Paraguay, a movement of agrarian reform under President Rafael Franco, hero of the Chaco War, was nipped in the bud by an army revolt. Army-dominated regimes, resembling in some respects that of *peronismo*, have followed. Ecuador has enjoyed relative political stability since 1948 under the constitutional regimes of Galo Plaza and José María Velasco Ibarra. Their governments have moved cautiously in the direction of economic development guided by the state.[25] The Cuban Revolution of 1934 initiated a complicated and at times turbulent polit-

---

[24] The social and political ideas of Arévalo may be found in his *Escritos políticos* (Guatemala: Tipografía Nacional, 1945) and *La filosofía de los valores en la pedagogía* (Buenos Aires: Imp. López, 1939). See also Marie-Berthe Dion, "The Social and Political Ideas of Juan José Arévalo and Their Relationship to Contemporary Trends of Latin American Thought" (M.A. thesis, The American University, Washington, D.C., 1956).

[25] Galo Plaza's explanation of his purposes and politics may be read in his *Problems of Democracy in Latin America* (Chapel Hill: University of North Carolina Press, 1955).

ical era of contradictory trends and ideas. The principal issues center around efforts to transform an agrarian sugar-centered economy into a more balanced economic system capable of improving the living standards of urban workers. The various political parties represent divergent approaches to this basic problem, and the several presidential administrations seem to have differed not so much in economic and social objectives as in the political methods and measures employed.

The Dominican Republic and Haiti have also felt the impact of twentieth-century economic and social nationalism, although in differing ways. In the former, an authoritarian regime dominated by the personality of General Rafael Trujillo has pursued some of the objectives of the welfare state, but has in general avoided any basic alteration in social and political structure. Because of her unique history, Haiti has not required reform of the land system so much as basic agricultural development and the improvement of public health. The ruling class seems to have lessened, though not entirely ceased, its traditional factional violence in its pursuit of limited national development objectives. The autonomous government of Puerto Rico, in its "Operation Bootstrap," a movement which stems basically from the New Deal, has given a dramatic example of the way in which the state may bring about rapid improvement in living standards. Its significance has not been overlooked elsewhere in Latin America.

Trends and Conclusions

On the whole, the vigor of these twentieth-century political movements reflects the dynamic character of the forces at work in contemporary Latin American society. There can be little doubt that the tempo of social and political change has speeded up since World War II. The most obvious change has been growth in the structure and functions of government, accompanied by an increased hold of the political institution upon the lives of people. These movements of change differ in the various countries, but are alike in urging greater state activity to ensure the health, education, productivity, and general well-being of workers. The scope of this state activity will be treated more fully in later chapters.[26] It has included national health and educational programs, the building of highways and railroads, financing of new industries, expansion of credit structures, technical improvement of agriculture, land reform, and the raising of levels of real wages. Sometimes the

[26] See Chapter 7, Organized Labor and Politics, Chapter 15, Government and the Economic Order, and Chapter 16, Government and the Social Order.

plight of landless agricultural workers has been lost sight of in the pursuit of measures more closely akin to the interests of urban workers and enterprisers. Frequently, too, the precarious political power of the "middle class," as it was exercised through the older political parties, has been ground out between powerful political forces of right and left in the sometimes violent struggle accompanying these movements. But if the Mexican example is valid, and there is reason to believe it is, the ultimate outcome may be the strengthening of a broader and more generalized "middle class" social and political outlook as a result of the contemporary trends.

Latin America is generally moving toward a structure and concept of society which has many aspects of state socialism. In this emerging system the political institution plays an enlarged social role but is not given complete power over other social institutions. The essentials of democratic process—freedom of association in political parties, free elections to express the general will, free speech, freedom of religion, and a free press—are assumed, almost without question, to be the necessary basis of this welfare state. These freedoms are often denied by arbitrary power and violence, but the vitality of Latin America's insistence upon them is just as frequently asserted in the overthrow of authoritarian regimes.

It would be hazardous to predict that democratic practices will be generally strengthened in the years immediately ahead. The situation is too full of contradictory trends to speak with that much assurance. But the movements of the twentieth century have strengthened in many ways the economic and political elements essential to the practice of political democracy.

The debate over policy and theory has been at its best in sociology (the sociology of politics) and, perhaps next, in the philosophy of history. Although outstanding books have appeared in other countries, the literature emanating from Mexico, despite its diffuse, contradictory, and frequently polemic character, best represents the general political movement of the century. Much of the argument has, of course, been carried on in the clichés and threadbare concepts of the warring political and economic doctrines of the twentieth century. Yet here and there the ideas of a Mariátegui, Haya de la Torre, José Vasconcelos, Molina Enríquez, Augusto Mijares, Gilberto Freyre, or Antonio Caso contain something of the living, vital reality of the Latin American scene. Economic theory, until recent years, has been largely oriented to the Franco-German historical school, especially the economics of Say, but it has taken most of its concepts ready-made, without probing deeply into Latin American economic history. The second influence in importance has been that of Marxist theory. Only occasionally, where British financial influence was strong, did the classical British economic doctrines prevail.

On the whole, however, the greatest intellectual weakness in this debate over national policy has been in more strictly political theory. With the exception of obviously Marxist or fascist works, some of which have been mentioned in this chapter, little writing of significance has appeared from Latin American pens on this subject, despite the voluminous writings on democracy and upon legal subjects, both national and international. The writing of Haya de la Torre is the most obvious exception.

Suggestions for Reading

Brief but reliable general accounts of twentieth-century political movements may be found in Harry Bernstein, *Modern and Contemporary Latin America* (Philadelphia: J. B. Lippincott Co., 1952). W. Rex Crawford, *A Century of Latin American Thought* (Cambridge, Mass.: Harvard University Press, 1944) sketches the ideas of numerous writers. Further light on trends in thought may be found in works by Harold E. Davis, including *Latin American Leaders* (New York: H. W. Wilson Co., 1949), and *Social Science Trends in Latin America* (Washington: The American University Press, 1950). Gerhard Masur has written with much insight on the influence of Miguel Unamuno in Latin America in *The Americas*, XII, No. 2 (Oct. 1955).

On Argentine *peronismo*, see Robert J. Alexander, *The Perón Era* (New York: Columbia University Press, 1951) or George I. Blanksten, *Perón's Argentina* (Chicago: University of Chicago Press, 1953). On the Mexican Revolution there are many useful books, but Howard Cline, *Mexico and the United States* (Cambridge, Mass.: Harvard University Press, 1952) is recommended. On Uruguayan *batllismo*, see Russell H. Fitzgibbon, *Uruguay* (New Brunswick, N.J.: Rutgers University Press, 1954). Peruvian *aprismo* is best treated in Harry Kantor, *The Ideology and Program of the Peruvian Aprista Movement* (Berkeley, Calif.: University of California Press, 1953). For developments in Chile, consult John Reese Stevenson, *The Chilean Popular Front* (Philadelphia: University of Pennsylvania Press, 1942). T. L. Smith, *Brazil: People and Institutions* (Baton Rouge: Louisiana State University Press, 1946), is a good introduction to Brazilian trends.

Chapter 5

Revolutions

The Concept of Revolution

Two general observations should be made about revolutions in Latin America. First, it is almost a truism that so-called revolutions occur frequently. Indeed, in some of the countries governments change by "revolution" more often than through procedures provided for in written constitutions. Second, the word "revolution," especially in Latin America, is generally employed loosely and imprecisely. One word has been used to refer to a number of different types of social and political phenomena.

TYPES OF REVOLUTIONS. Let us consider a few illustrations of the wide variety of occurrences which have gone by the name of "revolution" in Latin America. Take, for example, the movements which resulted in the national independence of many of the countries early in the nineteenth century. In some of these, as one Latin American writer has put it, "we accepted the proposition that sovereignty or the power to command resided in the people, just as we had formerly been convinced that the sovereignty of kings came from God. But we had only substituted one dogma for another." Thus national independence was achieved on "the last day of despotism and the first day of the same thing."[1] This, then, represents one type of Latin American revolution.

In a second type, a president may be forced out of office by a political rival. In this case, the identity of the chief executive changes—in a manner and on a date not stipulated by the written

[1] Pío Jaramillo Alvarado, *El régimen totalitario en América* (Guayaquil: Editora Noticia, 1940), pp. 24, 71.

119

constitution—but much else in the country remains as before, with the basic social and political structure intact. This is the most frequent form of revolution in Latin America. "Since the turn of the present century," according to a recent study of the area, "the governments of the nations to the south have been overthrown . . . seventy-six times. . . . Revolutions are still the order of the day. . . . Bolivia, for example, has had violent changes of government in 1920, 1930, 1934, 1936, 1937, 1943, 1946, and 1952."[2] The celebrated Brazilian Emperor Dom Pedro II is said to have remarked, when he visited the Philadelphia Exposition in 1876, that many of the Latin American countries had more revolutions per minute than the machines he saw on display at the exposition.

In a third, and far less frequent, type of revolution, a nation may experience a vast and impersonal movement of considerable proportions. This may recast the entire social order, bringing far-reaching changes affecting virtually all sectors of society. "The revolution is like a hurricane," a Mexican novelist, Manuel Azuela, has said of this kind of revolution. "If you're in it, you're not a man . . . you're a leaf, a dead leaf blown by the wind."[3] Violence, to be sure, may accompany such a cataclysm, but violence or the violation of constitutional provisions is not the most important characteristic of this type of revolution. Far more significant is its restructuring of the social order.

SOCIAL REVOLUTIONS. Obviously, the above instances represent widely varying classes of social and political phenomena, although the same word—"revolution"—has been applied to all of them. It is unfortunate that the word has been used so promiscuously, because such loose usage tends to obstruct analysis and understanding of revolution in Latin America. More than one lecturer on Latin American politics or history has said something like this to his classes: "Revolutions occur frequently in the area. But most of these so-called Latin American revolutions are not real revolutions. As a matter of fact, real revolutions are at least as rare in the Western Hemisphere as in other parts of the world."

The implications of this proposition are worth exploring. What is a "real revolution"? How does it differ from the so-called typical revolution which occurs so frequently in Latin America? And why do revolutions, regardless of category, take place in the area at all?

It is interesting to note that the author of one of the most per-

[2] Austin F. Macdonald, *Latin-American Politics and Government* (2d ed.; New York: The Thomas Crowell Co., 1954), pp. 11–12.

[3] Quoted in Russell H. Fitzgibbon, "Revolutions: Western Hemisphere," *The South Atlantic Quarterly*, LV (July 1956), 263.

ceptive and provocative studies of revolution chose "to dodge a good deal of unprofitable debate over the definition of 'revolution,' "[4] and therefore gave none.   Other students have been more venturesome.   A revolution has been defined as "a fundamental change in the political organization of a nation" and as "a forced transfer of power within a nation from one class, group or individual to another."[5]   Revolutions involve "abrupt changes which may be either temporary disturbances in a long-term trend or the beginning of a new epoch in the life of a nation."   Moreover, "the most fundamental transformations" with which revolutions are concerned "are long drawn-out movements in which wealth is gradually redistributed, social relations are materially altered and new groups acquire a dominant position in matters of State."[6]   In his penetrating study of the subject, Alfred Meusel pointed out that in a revolution "a major change in the political order—not merely a shift in the personnel of the government or a reorientation of its concrete policies —must be preceded or accompanied by a drastic change in the relation among the different groups and classes in society.   Thus a recasting of the social order is . . . a far more important characteristic of revolutions than a change in the political constitution or the use of violence in the attainment of this end."[7]

The Anatomy of Revolution

A number of comparative studies of revolutions have been attempted.   These works, while not conclusive, appear to suggest that all major revolutions, during the course of their development, pass through a more or less uniform set of steps or stages.   While these intriguing analyses differ in details, they generally agree that all "real" revolutions experience a common progression through seven or eight stages.

EARLY STAGES.   The first of these is a period of social unrest, frequently attributed to economic causes—serious crop failures, bankruptcy of the government, a depression, or some similar misfortune.   From this initial stage of unrest emerges what has been called the desertion or the defection of the intellectuals.   During this second period, the output of the writers, artists, teachers, and preachers of the affected society sets up a running attack against

[4] Crane Brinton, *The Anatomy of Revolution* (New York: W. W. Norton & Co., Inc., 1938), p. 35.

[5] Robert Hunter, *Revolution: Why, How, When?* (New York: Harper & Brothers, 1940), p. x.

[6] *Ibid.*, pp. xii–xiii.

[7] Alfred Meusel, "Revolution and Counter-Revolution," *Encyclopaedia of the Social Sciences* (New York: The Macmillan Co., 1937), VII, 367.

the existing order. Rather than defend or apologize for the government or other agencies of the established social system, the intellectuals seek out, give dramatic emphasis to, and frequently distort that system's weaknesses and injustices. This negative activity is followed by a stage, the third in the revolution, characterized by a more positive product of the intellectuals. It is this stage in the revolution that witnesses the emergence of the social myth, the beginnings of the ideology of the revolution. It is this stage that provides the rudiments of a political philosophy or a system of ideas justifying the overthrow of the established order.

The next, or fourth, phase is characterized by the failure, for one reason or another, of the armed forces to defend the existing government. This is usually due to inefficiency, a breakdown in the morale of the troops, or the desertion of a significant portion of them to the cause of the revolution. Then, in the fifth stage, the moderates rise briefly to leadership, seeking a formula for compromise between the revolutionary forces and the tottering old regime.

LATER STAGES. Next, violence breaks out on a usually intense scale. In this sixth phase there is a physical change in government, generally accompanied by bloodshed and a *coup d'état*.[8] The revolution then enters its seventh stage, which may bear any one of several labels. It has been called the accession of the extremists, the reign of terror, the era of virtue, or the period of revolutionary dictatorship. Whatever the designation, this is the time when power is held by those revolutionists who are dedicated, often fanatically, to the social myth or the political philosophy of the revolution. They are, by their lights, rigidly righteous men. They accept no compromise in the social myth, for they believe it immoral to compromise on political principles. Those who question these principles are ruthlessly dealt with; in the reign of terror the philosophical purity of the revolution cannot be attacked with impunity.

Finally, the revolution reaches the stage of Thermidor. During

---

[8] Authorities disagree in defining *coup d'état*. Brinton and Hunter regard it as any violent and unconstitutional change in government. Others are more rigid, defining *coup d'état* as an unconstitutional governmental change made by people already in office. In this view, the classic *coup d'état* was made in France by Louis Napoleon in 1852, when he unconstitutionally changed his status from president to emperor, thus prolonging his period in power. Illustrations of this interpretation of *coup d'état* abound in Latin America, particularly in Central America (there the phenomenon is called *continuismo*), where presidents resort to variously unconstitutional devices to remain in power after the expiration of their formal terms of office. For expositions of this latter view of *coup d'état*, see Henry R. Spencer, "Coup d'État," *Encyclopaedia of the Social Sciences* (New York: The Macmillan Co., 1937), IV, 508–510; and Carl J. Friedrich, *Constitutional Government and Democracy* (New York: Ginn & Co., 1946), pp. 127, 150 ff.

the Thermidorian period, the extremists or purists have fallen from power, and are replaced by a new breed of moderates. Under this moderate leadership the revolution compromises and reinterprets its social myth. When this process has run its course, the revolutionary principles are compromised though not undone. The line between these two conditions is, admittedly, subtle and sometimes thin, but it is nevertheless very important that the distinction be recognized. Revolutions are always compromised. They are almost never undone.[9]

The reader may argue that what has been said here might well apply to the French Revolution or to the Russian Revolution, but to very few, if any, Latin American revolutions. This argument is, no doubt, right, for as many students of Latin American history point out, most of these so-called Latin American revolutions are not real revolutions. Real revolutions are at least as rare in the Western Hemisphere as in other parts of the world.

A Revolution Unrealized

INDEPENDENCE NOT A SOCIAL REVOLUTION. The confusing Latin American habit of designating as "revolutions" occurrences which are not really revolutions may be said to date from the early years of the nineteenth century. During the course of sporadic and occasionally bloody hostilities which began about 1810 and were generally ended by 1825, the various states of Latin America achieved political independence from their respective mother countries of Spain, Portugal, and France.[10] That fighting, and the political movement of which it was a part, have frequently, and inaccurately, been referred to as one or more revolutions. The events of the independence movement have also been called the Wars of Independence and even "civil wars."[11] Either of these two latter designations is more valid than "revolution." The Wars of Independence were not a revolution. It has been said that the circumstance that they were not a revolution is one of the major factors underlying present-day political instability in Latin America;[12] indeed, many

[9] See Brinton, *op. cit.* A similar scheme is advanced in Lyford P. Edwards, *The Natural History of Revolution* (Chicago: University of Chicago Press, 1927).

[10] Three exceptions to this generalization should be mentioned. Haiti won its independence of France in 1804; Panama did not become an independent state until 1903; and Brazil acquired national independence of Portugal in 1822 without benefit of bloodshed.

[11] See Laureano Vallenilla Lanz, *Cesarismo democrático* (Caracas: Empresa El Cojo, 1919).

[12] This intriguingly significant thesis is developed in the late Professor Vernon L. Fluharty's as yet unpublished manuscript, "Problems of Governing and Government in Latin America."

have argued that the revolution which did not come in the nineteenth century is now long overdue and may be expected to arrive in the twentieth. Both of these propositions are highly important to an understanding of the problem of revolution in Latin America. Both, of course, merit more than passing mention and are examined at a later point in this chapter.

The Wars of Independence were not a revolution in the sense that they brought with them a significant recasting of the social order. In order to understand the meaning of this statement, however, it is necessary to inquire into the nature of the social and political system of colonial Latin America.

COLONIAL SOCIAL ORDER. Spain[13] established its empire in the Western Hemisphere early in the sixteenth century and remained the governing power there for some three hundred years.[14] During those centuries the basic social and political structure of Latin America took shape. That structure was composed of many elements, five of which may be isolated as major characteristics of the colonial order.

First among these was an essentially authoritarian political system. Spain—and France and Portugal—were governed by absolute monarchs during most of Latin America's colonial life, and virtually no opportunity for self-government existed in the colonies. Virtually all colonial officials with decision-making powers were appointees of the crown, responsible to their home governments rather than to the people of the colonies. At one time, certain scholars regarded the *cabildo,* the town council of colonial Spanish America, as a kind of cradle of Latin American democracy, but subsequent research suggests that what the *cabildo* cradled was not overly democratic. Essentially, government in the colonies was authoritarian, regardless of level.

Further, the Latin American class system which developed in the wake of the Spanish conquest was crystallized by the end of the eighteenth century. At the top of this system in most of the colonies were the creoles, the American-born descendants of the Europeans. The creoles, a small minority of the population, lived as an upper class and were at times involved in an acrimonious rivalry with the *peninsulares,* the aristocrats who could boast of European birth and who enjoyed the greatest social prestige. A

[13] Brazil was a Portuguese and Haiti a French colony. Their situations were not identical with the Spanish American. Where significantly at variance with the Hispanic American pattern as discussed in these paragraphs, the Brazilian and Haitian cases are noted.

[14] Two exceptions are Cuba and Puerto Rico, which remained under Spanish sovereignty until 1898.

lower group were the mestizos, a cultural mixture of Spanish and American Indian elements. Early in the colonial period, the mestizos were few in numbers. But with the passing of generations they came to be far more numerous than the creoles, constituting a landless proletariat of workers on plantations or cattle ranches and in mines. In much of Latin America, the Indians stood at the bottom of the social ladder. In many places,[15] they comprised the majority of the population. Finally, Negroes were introduced into plantation and mining areas as slaves. Where this was the case, particularly in the Caribbean area and in Brazil, they constituted a lower social class, although closely attached to the creoles. By the end of the colonial period, this class system was well entrenched.

An amazing social distance separated the various classes from each other. Little conscious contact occurred among them; each class possessed its own universe of discourse, each lived its own life. This cultural isolation of the classes was especially noteworthy in the areas with large Indian populations. Few of the Indians in such regions even spoke Spanish. Rather, they clung to their own languages and cultures, their own customs and traditions. The conquered Indians lived as an isolated and often exploited lower class.

Third among the major characteristics of the colonial social order was a system of land tenure which came to lie at the heart of the economy of Latin America. The Spaniards brought with them to the Western Hemisphere the land system they had known at home. This was a variant of feudalism, which at the time of the Spanish conquest was already dying out in much of Europe. Disappearing in Europe, this system came to prevail in the Americas. *Repartimientos,* or divisions of the land and certain power over the people living on it, were made, with Spaniards who may or may not have merited such bequests receiving sizable parcels of land to rule as quasi-feudal estates. From this grew the *encomienda* system of colonial society. Although *encomiendas* were later abolished by law, the large landed estate reminiscent of feudal Europe remained. In colonial Latin America the heirs of the *encomenderos* became a landowning aristocracy, a ruling class; and it was characteristic of the colonies that less than 5 per cent of their populations owned over 70 per cent of their land surface.

Moreover, the Roman Catholic Church played a strong temporal role in the life of colonial Latin America. In a sense, Spain

[15] *E.g.,* in what are now the republics of Bolivia, Ecuador, Guatemala, Mexico, Paraguay, and Peru.

was involved in a religious crusade at the time of the consolidation of its overseas empire. The persecution of the Jews and of the non-Christian Moors at the time of Columbus' voyages of discovery came in the midst of political struggles with strongly religious overtones. In the same era Spain, France, and Portugal girded themselves to defend the Church again, this time against the threat launched by Martin Luther in northern Europe. In Spanish eyes, the discovery of the American Indian meant initially the discovery of heathen souls in need of spiritual conquest.[16] The Spanish Inquisition came to the Americas with the *conquistadores*. A major temporal institution in the colonies, the Church was an arm of government and a major landowner, giving course and character to much of Latin American colonial life.

Finally, transportation and communication were painfully difficult in the colonies. Immense jungles and mountains separated the settlements from each other, while confusing and uncharted river systems were often as much a barrier as an avenue of transportation. The colonial settlements, thus largely isolated from outside intellectual and social influences, developed a curious regionalism. The colonists tended to harbor stronger sentiments of loyalty to neighborhood, province, or region than to such vague, distant, and hazy concepts as the colony as a whole or the empire, which were beyond the reach of the reasonably available means of transportation and communication.

NATURE OF THE INDEPENDENCE MOVEMENT. The preceding analysis is, perhaps, an oversimplified abstract of the colonial social order as it stood on the eve of the independence movement. It cannot be said that this movement was caused by any one condition or grievance arising from the colonial system. Rather, the factors encouraging the quest for independence were many and varied,[17] including events and conditions in Europe as much as those in Latin America. It has been said that "the interdependence of the Latin-American nations was precipitated prematurely by events in Europe."[18] In the wake of the French Revolution came the Napoleonic Wars, during the course of which both Spain and Portugal were occupied by France. The court of King João VI

---

[16] See, for example, Charles S. Braden, *Religious Aspects of the Conquest of Mexico* (Durham: Duke University Press, 1930).

[17] Brief summaries of the "causes" of the wars of independence may be found in Donald E. Worcester and Wendell G. Schaeffer, *The Growth and Culture of Latin America* (New York: Oxford University Press, 1956), pp. 405–426; and in William W. Pierson and Federico G. Gil, *Governments of Latin America* (New York: The McGraw-Hill Book Co., Inc., 1957), pp. 83–91.

[18] Worcester and Schaeffer, *op. cit.*, p. 423.

established a Portuguese government-in-exile at Rio de Janeiro in the Brazilian colony, while Spain, but not her colonies, fell under the rule of Napoleon Bonaparte's brother, the "Intruder King" Joseph. Dismayed by the mother countries' military weaknesses, the Latin American colonists nevertheless persisted in their habits of loyalty to Spain and Portugal. Rebellion, when it came, was initially directed not so much against the old system of empire as against Bonapartist attempts to exercise authority. Indeed, one of the first Latin American proclamations of independence expressed defiance of the "Intruder King." These rebels sought the restoration of a system of government "in conformity with the very principles of the ancient and wise constitution of Spain."[19]

On the whole, the Wars of Independence may be regarded as a conservative movement led largely by conservatives. "The Spanish-American revolutionaries were essentially conservative and aristocratic in their political leanings," two recent students have found. "The great majority of the *creoles* . . . were disinclined toward any move that might upset the social order. They sided with the independence leaders because Spain had been overrun and because of their class interest. . . . By stressing their continued allegiance [to Spain] they salved their conscience and at the same time stated their general acceptance and support of the old aristocratic social structure in which they now hoped to play a more prominent role."[20] It was not the intention of such leaders that the Wars of Independence become a revolution; under their leadership, independence was achieved, but no revolution took place.

THE PERSISTENCE OF ELEMENTS OF MONARCHISM. When the question of forms of government for the new states of Latin America arose, most independence leaders argued for the retention of monarchy. Augustín de Iturbide established a throne in Mexico, and General José de San Martín worked to retain monarchy in Peru. General Simón Bolívar championed a species of republicanism rather than monarchy, but Bolívar's "republicanism" was peculiar to his time and place. An intriguing insight into Bolívar's views may be gained from the Constitution of 1826, which he wrote for Bolivia. This document provided for a president with not only life-

[19] Quoted in Pierson and Gil, *op. cit.*, p. 88. The Haitian story, of course, differs. During an early phase of the French Revolution, slavery was declared abolished throughout the French Empire. This move was welcomed in Haiti, where a large proportion of the population had lived in slavery. In the later Bonapartist phase of the French Revolution, an attempt was made to restore slavery. The Haitians' protest against this was a major factor precipitating the independence movement in that colony.

[20] Worcester and Schaeffer, *op. cit.*, p. 417.

long tenure but also the authority to choose his successor. "The President of the Republic becomes in our Constitution the sun, which, firm in the center, gives life to the universe," Bolívar wrote. "This supreme authority should be perpetual." He felt that "a life-term president with the power of naming his successor is the most sublime addition to the republican system." This arrangement, he said, would have the advantage of avoiding "the changing administrations caused by party government and the excitement that too frequent elections produce." In defense of his "republicanism," Bolívar declared: "I have never been an enemy of monarchy, as far as general principles are concerned; on the contrary, I consider monarchies essential for the respectability and well-being of new nations. . . . The new states of America . . . need kings with the name of presidents."[21]

Reference has already been made to the Latin American scholar who recorded that, through the Wars of Independence, one dogma was substituted for another. National independence came on "the last day of despotism and the first day of the same thing."[22] He was, in a sense, quite correct. For most of Latin America, the Wars of Independence were not a revolution.

LACK OF BASIC SOCIAL CHANGE. In the preceding discussion, five major characteristics of the colonial social order in Latin America are mentioned. Revolutions, it will be remembered, generally bring with them a fundamental recasting of the social order. It may be well to inquire into the extent to which the colonial order has been altered since the Wars of Independence came to a close.

More than a century after independence, many of the social, economic, and political aspects of Latin American life still bear a striking resemblance to the colonial order. Consider, for example, authoritarianism in government. A fundamental element of the colonial system, this remains a major key to present-day Latin American life. Later chapters of this book will show that the contemporary scene reflects much that is indicative of continuing political authoritarianism in the area. Militarism is a chronic problem in many of the countries; dictatorship is frequent; and the strong executive common in much of twentieth-century Latin America is a variety of elected monarch in republican dress. Militarism is

[21] Víctor Andrés Belaúnde, *Bolívar and the Political Thought of the Spanish American Revolution* (Baltimore: The Johns Hopkins Press, 1938), pp. 243, 244, 246, and 283; Vicente Lecuna, *Cartas del Libertador* (New York: The Colonial Press, Inc., 1948), XI, 44, 50–51, 189, 222–223, and 267; and Pío Jaramillo Alvarado, *op. cit.*, p. 107.

[22] Pío Jaramillo Alvarado, *op. cit.*, p. 71.

somewhat more pronounced now than in colonial times,[23] and while the formal aspects of the monarchy of the pre-independence period have disintegrated, the basic pattern of authoritarianism in government remains.

Further, a rigid class system continues to characterize much of Latin American society today, as it did in colonial times. Some components of the class system have shifted; for example, the former struggle between the creoles and the *peninsulares* has given way to a more unified upper class. Social and cultural isolation, however, continues to separate that class from the mestizos and the Indians. Since winning independence, many Latin American countries have adopted written constitutions proclaiming the equality of all citizens—including the Indians—before the law, but in most of the countries with Indian populations this equality is not achieved in actual practice. In colonial times, the Indian was in a legally inferior but protected position. With the coming of national independence, he lost his protection, but only the legal aspects of his inferiority. Thus, in much of the area, the Indian's position "has produced the failure of all democratic reforms which have affected only the political, economic, and social periphery, establishing in fact an antagonism of classes. A nucleus, a minority . . . continues to dominate the Indo-American situation."[24] Such differences as have developed between the pre- and post-independence class systems hardly constitute a fundamental change in the social order.

Next, the system of large-scale land ownership, established in colonial times, has changed but little since independence. In one country, Mexico, there has been a fundamental—one may say truly revolutionary—change. A similar change seems to be occurring in Bolivia. And in Costa Rica, and a few other areas, small holdings have long been the rule. In much of the rest of the area, however, a small proportion of the population owns a large percentage of the land surface. New words (*hacienda, estancia, latifundio*) have replaced the old designation (*encomienda*) for the large landed estate, but the large estate remains. In the twentieth

[23] Pierson and Gil, *op. cit.*, p. 97.

[24] Pío Jaramillo Alvarado, *op. cit.*, p. 117. In recent times, the existing literature on the problems of the Latin American Indians has come to be impressively voluminous. The reader may be especially interested in W. Stanley Rycroft (ed.), *Indians of the High Andes* (New York: Committee on Co-operation in Latin America, 1946); Moises Sáenz, *The Indian, Citizen of America* (Washington: Pan American Union, 1946); and José Carlos Mariátegui, *Siete ensayos de interpretación de la realidad peruana* (Lima: Editorial Librería Peruana, 1934).

century, this system of land tenure has drawn increasingly critical attention on two scores. Not only has the problem been posed in terms of various conceptions of social justice, but also the blame for the underdeveloped nature of the economies of many states of the area has been laid, in part, at the door of the land system. Low standards of living, it is claimed, are integrally related to uneconomical and relatively unprofitable methods of working the land, and these methods, in turn, are tied to the system of tenure.[25]

Moreover, the Roman Catholic Church continues to play a major role in the temporal life of Latin America. Today this situation varies widely from country to country, but everywhere the influence of the Church in temporal affairs is evident. In a few countries, the Church enjoys a special constitutional position as the official religion. In others, Church and state have been separated for decades. In several countries, the Church actively sponsors and supports a political party, in some cases conservative and in some liberal in orientation. In Mexico no political party may bear a Christian label. "Man is essentially a religious being and religion, consequently, is a natural phenomenon," the leader of one conservative political party declared in expounding his group's *political* program. "The end of man is God, whom he should serve and adore in order to enjoy after death the beatified possession of divinity. . . . The purpose of the state is to facilitate religious action so that its subjects will not lack the necessities of the spirit and will be able to obtain in the next life the happiness which can never be achieved in this."[26] On the other hand, the Church is growing in strength under the influence of its new liberal philosophy of social action, based on the papal dogma contained in *Rerum Novarum*. Thus, whether it is conservative or liberal in its social and political view, its imprint on social and political structure is a leading characteristic of twentieth-century Latin America.

Finally, transportation and communication remain difficult. Isolation continues to breed regionalism and particularism as basic Latin American characteristics. Indeed, it is probably true that regional isolation has been a centrifugal political force since independence. One indication of this is the fact that the former eight Spanish colonies today comprise no fewer than *eighteen* separate

[25] Special Policy Committee on Technical Cooperation, *Technical Cooperation in Latin America* (Washington: National Planning Association, 1956); and Arthur T. Mosher, *Case Study of the Agricultural Program of ACAR in Brazil* (Washington: National Planning Association, 1955).

[26] Jacinto Jijón y Caamaño, *Política conservadora* (Riobamba: La Buena Prensa del Chimborazo, 1934), I, 26, 32. See also J. Lloyd Mecham, *Church and State in Latin America* (Chapel Hill: University of North Carolina Press, 1934); and Pierson and Gil, *op. cit.*, pp. 431–447.

sovereign states.[27] The persistence of this influence is thus quite apparent.

While it would not be true that independence brought no change at all in Latin America, it is nevertheless true that in many ways the alterations it brought in the colonial order were not fundamental. The number of twentieth-century writers and observers who use the word "colonial" in characterizing many aspects of contemporary Latin American life is impressive. "The root of [the area's] many difficulties," two recent observers have said, "is the colonial heritage of racial and class cleavages, failure to integrate the numerous Indian elements into national life, concentration of ownership of land and other forms of wealth, lack of economic opportunity, illiteracy, malnutrition, militarism, and inertia born of oppression. Each of the countries has made some gestures toward solving its basic problems, but only halfway measures have been tried."[28] For much of Latin America, revolution has not yet come.

A Revolution Realized: The Mexican Revolution

The proposition that true revolutions are rare in Latin America suggests, of course, that on occasion they do indeed take place. The number of countries which have experienced transformations sufficiently profound to be called revolutions is small. Mexico is certainly one of these; it is probably true that Mexico is the only Latin American state which has undergone what virtually all authorities would call a revolution. Less agreement exists with respect to the argument that one or two other countries in the area have also experienced revolutions, or that some others have made equal or even greater social progress.

The Mexican Revolution, discussed in the preceding chapter, first commanded Mexico's energies and attention in the early years of the twentieth century and is still in process.[29] One of the most

[27] Although the isolating factors discussed here play a major role in this centrifugal tendency, it should be noted that they do not constitute its entire explanation. A portion of this lies also in the nature of Spanish, as distinguished from French and Portuguese, culture. Haiti and Brazil, particularly the latter, also suffer from transportation and communication difficulties, but both, in sharp contrast with Spanish America, have remained territorially intact.

[28] Worcester and Schaeffer, op. cit., p. 916.

[29] See Chapter 4; also Henry Bamford Parkes, A History of Mexico (Boston: Houghton Mifflin Co., 1938), pp. 325–413; Anita Brenner, The Wind That Swept Mexico (New York: Harper & Brothers, 1943); Howard F. Cline, Mexico and the United States (Cambridge: Harvard University Press, 1953); Tomme Clark Call, The Mexican Venture (New York: Oxford University Press, 1953); and Frank Tannenbaum, Mexico: The Struggle for Peace and Bread (New York: Alfred A. Knopf, Inc., 1950).

significant and far-reaching Latin American social movements the twentieth century has seen, the Mexican Revolution is worth examining from two standpoints: its process and the extent to which a fundamental change in the social and political order has taken place.

The process of the Mexican Revolution coincides closely with the series of stages through which revolutions pass, as identified by writers like Brinton and Edwards and as mentioned earlier in this chapter. It may be in order at this point, therefore, to inquire into the applicability to the Mexican Revolution of this general formulation of the anatomy or natural history of revolution.

FIRST STAGE: SOCIAL UNREST. According to one formulation of revolutionary stages, the earliest phase of a revolution is a period of social unrest, frequently attributable to economic causes. This condition was especially evident during the closing years of the dictatorship of General Porfirio Díaz, who ruled Mexico from 1877 until 1911. During his regime large landed estates came to be concentrated in the hands of a small aristocracy—in 1910 only 1 per cent of the population owned 70 per cent of the land surface of Mexico. ". . . of the ten millions of Mexicans engaged in agriculture more than nine and a half millions were virtually without land. . . . Scarcely any had sufficient land for their needs, and the majority were compelled to become laborers on the *haciendas*. . . . Mexico, in which three quarters of the population were engaged in agriculture, was . . . unable to feed itself." Many of the farm workers lived under a system of peonage or debt servitude, which was subjected to scandalous abuses late in the Díaz regime. The administrators of the *haciendas*, in dealing with the peons, "would beat them and torture them and claim feudal rights over their wives and daughters. . . . The Mexican agricultural laborers existed, during the Díaz regime, in a condition of sodden and brutish misery probably unmatched by the proletariat of any other country."[30] The organization of labor, begun in the early years of the twentieth century, was violently suppressed by the government. Under Díaz, the temporal interests of the Church again increased, and foreign investors, particularly from the United States and Great Britain, came to control increasingly large sectors of the Mexican economy. Popular unrest was aggravated by a depression in 1907 and by widespread crop failures in the same year and again in 1908.

DEFECTION OF INTELLECTUALS. If the Mexican Revolution conformed to the classic pattern in its first stage, this may appear at first glance to be less true of the second, the defection of the intel-

[30] Parkes, *op. cit.*, pp. 306, 307.

lectuals. Many of the country's artists, teachers, novelists, and poets avoided criticism of their environment, perhaps because of their attachment to the modernist movement. The Nicaraguan poet, Rubén Darío, was the great creative spirit of this movement, and its leading Mexican exponents were Manuel Gutiérrez Nájera and Amado Nervo. Modernism has been described as "the highest literary achievement of the Indo-Hispanic peoples."[31] Mystical and aristocratic, it dominated an Augustan period in Mexican literature. Its cosmopolitan and pessimistic practitioners were deeply concerned with technical perfection and literary style, but showed little interest in the Mexican scene and little social consciousness. It has been said of their work that it "could have developed only at a time when all idealism had departed from politics and when sensitive persons were driven to look for their ideal not in a reformed society, but in mystical contemplation and self-discipline."[32]

But voices of protest were heard. Felix Requelme, in 1893, criticized the *hacienda* labor system as one of slavery. Juan Pedro Didapp (1904) attacked the Díaz administration, calling for political changes, if not revolution, in his *Explotadores políticos de México*. Socialists like Ricardo Flores Magón were organizing workers. Andrés Molina Enríquez, in his *Los grandes problemas nacionales*, dwelt upon the twin problems of Indians and land, while the ideas of Antonio Soto y Gama later took form in the Zapata agrarian reform. In the last years of the Díaz regime a small band of intellectuals gathered around Antonio Caso in the *Ateneo de Juventud*, or Youth Athenaeum, to criticize the philosophical, economic, and esthetic principles prevailing in the university. This group included José Vasconcelos, the painter Diego Rivera, the poet Alfonso Reyes, and the literary critic Pedro Henríquez Ureña. Their general questioning of the old regime created the environment in which Francisco Madero's rather unsensational book, *The Presidential Succession in 1910*, could set off a general popular revolt.

EMERGENCE OF THE SOCIAL MYTH. The Mexican Revolution also presents a departure with respect to the third stage in the anatomy of revolution—the emergence of the social myth. The doctrine or ideology of the Mexican movement was not controlled by a closely disciplined party and was less coordinated than that of certain other revolutionary movements. The Russian Revolution, for example, exercised tightly centralized control of the revolutionists' doctrine. And even the French and American revolutions

[31] *Ibid.*, p. 302.
[32] *Ibid.*, pp. 302–303.

had a more unified ideology, more agreement in philosophical terms among the rebels as to what their movement was about, than Mexico has shown. The Mexican Revolution was a decentralized and loosely coordinated movement in many other aspects besides the ideological. Its leaders rarely agreed among themselves as to their objectives. Thus, Francisco Ignacio Madero, its initial leader, thought primarily in legal and constitutional terms. Porfirio Díaz had evidently intended to control the election of 1910, as he had controlled previous elections, to return himself to the presidency. Madero raised the standard of revolt with the slogan "Effective Suffrage; No Reelection," which has since been official in revolutionary Mexico.

Other revolutionists, however, had other ideas. Some rallied behind the banner of "Land and Liberty," believing that land reform was the major objective and meaning of the revolution. Still others thought of the movement as fundamentally anti-clerical, its basic objective being the disestablishment of the Church. Other revolutionary groups urged improvement of the social and class status of the Indian, while still others, in Marxist fashion, championed the cause of organized labor and called for the expulsion of foreign "imperialists" from Mexico. All of these ideologies were fundamental to the Mexican Revolution, and all had their influence. But, since the revolutionists never thoroughly agreed among themselves, the Revolution was carried forward in the name of not one but many ideologies. Not until the 1940's and the 1950's could it be said that a more unified revolutionary "Mexican mind" was beginning to emerge.[33]

FAILURE OF ARMED FORCES. With respect to the fourth phase—inability of the armed forces to defend the established regime—the Mexican Revolution adhered to the classic pattern quite closely. Díaz's troops suffered from disadvantages reminiscent of the difficulties of the armies of Louis XVI. (Nicholas II was shortly to find his soldiers in similar situations.) Inefficiency and low morale characterized the Mexican army in 1910. "Díaz had failed to introduce new blood. . . . The majority of the generals . . . were . . . senile; Navarro, who commanded at Ciudad Juárez, was a veteran of the War of Reform.[34] The army had been steadily weakened; nominally thirty thousand, it actually contained only eighteen thousand men, and these were unwilling conscripts badly equipped by grafting war department officials. . . . There was nobody among [Díaz's

[33] Cf. Patrick Romanell, *The Making of the Mexican Mind* (Norman: University of Oklahoma Press, 1954).
[34] This conflict had taken place in the 1850's.

officers] whom he could trust; some were too old and feeble, others already planning to leave the sinking ship."[35] Such is the story of almost every revolution.

RISE OF MODERATE LEADERSHIP. In the next stage in the general formulation of revolution, the moderates rise briefly to leadership, seeking a formula for compromise between the revolutionary forces and the tottering old regime. Here, too, Mexico ran largely true to form. Indeed, for a brief time, Francisco Madero was his own Lafayette or prototype for the later Kerensky. "Madero was easy to deal with. His father and his uncles, who had opposed his revolutionary activities until they began to be successful, had taken control of him; and in deference to their wishes he was willing to accept a compromise. . . ."[36] It is interesting to note that Madero went so far in this direction that some revolutionary leaders came to regard him as a traitor to their cause and to seek his arrest. He was, however, able to extricate himself from this predicament and to regain the leadership of the movement.[37]

Mexico deviated, however, from the classic revolutionary pattern in this stage at two points. First, this moderate period was briefer in the Mexican Revolution than in most others; and, second, whereas this phase normally brings a change of leadership personnel, in Mexico Madero was his own moderate. On other, and more fundamental, counts, the Mexican Revolution conformed at this stage to the general pattern.

OVERTHROW OF THE GOVERNMENT. A similar conformity may be found in the next step, the actual overturning of the government. This came at the chronological point in the Mexican Revolution which conforms to the general formulation of revolutionary stages. This event was also accompanied by the customary violence, such as troops firing on revolutionary crowds. As revolutions go, however, the number of fatalities was small in this phase of the Mexican Revolution. It is estimated that only about two hundred corpses were found in the plaza near the National Palace and the cathedral at daybreak on May 25, 1911, when Díaz was at length forced to resign. Nor had the military actions of the revolutionary armies resulted in many casualties.

REIGN OF TERROR. The literature on revolutions suggests that the next, or seventh, is usually the most dramatic and violently bloody revolutionary phase. This period is variously known as

[35] Parkes, op. cit., p. 320.
[36] Ibid., pp. 320–321.
[37] Eventually, Madero was assassinated. This came at a later stage in the Revolution, and in another context.

that of the accession of extremists, the reign of terror, the era of virtue, or the period of revolutionary dictatorship. It comes when power is held by those revolutionists who are dedicated to the social myth or ideology of the revolution, often fanatically, and who accept no doctrinal compromises. Typically, during the reign of terror those who question this ideology are ruthlessly and brutally dealt with by the extremists. This is a time of guillotines and firing squads, of concentration camps and exile.

This was also the most dramatic and hectic phase of the Mexican Revolution. It cannot be said, however, that Mexico conformed at this stage to the general revolutionary pattern. Rather, some of the most significant deviations from the pattern occurred here.

The Mexican reign of terror (*La Tormenta*) was divided into two periods, the first of which deviated markedly from the general formulation, while the second tended to conform to the pattern. The first period in this reign of terror was one in which the ideology of the Revolution was uncoordinated, with the revolutionary leaders openly disagreeing among themselves as to the objectives of the movement. Some thought in constitutional, some in agrarian, some in anti-clerical, some in class, and some in anti-"imperialist" terms. The bitter rivalries and mutual suspicions of revolutionary leaders kept them constantly at odds with each other. They were reluctant to accept definitions of the aims of the Revolution other than their own or to place themselves under each other's leadership. In this first period of the reign of terror, revolutionists engaged in widespread hostilities among themselves, and Mexico was for a time in a generalized condition of civil warfare. This was the period in which Madero was assassinated (1913) and Victoriano Huerta rose to uneasy power, the era in which the redoubtable Francisco ("Pancho") Villa struggled against Venustiano Carranza and Emiliano Zapata was killed.

Not until the rise of Álvaro Obregón in 1920 did the "reign of terror" enter its second, or more unified, period. The unification which took place, however, and it was considerable, lay more in the field of political power than in ideological or doctrinal consensus. When Álvaro Obregón assumed the presidency in 1920, a more tightly controlled political group, later to become a well-organized official party, assumed command of the Revolution, giving stronger central direction to an increasingly stable government. In 1924 Obregón gave way to Plutarco Elías Calles, who dominated the revolutionary party for a decade following, in which the revolutionary dictatorship was stiffened. At length, the reign of terror came to a close during the presidency of General Lázaro Cárdenas (1934–1940).

Despite the political unification during this second period, ideological unification was not achieved. Different administrations gave emphasis to different facets of the revolution during the period. Obregón was anti-clerical, and gave some support to measures directed toward land reform. Calles gave less emphasis to the land problem, but pushed measures against the Church and regulation of the foreign-owned petroleum industry. Cárdenas stressed the place of the Indian and of organized labor in Mexican society and carried out an extensive agrarian reform. During the second period of the reign of terror, those facets of the Revolution which were stressed were pushed vigorously while they enjoyed emphasis. When the administration of Cárdenas brought to a close the "reign of terror," it was in the sense that he was the last of the revolutionary presidents to give vigorous implementation to these revolutionary reform programs.

THE LAST STAGE: THERMIDOR. Finally, Thermidor arrived during the presidency of Manuel Ávila Camacho (1940–1946). Mexico's Thermidor period has conformed remarkably to the classic pattern. The extremists have fallen from power and the Revolution has come to accept compromises. Revolutionary ardor has subsided, reform programs have tapered off, and principles have been compromised. Thus, agrarian reform has not been notably emphasized since the 1940's. In 1946, the revolutionary party's (PRI) presidential candidate, Miguel Alemán, made political capital of the fact that he was a practicing Catholic, and was elected. And Adolfo Ruíz Cortines, who collaborated at Vera Cruz with the foreign "imperialist" invaders during the reign of terror, was later elected president (1952 to 1958) and thus the head of the revolutionary party.

SOCIAL EFFECTS OF THE REVOLUTION. All revolutions eventually end in compromise, and this is true of the Mexican Revolution in its period of Thermidor. But compromise does not mean rejection of principles, and the Revolution is by no means undone. Indeed, the Mexican Revolution has brought lasting results in its recasting of the social order. The system of land tenure has been materially changed. Several million individuals own small parcels of land, and *ejidos,* lands held collectively by communities, stand on the ruins of the landowning aristocracy of the Díaz era. Even the legal basis of land ownership has changed. Moreover, revolutionary Mexico has forced the Church to accept its place in a secular society.

The Church has lost much of its wealth and Church officials are forbidden to vote or to present themselves as candidates for public office. The Revolution, even in Thermidor, remains anti-clerical.

Revolutionary Mexico has also provided a new place for Indians and mestizos in national life. It has campaigned against illiteracy and even tried to engineer a renaissance of Indian culture. While this Indian renaissance was artificial, it stimulated other developments in national culture. Class stratification has been made more flexible, and the older class system has been modified to multiply the opportunities available to the lower classes. Restrictions have been placed upon the right of foreigners to acquire property in the country. Expropriation and other revolutionary measures have deprived non-Mexicans of their holdings in such areas of the national economy as land, oil, and transportation. Nationalistic laws discriminate against foreigners doing business in Mexico.

Such has been the Mexican Revolution. It has been a revolution in as real and as profound a sense as the upheavals of France and Russia. A famous story is told about the Abbé Sieyès, a prominent revolutionary, who when asked about his personal achievements during the reign of terror in France, replied simply, "I lived." It was also a noteworthy accomplishment to live through *La Tormenta* in Mexico. One must not underestimate the experience of being, not a man, but rather "a leaf, a dead leaf blown by the wind," when the wind is a real revolution.

Near Revolutions

Two other Latin American developments containing many of the ingredients of revolution deserve examination here. One of them, in Guatemala, could well have been a full-blown revolution if the process had not been cut off before it had an opportunity to run its course. The other, in Bolivia, may actually prove to be a revolution, but its development is too recent to afford a sufficient basis upon which to evaluate it.

GUATEMALA. General Jorge Ubico, who ruled Guatemala from 1931 to 1944, was the Díaz of the Guatemalan revolution. Unrest was widespread during the early 1940's, but was restrained by the crisis of World War II. The country's publicists, as soon as they were freed from the rigid restraints of the dictatorship, built on that unrest in a fashion conforming to the stage of the defection of the intellectuals. They attacked the Ubico dictatorship as a tool of the "foreign imperialists," as symbolized by the United Fruit Company, a United States corporation doing large-scale business in Guatemala. The social myth arrived in due course. It was called "National Liberation," and comprised two major elements. One was "political liberation," meaning the dismantling of the machinery of dictatorship. The other was "economic liberation," or the expulsion of "foreign imperialists." In the fourth stage—ineffectiveness of the armed forces—Guatemala deviated somewhat from the general pattern. At first the army tried vigorously though unsuccessfully to defend the established order. Violence occurred twice in 1944. The forced resignation of Ubico in that year was followed by the classic rise of the moderates, headed by General Federico Ponce Valdés, a moderate who tried to protect the old order. His unstable regime endured from June to October of 1944, when a second and more intense outbreak of violence brought a more basic change in the government.

The ensuing reign of terror, or era of virtue, may be divided into two periods, coinciding with the administrations of Juan José Arévalo (1945–1951) and Jacobo Arbenz Guzmán (1951–1954). Both presidents clung stubbornly to the myth or ideology of the "revolution," though with different emphases. Arévalo devoted his administration to the "political liberation" of Guatemala. A new constitution, stressing civil rights, was written. Political parties, which had been outlawed under Ubico, were allowed to form, and the press became somewhat more free. Arévalo's successor, President Arbenz, dedicated his administration to the "economic liberation" of Guatemala, emphasizing agrarian reform and measures against the "foreign monopolies." Under Arbenz, the reign of terror reached its peak in 1953. He accepted the participation of Communists in his program of economic liberation, and Communist influence became evident in labor unions and his administration.

The Guatemalan "revolution" was cut short during what may be called its reign of terror, and had no opportunity to move on to the stage of Thermidor. A rebellion led by the exiled Colonel Carlos Castillo Armas, apparently with outside support, overthrew the Arbenz regime in mid-1954. The Castillo Armas government was in some respects a counter-revolution, dedicated to undoing the revolution of 1944. Whether it was a temporary interruption of the larger revolution or a final ending of it remains to be seen.[38]

[38] Some revolutions also include counter-revolution among their stages, but counter-revolution is not as common as the seven phases mentioned in this chapter. Where counter-revolution does take place, it frequently follows the reign of terror and precedes Thermidor. See Meusel, op. cit., and Edwards, op. cit.

It is clear, however, that the revolutionary process has not run its full course in Guatemala.[39]

BOLIVIA. Lack of proper perspective still precludes any final judgment as to whether or not a full revolution is in process in Bolivia, although a number of the ingredients undoubtedly are present. It could be said that Bolivia's Porfirio Díaz was General Enrique Peñaranda del Castillo, president of the republic from 1940 to 1943. Unrest was rife during his administration, particularly among the tin miners, and this discontent was fanned by the intellectuals, especially in the wake of the "Catavi Massacre" of December, 1942, when a number of striking miners were killed by government troops.

A clearly structured ideology or myth did not, however, develop, although a Bolivian scholar has called attention to an interesting literature of protest, compounded of Marxism, *indigenismo*, and a peculiarly Bolivian *mystique* of the land.[40] A strong antipathy arose against landowners and mining interests. When the time came, the Bolivian army demonstrated the inability or unwillingness to defend the Peñaranda regime to be expected in this phase.

The fifth revolutionary phase, the rise of the moderates, did not materialize in the Bolivian situation. Rather, events moved directly to the *coup d'état* in which President Peñaranda's government was violently overthrown on December 20, 1943.

The reign of terror, or period of revolutionary dictatorship, endured for the following three years. During that turbulent stage, power was held and ruthlessly exercised by the Nationalist Revolutionary Movement, known to Bolivians as the MNR.[41] Its leader, Víctor Paz Estenssoro, did not become chief of state during this period, but served as minister of finance in the cabinet. President Gualberto Villarroel was in many ways a figurehead, virtually a prisoner of the MNR during the dictatorship he nominally headed. Terror and violence approached an extreme stage in the Villarroel regime, with numerous opposition leaders assassinated, imprisoned, or exiled.

The Bolivian movement had its counter-revolution, resembling the Guatemalan experience. President Villarroel was killed in the

[39] See K. H. Silvert, A Study in Government: Guatemala (New Orleans: Middle American Research Institute of Tulane University, 1954), *passim*, especially pp. 6-25; Philip B. Taylor, Jr., "The Guatemalan Affair: A Critique of United States Foreign Policy," American Political Science Review, L (September, 1956), pp. 787–806; and Fitzgibbon, *op. cit.*, pp. 274–275.

[40] Guillermo Francovich, El pensamiento boliviano en el siglo XX (Mexico: Fondo de Cultura Económica, 1956).

[41] Movimiento Nacionalista Revolucionario.

spectacular violence which overthrew his government in 1946, and counter-revolutionary regimes remained in power for the ensuing six years. In 1952, the revolution was resumed in a successful armed uprising which brought the MNR back to power, this time under Paz Estenssoro's open leadership. During his presidency (1952–1956) the tin mines were expropriated and a far-reaching land reform program was launched. President Hernán Siles Zuazo, also of the MNR, was inaugurated in 1956 for what was to be a four-year term. Early in his administration, this renewed radical phase of the revolution appeared to be undergoing mitigation, although it could not yet be said that Thermidor had arrived.

"Typical" Revolutions

Let us return to the proposition that while so-called revolutions occur frequently in Latin America, most of them are not really revolutions. The use here of the word "frequently" may be an understatement. So-called revolutions take place in the area so often, one student remarked as recently as 1954, that "the governments of the nations to the south have been overthrown . . . seventy-six times" in the twentieth century, and "revolutions are still the order of the day."[42] Most of them might be called "typical Latin American revolutions," and two questions may be raised about them. If they are not really revolutions, what are they? In either case, why do they occur?

The "typical Latin-American revolution" may be defined as a change in government brought about by other than constitutional means but not accompanied by a fundamental change in the social order. Violence, or the threat of it, is frequently present in such a revolution. As in the case of "real" revolutions, however, the presence or absence of violence is not the important fact. What is more basic to the "typical Latin-American revolution" is the unconstitutional change in government. Such revolutions, and they are fairly frequent in Latin America, do not normally bring fundamental social and political changes, not even basic changes in governmental policies, but leave the economic and political structure essentially as it was before. Only the president of the republic and his immediate aides change in these "typical Latin American revolutions."

The pattern of such "revolutions" is always much the same. A *junta,* including key military commanders and those who will hold strategic posts in the new government, will have been organized in

[42] Macdonald, *op. cit.,* pp. 11–12.

advance, under pledge of secrecy. Agents will be ready, in foreign countries, to negotiate for speedy recognition of the new regime. Attacks upon the government in power, as vitriolic as possible and often slanderous, will have been given as wide circulation as possible, on the theory that at least some of the promiscuously made charges will stick. Charges always include graft and corruption, nepotism, favors granted to special business interests, especially foreign-owned enterprises, and often include attacks on the character and integrity of the president.

The uprising is usually set for a holiday or Sunday, because offices will be closed and communication will be more difficult. At the appointed hour, insurgent leaders appear at key military garrisons, including the one nearest the capital if possible. These leaders announce the deposition of the president, and immediately move to take over telephone, telegraph, and broadcasting centers, and to occupy other major government buildings. A group calls upon the president to demand his resignation in exchange for safe conduct out of the country. A mishap in planning, or unexpected resistance from loyal army officers, may lead to more violence, even civil war. But these "revolutions" have often been carried out with little or no loss of life, and Latin Americans generally respect the daring with which military and political leaders have wagered their lives in such gambles for political power.

In seeking an explanation of these so-called revolutions, the student should bear in mind two major considerations. The first has to do with the nature of Latin American constitutions, and the second with the structure of society.

EASE OF CONSTITUTIONAL CHANGE. A later chapter of this book deals extensively with constitutional problems. It may be well, however, to point out here that Latin American constitutions relate to "revolutions" in two ways. In the first place, these constitutions tend to be normative or anticipatory. That is, their texts often provide for what the constitution-writers hope will eventually come to pass rather than what the structure is or can be in reality. Insofar as constitutions exhibit this feature, they are appropriately called unrealistic. Next, it should be noted that much of the content of the constitutions of Latin America is derived largely from foreign—chiefly French and United States—experience and example; Latin American experience is drawn on only to a much lesser degree. The typical "revolution" is, essentially, the violation of a constitution. But this violation chiefly proclaims that tomorrow's ideals have not yet been achieved, or that constitution-writers have been unsuccessful in stretching Latin America on a European or North American frame.[43]

INFLUENCE OF SOCIAL STRUCTURE. The structure of Latin American society provides a second key to the typical "revolution." As noted earlier, social structure usually embodies a highly stratified class system. In Indo-America, a small upper class may consist largely of creoles or whites, the middle group of mestizos, and the lower class of Indians. The division follows similar ethnic lines in Negro America. Elsewhere class lines may follow something like the European lines. But everywhere in Latin America, an impressive social distance separates the classes from each other, however fluid the lines separating them may be.

In many of the countries, those in which the social revolution of the twentieth century has not occurred, a class-oriented differentiation of social functions operates to confer upon the upper class a virtual monopoly of active participation in national government and politics. Indians are virtually excluded from this area of action in most countries. Mestizos play a somewhat more active role in politics, but usually as followers. Indians and mestizos together constitute a majority of the population in many of the countries, so a good deal of the political activity, including the "revolutions," is conducted with little more than passive participation of that majority. The "typical Latin American revolution," therefore, has not been a mass movement and normally does not affect the way of life of the lower classes. Indeed, the usual failure of the Indians to participate in "revolutions" and other political activity is a part of what is meant when it is said that this class is isolated and separated from the national life of many of the states of Indo-America.

Since many of the "revolutions" of Latin America are primarily the work of the upper class and stem from political conditions within that class, it will be worth while at this point to examine some of the patterns of political activity within this ruling group.

Considerable freedom characterizes the political interaction within the upper class. It has been said that the political life of these countries resembles the democracy of the ancient Greeks, in which the ruling class enjoyed liberty of political expression and activity while such privileges were generally denied to the lower classes. Where such conditions prevail in Latin America, a constant struggle for political power goes on within the ruling class.

[43] See Chapter 9.

This often bitter contest within the upper class normally coalesces around one or more of three major lines of division. One of these is personal rivalry among politically prominent figures in the same class. Personalities and family traditions play a much stronger role in the politics of Latin America than elsewhere in the world, so that *personalismo* is a general characteristic of the Latin American pattern. *Personalismo* may be defined as the tendency of the politically active sectors of the population to follow or oppose a leader for personal, individual, and family reasons rather than because of the influence of a political idea, program, or party. One study of the politics of the area, for example, points to "the high value placed on the individual and personal leadership" which promotes "a disposition to vote for the man rather than the party or the platform."[44] Another commentator has said: "From earliest days the Latin Americans . . . have always been more interested in their public men than in their public policies. They have tended to follow colorful leaders, to the subordination of issues. . . . A picturesque demagogue is virtually assured a large following."[45]

The widespread influence of *personalismo* has inspired the political axiom that "in Latin America, almost every 'ism' is a somebody-ism." "Somebody-ism" indeed abounds in recent Latin American politics. Argentina saw *peronismo*, Paraguay has known *franquismo*, based on support of General Rafael Franco,[46] Brazil had its *querimismo*,[47] and Ecuador its *velasquismo*, the following of Dr. José María Velasco Ibarra. Even Uruguay, the most democratic of the Latin American states, has its *batllismo*, derived from José Batlle y Ordóñez. Since not only the "somebodies" who lead the "isms" but many of the "somebody-ists" who make up the movement come from the upper class, *personalismo* is a divisive factor within the class. And the point to be stressed, of course, is that in *personalismo* the "somebody" is of far higher significance than his "ism."

A second major force dividing the upper class is regionalism. Regionalism arises from many factors, one of which is the simple difficulty of transportation and communication in much of Latin America. Where two or more regions of a country are separated from each other by mountain ranges, jungles, or other types of difficult terrain, Latin Americans have developed historical loyalties to their regions, and these loyalties on occasion take prece-

---

[44] Pierson and Gil, *op. cit.*, p. 31.
[45] Macdonald, *op. cit.*, p. 2.
[46] Not to be confused with Spain's General Francisco Franco.
[47] Literally, "we-wantism," a popular abbreviation of "We want Vargas."

dence over national sentiments. When the ruling class in one region of a country develops this type of loyalty, it operates as a divisive factor, encouraging the political opposition of the dominant group of the first region against the corresponding class of another region of the same country. This political function of regionalism can be seen, for example, in the politics of such countries as Bolivia, Brazil, Ecuador, Paraguay, and Peru.

A third major divisive factor within the upper class is doctrinal or ideological. That is to say, the politically active sector of the population may be divided within itself because of intellectual or doctrinal disagreement on questions of political principle. Ideological conflicts are not as frequent a source of factional division as *personalismo* in Latin America, but situations have existed and do exist where ideological differences are significant. Illustrations of serious division on the question of the temporal role of the Church, and the importance of this division as a political factor, can be found in Ecuador and Colombia. Occasionally, the upper class may divide within itself on issues of government policy or, when new constitutions are to be written, on forms of government.

Conclusions and Trends

In summary, then, it may be noted that the "typical Latin American revolution" is integrally related to two chief factors. The first of these is the ease with which written constitutions are violated. The second is the nature of the structure of society. The latter is such, in many countries, that the upper classes exercise a virtual monopoly of active participation in government and politics, from which the lower class, especially in those countries where it consists chiefly of mestizos and Indians, is largely excluded. Moreover, the sometimes anarchic or chaotic "democracy in the Greek sense" to be found in the dominant group contributes to divisions and struggles within that class which are sometimes acrimonious and violent.

Thus the "typical Latin American revolution" is normally the product of the political activity of the upper class. Usually the lower classes do not participate in it actively, and this so-called revolution does not affect the status or the way of life of the Indians, mestizos, and others of lower social class. Such a "revolution," then, does not bring with it a change in the structure of society or a recasting of the social order.

In short, the "typical Latin American revolution" is not a revolution at all. In a sense it is a proclamation that true revolution has not yet come. The Mexican Revolution is a noteworthy exception, a true revolution, and it may be argued that such revolutions have also taken place in a few other countries.

For much of Latin America, however, fundamental revolution has not yet come. It accompanied neither the wars that brought national independence nor the subsequent political instability which has been frequently manifested. This failure, in most of the countries, to experience the basic social revolution of the twentieth century is central to any consideration of current trends in Latin America. Many have argued that revolution is overdue in the area, and some observers believe that they now see the first stages of revolution in twentieth-century Latin America, or at least its ingredients. Essentially, these remain propositions that cannot yet be validly tested. It may well be that the frequency with which so-called "revolutions" occur means primarily that in most of the countries involved there has as yet been little or no revolution. It may, however, be the ferment producing some larger change. On the other hand, one may read into recent developments in Guatemala and Bolivia the probability that in some of the less developed countries of the hemisphere the movement toward true revolution has already begun, and that the latter half of the twentieth century may be expected to see further steps in that direction.

Suggestions for Reading

Useful works dealing with the general concept of revolution include Crane Brinton, *The Anatomy of Revolution* (New York: W. W. Norton and Co., Inc., 1938), in which the mainsprings of revolution are sought out, and Lyford P. Edwards, *The Natural History of Revolution* (Chicago: University of Chicago Press, 1927), an intriguing attempt to spell out the universal steps or stages of revolution. Students grappling with problems in terminology should find stimulating assistance in Robert Hunter, *Revolution: Why, How, When?* (New York: Harper & Brothers, 1940) and in Alfred Meusel, "Revolution and Counter-Revolution," *Encyclopaedia of the Social Sciences* (New York: The Macmillan Company, 1937), IV, 259–262.

A number of works helpful in applying the general scheme of revolution to the Latin American environment include Donald E. Worcester and Wendell G. Schaeffer, *The Growth and Culture of Latin America* (New York: Oxford University Press, 1956); Víctor Andrés Belaúnde, *Bolívar and the Political Thought of the Spanish American Revolution* (Baltimore: The Johns Hopkins Press, 1938); and William W. Pierson and Federico G. Gil, *Governments of Latin America* (New York: McGraw-Hill Book Co., Inc., 1957), particularly pp. 135–159. Russell H. Fitzgibbon, "Revolutions: Western Hemisphere," *The South Atlantic Quarterly*, LV (July 1956), 263–279, is a useful and comprehensive survey of revolutionary development in Latin America as of mid-century.

Chapter 6

The Army in Politics

The armed forces in Latin America frequently play an active role in political life. Usually it is the army that has been most active, though at times the navy and even the air force have also played key roles.

Importance of the Army in Politics

Some idea of the importance of the military in public affairs in Latin America can be gained from the fact that in January, 1957, for example, military men were presidents in nine of the twenty Latin American republics—Argentina, Chile, Colombia, Venezuela, Honduras, El Salvador, Guatemala, Cuba, and the Dominican Republic. Other statistics show that eight of the ten presidents of Argentina since 1930 have been army men and that they have ruled for all but four years of this period; that three of the five Peruvian presidents during this same period have also been military men; that Venezuela has been governed by army officers for all but three of the last fifty years. Some Latin American nations during this century have been under virtually continuous control of the armed forces, whether or not a military man has been the chief executive. Among these nations can be counted Venezuela, Paraguay, and several of the Central American republics.

Even when a military man is not president of a Latin American state, the ruling politicians must constantly anticipate the possible reaction of the army to any move they make. The exceptions to this rule are rare; in 1957, for instance, there were not more than three such cases: Bolivia, Uruguay, and Costa Rica.

EXAMPLES OF MILITARY CONTROL. Several outstanding cases of control of Latin American governments by the armed forces are worthy of special note. In Venezuela a military dictatorship under General Juan Vicente Gómez dominated the country for twenty-seven years, during the period from 1909 to 1935. After the death of General Gómez, the administration was taken over by his minister of war, General Eleázer López Contreras, who granted a few months of freedom but soon restored military control of the government. In 1942 he was succeeded by another general, Isaías Medina Angarita, who encouraged greater civilian participation in what was still essentially a military regime.

Not until the revolution of 1945, conducted by a coalition of young army officers and the country's leading civilian political party, Acción Democrática, did a civilian, Rómulo Betancourt, become head of the government. His two-year administration and the short-lived rule of his successor, Rómulo Gallegos, were constantly threatened by *coups d'état*. Finally, realizing that the Acción Democrática government's policy of encouraging political parties, trade unions, and peasants' organizations was challenging its role in political life, the army ousted President Gallegos in November, 1948, installing a military *junta* in his place. Since that date the army has continued to run the country, even after the election of Colonel Marcos Pérez Jiménez as president (1952).

Paraguay, too, has experienced an almost unbroken military dictatorship since the end of the Chaco War with Bolivia in 1936. A *coup d'état* at the end of that war installed Colonel Rafael Franco as president. His regime, which began extensive social and economic changes in the country, was overthrown a year later by another *coup d'état*. Since the overthrow of Franco, real power has remained in the hands of the military, although there have been several civilian presidents. Regimes have usually been overthrown by the garrison of the capital, Asunción, and most particularly by the First Motorized Cavalry Division.

Nicaragua has been controlled by its army since General Anastasio Somoza seized power soon after the withdrawal of the United States Marines from that country in the early 1930's. He maintained control, though he was not always officially in office, until his assassination late in 1956. The power of the army (the National Guard) was demonstrated in 1947 when an elected civilian president, Leonardo Arguello, sought to undermine the position of General Somoza. The result was that the general, who had been careful to retain this position as commander-in-chief of the National Guard, ousted President Arguello after only twenty-seven days in power, installing another civilian in his place. A year later General Somoza was again elected and remained president until his death. His son Luis, not of the army, then took over the reins of office, but Luis' tenure in office depends largely upon his remaining in the good graces of his brother, Colonel Anastasio Somoza, Jr., commander-in-chief of the National Guard.

METHODS OF MILITARY INTERVENTION. The methods of military intervention in Latin American politics are varied. Perhaps the most frequent, and certainly the best-known, method is that of *coup d'état*. The *coup d'état* is by no means a standardized procedure. Not infrequently, a coup (or *golpe de estado* as it is known in Latin America) is staged by the highest officials of the armed forces. They simply agree that the current chief executive must be ousted and decide upon who is to succeed him. Thereupon they order the troops in or near the capital to take the necessary steps. This procedure occurred at the time of the 1943 revolution in Argentina and the 1953 coup in Colombia. This sort of coup is generally bloodless, or nearly so.

Frequently, however, a coup is engineered by only a faction of the armed forces. Such was the case in Venezuela in 1945 and again in 1948. Whether or not this kind of *golpe* will result in bloodshed depends on whether or not those loyal to the regime think resistance worth while. Often, when a large or strategic part of the armed forces remains loyal, such coups are defeated.

Sometimes an uprising of a faction in the armed forces may result in a civil war of longer or shorter duration. Such an uprising occurred in Argentina when the revolt of army and air force units in Córdoba and naval units in the south was resisted for several days by principal elements of the army, which surrendered only after they were abandoned by President Perón.

Not infrequently, the ambitious commander of some key military post will proclaim a *golpe* on his own authority, naming himself provisional chief executive, then hoping for the best. This was illustrated in Peru in October, 1948, when General Manuel Odría, the commander in Arequipa, proclaimed a revolution and was soon supported by armed forces elsewhere in the republic.

Perhaps the most bizarre instance of this last type of *golpe* was executed by General and ex-President Fulgencio Batista of Cuba on March 10, 1952. Although he had been in retirement from active duty, General Batista suddenly appeared at Camp Columbia, the principal army base outside Havana, at two o'clock in the morning. There he was met by some junior officers who were in on his plans. He proceeded to place the commanding officers of the post under arrest, and at the same time announced that he was assuming command. By five o'clock he had the camp fully under control and began to move to seize the capital. He would undoubtedly have been thwarted had President Carlos Prío Socarrás taken firm action against him, since all other garrisons remained loyal, awaiting orders from Prío and only going over to Batista after the president gave up the fight.

Once having seized power, the military men may choose to exercise it themselves or through civilians who are willing to work with them and under their control. The latter method has frequently been used in Paraguay and was employed by General Lott in Brazil from November, 1955, until the inauguration of President Kubitschek at the end of January, 1956. There are also numerous cases of the direct exercise of power, however. The regimes of Generals José Uriburu, Pedro Ramírez, Edelmiro Farrell, Eduardo Lonardi, and Pedro Aramburu, during the last quarter-century in Argentina, were all of this kind. The government of General Gustavo Rojas Pinilla in Colombia has called itself frankly "the government of the armed forces."

Army intervention in politics is frequently exercised by means more subtle than the *coup d'état* and open military dictatorship. On several occasions, for example, during the administration of President Juscelino Kubitschek of Brazil, the president or Vice President João Goulart has felt constrained to "consult" General Lott, Minister of War, before taking some important political step. In Mexico, for a short while under President Lázaro Cárdenas, the armed forces were actually a constituent part of the official party (PRI).

Individual military men may participate in one or another political party. Although the laws of most countries require that officers leave the service before becoming active in a party or an election campaign, in Ecuador, officers in active service not infrequently belong to and participate in party meetings.

Undoubtedly, a great deal of political pressure exercised by the Latin American armed forces never becomes public knowledge. Since ministers of defense are generally active military men, they are constantly in a position to express their views and the views of their organizations to the president. They undoubtedly accompany this "advice" with appropriate warnings or threats when that seems convenient. Thus, in one way or another, the armed forces in most Latin American republics play a key role in making governments, influencing their policies, and unmaking them.

EXCEPTIONS TO A POLITICAL ARMY. As indicated, at present there are perhaps no more than three countries in Latin America in which the army does not constitute a political factor of major impor-

tance—Bolivia, Uruguay, and Costa Rica.   In Bolivia, the army
was destroyed as a result of the revolution of 1952, and the administrations since that time have not allowed it to be reconstructed
sufficiently to threaten civilian control of the government.   Most of
the conscripts of the Bolivian army, and their officers, have been
sent to the eastern tropical part of the country, where they are employed in road-building and other constructive economic activities.

In the case of Uruguay, the civilian control of political life probably owes its origin, as do most things in contemporary Uruguayan
politics, to José Batlle y Ordóñez (1903–1907 and 1911–1915).   As
president, Batlle gave strong and positive leadership to the nation,
setting it upon a path of constitutional democracy, stability, and
social and economic experimentation which was for long a model
in the hemisphere.   During the one period of strong-arm rule in
Uruguay since Batlle's days—under President Gabriel Terra from
1933 to 1938—the National Police Force, and not the army, was
the dominant influence.   In general, the armed forces (and since
1938, the police) have remained unobtrusive and aloof from politics.

In Costa Rica, the army has never in recent years been a powerful political influence.   It was kept small and ill-equipped, and
after the 1948 Revolution led by José Figueres, the 1949 Constituent Assembly decreed its abolition.   A small National Police Force
exists, but it is equipped with little more than side arms and its
main function is to provide a core of officers for the civilian militia
upon which the country depends for the defense of its frontiers.

Causes of Military Intervention in Politics

The political importance of the armed forces in the Latin American nations continues, in spite of the fact that the armies are of
constantly decreasing importance insofar as the classical duties of
national defense are concerned.   During the twentieth century
only two important international wars occurred within the American hemisphere—the long struggle between Paraguay and Bolivia
from 1932 to 1936 and a short border clash between Peru and
Ecuador in 1942.   The growing force and effectiveness of the
inter-American system of conciliation and adjustment of international differences promises to make such international conflicts even
less frequent in the future.

Nor has Latin America participated to any great degree in wider
international conflicts.   No Latin American nation sent troops into
World War I.   Only Brazil and Mexico were actively engaged in
World War II, the former sending land troops to fight in the Italian
campaign, and the latter providing some air force units for the

later phases of the Pacific struggle. Colombia sent a contingent to Korea and contributed to the U. N. forces for the Suez.

Hence, the explanation for the great importance of the militarists in Latin American politics cannot be found in a need for large forces to defend these countries from foreign aggression. On the contrary, most of the armed forces have become little more than heavily armed police forces, whose principal task is to "preserve order."

TABLE X.   SIZE OF LATIN AMERICAN ARMED FORCES

Country	Army	Navy	Air Force
Argentina	105,000	21,500	—
Bolivia	—	—	—
Brazil	200,000	26,500	—
Chile	20,400	13,000	—
Colombia	12–15,000	2,800	—
Costa Rica	1,200[a]	—	—
Cuba	13,000	5,200	235
Dominican Republic	12,000	2,000	2,400
Ecuador	—	3,780	—
El Salvador	—	—	—
Guatemala	7–8,000	—	—
Haiti	4,040	300	152
Honduras	2,500	—	—
Mexico	300,000	—	—
Nicaragua	3,220	—	—
Panama	3,370[b]	—	—
Paraguay	5,850	—	—
Peru	32,000	—	—
Uruguay	—	—	—
Venezuela	10,000	—	—

A dash indicates that data are not available.
SOURCE: *Statesman's Year Book, 1956* (London: Macmillan & Co., Ltd., 1956).
[a] National Guard.
[b] National Police.

For the most part, by the standards of modern warfare Latin American armies are poorly equipped. Their armament is generally heterogeneous, frequently "hand-me-down" from the major powers. In recent years, however, the armies have increasingly tended to acquire tanks of various sizes, rapid-fire weapons, and other relatively heavy equipment. Air forces and navies have followed the same trend, though generally in a more modest fashion.

It is doubtful whether any of the Latin American armed forces could adequately defend their nation against a major military threat for any appreciable length of time. They might be able to wage war against each other, however, and one of the dangers in increasing the heavy armament of the Latin American military is that of precipitating an arms race. This danger is particularly acute in the case of Argentina and Brazil.

MILITARISM AND ITS ORIGINS. The reasons for the Latin American tradition of a political army must be sought elsewhere than in the needs of national defense. One of the original causes, undoubtedly, was the role of the national armies in the struggle for independence. These wars were long drawn-out affairs, and in some countries they were exceedingly destructive. When the struggles were over, the armed forces were almost the only institutions strong enough to maintain the cohesiveness of the nations. This became even more true as the destruction of the temporal power and influence of the Church proceeded during the nineteenth century.

Another important reason was that the former Spanish colonies lacked that tradition of separation of civil and military power so well established in the English-speaking world when the North American colonies achieved their independence. Thus few Latin American "liberators" were willing or able to follow the example of George Washington in refusing to seize civil control of the nation when they possessed the military force to do so.

In this connection, the parallel between the history of the former Spanish colonies and their mother country during the nineteenth century may suggest another cause of Spanish American militarism. The Spanish army, like the armies of Spanish America, intervened frequently in the political affairs of that nation throughout the century, making and unmaking governments with great frequency; indeed, this tradition has carried down to the present day.

SOCIAL AND ECONOMIC FACTORS. Also contributing to the political role of the military have been certain social and economic factors. Latin American economic and social life during much of the nineteenth century and even the early twentieth century was highly stratified. An individual had comparatively little chance to rise from the bottom of the social scale to a higher social position. The army presented one exception to this static social structure. A lower-middle-class boy who was able to receive training in a military academy, and thus gain a foothold on the lower rungs of the army's hierarchical ladder, might reasonably expect to become a high-ranking officer. Thus a humble peasant or ranch hand who had the strength of character, the ability, and the determination to command might join one of the rough-and-tumble armies in the Latin American civil wars of the nineteenth century with some expectation of rising high in the ranks of the military and of proceeding from there into politics, perhaps ending up as president of his country. Even the underprivileged ethnic groups of Latin America could use the army as a means of climbing the social ladder. The Indian recruit, for instance, entered the army as a conscript Indian but emerged as a cultural mestizo. A revolution might even bring an Indian boy to the top through the army.

The Latin American army officer, particularly one of high rank, has since independence always been in the upper social stratum, however plebeian his origin. In recent years the officers in most Latin American armies have not only enjoyed high salaries, but have been given opportunities to obtain automobiles and other perquisites of office. They have been able to buy goods below market prices in special commissaries, have had travel privileges, and have enjoyed exclusive and sometimes aristocratic officers' clubs. The officers' club of Caracas, Venezuela, is said to be the most expensive edifice of its kind in the world. In some instances, the officers have not only enjoyed these more or less legitimate benefits of office, but also have been in positions to make illicit gains in corrupt regimes.

INFLUENCE OF GERMAN TRAINING. Beginning in the latter years of the nineteenth century, many of the Latin American armies were trained by German military missions. This Prussian junker training reinforced already existing beliefs of the military men in their peculiar destiny and their right to be the final arbiters of national affairs. The Prussian officers believed even less than their Latin American protégés in the supremacy of the civilian branch of government over the military. The growing influence and prestige of the German military in the world tended to destroy whatever lingering doubts any of their pupils might have had on the subject.

PSYCHOLOGICAL FACTORS. Finally, a psychological factor in the development of Latin American militarism cannot be overlooked. For the Latin American army officers, intervention in political affairs became a habit, a custom. It became almost routine for military men who were dissatisfied with the political situation to try to do something about it. It became equally routine for politicians who were disgruntled with the regime in power to look for allies among the leaders of the armed forces. A British or North American general would never contemplate the ouster of the chief executive, or even the issuance of an ultimatum to him. But there was little "psychological block" against such action in the minds of the military leaders in many Latin American countries; in fact, it was a common occurrence.

Thus, the army in most countries of Latin America has become an independent political force. It operates for reasons of its own and intervenes in the civilian militia upon which the country depends for the defense of its frontiers.

THE ARMY AS A NATIONALIZING FORCE.   The army played a key role during the nineteenth and the early twentieth centuries in developing a spirit of nationality, and subsequently of nationalism.   The military was the branch of government concerned particularly with maintaining independence and protecting a nation from its neighbors.   Not infrequently during the nineteenth century, the armies of the various countries were called upon to defend their territorial integrity and national sovereignty.   As a result, the armed forces were more conscious than much of the civilian community of the importance of the nation as a concept, an ideal, and an actuality. They came to feel that it was their duty not only to defend the frontiers, but also to defend the "national honor" of their homelands.

The Brazilian army furnishes a striking example of this tendency.   Although militarism was not of major importance under the Empire, the armed forces were principally responsible for overthrowing the aging Pedro II, and hence came to regard themselves as peculiarly "the defenders of the republic."   Not infrequently thereafter, when they conceived the republic to be in danger, they undertook to intervene to set things aright.

The Spanish American tradition of personalism in politics has also contributed to the key role of the armed forces in politics.   A successful military leader is usually in a strategic position to become a *caudillo,* a popular figure with the masses and at the same time a likely defender of the status quo.   The Latin American version of "the man on horseback" is a highly popular concept in Latin American politics.

The Army and the Power Structure

INCREASED ARMY POLITICAL INFLUENCE.   In many ways the importance of the army as a political factor in most Latin American countries has been strengthened in recent years.   The increasing firepower of weapons and the expanding technology of war in general have made the armed forces much more powerful in relation to civilians than they were several generations ago.   During the nineteenth century, when military armament consisted mainly of small arms, and when these arms were also widely distributed among the civilian population, it was a comparatively simple matter to oust even a military despot.   If a large enough group of people were sufficiently determined, it could take up arms, storm through the streets, and attack the local soldiery.   A musket or a rifle in the hands of civilians would kill or maim just as effectively as the same weapon in the hands of the military.

However, this balance has been destroyed in recent years. Machine guns, armored cars, tanks, and airplanes are weapons difficult for civilians to oppose. Only well-trained and equally well-armed soldiers can effectively combat those loyal to a regime. Thus a situation has been created in which it is virtually impossible to overthrow a military dictator without the defection of a sizable part of the armed forces supporting him.

Various instances might be cited to demonstrate this fact. The Batista regime in the 1950's in Cuba and the military dictatorship in Venezuela after 1948 lacked strong civilian support; yet as long as the armed forces remained united the unarmed populace could do little about the situation. The Odría military regime in Peru was finally forced out of office in 1956 when a split in the ranks of the military made it possible for important civilian elements to make their voices heard.

The position of the military has been further strengthened by the army's taking over jobs which in other nations are usually carried out by civilians. The army thus has often helped to carry out the periodic census, and in many instances it has stepped in to preside over elections, on the theory that it was "above" politics and would not favor any of the candidates.

CHANGED SOCIAL ROLE.   While the relative power of the armed forces in the nations as a whole has been increasing, new trends at work within the armies themselves in the last generation have altered the nature of their role in Latin American society. During most of the nineteenth and the early years of the present century the army's chief social role was that of preserving the status quo. Although the armies of some countries led in the fight against the power of the Church, army leaders showed little sentiment for changing the basic social structure of the Latin American nations. The economic and social aristocracy were generally able to depend on the armed forces to defend their privileges. This was particularly the case in countries where the gulf between classes was widest. In those countries in which the large landholding system and its consequent social stratification were complicated by a difference in race between the landlord aristocracy and the peasantry, the ruling economic groups relied particularly on the armed forces for the "preservation of order," that is, for the maintenance of existing social relationships.

In recent years, this close alliance between the military and the dominant social and economic groups has been less certain. In the

Mexican Revolution the old army was destroyed, and the new one which took its place was led by men who had helped overthrow the old regime and were thus pledged to preventing its return. A break between the old landed aristocracy and the army also occurred in Brazil. In the early 1920's, a group of young army officers, who came to be known as the *tenentes* (lieutenants), began to think of altering the status quo. Although they were defeated in two revolutionary attempts, they succeeded in the third, the revolution of 1930, which brought Getulio Vargas to power. Since then the Brazilian army has been the chief support of the movement for social and economic change which is shifting power from the landowning aristocracy to the growing urban middle classes.

More recently, an Argentine movement which began in 1943 as a military revolution little concerned with social and economic affairs evolved under the leadership of General Juan Domingo Perón into a broad movement for social and economic development. For more than a decade the Perón regime rested on a rather peculiar alliance of the army and the government-controlled trade union movement. The old alliance of the military with the landed aristocracy was thus broken and may never be restored.

Finally, there is the case of Bolivia, where the revolution of 1952 resulted in the destruction of the country's former army. In building up a new military group, the government has been careful to choose its officers from among those who have been closely associated with the governing revolutionary party. At the same time, the government has provided a counter-balance to the military by arming its worker and peasant supporters.

CIVILIAN FACTORS LIMITING MILITARISM. Growing social consciousness within the ranks of the military reflects the economic, social, and political changes in civilian society which have been in process since World War I. These changes, as pointed out in earlier chapters, have created or strengthened civilian groups which offer a natural challenge to the preponderance of the armed forces in these countries' political life.

In the first place, well-organized and disciplined political parties have arisen in many countries. For the most part, these parties advocate social and economic change to some degree, if not revolution. They speak for hitherto submerged classes in society. Many of them have a fairly coherent body of doctrine, and many of them have developed first-class leadership. They are generally suspicious of military intervention in politics. At moments of crisis, they may be able to rally the civilian population to resist encroachment of the military by means of passive resistance and public protest.

In the second place, hitherto small urban middle classes have been much strengthened by the growth of industrialization. The additions to the middle class include people who have the skills necessary for managing an increasingly complex civilian society. They have considerable economic power, and their power is increasing. The middle classes are generally desirous of a stable political atmosphere in which their enterprises can prosper, and they are opposed to the frequent change of administrations by *coups d'état*.

Of course, the middle classes are no match for naked force, but they have means of preventing a resort to such force, by bringing behind-the-scenes social pressure to bear on the military and by conducting national economic affairs in such a way as to prevent the development of the kinds of crises which military men so often exploit. Their influence can also be exerted through the increasingly large numbers of their class who are now entering the army as officers.

Also of key importance is the trade union movement which has come into existence with the growth of the urban working class. Trade unions, in fact, probably offer the most potent challenge to army political power. When all else fails, by means of a general strike the unions can bring even the armed forces to heel when necessary.

The growth of these new socio-political groups on the heels of a rising industrialization also has the effect of lessening the power of the old aristocratic landowning classes to resist change. At the same time it makes the military less willing to be the principal prop of the economic and social status quo. Thus the old alliance between the army and landowners becomes less important in national political life.

ALIENATION OF THE OLIGARCHY FROM THE ARMY. Furthermore, in at least two of the South American countries, Ecuador and Peru, developments during the 1950's seem to show that the old aristocracy itself is no longer as willing as in the past to depend upon military force to maintain its power. The decade of the 1950's in Ecuador has been remarkable because between 1948 and 1956 two successive administrations came to power and gave up office legally. This is the first time in twentieth-century Ecuador that such a phenomenon has occurred. All civilian parties and groups then resolved that Ecuador was to continue on the path of constitutional legality. Even the 1956 election of a Conservative president, for the first time in over sixty years, failed to produce more than a minor uprising by a provincial garrison, and this was easily subdued. None of the civilian political groups wanted to place the destinies of the country in the hands of the army chiefs any longer, because no one could be sure what direction an army-controlled regime would take.

The re-election of Manuel Prado Ugarteche as president of Peru in June, 1956 (after an absence from the presidency of eleven years), also indicated that the old alliance of the military and the aristocracy in that country had been seriously weakened. One of the richest men in Peru, and the representative of the landowning–commercial oligarchy of the nation, President Prado was elected with the votes of the Aprista party. This party, as noted in a previous chapter, has advocated revolutionary social and economic changes in the nation, including agrarian reform. It had been kept from power for more than a quarter-century (and had been illegal all but four years of that time) in spite of being the nation's majority party. During these years a series of military regimes had been backed by the landowning and commercial aristocracy. But the experience of the ruling economic groups with the last of the military dictatorships, that of General Manuel Odría (1948–1956) had not been a happy one for them. During most of his tenure in office, Odría had maintained a military dictatorship, cracking down on any and all dissidents. His regime had handled certain elements of the oligarchy as cavalierly as it had treated the *apristas*.

As a result, powerful elements in the oligarchical group, represented by Prado himself, the Beltrán family, and its newspaper *La Prensa*, had concluded by 1956 that it would be better for the nation and for themselves to trust to a democratic evolution, supported by and perhaps ultimately led by the *apristas*, rather than to attempt to continue to suppress this evolution by excessive reliance on a military group having no real ties with the aristocracy.

Perhaps the ruling Peruvian economic and social groups were influenced in this change of heart by events in neighboring Bolivia, where obstinate resistance to change had produced a violent explosion in the early 1950's in which effective political power was transferred suddenly to the largely Indian masses. They may have been convinced that changes were inevitable and hence that it was futile to try to bar them by a military dictatorship which, in any case, could not always be counted upon to support their interests. These dominant Peruvian elements seem to have concluded that relatively slow and democratic change in the country's economy and society, through the eventual triumph of the *apristas* at the polls, was to be preferred.

CHANGES WITHIN ARMED FORCES. The revolutionary doctrines of militant nationalism and social revolt have had repercussions within the ranks of the armed forces. Officers have become increasingly concerned with social problems, even in countries in which social change is still not rapid. They have been convinced that to be "preservers of order" does not necessarily mean to be guardians of the economic and social status quo.

This growing social consciousness in the ranks of the officer corps has been strengthened in some cases by a desire of the military to obtain or maintain popularity among the civilians. Resentment and hostility toward military men has frequently existed among the working classes, intellectuals, and businessmen. But army officers who have participated in recent movements for social change have found this hostility turn into acceptance, approval, and even popularity. Once they have obtained this approbation, many officers have been hesitant to jeopardize their new popularity with the populace by unpopular acts. This recognition of the need for popular acceptance was certainly a key factor in the Argentine army's long hesitation in moving against the Perón regime. It was probably important, too, in Venezuela in the period of the Acción Democrática regime (1945–1948) and in Guatemala in the early 1950's.

This new social consciousness and desire for civilian popularity has also presented a serious dilemma to the officer corps. When the armed forces support national economic diversification and the abolition of old class and racial cleavages, this results in the rise of trade unions, middle-class economic organizations, and political parties which are opposed to the military in political life. In time, such groups may be in a position, through organized passive resistance, to challenge the political role of the army, as already indicated. Such a situation has arisen in recent years in Argentina, Venezuela, Guatemala, El Salvador, and several other countries.

Within the armed forces themselves, significant antagonisms have also arisen. Modernization of the armies since World War I and the resultant improvement in the technical ability of the military academies to give more highly professional military training, plus opportunities for foreign training, have contributed to this antagonism. The younger officers, who are more highly trained, become discontented with their older, sometimes uncouth and unlettered superiors. Such discontent played an important role in military uprisings during the 1940's in several countries, including Venezuela, Guatemala, and El Salvador.

INTERSERVICE RIVALRIES. Another factor to be considered in
assaying the role of the armed forces in the Latin American power
structure is the rivalry among the armed services. This is nothing
new in Latin American history, because interservice rivalry played
a key role in the Chilean revolution of 1891. But in recent years
the increased armament of some of the navies, as well as their
ideological divergences from the armies, has given naval leaders
special political importance, particularly in Argentina and Brazil.
The government of General Juan Perón was overthrown largely
through the action of the navy and the air force. The government
of General Pedro Aramburu, which replaced the two-month
interim administration of General Lonardi, has depended largely
on the navy for its support. Argentine army officers have been
discontented because of this "usurpation" of their role as moderator
of the national destiny.

In Brazil, likewise, political rivalries between the army on the
one hand and the air force and navy on the other became important in the early 1950's. The air force took a leading role in the
events leading to the suicide of President Getulio Vargas in August,
1954. His successor, President João Cafe Filho, was fully backed
by the air force and the navy as well as by most of the army. When
the Army chief, General Lott, ousted President Cafe Filho in November, 1955, however, this action was sorely resented by the naval
and air forces, even though its purpose was to ensure respect for
the results of the popular election of a new president. President
Juscelino Kubitschek, elected at that time, has relied heavily on
army support. The naval and air forces have appeared to be in
somewhat sullen opposition.

Another internal development in the armed forces, not uncon-
nected with political and social developments, is the change in the
status of the enlisted man. During the last several decades the
tendency has been to improve the housing, education, and health
conditions of the common soldier, and particularly the non-com-
missioned officer. In Mexico this policy began as early as the Calles
administration of the mid-1920's. It has been notable during recent
years in Cuba, Venezuela, El Salvador, Guatemala, and Ecuador,
and particularly during the Perón administration in Argentina.
Undoubtedly, the general modernization of the armies has contributed to this. However, one of the reasons for this improvement in the position of the enlisted man has certainly been the
concern of the leaders lest the enlisted men become a political
force independent of their officers. Army officials have therefore
accepted and encouraged moves to improve conditions of service

for the enlisted man and to soften the harsh distinctions between officers and the other ranks. Generals Perón in Argentina and Batista in Cuba (the latter a former sergeant himself) have been famous as defenders of the enlisted man.

Perhaps the most striking example of this preoccupation with the rank-and-file soldier was given in Cuba by General Batista at the time of his seizure of power in 1952 (mentioned earlier in this chapter). On the morning of March 10, 1952, he is reported to have mustered together the garrison of Camp Columbia to announce that in taking over the government of the republic he was immediately raising the pay of the army enlisted man from 30 to 100 dollars a month. He then offered to let all of those who opposed him retire quietly from the scene. Few did so. Five years later Fidel Castro, leading an uprising against Batista, made a similar appeal.

The Military and Hemispheric Defense

HEMISPHERE DEFENSE POLICY. Another aspect of the role of the military in politics worth exploring is its part in the inter-American defense system that has grown up since World War II. It was that conflict which brought about close cooperation between the United States and Latin American armed forces for the joint defense of the hemisphere. During the war the United States was allowed to send troops to man key defense installations in a number of the American republics, and an Inter-American Defense Board was established. These wartime agreements were later consolidated in the Rio de Janeiro Treaty of Reciprocal Assistance (1947) and in the Charter of the Organization of American States, drawn up at Bogotá in 1948.

The Inter-American Defense Board, with headquarters in Washington, has continued with somewhat enlarged functions assigned to it by the Conference of Foreign Ministers at Washington in 1951. Recommendations of the Defense Board are made to the twenty-one individual governments, rather than to the Organization of American States, since the Board has never been made a formal part of the OAS machinery. The Latin American nations have not been anxious to give this Defense Board more formal authority, because they fear to lose any measure of national control over their armed forces.

Inter-American defense policy has attempted to standardize arms of the Latin American countries as well as to coordinate strategic planning. Prior to World War II, the Latin American

armed forces were equipped with a potpourri of armaments purchased at various times and in various places as the opportunity
presented itself. Since the war, the effort has been primarily to
equip them with United States arms of uniform make and to provide training by United States instructors in the use of these
weapons. The United States has also entered into a series of
bilateral pacts with many of the Latin American countries to
provide equipment and training.

OBJECTIONS TO THE POLICY. Some critics in both parts of the
hemisphere feel that this inter-American defense program has draw-
backs at least as important as the advantages. The feeling is widespread in Latin America that the inter-American defense policy is
really a United States policy, and that the Latin Americans are
being used for selfish purposes by their stronger northern neighbor.
The bilateral pacts have been criticized in particular on this ground
by nationalist elements in Latin America. Some nations fear that
this armament program may lead to arms races among the nations
of the hemisphere which might, in turn, cause future wars.

Finally, there are those both in the United States and in Latin
America who question, on purely political grounds, the direction
which the inter-American defense program has taken. It is claimed
that few Latin American nations could defend themselves against
a serious invasion from another hemisphere for the length of time
necessary for the United States to come to their aid, and that therefore it is a serious mistake to further arm these countries, particularly those controlled by military dictatorships. It is argued that
most of the Latin American armed forces are little more than large
police forces with a penchant for interfering in politics and that providing them with modern armament seriously alters the balance of
power between civilian and military elements within these nations.

POLITICAL EFFECTS. Those who view matters in this way, both
in the United States and in Latin America, point out that the
strength of the United States is, in the last analysis, the only real
assurance of the inviolability of the Latin American republics.
They add that the problems of Latin America are at the present
time economic, social, political, and perhaps psychological, rather
than principally military. The future of democracy in the Latin
American hemisphere is more imperiled at the present time by
military dictatorship, they argue, than by any menace from the
outside. Piling up armaments seriously weakens the civilian elements in the Latin American states while diverting important
resources which would be better spent on economic development

and on raising the standards of living of the Latin American peoples. Such are the contentions of those who remain skeptical of the inter-American defense trends of the late 1940's and early 1950's.

On the other hand, there are those who feel that deeper involvement in hemispheric defense plans and closer contact with the United States Army will tend to divert the attention of Latin American military men from political activities, while at the same time helping to convince them that it is not the military man's prerogative to make and unmake governments. (The author of this chapter can discern little tendency in this direction at the present time.)

Trends and Problems, In Summary

Militarism remains a key problem in the politics of Latin America. Having roots deep in the history of these nations, it has in many cases become a tradition. In recent years the problem has been made more complicated by the economic evolution and the urge for social change which has swept across the hemisphere, as well as by the problems of hemispheric solidarity and defense.

The principal trends and problems in respect to militarism in politics may be summarized as follows:

1. The armed forces continue to maintain, if not to increase, the importance of their role in Latin American political life, as the result of expanding military budgets and increasingly heavy armament. The army's role has also been strengthened by its frequent assumption of such special duties as supervising elections, conducting censuses, and carrying out literacy programs.

2. On the other hand, there is growing resistance on the part of middle-class civilian elements, political parties, and trade unions to army meddling in politics.

3. At the same time significant changes have taken place in the social role of the army. As the economic middle class grows apace with industrialization the importance of the army as a source of political mobility tends to lessen. The armies tend to become infected with the new ideas of social change characterizing the civilian part of the populace, and the old alliance between the armed forces and the economic powers-that-be tends to weaken.

4. Other changes are at work within the armed forces themselves. In some countries interservice rivalries pose a serious problem, politically and in other respects. Tension is increasing between the younger, more highly trained officers and their older confreres, while the general trend is one of improvement in the lot of the enlisted man, for professional as well as political reasons, reducing class differences within the services.

5. Finally, the role of the Latin American military men in hemispheric defense makes the problem of the military intervention in politics increasingly a hemispheric problem, while at the same time it may conceivably, in the long run, lessen the tendency of military leaders to intervene in domestic political life.

The future of democratic government in Latin America will depend to a marked degree on whether or not the new forces in the area's economic, social, and political life will be able to "send the soldiers back to the barracks" and convince the military that its role is one of national defense and not that of arbiter of the nation's political life.

Suggestions for Reading

The role of Latin American armies in politics, and particularly in revolutionary activities, is discussed in two chapters in A. Curtis Wilgus (ed.), *The Caribbean: Its Political Problems* (Gainesville: University of Florida Press, 1956): "Bases of Revolutions in the Caribbean," by Charles C. Cumberland, and "Some Observations on Military Coups in the Caribbean," by Stanley R. Ross. The subject is also treated in several chapters in Asher N. Christensen (ed.), *The Evolution of Latin American Governments* (New York: Henry Holt & Co., 1951): "Revolutions," by German Arciniegas, "Roots of Revolution in Latin America," by Donald M. Dozer, "The Technique of Coup d'État in Latin America," by Kurt C. Andrade, and "Democracy and Dictatorship," by R. A. Humphrey. The Spanish reader should turn to the brilliant essay of Jesús Silva Herzog, "La juntas militares de gobierno," in the Mexican journal *Cuadernos Americanos*, July–August, 1949. William W. Pierson and Federico G. Gil have an interesting chapter in their *Governments of Latin America* (New York: McGraw-Hill Book Co., Inc., 1956). Finally, German Arciniegas, in *The State of Latin America* (New York: Alfred A. Knopf, Inc., 1952), discusses the problem of the military intervention in politics in a thought-provoking manner. *

Several studies of the military problem in particular countries may be noted. Jesús de Galindez' excellent work, *La era de Trujillo* (Santiago: Ed. Pacífico, 1956) deals with this problem in the Dominican Republic. Robert J. Alexander's *The Perón Era* (New York: Columbia University Press, 1951) and George Blanksten's *Perón's Argentina* (Chicago: University of Chicago Press, 1953) discuss the role of the Argentine army in the Perón revolutionary regime. The peculiar role of the army in the Mexican Revolution is interestingly told in Frank Tannenbaum, *Peace By Revolution* (New York: Columbia University Press, 1933). Finally, the work of an ex-president of Venezuela, Rómulo Betancourt, *Venezuela: Política y petróleo* (Mexico: Fondo de Cultura Económica, 1956), presents an excellent survey of the role of the military in that country's recent history.

Chapter 7

Organized Labor
and Politics

Revolutionary Role of Labor

Labor's role in Latin American politics is revolutionary. The entry of the organized labor movement into the political life of the Latin American countries means a fundamental altering of the rules by which the political game is played in Latin America, for it means bringing the lower and hitherto despised social elements of the various nations into an active role in their civic life. It also brings to politics a civilian element able to challenge the age-old tradition that the armed forces should have the last word in the making and unmaking of governments.

SOCIAL REVOLUTION. The appearance of more or less strong trade union movements in virtually all of the Latin American countries during the past quarter-century is part of that vast sociopolitical upheaval which, for lack of a better title, we may call the Latin American Social Revolution.[1] The changes which it embraces result in large measure from modern industrialism.

LABOR AND POLITICS BEFORE WORLD WAR I. During the nineteenth century most of the people of the region lived by means of a primitive subsistence agriculture and were thus permitted only a very low level of material well-being. Large-scale manufacturing industry virtually did not exist in most of the countries. The only "working class" elements were railroad workers, scattered groups of miners, and the handicraftsmen of the cities, who still

[1] For further discussion of social and political movements see Chapters 3 and 4.

166

made most of the locally-produced "manufactured" goods. Although there was some semblance of trade union organization among these elements—and in a few countries such as Argentina, Uruguay, and Brazil they were increasingly vocal and were growing in influence—in no Latin American nation did they play a major role in the political life.

Power rested firmly in the hands of the landowning aristocracy and their allies and associates, the merchants of the coastal cities, engaged largely in the export–import trade. The source of the aristocracy's power lay in its control of the economy by virtue of its monopoly of the ownership of land, the principal natural resource then under exploitation, and in its control of the trade in products of the land.

The great majority of the people were semi-serfs, working on the landed estates of the aristocracy under conditions suggestive of Europe in the later Middle Ages. These peasants were ignorant, miserably poor, and were concerned principally with the problems of keeping body and soul together on a subsistence level. They had neither time for, nor interest in, politics. Furthermore, their patriarchal loyalty to the *patrón* made them little more than pawns, politically speaking, in the hands of their landlords.

Except for certain turn-of-the-century trends in Chile, Uruguay, and Argentina, politics during the century preceding World War I was a game played by the landholding elite. The vote was a privilege of the educated, who were a small proportion of the total population. Social issues played little part in the quarrels among contesting parties. The chief political importance of the economic issues raised appeared in the Church–state controversy, and this controversy became acute partly because of the landowners' interest in acquiring the Church's lands. This conflict provided the principal issue in the politics of pre-1914 Latin America, and the victory of the anti-clerical forces reinforced the dominant position of the landholding elite. If the majority of the people, the peasants, had been consulted, the result might well have been the opposite, a resounding victory to the forces of ultramontanism.

Only in the closing years of this period did the problems of the lower classes begin to play a role in the political life of the more economically advanced of the Latin American countries. In Argentina, Chile, Uruguay, and Brazil, socialist parties and anarchist labor movements appeared among the city artisans and the rising industrial working class laboring on the railroads, on the docks, and in the mines of these countries. In Mexico, a revolution which began as a political contest between elements of the aristocracy quickly got out of hand and gave the peasants and urban labor groups an opportunity to play the dominant role.

The World Wars and the Growth of Labor

WORLD WAR I. But the cases just discussed were exceptions. It was not until World War I gave a sudden impetus to industrialization that for the first time the urban working class began to play a significant role in the political life of many of these countries. The textile industry, in particular, owes its first firm foundations to World War I. Cut off from their sources of supply in Europe and the United States, the Latin American peoples found that they themselves had to provide clothing and the goods from which it is made. Some other industries, too, received a considerable impetus from this world-wide conflict. To the incipient metallurgical industry it was a shot in the arm; then, too, the processing of some foodstuffs prospered, and the construction materials industry also felt the impact of Latin American wartime isolation. The upshot was that by the early 1920's the weight of the workers in the new manufacturing industries was beginning to be felt, and the urban working class was beginning to become much more vocal.

BETWEEN THE WARS. Nowhere were these trends more evident than in the labor organizations themselves. The prewar labor movement had been largely anarchist in ideology, following a philosophy which seems to be peculiarly congenial to the small craftsman and artisan but not very attractive to the factory worker.

After World War I the influence of anarchists in the Latin American trade union movement declined sharply. By 1930 it had been virtually obliterated, except in such isolated cases as that of Uruguay, where some anarchist elements still exist in the nation's labor movement. The socialists, communists, and, a little later, various indigenous groups took over political leadership of the trade unions.

The Great Depression gave a further impetus to industrialization and hence to the trade union movement. Furthermore, in the political unrest arising from the Depression, the labor movement began for the first time to play an important, if subsidiary, role in the making and unmaking of governments. Since the Depression, industrialization has become the well-accepted creed of most politically thinking Latin Americans and the policy of most of the governments.[2] During the economic crisis, the Latin American countries were forced to produce many of the things which, owing

[2] See Chapter 15, Government and the Economic Order.

to lack of foreign exchange, they were not able to buy from abroad.

WORLD WAR II. Once again, during World War II, the Latin Americans were thrown to a considerable degree upon their own resources, pushing industrialization to the fundamental step of heavy industry. Governments found it necessary to adopt a more positive attitude toward industrialization. During the past fifteen years virtually every country in the region has established some sort of development corporation, whose job it is to plan for and stimulate the construction of new industries. Tariffs, exchange controls, and other methods of giving protection to the rapidly developing manufactures have also been generously used by the various governments.

The result of this emphasis on industrialization has been that the industrial working class—taken in its broadest sense to include not only those employed in manufacturing but those who work for railroads, airlines, steamship lines and ports, mines, and even great modern agricultural enterprises producing the "desert crops" and industrial raw materials for the United States and Western Europe—has grown by leaps and bounds. This increase in the size of the working class has been reflected in the growth of Latin American cities. Mexico City, for instance, has more than quadrupled its population since the beginning of the Revolution in 1910. São Paulo, Santiago, Medellín, and scores of other towns have enjoyed equally phenomenal growth since World War I.

Growth of Labor Organizations

This growth of the working class brought an impelling drive for organization, with the result that trade unions have grown with tremendous rapidity. In Chile, for instance, the organized labor movement grew from something over 100,000 members in 1939 to between 350,000 and 400,000 in 1945. In virtually every Latin American country, most of what would generally be considered the "organizable" workers have been brought into trade unions since World War II.

Official figures on the strength of the trade union movements of Latin America are not thoroughly reliable. Table XI provides a reasonable estimate of the membership of these unions.

Sometimes a question is raised as to whether the labor movement and social legislation have really improved the standard of living of the workers of Latin America. It is a fair judgment, however, that both have made significant contributions toward modifying the impact of industrialization on the working classes

TABLE XI. MEMBERSHIP OF LABOR UNIONS

Argentina	2,250,000
Bolivia (including peasants' unions)	500,000
Brazil	2,000,000
Chile	400,000
Colombia	125,000
Costa Rica	25,000
Cuba	800,000
Dominican Republic	25,000
Ecuador	50,000
El Salvador	15,000
Guatemala	10,000
Haiti	2,500
Honduras	5,000
Mexico	750,000
Nicaragua	15,000
Panama	5,000
Paraguay	10,000
Peru	100,000
Uruguay	100,000
Venezuela	25,000

NOTE: Different figures on labor union membership, from ILO and U.S. government sources, appear in Table VI, pp. 68–69.

of the area, if they have not actually improved their relative economic position in terms of income. In many countries trade unions have successfully inaugurated continuing pressure for increases in wage scales, thus helping to keep real incomes in line with the rising price level. These wage increases, however, have also contributed to further inflation. It seems probable, nonetheless, that inflation would have come in any case, and that without trade unions the workers would have suffered from it more than has been the case. The unions have also forced upon employers a greater awareness of the problems of their workers' welfare.

More important, perhaps, has been the success of the trade unions in helping to convert illiterate, subservient workers into active citizens. Workers have learned through their unions to deal with employers on a basis of more or less equality. They have practiced democracy at the grass roots level in their organizations. Through their unions they have also become aware of the social and economic problems facing their countries.

Perhaps the most serious weakness of the unions is their lack of effective techniques for dealing with the increasingly complicated problems involved in collective bargaining in an industrial society. The labor movement needs to be able to call on the services of economists, technicians, and engineers in drawing up demands on employers and in negotiating labor contracts. In such countries as Argentina, Mexico, and Cuba the labor movements have reached the stage where they are increasingly able to do this, but in others the labor movement lacks the financial resources to attain this technical character.

LABOR AND SOCIAL LEGISLATION. Since the labor movement has ramifications in many aspects of political life, certain of its activities are discussed elsewhere in this book. Before examining the political influence of the labor movement, it is appropriate, however, to sum up the legislative gains made by the organized workers as the sixth decade of the twentieth century draws to a close.

In all of the countries of the region the unions have gained at least token recognition of the right to organize and bargain collectively, though in dictator-ruled nations, and even in some of the democratic states, this right is not always respected. In most democratic nations of the hemisphere the state intervenes to conciliate labor disputes, though not to act as arbitrator, except in cases involving governmental and agricultural workers, whose rights to organize and bargain are frequently restricted.

The eight-hour day is almost universally provided for in the labor legislation. In most cases, the maximum hours laws provide for a six-day week, though some reduce this to five and a half days. Minimum wage laws are found in Argentina, Chile, Uruguay, Brazil, Mexico, and some other nations. The method of fixing these wages varies a great deal from one country to another, and the groups of workers covered by the legislation are also different.

Most of the countries place restrictions on the work of minors, including minimum school requirements, prohibit the work of juveniles in industries considered dangerous, and impose other similar limitations. In most of the nations, moreover, measures to protect children against the worst types of exploitation, such as work in mines and very dangerous industries, are adequately enforced.

Some kinds of labor legislation are encountered in Latin America which are not found in the United States. Several countries, for instance, provide dismissal pay for workers, usually amounting to from two weeks to one month's pay for each year the dismissed employee had worked for the firm. Several of the countries, including Argentina, Brazil, Chile, Mexico, and Venezuela, among others, have special labor courts where violations of labor laws are handled. Some of these special courts have representation among the judges from both workers and employers.

In recent years social security legislation has become general in Latin America, and by 1956 Honduras was the only nation without a social security system. Usually this kind of legislation is inaugurated with health insurance. Only a few nations have made provision for old-age pensions, and virtually none of this legislation contains unemployment compensation.

These legal provisions vary in effectiveness and still apply chiefly to urban industrial workers, service industry employees, petroleum workers, and miners. In most countries (the exceptions include Mexico, Bolivia, Argentina, Uruguay, Cuba, and the banana and sugar workers of Ecuador and some of the Central American countries) agricultural workers are not allowed to organize and are not usually covered by protective legislation or by social security.

The reason for this discrimination against rural workers lies in the fact that the control of the landlords over the rural sections of the nation has not yet been challenged in most Latin American countries. Even in Chile, where power over the nation in general has been in the hands of middle-class urban elements for more than a generation, the landlords are still supreme in the countryside. The organization of rural workers and the extension of social security and labor legislation to cover them would severely undermine the control of the landlords over the rural regions. It would certainly raise labor costs in agriculture, it would destroy the landlords' undisputed control of these regions, and it would inevitably lead to demands for agrarian reform. In most Latin American countries the power of the urban middle classes is not sufficient to allow them to challenge these elements in their own bailiwicks, even where power in the nation has long passed from the hands of the rural aristocracy.

CHANGING POLITICAL ATTITUDES. The growth in labor organization has brought a change in the nature of Latin American politics. Politicians and governments, realizing full well the potentialities of this new force for the political life of their nations, have sought both to encourage and to control the new trade union movements.

That the attitudes of Latin American politicians have been influenced by a variety of factors was brought home to the author of this chapter by a discussion of this problem with the late President Arturo Alessandri of Chile. When President Alessandri was asked why he sought to enact a labor code in the early 1920's, an effort finally successful in September, 1924, he replied that he was motivated by two considerations. First of all, he said, he knew the miserable conditions under which most of the urban and mining workers of Chile lived, and he felt that something should be done to improve their situation. In the second place, Chile had recently become a member of the International Labor Organization, which recommended certain minimum requirements in labor legislation. If Chile were to be a full-fledged member of this new international group, he said, she must fulfill her obligations by adopting some or all of the measures recommended by the ILO, including official recognition of the trade union movement.

No doubt these two motives, genuine sympathy for the plight of the new industrial workers and the necessity for "keeping up with the international Joneses," have induced more favorable attitudes in many of the Latin American governments and among politicians toward the organized workers and their demands.

Other motives, however, have also played an important part in this development. Latin American politicians have undoubtedly realized that their own fates lie in the hands of the organized workers. If a politician gains the support of this important new group, it can be of great value to him, for in those nations where governmental change is brought about by ballot rather than bullet, organized workers represent an important bloc of votes. Where cruder methods of altering the administration are the rule, the ability of the trade union movement to paralyze much of the national life by resort to partial or general strikes is peculiarly useful, whether the politico favored by the unions is in power and finds his regime in danger, or whether he is out of power and wishes to seize the government by force. In the latter case, the organized workers may be a source of civilian soldiers for the politician who has won labor sympathy.

The tendency of certain army officers to cultivate labor support in recent years, because of the importance of industrialization for a modern army, has also been noted in a previous chapter.[3]

For these various reasons many politicians, civilian and military alike, have shown unexpected sympathy for the trade union movement. At the same time, because they have realized the potential dangers of the movement, they have sought to hedge legal recognition and other workers' benefits with a kind of government control which the labor movements of the United States and most Western European countries would not permit.

Government and the Unions

POLITICAL SUPERVISION. Thus we find that many of the labor codes provide for government supervision of trade union elections and for some type of control over the use of labor funds. These restrictions usually prohibit the use of funds for political purposes, a prohibition more honored in the breach than in the observance. Often the labor codes specify the structure of the trade union move-

[3] See Chapter 6.

ment and provide government supervision of collective bargaining. They usually exclude certain kinds of workers, particularly government employees and agricultural workers, from legal trade union organization.

LABOR DEPENDENCE ON GOVERNMENT.   For their part, the workers have usually welcomed whatever help they could obtain from the government or from particular groups of politicians.   In the first place, this help provides legal recognition, almost eliminating in Latin America in recent years the kind of strike which was so common in the United States before the National Labor Relations Act—the strike for union recognition.   In the second place, in actual collective bargaining negotiations the unions have frequently appealed to friendly politicians, often to the president, to force employers to grant their demands.   In doing so, the unions have been fully aware of their own political importance to the government and the politicians.

Finally, the unions have needed the financial help received from a close alliance with politicians and the government.   Most Latin American industrial workers are still very poor by any standard and have little money to spare for the payment of union dues.   But, despite this poverty of their members, Latin American unions need considerable funds.   They need money for organizing, for the costs of transportation, for the costs of collective bargaining.   Like unions elsewhere, they need full-time, or nearly full-time, officials.   Hence, they have been more than willing to accept the support of middle-class politicians willing to offer their financial backing, or that of the government if they are in power, in order to gain labor loyalty.

Labor and Political Parties

The consequence of this political and financial dependence has been to wed the average Latin American trade union firmly to one or another political party and to deprive it of the independence of the government usually considered healthful.   Few Latin American trade union groups escape control by a political party.   Unfortunately, this has frequently meant that the trade union is sacrificed when the party is in difficulty.   A growing trend toward union independence of the government and politicians will be discussed later in this chapter, but it may be noted here that organizations really independent in the sense that they are in the United States are a small minority.

The growth of the labor movement has, of course, brought numerous new political parties which appeal particularly to organized workers.   Some of the older parties have also been transformed in their efforts to gain the support of the trade unions by including labor demands and aspirations in their programs.

SOCIALIST PARTIES. In the first place, there are the more or less orthodox socialist parties. The oldest of these is the Socialist party of Argentina. Founded in 1896, it fought with the anarchists for control of the infant labor movement in pre-World War I days. In the period between the wars it finally won control of most of the important labor organizations and the electoral support of a considerable element among the union membership. It met with a grave defeat, however, in the rise of the *peronista* movement and has declined greatly since. However, the Argentine socialists have been trying hard to recover influence over the worker since the overthrow of Perón.

The Socialist party of Chile arose in the mid-1930's as the center for all of those elements in the organized labor movement which were disgusted with the communists. Although it has suffered a series of splits since 1940, the socialist movement of Chile still represents the chief rallying point for the noncommunist workers of that country.

Other nations have had socialist parties of longer or shorter duration. Although the Uruguayan party has had varying success, it has never become a major political force in the country. Again, the Brazilian Socialist party, born after the end of Getulio Vargas' dictatorship seemed to mark the disappearance of his *Estado Novo*, has tried vainly to fill the vacuum created by the decline in the popularity of the Vargas and Communist parties. Cuba, Panama, Colombia, Ecuador, Peru, and Bolivia have also had socialist parties of some importance.

APRISTA PARTIES. Akin to the socialists in the Latin American political spectrum are the parties we may call *aprista*. These groups, which include the original Aprista party (APRA) of Peru, the Democratic Action party of Venezuela, the National Liberation party of José Figueres in Costa Rica, Luis Muñoz Marín's Popular Democratic party in Puerto Rico, the old Auténtico party of Cuba, the Bolivian MNR (Movimiento Nacional Revolucionario), and the Paraguayan *febreristas,* are indigenous groups accepting Marxist principles which they attempt to adapt to the peculiar atmosphere of their own nations.[4] They are socialistic in a general sense, nationalistic in economic matters, and democratic in their political aspirations. Like the socialists, they have won their principal support among the urban working class; unlike the socialists, however, they have not been avowedly labor parties.

[4] These movements are discussed more fully in Chapter 4.

Most of these *aprista* parties have embodied a strain of personalism. Their original popularity was clearly connected with the prestige of such leaders as Raúl Haya de la Torre, Rómulo Betancourt, José Figueres, Rafael Franco, Víctor Paz Estenssoro, and Luis Muñoz Marín. Unlike the more strictly personalist parties, however, they have attempted, with considerable success, to evolve an ideological basis for their respective movements, thus becoming more than a passing phenomenon depending on the popularity of one man.

They have not infrequently been in actual control of, or influential in, the governments of their respective countries. When in power, their success has ranged from the miserable failure of the Cuban Auténticos through the brilliant temporary success of the Venezuelan Democratic Action to the more lasting success of the National Liberation party in Costa Rica and that of the Popular Democrats in Puerto Rico.

COMMUNIST PARTIES. The communists, of course, have also made their principal appeal to the urban working class. Though from time to time they have sought the backing of the largely inert agricultural masses and of the middle class—and there are those who claim that the Latin American communists are now passing through a "Maoist" phase in which their principal appeal is to these groups—they have sought and won their principal support among trade unionists.

The Latin American communists are like their brethren elsewhere. They are the genuine revolutionaries. They are not "mere agrarian reformers," nor "really more Latin American than Communist." They are members of the world-wide Communist movement, and their principal objectives have been service to the interests of the Soviet Union and the establishment of totalitarian dictatorships in their respective countries. Although in the past they built substantial followings in several of the Latin American countries, their importance today is more potential than real.

ARGENTINE AND BRAZILIAN LABOR PARTIES. A fourth group of parties appealing particularly to the working class includes the *peronista* party of Argentina and the Labor Party (Partido Trabalhista) of Brazil. Both these parties were created from the top by dictators who gained the loyalty of the urban working masses by giving concrete economic benefits and enhancing labor's self-esteem by demagogic politics, in exchange for the abrogation of civil liberty and free trade unionism. Both Perón and Vargas enjoyed their principal civilian support in the labor movements. They controlled the trade unions of their respective countries much more rigidly than is the rule in Latin America, turning the labor organizations into virtual organs of the government. Yet they also introduced numerous benefits for the workers, enacted social security systems, supported those unions subservient to them in negotiations with their employers. They convinced a large segment of the working classes that Getulio and Perón were the principal supporters of the rights of the workingmen.

CHRISTIAN DEMOCRATS. A fifth group of new political parties which have sought support among the industrial working class is made up of the Christian Democratic parties. The best known of these is the Falange Nacional of Chile. This party, it is customary to point out, has nothing in common with, and in fact antedates, Franco's Falange in Spain. During the last twenty years the Chilean *falangistas,* starting as a small group comprised mostly of recent university graduates, have carved out a well-recognized place for themselves among the workers of Chile. Although it has not become a major party, even among the workers, it has gained a solid place in the trade union movement.

The Unión Cívica of Uruguay is more middle class in its appeal than the Chilean Falange, but it, too, has some working-class support. In recent years it has turned even more in the direction of labor. The Social Democratic party in Bolivia, also Christian socialist in outlook, attempted to exert influence on the Bolivian labor movement between 1946 and 1952, but without much success. Since the fall of Perón, two Catholic parties have appeared in Argentina, the Christian Democratic party and Unión Federal. The latter has become particularly active in trying to win support among the *peronista* workers.

LIBERALS. While the new political parties were taking advantage of the rise of the urban working class to a position of importance in the life of the Latin American nations, some of the older parties have also sought to move with the times by incorporating workers in their ranks. Thus, in the 1930's and early 1940's the Liberals of Colombia, particularly, were exceedingly active among the workers, controlling what was at that time the principal labor organization in the country, the Colombian Confederation of Workers (Confederación de Trabajadores de Colombia).

The Liberals of Honduras, who in 1954 returned to the political wars of that country after a lapse of almost twenty years, have welcomed the birth of a labor movement there. They are seeking to include workers' demands in their program and to gain the support of the still small trade union movement of the cities as well as the newly powerful labor organizations of the banana plantations.

ARGENTINE RADICALS. The Radical party of Argentina is one of the most notable among the older parties for the degree to which it has sought to take up the banner of the workers in the political arena. Although the Unión Cívica Radical, as the party is officially known, has always had the electoral support of a large part of the urban proletariat, it was essentially middle class in its control and outlook. Because of this, it failed to satisfy working-class demands when it was in power, and its failure to capture labor support did much to pave the way for the victory of the *peronistas* after 1943.

Under the whiplash of Perón, important elements in the Radical party came to realize their past errors. They came to understand the power of the urban worker's vote, as well as the potentially destructive power of the trade union movement in the political arena. They therefore decided to develop a program and a policy to win back to Radical allegiance those workers who had followed Perón. Shortly before the latter's fall the Radical party commenced to organize its supporters in the trade union movement, hoping to be able to capture the labor movement once Perón was out of the way. After the overthrow of the dictator, they became almost frantically active in the labor movement.

BATLLISMO. Finally, one cannot pass over the Batllista party in Uruguay when discussing the efforts of older political groups to win the backing of the organized workers. The Batllista party is a faction of the traditional Colorado party. Formed under the leadership of the late President José Batlle y Ordóñez, it launched the nation on a series of social experiments which included an extensive social security system, the application of the "yard-stick principle" to public utilities, and encouragement, though comparatively little regulation, of the trade union movement. Ever since the time of Batlle it has kept the voting loyalty of the majority of the urban working class.

Labor, a New Political Force

The impact of the rise of organized labor on Latin American politics is not confined, however, to new political parties and the alteration of old ones. Of equal or more importance, in the long run, is the fact that the trade union movement presents the Latin American republics, for the first time in a century and a quarter of national existence, with a potential rival to the armed forces as the ultimate determinant of power in political life.

The potency of the Latin American unions as a power factor is likely to increase as industrialization proceeds. The power of a labor movement is strictly limited in an economy in which most of the people grow their own food, make their own clothing, and construct their own houses. Although it may be able to damage individual urban employers or mining interests through strikes, it cannot cripple the entire economic life of the nation. The great majority of the people will continue to live more or less normally, despite anything the labor movement might be able to do. In a more highly industrialized economy, however, the situation is entirely different. In such an economy there is great interdependence. No individual or family group is self-sufficient, economically speaking. Large cities must be fed by a constant inflow of agricultural produce from the interior. The power of labor is increased by the fact that a general strike can bring the life of a community virtually to a standstill. Furthermore, as the organized urban working class becomes larger and larger, it tends to become an important pool of recruits, already accustomed to the discipline of factory life and trade union activities, for participation in armed rebellion.

In recent years Latin America has provided a number of striking examples of the power of this new political force. Three nations in which labor has thus gained considerable power will be discussed.

The earliest development was that of Mexico. As far back as 1915, Venustiano Carranza and his advisers, then engaged in civil war with the forces of Pancho Villa and Emiliano Zapata, became aware of the military and political potentials of the trade union movement. Carranza made an agreement with the still weak Mexican labor movement, granting the workers freedom to carry on their activities behind the lines of the Constitutionalist Army, in return for which they agreed to provide badly needed battalions for Carranza's hard-pressed forces. These Red Battalions, as they were called, played a key role in the triumph of Carranza's forces over his two rivals.

Twenty years later, President Lázaro Cárdenas, pushing hard for the completion of his land reform and the nationalization of the Mexican economy, began to doubt the political dependability of the army, previously loyal to ex-President Plutarco Elías Calles, who had now become a political opponent. In this situation, Cárdenas fell back on the organized labor movement and armed the organized peasantry to strengthen his regime against attempts at subversion by the military.

Not only did Cárdenas and his lieutenants unify most of the hitherto badly divided Mexican trade union movement into the Confederation of Mexican Workers (Confederación de Trabajadores de México), but he also provided arms to his labor cohorts, encouraging the formation of a labor militia under the control of the new Confederation. Thus the government had at its command a powerful force able to paralyze the economic activity of the urban centers and able also, if necessary, to enter the field against any potential military foe. Organized labor thus greatly strengthened the hand of the Cárdenas regime. In return labor received many benefits in the form of labor laws and wage increases.

A spectacular exhibition of the power of the trade unions vis-à-vis the armed forces was furnished by the Argentine workers in October, 1945. At that time Perón had already become the idol and boss of the trade union movement, but was temporarily overthrown by a faction of the army opposed to his personal ambitions. The workers in the unions loyal to Perón went out on a virtually spontaneous general strike throughout the country, thus hampering the efforts of the new regime to re-establish order. At the same time, laborers from Buenos Aires and its suburbs, led by the packinghouse workers from nearby La Plata and Avellaneda, marched on the capital city. Within a few days of Perón's overthrow, the streets of Buenos Aires were in the hands of his labor supporters. Although the army could probably have put down this insurrection, the cost in lives of Argentine workers would have been great, and great hatred would have been inspired in the masses of the urban population. The army did not think it worth this price to prevent Perón's continuance in power and hence it permitted him to return from the prison island of Martín García on the night of October 16. The next day he triumphantly addressed his supporters from the balcony of the Casa Rosada.

From October 17, 1945, until June 16, 1955, Perón governed with the support of organized labor and the armed forces, the latter held in check by the menace of a repetition of the nightmare of October 17. This power structure lasted until the labor movement was caught off guard by the naval mutiny of June 16, 1955. The army, by remaining "loyal" to Perón and suppressing the revolt, was able to seize the upper hand once more in Argentine politics. The unions were strangely quiet in the events of September, 1955, which drove Perón from power.

Peronista leaders in the labor movement subsequently received at least temporary setbacks. They attempted a revolutionary general strike against General Pedro Aramburu a few days after he seized the government from General Lonardi in November, 1955. Aramburu crushed the general strike and proceeded to "intervene" in the CGT and all of its constituent unions, placing army, navy, and air force officers in charge of union affairs until elections could be held throughout the labor movement.

A third example of the power of the trade union movement may be seen in the April, 1952, revolution in Bolivia. That conflict began as an insurrection of the National Police in alliance with the outlawed MNR party, but was turned into a struggle of the organized workers of La Paz and the mining centers against the national army when the National Police seemed to be beaten in the fighting two days after it began. The trade union forces, led by the tin miners' chief Juan Lechín and Hernán Siles, decided to continue the struggle and in the end they were victorious. They triumphed over the armed forces, placing Víctor Paz Estenssoro and the MNR in power. The MNR regime thus rested squarely on the trade unions. After the beginning of the agrarian reform in 1953, the growing forces of the peasantry, anxious to defend their newly acquired land, came to share power with the workers.

FAILURES TO USE THE POWER OF LABOR. Events of recent years have also provided at least three examples in which ruling political groups that commanded the support and loyalty of the trade union movement were unable or unwilling to bring its weight to bear in defense of their regimes. These failures occurred in Venezuela, Cuba, and Guatemala, and can be briefly summarized as follows.

In November, 1948, President Rómulo Gallegos of Venezuela was unwilling to call upon the nation's trade union movement to defend his regime against the attempt of the army to oust him. Although the intentions of the top military officers were widely known throughout the country for at least three weeks before his ouster, President Gallegos insisted on trying to settle the problem "without violence." As a result, although sporadic strikes in defense of the regime occurred in different parts of the country, they proved futile because they received no encouragement from the presidential palace. Had Gallegos used the radio to call upon the workers to declare a general strike and to join with military elements still loyal to the regime, he might well have saved his government, according to competent observers, thus sparing Venezuela the experience of the military dictatorship which followed.

President Carlos Prío Socorrás of Cuba showed the same kind of vacillation on March 10, 1952, when faced with the military coup of General Fulgencio Batista. Prío made no attempt to notify the trade union leaders, virtually all of whom were his loyal supporters, that a military movement against the government was afoot. Although the trade unionists called a nationwide general strike when they learned of the coup at nine o'clock on the morning of March 10, it was already too late. The strike fizzled out because it had no support from the president. Both trade union and student leaders offered to fight for the regime if Prío would give them arms which he still had in his control. Here again, had Prío acted with decision, calling the workers to a general strike and arming his labor and student supporters, he could probably have snuffed out the Batista coup.

Finally, there is the case of Guatemala. Here, too, the trade unions, though of less importance than in Venezuela or Cuba, were loyal to the government of President Arbenz. His failure to bring to bear either the economic or military potential of the labor movement, was one of the principal causes of his overthrow by the forces of Carlos Castillo Armas in 1954. Communist influence in the Arbenz regime made the situation in Guatemala different from those in Venezuela and Cuba, but the lesson is the same.

Labor's Future Political Influence

What of the future influence of labor in Latin American politics? Conflicting tendencies are presently at work. The labor movement will undoubtedly play an increasingly important direct role in those countries which have not yet experienced revolutionary social changes, or where these changes have temporarily been thwarted. One can expect more examples of the power of labor such as those of April 9, 1952, in Bolivia and October 17, 1945, in Argentina. So long as the Latin American social revolution has not occurred in a given country, one of the principal tasks of the trade union movement will continue to be the achievement of fundamental changes in the social and political structure of the nation. And the labor movement will continue to be a force of tremendous revolutionary political potential.

Paradoxically enough, however, once the social revolution has occurred in a given country, we may expect a lessening of the direct political importance of the labor movement. Forces which are at work will make the trade unions turn increasingly in the direction of economic rather than political activity. As Latin American industrialization continues, as the living standards of the workers rise, and as workers become more capable of paying the costs of their trade union movements, labor unions will acquire increasing political independence. They will rely less on the government and politicians, more on their own resources. As they become stronger financially and more independent politically they will become increasingly concerned with the basic economic problems of wages, hours, working conditions, and productivity—less directly concerned with the political framework within which these economic problems are to be resolved.

There are evidences of this trend toward political independence in some of the Latin American countries. In Mexico, since 1950 unions have increasingly demanded the checkoff of union dues, the compulsory deduction by employers of dues which are then paid directly to the union. Increasingly, the unions depend on members' contributions for their finances. At the same time, the unions are increasingly concerned with day-to-day collective bargaining. Collective contracts are becoming long and more detailed, tending to include seniority rights, grievance procedures, and other such provisions which are still alien to most of the Latin American unions.

In Cuba the trade union movement has acquired considerable political independence during the period since 1952. As a result of the armed truce between the Batista government and labor, the trade unions have turned more and more to economic issues. The demand for the checkoff is growing, and the unions are gaining a financial independence never before enjoyed.

Finally, in Colombia, the rise of the Colombian Workers Union (Unión de Trabajadores de Colombia) since 1946 has presented a new phenomenon. The UTC is not politically affiliated with any party. It has, in fact, had to fight off attempts by Conservative party politicians to infiltrate and take over control of the organization. The UTC is largely financed by the dues of members and has been anxious to be granted the checkoff. It has attempted to build up in the ranks of its members a consciousness of being good trade unionists first and members of one or another political party second.

Conclusions

One should not overstate the case, of course. Latin American labor legislation over the years has tied the unions more closely to the ministry of labor than is customary in the United States or Western European countries, so that traditionally in Mexico, Cuba, and Colombia the unions tend to take their difficulties to the government for solution to a much greater degree than in the United States. However, the evidence of the Mexican, Cuban, and Colombian labor movements would seem to indicate that the trade unions in those countries, at least, are becoming more like those of the United States than has been true in the past.

As this new trend continues, the trade unions will undoubtedly find that they must supplement their collective bargaining activities by participation in politics. They will want friends in the government and in the halls of congress in order to protect themselves from legislation unfavorable to labor. But these political activities are likely to be subordinated to their collective bargaining functions, as they become principally economic organizations rather than partisan political groups.

In those countries in which an extensive social revolution has been taking place, factors other than the tendency of unions to concentrate on economic rather than political matters will reduce the direct political importance of Latin American trade unions. In Mexico and Bolivia, for instance, the increasing political role of the peasantry will lessen the relative importance of the votes of urban workers. The growth of the middle class as a result of industrialization will have the same effect.

Thus emerges a picture of the Latin American trade unions playing a key role in the social, economic, and political revolution now under way. As compact organized bodies in the principal centers of population these unions are playing a role out of all proportion to their size or to the wealth or individual influence of their members. Organized labor is truly a revolutionary force in Latin America, promoting further industrialization, altering the relationship of classes, increasing the pressure for the democratization of political life, giving rise to new political parties and profoundly modifying some of the old. Yet if present trends continue, the labor movement is likely to play in the future a role of somewhat less direct political importance in those countries which have experienced the social revolution, although it will continue to be of great importance in the preparation for this transformation.

Suggestions for Reading

There is no adequate general work on this subject in English. Marjorie R. Clark's *Organized Labor in Mexico* (Chapel Hill, N. C.: University of North Carolina Press, 1934) is an early but very good history of the first two decades of Mexico's labor movement. Archer C. Bush's "Organized Labor in Guatemala" (mimeograph) (Hamilton, N.Y.: Colgate University, 1950) is also to be noted. In Spanish, the work of Moisés Poblete Troncoso, *El movimiento obrero Latinoamericano* (Mexico: Fondo de Cultura Económica, 1946), while often inaccurate, is one of the few over-all histories of Latin American trade unionism. In his *Le Mouvement ouvrier en Amérique Latine* (Paris: Les Editions Ouvrières, 1953), Victor Alba has given a somewhat sketchy account of the general movement. The book of Guadeloupe Rivera Marín, *El mercado de trabajo—relaciones obrero-patronales* (Mexico: Fondo de Cultura Económica, 1955), contains statistical information on Mexican trade unions, but shows little insight into how collective bargaining is carried on in Mexico.

Other published works of Robert J. Alexander, the author of this chapter, include three pamphlets: *Labor Parties of Latin America* (New York: League for Industrial Democracy, 1942); *Labour Movements in Latin America* (London: Fabian International Bureau, 1947); *Reseña del movimiento obrero en la América latina* (Washington: Pan American Union, 1950); and two books: *The Perón Era* (New York: Columbia University Press, 1951), explaining Perón's use of labor to seize power in Argentina; and *Communists in Latin America* (New Brunswick, N.J.: Rutgers University Press, 1957), which discusses labor's role in the Latin American social revolution, and the Communists' role in the labor movement in Latin America.

The report of the commission sent by the International Labor Office to study changes of the suppression of trade unionism by the government of Venezuela may be read in *Freedom of Association and Conditions of Work in Venezuela* (Geneva, 1950). It gives a good picture of legislation and national labor relations. The Venezuelan government replied in *Freedom of Association and Conditions of Work in Venezuela —Reply of Venezuelan Government* (Geneva, 1951).

The student may follow current developments in the *Inter-American Labor Bulletin,* published by the Inter-American Regional Organization of Workers (ORIT) at Washington, D.C.; in the *Free Labor World,* monthly magazine of the International Confederation of Free Trade Unions (published by ICFTU, Brussels, Belgium), which frequently has articles on Latin America; and in *World Trade Union Movement,* a monthly magazine of the Communist-controlled World Federation of Trade Unions, published in English in London and in Spanish in Mexico.

Chapter 8

Political Parties
and Elections

General Aspects of Political Parties in Latin America

Single-party and ineffective multiple-party systems are as characteristic of Latin American nations as two-party systems are of the United States and Great Britain. An understanding of this simple fact is essential to the proper study of political parties and popular elections. For the pattern of one-party or, more properly, no-party government was imposed upon Latin Americans by their European overlords, and few truly effective multi-party systems have appeared during more than a century of independent nationhood. While most nations still reflect traditional practices, political party behavior in a few of these nations does compare favorably with the best democratic procedures in the United States and Great Britain. Even for these chosen few, experience suggests that what appears at the moment to be a relatively effective multiple-party system may be destroyed very suddenly. But experience furnishes no precedent for socio-economic changes of the magnitude now transforming much of Latin America, and it is these new forces that may lead to the creation of effective party systems. Nevertheless, as of today, a basic pattern of one-party and relatively ineffective multi-party systems persists and is likely to do so for years to come.

INEFFECTIVE PARTY SYSTEMS? Students of political processes in Latin America advance various reasons for the absence of effective party systems.[1] Some argue that broader party development is

[1] For further discussion of the broader problem of a rationale or theoretical systemization of the entire political process, of which political parties comprise only one part, see Chapters 1 and 4.

precluded by an authoritarian tradition connected with the dominance of the Roman Catholic Church. Others contend that the real barrier is a penchant for violence, "the normal and inevitable action through which the innermost social and psychological forces of these people express themselves."[2] Not a few observers point the finger at a lack of enlightened leadership and an electorate inexperienced in the ways of representative political parties.

These theories fail to satisfy other observers who insist upon more historical perspective. The cause of the persistence of one-party systems, they say, is not Latin America's lack of acquaintance with American and European laws and practices. Since the dawn of independence, leaders in Latin America have, in fact, been familiar with foreign processes, and through the years they have incorporated into their fundamental laws the best features of American, French, and British thought. Neither do they persist just because the people have failed to set the observance of the democratic principle as a prime objective. Even the most ruthless dictators must pay at least lip service to the ideal of democracy. Nor do they persist merely because a two-party system has never been tested. Not a few elections have been eminently honest during periods when rival political parties enjoyed freedom of organization and expression. If enlightened leadership, a desire for democratic procedures, and successful experience have failed to bring into being effective parties and honest elections, then how are shortcomings in this respect to be explained?

From the record of Latin American achievement it can be observed that an enlightened leadership, even when supported by public opinion, often failed to establish representative parties because policy and program alike were not adjusted to the socioeconomic realities of a country. Parties used too many words and showed too little respect for changing class stratification, the encumbrances of geography, existent systems of land tenure, economic productive capacity, the nature of foreign investments, and the advancements of industrial technology. Political parties were confronted by insuperable tasks of overcoming debilitating ethnic tensions, illiteracy, a lack of communication and transportation media, poorly trained civil servants, and a pervasive lack of political confidence. Shackled by these stern realities, party programs consciously directed toward the development of representative and

[2] This thesis is developed by William S. Stokes in "Violence as a Power Factor in Latin American Politics," *The Western Political Quarterly*, V (September 1952), 445–468, and in "Violence: The South American Way," *United Nations World*, December 1951.

effective political parties could not be realized and, indeed, they often resulted in dictatorships.

UNIQUE ROLE OF POLITICAL PARTIES. Furthermore, even an enlightened leadership is confronted today by a political tradition that assigns political parties various functions not ordinarily associated with party activity in the United States. In the United States, parties are in business primarily to acquire and hold public office. In Latin America, they are frequently creatures of the controlling regime, receiving direct financial assistance from the government merely for presenting a façade of opposition. Parties in the United States exercise no police functions. Those in Latin America sometimes serve as police agents, investigators, and quasi-military forces. What Latin Americans sometimes call political parties, North Americans would call factions, pressure groups, fraternal organizations, or lobbies. The opposite is also true: nominally non-party groupings in Latin American nations frequently exercise functions ordinarily performed by political parties in the United States.

PERSONALISM. Political parties of the two Americas differ in their relations with party leaders. Latin American parties tend to identify themselves more intimately with the personality of prominent leaders. This personalism which has long characterized Latin American politics may seem on the wane in certain nations, but party and faction labels still reflect the magnetism of the leaders. In Argentina, lingering *peronistas* still boast loyalty to Juan Perón, just as *irigoyenistas* earlier followed their Radical party leader Hipólito Irigoyen. In Mexico, the dominant Institutional Revolutionary party counts in its ranks such factions as *alemanistas* and *cardenistas* (followers of former presidents Miguel Alemán and Lázaro Cárdenas) as well as *ruizcortinistas* (adherents of President Adolfo Ruiz Cortines). In Guatemala, opposition to the party of the late president Carlos Castillo Armas and his *castillistas* is led by *arbenzistas* (disciples of former president Jacobo Arbenz Guzmán).

EXCESSIVE LOYALTY TO CLASS INTERESTS. Moreover, political parties frequently seem to subordinate the general welfare to class loyalty. An astute observer of Latin American politics has described the adverse effects upon democratic processes of placing the interests of class above those of the nation:

Democracy presupposes a tough-minded and tenacious acceptance of the nation as deserving a continuing loyalty which transcends loyalty to class. Democracy assumes that the proper adjustments and accommodations among classes, probably accompanied by vigorous debate and pulling and hauling, will be made peacefully within the framework provided. If loyalty to a class, whether a proletariat in the professional sense or an elite group, supersedes the common loyalty, then democracy suffers correspondingly.[3]

Modern Uruguay, one of the most democratic states in Latin America, differs in this respect from those nations plagued by excessive loyalties to class. This first "welfare state" of South America appears to have found a stable balance between class interests and the general welfare. In standing united on the desirability of government ownership and regulation of competition in the business world of their nation, the major parties in Uruguay serve as a buttress against inroads from extremist interests attempting to overpower the nation on behalf of either labor or capital.[4]

GOVERNMENT DOMINATION OF PARTIES. Another difference arises from the fact that governments in Latin America play a very active role in party activities. Even when a Latin American government adopts a benevolent policy toward opposition parties, it is likely to abide by this policy only so long as the interests of the administration party are not jeopardized. Moreover, criticism of an official party may call for reprisal. When a president is also the nominal official party chieftain, he may decide to employ the full weight of his government against the opposition. With such support, it is not strange that leaders of official parties should believe that fulfillment of their ambitions depends not only on the preservation of their own party machinery, but also on the destruction of that of rivals.

Given the heritage of Latin American politics, an in-party has good reason to suspect that an out-party will show little mercy if it gains control of the public offices. Unfortunately, this manner of thinking tends to erase the lines separating the official party and the government. In losing its separate identity, an official party looks more and more to the government for assistance which free parties elsewhere, and particularly minority parties, would find repulsive.

THE SPOILS SYSTEM AND POLITICAL PARTIES. The tendency of official parties to identify themselves with the government raises the question of the relationship of the bureaucracy to political parties. Most governments permit their civil servants to join political organizations, but of course this applies only to those groups supporting

[3] Russell H. Fitzgibbon, "The Pathology of Democracy in Latin America: A Political Scientist's Point of View," *The American Political Science Review*, XLIV (March 1950), 122.
[4] For an appraisal of this phenomenon of Uruguayan politics, see Philip B. Taylor, Jr., "The Electoral System in Uruguay," *The Journal of Politics*, XVII (February 1955), 19–42.

the administration. In fact, support of the official party is ordinarily a prerequisite for continued employment. Career civil services are the exception in Latin America, and discrimination in public employment against members of political parties opposing the administration is a regular practice. In some countries, this discrimination has taken the form of issuing lists of the names of rival party members to guide civil servants in the day-by-day conduct of routine government business.

UNREGULATED PARTY FINANCE. Moreover, governments have done little to regulate party finances. Parties are permitted nearly complete freedom of action in soliciting funds. Some parties insist that all contributions must reach party headquarters. Others permit their candidates to gather and spend funds without special accounting to the party. Still others give no financial assistance, leaving the whole problem of fund-raising to the candidates. Some pay all expenses from the public treasury. Legal limits on the amount which an individual, group, or corporation may contribute are virtually unknown. In some countries, deductions from the pay of labor union members help to finance the party. Sometimes public officials collect "compulsory" membership dues for an official party. For example, a civil servant employed by one of the states of Mexico must contribute to the official party one day's salary for each thirty-one-day month in the year. If he fails to pay, a reminder from a party official (who naturally enjoys the favor of the governor) ordinarily suffices to convince him.

ACCESS TO THE ELECTORATE. Another distinguishing feature of Latin American parties may be observed in the degree to which opposition parties have access to media of communication. Even when a political group is not hampered in its propaganda appeals by cultural prejudice or language barriers, it frequently runs into other obstacles to the free expression of its appeals. In many countries an opposition party simply cannot always reach its members, to say nothing of reaching potential members or potential voters, because the peaceful media of communication—radio, television, motion pictures, billboards, and newspapers—may be closed to anyone unfriendly to the incumbent party. To oppose and to organize, to hope eventually to become the dominant majority, these normal functions and goals of political parties presume a free access to the general public. Without freedom of the press, speech, and assembly, a party may understandably turn to nonpeaceful means of gaining office.

MANIPULATION OF ELECTION MACHINERY. A final distinction between party practices in the two Americas appears in the different light in which political parties in Latin America and those in the United States regard the electoral process. Latin American political parties have often found themselves cheated by falsification of registration lists and penalized by tactics that prevent the voter from reaching the polls. Moreover, the voter has less assurance than a North American voter that his vote will be counted, or if counted, that the voting box will be undisturbed in case of any challenge of the ballot tally. The regularity with which election machinery has been manipulated is, in fact, an additional reason why political parties have often devoted their energy to devising schemes to capture public offices by violence.

After this description of Latin American party characteristics it should be unnecessary to point out that even when political parties unfold platforms which read like planks in the Republican and Democratic platforms in the United States, tradition and environment give them distinct meanings. *Personalismo,* subordination of nation to class, bureaucratic interference and injustice, the spoils systems, unregulated financing of parties, barriers to reaching the electorate, fraudulent elections—these are party characteristics and they reflect the illiteracy, the low living standards, the ethnic and socio-economic tensions, the encumbrances of geography, and the meager means of communication and transportation encountered in much of Latin America. These factors influence the nature and perspective of political parties. It is this background, therefore, and not such matters as local conditions in Philadelphia, Keokuk, or Spokane, that a student should keep in mind if he is to understand the platforms, organization, and procedures of Latin American parties.

The Traditional Parties

By the mid-nineteenth century two relatively homogeneous party traditions had emerged. They originated partly in the divisions between loyalists and rebels during the Wars of Independence, partly from the bitter conflicts between Church and state during the nineteenth century, and partly from basic differences of opinion as to how government should be organized and conducted for the general welfare. These two traditional parties were—in the Latin American terminology of the time—Liberal and Conservative.

These Liberal and Conservative parties were really factional groupings within a small, wealthy ruling class. Yet this does not mean that they lacked issues. The Liberals generally advocated encouragement of commerce through free trade, freer immigration, free secular schools, a broader suffrage, and republican government. Conservatives also favored some of these things at times as well as regularly upholding the Church's interests, strong unitary forms of government, the Spanish or Portuguese connection through loyalty to monarchism, and the interests of large landowners.

A notable exception to this party division occurred in Argentina, where the Rosas Federalists were actually the Conservatives and pro-clerical. As the century wore on, such nationalist parties as those led by Rafael Núñez in Colombia and José Balmaceda in Chile tried to bury the old issues in programs of national development, splitting the traditional Liberal parties, which always tended to splinter more than the Conservatives anyhow.

While party alignment in most nations today tends to follow socio-economic lines rather than the older lines of division over the issues of the separation of Church and state and centralism versus federalism, the traditional party division is still observed in some countries. In Colombia, the Conservatives held power from 1900 to 1930 and, after a sixteen-year reign of the Liberals, again from 1946 to 1953. Splintering tendencies within both parties contributed to the major shifts in political control in 1930, 1946, and 1953.[5] The party alignment under the subsequent military dictatorship of the Rojas Pinilla regime, overthrown in 1957, was difficult to appraise. In Uruguay, the Colorado and Blanco parties typify the traditional division to a small degree: the Blancos prefer a greater influence for the Church and, though not entirely opposed to state regulation, tend toward support of vested private interests.[6] The traditional split has also characterized political parties in Ecuador and Honduras.

Twentieth-Century Parties

Whenever the social and economic organization has been challenged by new economic trends in the twentieth century, the old pattern of two political groupings has tended to give way, in most nations, to one reflecting the changing patterns of economic interests and social stratification. During the late decades of the nineteenth century, commercial and industrial groups had successfully challenged the supremacy of landed agricultural interests. Yet despite

[5] The party system in Colombia is described in two unpublished dissertations: Ben G. Burnett, "The Recent Colombia Party System: Its Organization and Procedure" (University of California at Los Angeles, 1955); and Abelardo Patiño, "The Political Ideas of the Liberal and Conservative Parties in Colombia During the 1946–1953 Crisis" (The American University, Washington, D.C., 1955).

[6] Philip B. Taylor, Jr., "Interparty Co-operation and Uruguay's 1952 Constitution," *The Western Political Quarterly,* VII (September 1954), 391–400.

the growth in industry, and of urban areas in general, neither of the traditional parties spoke on behalf of the industrial and white-collar worker. Liberals of the urban centers remained liberal only in their opposition to the vested rural interests, and conservatives frowned indiscriminately on all laborers.

As the economic self-interest underlying this political grouping became more evident, a few intellectuals and labor leaders began to repeat the charge that the old parties really represented nothing at all. Instead, they asked, why not unite the urban industrial laborers with the rural agricultural workers? This Marxist-like approach to political organization, pitting the "haves" against the "have-nots," radically altered the traditional bases of political parties. Lines of party affiliation became even more confusing when these economic determinists divided on issues of timing and methods. Some preferred immediate, revolutionary, and violent action; others insisted on evolutionary and peaceful means of acquiring control; and a few opposed all authority merely because it was authority. Most preferred new parties, but some, as in Uruguay, proposed to revolutionize an older party.

THE ARGENTINE EXPERIENCE. Perhaps the earliest expression of these twentieth-century forces appeared in two new political parties—the Radical and the Socialist—which unfolded their banners in Argentina in the decade of the 1890's. The Unión Cívica Radical (the Radicals) advocated foreign trade controls, economic nationalism, and government intervention in Argentina's domestic economy to ensure greater social justice. The Socialists put forward a similar platform with a more Marxist orientation. To the Socialists, only the workers really merited higher social benefits. Their party membership was accordingly limited largely to this class. The Radicals, on the other hand, appealed more to the growing middle classes.[7]

Gaining control of the government in 1916 through what is generally regarded as one of the most honest elections in Latin American history, the Radicals had an opportunity to put into

[7] Argentina was by no means typical. The socio-economic forces unleashed in other countries have produced different results. Moreover, the virtual extinction of the Indian made Argentina one of the few Latin American nations no longer confronted by major ethnic-racial problems so common elsewhere. On Argentine political parties see José Luis Romero, *Las ideas políticas en Argentina* (Mexico: Fondo de Cultura Económica, 1946); A. Hasbrouck, "The Argentine Revolution of 1930," *Hispanic American Historical Review*, XVIII (August 1938), 285–321; Robert Alexander, *The Perón Era* (New York: Columbia University Press, 1951); George I. Blanksten, *Perón's Argentina* (Chicago: University of Chicago Press, 1953); and Arthur P. Whitaker, *Argentine Upheaval* (New York: Frederick A. Praeger, Inc., 1956).

practice what they had been preaching for more than two decades. The man in the street and the man in the field could look forward to an end to the large landowners' monopoly of political life. Since the earliest days of national independence the landowners had regarded public offices as their property, rightfully beyond the reach of other classes. Unfortunately, the Radicals also had within their ranks elements of the traditional ruling class, an influence which soon subjected them to the corrupting influences of power and alienated the classes which they avowedly represented. The Socialists, on the other hand, although they maintained the class basis of their party, never gained control of the government. The Radicals lost popular support after 1928 and became easy victims of the *cuartelazo* led by General Uriburu in 1930. The people had been "sold short," but apparently, in view of what happened later, they had gained new insight into political parties.

Conservative party interests once more assumed a prominent role after the revolution of 1930. Although some Radical and Socialist party members had joined forces with the Conservatives to form the *Concordancia,* the political coalition supporting the new government, antiadministration Radicals and Socialists became the object of reprisal for criticism of the ruling group. Political conditions changed somewhat after 1936. Constitutional party government was restored, but the parties and even many army leaders became disillusioned with the government. Radicals, Socialists, and Conservatives alike were soon to lose out to the fascist politics of a movement which shortly arrived in Argentina, reducing in true authoritarian fashion the influence of all opposition groups.

The Perón system was based on an alliance between the less privileged classes and an Argentine army which traditionally had shown a preference for the wealthy vested interests. Perón built up his party on the pledge of improving the lot of the "shirtless ones"—a pledge largely redeemed—while keeping the army content. Thus, when challenged by opposing groups, Perón frequently threatened to evoke the support of the army or labor organizations; failing to achieve his ends by threats, he actually deployed organized labor or army troops to crush the opposition. Sometimes he played labor against the army. After Perón pushed through a constitutional amendment to pave the way for his re-election, the Radicals sometimes boycotted elections. At other times they participated, though under adverse conditions. Perón's overthrow brought once again into public view parties of all shadings,[8] parties

8 Whitaker, *op. cit.,* identified eight parties on the post-Perón political scene: the *peronistas;* the Radical party (established 1892); Christian Democratic Federal Union

which seemingly have one important feature in common—they all lay great emphasis on economic issues.

ARMY–LABOR PARTIES. Developments in Argentina illustrate a twentieth-century trend toward parties based on coalitions of labor and army leaders. The fact that the army prefers or condones an alliance with labor, instead of supporting other groups, does not generally affect the favored position which the military traditionally enjoys in Latin American political life. One or another army leader may profit more than his fellows from a realignment of political parties, but the armed forces, and particularly the career officer class, usually receive a substantial share of the national budget and of other patronage. Otherwise, they soon look around for a new president and, when necessary, form new political alliances for this purpose. The army can usually renew its commanding position in short order. Faced with a similar crisis, labor has not been able to recover so quickly.

Two aspects of these army–labor coalitions are to be noted. First, governments based on the support of army leaders and organized labor have tended to bestow on labor such significant benefits as social security, minimum wages and hours, and sometimes even profit-sharing arrangements, or direct ownership of industries. Second, to keep both groups in line, the chief executive has played one group against the other.

In what nations have these coalition parties appeared? In Mexico, under Lázaro Cárdenas (1934–1940), labor groups and the military were major props of the Mexican Revolutionary party. In Argentina, the *peronista* party drew its basic strength from labor and the army. In Brazil, Getulio Vargas sustained his earlier regime in the 1930's by an official party, the Brazilian Labor party, composed primarily of organized labor and backed by the military. In Cuba, General Fulgencio Batista also combined the army and labor into a party that sustained his rule during the 1933–1944 era and supported his return to power in 1952. Common to all these experiences, as noted in the previous chapter, was the dependence of the labor movement on the official party organization.

SOCIALIST PARTIES. Though writers differ in categorizing the features of socialism, as distinct from communism, most agree on the following elements of socialist ideology: political tolerance, state economic planning, social security, and social ownership and control of the major means of production and distribution. In this

(founded July, 1955); Argentine Socialist party (created 1894); Communist party; National Democratic party (commonly identified as the Conservative party); Christian Democratic party (founded May, 1955); and the Progressive Democratic party.

sense, socialist parties were virtually unknown in Latin America until the last decade of the nineteenth century.

The first truly socialist party following the pattern of European parties was the Argentine Socialist party. Although it never gained control of the nation, owing in part to the fact that its power was largely confined to Buenos Aires, its influence in the Argentine labor movement was impressive until the advent of Perón in 1943. With Perón's overthrow, the socialists have again sought public office.

Socialist parties also appeared early in Chile and Uruguay. Since the 1930's, socialist political groups have appeared in Bolivia, Brazil, Colombia, Cuba, Ecuador, Panama, and Peru. Some students contend that the Revolutionary party in Mexico, at least during the days of Lázaro Cárdenas, also belongs in the list. In any case, save for the Mexican party, socialists have rarely captured public office.

The *aprista*-type parties, though indigenous, constitute another twentieth-century group with general Marxist orientation.[9] Modeled on the party founded in Peru by Víctor Raúl Haya de la Torre,[10] these *aprista* parties include the Auténtico party in Cuba, the Democratic Action party in Venezuela, and the Social Democratic party in Costa Rica. They may be considered as a homogeneous group because of the basic objectives which they advocate. On the international scene, they oppose "imperialistic" penetration and advocate Latin American political and economic union. In national affairs, they advocate objectives which one authority has summarized as follows: political democracy, agrarian reforms, over-all economic planning, industrialization, socialization of industry, social security, education, nationalism, and inter-Americanism.[11]

What success have the *aprista* parties attained? In general, their success has been limited. But they have at least surpassed the traditional socialist parties in respect to gaining public offices and even, on occasion, control of governments. In Peru, where *aprista* successes have fallen far short of the party's popularity, they claim to have won the presidential elections of 1931 and 1936, although they were prevented by force from taking office. The Aprista party was outlawed until 1945, when their candidate Manuel Bustamante

---

[9] For an account of these parties, see Robert J. Alexander, "The Latin American *Aprista* Parties," *Political Quarterly*, XX (July–September 1949), 236–247, and Chapter 7 above, by the same author.

[10] See Chapters 4 and 7. Literature on Haya de la Torre and the *aprista* movement in Peru is fairly abundant. A standard guide to the *aprista* program for the hemisphere and for Peru itself is Harry Kantor, *The Ideology and Program of the Peruvian Aprista Movement* (Berkeley: University of California Press, 1953).

[11] Alexander, "The Latin American *Aprista* Parties," *op. cit.*

(not an *aprista*) was elected, with an *aprista*-dominated majority in both houses of congress. *Aprista* inability to translate principles into sound political action crippled the Bustamante government, and when a member of this government, Manuel Odría, drove the president from power three years later, the party was again outlawed.[12] Not until 1956 did the *apristas* in Peru again enjoy legal status. In the election held that year their support of Manuel Prado Ugarteche won him the election.

In Costa Rica, the *aprista*-like Social Democratic party came to power in 1948 and became the principal support of President José Figueres. In Cuba, the Auténtico party controlled the government for eight years until Fulgencio Batista seized the presidency in a military coup on the eve of presidential elections in 1952. In Venezuela, the Democratic Action party carried out three years of reform based on *aprista* principles, only to fall before a military coup in 1948. After that date, the government of Pérez Jiménez offered little concession to this chief opposition party.[13]

COMMUNIST PARTIES. Communist parties have changed their tactics with the changing international situation, but their strategy in Latin America has always remained in line with the communist strategy for world domination.[14] The split in socialist parties initiated by the Russian Revolution of 1917 initiated communist activity in Latin America. The Communist party was a revolutionary party from the outset, "working through intellectuals, artists, students, and laborers to spread discontent and to subvert established governments." Their plan has been to champion the aspirations and programs of the groups they strive to influence. This strategy they have employed in their relations with agrarian and industrial labor unions, first in Argentina, Chile, Cuba, Mexico, and Peru, and later in Bolivia, Brazil, and Guatemala. They sought to arouse old antagonisms based on the "Big-Stick Policy" and supported attempts to wrest from American and European hands concessions of natural resources and public utilities.

During World War II the overtones of the fascist–communist struggle in Europe brought tactical changes in the communist fight against "imperialism" in Latin America. There was to be no sub-

---

[12] Kantor, *op. cit.*, pp. 13–21.

[13] On the prospects for legally recognized party opposition in Venezuela, see Leo B. Lott, "Executive Power in Venezuela," *The American Political Science Review*, L (June 1956), 422–441.

[14] For a more extensive commentary on communism in Latin America, see Frank R. Brandenburg, "Communism and Security in Latin America," *The Yale Review*, XLVI (Spring 1957), 413–424, and Robert J. Alexander, *Communism in Latin America* (New Brunswick, N.J.: Rutgers University Press, 1957).

version, no discontent, no antagonism—nothing that might alienate the people of the hemisphere and lead them to reduce the supply of goods flowing to the eastern front. At the end of the war, activity was renewed against established governments, from the Rio Grande to Tierra del Fuego. Soldiers in civilian uniforms arrived on the scene to direct subversive programs, to exploit antagonisms existing within the Latin American republics and between them and the United States, and even to whip up some new and pernicious issues. Once again such Marxian terms as "the class struggle," "imperialist war," and "proletariat" became commonplace in political discussion. In seeking to overthrow unpopular governments, local communists exploited ready-made tensions between businessmen and industrial labor and between landowners and agricultural workers. Not until official policy-makers in the United States fully grasped the global character of the objectives of communism were the Latin American governments alerted to the dangers they confronted. These warnings came late to nations long beset by concerted communist activity.

Events of the past decade suggest that communist activity is unlikely ever again to transcend the stage of friction-producer and reach a level of generating major tensions. Nevertheless, the Guatemalan interlude which brought the communists into high favor during the Arbenz Guzmán regime should arrest indifference before the communist threat.[15] Today, practically everywhere in Latin America the Communist party is outlawed. Only Uruguay, where democratic institutions are firmly established, has desisted from taking action to uproot the communists. The dimness of communist prospects is thus mirrored in the fact that the party can no longer expect vindication through identification with "popular front" groups. Communist weakness is further reflected in their failure to sustain pro-communist regimes in Guatemala and British Guiana. It is exposed also in the rupture of diplomatic relations between many Latin American republics and the USSR. Only Argentina, Mexico, and Uruguay exchanged ambassadors with the Soviet Union in 1957. Despite legal prohibitions of their party, however, communists still participated in elections, sometimes by open declarations, other times by identifying themselves with popular groups or by setting up "front" organizations.

Reliable statistics on the hard-core membership of the Com-

---

[15] A good analysis of the communist interlude in Guatemala may be found in Philip B. Taylor, Jr., "The Guatemalan Affair: A Critique of United States Foreign Policy," *The American Political Science Review*, L (September 1956), 787–806; also see Daniel James, *Red Design for the Americas* (New York: John Day Co., Inc., 1954).

munist party in the twenty republics of Latin America are difficult to obtain because reliable sources of information are not publicly available. Neither the United States government nor the Organization of American States has released any statistical data on the strength of Latin American communist parties. In addition, evaluation of these statistics is difficult because some governments tend to consider as a communist anyone who criticizes the status quo. Vested interests frequently are guilty of the same offense against government officials who suggest or undertake social and economic reforms. By necessity, therefore, the figures which follow are estimates compiled by the author or calculations of other observers.[16]

Communist strength is distributed so unevenly in the various countries that the countries may be classified best as those of greatest, medium, and least communist influence. Four nations fit into the first category. Argentina has 25,000 to 35,000 members, plus a considerable number of fellow travelers in industrial labor unions; Brazil has 60,000 to 75,000 members, augmented by twice this number of sympathizers in the ranks of organized labor; Cuba has 20,000 to 25,000 members; and Mexico has 25,000 to 40,000 members, besides some 100,000 sympathizers in agricultural labor unions and student groups. The nations where medium communist influence prevails have a total of approximately 50,000 hard-core members. Though seven nations—Guatemala, Panama, Colombia, Venezuela, Peru, Chile, and Uruguay—reveal this level of communist strength, in each nation the tactical approach is different. The hard-core membership in the nine remaining countries combined probably does not exceed 20,000. This means a minimum of 200,000 hard-core members for Latin America as a whole, or little more than one member per thousand inhabitants. Since earlier estimates placed membership somewhat higher,[17] it may be assumed that the brutal suppression of the Hungarian revolution has reduced the Latin American affinity for Communist appeals which had been growing since the apparent Soviet retreat from rigid Stalinism.

Communism's few successes and many failures during more than thirty-five years of activity in Latin America suggest that in the future Moscow is apt to pursue different approaches. Trade between Latin America and the Soviet Union has always been negligible, and there are few indications that mutually satisfactory commercial relations can be established to alter this pattern. The

---

[16] Estimates of communist party membership are for early 1957.

[17] On March 7, 1954, *The New York Times* estimated membership to be in excess of 240,000.

Kremlin may enhance its reputation, however, by helping to satisfy the Latin American appetite for technical assistance. It may also achieve this result through cultural activities, a field in which the communists have already utilized propaganda techniques through the press, billboards, radio–TV, paintings, and concerts. Latin Americans are highly appreciative of the *bellas artes* and frequently boast of superiority in art, literature, and music. Communists exploit this sentiment, particularly against the United States, and tend, in general, to emphasize appeals to the cultural side of Latin American life, although economic appeals are not neglected. Nor does this mean that the communists will abandon time-tested methods in other fields of activity.

Wherever Latin Americans have been offered a choice between the Communist party and a non-communist party truly representing the interests of the popular classes, they have shown a clear preference for the latter. The nations in which Communists have been the only political party promising social and economic reforms have generally been those in which the ordinary worker has lived in abject poverty, convinced that relief from his peonage would come only with death. Political leaders, whether liberal or conservative, are slowly coming to recognize, however, that the common man expects them to hold out some promise of help in achieving a better life. But illiteracy and low standards of living do not explain the communist appeal entirely. Lack of liberal party leadership is an equally important cause.

FALANGE PARTIES. *Falange* (phalanx) parties in Latin America are a by-product of the Spanish Civil War. Fascist-like parties, patterned on models provided by Nazi Germany and Fascist Italy, rallied to the support of Franco and the Spanish Nationalist cause, and their growth was greatly enhanced by the victory of the Generalísimo in Spain.

Falange ideology is based on a triad of *hispanidad* (loyalty to Spain and the Spanish inheritance), militarism, and intense Catholicism. It appeals to nationalistic sentiments and denounces both the "imperialism" of the United States and communism. Falangist popularity ran highest during the years immediately preceding the emergence of inter-American solidarity in 1942. *Falange* or similar parties appeared in almost every nation during those years, though notable success escaped all of them. Perhaps Chile experienced its greatest impact. Two parties in this mold were extremely active in the mid-1930's. The failure of the Chilean Nazi party of Jorge González von Marées to carry out a *coup d'état* in 1939 led to the virtual extinction of both parties.[18]   The defeat of the Axis powers dealt another blow to falangist popularity in Chile and elsewhere. The governments of Trujillo, Perón, and other rightist authoritarians have shown some sympathy for the *Falange*, but no Latin American government has yet relied for its principal support on a falangist party organization.   During the 1950's the Bolivian Socialist Falange has plagued the Siles administration in Bolivia, but in general, their influence throughout Latin America shows little promise of appreciable growth.

A political movement of falangist orientation which arose in Mexico in the late 1930's still persists in Mexican political life.   Its principles center in a doctrine called *sinarquismo* ("with order," the opposite of anarchy).   Advocating the establishment of a true "Christian Order," *sinarquistas* exalt the Spanish inheritance and denounce both the United States and communism.   They enjoyed considerable success during the late 1930's and early 1940's among Catholic youth groups, peasants, and others disillusioned with excesses of the Mexican Revolution.   National Sinarquista Union headquarters in Mexico City, their central base of political operations, directs *sinarquista* participation in electoral campaigns.   They first entered elections under the banner of the Popular Force party and, later, of the Party of National Unity.   Since 1948, when the ministry of government (*Gobernación*) cancelled their legal registration after five young *sinarquistas* had draped in black the statue of Juárez on the avenue dedicated to the great liberal in Mexico City, the National Sinarquista Union has generally backed candidates of the Party of National Action (PAN).   They failed to gain official status as a political party for the congressional elections of 1955, but once again contend for recognition in the presidential election of 1958.   *Sinarquista* strength today centers in the central states of Guanajuato, Querétaro, Michoacán, San Luis Potosí, and Jalisco.   Their prospects of strengthening their position in national politics are dim.[19]

CATHOLIC SOCIAL ACTION PARTIES.   Several parties of more liberal social orientation advocate principles based on the papal encyclicals *Rerum Novarum* and *Quadragesimo Anno*, although none has yet

[18] Jorge González von Marées, *El mal de Chile* (Santiago: Talleres Gráficos Portales, 1940).

[19] For an account of *sinarquismo* by one of its outstanding advocates, see Juan Ignacio Padilla, *Sinarquismo: Contrarevolución* (Mexico: Editorial Polis, 1948); also see Harold E. Davis, "Mexican Sinarquism," *Free World*, V (May 1943), 410–416; and Frank R. Brandenburg, *Partidos políticos* (Mexico: Problemas Agrícolas e Industriales de México, 1957), Chap. 2.

attained significant political power in any Latin American country. They resemble the Christian Socialist parties in Europe. Two parties of this kind, the Christian Democratic party and the Christion Democratic Federal Union, have been organized in Argentina. The National Falange party in Chile, in existence for more than two decades and not to be confused with the fascist-like *falange* parties elsewhere, is perhaps the oldest of these Catholic Social Action parties. But the most successful has been the Civic Union (or Catholic) party in Uruguay, which obtained 4.2 per cent, 5.4 per cent, and 4.3 per cent of the votes cast in the 1942, 1946, and 1950 presidential elections, respectively.[20] It held four of the ninety-nine seats in the Uruguayan Chamber of Representatives when the collegiate system was adopted in 1951.[21] Another of the Catholic parties is the Social Democratic party of Bolivia; it has had little success, however. Elsewhere, in Brazil, Colombia, Costa Rica, Ecuador, Guatemala, and Mexico, groups based on *Rerum Novarum* principles, and consisting primarily of youths and industrial and agricultural laborers, act more as pressure groups than as political parties. It may be expected that more parties of this nature will appear in response to a growing recognition among many younger priests that the Church must encourage lay movements dedicated to the social and economic improvement of the working classes.

Party Issues: Retrospect and Prospect

The experience of political parties during the preceding decades of this century offers some insight into the issues which bid fair to occupy political parties in the future. One striking characteristic of party platforms during these years has been their dedication to socio-economic considerations. First articulated in the programs of the Radical and Socialist parties in Argentina, this concern for socio-economic matters has marked the policies of army–labor parties, *falange* parties, and Catholic parties, as well as of socialist and communist parties. To a substantial degree, party membership has also changed. Sometimes these new parties have moved forward too rapidly in their effort to break down class stratification and to transform popular aspirations into realities, with the result that forces of reaction united and ousted them from power. This seems to have been the case with the *aprista* parties and perhaps

[20] Philip B. Taylor, Jr., "Interparty Co-operation and Uruguay's 1952 Constitution," *op. cit.*, p. 396.

[21] Russell H. Fitzgibbon, "Adoption of a Collegiate Executive in Uruguay," *The Journal of Politics*, XIV (November 1952), 624.

even with the army–labor parties of Perón and Vargas. Meanwhile, certain groups in some of these countries have begun to re-examine their position in society in terms of long-range interests. The appearance of Catholic Social Action underscores this recognition within traditionally conservative ranks of the urgent need to show more attention to the growing socio-economic demands of the lower classes.

These new parties and the dynamic nature of Latin American political life point up eight issues which should occupy political leaders during the years ahead. Stated briefly, these are: (1) the degree of state intervention in economic affairs—free enterprise versus public ownership; (2) the maintenance of large *haciendas* or their breakup into small privately owned farms, co-operatives, or communal forms; (3) controlled or unrestricted exports; (4) agriculture versus industry; (5) labor pitted against capital; (6) public- or Church-controlled education; (7) a more effective suffrage and freer elections; and (8) the role of the middle classes.

Party Organization

Latin American constitutions contain few direct references to the organization of political parties. Until recent decades, statutory enactments also ignored this aspect of political life. Even today election laws present few guideposts to party organization. Legislation emphasizes the requirements for obtaining legal status as a party, the grounds for losing this status, and general party organizational structure. To acquire legal party status, the laws generally require that a political group produce evidence of a fixed minimum number of members. The basis upon which this number is calculated varies from country to country. Argentina and Cuba set the minimum at a fixed percentage of the total registered voters in the general electorate. Others, like Brazil and Mexico, establish an arbitrary minimum that bears no direct relationship to the size of the electorate.[22]

A group aspiring to party status is also required to advance a program for the solution of their nation's problems. This restriction is no significant impediment, since most political groups in Latin America readily develop such platforms. Legal restrictions on party membership often ban clerics, members of the armed forces, and persons advocating a foreign creed or owing allegiance to a foreign government. Moreover, a party may lose its legal status by failing to obtain a minimum number of the total votes cast in

[22] Much of the following discussion is based upon an examination of national election laws. See the Suggestions for Reading at the end of this chapter.

an election, by resort to violence, or by advocating the forceful overthrow of an established government.

The organizational structure of political parties is fairly uniform, despite the paucity of legal provisions and despite such diversifying factors as custom, geography, the nature of party membership and leadership, the socio-political environment, and considerations of political expediency. Since parties perform the function of placing candidates in public office, and since these candidates, once elected, usually represent a defined geographical area, party organizational structure tends to correspond to the territorial political divisions.

At national, state (in federal systems), district, and local levels, parties, when well organized, are likely to consist of four agencies. First and foremost is a party president, second is a central executive committee, third is a convention or assembly, and fourth is an administrative staff or secretariat serving the three other agencies. Party presidents and central committees are nominally chosen by the convention and serve for specified terms of office. While all levels of party organization concern themselves with national elections, the national agencies rely on the state, district, and local organs to direct party machinery for the winning of elections of senators and deputies, of mayors (*alcaldes, jefes políticos, intendentes, presidentes municipales*), councilmen (*regidores*), and public attorneys (*síndicos*), and, in the federal states, of governors and state congressmen as well. At the local level, party organization is sometimes structured into precincts (*barrios*), which in the larger cities may encompass no more than one city block (*manzana, cuadro*) or merely a large building (*edificio*).

Federal and unitary governments have different patterns of party organization only insofar as the federal form actually disperses political power among different levels of government and provides for a greater number of elective offices. In reality, these considerations have not altered the general pattern of party structure in the federal states. Elections are still held on several levels in both federal and unitary systems, thus necessitating similar party structure in both.

In all unitary governments, members of the lower chamber of the national congress or the unicameral legislature are elected by direct popular vote. The fourteen nations having an upper chamber, whether federal or unitary, elect national representatives by popular vote. Five nations elect state or provincial governors by popular suffrage.[23] Organizational machinery at the state and

---

[23] Argentina, Brazil, Cuba, and Mexico elect single executives. Uruguay elects its plural executive at the provincial level.

local levels nominates candidates to senatorial, congressional, and, in federal states, to gubernatorial and state legislative posts. Since World War II, this local party organization has seemingly been no less extensive or free from control by national organs in unitary states such as Costa Rica, Ecuador, Chile, and Uruguay than it has been in the federal states of Argentina, Brazil, Mexico, and Venezuela. Although some observers have seen a tendency toward greater party centralization in unitary states, the parties of Perón (Argentina), Vargas (Brazil), and Pérez Jiménez (Venezuela) since 1940 belie this claim.

Party organization throughout Latin America has certain other common characteristics. Since membership increasingly follows socio-economic and occupational lines, party organization tends to divide into such groups as organized labor, agricultural workers, bureaucrats, and intellectuals. Another rather uniform characteristic is that party organs below the national level generally operate only during electoral campaigns, remaining dormant the rest of the time. Still another trend is the personalism which magnifies the *líder*. President Perón of Argentina, for example, changed the name of his following from the Labor party to the *Peronista* party. Finally, the party and its organs invariably overshadow issues.

The Party System in Mexico

The constitutions of Mexico, both federal and state, contain few direct references to political parties, reflecting a traditional Mexican preference for unwritten and informal rules in party matters. Not until the election laws were redrafted in 1945 were Mexican political parties bound by uniform regulations. Today a federal election law governs political parties that participate in federal elections, while state laws patterned on the federal model regulate state and local party organization and activity.[24]

The law defines a political party as an association of political orientation, established for electoral ends, and composed of Mexican citizens in full enjoyment of their political rights. To qualify as a national party, a political group must register with the ministry of government (*Gobernación*). To be approved, it must number at least 75,000 qualified voters, of whom more than 2,500 must reside in each of two-thirds of the nation's twenty-nine states, two terri-

[24] This summary of Mexican political parties is based on Brandenburg, *Partidos políticos,* previously cited. For a careful estimate on political affairs, also see Howard C. Cline, *The United States and Mexico* (Cambridge: Harvard University Press, 1953). For political parties from Carranza to Ruíz Cortines, see Vicente Fuentes Díaz, *Los partidos políticos en México* (Mexico: n. p., 1956), vol. II.

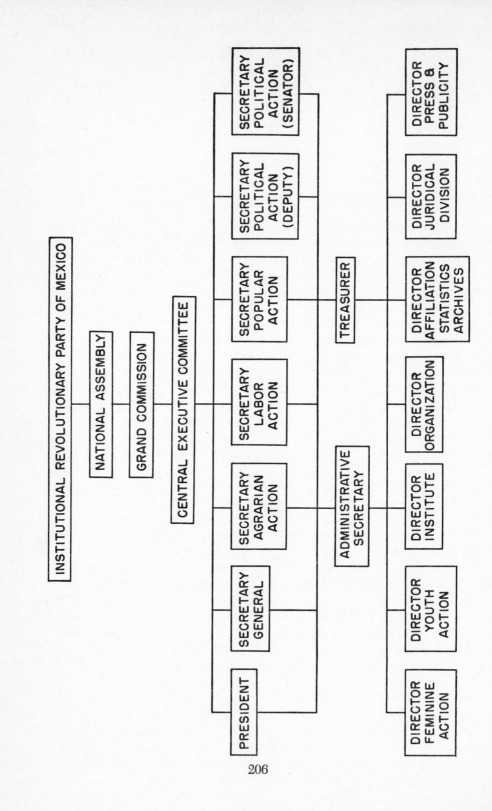

INSTITUTIONAL REVOLUTIONARY PARTY OF MEXICO

NATIONAL ASSEMBLY

GRAND COMMISSION

CENTRAL EXECUTIVE COMMITTEE

PRESIDENT

SECRETARY GENERAL

SECRETARY AGRARIAN ACTION

SECRETARY LABOR ACTION

SECRETARY POPULAR ACTION

SECRETARY POLITICAL ACTION (DEPUTY)

SECRETARY POLITICAL ACTION (SENATOR)

ADMINISTRATIVE SECRETARY

TREASURER

DIRECTOR FEMININE ACTION

DIRECTOR YOUTH ACTION

DIRECTOR INSTITUTE

DIRECTOR ORGANIZATION

DIRECTOR AFFILIATION STATISTICS ARCHIVES

DIRECTOR JURIDICAL DIVISION

DIRECTOR PRESS & PUBLICITY

tories, and the Federal District. It must present a program for the solution of national problems without alluding to religious or racial matters. It must not be affiliated with any international or foreign political organization.

Four political parties presently enjoy national status. These are the middle-of-the-road Institutional Revolutionary Party (PRI), the moderately conservative Party of National Action (PAN), the pro-clerical, moderate Mexican Nationalist Party (PNM), and the Marxist-oriented Popular Party (PP). The greatest obstacle to obtaining party status has been the requirement of 2,500 members in each of twenty-two entities. Of the four registered parties, it is questionable whether either the PNM or PP actually meets this requirement. Informed opinion contends this applies equally to the unregistered fascist-like *sinarquistas*, who now call themselves the Party of National Unity (PUN), and to the Mexican Communist Party (PCM).

Still another political party, though not permanently established in the sense of the PRI, PAN, or PP, nevertheless plays an important role in the Mexican party system. This is the major opposition party in each presidential election. In 1940, General Juan Andreu Almazán led the party, in 1946 Ezequiel Padilla, and in 1952 General Miguel Henríquez Guzmán. And there is every reason to suspect that a similar party will appear in 1958. What are the characteristics of this major opposition party which changes with each presidential election? First, the party's presidential candidate is a former member of the official party. Second, unlike other opposition parties, he has not campaigned against the Mexican Revolution, but merely against the interpretations placed on it by the official party. Third, he has attracted a substantial number of voters from within official party ranks, though not enough to win the election. Finally, each of these opposition groups has forthwith given up or lost its legal status as a political party after the election is over. Many political leaders contend that short of institutionalizing this periodic party into a permanent national party there is little prospect for an effective two-party system in Mexico.[25] The official party (PRI) rejects this contention, but their attitude may be colored by the fact that this opposition party—not the PAN, PP, *sinarquistas*, or communists—has constituted the greatest challenge to PRI dominance.

Control of party membership is left largely to the parties themselves. In the PRI, membership is regulated primarily by its affili-

[25] See, for example, "La revolución, los partidos políticos y la sucesión presidencial," *La política mexicana* (Mexico: Buro de Investigación Política, 1956).

TABLE XII. GROUPS CONSTITUTING MEXICAN INSTITUTIONAL REVOLUTIONARY PARTY

LABOR SECTOR

Confederación de Trabajadores de México (founded 1936)	1,150,000[a]
Sindicato de Trabajadores Ferrocarrileros de la República Mexicana (founded 1935)	100,000
Confederación Revolucionaria de Obreros y Campesinos (founded 1952)	86,000[b]
Sindicato de Trabajadores Mineros, Metalúrgicos y Similares de la República Mexicana (founded 1938)	80,000
Confederación Regional Obrera Mexicana (founded 1918)	35,000[c]
Confederación General de Trabajadores (founded 1921)	20,000[d]
Confederación Revolucionaria de Trabajadores (founded 1954)	20,000[e]
Sindicato Nacional de Trabajadores del Seguro Social (founded 1944)	7,000
Sindicato de Telefonistas de la República Mexicana (founded 1951)	7,000
Sindicato de Trabajadores de la Producción Cinematográfica (founded 1947)	6,000
Sindicato Mexicano de Electricistas (founded 1914)	5,000
Small independent unions	10,000
TOTAL	1,526,000

AGRARIAN SECTOR

Confederación Nacional Campesina	1,650,000[f]
Sociedad Agronómica Mexicana	3,500[g]
TOTAL	1,653,500

POPULAR SECTOR

Civil Servants

Federación de Sindicatos de Trabajadores al Servicio del Estado	250,000[g]
Sindicato de Trabajadores de Puertos Libres	1,000
State civil servants' unions	18,000
Municipal civil servants' unions	40,000
Teachers' unions outside civil servants' unions	6,000

Cooperatives

Confederación Nacional Cooperativa de la República Mexicana	250,000[h]
Liga Nacional Cooperativa	2,000[h]

Small Farmers

Confederación Nacional de la Pequeña Propiedad Agrícola	750,000[i]

Small Industrialists and Small Merchants

Federación del Comercio y la Industria en Pequeño del Distrito Federal	25,000
Confederación de Comercio, Industria y Agricultura en Pequeño	6,000
Confederación Nacional de Comerciantes en Pequeño	5,000

Professionals and Intellectuals

Confederación Nacional de Trabajadores Intelectuales	25,000[j]

Youth

Confederación de Jóvenes Mexicanos	40,000
Instituto Nacional de la Juventud Mexicana	10,000

Women

Consejo de Mujeres (Distrito Federal)	120[k]

Artisans

Federación de Organizaciones de Trabajadores No Asalariados	48,000
Independent Union of Artisans in Pachuca, Hidalgo	6,000
Other small independent artisan unions	25,000

Diversified

Confederación Nacional de Jóvenes y Comunidades Indígenas	75,000
TOTAL	1,582,120

SOURCE: Frank R. Brandenburg, *Partidos políticos* (Mexico: Problemas Agrícolas e Industriales de México, 1957), chaps. 4, 5, 6.

[a] Includes 100,000 *ejidatarios* affiliated also with the Agrarian Sector. [b] Includes 7,000 *ejidatarios* affiliated also with the Agrarian Sector. [c] Includes 12,000 *ejidatarios* affiliated also with the Agrarian Sector. [d] Includes 10,000 *ejidatarios* affiliated also with the Agrarian Sector. [e] Includes an indeterminate number of *ejidatarios* affiliated also with the Agrarian Sector. [f] Includes approximately 130,000 also affiliated with the Labor Sector and 100,000 affiliated with Cooperatives branch of the Popular Sector. [g] Virtually all 3,500 also hold membership in the Professionals and Intellectuals branch of the Popular Sector and approximately 15,000 federal civil servants also hold dual membership within the Popular Sector through this branch. [h] Includes 100,000 affiliates of the Agrarian Sector and an additional 25,000 who also hold membership in either the Labor Sector or in another branch of the Popular Sector; virtually all members of the *Liga Nacional Cooperativa* hold dual membership. [i] Includes 250,000 *ejidatarios* who belong to the Agrarian Sector but also possess private agricultural properties. [j] Includes 20,000 who hold dual memberships (civil servants, agronomers, women, *et al.*). [k] All hold additional membership in the Professionals and Intellectuals branch; many similar Councils of Women are in process of formation in other parts of the Mexican Republic.

ated industrial and agricultural labor unions, confederations of middle-class elements, and other socio-economic groups (see Table XII). Thus, when a mass rally is needed for discipline or for assistance in a campaign, the PRI leadership generally calls upon the heads of the party's labor, agrarian, and popular sectors. The effect of placing this responsibility in the hands of persons who are simultaneously party leaders and occupational bosses is to make party members consider their responsibilities to the party as part of their jobs. Opposition parties also tend to relate party duties to job security.

Neither state nor federal law regulates party finances. Mexican parties on the right—the PAN, PNM, and the unregistered *sinarquistas*—draw their financial support chiefly from wealthy businessmen, from large landholders, and to some extent from religious fanatics among the rural laboring class. Parties on the left—the PP and the outlawed Communists—solicit funds from laborers, students, and intellectuals. They probably receive additional support from abroad. The official Institutional Revolutionary party (PRI) collects "participation dues" from high-ranking government officials, from industrial and agricultural labor unions, from wealthy businessmen, and from civil servants in the state and local governments.

Mexican laws thus provide the basis for a fairly sound multiple-party system. But the discrepancy between these laws and Mexican political reality appears in the dominant position of the official party,[26] avowedly representing the great social upheaval which began with the Mexican Revolution of 1910-11. From its inception in 1929, the official party has controlled the presidency, the federal legislature, the governorships, and the state legislatures. This does not mean that all or even most candidates have been imposed on the electorate. At least in recent years the reverse has been true. Since the remodeling of the official party in 1942, in more than nine-tenths of the elections held the candidate declared winner probably did receive the largest vote, if not always the number officially released. But the persistence of the general belief that the official party has the power to impose a losing candidate makes it impossible to say without qualification that Mexico has an effective multiple-party system.

In comparison with official parties elsewhere in Latin America, however, Mexico's official party deserves special credit for the

[26] Since 1946, it has been called the Partido Revolucionario Institucional; in earlier years it was known as the Partido de la Revolución Mexicana (1938–1946) and the Partido Nacional Revolucionario (1929–1938).

immunity it gives to its critics. Opposition parties publicly censure PRI members and practices, and Mexicans generally enjoy freedom of speech, freedom of press, and freedom of assembly during electoral campaigns. All sectors of the official party are relatively united in upholding the principles of the Mexican Revolution, contending that the hegemony of the party that has given these principles realization is a prerequisite for continued national progress. As long as the dynamism engendered by the Revolution assures the acceptance of the PRI by organized industrial and agricultural laborers, the middle classes, the bureaucracy, and the army, opposition parties will not make serious inroads into national and state governments in Mexico. The official party has been guilty of some flagrant abuses of representative government, but effective opposition organization is lacking, partly because the present opposition parties, the PAN, PP, and PNM, and of course the *sinarquistas* and communists, all represent principles uncongenial to a majority of the Mexican people. Perhaps the most legitimate criticism which may be aimed at the leaders of the official party is that they prevented Almazán, Padilla, and Henríquez Guzmán from keeping their opposition parties intact after the elections were over. It seems obvious that PRI leaders recognize that the real challenge to their apparent invincibility will come from just such a party dedicated to Revolutionary principles.

Elections

SUFFRAGE QUALIFICATIONS. An effective suffrage and free elections are inseparable twins. Fraudulent balloting and dishonest vote-tallying submerge a republican government in authoritarianism. Laws may define an electorate, but the effectiveness of this electorate depends less on the legal right to vote than on the procedures adopted to ensure honest elections and on the good faith of officials. The electoral process thus includes three major elements: legal provisions defining the electorate, laws governing elections, and electoral practices.[27] Attention can now be directed to the first of these. What are the qualifications for voting in Latin American elections?

1. *Sex.* In all nations of Latin America, the ideal of universal popular suffrage has experienced steady progress toward fulfillment in reality. Property and literacy qualifications which limited voting to a small segment of the population during the nineteenth century were removed in most nations, thus granting suffrage to all adult

[27] Data on suffrage and elections is based on the most recent electoral laws, all of them, incidentally, passed since 1946.

TABLE XIII. VOTING QUALIFICATIONS FOR NATIONAL ELECTIONS

Country	Minimum Age	Year Women Granted Suffrage	Literacy	Registration	Identification Credentials
Argentina	18	1947	No	Yes	Yes
Bolivia	21	1952	Yes	Compulsory	Yes
Brazil	18	1932	Yes	Yes	Yes
Chile	21	1949	Yes	Yes	Yes
Colombia	21	1954	Yes	Yes	Yes
Costa Rica	21	1949	No	Yes	Yes
Cuba	20	1934	No	Compulsory	No
Dominican Republic	18[a]	1942	Yes	Yes	Yes
Ecuador	18	1929	Yes	Yes	Yes
El Salvador	18	1939	No	Yes	Yes
Guatemala	18	1945	No	Yes	Yes
Haiti	21	1958	No	Yes	Yes
Honduras	21[b]	1954	No	Yes	Yes
Mexico	21[b]	1953	No	Yes	No
Nicaragua	21[b]	1955	No[c]	Yes	Yes
Panama	21	1946	No	Yes	Yes
Paraguay	18	–	No	Yes	Yes
Peru	21[b]	1955	Yes	Yes	Yes
Uruguay	18	1932	No	Yes	Yes
Venezuela	21	1947	No	Yes	Yes

[a] No minimum age for married persons.
[b] Minimum age is 18 for married persons.
[c] Unmarried persons may vote at 18 if literate, otherwise at 21.

male citizens.   Until well into the twentieth century, however, women were denied the right to vote, not only because men believed that a woman's place is in the home, but also because the fairer sex was considered susceptible to clerical influence.   By 1957, however, women had been given the right to vote in every nation except Haiti and Paraguay.   Even in Haiti women have been promised suffrage in 1958.

2. *Citizenship.*   Citizenship is prerequisite to voting in all countries, although resident aliens are permitted to vote in some municipal elections.   Naturalized citizens of Argentina, Costa Rica, and Uruguay must wait one year, three years, and five years, respectively, before they are eligible to vote.   Citizens who have temporarily lost their citizenship rights, through conviction for crime for example, are also ineligible.

3. *Age and Marital Status.*   Twenty-one years is the minimum voting age in eleven nations.   Twenty years is the minimum in Cuba, and in the eight other nations it is eighteen.   Five countries take special cognizance of marital status in setting the legal voting age.   In Honduras, Mexico, Nicaragua, and Peru married persons may vote at eighteen, while in the Dominican Republic any married person may vote, regardless of his age.   Nicaragua lowers the voting age from twenty-one to eighteen for anyone who possesses an academic degree or who can read or write.

4. *Other Qualifications.*   Residence in a specific electoral district immediately prior to a national election is not usually required, but Bolivia, Brazil, Colombia, Haiti, and Paraguay have such a requirement, the period ranging from one month to two years.   Six countries—Bolivia, Brazil, Chile, Colombia, Ecuador, and Peru— require literacy.   The lower voting age for literates in Nicaragua has been noted previously.   There is no poll tax in any Latin American nation.   Nor is the ownership of property usually a requirement, although some nations deny the suffrage to vagrants. Finally, clerics are excluded from suffrage in Peru, as are members of the armed forces in Argentina, Brazil, Colombia, Cuba, the Dominican Republic, Ecuador, Guatemala, Paraguay, Peru, and Venezuela.

These suffrage qualifications may be thus summarized as follows. Citizenship is uniformly required, but property ownership and poll taxes are not.   Women are permitted to vote in eighteen nations, and in Haiti provision has been made to permit women suffrage in 1958.   A minimum age is set in every country, but married persons of any age may vote in the Dominican Republic.   Marriage reduces the minimum voting age in five other countries.   Residence and literacy qualifications affect suffrage in no more than one third of the Latin American nations.   (See Table XIII.)

ELECTORAL LAWS. Although regular court systems or an agency in the executive branch is sometimes entrusted with the enforcement of election laws, this responsibility generally rests with special electoral organs, variously called assemblies, commissions, committees, councils, juries, and tribunals. In Costa Rica this body is called the Supreme Electoral Tribunal, in El Salvador the Central Council of Elections, in Peru the National Electoral Jury, and in Mexico the Federal Electoral Commission. Subordinate organs are also provided, reaching down to electoral districts. The number of members and their qualifications, duties, and powers vary from country to country.

These various electoral organs fall into two general types: administrative boards, resembling those used for elections in the United States; and election tribunals, resembling regular courts. Legally, both types are independent of the executive, legislative, and judicial branches of government. The laws usually provide, however, that at least one of the three principal branches of government will resolve those electoral disputes not resolved by regular election organs. In the case of elections involving legislators, the legislature concerned may possess the final power to determine whether fraudulent electioneering should nullify an election of its members-elect.[28]

One of the principal duties of these electoral organs is to make certain pre-election arrangements. This duty includes setting a date and the hours for elections, establishing voting sites, making a definitive list of voters, and preparing ballots. In setting a time, authorities are generally bound by explicit instructions in constitutional or statutory mandates. The location of voting places is not so easily determined, because in some countries political parties or candidates have the right to protest the designation of a site which does not conform to law.

Preparing and keeping current a list of voters is even more complicated. Each voter's name is usually placed on a permanent voting register which indicates the province, electoral district, and section of his residence. Although the citizen must usually take the initiative in registration, persons in charge of the register receive considerable assistance from local officials who notify them of marriages, judicial proceedings, deaths, and other changes affecting voting status. Ministries of foreign affairs and of the interior sometimes assist by informing the register of the issuance and cancella-

[28] On electoral boards and courts, see Helen L. Claggett, *Administration of Justice in Latin America* (New York: Oceana Publications, Inc., 1952).

tion of naturalization papers, as do ministries of defense by sending in the names of inductees.

Since a citizen desiring to vote cannot ordinarily obtain a ballot unless his name appears on the list, it is vitally important for him to register. At the time of first registration (the Dominican Republic and Nicaragua excepted) he receives a voting credential variously called *carnet de identidad* (Bolivia), *cédula electoral* (Colombia), *cédula de identidad* (Costa Rica and Honduras), *carte d'electeur* (Haiti), or *libreta cívica* (Paraguay). Unless this identification is produced when demanded at the polls the voter may be denied a ballot.

The electoral organ is also called upon to design a model ballot. This ballot is usually not official, as in the United States, for the political parties or the candidates usually prepare the ballots used at the polls. In conformity with this model, a ballot will contain the name of the candidate, the office sought, and a special mark of identity for each candidate or party, such as a ballot of particular color.

Preliminary election arrangements completed, election day is now at hand. If the written word of the electoral laws is our guide, the voter approaching the polls may find several soldiers posted outside to assure that every person entering is unarmed and orderly. Upon entering he should find the election officials as well as representatives of political parties. The voter now presents his credential card, which is checked against the register. If everything is in order, he is given a ballot, or probably more than one, because a separate ballot is frequently provided for each office. In more than half of the Latin American nations a voter has the legal guaranty that he may cast his ballot under conditions to ensure secrecy. In a few urban centers he may manipulate the levers of a voting machine. Usually he merely marks an × opposite the name of the candidate of his choice. He completes his role in the electoral process by depositing his ballot or ballots in the corresponding urns.

The next stage is the tabulation of ballots. Election procedures legally provided emphasize accuracy in counting ballots. The tallying process generally begins at the voting booth level and proceeds through district electoral organs up to the final board of review. As we shall see, it is during this procedure that the theory of honest elections often degenerates into dishonest practices.

Finally, all nations provide legal safeguards against irregularities in election procedure. Stiff penalties are provided by law for the miscount of votes, and an election may be nullified for fraud. Parties accused of misconduct or fraud are, at the discretion of electoral organs, generally subject to trial before regular courts. In practice, however, these electoral organs are overweighted with members sympathetic to the administration responsible for their appointments and are therefore indisposed to rule against parties enjoying official favor. The consequent failure of opposition parties to secure redress for election grievances, despite the legal provisions, frequently leads them to seek justice by non-peaceful methods. This question of the conduct of lax and dishonest officials, however, leads us to the whole matter of electoral practices.

ELECTORAL PRACTICES. In many countries there is considerable discrepancy between the electoral procedures legally prescribed and those actually followed.[29] Many of these inconsistencies are generated by official parties and regimes such as the recent governments in Nicaragua and the Dominican Republic that seem to impose their will on the electoral procedure. The written word is often refuted in other nations also by the imposition of losing candidates, or by actions which prevent a winning candidate from taking office. Observers generally agree that in the Peruvian elections of 1931 Víctor Raúl Haya de la Torre won the presidential office given to Luis Sánchez Cerro, that Víctor Paz Estenssoro really carried the Bolivian elections of 1951, and that Jovita Villalba was the legitimate victor in the Venezuelan elections of 1952. And in gubernatorial and congressional elections, losing candidates are more often imposed than in presidential contests.

Evidence of the divergences between electoral laws and political practice appears in the general failure to apply the prescribed penalties for violations of the law by voters, candidates, political parties, and officials. Because of this general disrespect for election laws, opposition parties frequently regard an election as an opportunity to overthrow an existing regime by force, rather than as a dependable avenue to power. This attitude has been especially prevalent in nations where one man or a single party has enjoyed a long hold on public office. Devices which have made a mockery of elections in the past—imposition tactics in nominating candidates, illegal obstruction of opposition in electoral campaigns, partisanship in selecting election officials, and dishonesty in tallying votes—are still common in many coutnries. In spite of the electoral reforms of the past decades, the day when all Latin Americans will

[29] Certain matters relating to the election of presidents, the presidential role in selection of successors, and the principle of no re-election will be discussed in Chapter 10. The present chapter discusses election procedures and practices.

accept the suffrage as both a right and a function in representative government is still distant.[30]

A THEORY OF VIOLENT ELECTIONS. The persistence of electoral irregularities has led some students to offer hypothetical explanations of the real functions of Latin American elections. Defending the thesis that a violent struggle for personal power is central to political life of the region, one student has asserted that elections are merely the last resort after other methods of selecting officials have failed:

. . . elections in the Anglo-American sense for the determination of executive leadership are resorted to mainly in Latin America when more satisfactory methods have for one reason or another proved inadequate. Election under such circumstances is not likely to produce a strong, popular leader, but the technique may provide time for reassembling and again bringing into play the more fundamental bases for determining political power.[31]

The point is proved, this student claims, by the fact that "the electoral method of organizing power has been employed at least once in all of the Latin American countries."[32] Only by accepting this peculiar theory of violence does the quoted statement make sense, because the phenomenon of dishonesty in elections in itself hardly justifies the contention that elections are a last resort.

Persistent fraud and dishonesty in elections may in fact obscure the more important point that Latin Americans increasingly look to honest electoral procedures as the most satisfactory technique for organizing and changing administrations. One of the best evidences of this trend is the number of laws in recent years reforming antiquated electoral procedures. Several recent administrations have given moral support to more honest elections by measures which ensure the freedom of suffrage provided by law. Women as well as men may now vote in almost every nation. Literacy and property restrictions on the suffrage have been removed. Systems of registration have been reformed. Election boards have been reformed and electoral courts established. Improved media of transportation and communication permit candidates to reach people heretofore outside the effective voting public, and popular election campaigns tend to become the rule. Many defeated candidates have shown themselves to be good losers, accepting the results of the balloting, while victorious candidates have often expressed magnanimity toward their opponents. In several recent

[30] For a critical evaluation of the suffrage in Mexico, see Emilio Rabasa, *La constitución y la dictadura* (Mexico: Editorial Porrúa, 1956), pp. 117–137.

[31] Stokes, "Violence as a Power Factor in Latin American Politics," p. 465.

[32] *Ibid.*

elections, incumbent presidents have permitted free campaigns, demanded honesty from election officials, and, regardless of party affiliations, turned over the reins of government to winning candidates.

RECENT ELECTIONS IN ECUADOR.   In 1948, in an honest election, the liberal Galo Plaza rolled up more votes than his opponents and assumed the presidential office in Ecuador.   During four years crowded with achievements for the general welfare of the nation, Plaza faced several armed uprisings, all of which he suppressed. He thus became the first popularly elected president in more than twenty-five years to complete his full term of office.   He scrupulously observed his pledge of free elections, in spite of the basic ideological differences separating him from one of the candidates, José Velasco Ibarra.   Although he had reason to suspect that Velasco Ibarra, if elected, would disregard democratic procedures as he had done during two previous presidencies, Plaza held fast to his promise of nonintervention in the election.   When Velasco Ibarra received enough votes from Liberal party members who crossed party lines to put him into office, Plaza accepted the outcome and saw his opponent duly installed in office.

As the election of 1956 approached, there was speculation that Velasco Ibarra might hand-pick his successor.   But he apparently did not do so.   Neither Camilo Ponce Enríquez nor Raúl Clemente Huerta, the two major candidates, had been chosen or otherwise supported by the president.   The one-time *caudillo* deserves further praise for his hands-off policy in the campaign, making this election day one which merits inclusion in the history of free elections.   The Liberal party lost because its vote was divided between liberal, moderate, and conservative factions.   The greatest number of Liberal votes went to Clemente Huerta, but they were not sufficient to match the total polled by the Conservative party coalition that supported Ponce Enríquez.   Although the combined vote of the Liberals was a majority, the Liberals abided by the popular mandate which gave Ponce a plurality, permitting him to assume office.[33] They did not, apparently, think of the election merely as "a last resort."

ELECTION OF 1956 IN PERU.   Peru also deserves recognition for its presidential election in 1956.   Manuel Odría took control of Peru's government in 1948 by the use of force.   Ruling out any serious opposition parties, he managed to have himself elected president

[33] For earlier elections, see George I. Blanksten, *Ecuador: Constitutions and Caudillos* (Berkeley: University of California Press, 1951).   For the 1956 elections, see reports in *The New York Times* and "Ecuador: A Case Study in Politics," *Latin American Report,* I (July 1956), 24–29.

in 1950 for a six-year term.   This regime was notable for its lack of civil liberties.   After the campaign of 1956 was under way, Odría indicated his preference for Hernando de Lavalle, and it was assumed that the two other candidates in the race would meet with government opposition.   From time to time, Odría entered the campaign to support his candidate.   But Lavalle's two rivals, former president Manuel Prado Ugarteche and Fernando Belaunde Terry, conducted extensive speaking campaigns across the nation, appealing to the electorate.   Lavalle did likewise.   If some doubts had arisen during the campaign concerning the fairness of the government's tactics, they were overshadowed by the fairness and honesty of election day.   In what was interpreted to be a direct repudiation of Odría's eight-year rule, Lavalle was defeated by a majority of landslide proportions, Prado and Belaunde each receiving more than three times the number of votes cast for Lavalle.   With the support of the *apristas,* who had been permitted to resume political activity but not to nominate candidates, Prado edged out Belaunde and assumed the presidency without opposition.[34]

OTHER FREE ELECTIONS.   Other recent elections have been noteworthy for their fairness and freedom.   Observers generally concur that the Cuban elections of both 1944 and 1948 were honest.   In the former, President Fulgencio Batista left Cuba voluntarily after his candidate, Carlos Saladrigas, was defeated by Ramón Grau San Martín.   In the 1948 contest, the Auténtico party stalwart, Carlos Prío Socarrás, won the confidence of the voters in an honest contest with Ricardo Núñez Portuondo and Eduardo Chibás.   Uruguay has given dignity to democratic procedures for many years, so that the Tomás Berreta–Luis Batlle Berres victory in 1946 and that of Andrés Martínez Trueba in 1950 were no exceptions.   In Venezuela, Rómulo Gallegos is generally credited with winning a fair electoral contest in 1947.

The same observation can be made for the Chilean elections of 1946 and 1952 which brought, respectively, Gabriel González Videla and Carlos Ibáñez del Campo into office, as well as for the Bolivian elections of 1947 and 1956 which seated, respectively, Enrique Hertzog and Hernando Siles in the presidential chair, and for the Costa Rican election won by José Figueres in 1953.   The victory of Eurico Dutra in 1945 may have been the most honest election in Brazilian history.   In the 1950 presidential election of Brazil, acceptance of the clear mandate expressed for Getulio Vargas accorded similar confirmation to the principle of free elections, as did the election in 1955.   Opposition parties and impartial

[34] For a report on the elections, see *The New York Times,* June 19, 1956.

observers alike usually concur that both Miguel Alemán and Adolfo Ruiz Cortines became presidents of Mexico by virtue of free and honest elections.[35]

As these experiences seem to show, Latin American elections do not easily fit any systematic "theory of violence." To be sure, political parties do not always accept the adage that "counting heads is better than knocking them together." Moreover, fraud and dishonesty occur regularly in campaigns and electioneering, in registration and balloting, in the selection of poll officials, and in vote-counting. But the theory that dishonest elections are an "intrinsic" characteristic not only overlooks the Latin American belief to the contrary, as evidenced in the present wave of electoral reform, but also some rather important cases of fair and free elections.

Trends

A basic pattern of one-party and relatively ineffective multi-party systems persists in Latin America and is likely to do so for years to come. Within the context of this traditional pattern, however, several changes have occurred in the twentieth century. These changes grew out of the powerful socio-economic forces transforming Latin American life. In many countries political parties no longer have a narrow membership base. Witness developments in the official party in Mexico, in the Colorado party in Uruguay, indeed, in all nations where army–labor coalitions, Catholic Social Action parties, and socialist parties have appeared. Improved systems of communication and transportation have carried party organization outside the large cities. More people, better educated and better clothed and fed, have begun to participate actively in politics. Industrialization and the rise of commercial and middle classes continue to accelerate party development. All these forces should have a greater impact on party membership and party organization in subsequent decades. Parties with a broad membership basis, coupled with enlightened leadership, may go far in advancing representative government in Latin America. Until such political parties have grown to assume a more responsible role in the political processes of Latin American nations, however, charismatic personal loyalties will continue to overshadow issues and group interests.

Party growth during recent decades has brought electoral im-

---

[35] Many of these recent elections are described in Austin F. Macdonald, *Latin American Politics and Government* (2d ed.; New York: The Thomas Crowell Co., 1954) and Miguel Jorrín, *Political Instability in Latin America* (Albuquerque: University of New Mexico, 1953).

provements in the form of better legal provisions and laws which attempt to correct electoral abuses. The incidence of dishonest elections seems highest in those countries where the base of party membership is most restricted. But these dishonest elections are by and large the product of irresponsible political leaders rather than of poor election laws. While the improved electoral laws are still too frequently honored only in the breach, is it too much to hope that in the decades ahead, political leaders will see the way to translate these legal provisions into increased party responsibility and more honest elections?

Suggestions for Reading

There is no good general work in English or Spanish. Election statistics published by the governments often demand close scrutiny. A few works of a general character treat political parties and offer suggestions for further reading. Among these are: Austin F. Macdonald, *Latin American Politics and Government* (2d ed.; New York: The Thomas Crowell Co., 1954); W. W. Pierson and Federico Gil, *Governments of Latin America* (New York: McGraw-Hill Book Co., Inc., 1957); and Robert J. Alexander, *Labor Parties of Latin America* (New York: League for Industrial Democracy, 1942). The short monograph by Miguel Jorrín, *Political Instability in Latin America* (Albuquerque: University of New Mexico, 1953), offers valuable data on the years immediately preceding its publication. There are three short studies that contain sound analyses of political parties: Russell H. Fitzgibbon, "The Party Potpurri in Latin America," *The Western Political Quarterly*, X (1957), 3–22; Federico G. Gil, "Responsible Parties in Latin America," *The Journal of Politics*, XV (1953), 333–348; and Robert J. Alexander, "The Latin American *Aprista* Parties," *The Political Quarterly*, XX (1949), 236–247.

On specific political movements there are Harry Kantor, *The Ideology and Program of the Peruvian Aprista Movement* (Berkeley: University of California Press, 1953); Robert J. Alexander, *Communism in Latin America* (New Brunswick, N.J.: Rutgers University Press, 1957); and Víctor Alba, *Historia del comunismo en América Latina* (Mexico: Ed. Occidentales, 1954). A few works on political parties of a specific nation may be mentioned: José Luis Romero, *Las ideas políticas en Argentina* (Mexico: Fondo de Cultura Económica, 1946); Santiago Távara y Hernández, *Historia de los partidos* (Lima: Ed. Huascarán, 1951); Alfredo Hernández Urbina, *Los partidos políticos y la crisis del Apra* (Lima: Ed. Raíz 1956); and Frank R. Brandenburg, *Partidos políticos* (Mexico: Problemas agrícolas e industriales de México, 1957). Philip B. Taylor, Jr., has written on "The Electoral System in Uruguay" in *The Journal of Politics*, XVII (1955), 19–42. For details concerning electoral provisions it is necessary to refer to the various national laws, all of them, incidentally, adopted since 1946.

II

THE STRUCTURE AND FUNCTIONS OF POLITICAL POWER

Chapter 9

Constitutions and the Structure of Power

Constitutional Instability

The constitutional instability prevalent in much of Latin America may impress sharply—even shock—the student who tends to think of a written constitution as a reasonably long-lived political instrument. Comparison is inevitably made with the experience of the United States which, during its national history, has had two constitutions. While one of these, the Articles of Confederation, enjoyed less than a decade of life, the other has endured for more than a century and a half. From the standpoint of constitutional longevity, the first of these North American experiences is more comparable with the Latin American than the second. The written constitution which lives for more than a quarter of a century is rare in Latin America, where no fewer than eight countries[1] have had ten or more constitutions. Indeed, two states, the Dominican Republic and Venezuela, have each had more than twenty.

This transient nature of written constitutions gives rise to three questions. First, how real, how profound a condition of political instability underlies this relatively rapid turnover of constitutions? Next, why does this turnover occur? Finally, in view of this impermanence of documents, why do the states of Latin America bother to write constitutions in the first place? While these questions have been discussed in previous chapters, it is necessary to return to

[1] Bolivia, Colombia, the Dominican Republic, Ecuador, Haiti, Honduras, Peru, and Venezuela.

them here to see what light their exploration may throw on the constitutional problems of Latin America.

With respect to the first question—how profound is the constitutional instability?—it should be noted that, typically, a Latin American state undergoes an essentially superficial change when it abandons one constitution to adopt another. Normally, the change involved is far more apparent than real. At least three considerations underlie this general proposition. One lies in a contrast between United States and Latin American constitutional practices. Illustrations of this contrast can be found in such matters as the adoption of a bill of rights, a change in the manner of choosing a president, or redefinition of an incumbent executive's eligibility for re-election. These questions have been met in the United States through constitutional amendment; typically in Latin America, they bring new constitutions. The United States Civil War is a dramatic case in point. That struggle stimulated profound changes in a nation's way of life—and three amendments to an existing constitution. Any Latin American state experiencing a similar crisis would almost certainly have acquired a new constitution in the process.

Moreover, the substantive content of a new constitution adopted by a given Latin American state is normally essentially similar to the provisions of the preceding document. More frequently than not, both provide for the same structural scheme of government, the same or similar political institutions and practices, and like systems of private rights. The date on which the new president is to take office or the circumstances under which he may be eligible for re-election change from one constitution to the next, to be sure; but the presidential system of government,[2] as well as the complex of legal norms administered by the courts in the typical Latin American state, antedates its present constitution and will probably outlive it.

A further factor in the superficiality of Latin American constitutional instability appears in the frequency of the so-called "revolutions." This question was discussed in an earlier chapter, but two observations may be made here. In the first place, the typical Latin American revolution is not a real revolution, either in the sense of involving a recasting of the social order, or in the sense of a restructuring of a nation's political system. Fundamental revolutions in this sense have indeed occurred in Latin America, for example the Mexican Revolution,[3] which began in 1910, but

---

[2] For a discussion of presidential government, see Chapter 10.
[3] See the discussion later in this chapter; also Chapters 4 and 5.

they are rare. The usual Latin American "revolution" involves little more than an extraconstitutional change in administration without affecting the national order substantially.

The second observation to be made about the constitutional effects of these so-called "revolutions" is that they are normally occasions for the writing of new constitutions. Since the "revolutionary" government usually presides over the same political order as the overthrown regime, the new constitution will contain provisions essentially similar to the previous text. This constitution-making is thus a method of regularizing a revolutionary regime and is a familiar Latin American practice. "A new fundamental law of his own drafting (though perhaps little changed from its predecessor) gave a president who came into office by a coup or a revolution a feeling of greater legal security and solidity."[4] It may thus be concluded that the Latin American tendency to abandon old and adopt new constitutions in sometimes rapid succession does not of itself point to a condition of deep or profound instability.

The second question—why do these relatively rapid constitutional changes occur in Latin America?—reaches more fundamental ground. It is probably helpful to distinguish between a "real" and a "written" constitution. The former can be defined as the existing system of power relationships operating within a political community, or the "arrangement of the inhabitants of a state."[5] The latter refers to that document which has been declared by the legally competent authorities to be the supreme law of the land. In much of Latin America a wide gulf separates the real from the written constitutions. Indeed, an Ecuadorian writer has said:

It can happen that the system of rules set forth in the [written] constitution does not coincide with the existing political conditions in the state, in which case the objective law created by [written] constitutional norms cannot have actual, effective validity. In such a case there is produced a frank discrepancy between the constitutional order and the political order. . . . This discrepancy, if not adjusted in logical and realistic terms, can produce changes and unrest in the social order, to the extent that passive as well as active resistance movements result in the reform or the elimination of the written constitution.[6]

In most cases of conflict or discrepancy between the real and the written constitution the former prevails, with the result that the latter is upset or violated.

[4] Russell H. Fitzgibbon, "Constitutional Development in Latin America: A Synthesis," *American Political Science Review*, XXXIX (June 1945), 517–518.

[5] Aristotle, *Politics*, translated by Benjamin Jowett (London: Oxford University Press, 1920), p. 100.

[6] Aurelio García, *Ciencia del estado* (Quito: Imprenta de la Universidad Central, 1947), II, 259–260.

It is probably true that no constitution, Latin American or any other, functions wholly in the manner that its writers intended. However, the consistently wide divergence between the real and the written constitutions may well be peculiar to Latin America. One reason for this may be that, for Latin America, the two derive from widely separated sources. The real constitutions of the various states of the area originated in their own experiences, not only during the colonial period but also since the achievement of independence. Yet few aspects of this experience have been written into Latin American constitutions. The explanation of this phenomenon lies partly in the fact that Latin American independence was achieved in a movement against the political system which had obtained during the colonial period, and partly in the fact that Latin American written constitutions have tended to be normative or anticipatory, addressed to ideals not yet achieved rather than to existing political conditions. Thus, relatively few of the "real" constitutions of Latin America are written.

What, then, are the sources of the material embodied in most of the written constitutions of the area? The answer is that much of this material is derived, not from Spanish or Latin American experience as one would expect, but rather from the constitutional norms and practices of France and the United States. From the French, Latin American constitution-writers have borrowed philosophical and theoretical propositions developed by such writers as Rousseau, Voltaire, and Montesquieu; they have also drawn constitutional and administrative arrangements such as parliamentary interpellation, decree legislation, police organization, some forms of proportional representation, and a number of fundamentals of municipal administration. From the United States, Latin Americans have borrowed such constitutional ideas and practices as federalism, the separation of powers, and certain protections of private rights. Thus it is not surprising that Latin American "written" constitutions, frequently exhibiting ill-considered imitation of foreign models, are often in conflict with the "real" constitution.

Why do the Latin Americans bother to write constitutions at all? Comparisons with the development of the United States are frequently made for the purpose of pointing up contrasts with Latin America. In this case, however, a basic similarity is also worth noting. The United States and the other American republics achieved their political independence during the same half-century —from 1775 to 1825. This period in the history of Western civilization was one of ferment in political philosophy, an era which endowed the political movements of the time with a certain unity.

The movements of independence, whether American, French, or Latin American, partook alike of the political and philosophical content of the Enlightenment. This content, embracing as it did the notion of constitutionalism, was as much an integral part of the *raison d'être* of Latin American independence as it was of the independence of the United States. In this sense the two Americas share a common political and constitutional tradition. In this context it is no less unthinkable for Latin America to abandon the idea of constitutionalism than it would be for the United States. To do so would be to abandon national independence as it has been understood in the tradition of Franklin, Jefferson, Miranda, Bolívar, and San Martín. In this sense a written constitution is as much a part of the Latin American as of the "North American" way of life. However, the fact that the twenty countries of the area, according to some computations, have had more than one hundred and eighty such documents stands as evidence that troublesome constitutional problems abound.

Major Constitutional Problems

Constitution-writers in Latin America typically face four major types of problems in the drafting of texts. The decisions rendered on these problems by a given constituent authority are generally reflected in the provisions of the written constitution produced by that authority. These four major problems are centralization versus decentralization, the power of the executive, the feasibility of parliamentary government, and problems of social welfare. As they occur in the Latin American scene, they present complexities which it may be useful to examine here.

CENTRALIZATION VERSUS DECENTRALIZATION. It is an elementary proposition in political theory that governments may be internally organized in any one of three possible ways. The national or central government may have unlimited legal power over all territory within the state, in which case it is said that the organization is unitary. Political authority may be divided by the constitution between self-governing parts and the central whole; then the state is designated a federal one. Or legal power may belong to parts which are loosely associated through a weak central organ, in which case the arrangement is termed confederate. Constitution-writers, in the Western Hemisphere or elsewhere, must choose among these alternatives. For historical and other reasons, Latin American constituent authorities have rarely selected the confederate formula, except as they have thought of some larger union of states. To them the choice, for most practical purposes, has been between the unitary and federal approaches.

In Latin America the actual difference between the two systems in operation is not as great as the uninitiated might expect. Latin Americans normally live in a crossfire between centripetal and centrifugal political forces—forces that have been involved in age-old conflict in the area. Essentially, the issue facing the constitution-writer is which side in this struggle will be supported by the document he produces. Inasmuch as the opposing forces are often relatively evenly matched—and since the written constitution does not carry enough weight to be decisive in the matter—the written instrument, in the last analysis, is but one more factor buttressing one camp or the other. The tug of war between centripetal and centrifugal political forces has never yet been decisively terminated by a constitution anywhere in Latin America.

The components of both camps are impressive in their strength. Among the forces making for centralization have been the strong authoritarianism of the Spanish and the Bourbon political tradition; administrative, legislative, and judicial uniformity springing from the French Revolution and represented in Latin America by such practices as administrative centralization and judicial application of code law or the Roman law; and the unifying influence of the Roman Catholic Church. Taken together, these are weighty forces in Latin America. They may be supported by a unitary constitution, or they may be mitigated somewhat—but not entirely overcome—by a federal document.

Decentralizing forces are also very influential. They include regionalism or particularism, frequently reaching impressive extremes in Latin America; the lack of national cultural cohesion in many states of the area, especially those with large Indian populations; the difficulty of transportation and communication among regions separated by jungles, mountains, and other physical barriers; and the tradition of municipal autonomy strong in much of Latin America. These may be abetted by a federal constitution. It is unlikely that they would be overcome by a unitary instrument.

The constitution-writer must therefore decide which of these formidable camps his document will support. The selection itself is normally governed by the political situation prompting the promulgation of a new basic law. Hence, in a nation where the centralizing forces are widely regarded as evils or ills afflicting it, a federal constitution is likely to result, even though it will not cure those ills. If, on the other hand, the decentralizing forces are regarded as basic difficulties of the country, a unitary constitution may result. In any case, the resultant document, whether federal or unitary, does not resolve the question. Normally it merely adds more weight, usually small, to one side of the scale or the other.

At present, sixteen of the twenty states of Latin America have unitary constitutions. Their authors have generally sought to combat regionalism, to instill national cohesion into a culturally and geographically divided state, or to offset excessive municipal autonomy. Typically, the unitary constitution makes regional and local units of government the servants or creatures of the central authorities, operating as agents of the national government and reflecting its interests rather than those which are primarily regional or local. Governors and other officers of regional or local government in the unitary state are designated by the national authorities, hold office at the pleasure of these authorities, and carry out orders and instructions from the national capital.

Only four Latin American states, Argentina, Brazil, Mexico, and Venezuela, currently have federal constitutions.[7] These provide for a division of constitutional authority between the national and state or provincial levels of government, with the governors and other officials of the latter popularly elected and representing regional rather than national interests. The framers of these constitutions sought to offset the centralizing forces in their respective countries. But these forces are not dormant in any of the four countries, though they may be mitigated somewhat by the constitutional provisions.

Many of the states of Latin America, whether their constitutions be federal or unitary, display impressive degrees of municipal autonomy. The roots of this condition are deeply embedded in the history of the area. In colonial days, the cities were the chief centers of political activity of the upper classes and, indeed, the only community levels where they, rather than the home government in Europe, could exercise power. The *cabildos,* or town councils, of colonial Latin America thus became major centers of colonial politics. It is worth noting that in many nations the *cabildos* launched the movements leading to national independence. Moreover, in those countries with large Indian populations, the Indian majority has comprised the lower rural classes; it has been the urban dwellers who have been the more politically articulate group. Against this historical and cultural background,

---

[7] Two of these federal states, Argentina and Mexico, are discussed later in this chapter.

municipal autonomy continues to be a major characteristic of the area.[8]

It has already been pointed out that in Latin America written constitutions are frequently anticipatory, normative, and corrective in character. It should thus be borne in mind that the presence of a unitary constitution may well signify that its drafters viewed regionalism, cultural diversity, geographic fragmentation, and municipal autonomy as major problems of their country. Similarly, the authors of federal constitutions have frequently seen their nation's chief ills as encompassing the tradition of central authority, administrative uniformity, and the temporal influence of the Roman Catholic Church.

The insight and vision of these men are not to be discounted. Although the constitutions of Latin America tend toward the unitary form, political fragmentation is a major problem, as evidenced in the existence of twenty, mostly small, republics. These two phenomena are not unrelated, and the lack of larger political units in federal or other form explains much of the political weakness of the area.

THE POWER OF THE EXECUTIVE. Among the classic problems faced by the writers of Latin American constitutions is the great power traditionally exercised by the chief executive. Presidential authoritarianism is common. Military dictatorship is its most dramatic form, but it may also be present in other guises. Several factors contribute to produce this result. Authoritarianism in government is deeply embedded in the Spanish political tradition. Brought to the Americas by the *conquistadores,* this tradition continues to flourish in the area. It is frequently forgotten that the Indian political tradition embraced a similar element, which is still operative in the countries where indigenous peoples form a major sector of the population.[9] Authoritarianism has likewise been nurtured in the past by the Roman Catholic Church, which plays a large temporal role in Latin American life. Militarism, a chronic political problem in the Americas, also contributes to the problem, since at any given time approximately two-thirds of the presidents in Latin America are likely to be army officers. Indeed, it is still a frequently heard political maxim in some of these countries that

[8] Argentina is an exception here, since in that country regional autonomy has been the historical role of the provinces rather than of the cities. See George I. Blanksten, *Perón's Argentina* (Chicago: University of Chicago Press, 1953), pp. 133–158.

[9] See, for example, George I. Blanksten, *Ecuador: Constitutions and Caudillos* (Berkeley: University of California Press, 1951), particularly pp. 14–57 and 141–168.

"the last step in a *military* career is the presidency of the republic."[10]

Finally, the presidential system of government, as implemented in the countries of the hemisphere, itself contributes to the power of the executive. It has already been suggested that some of the borrowing by Latin Americans of constitutional practices of foreign sources is ill-considered. One of these, as noted in Chapter 10, is the presidential system, a "North American" device widely imitated in the other American republics. A cardinal feature of this arrangement is the separation of powers, presupposing a balanced apportionment of authority among the executive, legislative, and judicial branches of government. This apportionment rarely exists in fact in many states of Latin America. Some of the factors adding to the strength of the executive have already been mentioned; to these must be added elements detracting from legislative and judicial authority. Legislative bodies are weakened by an electoral process tying legislators to the president's coat tails and by the typical infirmity of political parties in Latin America. As for the judiciary, it should be remembered that the common law, known in England and the United States, does not hold sway in Latin America, which follows the civil or Roman law. Courts enjoy a different scope of authority and much less independence than in the United States or Britain.

As will be noted in later chapters, executive domination has long been recognized as a major constitutional problem of Latin America. Yet little success can be expected or claimed for the extensive provisions written into the basic documents in an attempt to remedy this situation. The terms of office of presidents have been limited; their eligibility for re-election has been restricted, even prohibited; legislative bodies and courts have been given authority to curb executive actions; and cabinet ministers have been empowered to grant or deny legality to presidential measures. The effectiveness of such measures remains unimpressive, and presidential domination remains an essentially unsolved constitutional problem.

PARLIAMENTARY GOVERNMENT. Constitutional fluidity in Latin America has permitted considerable experimentation with governmental forms and processes. Parliamentary systems, while they have never enjoyed a widespread vogue in the area, have on occasion emerged from the pens of the constitution-writers. Latin American advocates of parliamentary government advance a number of arguments in support of that arrangement.

---

[10] It is an indictment of the Latin Americanists among political scientists that, although the problem has long been recognized, no satisfactory study of militarism in the Western Hemisphere has yet been published.

It is contended, in the first place, that the parliamentary system might meet the chronic Latin American problem of the strong executive by rendering the president and the executive ministers more responsible to the legislature. It is suggested, further, that legislative interpellation and the fall of administrations through no-confidence votes—legal and constitutional under many parliamentary arrangements—might provide many of the psychological and some of the political equivalents of constitutional instability and so-called "revolution," while at the same time preserving an institutional fabric, thus killing two Latin American birds with one constitutional stone. It is also argued that such an arrangement might bring about more generally responsible and responsive government, and that parliamentary forms would stimulate greater popular interest and participation in government and politics. Finally, since the separation of powers associated with the presidential system is sometimes vitiated in Latin America anyway, parliamentary forms are urged as ready alternatives for states prepared to abandon the presidential arrangement.

The Latin American experience with parliamentary government has neither supported nor disproved the above contentions. At one time or another, Chile, Brazil, Bolivia, Haiti, and Honduras have adopted the parliamentary system. Thirteen others[11] have experimented with certain aspects of that arrangement. Constitutional instability has nevertheless persisted; and the record does not justify a contention that the parliamentary form has been either more or less stable than the presidential.

Chile enjoyed the most nearly successful experience with parliamentary government in Latin America, during the period from 1891 to 1925. It is significant that this successful episode grew from a constitutional crisis in Chile, and was not a conscious attempt to imitate a system from abroad. And though the Constitution of 1833—a charter that had provided for the essentials of presidential government—remained in effect, under it the parliamentary system developed and flourished until 1925.

Chilean electoral reform early in the 1860's created a political situation during the ensuing thirty years in which the national congress represented interests different from those giving their support to the executive. The result was a conflict between the legislative and executive branches of the government, a struggle which dominated Chilean national politics until the revolution of 1891. President José Manuel Balmaceda inherited this problem

[11] Uruguay, Cuba, Peru, Costa Rica, Mexico, Panama, Argentina, Colombia, Ecuador, Guatemala, Nicaragua, El Salvador, and Venezuela.

when he assumed office in 1886, and the overthrow of his government in 1891 marked the victory of the legislature over the executive. "The revolution of 1891 was a serious incident in the constitutional life of the republic," one Chilean historian has written. "With it there fell not only a president but also the presidential authority. It was an entire political system that collapsed."[12]

During the ensuing decades of parliamentary government, the Chilean government was characterized by a congressional supremacy in which "the real governors were not the chiefs of state, but the leaders of parties through whose committees must pass all public business." During this epoch, "it was planned to make the presidency of the republic a purely decorative office, or at most a conciliatory element. The government lost its unity. There was no one man responsible for its operation. It was impersonal and divided."[13] Political parties in Chile's multi-party system became powerful agencies of government, with the basic locus of authority in the national Congress.

Although the Chileans stumbled upon it largely by accident in a crisis, the parliamentary system functioned relatively well for more than thirty years. But the parliamentary structure finally disintegrated during the first administration of Arturo Alessandri Palma, the "Lion of Tarapacá," who came to the presidency in 1920 with a "program of rebellion." President Alessandri's first term was characterized by excessive cabinet instability; indeed, there were no fewer than sixteen cabinet crises in the four-year period ending with Alessandri's resignation in 1924.

Far from easing the situation, Alessandri's resignation ushered in a period of even greater instability. The army, under the leadership of Colonel Carlos Ibáñez del Campo, assumed the reins of government in 1925. It was thought at the time that this would be an interim caretaker arrangement, to endure only until the political parties could reorganize to resume civilian government. By 1927, however, Ibáñez apparently had come to believe that such a solution was not likely to be possible in the immediate future. Accordingly, he reorganized his regime as a frank military dictatorship, and it prevailed until its overthrow by revolution in 1931. Nor was a solution even then at hand. The chaotically unstable political situation resulted in no fewer than *six* presidents in the one-year period ending in late 1932!

The Constitution of 1925, Chile's basic law today, had been

---

[12] Luis Galdames, *A History of Chile*, translated by Isaac J. Cox (Chapel Hill: University of North Carolina Press, 1941), p. 361.
   [13] *Ibid.*

written during a period of political instability and consequent disillusionment with parliamentary government. The blame for the
instability was laid at the door of congressional supremacy, and the
new constitution was written as a frank reaction against the parliamentary system. Because of this historical background, perhaps,
Chilean government as it has developed under the Constitution of
1925 exhibits a mixture of both parliamentary and presidential
forms and procedures. Political parties remain powerful, their
basic authority exercised through the congress. There are twelve
executive ministries. But from time to time the president presides
over a cabinet of more than this number of members, the additional
"ministers without portfolio" being appointed, in parliamentary
fashion, to strike an executive balance with the political composition of the legislature. Although the cabinet is appointed by, and
is theoretically responsible to, the president, its members can be,
and are, questioned on the floor of either house of the congress.
The legislature, however, cannot force the dismissal or resignation
of members of the cabinet. The executive ministers have more
power than is generally the case in presidential systems, since presidential orders lack the force of law unless signed by the ministers
heading the agencies of government expected to administer or
enforce the measures.

This unusual mixture of parliamentary and presidential features
under the Constitution of 1925 has become somewhat institutionalized in accordance with the views of the various presidents who
have held office under it; that is, according to whether they have
favored the parliamentary or the presidential aspects. Thus, Alessandri, when he returned to the presidency (1932–1938), tended
to fortify the presidential features, endeavoring to strengthen his
office against the legislative branch of the government. President
Pedro Aguirre Cerda, who succeeded him in 1938, presided over a
popular front—the only such government to come to power in the
Americas. The popular front consisted of a coalition of the Radical,
Democratic, Socialist, and Communist parties of Chile. As the
leaders of this coalition were in the congress rather than in the
executive branch, Aguirre Cerda tended to turn to the legislators
for advice and even leadership. His administration thus heralded
a return to the usages and practices of the parliamentary period.

President Aguirre Cerda died in 1941. He was succeeded by
President Juan Antonio Ríos (1942–1946), who incurred considerable opposition from the congress because of his effort to dissociate
his Radical party from its popular front collaboration with the other
parties of the left. Yet, although the Ríos administration was char-

acterized by renewed struggles between the legislature and the executive, its general effect was to reassert presidential authority, thus fortifying the nonparliamentary features of the constitution. Like Aguirre Cerda before him, President Ríos died in office. Gabriel González Videla (1946–1952), who followed Ríos, achieved an administration characterized by an internal balance of parliamentary and presidential features.   But Carlos Ibáñez, who returned to power as president in 1952, revealed a tendency to favor the presidential over the parliamentary aspects of the Chilean system and soon was involved in a conflict with the congress.

Thus, although Chile is today regarded as one of the more democratic of the states of Latin America,[14] the case for the parliamentary system is hardly proved by her experience.   It is still asserted in many quarters that the parliamentary arrangement offers a solution for many of the constitutional problems of the area, but in view of the brief and sporadic nature of Latin American experimentation with the system both the virtues and vices claimed for the arrangement must remain in the realm of speculation.[15]   It is at least questionable whether real, as distinguished from written, constitutional trends lie in that direction.

SOCIAL WELFARE. The classic view of written constitutions is that they are designed to perform three functions: to limit the power of government, to set forth the basic outlines of its structure, and to state certain of the broad hopes and aspirations of the constitution's framers.   Today many of the constitutions of Latin America attempt a fourth function: to render mandatory certain operations of government designed to contribute to the social welfare.   The social forces behind this trend have been discussed in earlier chapters.   Here we may note two influences affecting this changed concept of the constitution: the Roman Catholic Church, and world-wide trends in constitution-writing since World War I.

The temporal role of the Roman Catholic Church has been a center of political controversy in Latin America ever since independence.   This is not the place to explore the ramifications of this conflict.   Let it suffice to note that the Church exercised a vigorous political role at the time of the Spanish conquest of the

[14] See Russell H. Fitzgibbon, "The Measurement of Latin-American Political Phenomena: A Statistical Experiment," American Political Science Review, XLV (June 1951), 517–523.   Confirmed in a 1955 poll.   See also the same author's "How Democratic Is Latin America?" Inter-American Economic Affairs, IX (Spring 1956), 65–77.

[15] The reader may wish to consult Paul S. Reinsch, "Parliamentary Government in Chile," American Political Science Review, III (November 1909), 507–538; and William S. Stokes, "Parliamentary Government in Latin America," American Political Science Review, XXXIX (June 1945), 522–536.

New World, that today the overwhelming majority of the people of Latin America are Roman Catholics, and that Church doctrine has, traditionally, colored many of the social welfare provisions written into the constitutions of the Americas. Indeed, some Latin American constitutional lawyers, influenced by contemporary Catholic thought, have argued that the function of the state is primarily religious.

During the last century and a half, almost two hundred written constitutions have been promulgated in the various states of Latin America.[16]   Read chronologically, these documents trace, among other things, a troubled trend toward the gradual separation of Church and state.[17]   In their handling of Church–state relationships, the twenty states of Latin America may be divided into three general groupings.   The first of these groups embraces eight states, Argentina, Bolivia, Costa Rica, Ecuador, Peru, Paraguay, Colombia, and Venezuela, whose constitutions in one way or another provide for or imply a degree of union between Church and state.   This may range from a constitutional stipulation of formal union, through governmental exercise of Church patronage, through constitutional requirements that presidents or other government officials be Roman Catholics, to provision for a species of religious freedom under which the Roman Catholic Church enjoys an officially privileged position.   The second group embraces eleven states, Brazil, Chile, Cuba, the Dominican Republic, El Salvador, Guatemala, Haiti, Honduras, Nicaragua, Panama, and Uruguay, in which Church and state are constitutionally separated, much as in the United States.   Mexico's Revolutionary Constitution of 1917 is in a class by itself in providing for official anti-clericalism.[18]

Church-oriented social welfare provisions, representing the influence of Catholic Social Action, are found in the constitutions of many of the eight states in the first group noted.   These stipulations include such matters as protection of the family as the basic social unit by rendering divorce difficult or even legally impossible.[19]   In this group of states, and in some others, public schools may be

[16] See Russell H. Fitzgibbon (ed.), *The Constitutions of the Americas* (Chicago: University of Chicago Press, 1948), pp. 1–13, 32–33, 58–59, 137–138, 164–165, 202–203, 226, 297–298, 321–322, 366–367, 397, 442–443, 467–468, 496–497, 554–555, 604, 652, 666–667, 713–714, and 762–763.

[17] See J. Lloyd Mecham, *Church and State in Latin America* (Chapel Hill: University of North Carolina Press, 1934).

[18] See Miguel Jorrín, *Governments of Latin America* (Princeton, N. J.: D. Van Nostrand Co., Inc., 1953), pp. 23–27, 64, 205, 206.

[19] See Gordon Ireland and Jesús Galíndez Suárez, *Divorce in the Americas* (Buffalo: Dennis and Co., Inc., 1947).   For a case study of divorce law under the constitution of one of the states in this group, see Blanksten, *Ecuador: Constitutions and Caudillos,* pp. 131–136.

directly or indirectly administered by the Church. And even where the Church–state relationship is less intimate, instruction in the Roman Catholic religion may be compulsory in the public schools. In many of the states of the first group, tithes or taxes for Church revenue are levied and collected by the various governments.

A second kind of social welfare provisions, largely unrelated to the Church, is to be found in many Latin American constitutions. The general post-World War I trend has been to write social legislation into the texts of constitutions. Since sixteen of the twenty constitutions now in force in Latin America[20] have been written since World War I, many of them naturally reflect this recent trend. Such social welfare provisions are notable in the present constitutions of Brazil, Cuba, Mexico, and Uruguay. Their provisions include measures designed to protect workingmen, women, children, the aged, the unemployed, and the otherwise infirm or underprivileged.

Whether or not such matters properly belong in a constitution is a question familiar to students in the United States who have studied the constitutions of its various states. Those who argue against including such provisions generally claim that constitutions, because of their very nature, should be limited to the three classic functions of restricting the power of government, setting forth basic outlines of its structure, and stating general purposes or aspirations. Constitutions, they maintain, are expected to be long-lived, and soon-dated welfare provisions, particularly if spelled out in detail in the written text, defeat this objective.

As applied to Latin American constitutions, neither of these contentions is especially impressive. With respect to the classic functions of constitutions, it may be pointed out that, despite the existence of almost two hundred written constitutions, many of the nations have thus far generally failed to produce even the most fundamental constitutional function: genuine constitutional, limited government. Yet it would be difficult to attribute this political defect, should it continue, to the effects of minimum wages for the workingman or state aid for the aged or poverty-stricken. As for the lack of constitutional longevity, Latin American constitutions have been so short-lived ever since independence that it would make little sense to assign to social security provisions more than a minor share of the responsibility for the fact that but four of the current Latin American constitutions antedate World War I.

[20] Of the present constitutions, only those of Argentina (1853), Colombia (1886), Costa Rica (1871), and El Salvador (1886) antedate World War I.

Constitutions in Action

THE MEXICAN CONSTITUTION. Of the twenty states of the area, Mexico, Argentina, and Uruguay present constitutional problems of particular interest and significance and will therefore be discussed at greater length. Because of its basic importance, the Mexican Constitution will be discussed first.

Mexico's current Constitution of 1917 represents a remarkable attempt to cope with the basic issues which have been central problems throughout her national history. These are the question of centralization versus decentralization of government, the land problem, the Church issue, the ethnic problem of Indians and mestizos, and the issue of foreign economic influence in the country.

It has been pointed out that, while many so-called revolutions have occurred in Latin America, relatively few of these have been real revolutions. However, the storm that swept Mexico beginning in 1910 was, as we have seen in Chapter 5, a "real" revolution in as profound a sense as the French and Russian upheavals. The Mexican Revolution has met many basic national issues squarely, and the pattern of its approach is spelled out in the text of the Constitution.

The question of centralization or decentralization has been a general problem in Latin America. In 1857, Mexico adopted a federal constitution favoring the decentralized approach. During the regime of General Porfirio Díaz (1877–1911) the trend was toward greater centralization. The Revolution continued this trend in some respects, while in others it attempted to return to the federal arrangement. The Constitution of 1917 is federal, and contemporary Mexico is committed to decentralization in government.

The Revolution's approach to the land question is also set forth in the Constitution, which has effected a fundamental change in the legal basis of property ownership, establishing greater social control over land use. The Revolution is committed to replacing the system of large landed estates of the prerevolutionary period with other systems of land ownership. One of these is designed to create a large group of individual owners of small parcels of land, in the tradition of President Benito Juárez' unsuccessful program of the 1850's and 1860's. Another is the *ejido* system of collectively owned lands, designed especially for Indian communities. Particularly in the early years of the Revolution, Mexico sought a solution to its land problem through these devices, notably the *ejido* system.[21]

[21] See Eyler N. Simpson, *The Ejido: Mexico's Way Out* (Chapel Hill: University of North Carolina Press, 1937), and Nathan L. Whetten, *Rural Mexico* (Chicago: University of Chicago Press, 1948).

The Revolution's approach to the Church question is also set forth in detail in the text of the Constitution. Revolutionary Mexico has reaffirmed the disestablishment of the Church. Renewed restrictions have been placed on the ability of the Church to acquire land, and Church officials are forbidden to vote or to present themselves as candidates for public office. Christian political parties are also forbidden. In short, much of the Revolution has been distinctively anti-clerical.

Moreover, the Revolutionary Constitution seeks a redefinition of the place of the Indians and mestizos in the national life of Mexico. A part of this quest is to be found in the *ejido* system of communal land ownership, but the land program is only a part of the approach to the problems of the lower classes. The Revolution has also striven to eliminate illiteracy and has stimulated a renaissance of Indian culture. It has also tried, with some success, to destroy the older class system with a view to multiplying the opportunities available to the lower social classes.

The Revolution has likewise attacked the problem of foreign economic influences in the country. The constitution has placed restrictions and limitations upon the right of foreigners to acquire property in Mexico. Especially affected by these measures have been large "North American" and British interests. Expropriation and other measures of the Revolution have deprived them of their holdings in such segments of the Mexican economy as land, oil, and transportation. Foreigners attempting to do business in Mexico frequently find themselves discriminated against by the pattern of the Revolutionary Constitution and laws.

Thus, we may say in general that Mexico's remarkable Revolutionary Constitution of 1917 has institutionalized the precepts, content, and process of what is probably Latin America's most profound revolution of the twentieth century.

CONSTITUTIONAL PROBLEMS IN ARGENTINA. Argentina's political experience is unique in many ways. As far as constitutional problems are concerned, the fate of the country's celebrated Constitution of 1853 certainly merits attention here. The promulgation of that document signified the termination of a generation of civil war and military dictatorship and the inauguration of three-quarters of a century of relatively stable and orderly constitutional government.

Frankly modeled after the Constitution of the United States, yet differing from it in some respects, the Argentine Charter of 1853 provided for a federal system and presidential government. During the seventy-seven year period which ended in 1930, Argentine constitutional forms and practices closely resembled those of the United

States. Although these years after 1853 were, on the whole, years of constitutional government and a measure of democracy, national life was essentially dominated by the landowning class. Less privileged Argentines, though they enjoyed many civil and political liberties, remained essentially outside the processes of government. Politics seemed to be the monopoly of a social class, the landowning *estancieros*. Within this class, perhaps no more than two hundred families exercised the controlling voice. Imperfect as this picture of constitutional government and democracy may be, it is worthy of note, because Argentina's record on this score from 1853 until 1930 is not easily matched elsewhere in Latin America.

Two rebellions, one in 1930 and the second in 1943, dealt staggering blows to constitutional government in Argentina. The first of these, the revolution of 1930, was led by General José F. Uriburu, who overthrew the government of President Hipólito Irigoyen. At the time, Uriburu's revolt appeared to many Argentines to be a minor matter. "My personal impression was that the so-called revolution consisted of a twelve-hour parade of cadets from the Military School," one eyewitness wrote. "With the exception of a bloody incident at the Plaza de Mayo,[22] where two cadets and a civilian lost their lives, the parade met with no resistance."[23]

Unimpressive as the revolution of 1930 may have seemed at the time, it came to affect Argentine national life in four ways, each of them of some lasting significance. First, the rebellion seriously interrupted the constitutional stability the nation had enjoyed during much of the preceding three-quarters of a century. Second, the coup raised militarism from the status of a covert to an overt and dominating force in Argentine politics: between 1930 and 1957 the country had ten presidents, eight of whom were army officers.[24] Third, Uriburu's rebellion brought the *Concordancia* to power. The *Concordancia* was a political coalition of the military with the Conservative party, the latter embracing the large landowners. This combination has had remarkable durability, endowing post-1930 Argentine politics with a flavor which came to be a major element of the national scene. Finally, European fascist systems were at

[22] This is the huge open square at Buenos Aires faced by the Casa Rosada (the Pink House), Argentina's White House.

[23] Quoted in Blanksten, *Perón's Argentina*, p. 36.

[24] These officer-presidents were General José F. Uriburu (1930–1932), General Agustín P. Justo (1932–1938), General Arturo Rawson (1943), General Pedro P. Ramírez (1943–1944), General Edelmiro J. Fárrell (1944–1946), General Juan Domingo Perón (1946–1955), General Eduardo Lonardi (1955–1956), and General Pedro Aramburu (1956–). The two civilian presidents after 1930 were Roberto M. Ortiz (1938–1940) and Ramón S. Castillo (1940–1943).

first admired and later imitated in Argentina in the wake of the 1930 revolution.

The second upheaval, in 1943, is generally known as the "Perón Revolution." Although Juan Domingo Perón, who was a colonel in 1943, did not become president until three years later, he was the central figure in the rebellion and dominated national politics from that date until his overthrow in 1955. The Perón era is still so recent in Argentine affairs that it is difficult to view it with sufficient perspective to evaluate its long-range significance. It seems fairly obvious, however, that Perón's regime has left three major marks on the constitutional life of Argentina.

In the first place, Perón's movement was another interruption in constitutional stability. The revolution of 1930 had a similar effect, to be sure, but *peronismo* was a far more severe blow to constitutional order. Uriburu and his associates had paid great lip service to the Constitution of 1853, and had gone to considerable lengths to appear, at least, to be governing in accordance with its precepts. Perón, on the other hand, sought extensive revision of the constitution, obtaining it in 1949. This was done, he said, "in order to: (1) bring it up to date, and adjust it to the evolution of the world; and (2) make it complete in the different aspects in which it evidently is not, in accordance with the life we lead today."[25] Given what he demanded in the constitutional field, Perón was able to preside over the second major disruption of Argentina's constitutional development within a generation.

Secondly, the Perón regime severely curtailed civil and political liberties. Not since the government of Juan Manuel de Rosas (1829–1852) had Argentines seen a dictatorship so destructive of freedom as that of Perón. During his presidency, opposition political parties, while permitted to exist, were rendered ineffectual. Only the *peronista* party was able to win elections. Both of the presidential election campaigns during the Perón period were conducted under states of siege, with many of the ostensible civil and political liberties suspended. Neither the press nor the schools were free; and radio and the theater were placed under a thoroughgoing censorship.

Finally, the Perón regime brought a social revolution to Argentina. For Perón came to power in an essentially agricultural country, a nation traditionally ruled by the landowners who showed little concern for the welfare or grievances of the lower classes. Yet Perón proclaimed himself the champion, not of the oligarchy, but

[25] Quoted in Blanksten, *Perón's Argentina*, p. 73.

of the lower classes. During his stewardship, a new class of "uncultured" folk, men of little social status, rose to political power. These people, many of them labor organizers, threatened the landowning "oligarchy" with social changes reminiscent of those of the Jacksonian movement in the United States more than a century before.

Many of the constitutional problems of post-Perón Argentina result from the necessity of coping with the *peronista* legacy. The situation no longer presents the picture of constitutional stability once found in Argentina, and so envied by other countries. From this standpoint, the nation's constitutional fabric cannot now be said to be the same sturdy stuff discussed in Leo S. Rowe's *The Federal System of the Argentine Republic*, published in 1921, or even in Austin F. Macdonald's *Government of the Argentine Republic*, published in 1942. Post-Perón Argentina is accustomed to living in prolonged periods of what has euphemistically been referred to as "constitutional abnormality." The Constitution of 1853 has been restored, to be sure; but the Argentine constitutional tradition is no longer what it was before World War II. That tradition, after all, now includes Perón.

Furthermore, just as Argentine political life is now more unstable constitutionally, so too does it involve more of dictatorship, more of limitations on civil and political liberties. Where once "every man was his own political party," where the theater brilliantly lampooned the political personages of the day, and the press severely criticized them, restrictions on such freedoms remain an integral part of the post-Perón atmosphere. For every Argentine who can remember the liberty with which President Irigoyen was criticized and caricatured, hundreds remember the days when "plainclothesmen circulated in bars and public places, listening for public expressions of disagreement with the regime. . . . People looked over their shoulders before expressing a critical opinion. The waiter might be a spy."[26] This ingredient is also a part of the Argentine constitutional tradition as it moves into the latter half of the twentieth century.

Let it not be forgotten, moreover, that in one significant sense Perón did contribute something to the democratization of Argentina. The "uncultured" folk, the men of little social status, who enjoyed Perón's day with him cannot be expected to resume their pre-World War II political roles. As Argentines face and attempt to solve their continuing constitutional problems, however difficult,

[26] Ysabel F. Rennie, *The Argentine Republic* (New York: The Macmillan Co., 1945), p. 351.

this very process will itself take place in an environment in which more citizens of all classes can exercise a growing voice in the decisions taken by the nation.

THE CONSTITUTION OF URUGUAY. It is difficult to find anywhere in the world another pair of states so culturally similar yet so politically dissimilar as Argentina and Uruguay. Not only is Uruguay generally regarded as the most democratic nation in Latin America,[27] but its present constitutional arrangement is also unique in the Western Hemisphere.

Since the achievement of national independence in 1828, Uruguay has had a number of written constitutions. The first of these, adopted in 1830, provided in orthodox fashion for the presidential system common in the Americas. The second, which became operative in 1919, was peculiarly the product of the ideas of one man, José Batlle y Ordóñez, a gifted statesman whose career has left a lasting impression upon the small republic. The Constitution of 1919 introduced the plural executive to Uruguay, providing for a governmental system rarely employed by the states of the world. This experiment was abandoned temporarily in 1934, when Uruguay adopted its third constitution; but the plural executive has been resumed under the 1952 constitution.

The resumption of the plural executive, which Uruguayans call the *colegiado,* was the fruition of a campaign launched in the mid-1940's. Tomás Berreta was elected president in 1947, while the constitution of 1934 was in force, with a program calling for a return to the *colegiado* system. President Berreta's untimely death a few months after his inauguration brought Vice-President Luis Batlle Berres into office as his successor. Although Batlle Berres himself was comparatively unknown at the time, he was the third member of his family (the others being General Lorenzo Batlle and the redoubtable José Batlle y Ordóñez) to be president of the republic. Popular interest intensified during the Batlle Berres administration (1947–1951) in the career of Batlle y Ordóñez and in the plural executive system he had introduced earlier in the century (partly because of a family political feud between the latter's sons and Batlle Berres). This increase in popular sentiment favoring a return to the *colegiado* was sufficient to support the steps necessary to incorporate the plural executive in the new constitution adopted a year after the expiration of Batlle Berres' term.

The plural executive system in the 1952 document resembles the

[27] See Russell H. Fitzgibbon, "The Measurement of Latin-American Political Phenomena . . ."; and Fitzgibbon, *Uruguay: Portrait of a Democracy* (New Brunswick, N. J.: Rutgers University Press, 1954), particularly pp. 122–184.

presidential system in that both retain the principle of the separation of powers, carefully demarcating the legislative, executive, and judicial branches of government.   Indeed, the constitutional positions of the national legislature and of the judiciary are essentially the same under the *colegiado* as under the presidential system. The difference resides in the internal structure of the executive branch.   Whereas the executive branch is headed by one man under the presidential arrangement, the plural executive in Uruguay's constitution of 1952 is composed of a nine-man council.   Under the new constitution, the party receiving the majority of the votes when the *colegiado* is elected names six of its members to that body. The minority party controls the other three seats.   (In 1957 Uruguay and Colombia were the only Latin American countries with two-party systems.)   The chairmanship of the plural executive rotates annually among the members.

It is perhaps still too early to attempt any final judgment on this revival of the *colegiado*.   But in any event, the plural executive continues to engage the excited attention of Uruguayans, who persist in debating its advantages and shortcomings.   Some have argued that the system checked the chronic Latin American tendency toward a strong executive, and would, therefore, prevent dictatorship.   Skeptics have replied that it did not do so in 1933 when the *colegiado* was upset through a *coup d'état* led by General Gabriel Terra,[28] who presided over a dictatorship for five years thereafter.   The influence of the plural executive upon the political party system has likewise been examined.   The collegiate arrangement, it urged, tended to strengthen the two-party tradition, discouraging divisions within the two major parties[29] and the formation of third parties.   Among other points, it has been suggested, for example, that the collective nature of the executive branch tended to shift its functional emphasis from politics to administration.   It is also alleged that, since the executive could never be monopolized by any one political party, the other party was always a watchdog against corruption and other irregularities, and thus it minimized the need for later congressional investigation, coming long after the supposed misdeeds.

Whether or not Uruguay's second experiment with the *colegiado* will be more successful than the first remains an open question. During the first years under the new constitution of 1952, Uru-

---

[28] See Philip B. Taylor, Jr., "The Uruguayan Coup d'État of 1933," *Hispanic American Historical Review*, XXXII (August 1952), 301–320.

[29] Many quite formal divisions have long existed within the Colorado and Blanco parties.

guayans differed as to whether its virtues outweighed its defects.[30] One thing, however, appears certain. The small republic, with its plural executive, continues to enjoy the same good reputation as the most democratic Latin American state which it had during most of the life of the presidential constitution of 1934.

The Structure of Power

A distinction was drawn earlier in this chapter between a "real" and a "written" constitution. The first may be defined as the actual structure of power within a state. The second is the document promulgated as the supreme law of the land. In much of Latin America, as we have seen, a wide gulf separates the two. When they come into conflict in a given situation, the documentary normally yields to the real constitution.

The structure of power, that is, the real constitution, is intimately associated with the class systems of the various countries, discussed in earlier chapters of this book. On the whole, as we have seen, the social structures in Latin America are substantially more formalized and rigid than in the United States. In many nations, particularly in Bolivia, Peru, Ecuador, Mexico, and portions of Central America (notably in Guatemala), Indians constitute an appreciable portion, in some cases the majority, of the population. The upper classes, creoles or whites in most of these countries, are European[31] in cultural and historical orientation. The Indians tend to form the lower classes. In between stands the group variously called mestizo or *cholo,* a cross or fusion of the European and Indian cultures.[32] Negroes are rare in many of the nations, practically nonexistent in some, but are numerous in the Caribbean island republics[33] and in Brazil. Where they exist in appreciable numbers a similar social structure appears, except perhaps in Haiti, in which Negroes tend to be found in largest numbers in the lower classes. In these states a structure of power sometimes called "colonial" is marked by the survival of political relationships which have their roots in the conquest of the native peoples and in the previous slave status of the Negroes.

In such ethnically homogeneous nations as Chile, Argentina,

[30] See Russell H. Fitzgibbon, "Adoption of a Collegiate Executive in Uruguay," *Journal of Politics,* XIV (November 1952), 616–642.

[31] Portuguese in Brazil, French in Haiti, and Spanish in the other eighteen states, plus recent immigrants from other European countries.

[32] The mestizos are a middle class in an ethnic rather than the classic economic sense of the term. The economic middle class is small and weak. In some countries is is virtually nonexistent.

[33] Cuba, the Dominican Republic, and Haiti.

Uruguay (and southern Brazil), having predominantly immigrant populations, the social structure more nearly resembles that of the European countries of origin. The relationship of the dominant power groups to the society in these nations tends to follow lines more like those of Europe. In Brazil, because of its regional complexity, social structure and power structure in the northern states differ greatly from those in the southern states, where mestizos (*caboclos*) or European immigrants make up the population base.

The socio-political structure has sometimes been described as feudal, but this is a misleading oversimplification. Many elements of the hierarchical structure can be seen, but Latin American students of the sociology of politics have frequently called attention to the fluidity of their society. This fluidity is characterized by the absence of the stabilizing influence of a peasant class closely attached to small land holdings, except in the Indian towns, as well as by the lack of a class of small free-holders, save in a few areas. A proletariat of landless agricultural workers, whose existence explains much of the social instability, has often provided the basis upon which demagogic militarists or politicians have created dictatorial power structures. At other times the fear that such regimes might arise has led the ruling class to support arbitrary militarist regimes.

Rapid population increase today, even though coupled with growth in economic productivity, has increased the pace of social change and the sense of instability which enables small ambitious groups to erect power structures which rule with thinly veiled force. Urbanization and industrialization, giving agricultural nations like Mexico an urban population of perhaps 50 per cent and others, like Argentina, an even higher urban proportion, have also changed the social structure upon which actual political power rests. Labor organizations tend to stabilize the political expressions of this dynamic social change, channeling it into more orderly political movements. Increase in the numbers of the urban middle class tends to increase stability. But the labor movement, as noted in an earlier chapter, has often been misused politically during the decades since 1930, while the urban middle class has seldom been able to exert its potential stabilizing influence.

BASIC CONSTITUTIONAL ELEMENTS. Thus, the structure of power or real constitution comprises the following basic elements in much of Latin America.

1. An upper class, in Indian countries the white or creole, controls the organs of public power and the avenues of approach to it. This group, which includes the large individual landholders, pro-

vides political leaders and government officials (either from their own members, or by adopting them from lower social strata) and sometimes even most of the voters. The overwhelming majority of the formally educated people of Latin America are associated with this class, which normally enjoys a virtual monopoly on the liberal professions and the higher ranks in the armies.

2. As we have seen, this upper class is often divided on issues arising out of conflicting regional interests, personal and family loyalties, sentimental residues from historic political crises in the respective countries, and, to a lesser extent, political doctrines and programs. These divisions within the ruling class underlie the traditional political parties and the basic patterns of national politics, particularly in those countries with large indigenous populations. Even in nations with powerful labor movements, the upper class seems not to have been effectively replaced by systems based upon such new urban elements.

3. The middle and lower classes, in some cases constituting up to 85 per cent of the national population, are largely excluded from active participation in government and politics. In Indian America, Indians rarely vote. Their contacts with government are primarily through tax collectors, police officials, and military recruiting officers. The tidings brought by these people are rarely regarded as good news by the Indian. Mestizos participate in the political "national life" on a somewhat larger scale, depending upon the country, than do Indians. In homogeneous mestizo countries, or those more largely European in population, the pattern differs. In some of these countries the real power structure is today undergoing significant change, as noted in the earlier chapter on revolutions. But even here the dominance of a ruling class is still evident.

4. This structure of power is supported by the patterns of land-ownership, the attitude of the Church, armed force, the class distribution of literacy, and other social institutions and interests. To a lesser extent it is written into constitutions and other laws.

5. The tradition of monarchy is so deeply embedded in both the Spanish and Indian cultures that it enhances a continuing authoritarianism in government, in the sense in which Vilfredo Pareto spoke of cultural residues. As will be seen in the next chapter, this tradition helps to explain the phenomenon of the strong executive typical throughout Latin America.

6. Although the hereditary principle in selecting new rulers has now been abandoned, electoral systems frequently do not perform this function effectively in many states. Thus, in some countries, succession in power is achieved by an informal process through

which a *caudillo*, the "natural" leader, the "man with a mission," is produced by a socio-political interaction within the ruling class.

This *caudillo* possesses a number of more or less well-defined characteristics. He is usually, but not necessarily, an army officer. He is frequently regarded as an indispensable man, the only one who can "save the country." He bears a striking resemblance to Max Weber's "charismatic" leader, who feels an "inner call" and is recognized by his followers as the "innerly 'called' leader of men." "Men do not obey him by virtue of tradition or statute, but because they believe in him. His divine mission must 'prove' itself in that those who faithfully surrender to him must fare well. If they do not fare well, he is obviously not the leader sent by the gods."[34] This is the *caudillo* called for by Simón Bolívar when he declared: "The new states of America . . . need kings with the name of presidents."[35]

CONSTITUTIONAL APPROACHES TO THE STRUCTURE OF POWER. A written constitution may make any one of several approaches to the structure of power. It may ignore the real structure. This is the "paper" constitution. A number of these are currently on the books in Latin American countries, among them Ecuador. One Ecuadorian political leader has said: "Our idiosyncrasy has been to omit from our constitutions any traces or indications of the complex which characterizes our nationality."[36] Or the document may recognize the elements of the real constitution and rest on or protect them. Such a charter may be styled a "conservative" constitution. It is perhaps significant that few of these are found in Latin America today. The charter may also combine the qualities of the two approaches already mentioned, in what might be dubbed a "paper–conservative" instrument. Examples of this type are the current written constitutions of the Dominican Republic and Nicaragua. Another type of charter may endeavor to alter the elements of the structure of power. This may be called a "revolutionary" constitution; contemporary Latin America furnishes several examples, the most outstanding of which is Mexico's Revolutionary Constitution of 1917. A charter may also unite the characteristics of a "paper" constitution and a "revolutionary" one, in what may be called a "paper–revolutionary" document, because it is largely a legal "cover" for revolutionary change by arbitrary means. And finally, a "revolutionary–conservative" com-

[34] Max Weber, *From Max Weber: Essays in Sociology*, translated by H. H. Gerth and C. Wright Mills (New York: Oxford University Press, 1946), pp. 79, 249.

[35] Quoted in Pío Jaramillo Alvarado, *El régimen totalitario en América* (Guayaquil: Editora Noticia, 1940), p. 107.

[36] *Ibid.*, p. 73.

bination is theoretically possible, though none of this type is found today in Latin America.

It is probably true that no constitution anywhere functions exactly as written. It is also probably true that the divergence between written constitutions and actual political systems is wider in Latin America than in most areas of the world where attempts at constitutional government have been made for a comparable period of time. This situation stems not so much from cynicism on the part of the architects of these constitutions as from extremely difficult problems in the relationship of government and politics to culture. Hence, in analyzing Latin American political systems, the student should address his attention to the cultural bases of the structure of power more than to the texts of written constitutions, since constitutional texts, as the foregoing pages may have helped to explain, at best afford limited insight into the real constitutions.

Suggestions for Reading

English translations of many of the constitutions may be found in Russell H. Fitzgibbon (ed.), *The Constitutions of the Americas* (Chicago: University of Chicago Press, 1948), and in a series published by the Pan American Union. Texts in Spanish may be consulted in Andrés María Lazcano y Mazón, *Las constituciones políticas de América* (Havana, 1942).

Fitzgibbon has given one of the best brief discussions of the subject in his "Constitutional Development in Latin America: A Synthesis," *American Political Science Review*, XXXIX (June 1945), 500–522. Two other articles in this journal have special value: Arthur P. Whitaker, "The Pathology of Democracy in Latin America: A Historian's View," XLIV (March 1950), 101–118; and W. Rex Crawford, "The Pathology of Democracy in Latin America: A Sociologist's Point of View," in the same issue, pp. 143–147. Kingsley Davis discusses the relation of social structure to political structure in "Political Ambivalence in Latin America," *Journal of Legal and Political Sociology*, I (October 1942), 127–150. These four articles are reproduced in Asher N. Christensen (ed.), *The Evolution of Latin American Government* (New York: Henry Holt & Co., 1951).

For the fundamental question of Church–state relations see George P. Howard, *Religious Liberty in Latin America* (Philadelphia: Westminster Press, 1944), and J. Lloyd Mecham, *Church and State in Latin America* (Chapel Hill: University of North Carolina Press, 1934). The Latin American classic by José Carlos Mariátegui, *Siete ensayos de interpretación de la realidad peruana* (Santiago, Chile: Editorial Universitaria, 1955), gives a Marxian, but not strictly dialectical, analysis of social elements in Peruvian political structure. Óscar Morales Elizando discusses the applicability of the classic separation of powers in *El principio de la división de poderes* (México, 1945). The reader may also consult George I. Blanksten, *Ecuador: Constitutions and Caudillos* (Berkeley: University of California Press, 1951).

Chapter 10

The Presidency

General Aspects

The Spanish American nations experimented with several forms of organization of the executive power in some of their early constitutions. These experiments ranged from centralized monarchy to weak committee executives. Portuguese-speaking Brazil, on the other hand, enjoyed more than half a century of success with constitutional monarchy before turning to a presidential system in her republican constitution of 1891, and French-speaking Haiti experienced several monarchies much less successfully, during its first half-century of independence. Sooner or later, however, all the Latin American nations adopted the strong presidency, concentrating the executive power in the hands of one official, elected for a fixed term of years and usually not eligible for immediate re-election.

As in the United States, the strong executive everywhere in Latin America has been premised on the tripartite separation of powers. An independent judiciary and congress have been expected to check abuses of executive power, while a strong presidency, an independent court system, and a conservative upper chamber in the legislature are to protect the rights of minorities against the excesses of popular assemblies. Also, following the example of the United States, many countries experimented with various patterns of political decentralization, which they usually called federalism, to check excessive power in central government. Certain federalist concepts peculiar to this Latin American experience appear in the constitutions of four of the nations today, as noted in the preceding chapter. Yet neither the theoretical balance of power, nor federalism where tried, has much deterred an apparently natural tendency toward

252

concentration of power. As a result, the presidency has usually monopolized the power structure, dwarfing the other branches of government into relative insignificance.

It has been suggested that this exaggerated presidentialism of the Latin American republics is due to the exotic character of the presidency, an institution of government copied especially from the United States. It has also been attributed to the adoption of the equally novel doctrine of the separation of powers. Each of these doubtless had its effect, but other factors, as we shall see, also contributed to giving the presidency the peculiar character of presidential dictatorship it has frequently assumed.[1]

Some writers have urged that the very nature of the presidential system tends to make the president supreme.[2] One such critic asserts that its success in the United States has been a miracle. "Those more charitably inclined," he asserts, "will ascribe the happy results to the integrating and moderating influence of public opinion which, in turn, is conditioned by the relatively high standards of political education. But history does not repeat itself and, transplanted to a less favorable environment, the North American system has failed to give either good government or personal security."[3]

The presidency, more than some other forms of organization of the executive power, may well carry within it the possibility of dictatorship unless limited by a successful division of powers. The ideal president, as Lord Bryce observed, is "a strong man, resolute, prudent, and popular."[4] During a severe political crisis such a man may well be persuaded that only the power of his office stands between the nation and political chaos. In the United States, presidents Lincoln, Cleveland, Wilson, and Franklin Roosevelt employed extraordinary powers at such times. A less prudent or more personally ambitious man may be led to arbitrary exercise of power, perhaps even welcoming the opportunity it provides. The *coup d'état* of President Gabriel Terra of Uruguay in 1933 may perhaps be explained in this fashion.[5] However much the nature of the

[1] See James Bryce, *South America* (Rev. ed., New York: The Macmillan Co., 1916), p. 538; Annibal Freire da Fonseca, *Do poder executivo na república brazileiro* (Rio de Janeiro: Imp. Nacional, 1916), p. 15, and his significant quotation of Ruy Barbosa, *Actos inconstitucionaes do congresso e do executivo* (1892), on p. 11; Karl Lowenstein, "The Presidency Outside the United States," *Journal of Politics*, XI (August 1949), 447–496 (also Spanish trans. in *Boletín del Instituto de Derecho Comparado de México*, II (May–August 1949), 15–64.

[2] Émile Giraud, *Le pouvoir exécutif dans les démocraties de l'Europe et de l'Amérique* (Paris: Librairie du Recueil Sirey, 1938), p. 64.

[3] Karl Lowenstein, *op. cit.*, p. 452.

[4] *The American Commonwealth* (New York: The Macmillan Co., 1926), I, 227.

[5] See Philip B. Taylor, Jr., "The Uruguayan Coup d'État of 1933," *Hispanic American Historical Review*, XXXII (August 1952), 301–320.

office may be the cause, not only the worst but some of the best presidents in Latin America, from Simón Bolívar and José San Martín to those of the present day, have felt obliged to assume dictatorial powers for greater or lesser periods of time.

Certain elements in Latin American culture and social structure have also encouraged what has been appropriately called an "exaggerated presidentialism." Bolívar was early convinced that what he called *pardocracia*, the demagogic exploitation of racial-cultural tensions and unrest, required a strong executive. "The diversity of racial origin," he said, "will require an infinitely firm hand and great tactfulness in order to manage this heterogeneous society."[6] He ascribed the defeat of the first Venezuelan republic to the weakness of its committee-type executive and recalled how Spanish loyalists had turned the half-breed *castas* against the republican leaders. Like other independence leaders, he may also have been influenced by the example of the French Revolution and by Rousseau's idea that dictatorship sometimes became necessary in a democracy.

At all events, the history of the presidency in Spanish America has fulfilled Bolívar's prediction. The most successful presidents, even those most firmly addicted to constitutional government, have dominated their legislatures and have often resorted to the exercise of extraordinary powers in suppressing armed opposition. One sympathetic interpreter of Mexico even goes so far as to write that her president has always had to be something of a dictator.[7] This is an obvious overstatement, for not all Mexican presidents have really been dictators, unless that term is used so broadly as to have little meaning. Moreover, not all those who have acted in an authoritarian manner have had to do so. Yet something in the conditions governing Mexican political life causes the political process to center in the president to an extraordinary degree. The same tendency appears to such an extent throughout Latin America that the thoughtful student in the United States may well be led to marvel at the form assumed by the presidential institution when transplanted into another environment.[8]

Lord Bryce mentioned three forms of political organization which he believed might have been better adapted than presidentialism

[6] Address to Congress of Angostura, February 15, 1819, in Vicente Lecuna and Harold A. Bierck, Jr., *Selected Writings of Bolívar* (New York: Colonial Press, 1951), I, 182.

[7] Frank Tannenbaum, *Mexico: The Struggle for Bread and Peace* (New York: Alfred A. Knopf, Inc., 1950), p. 686. See also his "Personal Government in Mexico," *Foreign Affairs*, XXVII (October 1948), 44–57.

[8] "Elle [l'étude du régime presidential dans l'Amérique latine] montre combien différentes peuvent être les fruits d'un même régime quand il est transplanté sous un autre climat." Émile Giraud, *op. cit.*, p. 56.

to then existing social and economic conditions, especially among what he called "the aboriginal peoples in the tropical regions."[9] But no one familiar with the political history of Latin America imagines that the alternatives he suggested—tribal government, monarchy, or a constitutional class oligarchy—would have had much chance of success. With the exception of Uruguay, which in 1952 re-adopted the collegiate executive, and the possible exception of Cuba, whose modification of the parliamentary system is currently in abeyance, every Latin American nation which has experimented with other forms of the executive (Haiti, lifetime presidency and monarchy; Brazil, monarchy; Mexico, monarchy; Paraguay, the lifetime consulate of Francia; and Chile, parliamentary government) has returned to the unipersonal executive, elected for a fixed term of years. Experience suggests at least the possibility that Uruguay and Cuba might some day return to the type. Thus a century and a quarter of republican government in Latin America, while revealing in so many ways the agony of the ordeal predicted by Bolívar and later observed by Alberdi, seems also to have shown the presidential regime, whatever defects and shortcomings it may have had, to be the one best suited to Latin American needs.[10]

Like the United States, Latin America has its advocates of the superiority of the parliamentary system. One of these, a Mexican, has recently written, with unnecessary condescension, that the presidential regime is better suited to Mexico because of the "backwardness" of its people.[11] The experience of republican government in Mexico, or in the Americas generally, hardly proves such a broad causal principle. Indeed, if one is looking for causes in the Latin American scene, it would seem more logical to assume that complicated ethnic problems in many countries and the rapidly changing social basis of politics everywhere have necessitated a strong executive both to restrain forces of disorder and to institute neces-

[9] *Modern Democracies* (New York: The Macmillan Co., 1931), I, 203–207. See also Giraud, *op. cit.*, pp. 56, 64.

[10] "Necesitamos un estado fuerte, bien organizado. Dentro del estado, una administración formada por hombres capaces y que conozcan nuestro problema humano. Necesitamos un Poder Ejecutivo fuerte, no solo desde el punto de vista político, sino fuerte también por los elementos con que cuente y por las amplias facultades que lo coloquen en condiciones de solucionar enérgica e inmediatamente los problemas del país. Que esté en posibilidad de asumir poderes dictatoriales, principalmente en algunos aspectos de la vida económica. Que pueda obrar con mano de hierro para detener el desbarajuste ocasionado par el egoismo individual." Hector Ornelas K., *¿Hacia dónde va la administración pública mexicana?* (Mexico: Universidad Nacional, 1943), pp. 20–21.

[11] Herminio Álvarez B., *La eficacia de las atribuciones del poder ejecutivo en los regímenes parlamentario y presidencial* (Mexico: Universidad Nacional, 1943), p. 33.

sary reforms. Lord Bryce, confirmed believer in parliamentary government that he was, spoke more to the point when he concluded that it was not necessary to discuss the presidency "as a danger to democracy," since it was "only in countries where constitutional government is not well settled, as is still the case in most of the republics of Spanish America . . . , that the head of the executive can venture to aim at a dictatorship. . . ."[12]

Evolution of the Presidency

Three groups of factors shaped the presidency in Latin America: (1) those derived from the Iberian tradition, both national and colonial, (2) the events and ideas of the independence movements, and (3) the political experience of the nations after independence.

THE IBERIAN TRADITION. A deep-rooted tradition of political absolutism and personal government was inherited from the nations of the Iberian Peninsula and especially from Spain, where limited monarchy had disappeared under the Hapsburgs and Bourbons. The leaders of independence felt a strong antipathy toward all things Spanish and tended to improvise political institutions or to copy those of other nations. Yet after initial experiments with weak executives in Mexico, Venezuela, and Chile, they gave to the Spanish American president many of the attributes and characteristics of the Spanish monarch, or, more specifically, of his representative in America, the viceroy. The tradition of an absolutism supported by a close union of Church and state militated against the success of a division of powers. The popular concept of political power as personal, derived from colonial paternalism, also tended to identify the head of the state with the state itself. The anecdote, commonly heard, of the peon who points to the president saying, "There goes the government," may express merely a folk idea of the personal nature of political power, inherited from the Iberian tradition, which persists after a century and a quarter of republican government. But the idea is deeply embedded in legal thought, for example, in the juridical concept found in the constitution of Peru that the president of the republic "personifies the nation." Bolívar expressed a similar concept of the office in his message to the congress of Bolivia (1826) when he described the life-term presidency as "the sun which, fixed in its orbit, imparts life to the universe."

INFLUENCE OF INDEPENDENCE MOVEMENTS. The bitterness and frustration of the long struggle for independence in Spanish America accentuated this tendency toward a powerful executive by giving

[12] *Modern Democracies*, II, 358.

pre-eminence to the successful military leaders, whether citizen-soldiers like Simón Bolívar or professionals like General San Martín. Congresses were not strong enough to counterbalance this power of the military leaders. For although they played an important role in Latin American independence, nowhere did their role equal in autonomy that of the Continental Congress in the United States.

Another influence favoring the strong executive was the Spanish Constitution of 1812, in effect in America from 1812 to 1814 and again from 1820 to 1823. The political norms of this constitution—its lack of anti-clericalism, its provision for a regency elected by the Cortes, its council of state appointed by the crown upon proposal of the Cortes (Arts. 231–241), its declaration that the king was not subject to responsibility (Art. 168), coupled with provisions for the responsibility of ministers (Arts. 225–229)—were echoed frequently in the constitutional controversies of Spanish America, especially, but not exclusively, by those elements tending toward monarchism. Such provisions appealed to many statesmen as logical means for making the transition from Spanish absolutism to constitutional government, whether monarchical or republican.[13]

Historical studies have shown that the reaction against the Bourbon policy of political centralization was one of the causes of the independence movements. Because of the strength of this sentiment, early constitution-makers in Venezuela, Chile, Mexico, and Argentina limited the executive even more strictly than had been the case in the Spanish Constitution of 1812. Bolívar, as previously noted, explained the failure of the first republic in Venezuela upon this basis, and in Mexico Morelos complained similarly of the weakness of the executive power under the constitution of 1814. Many Spanish American liberals, on the other hand, considered the Spanish charter a model for the relationship of the executive to the congress, while their more conservative countrymen who leaned toward monarchism saw in it the way to make monarchy acceptable in the New World.

Bolívar recommended to the Venezuelan Congress of Angostura (1819) careful examination of the "republican features" of the British constitution. He seems not to have fully understood the system of cabinet government growing up in Britain at the time, but what impressed him, in respect to the executive power, was the stabilizing role of the monarch in a hierarchical society, a role which he was certain would be even greater in one which was non-hierarchical. Seeking the republican equivalent of the monarch who governed

[13] For the Constitution of 1812 see Arnold R. Verduin, *Manual of Spanish Constitutions, 1808–1931* (Ypsilanti, Mich.: University Printers, 1941).

through others, he came to believe that a life-term presidency would reconcile the strong executive with the needs of a democratized social order.

French constitutions also influenced Latin American concepts of the executive power. That of Napoleon's Consulate found an echo in the Paraguay of Francia and, to a lesser degree, elsewhere. The later French failure to develop a strong elected executive served chiefly, however, to highlight the success of the presidency in the United States, making the latter the outstanding example to be emulated by republics. Thus, while later in the nineteenth century parliamentary government in Chile and elsewhere derived inspiration from the example of the French Third Republic, in the main the executive in Spanish America followed the northern model. This was true, at least, of the provisions written into constitutions, although the real structure of the executive power was often quite different. Many aspects of the traditional Spanish structure of absolute and personal power persisted in practice, while nineteenth-century experience brought still further divergences from the model.

NINETEENTH-CENTURY EXPERIENCE. As already noted, because the nations of Latin America lacked well-established legislative bodies such as those which waged the successful war for independence in the English colonies of North America, power gravitated into the hands of the military leaders. Unsettled political conditions following the war accentuated this tendency toward militarism and personalist politics. These conditions resulted in part from basic social and ethnic problems, but they also stemmed from a severe economic depression brought about by the disruption of international trade and the interruption of the essential flow of investment capital from Spain. All the new nations faced financial crises because of these economic conditions, and because of their inability to raise sufficient revenue by taxation and their consequent failure to establish the financial credit of their governments. A disastrous conflict between the Church and the state further weakened general confidence in government, giving rise to bitter factional rivalry within what was in most countries a small ruling class, while opening the way for military adventurers to seize power almost at will.

The social changes accompanying independence, especially the liberation of the Negro slaves and the growth in numbers and influence of the mestizos, led Bolívar to conclude that "the most perfect form of government is that which provides the greatest degree of social security, the greatest amount of political stability."[14] In his constitution for Bolivia (1826) he sought this stability through a lifetime president, whom he thought of as heading a hierarchy of power built around an aristocracy of veterans of the armies of independence. A vice-president appointed by the president was to be the acting executive and was to succeed the president upon the latter's death. These officials were strictly limited in their powers in order to ensure that the actual execution of the laws would rest in the hands of other magistrates. Thus, by avoiding the tumults incident to popular presidential elections, Bolívar hoped to establish a regime of law more consistent with Spanish political tradition and more in accord with the needs of the new republics.[15] Latin Americans rejected his proposed lifetime presidency. But the violence which accompanied the transmission of the executive power in many of the Spanish American nations during the nineteenth century led many thoughtful men to believe that his analysis was in many respects correct, even though the remedy he proposed was unacceptable.[16]

Those countries which enjoyed the earliest success in achieving stable constitutional government—Chile, Colombia, Argentina after 1853, and Brazil (under monarchy until 1889)—did so under strong executives. Where political and social conditions were less stable and institutions of government weak, revolution by armed force became almost a fixed habit. In the unhappy political history of Mexico, although there were several notable constitutional regimes prior to that of Benito Juárez, and although Porfirio Díaz maintained political stability by a rule of iron from 1876 to 1910, examples of the peaceful transmission of the presidency were few until after 1920. The first peaceful transfer of the presidential office in Bolivia occurred in 1855, when President Manuel I. Belzú managed to hand over the office to his own choice as a successor, General Jorge Córdoba. In many countries, efforts were made to control presidential power with strict constitutional limitations, although the outcome often was that the president, once in office, seized

[14] Víctor Belaúnde, *Bolívar and the Political Thought of the Spanish American Revolution.* Quoted by Russell Fitzgibbon in the *American Political Science Review,* XLIV (March 1950), 120. Belaúnde's translation of the Address to the Congress of Angostura (1819) differs somewhat from the translation by Lecuna and Bierck, *op. cit.*

[15] Message to the Congress of Bolivia, May 25, 1826, in Lecuna and Bierck, *op. cit.,* II, 596–606.

[16] For a recent reflection of this view see the study of Antonio Leocadia Guzmán Blanco of Venezuela, by Ramón Díaz Sánchez, entitled *Guzmán: Elipse de una ambición de poder* (Caracas, Venezuela: Ministerio de Educación Nacional, 1950).

dictatorial powers "either in a frank and open form or covertly, with apparent clothing of constitutional precepts."[17]

Émile Giraud's comment that the presidential regime is well calculated to deal with the threat of revolutions[18] seems to be borne out by the facts. The overwhelming power of the Latin American presidents, in comparison with the other branches of government, stems largely from this nineteenth-century experience of revolutionary violence. As Lord Bryce remarked, "In such circumstances, power inevitably fell to the executive head, the person whom the people could see and know, and to whom belonged the command of the army. The interest of the community required that this power, needed for the maintenance of order within and defense against aggression by violent neighbors, should be lodged in one strong hand."[19] Whether he gained power by election or at the head of an armed force, the president's power always depended largely upon his ability to control the army. Even in Argentina, where one president succeeded another constitutionally from 1862 to 1930, practically every administration was called upon to suppress an armed uprising. Constitutional government could be maintained because the presidents were able to depend on a loyal army to defeat the rebellions against their authority.

Late nineteenth-century liberalism, as noted earlier in this book, drew its support largely from urban business and professional middle-class groups. Its immediate aim was to secularize society, separating Church and state. Civilian parties strong enough to challenge the army's predominance had emerged in some countries by the early years of the twentieth century. Some of these *civilista* parties tended theoretically toward congressional supremacy or parliamentarianism, as in Chile. More often, however, they tended to strengthen the presidency, sometimes in alliance with the now more professionalized military. Nor did the success of the presidency always improve political stability, at least in the sense of orderly transfer of the power structure. The history of almost every country furnishes at least one instance in which civilian reformers turned to some popular military leader in order to gain or to retain political power. In fact, some of the worst military dictatorships resulted from just such combinations. Nor has the tendency disappeared completely in the twentieth century. In recent years, agrarian and labor forces in Cuba, El Salvador, Mexico,

---

[17] René Canelas López, "El problema del gobierno federal en Bolivia," *Revista Jurídica* (Cochabamba, Bolivia), XII, No. 46 (1948), 8–86.

[18] Giraud, *op. cit.*, p. 63.

[19] *Modern Democracies*, I, 204.

and Argentina have supported presidents in giving an extraordinarily broad scope to presidential powers.

Nineteenth-century Latin American presidents typically acted with a high degree of loyalty to the small, faction-ridden, but on the whole coherent political class. Occasionally, however, political leaders frankly sought more popular sources of support to further the interests of faction or party. Precedents for this demagogic political leadership are found as early as the independence movements, and *caudillos* leading popular military-political movements furnish many of the most colorful chapters of nineteenth-century politics. Such movements helped to spread democracy by extending the suffrage and by urging the popular election of presidents, as well as by increasing the participation in the political process of larger numbers of the emerging urban middle class.

TWENTIETH-CENTURY TRENDS. By the early years of the twentieth century, the very type of presidents elected in most countries changed because of the democratic tendencies. Earlier trends toward parliamentarianism and ministerial responsibility had also been arrested. The president, whether a constitutional executive or an irresponsible dictator, now tended to become the spokesman for more popular movements in national politics. Chile, which turned to parliamentary government as a result of the Balmaceda revolution of 1891, seems to be in some respects an exception which proves the rule. For the popular forces which Balmaceda had led arose from defeat in 1891 to triumph under Arturo Alessandri thirty years later. On the whole, the popular political movements of the twentieth century seem to have embedded the strong presidency in Latin American political mores so firmly as to defy change.

One important exception is to be noted—the movement led in Uruguay by José Batlle y Ordóñez, who served as president from 1903 to 1907 and from 1911 to 1915. As noted in the preceding chapter, Batlle became convinced that the presidency was a major cause of his country's political instability. Influenced by the success of a commission in the government of Switzerland, he urged upon his country the substitution of a collegiate executive. The idea was that each member of this executive commission would be responsible for the administration of one of the major departments of the government, including the key responsibility for appointments in the department. The political essence of the system lay in the bipartisan character of the nine-member commission proposed—each of the major parties would have its share in the political spoils. The principle was accepted partially in the constitutional revisions adopted in 1919, but abolished as the result of a *coup d'état* during the crisis of 1933. In 1951, however, both major political parties agreed to restore the system completely, except that council members were not made individually responsible for the ministries. Its bipartisan character seems to have lessened the intense party competition for political jobs, although some observers feel this has been accomplished at the price of an overdevelopment of the evils of bureaucracy. The Uruguayan experiment will well bear watching, however. Like the commission form of city government, its importance may not be so much in the form itself as in the attention it directs to the problem of effective organization and the use of the executive power.[20]

The Vice-Presidency

The vice-presidency, filled in the same manner and for the same term as the presidency, has been less successfully developed in Latin America. The reason lies within the Latin American political scene. In the early years, the Spanish American vice-president all too frequently represented a political party or faction opposed to the president and became the center of some revolutionary conspiracy or uprising to replace him. Consequently, of the twenty republics, only eight have retained the elective vice-president.[21] El Salvador, Costa Rica, Nicaragua, and Colombia have one or more official "designates" (*designados*) elected in advance by the congress (a device which strengthens the congress, while lessening the political danger of the "designate"). But most of the present constitutions in those states which have no vice-president provide for the immediate election of a successor by the congress if the president should die in office. The president of the supreme court, the president of the assembly, or a minister acts as president until this successor is chosen. El Salvador is unique in having both an elected vice-president and "designates" chosen by the legislature.

The history of the vice-presidency in Mexico illustrates the difficulties associated with the office. Under the constitution of 1824 the person receiving the second highest number of votes became vice-president. The constitution of 1836 abolished the office, authorizing the senate to select an interim president (*interino*) from a list prepared by the chamber of deputies. During temporary

---

[20] On the constitutional change in Uruguay, see Russell H. Fitzgibbon, "Adoption of a Collegiate Executive in Uruguay," *The Journal of Politics,* XIV (November 1952), 616–642.

[21] Argentina, Bolivia, Brazil, Cuba, Ecuador, Honduras, Panama, and El Salvador. Panama elects two. Chile elects no vice-president, but the minister designated assumes that title.

lapses the president of the council of state was to serve. The *Bases Orgánicas* of 1843 retained essentially the same arrangement, providing for election by the senate. The Reform Act of 1846 also rejected the vice-presidency, returning to the provision of 1824 for the selection of an interim executive in the event of disability of both president and vice-president. The chamber of deputies, if in session, chose an interim president. If this body was not in session, the president of the supreme court and two members chosen by the council of government were to serve until an interim executive was chosen.

The Constitution of 1857 provided that the president of the supreme court, who was elected by the congress, would succeed to the presidential office. This system worked little better than that of 1824 for, as under the earlier charter, the president of the supreme court became the political rival of the president.[22] A reform adopted in 1882 provided for the succession of the president of the senate, or if this body was not in session, the president of the permanent commission of congress. Another amendment in 1896 provided that the secretary of foreign affairs or, should he be unable to assume the office, the secretary of government (*gobierno*) should serve until the congress designated a successor. Then in 1904 the elective vice-presidency was restored. But the restoration of the office was so thoroughly identified with the Díaz dictatorship, and so thoroughly discredited by former experience, that it was abolished by the Constitution of 1917. No serious effort to restore it has since been made.

Under the present constitution, congress or its permanent commission elects the substitute if the presidential vacancy occurs during the first two years of the six-year term, and a new election follows. If the vacancy occurs during the last four years, a substitute president is selected by the congress to fill the unexpired term. The most recent Mexican study of the problem reaffirms the view that the experience with the vice-presidency in Mexico demonstrates its unsuitability. Summing up the history of the subject, the author of this study writes: "Our entire history condemns the existence of the previously chosen substitute . . . that institution which, among other peoples, emanates properly from the basis of its nature."[23]

[22] For an example of difficulties under this provision see Ivie E. Cadenhead, Jr., "González Ortega and the Presidency of Mexico," in the *Hispanic American Historical Review*, XXXII (August 1952), 331–346.

[23] Jaime Vega Hernández, *La sucesión presidencial en México* (Thesis, Universidad Nacional Autónoma, Mexico, 1949), pp. 83–87. See also Felipe Tena Ramírez, *Derecho constitucional* (Mexico: Porrúa, 1944), p. 388.

Presidential Elections

QUALIFICATIONS.   All the Latin American constitutions require that the president be a native-born citizen and all require a period of residence in the country prior to election.   The required residence varies from one year in Mexico to ten years in Peru (Art. 136). These residence provisions had their historical origin in an effort to prevent the candidacy of political exiles.   A minimum age of thirty is set by seven states,[24] nine require the age of thirty-five,[25] and two (Haiti and Paraguay) require that the president be forty years of age.[26]   Haiti (Art. 31) requires ownership of real property in Haiti.   Paraguay (Art. 46) and El Salvador (Art. 96) establish "moral and intellectual" qualifications.   Six nations require that the president should not have belonged to the active armed forces during the previous six months or year.[27]   Eight nations prohibit the election of a priest to the presidency.[28]   Most of the other constitutions are silent on the question of religious qualifications. Argentina and Paraguay, however, require that the president ascribe to the Roman Catholic Apostolic Faith.   Panama is unique in its provision (Art. 141) that a president-elect *who has no religious belief* may dispense with the invocation to God in his oath of office.

Popular attention has too frequently been directed to the examples of political adventurers who have "captured" the presidency by force and who have had no apparent qualifications except a certain unscrupulousness and the ability to retain the loyalty of their armed followers.   Unfortunately, there have been such instances.   But it would be a mistake, even in these cases, always to accept the criticisms of their political enemies at face value or to infer that such presidents always lack completely the requisite ability.   On the other hand, the men elected to the office under more normal conditions have generally been men of high character and ability, sometimes exceptionally so.   They have usually been university graduates, lawyers, soldiers, and in more recent years often journalists or engineers, with experience in politics and a high reputation for probity and leadership ability.   And in spite of the

[24] Chile, Colombia, Costa Rica, El Salvador, Honduras, Nicaragua, and Venezuela. This reference, and those which follow are based on constitutions in effect in 1957.

[25] Ecuador, Guatemala, Bolivia, Brazil, Cuba, Mexico, Panama, Peru, and Uruguay, as of 1957.

[26] Argentina makes no provision as to age, and the Dominican Republic (Art. 45) seems to require only the age for voting (eighteen).

[27] Bolivia, Cuba, Guatemala, Mexico, Nicaragua, and Peru, as of 1957.

[28] Bolivia, Costa Rica, El Salvador, Guatemala, Mexico, Nicaragua, Peru, and Venezuela.   Note the concentration in Mexico and Central America where the nineteenth-century conflict of Church and state was especially intense.

low opinion Latin Americans frequently express of politicians, the office of president is generally regarded with respect.

DIRECT AND INDIRECT ELECTION. During the nineteenth century, presidents were generally elected indirectly by electoral congresses, by state or provincial assemblies, or by national congresses. In many nations property or literacy qualifications, limiting the suffrage to a small part of the population, further restricted the popular character of the office. As the century progressed, however, direct election became increasingly the rule, although as late as the 1920's almost half the republics retained some aspects of indirect election.[29] Today, direct popular election is the rule. Venezuela's constitution provides for direct election. Argentina, one of the last to fall in line, adopted direct election in 1949, but her electoral college, like that of the United States, had long been largely a fiction.[30] Haiti has given up election by congress (Art. 88). In Cuba a holdover from the system of indirect election may be seen in a constitutional provision (Art. 140) that votes be cast by provinces and that the party carrying each province receive all the electoral votes of that province.

TERMS OF OFFICE. Presidential terms range from four to six years. In seven nations the term is four years: Colombia, Costa Rica, Cuba, Ecuador, Panama, El Salvador, and Uruguay. Five have terms of five years: Brazil, the Dominican Republic, Paraguay, Peru, and Venezuela. Eight elect their presidents for six years: Argentina, Bolivia, Chile, Guatemala, Haiti, Honduras, Mexico, and Nicaragua. The terms of office for vice-president, where that office is established, correspond to those of the president. "Designates," where they are provided for, are usually chosen for shorter terms. The question of eligibility for re-election, closely related to the term of office and a very controversial matter in Latin American constitutional history, will be discussed later in this chapter.

THE PRESIDENT AND THE SUCCESSION. The conduct of elections was discussed in an earlier chapter, but the role of presidents in the selection of their successors requires special comment here. The process seems to vary greatly from one nation to another and even from one election to another within the same nation, depending

[29] Examples: Argentina (electoral college), Costa Rica (election by electoral assemblies), Cuba (electoral college), Haiti (election by congress), Venezuela (election by congress), Paraguay (*junta* of electors).

[30] As of this writing, the Argentine constitutional changes of 1949 have been abolished by the interim regime of President Pedro Aramburu, and the provisions of the 1853 constitution restored. Presumably this restores the electoral college system, unless the constitutional assembly elected in 1957 abolishes it.

upon the character of the candidates, the issues of the day, the strength and nature of party organization, and the determination of the administration in power. The degree of the latter's willingness or ability to permit free campaigning and to conduct fair elections is always an important factor.

In all countries, attention centers upon the selection of the official candidate, and within the limits of political realities, the president, if he has been successful, is able to nominate his successor. It is not always a simple matter, however, and complicated and intricate political maneuvers must often precede this choice. Cabinet members are changed and other important civil and military appointments are made. The prospective candidate is usually moved into a key political position in the cabinet, or conspicuously freed from office in order to campaign. These moves are aimed at satisfying various factions and interests upon which the president's strength rests, at checkmating others, and at drawing as much support as possible away from potential opposition candidates. In such federal countries as Brazil, Argentina, and Mexico, the governors of certain key states are likely to be changed. Usually it is also essential to select a candidate whom the army will support, or at least not oppose. This means a more or less open endorsement by high military officers, and results, in many cases, in the selection of military candidates.

In nations where political parties are highly organized, as in Mexico, much of this discussion and negotiation goes on within the party organization, culminating in the selection of the official candidate in a party convention. Before this official selection takes place, however, labor unions and similar groups will usually have acted to proclaim the person who is evidently to be the choice, so that the convention becomes a gala proclamation of a candidate who has, in fact, already been selected. Where parties are less well developed the outcome of the process is similar, but popular participation is much less in evidence.

Selection of an official candidate by an outgoing president is not in itself as surprising as it may at first appear. It seems, in fact, to be characteristic in certain respects of the presidential system everywhere. In the United States, most presidents, if not candidates for re-election themselves, try to dominate the party convention in the selection of a candidate. Even under the parliamentary system, a strong leader may sometimes designate his successor, as William Lyon Mackenzie King did in recent years in Canada, and as Winston Churchill did in Britain. The significant points about the Latin American practice, however, are the manner in which it is dominated by the military and the lack of a real, as distinguished from a *pro forma,* confirmation by a party organization which feels that it has the necessary freedom to accept or reject.

The official candidate usually wins, but not always. One may, perhaps, see a wholesome democratic trend in Latin America in the fact that opposition parties won presidential elections in four countries from 1945 to 1952.[31] In two additional cases the popular choice became effective indirectly. In Bolivia, in 1951, the prospect that opposition candidate Víctor Paz Estenssoro would obtain a plurality, thus forcing the election into congress, brought a *coup d'état* to forestall the revolution likely to occur if the congress failed to choose this popular opposition candidate. A successful revolt later brought Paz Estenssoro into office. In Costa Rica, in 1947, Otilio Ulate apparently won the election, but an armed uprising was required, in a normally peaceful country, to place him in office.

TRANSFER OF THE OFFICE. The violence and personalism of Latin American politics is what makes the selection of a nominee (in most cases the real successor) such a key function of the president. Even where the selection is made in accordance with the criteria of a democratic constitution, the Latin American president is still expected to manage a free and orderly election in such fashion that the victory will be ensured for his party's candidate. In any case, the exercise of this function requires great political finesse if a strong political structure is to be maintained. Whether the election is to be controlled or free, the successor is likely to be groomed in a cabinet post which is recognized as politically strategic. In Mexico, for example, it has frequently been that of *gobierno,* which handles the important relations with the states and their political bosses, national defense, or sometimes the ministry of public works. The more a regime relies upon the army for its support, the more likely it is that the ministry of war or defense will be the key political post.

Most of the constitutions provide that the congress shall examine the results of the election and declare elected the candidate having the prescribed majority. In some recent constitutions, as noted in an earlier chapter, this function has been assigned partially or completely to special electoral courts. In most countries, the congress elects between the highest candidates in the event no candidate receives a legal majority. Approximately half the constitutions give this right to the full congress, but a considerable number authorize the lower house to make the selection, as in the United States. In

[31] Peru, Cuba, Brazil, and Chile. Also, between 1952 and 1956, Peru, Brazil, and Ecuador.

Costa Rica, the older candidate receives the election in the event of a tie vote (Art. 138), while Ecuador provides that in such a case the choice shall be by lot.[32]

Many of the Latin American constitutions are meticulous in specifying the day and even the manner in which the incumbent shall turn over the office to his successor, what shall be done in the event the president-elect fails to qualify, and the form of his oath of office. This oath is usually taken before the full congress. Paraguay, however, specifies (Art. 50) that it shall be before the chamber of deputies, the council of state, and the supreme court. Honduras (Art. 116) and Mexico (Art. 87) provide that it may be before the supreme court or the congress, while Cuba (Art. 141) prescribes an oath before the supreme court. A natural first impression of such provisions is that they are excessively legalistic— at worst that they are devices which help arbitrary regimes to keep up the appearance of constitutionality. It may just as readily be concluded, however, that such meticulous provisions are inspired by the prevalence of irregularities in the transmission of political offices and not just by Latin American love of formality. Moreover, another interpretation is at least possible. The thoughtful student, who considers these provisions against the background of the changing cultural context of Latin American society, may see in them norms significant for the formulation of that political will to act in relation to the selection of the chief executive which is so basic an ingredient of political stability.

The Principle of Non-re-election

Bitter Latin American experience with presidents perpetuating themselves in office and, perhaps, some influence from Spanish constitutional examples explain the almost universal rule against re-election. Almost all of the constitutions forbid re-election under any circumstances. The exceptions occur in the Dominican Republic, in Paraguay which permits re-election for one term, and in Argentina which, under a *peronista* amendment in effect from 1949 to 1954, permitted re-election after having forbidden the practice for nearly a century.[33] The Brazilian constitution has no clause

---

[32] Art. 72. For a discussion of this question see Oswaldo Miranda Arenas, *El jefe del estado en las constituciones americanas* (Santiago: Imp. de Carabineros, 1944), pp. 14–19.

[33] Bartolomé Mitre, president 1862–1868, was several times an unsuccessful contender in later years for the office. Julio Roca (1880–1886 and 1898–1904) and Hipólito Irigoyen (1916–1922 and 1928–1930) are the only Argentines who had twice held the office of president prior to Perón's re-election in 1952 after the change in the national constitution.

specifically forbidding re-election, but prior to Getulio Vargas no president of Brazil had served more than one term, even nonconsecutively, except Francisco de Paula Rodrigues Alves (1902–1906, 1918–1919) who died less than a year after assuming office the second time.[34] After the long presidency of Augusto B. Leguía, Peru adopted (1933) a constitutional provision typical of the rules against immediate re-election:

ART. 142. There is no immediate presidential re-election. This prohibition cannot be amended or repealed. The author or authors of the amending or repealing proposal, and those who may support it, directly or indirectly, shall cease effectually in the discharge of their respective offices and shall be permanently incapacitated for the exercise of any public function.

Mexico, still recalling the long presidential dictatorship of Porfirio Díaz from 1876 to 1910, provides in its constitution (Art. 83): "Any citizen who has discharged the office of President of the Republic, popularly elected or in the character of interim, provisional, or substitute, may in no case and for no reason again hold this office." Since 1910 no person has twice held the presidential office. Álvaro Obregón was re-elected in 1928, after an intervening term, but was assassinated before he was installed.

The rule of the one-term presidency, adopted by Chile in 1871, was a major step in the process by which the Chilean congress successfully challenged the supremacy of the presidency in the national government. In this, as in a number of other constitutional provisions, the example of Chile has doubtless influenced other nations of Spanish America. Even more challenging in recent years has been the apparent success of the rule of no re-election in bringing political stability in Uruguay and Mexico.

Many Latin Americans consider this rule of no re-election one of their greatest constitutional achievements and believe its maintenance is essential to constitutional government. "Continuism" has been due to personalist politics, to personal abuse of political power, in some cases to militarism, but more basically to the weakness of political institutions, including political parties, and to the lack of patterns and standards of political behavior suited to the needs of republican constitutions. As the functions of government

[34] Vargas came into office as leader of a successful revolution in 1930 after his defeat in a presidential election. He ruled as provisional president for nearly four years, then was elected president by the constituent assembly which drew up a new constitution in 1934. In 1937, by a coup d'état, he suspended the new constitution and the forthcoming elections, proclaiming a new constitution under which he ruled until 1945. He was forced by the army to resign in that year, and Eurico Dutra was chosen constitutional president. In 1950 Vargas was again elected (for the first time in a popular election).

have increased in the twentieth century, and with them the powers and duties of the president, it has become increasingly difficult for one man to retain the reins of power in his own hand sufficiently to ensure his continued succession.   Moreover, a president's perpetuation in office in the twentieth century usually means resort to the practices of the police state.   These practices few have seen fit to try, because the dynamic vigor of Latin American political life has usually driven self-established dictators from office, often with great violence.

The principle of no re-election is not an unmixed blessing, however.   Political leaders find ways of bending any constitutional provision to their own purposes, and this one is no exception.   The president who installs in office his personally selected successor may continue as the real political chief, as President Calles of Mexico did from 1928 to 1934, controlling the basic political decisions from behind the scenes.   As we have noted earlier, there are precedents for this power structure built around some figure behind the scene, both in the colonial vice-royalty, in which the king overseas served this function, and in the example set in the early years of independence by Bolívar in Colombia, Santa Anna in Mexico, Portales in Chile, and others.   In fact, experience with the rule of no re-election seems to show that at times its seeming success has been possible only because of such a political "strong man."   The fact that a president cannot succeed himself also limits his political influence upon the ever-continuing process of renewing the power structure, encouraging resort to intrigue or abuse of power.   This latter argument was used by President Perón in Argentina to justify repeal of the no re-election rule in 1949, even though he had unequivocally endorsed the no re-election principle at the beginning of his term of office.

On the whole, however, it may be concluded that the principle of no re-election is thought to be an effective way of limiting undue growth of the presidential powers and that it is firmly embedded in Latin American political mores and ideology.   It was a measure especially favored by the creole *civilismo* of the late nineteenth and early twentieth centuries.   What effect the new army–labor parties will have upon a rule which they have sometimes described as merely a survival of the "tired *criollo civilismo*" remains to be seen. Perón's re-election can hardly be said to have challenged the principle, even in Argentina, in view of his recent overthrow.

The experience of the presidency in the United States, which adopted a two-term rule only after Franklin Delano Roosevelt had broken the long-observed precedent of two terms set by George

Washington, throws little light on the Latin American problem. This United States experience might suggest that the need for the no re-election rule arises partly from the weakness of the Latin American parties and the consequent weakness in the power structure. On the other hand, the long six-year term, which is so common in Latin America, brings the situation closer to that in the United States, compensating for whatever weakness in the power structure results from the single term. This six-year term is slightly longer than the average incumbency of United States presidents, which has been slightly over five years, so that the typical Latin American president when he serves his term holds office about as long as the average president in the United States.

The Office of the Presidency

MAINTAINING THE POWER STRUCTURE. It should be clear from the preceding discussion that the presidency is the co-ordinating center of the power structure. All lines of political power and influence converge upon this office, and its functions reach to almost every aspect of government in some way or other. The president's position in respect to strictly executive functions corresponds more or less to that of the president of the United States, especially in that acts of secretaries or ministers are legally those of the president.[35] But in some respects his influence upon policy and action is greater because of the special nature of his political position. The latter requires him to dominate the political process of his country, eliciting from the changing political scene the elements of power from which he can knit together the general will to act. He must give this political force tangible form in the group of strong, shrewd political personalities with whom he surrounds himself. This function of consolidating the power structure he must perform whether he is leading the van of social and political change or heading a conservative political combination engaged in stemming the tide of change and maintaining the status quo. Failure to maintain his personal political position will almost certainly cost him the office.

PERSISTENCE OF PERSONALISM. The high degree of personalism still remaining in Latin American politics sometimes accentuates the personal character of this function of crystallizing the will to act within the political process. But in any case the essence of its exercise is not very different from the more impersonal performance of the same function by chief magistrates in other presidential

---

[35] Felipe Tena Ramírez, *Derecho constitucional* (Mexico: Porrúa, 1944), p. 376.

republics. The personalist view of the office often gives the impression, however, that the president's power and the scope of his functions are greater than they really are. For it is often an apparent requisite of politics in many countries that the president seem to make all the important decisions and to take all the decisive actions, even when they may actually emanate from someone else. Foreign observers are thus sometimes led to the erroneous conclusion that no political will exists other than that of the president.

In most cases, it must be pointed out, the political process is not that simple, even in the most rudimentary authoritarian structures which appear from time to time in some countries. On the other hand, there is little doubt that power and political influence are more highly concentrated in the hands of most Latin American presidents than in those of the president of the United States. The judgment of Lord Bryce in this respect is still true: "Legally the powers may seem the same; practically they are wider in the countries where constitutional traditions are still new and public opinion still weak or divided into sections by an economic or religious antagonism."[36]

The president spends much of his time in the public eye, although in recent years some presidents, for example in Mexico, have protected the privacy of their family life by refusing to live in the official residence. His life includes a constant round of official visits, ceremonies, appearances, speeches, and conferences with political, military, and other leaders. In some of the smaller republics, much of his time may be given to purely administrative matters. But this is obviously less possible in the larger and more complexly organized countries where the ministers increasingly assume most of the burden of administration. Where the minister of the treasury (*hacienda*) is responsible for formulating the budget, he may become a kind of administrative head. Frequently some one minister becomes a chief political aid. In Mexico, for example, it has often been the secretary of communications and public works or the secretary of government (*gobierno*). But the president cannot really delegate to anyone the basic responsibility for keeping the power structure intact.

When he owes his position chiefly to an army *coup d'état*, his political functions tend to recede into the background until the possibility of some workable party group or combination appears upon the political horizon. In such cases military influence is also much greater in administration. Under more normal conditions, especially in those nations in which the army is an important political force, and they are many, the president's relation to the armed forces falls within the sphere of his political rather than his administrative activity, and his task is to keep the army in the power structure. Thus, according to press reports, when President Velasco Ibarra of Ecuador was apparently told in December, 1956, to get rid of his minister of national economy or take the consequences, he responded with the adroitness of an experienced politician by firing both the minister of economy and the minister of defense.

RISKS OF THE OFFICE. Students familiar with the detailed manner in which every move of the president of the United States is watched and even planned by his secret service guards are surprised at the informality with which a Latin American president appears in public, mingling with crowds on thoroughfares and in general gatherings. The traveler is impressed with the ease with which one may approach the presidential residence in many countries. A recent European visitor in Chile reports that "the President sees his visitors to the door of his office and calls the next visitor. The waiting room, serious and unpretentious, circumspect but agreeably simple, seemed like the waiting room of a family physician."[37] It appears to be part of the tradition of the office for the president to take the obvious risks involved, thus demonstrating that he is not a dictator. Only dictators move surrounded by armed guards. Hence the political phenomenon, unthinkable in the United States, of a liberal president of Colombia (Alfonso López) being kidnaped by his political enemies in 1944.

There have been notable cases of presidential assassinations, of course, especially in Mexico in the early decades of this century. In 1913 President Madero and Vice-President Pino Suárez were shot while being moved from one prison to another after a *coup d'état*. President Carranza was assassinated in 1920 while fleeing the country after being driven from office. Then in 1928 president-elect Álvaro Obregón was shot during a political meeting in one of the suburbs of Mexico City. Controversial President Gabriel García Moreno of Ecuador was assassinated by his political enemies in 1875, and in 1911 Ecuador's great liberal president, Eloy Alfaro, met a similar fate. President José Balta of Peru was murdered by a dissatisfied army officer in 1872, and in 1933 Peruvian President Luis Sánchez Cerro was assassinated while reviewing troops. In 1946 President Gualberto Villarroel of Bolivia and some of his associates were lynched by a mob after his government had been overthrown by a rebellion. This lynching of a Bolivian president

[37] Tibor Mende, *América latina entra en escena* (Santiago: Ed. del Pacífico, 1956), p. 225.

shocked Latin American opinion, as an action of exceptional violence without precedent in the history of the presidency. Almost equally without precedent was the murder of President José Remón of Panama in 1955, under conditions which seemed to involve high political leaders. The assassinations of Anastasio Somoza of Nicaragua and Carlos Castillo Armas of Guatemala, both in 1957, suggest an increased tendency toward such violence.

The violent tensions which surround the presidential office have also produced a number of presidential suicides. Among the notable examples are those of President José Manuel Balmaceda of Chile (1891), President Germán Busch of Bolivia (1939), and President Getulio Vargas of Brazil (1954). On the whole, however, few of the many presidents in more than a century of the political history of twenty nations have met violent ends, despite the general lack of precautions taken for their protection and the turbulence of Latin American political life. Many have been saved, of course, by going into exile or by taking refuge in foreign embassies in accordance with the peculiar but well-established institution of political asylum.[38]

BROAD SCOPE OF POWERS. One of the clearest facts about the Latin American president is that his powers, both constitutional and real, exceed those of his prototype, the president of the United States, at least if one excludes what may more appropriately be called political influence. The usually discerning Lord Bryce seems to have overlooked the significantly broader constitutional powers granted to the Latin American chief executive when he assumed that the difference resulted merely from a broader interpretation given to presidential powers because of "racial and social conditions." The office of the presidency has constantly tended to receive greater constitutional powers, particularly in recent years, as the social functions of government have expanded. As a result, the determined efforts of Latin American constitution-makers to set constitutional limits to presidential powers often seem the labor of a mountain to produce a mouse.

Why has the Latin American presidency developed these greater powers, both in the real and in the written constitutions? The answer cannot be a simple one, for it involves socio-psychological aspects of Latin American life, social structure, historical experience and tradition, political mores, ideologies, even certain religious atti-

[38] The long period of political asylum of the Peruvian *aprista* leader, Víctor Raúl Haya de la Torre, in the Colombian embassy in Lima (1948–1954) became the center of a controversy between the two nations which was finally settled (1954) by an agreement, but only after several rulings by the World Court. See Carlos Urrutia, *El derecho de asilo diplomático* (Guatemala: Talleres Gutenberg, 1952).

tudes and beliefs. One Brazilian writer has recently argued that the growth of the presidential power, especially the regulatory or decree power, is a natural result of the president's popular election and independent position in relation to the parliament,[39] while a Mexican explains it, more pragmatically, as the result of the growth in administrative functions of the executive.[40] Perhaps the only conclusion which may be safely drawn is the very general one that the powers of the institution as it developed in the United States have proved inadequate in Latin America for certain reasons which scholars have not adequately explained and that a different structure of power, more appropriate to other aspects of the culture, has therefore evolved.

Certain pessimistic writers of Latin America in the early years of this century connected this phenomenon with a more general illness (*enfermedad*) of the body politic, an illness which they ascribed to factors of political disunity resulting partly from foreign intervention. As noted earlier in this work, some Americans, both North and South, insist upon speaking of the "pathology" of Latin American democracy, in spite of the obvious vigor and violent activity of the "patient." Francisco Calderón of Peru, on the other hand, argued that strong rulers of the *caudillo* type were essential to the social and political development of the southern republics. Other writers followed the lead of Anglo-Saxon commentators in laying the blame for the overly strong presidency on lack of political experience, political immaturity, illiteracy, lack of a well-developed body of public opinion—in short on socio-moral factors. In recent years it has often been explained as the result of the lack of a strong middle class.[41] None of these explanations is complete in itself, although each has some validity. For the authors of this volume, a better explanation is to be found in such factors as the fundamental ethnic and social transformation so many of the nations have been undergoing, the rapid economic change they have experienced, their rapid growth in population, and the urbanization of the past half-century.

COMMAND OF THE ARMED FORCES. The political importance of the president's relation to the army has already been pointed out. Invariably, the constitution makes him head of the armed forces of the nation. In spite of the fact that this power is usually not

[39] Carlos Medeiros Silva, "O poder regulamentar e sua extensão," *Revista de Direito Administrativo*, XX (April–June 1950), 1–5; also in *Revista Foren*, CXXX, ano XLVII (August 1950), fasciculo 566, pp. 339–441.

[40] Hector Ornelas K., *op. cit.*, p. 53.

[41] See Theo Crevenna (ed.), *Materiales para el estudio de la clase media en la América latina* (Washington: Pan American Union, 1950-51), 6 vols., mimeograph.

exercised personally, it is often the key to the effective exercise of all other powers. With the growth of the modern bureaucratic state, most rulers have given up the personal command of armed forces in combat which they once exercised. Since the days of George Washington, for example, no president of the United States has assumed personal command of an army. In many countries of Latin America, however, the practice continued during the nineteenth century. Presidents Mitre and Sarmiento of Argentina, for example, commanded armies personally. In the twentieth century, presidents of Mexico have usually assumed personal command of the armed forces when it was necessary to suppress armed rebellion. Numerous examples could also be cited of presidents gaining office as leaders of successful army revolts.

A provision in the Peruvian constitution which prohibits the president from taking personal command of the armed forces reflects the determined efforts of civilian elements in Peru to control this militarism. While it may have helped to lessen civil wars, it does not, of course, prevent the president from controlling the army when it is within his power to do so, or keep the army from intervening in politics. A different tendency may be seen in Colombia, where the appointment of those army officers not requiring congressional approval has recently been delegated to the minister of war. In any case, the president's function of maintaining an army which will defend the government when it is threatened by overt force is an important basis of his power. And, as pointed out in an earlier chapter, the recent increased military reliance upon expensive technological and mechanical equipment, for which the government is the only source of supply, also increases the president's power over the army and, hence, the general power of the presidential office.

PRESIDENTIAL APPOINTMENTS. Latin American constitutions uniformly grant to the president the authority to appoint and dismiss freely the members of his cabinet. A Latin American president, in point of fact, has greater appointive power than the chief executive of the United States. His appointments are subject to fewer constitutional limitations and checks, while various political factors help to concentrate this power in his hands rather than in those of party leaders.

The president's appointive power is particularly great in some of the unitary states, where it is not shared with state or provincial governors as in the federal republics. In some nations (for example Chile, Costa Rica, Ecuador, Mexico, and Paraguay) appointments of high military and naval officers require approval of the senate (or the council of state in Paraguay). In the Dominican Republic diplomatic appointments alone require senate approval, while in Honduras only military officers above the rank of captain must be approved by the (unicameral) congress. In Peru, high diplomatic officials must be approved by the council of ministers. Uruguay requires senate approval of the appointments of high military officers, the chiefs of diplomatic missions, and the attorney general. In most nations, the president shares with congress, or usually the senate, the appointment or election of judges. Many constitutions also require congressional concurrence in the selection of the attorney general. In Mexico, however, the constitution provides (Art. 73) that the president may freely appoint and dismiss the attorney general. In those nations (Argentina, Paraguay, Bolivia, Peru) in which the president appoints bishops, this power is usually exercised with the concurrence of the senate as well as of the appropriate Church bodies, and is generally thought of as *pro forma.*

The executive appointive power is further enhanced through the informal or political control of presidents over legislatures, which makes the latter's approval a formality, as well as through the lack of adequate provision for a merit system in the civil service. In the early years of this century, President Batlle of Uruguay concluded that the presidential monopoly of appointments, more than anything else, accounted for the frequent armed uprisings seemingly required to drive incumbent presidents and their appointees from office. In recent years, the tendency in most Latin American countries has been to bring appointments to positions below the policy-making level under civil service laws, new constitutions frequently requiring that presidential appointments be made in accordance with such laws.[42] But the realities of practice often fall short of these constitutional and legal provisions, leaving the president's control of appointments virtually unrestricted.

LEGISLATIVE FUNCTIONS. Despite the formal separation of powers in modern states, most national executives participate in some way in the legislative function. In Latin America the president's role in this respect, both constitutionally and in practice, is large. In all the nations his constitutional functions include sending messages to the congress or appearing personally before that body to request legislative action. Beyond that the functions differ somewhat in the various nations. In Venezuela, the constitution specifically author-

[42] For an example of a comprehensive constitutional provision of this kind see Title XII (Arts. 240–243) of the Panama constitution (1946) in Russell Fitzgibbon (ed.), *Constitutions of the Americas* (Chicago: University of Chicago Press, 1948), pp. 646–647.

izes the president to introduce bills into the congress, but in other countries the language of the charters is more ambiguous in this respect. The Argentine constitution, for example, speaks of the president sharing in the legislative process.

Political practice differs less, however, than these differences in constitutional provisions suggest. In all countries it is assumed to be a function of the president and his ministers to present projected legislation to the congress, including the annual budget in the form of an appropriation bill (the *presupuesto*). These projects may be approved, disapproved, or altered in congress, but they usually do not originate there. Only in Brazil does the executive seem to play a less important part in the initial formulation of legislation. In general, therefore, the relation of the executive to the legislative process in Latin America resembles that in Britain or Canada more than that in the United States.

THE ANNUAL BUDGET. Preparation and administration of the budget is one of the most important governmental functions everywhere, and in Latin America it contributes greatly to strengthening the presidential powers. In theory, the budget is prepared by the president with the cooperation of his cabinet, but in practice it is usually prepared in the ministry of treasury (*hacienda*). As will be pointed out in a later chapter, certain present tendencies in budgetary practice tend to increase the president's already great authority over government finances.

THE VETO POWER. In general, the veto power is broad, usually including the item veto on appropriation laws, for example. The majorities required to override it are often large, as in Cuba, where the requirement is a two-thirds constitutional majority. Such strict rules, together with the president's political influence over congress, greatly strengthen his hand in controlling legislation.

THE DECREE POWER. Any discussion of the president's powers must note that Latin American presidents enjoy a much broader power to legislate by decree and administrative order than the chief executives of many other modern republics. Constitutional provisions concerning this decree power and traditions concerning its use vary considerably among the states. Tradition also plays a large part in its exercise. One may discern in this power of the president an element traceable to his colonial antecedents, the viceroy and the king, for in the Spanish empire these officials were the source of most of the laws touching everyday life. Neither in Spain nor in Spanish America had legislatures preempted this power of decree legislation at the time of independence, as they had in the

Anglo-American constitutions. Nor have they done so since independence. It is taken as a matter of course that the president should dictate laws when necessary in times of crisis, and the frequency and seriousness of these crises doubtless explain in considerable degree the extent of this power and its continuance. Yet something in the general character of legislation in the Latin American countries also encourages its use. Laws are often formulated in more general terms than accords with the Anglo-American tradition, leaving broad powers to the executive to implement these principles by decree. These various factors combine to make the decree power one of the outstanding characteristics of the Latin American presidency. They also help to explain the president's traditional predominance over the other branches of government.

Uses of the decree power fall into two general categories: regulations to implement an existing law; and decrees issued in time of crisis, while congress is not in session. Decrees emanating from the presidential office or from the ministries, with presidential approval, often go to surprising lengths in including what might be considered new legislation. The decree usually has a legal form traceable to some law of congress which the president is in this way carrying out, even though in effect it may be legislation *de novo*. Courts have not been ready or very effective in checking the growth of the practice. Since these decrees often fall in the field of administrative law, they have contributed to the development of a great body of such law, as will be pointed out in a later chapter.

Decrees issued under the extraordinary powers exercised by the executive while congress is not in session have a more fundamental importance; it is these decrees which attract especial attention. A striking example was the establishment of the Republic in Brazil (1889) by decrees emanating from the revolutionary government. Constitutional provisions regulating such use of the decree powers vary from one nation to another. The constitution which gives the president the broadest authority is that of the Dominican Republic, in which the president is given virtual carte blanche to legislate to meet any emergency. In most of the others, provisions concerning presidential decrees are much more specific and careful. Some constitutions require that all decree laws appear automatically on the agenda of the congress when it reconvenes. If congress fails to act, however, the decree, in most nations, continues to be law. Obviously, since the president is usually able to confront congress with a *fait accompli,* little can be done about it by that body. Presidential decrees are rarely rescinded, unless a revolutionary change of regime intervenes.

Most of the liberal reforms of the Juárez period in Mexico were enacted by presidential decree. Nationalizing of the Church lands, for example, was carried out under the emergency war powers of the president while congress was not in session, thus ensuring the constitutionality of the measures. In a later period, remembering how land reform had bogged down in congressional debate during the Madero administration, Venustiano Carranza legislated agrarian reform by decree. When congress met after the law had gone into effect, its repeal would have been very unpopular.

The revolution which began in Argentina in 1943 brought a great amount of decree legislation. Congress was not in session and a state of siege had been declared. When it reconvened several years later, congress found a mass of decree legislation on labor and social security matters. In most cases congress did nothing about it until after the revision of the constitution in 1949, but meanwhile the revolutionary decrees remained in force.

EXTRAORDINARY POWERS. Most national constitutions provide in some form for emergency powers to deal with civil turmoil, territorial invasion, and other such crises. Democracies understand that the very continuance of law and order often depends upon a narrow margin of power exercised judiciously—upon the ability of government to act quickly and firmly in crises endangering the general peace. In the United States this power is exercised, when necessary, by either federal or state government. In Latin America, presidential abuse of these emergency powers has resulted in certain constitutional provisions intended to impose restraints upon their use.

All countries except Mexico provide explicitly for state-of-siege powers.[43] Haiti and Paraguay, for example, grant the executive the right to suspend constitutional guaranties, placing no constitutional restrictions upon this authority. This does not mean that courts recognize no constitutional limitations on the authority, but it does indicate the constitutional acceptance of the occasional need for concentrating all public authority in the hands of the executive. Other nations, the majority, prescribe the guaranties which may be suspended and limit the state-of-siege power in various ways. Under these emergency powers the president generally has the right to detain persons whose liberty he considers dangerous. Most

[43] The case of Mexico is not really different from the others, however, for Article 29 of the constitution provides for the suspension of constitutional guaranties in time of invasion or other national emergency, and the power was so used by President Ávila Camacho in 1942. José Aguilar y Maya, *La suspensión de garantías* (México: National School of Jurisprudence, 1945), pp. 46–50.

constitutions prescribe, however, that this detention shall not be in common prisons. Frequently the president is limited to transferring such persons from one point to another within the country. Peru (Art. 68) and Venezuela (under the 1945 constitution) permit exile in such cases. Bolivia (Art. 35) and Cuba (Art. 30), on the other hand, expressly forbid exile under state-of-siege powers. In Argentina, the person detained under these state-of-siege powers may elect between confinement and leaving the country.

In general, the basic constitutional authority to declare a state of siege rests in the congress. The president may declare such an emergency, however, when congress is not in session, with the approval of either the council of ministers or the permanent commission of congress, where such a body exists. Many constitutions require joint approval of the regulations by the council of ministers, and some declare the latter collectively responsible. Obviously, in some of the revolutionary disturbances, particularly after a military *coup d'état,* such constitutional approvals mean little and are used chiefly to "cover appearances" by preserving a fiction of constitutionality. Yet even this covering of appearances may serve a useful purpose in the minds of Latin Americans, because of the highly developed legalism and constitutionalism of their political psychology.[44]

In both theory and practice Chile has limited these extraordinary powers more strictly than most of the other nations. Its constitution (Art. 72, Par. 17) authorizes the president to declare a state of siege for a maximum of sixty days, but only if congress is not in session. Otherwise, the congress must act to declare the emergency and authorize the extraordinary powers. If a state of siege is declared while congress is not in session, this body must assemble within sixty days. When congress convenes, the presidential decree is before it as a proposed law. The president's state-of-siege powers are carefully prescribed. In dealing with political offenders, for example, he is limited to transferring them from one department to another or confining them to their homes; he may not imprison them. Moreover, these limitations have been respected by Chilean presidents, for example, González Videla during the state of siege proclaimed in connection with the strike in the nitrate mines (1946) which resulted in the outlawing of the Communist party.

In Brazil, the president has broad authority to proclaim a state of martial law when congress is not in session. Under this state of martial law his power extends even to "defining" crimes of treason.

[44] Rafael Errázuriz Edwards, *Los regímenes jurídicos de emergencia en las constituciones americanas* (Santiago: University of Chile, 1945), pp. 29–54.

Upon declaring a state of siege, however, he is obliged to reconvene congress within fifteen days. The Argentine constitution, profiting from the experience of the Rosas dictatorship, forbids the conferring of the sum of public authority upon either the president or provincial governors. The president may declare a state of siege upon his own authority only when congress is in recess. The *peronista* constitution (1949-1954) authorized him to proclaim a state of "prevention and alarm" whenever the public order was in danger, whether congress was in session or not. The frequent use of this proclamation of martial law was considered by Perón's opponents to have been one of his worst abuses of power.

It would be a mistake to assume that this extraordinary state-of-siege authority is usually abused. Abuses occur, to be sure, but they occur most frequently in the countries of least stable democracy. Because the possibility of revolutionary violence is always in the public consciousness in most countries, the president would be considered derelict if he did not take such extraordinary precautions when there is threat of disorder. Public confidence normally responds with approval to measures obviously taken to maintain peace and order, and presidential abuse of the power is an abuse of this public confidence. The wise executive who has consolidated his political position upon a broad basis of support will find a way to keep arbitrary measures to a minimum, as President Carlos Ibáñez of Chile did during the crisis of 1955, inspiring greater public confidence and support by declining to suspend the customary liberties. He will mobilize public opinion to meet the crisis by effective use of the radio and press, as President Manuel Ávila Camacho did effectively in Mexico immediately after the Pearl Harbor attack. At the same time he will take energetic measures to ensure that the armed forces and the police are properly prepared and alerted to deal with any disorders which arise, making sure that the public knows of these measures.

INTERVENTION IN PROVINCIAL GOVERNMENT. In the federal states, the power to intervene in provincial governments has become in practice another form of extraordinary presidential power. Between 1860 and 1930, Argentine presidents intervened one hundred and one times in state governments. About two-thirds of these interventions were requested by provincial governments, while in the other cases the federal government decided that intervention was necessary. Nearly half of the interventions arose out of quarrels between governor and legislature, with one of them appealing to the federal government against the other. Under the constitution, congressional approval was required, provided congress was in session, but sixty-four of these interventions were initiated by presidential decree while congress was not in session. Thirty-seven were authorized by laws of congress, but, in general, these came during the earlier years. Usually, in recent years, the president has simply waited until congress adjourned and then acted on his own authority. Out of these sixty-four presidential interventions only six were later sanctioned by the congress.[45] President Perón made extensive use of intervention, both before and after his election as constitutional president.

In Mexico intervention takes place either at the request of the state authorities (Art. 122) or when the senate determines that "all the constitutional powers of any state may have disappeared" (Art. 76). In the latter case, the senate elects a provisional governor, choosing from a panel named by the president. But in either case, because of his position as leader of the predominant single party and because of the tradition of the presidential office, a strong executive is almost certain to hold in his hands the power to make the real decisions concerning intervention. The secretary of *gobierno*, because he is responsible for federal relationships, usually handles these matters. Hence, the decision as to intervention is likely to be made with political purposes in view. It is often said that Mexican presidents have used the power of intervention to establish the predominance of the executive office.[46] But it would probably be more accurate to say that it has been used to maintain or strengthen the party's position or that of some group within the party.

The situation is similar in Brazil and Venezuela. Getulio Vargas used the broad powers of intervention lodged in the president's hands by the Brazilian constitution (Arts. 7–14) to intervene in both state and municipal governments during the 1930's in order to ensure his political control and to carry out federal measures of economic and administrative reform. The Venezuelan constitution extends the power of intervention even further than that of the other federal states, giving the president the right to declare a visitation of a state. This provision, reminiscent of the Spanish colonial institution of the *visita* (an inquiry into the conduct of any colonial official during his term of office by a higher authority), suggests the persistence of inherited ideas of the executive office.

[45] R. A. Gómez, "Intervention in State Governments in Argentina, 1860–1930," *Inter-American Economic Affairs*, December, 1947.

[46] Frank Tannenbaum, *Mexico, the Struggle for Peace and Bread*, p. 86.

It is even more significant as an indication of how the Latin American concept of federalism differs from that of the United States.

GOVERNMENT OF THE CAPITAL. Another important duty of the president as the chief executive, that of governing the capital city, will be discussed in the chapter on local government. In the federal republics, where the capital constitutes a separate federal district, this is a key political function, and the power is exercised through an appointed governor or a minister. In most of the centralized states, also, the executive of the capital city is a presidential appointee.

The President and Administration

PERSONALISM IN ADMINISTRATION. Public administration is the subject of a later chapter, but the role of the president as the head of the administrative structure will be discussed here briefly. It is easy for the student to misinterpret the frequent interventions of the president in obviously minor aspects of administration. The tradition of personalism is so strong, even in some of the most stable Latin American democracies, that the president will often act personally to appoint a friend to some office, to secure his relief from the application of some law or decree, or to authorize expenditures of funds for some specific purpose in his interest. It is not unheard of for the president to intervene in the administration of justice, but this is much less common than might be thought. Nepotism is quite general in the civil service, and political debts to those outside the family are also repaid frequently with administrative favors.

Most of this personalism in administration is not really necessary, even in the atmosphere of Latin American politics. Many of the most successful presidents have rigorously opposed it, and the trend today is toward more impersonal administration. Presidents are quickly judged on the basis of their susceptibility to the constant pressure for such personal favors, and much of the reputation for morality, integrity, and civic virtue, or their opposites, with which they are invariably tagged, stems from this particular aspect of administration. For our purpose, however, the important thing is to notice that this personalism in administration chiefly represents the president in the exercise of his political functions, not as an administrator.

It generally is true that presidents supervise the public administration personally to a greater extent than in the United States, but this is most likely to occur in the smaller nations and, above all, in those controlled by dictatorial presidents. Moreover, personalism in the civil service in the more general sense of the spoils system is still one of the major evils of Latin American politics, although in some states progress has been made toward a merit system. As we shall see later, the rapid growth of bureaucracies in recent years, whether or not accompanied by growth of the merit system, tends to decrease the element of personalism in appointments, as it becomes more difficult for the president to give personal attention to the many agencies of government.

Honesty and efficiency in administration inevitably depend to a considerable extent upon the tone set by the chief executive. One of the most serious charges to be made against many Latin American presidents is that they have not realized the extent to which their success depends upon using the resources of the presidential office to the full for the improvement of efficiency and honesty of administration. The administration of Carlos Prío Socarrás (1948–1952) in Cuba came to grief partly on this account, as did the reforming *aprista* government of José Bustamante Rivero (1945–1948) in Peru. The secretaries or ministers of state are directly responsible to the president, as already noted, and their acts are his from the standpoint of law. Practically, his freedom to achieve efficient administration varies widely according to the nature of the political and administrative structure in the various states. But in all cases he is constitutionally and legally free to act. The effective limitations to his action for this purpose are his political strength and his personal ability to use the powers given him.

Increase in the size of government clearly necessitates the development of a professional spirit and morale among public employees. Such a spirit requires freedom to execute the functions of office according to law without arbitrary political interference. A number of national constitutions authorize the merit system in public service, and a few nations have adopted general laws for this purpose. But adequate provision is not made for enforcement, and until this is done the president will often be his own worst enemy in undermining the efficiency of his administration. Ambitious training programs have also been launched, as we shall see, to improve the professional competence of civil servants. But all of this progress will be illusory until presidents who are determined, and strong enough politically to do so, make adequate provision for the recognition of merit. Latin American presidents must learn to say to their friends what Fiorello La Guardia is reported to have told his supporters in New York: "My first qualification for this great office is my monumental ingratitude."

MINISTERIAL RESPONSIBILITY.   The president, as the chief administrator, generally acts through ministries, which are usually declared by the constitutions and the various regulatory laws to be legally responsible for all their actions and subject to legal process through various administrative courts for any illegal acts.   Behind this concept of legal responsibility lies the Hispanic tradition of administrative and constitutional law.   Many of the newer constitutions specify this responsibility in considerable detail, in an effort to curb venality and at the same time strengthen the independence of the bureaucracy.   A 1939 law of Venezuela and a 1940 law of Mexico fix this legal responsibility of officials in typical fashion.   Mere legislation is not enough, of course, to correct Caesarism or venality. In the final analysis, more depends upon developing a tradition of administrative probity.

Problems and Trends

Generally speaking, presidents seem to succeed or fail more in the political than in the administrative realm of their functions. But administrative success or failure often has political implications.   Although the expanding functions of government in Latin America have been administered successfully on the whole, the twin evils of militarism and Caesarism continue to plague the presidency from the standpoint both of effective public administration and of political leadership.   In only a few nations, such as Uruguay, Costa Rica, and Chile, can it be said truthfully that the executive (in Uruguay, of course, the executive is a commission) is free to staff public offices without considerable deference to military leaders.

Perhaps more frequently in the twentieth than in the nineteenth century the presidents seem to be men who are prepared by experience to deal with the increasingly complex and technical problems of government.   But they must often deal with lieutenants whose political ambitions fall into the traditional pattern of *caudillismo*. Two of the most tragic failures to remain in office by Latin American presidents in the twentieth century, both great presidents— Venustiano Carranza of Mexico (driven from office and assassinated in 1920) and Hipólito Irigoyen of Argentina (overthrown by the army in 1930)—were due in considerable measure to a kind of Caesarism which, in the case of Carranza, at least, was too largely military.   Both insisted upon keeping the reins of power so tightly in their own hands, making even the most ordinary day-to-day decisions, that eventually they became isolated from the real sources of power in the nation.   They were surrounded by a ring of sycophants who dammed up the essential channels of communication and criticism, while contributing little or no political strength in their own right. Thus, what was in essence a weakness of administration became the cause of political failure.

A second major problem facing presidents results from the weakness and changing character of political parties. The gist of the party problem is that the president, to succeed, must consolidate his position as the leader of a party, but must also control, or at least satisfy, the army, which represents order and stability. Thus he often faces the harsh alternative of governing with a party and running the risk of conflict with the army, or of being ruled by the army and so failing politically. It is a cruel, bitter dilemma. Getulio Vargas twice found himself facing such a choice in Brazil —in the 1930's and again in the 1950's. In the 1930's, with army support, he resorted to dictatorship. His tenure of office continued to 1945, but he was ultimately overthrown when the army turned against him. Moreover, resort to dictatorship is failure, or the prelude to failure, as even the most hardened dictator will admit when he faces the realities of transmitting power to a successor. In 1954 Vargas chose suicide rather than submit a second time to the army's ultimatum.

In Peru, José Luis Bustamante followed an equally tragic course after his election to the presidency in 1945 with the backing of the National Democratic Front, of which the largest element was the Aprista party. By 1948 he found himself without a party, supported only by the army, and within a few months was overthrown by an army *coup d'état* which forced him into an unhappy exile. Although he had the best intentions of ruling constitutionally, he failed in the most fundamental task of a president—that of organizing, consolidating, and directing the party with which he gained office.[47] Although the Latin American party, as we have seen, is ordinarily a weak reed to lean upon, the president must somehow galvanize it into effective action.

But this is far from being a simple or easy task. The greatest difficulties often arise from within the party itself. As one critic has said, a malady of the presidency is the loyalty of good presidents to a party which, on the other hand, relies too much upon him. Since parties sometimes do not really depend upon the sup-

[47] A good brief account will be found in Macdonald, *Latin American Government and Politics* (2d ed.); (New York: The Thomas Y. Crowell Co., 1954), pp. 363–369. See also Harry Kantor, *Ideology and Program of the Peruvian Aprista Movement* (Berkeley: University of California Press, 1953). Bustamante has told his own story in *Tres años de lucha en defensa de la democracia peruana* (Buenos Aires: Bartolomé U. Chiesino, 1949).

port of an electorate, they are likely to be flabby, incompetent, unorganized, and tolerant of all forms of dishonesty. It is a fact of considerable significance that in most countries political jobs do not depend upon success with the electorate so much as upon the president's personal success. The "good" president is expected to show his loyalty, courageously, to his friends. He either delegates power sweepingly to them or, to protect them, delegates very little. Either path is likely to be fatal to administrative success in the modern bureaucratic state.[48]

A third basic problem confronting most presidents, like the first essentially political, is that of consolidating the "interests," the real elements of power, within or outside the party. This problem centers particularly, although not exclusively, around the task of selecting a successor, because this selection helps to form a new political combination—a new structure of power to exercise the functions of government. Former president Miguel Alemán of Mexico almost failed at this point in 1953. He was saved chiefly by the strength of party discipline of the Partido Revolucionario Institucional, which Alemán himself had changed in some fundamental respects during his administration. The party selected Adolfo Ruiz Cortines, after the president's candidate failed to gain acceptance by the party. In many, perhaps in most, Latin American countries such a mistake might have brought more fatal consequences, even open rebellion.

As has been pointed out, the president must dominate the army if he is to succeed. Otherwise he will be ruled by the army and fail. Basically, this comes about because the army, in spite of all its defects, is still the most reliable institution in providing for political continuity in these countries.

In most nations today, the president must also deal in some way with the growing bid of organized urban workers for political power. In such a changing and increasingly complicated political scene, it clearly is not enough for a president to possess integrity and honest intentions in order to succeed, as the tragic failure of President Bustamante of Peru well illustrates. The example of Juan Domingo Perón of Argentina, on the other hand, shows that a president who understands the potential strength of the labor movement may attain great success even though he is unscrupulous politically. The two basic essentials seem to be that a president must somehow galvanize a cohesive political party into effective action and that he must form within that party a structure of

[48] See Carlos Goyeneche, "Cambios presidenciales en Centro y Suramerica," *Política Internacional* (Madrid), April–June 1950.

really dynamic elements—"interests." Thus he can give assurance to the army and to effective public opinion, however broad the latter may be, of his ability to maintain a structure of power strong enough to carry out national policies and to effect a peaceful transition of this power to an acceptable and reasonably popular successor.

Such a president understands the meaning of his times and the nature of his people's aspirations and needs. He can bring peace, freedom, and prosperity, as did William III to the corrupt and revolution-ridden government of England in the late seventeenth century, through the confidence inspired by imperturbable rectitude, combined with skillful and timely measures clearly within the accepted scope of his authority. Perhaps this is what a former president of Chile meant when he observed to the present author that the presidency throughout Latin America is a powerful enough office to deal constitutionally with any problem which may arise. Certainly the examples of Mitre and Sarmiento in Argentina, of Batlle in Uruguay, and of Juárez in Mexico, to mention only a few, show that moral leadership can be successful in the Latin American presidency when combined with vigor, political intelligence, and courage. Is it, perhaps, one of the important signs of the times, that President Adolfo Ruiz Cortines of "Revolutionary" Mexico was elected to office on a platform of restoring political morality to that country's government? Or that a president of Bolivia, by a hunger strike, should be able in 1957 to bring recalcitrant political elements into line?

Suggestions for Reading

There is no general work in English. Karl Lowenstein's article, "The Presidency Outside the United States," *Journal of Politics*, XI (August 1949), 447–496, is a good brief discussion. The article by Frank Tannenbaum, "Personal Government in Mexico," *Foreign Affairs*, XXVII (October 1948), 44–57, is stimulating, but one-sided. Russell Fitzgibbon has written of the collegiate executive in Uruguay in "Adoption of a Collegiate Executive in Uruguay," *Journal of Politics*, XIV (November 1952), 616–642. Philip B. Taylor, Jr., has written of Gabriel Terra's restoration of the presidency in Uruguay in "The Uruguayan Coup d'État of 1933," *Hispanic American Historical Review*, XXXII (August 1952), 301–320; his unpublished thesis, "Executive Power in Uruguay" (University of California, Berkeley, 1951), is useful but rather inaccessible. Ernest Hambloch's *His Majesty the President* (London: Methuen & Co., Ltd., 1935) is useful for Brazil.

The best work in French is that of Émile Giraud, *Le pouvoir exécutif dans les démocraties de l'Europe et de l'Amérique* (Paris: Recueil Sirey, 1938). One general work in Spanish may be mentioned: Oswaldo E. Miranda Arenas, *El jefe de estado en las constituciones americanas* (Santiago, Chile: Impr. de Carabineros, 1944).

Chapter 11

Legislatures and
Legislation

Every year on a constitutionally appointed date the elected lawmakers of each Latin American country meet to inaugurate the annual session of its national congress, unless prevented by some untoward cause such as civil strife.[1] The opening day of a legislative session often is a festive occasion, marked by more formal and public activities than attend the first meeting of the congress in the United States. The president of the republic, accompanied by his cabinet, may lead a small parade through the crowded, flag-decorated streets of the capital to the meeting place of the legislature, usually an impressive building constructed specially to house the lawmakers. Here the president opens the session, presenting to the congress a message outlining his administration's legislative program. He then retires from the halls of congress, confident that the legislators will consider his remarks carefully, investigate the bills he introduces in a sympathetic manner, and—most of the time—supply him with the appropriations, the laws, and the authority he has requested.

The man on the street learns what the president has recommended to the congress, because the speech is broadcast throughout the nation. Loudspeakers are often set up in the main plaza of each city so that workers who have been released from their jobs may hear it. The politically aware citizen listens most attentively, for in most countries he knows by experience that much or all of

[1] For dates of congressional sessions in each country and other information concerning legislatures, see Tables XIV and XV.

the president's program will be adopted, usually without major changes by the congress. On the other hand, he appears little concerned with the reaction of the members of congress to the president's message. Sometimes, in fact, it seems to the casual observer that the least important participants in the festivities centering on the reopening of the congress are the legislators themselves.

In view of the importance attributed to legislative functions in most modern states and the rather broad formal powers granted to Latin American congresses by the constitutions, this situation may appear somewhat surprising unless one understands the position of the legislature in the political process of most of these countries. Previous chapters have suggested that political practice sometimes departs rather markedly from the system of government described by the constitution. This applies to the functioning and operation of legislatures at least as much as it does to any other formal instrumentality of constitutional government.

Constitutional Role of the Latin American Legislature

THE LEGISLATIVE FUNCTION. The trend in Latin America is toward increased government activity, and in most countries the formal activities of the legislature have grown apace with the trend. It would be incorrect, however, to assume a corollary growth in the importance of congress or the effectiveness of the legislative function. In almost every country there is a measurable lag between expansion of government and increased stature for congress.

This lag is attributable in part to the lack of a tradition of legislative independence and in part to social and economic conditions. Iberian tradition explains an overly strong executive but at the same time it fails to provide the basis for a strong legislature. In the inevitable give-and-take relationship engendered by the presidential system of government, the chief executive has taken upon himself many of the old vice-regal attributes, becoming a kind of uncrowned monarch. The legislatures, on the other hand, have constitutional functions very unlike those of the Spanish *cortes* at the time of independence, functions which were mainly advisory and representative of a small group of vested interests. Instead, their formal constitutional role is patterned to a great extent upon that of the United States Congress. In structure, in their manner of representing territorial and population interests, in the general powers granted them by the constitution, even in their internal rules and committee structure, they resemble that model. These legislative bodies are supposed to act as agencies equal and coordinate with the executive branch. But the formal constitutional relationships break down in the face of political realities, making the theoretical concepts of legislative independence very nearly meaningless.

The Iberian heritage is not the sole cause of the frequent failures of the legislature to attain increased effectiveness as the scope of governmental activities has broadened. Many of the same factors which tend to make formal constitutional provisions ineffective in other fields of government affect the congress, too. Illiteracy, localism, the absence of a general national will—all of the social and economic problems which beset the political system as a whole also lessen the effectiveness of the congress.

The principal function of a legislature in most systems of government is to determine basic public policy by the enactment of laws. Legislative policy-making is so fundamental in the process of government that most democratic systems attempt by law to deny to the executive agencies the right to decide policy questions; equally binding restrictions are also placed upon the competence of the courts in this respect. The formal adoption of policy, even though most of it may originate with the executive, is the primary duty, though not necessarily the only activity, of separate lawmaking bodies. In this way, it is thought, citizen electors can hold legislators responsible for policies adopted without being confused by questions of the success or failure of individual executives or administrative agencies in applying the policies. The government may be unitary or federal, presidential or parliamentary; the activities of the legislature may be controlled by tradition and usage, as in Britain, or by a written constitution describing the relationship and responsibilities of the several branches of government, as in the Americas. But in order to be effective the legislative body must be able to act with relative independence when considering and adopting governmental policies and it must have a reasonable expectation that these policies will be carried out.

This is not to say that the other branches of government, especially the executive, have no proper constitutional or political part in the policy-making process. Because of the indivisible nature of government activities, it would be unwise and, indeed, impossible to deny them a degree of participation. But the democratic system requires that they should not encroach upon the peculiar responsibility of congress to make final determination of policy, subject only to constitutional limitations and the popular mandate.

The legislative function must be interpreted as part of the general political process. In practice, the constitutional roles of the several branches of government are influenced by the habits and thought patterns of the politically active citizens—patterns which reflect their understanding of the political system. This understanding, in turn, depends to a great extent upon the political traditions and values current in the society, no matter what the formal constitution may stipulate.

In a region such as Latin America, where social conditions and political institutions have developed within a more or less common cultural background and with roughly similar political experiences, the political process and the role of the legislature in it are likely to be quite similar from country to country. Thus the constitutional provisions establishing the formal structure of government are much alike in the various countries because they were adapted from the same sources. But differing local conditions and historical influences, not to mention the influence of *personalismo*, stamp the political process in each country with its individual characteristics.

LEGISLATIVE–EXECUTIVE RELATIONS. Most of the time in most of the countries of Latin America the legislators go through the formal steps of lawmaking, but their acts frequently are dictated by presidents. The policy-making functions of the legislature are most highly developed in such countries as Chile, Costa Rica, and Uruguay. That is, the political habits of the greater part of the citizens, the governing group as well as the governed, tend to reinforce the constitutional decision-making role of congress. At the other end of the scale, in such states as the Dominican Republic and Paraguay, the legislative branch seldom exercises an independent policy-making power. In point of fact, the constitutions of these two particular countries actually extend broader authority in this realm to the president than to congress. Between these two extremes lie the majority of states, in which legislators occasionally demonstrate independence in exercising the policy-determining power granted them by the constitution, but more regularly yield to the executive's influence.

Constitutional norms and actual political practice in respect to the legislative function occasionally merge in almost every country. During such periods congress becomes the policy-making body, at least temporarily. The administration of Galo Plaza Lasso in Ecuador (1948–1952) is an example. Plaza's administration was one of constitutionalism, during which the national congress exercised its lawmaking function much as the constitution conceived it.[2] Under his successor, José Velasco Ibarra, this formal relationship broke down in the course of an executive–legislative struggle for

[2] See Galo Plaza, *Problems of Democracy in Latin America* (Chapel Hill: University of North Carolina Press, 1955).

domination. The constitutional history of Ecuador furnishes a number of such instances of the fluctuation between constitutional balance and struggles for power between the political branches.[3]

To some degree this kind of "fluctuating constitutionalism" appears throughout Latin America. Even those countries in which normal congressional functions are most respected find difficulty in maintaining a long-term balance between the political branches of government. It is true, of course, that every country in the world experiences realignments in the distribution of power among the several branches of government. But in Latin America the shifting roles of president and congress seem more pronounced, and the executive power, with deadly regularity, breaks through its limits set by the constitution.

Because the ability of the legislature to carry out its legal role tends to rise and fall in response to transitory political considerations, it is difficult to rank the Latin American congresses according to their effectiveness in fulfilling the legislative function at any given time. The reader can, however, form some judgment of the legislature of a particular country by noting the prevalence or lack of the essential components of democratic and responsible government. It may suffice here to point out that such factors as freedom of speech, press, and assembly, free elections, freedom of party organization, genuine and effective party opposition in lawmaking bodies, and congressional scrutiny of the executive are as vital to effective legislative functioning as they are to constitutional and democratic government in more general terms. Without them a congress can scarcely be expected to perform in more than a perfunctory and formalistic manner.

The high degree of correlation between these factors and the degree of responsibility displayed by the congress appears in the case of the legislatures of the ten nations ranked highest in democratic tendencies in a survey by a group of specialists in 1955.[4] Of these ten countries,[5] only one, Colombia, did not have a legislature elected in the ordinary manner provided by law. It had an elected

[3] George I. Blanksten, *Ecuador: Constitutions and Caudillos* (Berkeley: University of California Press, 1951), particularly chapters 5 and 6.

[4] This survey by political scientists and journalists specializing in the area was discussed in Chapter 3, and has been reported in two articles by Russell H. Fitzgibbon: "How Democratic Is Latin America?" *Inter American Economic Affairs*, IX (Spring 1956), 65–77; and "A Statistical Evaluation of Latin American Democracy," *The Western Political Quarterly*, IX (September 1956), 607–619.

[5] The survey ranked the countries for democracy in the following order: Uruguay, Costa Rica, Chile, Mexico, Brazil, Colombia, Cuba, Argentina, Panama, Ecuador, El Salvador, Honduras, Venezuela, Guatemala, Bolivia, Peru, Haiti, Nicaragua, the Dominican Republic, and Paraguay.

constituent assembly that was to convert itself into the legislative body but failed to do so for several years, allowing the president a free hand. Only two others, Argentina and Mexico, had what were, in effect, one-party congresses. And in most of the ten countries the members of congress were reasonably independent in carrying out their legislative activities, at least if measured in terms of the traditionally stronger role played by the executive in the politics of the area.

In the ten countries considered less democratic, on the other hand, numerous irregularities had occurred in the selection or functioning of the legislative bodies, particularly in Bolivia, Guatemala, Honduras, and Venezuela. In four others—the Dominican Republic, Nicaragua, Paraguay, and Peru—the existence of a single-party system, or a "shadow opposition" in congress, permitted almost unlimited executive domination of the legislature.[6]

Many Latin American nations have made marked improvement in literacy, communications, and some of the other basic components of popular and responsible government. On the other hand, the social ferment and the new political movements since World War II have resulted in the paradox of increased influence of the executive office. Some improvement in general political maturity has come about during the years since 1945, but civilian control of government has become less effective, as have congressional controls over the executive in numerous instances.[7] Until the new ideas which have led to the present political ferment and disequilibrium can really take root, forming a more stable and broadly based political society, congress will continue to exercise a largely formal role, while the president remains the real source of political action.

How could it be otherwise? Deep-seated habits of political action in many countries tend to overwhelm the formal constitutional provisions for balanced legislative–executive relations, exalting instead an all-powerful leader as the only alternative to the parliamentary anarchy that tends to result when congressmen are left to themselves. For even when congress performs its legislative function without interference from the president, it is not highly efficient in meeting its responsibilities. Most legislatures lack internal cohesion; there is very little display of a sense of political responsibility on the part of individual legislators, and leadership from within the chamber itself is often ineffectual. The legislature, like the political society, has no hard core of shared values, no sense of

---

[6] Observations on the political status of legislatures during 1955 are the author's and not those of Professor Fitzgibbon's study.

[7] Fitzgibbon, "A Statistical Evaluation of Latin American Democracy," p. 615.

a general, as opposed to individual, welfare, no tradition of compromise which could unite legislators into a cooperating and effective congressional majority.

PRESIDENTIAL LEADERSHIP. In general, the president uses his influence to discipline recalcitrant legislators, reduce the struggles among competing factions, and integrate congress into a functioning body. Where he does not, little positive legislative activity can be anticipated. Sad experience has convinced the rank-and-file citizen that without this unifying force exercised by the president the personalist tendencies in the political culture tend to reduce the congress to irreconcilable factions. He recognizes that, without the integration supplied by presidential leadership, the legislature would find it difficult even to complete the mechanical steps by which laws are passed; much less could it exercise the full legislative function.

The legislator, himself a product of the political environment, tends to accept this reasoning and adapts his actions to it. If he is personally loyal to the chief executive, he is receptive to the president's leadership. Seldom will he oppose presidential desires for legislation, appropriations, or authority; and almost never will he question the administrative or political acts of his leader. If he is in opposition, on the other hand, a member of congress will do everything in his power to thwart the administration, embarrass or attack the president, unhampered by a greater loyalty to a constitutional system, respect for the office of the presidency, or responsibility for any concept of national welfare. The concept of the "loyal opposition" is largely unknown. To a member of the opposition, the interests he represents are best served by weakening or even removing the president, rather than by working with him.

A strong president can, and a successful president must, manipulate the legislature. If it rebels he may suspend its operations "temporarily," as Fulgencio Batista did in Cuba when assuming power in 1952, or he may dismiss it entirely, as Ospina Pérez of Colombia did when congress threatened to impeach him in 1949. Even a constitutional provision, such as that in Ecuador which specifically prohibits a president from dissolving congress, has not prevented strong executives from dominating the legislative branch.

CONGRESSIONAL CONTROLS OVER THE PRESIDENT. Many thoughtful citizens realize that presidents too often and too speedily resort to force or other unconstitutional acts in their relations with congress. As they point out, Galo Plaza Lasso demonstrated in Ecuador that when a president places confidence in the legislative body it may respond in kind, to the general strengthening of constitutional government. Many Latin Americans believe that confident, intelligent leadership in any country could make its legislature an effective instrument of government. Certainly, without opportunities to assume responsible roles in the political process the legislators will never learn the hard lessons of compromise and responsibility which are fundamental to a working democratic system.

Even in those few countries where the legislative power traditionally is more nearly equal to that of the executive, fear that the balance will be upset lies behind frequent efforts to maintain it by mechanical means. Uruguay is a case in point. After turbulent, partisan struggles involving frequent breakdowns between the branches of government, the Uruguayans achieved a more stable political system, with working majorities and "loyal" minorities in congress free from presidential domination. But even here, in order to reduce the danger of expanding "personalist" power in the presidency, authority has been dispersed among a plural executive, so that no one person can dominate the presidential office and, indirectly, the legislature.[8]

PERMANENT COMMITTEES OF CONGRESS. Efforts of some countries to control presidential power by resorting to the parliamentary system, or certain aspects of it, were discussed in the previous chapter. In recent years, another interesting device to strengthen the hand of the legislatures has been a permanent committee of congress. The constitutions of El Salvador, Guatemala, Mexico, Panama, and Uruguay provide for a committee composed of representative members of congress to exercise some of the functions of the legislature when that body is not in session. These "watchdog" committees are supposed to check on executive activities; they are authorized to approve interim appointments, to declare a state of siege when necessary, and to call special sessions of congress.

Establishment of permanent committees in congress is not a new idea, but seems to have been imported to the New World from Spain, where the ancestor of such a committee existed in Aragon in the thirteenth century. In the New World it first appeared in the Mexican constitution of 1824. It is not an idea that has increasingly gained acceptance, however. In fact Paraguay, after trying the idea, has dropped it.[9]

Experience proves that the existence of such committees does not in itself change the position of congress in the government.

[8] Russell H. Fitzgibbon, *Uruguay: Portrait of a Democracy* (New Brunswick, N.J.: Rutgers University Press, 1954).

[9] Felipe Tena Ramírez, *Derecho constitucional mexicano* (Mexico: Ed. Porrúa, 1944), pp. 365–366.

What is required is some alteration in the fundamental power relationship between president and congress, as in Uruguay. For the permanent committee of congress can be no more effective as a check on the president than is its parent legislative body.

LEGISLATIVE–EXECUTIVE STRUGGLE IN CHILE. The recent political history of Chile illustrates the difficulty in attempting to restrain presidential influence over congress when legislative cohesion is lacking, even in a country politically mature and stable. When Chile re-adopted presidential government in 1925, it carried over from the previous parliamentary system a tradition of parity between the political branches of government. Unfortunately, it also carried over the multi-party system, because the particular interests which the various parties represented could not find a basis for common cooperation. Restoring the separation of powers did not, therefore, bring congressional cohesion. Nor could it make a majority of the legislators willing to accept executive leadership, because no president could satisfy the conflicting demands of all of the factions actively represented in congress.[10]

Under these conditions, unless Chile's president commands a strong enough personal following to assure an absolute majority in the two chambers, he finds great difficulty in uniting the numerous parties sufficiently to obtain passage of a legislative program. In 1954 the executive–legislative conflict became so serious during the course of a lingering economic crisis that President Carlos Ibáñez del Campo appointed a constitutional commission to explore measures for strengthening the presidency in its relations with the congress.

The congress protested violently against this move, which it considered an invasion of its constitutional rights. Much of the protest, however, originated with groups of legislators who feared that strong action might harm the specific interests they represented. Ex-president Gabriel González Videla, on the other hand, voiced the opinion that the president already had ample powers, if properly used, to meet the crisis. Whatever the merits of the question, the commission could not act to expand the president's power; and President Ibáñez was unable to get action from the badly split legislature, despite twelve cabinet reorganizations during the first two and a half years of his term, a total that had grown to nineteen two years later.

Not until 1956, when economic conditions became so dangerous

---

[10] John Reese Stevenson, in *The Chilean Popular Front* (Philadelphia: University of Pennsylvania Press, 1942), chaps. 2–4, describes problems of executive–legislative relations under the presidential system re-established by the constitution of 1925.

that even the irreconcilables were frightened into cooperation and compromise, did congress grant the president authority to attack the crisis. The congress then assumed its constitutional responsibilities in the matter, for initiative for reform came from within the two chambers. Unfortunately, the authority granted was insufficient to avoid the disorders resulting from inflationary pressures which took place during April and May, 1957. Only then did congress give President Ibáñez sufficient authority to cope with the situation.

This inability to achieve prompt and effective legislative action in Chile is similar to that in postwar France, where numerous parliamentary groups also have found it impossible to merge individual interests in the national welfare and have refused to grant any premier the extraordinary powers necessary to solve the country's economic and political difficulties. In most other Latin American countries, as we have seen, strong presidential leadership traditionally supplies this political integration when congressional leadership fails.

FISCAL CONTROLS. In some countries the congress has also tried to control executive actions by fiscal measures. In both Chile and Uruguay an independent office or tribunal of accounts, appointed by and responsible to the legislature, supervises expenditures and conducts regular audits. In these countries legislative controls over presidential financial activities are relatively successful, because the political system recognizes the right of congress to fulfill its constitutional function. In Mexico, however, where much the same machinery exists, fiscal controls are little more than a matter of form, observed in theory but in no way effective.[11] Similarly, the 1953 Venezuelan constitution establishes the office of comptroller of the nation, selected by and responsible to the congress. But it also allows the president "to decree credits in addition to those provided in the Law on the Budget of Public Revenues and Expenditures." Moreover, if congress has not approved the budget submitted by the executive by July 1, it automatically goes into effect.

Congressional Powers

BROAD FORMAL POWERS. Latin American constitutions generally grant more power to government than the United States constitution assigns to the federal government. As noted in Chapter 9 and else-

[11] Congressional fiscal activities will be discussed later in this chapter; other aspects of government finance are discussed in Chapters 15 and 17. On the weakness of Mexico's congressional fiscal controls, see Robert E. Scott, "Budget Making in Mexico," *Inter-American Economic Affairs*, IX (Autumn 1955), 3–20.

where, this trend is consistent with Spanish-Portuguese tradition, and was not reversed by Latin American political experience after independence. Governmental authority also has been increased in recent years because of the extension of government activity into important social and economic activities. Generally speaking, however, the powers and functions assigned to Latin American congresses do not differ substantially from those granted to legislative bodies in most constitutional systems.[12]

LAWMAKING. The most important powers are legislative in character. Legislatures in Latin America have most of the powers granted to the congress and to the state legislatures in the United States. Typically, these powers include authority to levy taxes, to borrow and spend money, to coin money, to regulate foreign and domestic commerce, to declare war, and to make policy concerning all of the activities which concern the modern state. Legislative power reserved to local governing bodies is relatively small, even in the four nations with federal governments.

The detailed grants of legislative power in Latin American constitutions resemble the itemized provisions of some state constitutions in the United States more than the general statements in the federal constitution. The habit of detailing legislative powers reflects a determination of Latin American constitution-writers, emanating from some of their unhappy political experiences, to prevent executive inroads on legislative policy-making, as well as certain influences of the legal system.

In spite of the detailed provisions, both juridical thought and political practice are so distinct from that of North America that specific elaboration of legislative authority does not restrict congressional freedom of action as it does in some states in the United States. Even in those countries where the doctrine of judicial review has been accepted, when congress enacts a program sponsored by the president, judicial restraints are unlikely to hamper a broad interpretation of the constitution.

One factor limiting congressional independence in lawmaking must be mentioned here briefly, although it was discussed in the last chapter. This is the power of the executive in many countries to issue decree laws as well as administrative rules. Since these countries generally follow the civil law, the extent of administrative rule-making is much greater than in a country with common law. This also is in accord with political reality, since the power struc-

---

[12] For the constitutions see Russell H. Fitzgibbon (ed.), *The Constitutions of the Americas* (Chicago: University of Chicago Press, 1948); for those since 1948, see the *Law and Treaty Series* of the Pan American Union.

ture tends to center around the president. Most constitutional systems in the world recognize the necessity for executive rule-making power, but normally this authority does not include legislation on the level of high policy-making.

In many of the Latin American states, however, the constitution or accepted practice allows the president to legislate by decree in times of national emergency if the congress is not in session. These decrees have the same legal effect as acts of congress, unless subsequently repealed by that body. Of course, repeated resort to legislation by presidential decree, arising out of the frequency of political disturbances in many countries, constitutes an extensive usurpation of legislative power, which constitution-makers have attempted to restrain. The Mexican constitution, for example, forbids general delegation of decree powers to the president. Despite this provision, practice had gone so far by 1938 that it was felt necessary to amend Article 49 of the constitution to restate the prohibition. Ironically, amendment to Article 131 a few years later extended presidential power to issue decrees in customs and foreign exchange matters.

CONSTITUTION-MAKING. While the main business of the legislatures is lawmaking, they have other functions as well. One of these is the constituent power, relatively more important in Latin American countries than in some other parts of the world. As noted in Chapter 9, written constitutions do not always represent political realities. Not infrequently, leaders of a successful political upheaval will seek to erase the past with a new constitution, even though its provisions may differ but little from those of the previous charter. Moreover, detailed constitutions such as those common in Latin America require more frequent changes than do documents drawn in more general terms. The Mexican Constitution of 1917, for example, has been amended more than a hundred times since its promulgation.

As a general rule, constitutions are amended easily and speedily in Latin American countries, despite elaborate provisions to discourage such changes. The laws of Argentina and the Dominican Republic require congress to call a constituent convention, but the ease with which such a convention may be manipulated by a strong leader has been demonstrated in both countries. Generalissimo Trujillo imposed a new constitution on his people in 1955, and the 1853 Argentine charter was greatly changed by a convention under Perón (although it was restored after his fall). The federal states of Brazil, Mexico, and Venezuela (like Argentina) require participation of both congress and the member-states in constitutional changes, but in none of them has this requirement prevented ready change in the fundamental law.

Nine countries place all or most of the amending power in the hands of congress, though usually approval by an extraordinary majority (often two-thirds) and adoption in two separate congressional terms are required.[13]   Six other states stipulate that congress must call a special constituent convention when general rather than specific revision is contemplated.[14]   Three constitutions require that a fixed number of years elapse before general revision may be attempted.   Finally, several states require some form of popular initiative and referendum, or a combination of these and congressional action, for amending the basic law.[15]

Political history has demonstrated repeatedly that however specific the grant of constituent power to the legislature or the formal restrictions upon precipitate action, such factors as political unrest, the emergence of a new national leader, or a change in government frequently cause changes in all or part of the constitution.   If congress itself cannot find a way to bring about these changes, it may be dissolved in order to allow a new constituent assembly to act. Thus, in recent years, either the congress or a special constitutional assembly has adopted basic constitutional changes following unconstitutional political changes in such states as Argentina (1955), Brazil (1946), Costa Rica (1949), El Salvador (1950), Guatemala (1954), Haiti (1950), and Venezuela (1952).

REGULATION OF LOCAL GOVERNMENT.   In the four federal states, Argentina, Brazil, Mexico, and Venezuela, congress admits new states or provinces into the union.   During the early 1950's the state of Baja California Norte in Mexico and two new provinces in Argentina were set up by the legislatures of those countries.   In the case of Mexico, at least, the congress had at an earlier date returned parts of states to territorial status.

These federal states also endow the national congress with extensive legislative authority over national territories and national capital cities.   Two of the latter, México, D.F. (Mexico City) and Buenos Aires, are separate administrative districts, subject to acts of congress and without elective local governments, much like Washington, D.C.   The other two, Rio de Janeiro and Caracas, have some form of local representation.   As will be noted in a later chapter,

---

[13] Bolivia, Colombia, Cuba, Ecuador, Guatemala, Haiti, Honduras, Panama, and Peru.

[14] Argentina, Costa Rica, Cuba, El Salvador, Honduras, and Uruguay.

[15] Guatemala requires that its constitution be in effect six years, Nicaragua five years, and Paraguay ten years before general revision.   Some form of popular participation in constitution-making is provided for in Cuba, Peru, and Uruguay.

some of the unitary states also place their capital cities in some sort of special status; among these states are Colombia, Costa Rica, Nicaragua, Paraguay, and Uruguay.

ELECTORAL POWERS. Latin American legislative bodies have broad responsibilities regarding elections. In the federal as well as the unitary states, the constitutional and political systems give the national government great responsibility for control of elections. Qualifications for voters as well as candidates, standards and methods of conducting elections, and other matters of election procedure come under the national legislative authority.

Each chamber of congress is usually authorized to judge the qualifications and pass upon the election of its members. Because of the inadequacy of electoral safeguards and frequent lack of guaranties of free suffrage, disputed elections are numerous. This congressional function is, therefore, an important one, and much depends upon the way it is exercised.

In recent years congress has tended to assume a larger role in presidential elections. The legislatures of most countries have long been responsible for scrutinizing ballots and proclaiming the election of the president. In practice this has sometimes caused difficulty, however, for if opposition parties control the legislature they can invalidate the election result without just cause, as they did in Costa Rica in 1948. Or, if they are in a minority, the opposition members may refuse to perform their constitutional function, as did the Liberals in Ecuador, who conducted a congressional strike after the presidential election of 1956 to prevent a legislative quorum.

The congressional function of deciding contested presidential elections has taken on new importance lately, because of the increasing number of active political parties and broader popular participation in elections. Constitutions frequently require that a presidential candidate receive an absolute majority of the popular votes cast, a provision which throws many elections into the legislature for final determination. Such contested elections occurred in Bolivia in 1947, and in Chile in 1946 and 1952. In these three cases the candidate with the plurality was selected. But in Honduras, in 1954, the national congress failed to agree, whereupon the acting president seized control of the government, transforming the congress by decree into an "advisory" council without legislative powers.

Congressional selection of presidential "designates" in those countries having no vice-president, the election of provisional presidents, and congressional participation with the president in the appointment of certain high government officials were discussed in the previous chapter. Obviously, congressional independence in carrying out this function depends largely upon the relationship with the executive.

THE STATE OF SIEGE AND INTERVENTION. Latin America's legislatures also exercise two other powers which reflect the frequent experience with civil disorder. One is the power, exercised in some respects jointly with the president, to proclaim a state of siege or national emergency, authorizing the executive to suspend certain constitutional guaranties. The importance of this function is indicated by the fact that this power is usually granted in a separate and independent constitutional clause, and not included as an aspect of martial law, which is a component of the power to declare and wage war; nor is it to be confused with martial law and its application.

Experience has shown, however, that in the exercise of the siege power the initiative has usually come from the president. While in some respects this is natural under the presidential system of government, it also reflects the weak position of Latin American legislatures. Few congresses are strong enough to oppose a presidential request for extraordinary powers to deal with a national crisis, although the Chilean congress did so in 1954. In the federal states of Latin America the congress (or, in the case of Mexico, the senate) must authorize intervention by the central government in the states or provinces. Not unexpectedly, the president seldom finds much difficulty in obtaining such authorization. The use of this power for political purposes as well as the control of civil disorders has been described previously, particularly in Chapter 10.

JUDICIAL POWERS. In most of the bicameral legislatures the lower house impeaches and the upper house tries high government officers for official and other offenses. Removal from office and disqualification from office for a given period are usually the only punishments applied by the legislatures, criminal trials here being left to the courts.

Unicameral legislatures also have this power to try official offenders, often with some kind of unusually large majority required for its final decisions. In El Salvador, Honduras, and Venezuela trial after impeachment is by a judicial court rather than by an upper legislative chamber.

Threats of impeachment are not uncommon in Latin America, but presidents seldom are removed from office by this process. Impeachment proceedings invariably are colored by political considerations and, given the predominance of presidential power, it is quite unlikely that such action will be taken against a strong president. When a president is not all-powerful, threats of impeachment may, of course, force him to adjust his differences with congress, as Alfonso López was forced to do in Ecuador during 1945.

Some presidents actually have been removed from office. This happened to President Balmaceda of Chile in 1891 and to Eloy Alfaro in Ecuador during 1933. In 1955, President José Ramón Guizado of Panama was removed from office and imprisoned on the grounds that while vice-president he had conspired in the murder of President José Antonio Remón. In 1848, on the other hand, President Monagas of Venezuela instigated mob action against a congress that tried to impeach him, causing the death of three deputies.

Lesser officials occasionally are removed from office by impeachment, but usually cabinet-level ministers are protected by their identification with the president's program. If the president decides to throw one of his close colleagues to the wolves he is more likely to fire him or force his resignation than to yield to congressional proceedings. The impeachment of judges is somewhat more common, however, probably because of their fixed terms and the difficulty at times of reconciling law with the political desires of the executive. Justices of the highest court were impeached and removed by president-dominated congresses in Argentina (1947) and Guatemala (1953) after those judicial officers had declared unconstitutional certain measures sponsored by the government.

Moreover, threats of impeachment against judges for political reasons are not uncommon and reflect the relatively dominant role of political officials in Latin America's constitutional–political systems. A special provision of Article 111 in the Mexican Constitution allows the president to request the two chambers of congress to remove judicial officers by absolute majority vote, a less difficult process than formal impeachment. This provision, or threats to apply it, have been used several times to influence the courts when they are deciding controversial matters.[16]

INVESTIGATING POWERS. A lawmaking body must have investigatory powers in order to legislate and implement its constitutional powers. In some countries these powers include authority to summon and to question ministers of state (Argentina, Bolivia, Colombia, Ecuador, Guatemala, Honduras, Nicaragua, and El Salvador). In others the ministers may attend and participate in debates (Costa Rica, Chile, Haiti, Mexico, Peru, and Venezuela). In some countries interpellation may lead to votes of censure and result in the

[16] See Robert E. Scott, "Some Aspects of Mexican Federalism, 1917–1948" (Unpublished thesis, University of Wisconsin, 1949), chapter 5.

removal of ministers from office. Such removals have occurred from time to time in Brazil, Bolivia, and a few other states. But, with the exception of Chile, these removals have not been regular occurrences. Presidential influence discourages such assertions of congressional power.

In recent years special congressional investigating committees have been established in some countries, but they are not common and generally their effectiveness is not great. During 1949, for example, the *peronista*-dominated Argentine congress appointed such a committee to investigate reports that political prisoners were being subjected to physical torture. This committee complied with its duty by subjecting the newspapers and wire services which carried the reports to a thorough investigation, but stated that it was not "convenient" to report on the matter of torture.[17] The two special committees established by the legislative chambers in Peru during 1956 to investigate constitutional infractions by the Odría regime, on the other hand, were more effective. Because they had been appointed after Odría left the presidency, they had the co-operation and support of the new president, and so were able to act with relative impunity.

The normal investigative function of congressional committees as part of the legislative process will be considered presently. Here it need only be noted that in Argentina before the days of Perón, in Chile, Costa Rica, Brazil, or Uruguay, nations where traditionally the legislature has been more powerful, such activities have been more successful than in countries dominated by a strong president at the expense of the constitutional status of congress.

DISCIPLINARY AND RULE-MAKING POWERS. Normally, each legislative chamber has disciplinary authority over its own members and over persons within its physical or legal jurisdiction. Typically, the constitution provides that the legislature shall have its own police officers, or the right to request aid from other police or military forces, in order to enforce this authority. All of the legislatures have legal authority to make rules governing their procedure and internal administration, although their freedom of action in these matters sometimes is limited by overly detailed constitutional provisions establishing fixed procedures or requirements for extraordinary quorums. Within their competence, however, the legislatures adopt the necessary parliamentary rules.

RATIFICATION AND CONFIRMATION. Because they have been modeled upon the United States' presidential system of government,

---

[17] George I. Blanksten, *Perón's Argentina* (Chicago: University of Chicago Press, 1953), pp. 119–120, 182–185.

with its concept of checks and balances, most Latin American constitutions place responsibility for ratifying foreign treaties and confirming appointments of high civil and military officers in the hands of the senate or the congress. Cases of congressional refusal to approve a president's action in these matters are very rare, however, though cases in Chile, Ecuador, and a few other countries could be cited. The Mexican senate once held up the appointment of three members of the supreme court of justice for an entire day because it felt that they were old and that older men are apt to be "too conservative."[18]

FISCAL POWERS. Following the North American model of checks and balances, in most bicameral legislatures the lower chamber has precedence in the initiation of money bills. The only exceptions are Venezuela, where both houses of congress have equal authority, and Mexico, where the chamber of deputies approves the budget of expenditures without action of the senate (Art. 74). As indicated in the earlier discussion of fiscal controls, however, the degree to which legislatures really exercise the power of the purse depends more upon political factors than upon constitutional provisions.

Congressional Structure and Membership

BICAMERALISM OR UNICAMERALISM? Fourteen of the twenty national legislative bodies are bicameral. The exceptions are Costa Rica, El Salvador, Guatemala, Honduras, and Panama in Central America, and Paraguay in South America. The reader may well wonder what useful purpose bicameralism serves in the ten non-federal states. In the four federal states two legislative chambers have found theoretical justification in the necessity of representing both population and the separate entities which unite to form the union. And historical precedent for the arrangement can be cited also for a few unitary states, such as Colombia and Peru, which once had federal systems. As for the other unitary states, most of them adopted bicameralism for yet other reasons. Some modeled their congressional system on the North American constitution or on the short-lived Spanish document of 1812, which provided for two chambers; in others the ruling classes sought to introduce a conservative influence, much in the terms of the original concept of the senate in the national government of the United States.

Whatever the reason bicameralism was adopted, the two-house system has not developed along the same lines in Latin America as it has in the United States. Even when their pattern of representation differs, the two chambers seldom speak for different

[18] *Excelsior* (Mexico City), December 28/29, 1940.

regional or population interests. Their failure to do so doubtless reflects their usual political role of subservience to the president rather than the manner in which they are constituted.

But the idea of two legislative houses is well established and no trend away from bicameralism is apparent. Even when so basic an alteration in legislative power as adoption of parliamentary government occurs, as in Cuba's constitution of 1940, the two houses have been retained.

THE SENATE. The upper chamber in bicameral legislatures is always called the senate (*senado*). Its size is determined in the federal states by a fixed number of senators per state or province. The unitary states tend to make senatorial representation more proportional to population. For example, in Chile, the twenty-five provinces are divided according to population into nine groups of from one to three provinces, each group electing five senators. Colombia distributes its senators according to the population in each department. In Ecuador the two most populous departments have two rather than one senator, and there are twelve functional senators, as will be explained shortly. Senate representation in Haiti is based strictly on population. Nicaragua elects one senator directly from each province, but ex-presidents are lifetime senators and the defeated runner-up in the presidential election holds a senate seat for six years. Uruguay elects its senators by proportional representation from the country at large.[19]

THE LOWER HOUSE. In bicameral legislatures the lower house is called the chamber of deputies (*cámara de diputados*), except in Colombia, Cuba, and Uruguay, where it is known as the chamber of representatives. The single chamber in unicameral legislatures is usually called the national assembly or the national congress. The number of deputies is always proportional to population, except where a territorial division of a country is assured a minimum representation of at least one, however small its population may be. The basis of representation ranges from a ratio of 1 per 15,000 in Costa Rica to 1 per 150,000 in Brazil and 1 per 190,000 in Mexico.

SIZE OF LEGISLATURES. Legislative bodies range in size from 40 to 389 members. Among bicameral congresses, that of Brazil is largest, with 63 senators and 326 deputies, while the 16 senators and 42 deputies in Nicaragua constitute the smallest. Guatemala's 53-member national congress is the largest unicameral body, and Paraguay's 40-member body is the smallest. Generally speaking,

---

[19] See Tables XIV and XV for the organization and structure of the legislature in each country.

Latin American legislatures are not disproportionately large, given the different kinds of geographic and social elements represented.

REPRESENTATION OF SPECIAL DISTRICTS. Usually all political subdivisions, including the capital city and any "national" district that may surround it, are represented in congress, even in the federal states. This is both fair and politically wise, considering the high degree of national control over these areas and their relative importance in the political and economic life of the countries.

In the federal states, the national territories often send representatives to congress. Brazil's territories, for example, elect one deputy each and Venezuela's elect two. In Mexico, politically incorporated states are guaranteed at least two deputies while the territories are assured of only one.

METHODS OF ELECTION. Most legislators are elected by direct popular vote. In Argentina and Venezuela, however, senators are elected by provincial or departmental assemblies, while in Ecuador 12 "functional" senators, representing the professions, economic interests, and cultural groups, share power with 33 conventionally elected senators. In Nicaragua, as noted above, ex-presidents and runner-up candidates in presidential elections are seated in the upper chamber. Peru has a constitutional provision for a functional senate, but it has not been implemented.

Deputies are elected either from single-member districts or as groups from provinces or other administrative subdivisions, in the latter case sometimes by proportional representation. Argentina, Brazil, Chile, Colombia, Costa Rica, Cuba, Ecuador, Uruguay, and Venezuela, either in their constitutions or by statute, provide for minority representation in one or both house of congress. This is accomplished by assigning a minimum quota of seats to the opposition, or by some form of proportional representation. The degree to which such opposition representation can serve as a watchdog upon the regime in power depends, of course, upon the political environment in which it operates. As shall be seen presently, in day-by-day operations the influence of the opposition is a great deal more effective in some countries than in others.

QUALIFICATIONS FOR OFFICE. Qualifications for membership in congress vary, but always include a minimum age and national citizenship. In three of the unicameral houses the legislators must be native-born. Similarly, members of six lower chambers and seven senates among the bicameral legislatures also must be native-born (see Tables XIV and XV). Argentina and Mexico specifically prohibit members of the clergy from sitting in congress, and many constitutions also require separation from military or executive

TABLE XIV.   BICAMERAL LEGISLATURES

COUNTRY	SENATE				
	No. of Members	Term	Method of Selection	Qualifications for Office	Party Members In Senate*
Argentina	34	9 years; ⅓ each 3 years	By legislature of province; in Fed. Dist. by electoral college. Two per province and Fed. Dist.	30 years old; citizen 6 years; 2,000-peso income; native or 2-year resident of province (or born in it.	Congress dissolved after military coup of Nov. 13, 1955. Constituent Assembly, 1957
Bolivia	18	6 years; ⅓ each 2 years	Direct election. Two from each of 9 departments.	35 years old; native-born; military service complete.	18 National Revolutionary Movement
Brazil	62	8 years; ⅓-1950 ⅔-1954	Direct election. Three per state and Fed. Dist.	35 years old; native-born.	22 Social Democratic; 16 Labor; 13 National Democratic Union; 4 Republican; 3 Social Progressive; 5 other parties.
Chile	45	8 years; ½ each 4 years	Direct election. Five from each of 9 groups of provinces.	35 years old; citizen; voter.	5 Agrarian Labor; 40 Senators from 10 non-presidential parties, some supporting president at times, others never.
Colombia	63	4 years	Election by P.R. Three to 9 senators per department. 1:190,000	30 years old; native-born; have held high political or admin. office, or be professor or professional with degree.	Congressional operations suspended in June, 1953. Constituent Assembly that assumed legislative power in July, 1955 dissolved self in 1957.
Cuba	54	4 years	Direct election Nine from each of 6 departments. (3 of 9 to opposition)	30 years old; native-born.	36 Coalition of four Batista parties; 18 Cuban Revolutionary (Authentic)
Dominican Republic	21	5 years	Direct election. One per province and Dist. of Santo Domingo.	30 years old; citizen 10 years and 2-year continuous residence.	21 Dominican Party

SOURCE: Information, for the year 1957, supplied by the Latin American countries' embassies in Washington, D.C.

* Administration supporters in senate indicated by underlining.

IN LATIN AMERICAN COUNTRIES

LOWER CHAMBER				
No. of Members	Term	Method of Selection	Qualifications for Office	Party Members in Chamber*
166	6 years	Direct election by population; province-wide districts; second party assured 10 seats.	25 years old; citizen 4 years; native or 2-year resident of province.	Congress dissolved after military coup of Nov. 13, 1955.
68	4 years; ½ each 2 years	Direct election from districts based on population.	25 years old; native-born; military service complete.	63 National Revolutionary Movement; 5 Bolivian Socialist Phalanx
346	4 years	P.R., by states; at least 7 per state. 1:150,000	21 years old; native-born.	119 Social Democratic; 76 National Democratic Union; 56 Labor; 37 Social Progressive; 21 Republican; 27 other parties
147	4 years	P.R., by districts. 1:30,000	Citizen; voter.	25 Agrarian Labor; 122 from 18 other parties, some supporting president at times, others never.
131	2 years	P.R., by districts; at least 3 per district. 1:90,000	25 years old; full citizenship rights; no felony convictions.	Congressional operations suspended in June, 1953. Constituent Assembly that assumed legislative power in July, 1955, dissolved itself in 1957.
130	4 years; ½ each 2 years	Direct election, by provinces. 1:35,000	21 years old; citizen 10 years.	114 Coalition of four Batista parties; 16 Cuban Revolutionary (Authentic)
47	5 years	Direct election, by provinces; at least 2 per province. 1:60,000	30 years old; citizen 8 years and 2-year continuous residence.	47 Dominican Party

* Administration supporters in chamber indicated by underlining.

Continued on next page

TABLE XIV.   BICAMERAL LEGISLATURES

COUNTRY	Sessions of Congress	Special Features of Congress	General Comments
Argentina	One session, May 1 to Sept. 30. President calls special sessions; fixed agenda.		
Bolivia	One session, Aug. 5 for 90 days, extended to 120 by congress or president.		
Brazil	One session, March 15 for 6 months. President or ⅓ of either chamber calls special sessions	Alternate elected for each senator and deputy.	
Chile	One regular session, May 21 to Sept. 18. President calls special sessions; fixed agenda.		Tendency toward numerous special sessions. Multi-party representation in both chambers.
Colombia	One session, July 20 for 120 days. "Government" calls special sessions; fixed agenda.	Each party supplies list of senatorial alternates in department. Every deputy has two personal alternates.	
Cuba	Two sessions of 60 days, starting 3rd Monday of Sept. and of March. President calls special sessions; fixed agenda.		
Dominican Republic	Two periods of 90 days starting in Feb. and August. President calls special sessions.	Alternates elected for senators and deputies as needed by chamber, from list supplied by incumbent's party.	President has very broad decree power to legislate on "emergency matters."

SOURCE: Information, for the year 1957, supplied by the Latin American countries' embassies in Washington, D.C.

IN LATIN AMERICAN COUNTRIES (*Cont.*)

COUNTRY	SENATE				
	No. of Members	Term	Method of Selection	Qualifications for Office	Party Members in Senate*
Ecuador	44	4 years	Direct election (2 from large, 1 from small provinces). Also 12 functional senators.	35 years old; native-born.	34 Right Center (Conservatives, Social Christians, Revolutionary National Association (ARNE), and Chiribogistas); 4 C.F.P. (Popular Front); 1 Democratic Front (Liberals and leftists); 1 Communist; 5 others.
Haiti	21	6 years	Assembly of voters in each department. Number elected based on department population.	35 years old; native-born; 2-year resident of department.	At time of 1950 elections, no "parties" as such permitted. Senate term extended after ouster of President in Dec. 1956.
Mexico	60	6 years; no immediate re-election	Direct election. Two per state and Fed. Dist.	35 years old; native-born; native or 6-month resident of state.	60 Institutional Revolutionary Party (PRI)
Nicaragua	16+	6 years	Direct election. One per province, plus ex-pres. for life and runner-up for 6 years	35 years old.	12 National Liberal; 3 Conservative; 2 ex-presidents; 1 defeated candidate (Conservative)
Peru	52	6 years	Direct election. Functional senate not operative.	35 years old; native-born; native or 3-year resident of department.	18 Pradistas; 7 National Union; 4 Belaundistas; 4 Christian Dems.; 19 Independent and others.
Uruguay	31	4 years	P.R., in the country-at-large, by slates.	30 years old; citizen 7 years.	16 Colorado Party; 11 Blanco Party; 1 Independent Colorado; 1 Independent Blanco; 1 Socialist; 1 Catholic
Venezuela	42	5 years	Indirect election by state legis. Two per state and Fed. Dist.	30 years old; native-born.	42 Appointed by president-dominated constituent assembly April, 1953; 5-year term.

SOURCE: Information, for the year 1957, supplied by the Latin American countries' embassies in Washington, D.C.

* Administration supporters in senate indicated by underlining.

Continued on next page

TABLE XIV. BICAMERAL LEGISLATURES

COUNTRY	LOWER CHAMBER				
	No. of Members	Term	Method of Selection	Qualifications for Office	Party Members in Chamber *
Ecuador	71	2 years	Direct election, by provinces. 1:50,000	25 years old; native-born.	50 Right Center (Conservatives, Social Christians, Revolutionary National Association (ARNE) and Chiribogistas); 15 C.F.P. (Popular Front); 30 Democratic Front (liberals and leftists)
Haiti	37	4 years	Direct election, by districts.	25 years old; native-born; 1-year resident of district.	At time of 1955 election, no "parties" as such permitted
Mexico	162	3 years; no immediate re-election.	Direct election, by districts. 1:170,000	25 years old; native-born; native or 6-month resident of state.	150 PRI, 5 National Action (PAN); 4 other parties; 3 vacant
Nicaragua	42	6 years	Direct election, by departments; at least 1 per department. 1:30,000	25 years old	28 National Liberal; 14 Conservative
Peru	156	6 years	Direct election, by districts.	25 years old; native-born; native or 3-year resident of department.	50 Pradistas; 38 National Union; 17 Belaundistas; 7 Christian Democrat; 71 Independents and others
Uruguay	99	4 years	P.R., in the country-at-large, but at least 2 per department.	30 years old; citizen 5 years.	49 Colorado Party; 35 Blanco Party; 2 Independent Colorado; 3 Independent Blanco; 3 Socialist; 2 Communist; 5 Catholic
Venezuela	104	5 years	P.R., by districts. 1:40,000	21 years old; native-born.	104 Appointed by president-dominated constituent assembly in April, 1953; 5-year term.

SOURCE: Information, for the year 1957, supplied by the Latin American countries' embassies in Washington, D.C.

* Administration supporters in chamber indicated by underlining.

IN LATIN AMERICAN COUNTRIES (*Cont.*)

Sessions of Congress	Special Features of Congress	General Comments
One session, Aug. 10 for 60 days. President or ⅔ of congress calls special session; fixed agenda.	Two alternates for each elected senator. Inter-government legislative committee prepares special status bills.	
One session, 2nd Monday of April for 3 months.	President may dissolve congress if "serious dispute"; new election in 3 months. Meanwhile president rules by decree.	President has exclusive initiation of fiscal bills.
One session, Sept. 1 to Dec. 31. Permanent Committee calls special session; fixed agenda.	Permanent Committee (15 deputies, 14 senators). Alternate elected for each senator and deputy.	
One session, April 15 for 60 days. Executive calls special sessions; fixed agenda.	Alternate elected for each senator and deputy.	Broad delegation of legislative power to président, including "emergency economic powers."
One session, July 28 for 120 days.		
One session, March 15 to Dec. 15, except when legislature elected; then Feb. 15 to Oct. 15.	Permanent Committee (7 representatives, 4 senators). Alternate elected for each senator and representative.	Only National Council (exec.) may initiate budget and some other fiscal bills.
One session, April 19 for 100 days. President calls special sessions; fixed agenda.	Permanent Committee (Pres. and v.p. of congress, 20 members). Alternate elected for each senator and deputy.	

TABLE XV.   UNICAMERAL LEGISLATURES

COUNTRY	No. of Members	Term	Method of Selection	Qualifications for Office	Party Members in Chamber*
Costa Rica	45	4 years; ½ each 2 years	P.R., by provinces. 1:15,000	21 years old; citizen 10 years	31 National Liberation; 14 Democratic and National Union
El Salvador	54	2 years	Direct election, by districts 1:39,000	25 years old; native-born; resident of or born in district	54 Revolutionary Party of Democratic Unity
Guatemala	66	4 years; ½ each 2 years	Direct election, by districts. 2 per district, + 1:50,000 if over 100,000	21 years old; native-born; secular	59 Nationalist Democratic Movement; 5 Guat. Christian Democrats; 2 Unity Anti-communist
Honduras	56	6 years	Direct election, by departments. 1:25,000	25 years old; citizen	Election for congress held Oct. 7, 1956, declared null by military
Panama	53	4 years	Direct election, by districts. 1:15,000	25 years old; citizen	47 National Patriotic Coalition; 6 National Liberal
Paraguay	40	5 years	Direct election, by districts.	25 years old; native-born	40 Colorado

SOURCE: Information, for the year 1957, supplied by the Latin American countries' embassies in Washington, D.C.

* Administration supporters in chamber indicated by underlining.

civilian positions for a stated period of time (usually three to six months) before election. Such provisions are intended to limit the practice of imposing official candidates and to limit army political activity. In practice, however, they do not seem to prevent persons in strategic political positions from winning election to congress.

TERMS OF OFFICE. Legislative terms of office in many Latin American countries are somewhat longer than in the United States, the most typical terms being four years in the lower and six years in the upper chamber. In the upper house, the term sometimes may run as long as eight or nine years. Argentina, Bolivia, Brazil, Guatemala, Chile, Costa Rica, and Cuba stagger the elections of one or both houses of the legislature. Where this is done, from a

IN LATIN AMERICAN COUNTRIES

Sessions of Congress	Special Features	Name of Legislature and General Remarks
Two sessions: May 1–July 1; Sept. 1–Nov. 1 Executive calls special sessions; fixed agenda.	One alternate for each 3 deputies.	The Legislative Assembly President may not veto regular budget law
Two sessions, Dec. 1 and June 1, for as long as necessary.	Alternate for each deputy. Permanent Committee (9 members).	The Legislative Assembly
One 3-month session, March 1. Permanent Committee or executive calls special sessions; fixed agenda.	Permanent Committee (9 members).	The National Congress
One session, Dec. 5 for 60 days. President calls special sessions; fixed agenda.	Alternate for each deputy.	The National Congress
One session, Oct. 1 for 90 days	Permanent Committee (5 members).	The National Assembly
One session: April 1–Aug. 31.	One alternate for each 3 deputies (18 alternates in all).	The Chamber of Representatives President has sole initiative in tax and military bills and absolute veto, except for item vetoes.

third to a half of each chamber is elected at some time during the presidential term. Thus, after mid-term elections, the reorganized congress is often a barometer of the political strength of the president. If his followers retain a comfortable majority in congress, the executive has retained his influence. Or a president's weakness may first become publicly apparent through the growth of opposition strength in the legislature after a mid-term election.

The Mexican constitution prohibits legislators from succeeding themselves in office. Although this provision is aimed at preventing a strong president from imposing his followers upon congress time after time in order to dominate congress, it has had exactly the opposite effect. No cadre of legislators has developed which understands the complexities of governmental programs and activities well enough to give continuity to legislative policy.

SUBSTITUTE LEGISLATORS.   Twelve Latin American constitutions provide a system for replacing legislators who for one reason or another cannot perform their duties.   The others either provide for special elections or allow the seat to remain vacant until the next regular election.   Automatic replacement avoids the expense and political turmoil of special elections, though at times it tempts the executive to find some way to remove a particularly recalcitrant member of congress in order to seat a more tractable person.

Brazil, Honduras, Mexico, Nicaragua, Panama, Uruguay and Venezuela elect a substitute (*suplente*) for each member elected to congress.   Paraguay and Costa Rica select a panel of *suplentes* equal to one-third of the congress.   In Colombia senatorial alternates selected in the departments by the winning party are designated in numerical order to replace any senator from that department who may default, while each deputy has two personal alternates.   Two *suplentes* are elected for each incumbent elected senator in Ecuador.   In the Dominican Republic the political party of the late incumbent nominates a panel and the chamber selects one of these persons as a replacement.

QUALITY OF LEGISLATORS.   It is worthwhile to note that although congresses lack independence in legislation in many countries, the quality of individual lawmakers is surprisingly high.   Inevitably, a few political hacks obtain office, but a high proportion of the members display the highest levels of professional and cultural attainment.   Lawyers, doctors, professional military officers, even university professors, proudly bear the title of senator or deputy.[20] In recent years, with the spread of suffrage for women, a few women legislators have been elected in such countries as Brazil, Chile, and Mexico, but their number is small.

PAY AND PERQUISITES.   The high level of education and culture among congressmen reflects in part the predominating influence of a social and economic elite and in part respect for the office and title.   It may also show that government plays a less neutral role in economic and social life in Latin America than in the United States.   Hence participation in government has its attractions, even in a legislative branch that may be subservient to the executive.   Perhaps the greatest appeal of congressional membership is its value as a stepping stone to a place in the executive branch.

[20] In Venezuela, for example, 55 per cent of the senators and 32 per cent of the deputies in the 1952 congress had the academic title of Doctor. *Gaceta Oficial,* April 17, 1952, quoted in Leo B. Lott, "Executive Power in Venezuela," *American Political Science Review,* L (June 1956), 423.   In some other countries military rank is more common, but the proportion of academic titles generally is high.

Certainly the rate of pay is not usually a primary inducement, for legislative salaries are quite low, ranging from the equivalent of 10,000 dollars yearly in Argentina to some 600 dollars in Ecuador. The amount of salary seems to depend neither upon the size nor the wealth of a country. The Dominican Republic pays its legislators about 6,000 dollars, while Brazil pays only the equivalent of 1,500 dollars. For many members of congress, especially those who are lawyers, fees for using their personal influence in legislation or within the administration offer a source of supplementary income. Unfortunately, simple graft is not unknown in this connection. This all too regular practice is one of the factors which limits the strength of the legislature in matters on which it might have an effective voice.

In many cases members of congress are expected to turn back a portion of their pay to the political party. Even in Uruguay, where lawyers who are members of congress are prohibited legally from having any practice before government agencies,[21] congressmen are expected to "kick back" 20 to 30 per cent of their salaries.

CONGRESSIONAL IMMUNITIES. Most constitutions provide special status for legislators, and those of Latin America are no exception. Immunity from arrest or civil suit during congressional sessions and immunity from responsibility for acts or statements made in pursuance of congressional duties are intended to assure the independent operation of the congress. These constitutional guarantees are respected for the most part, but numerous violations have occurred in times of revolutionary disturbance or under governments of dictatorial character.

Although legislators are guaranteed immunity for remarks made on the floor of congress, this guaranty does not, in some countries, extend to attacks upon the president or even his policies. The sanctions employed against congressmen may be merely political, as when the president of Mexico's chamber of deputies was removed from office in the early 1940's for suggesting, in a reply to President Ávila Camacho's speech opening the congressional session, that the elections of certain members of the official party had been rigged. Or the sanctions may be legal, under a law of *desacato* (disrespect). In Argentina, where congressional immunity was highly respected before the days of Perón, the *peronista* congress several times expelled Radical deputies who dared even to question policies or acts of the president on the floor of congress.[22]

[21] Fitzgibbon, *Uruguay: Portrait of a Democracy*, pp. 162–163.
[22] For further discussion of *desacato* see Blanksten, *Perón's Argentina*, pp. 81–82, 118–119, and Chapter 12 of this book.

Congressional immunity from arrest during sessions of congress generally does not protect a congressman caught committing a criminal act. In some countries he may also be tried for crimes or sued while congress is not in session; in others the chamber to which he belongs may have to extend permission for such prosecution. Because legislators have been known to take undue advantage of their immunity, in criminal as well as in civil matters, some countries have limited this protection. Mexico, for example, specifically excludes matters of civil liability from congressional immunity.

Congressional Organization and Operation

DURATION OF SESSIONS. The beginning date and duration of legislative sessions are prescribed in most Latin American constitutions. Length of sessions ranges from two months each year in Ecuador and Nicaragua to nine months in Uruguay, depending upon the term provided for in the constitution and sometimes upon the amount of legislative business. Most sessions last about six months, but a few constitutions call for two shorter sessions each year. Specific dates for opening and in many cases for closing the sessions, as may be seen in Tables XIV and XV, make the assembling of congress mandatory. But revolutionary governments sometimes ignore these provisions and operate without convening the legislature, at least until such time as a congress more attuned to the desires of the new regime can be seated.

SPECIAL SESSIONS. Because of the shortness of regular sessions, provision for convening special sessions often takes on added importance. Although the legislature has some voice in the matter, much of the initiative in calling and assigning tasks for extraordinary sessions, in practice as well as by law, lies with the executive. Only in Mexico and Venezuela does the permanent committee of congress have formal and exclusive authority to call special sessions, but in both countries presidential predominance is so marked as to negate this formal independence.[23] Six countries (Argentina, Costa Rica, the Dominican Republic, Haiti, Nicaragua, and Paraguay) assign this important function to the executive. Eight others permit either the executive or the legislative branch to act. In the latter case, the permanent committee (where it exists) or from one-fourth to an absolute majority of the legislators must request a special session. In thirteen countries only matters listed on the agenda for which a special session is called may be considered.

[23] See Lott, *op. cit.*, pp. 436–438, and Scott, "Some Aspects of Mexican Federalism, 1917–1948," *op. cit.*, chapter 3.

ORGANIZATION OF THE CHAMBER. Once in session, the legislature must organize itself for business by adopting rules of procedure, selecting officers in each chamber, and setting up standing committees. Rules governing congressional organization and procedure differ from country to country, but usually lean heavily on tradition and do not change much in any given session. It would not be consistent with Latin American constitutional principles and practice, however, to accord complete freedom of action in these matters to the congress. Most constitutions carefully provide for the internal organization of the houses of congress and detail the steps of the lawmaking process.

Some bicameral legislatures adopt rules jointly, others do not. In such countries as Chile, Costa Rica, or Uruguay, in which congress has a stronger role, the rules assure some degree of independence of action for the lawmakers. In most others they do not.

In those countries having vice-presidents, this officer usually presides over the upper chamber of congress. Otherwise, both chambers elect their own officers, generally including a president, vice-presidents, secretaries, committee chairmen, and other officials. In practice the majority party, or a coalition of parties, caucus beforehand to decide upon a slate. Where a multi-party system exists, the posts may be divided among a number of factions. In some countries the president's wishes may be a determining factor in the selection, and usually, unless the president is uncommonly weak, the naming of parliamentary officers is at least not contrary to his wishes.[24]

When the legislature is dominated by a single party, such as the PRI in Mexico or the former *peronista* party in Argentina, these elected parliamentary officers become key figures for ensuring control of congressional action by the president and his followers. Unanimous senatorial votes were not uncommon in Argentina under Perón, and divisions of one hundred and sixty deputies to four have been frequent in Mexico. In those countries where the legislature is less under presidential influence, the congressional officers enjoy correspondingly greater political influence.

Most Latin American lawmaking bodies, like modern legislatures everywhere, publish their actions and debates as a permanent record, usually called the *diario de debates*. This publication includes the official texts of bills introduced and passed in each chamber, reports of congressional committees, as well as

---

[24] For an example of presidential influence in naming legislative officers see William S. Stokes, "The Cuban Parliamentary System in Action, 1940–1947," *Journal of Politics*, XI (1949), 352–354.

reports of other congressional activities, such as the election of officers.

THE LEGISLATIVE PROCESS.   Latin American legislators have the right to initiate legislation, but not always as individuals.   In Venezuela and Ecuador three deputies must join to initiate a bill; in Chile five senators or ten deputies are required to join in a proposal.   The lack of more legislative initiative by members of congress is due less to these constitutional limitations, however, than to the general absence or inadequacy of bill-drafting and fact-finding agencies to assist legislators in the preparation of legislation.   Congressional libraries are adequate in Argentina and Chile, for example, but are largely lacking in other countries.   Even Mexico's library of congress is little more than a collection of miscellaneous books housed in an old church.   Legislative reference services are inadequate or entirely lacking.

Another cause for the lack of individual legislative initiative is the fact that members of congress often share the right to initiate bills with other agencies of government.   In Cuba, for example, under the 1940 constitution the judiciary and tribunal of accounts could originate bills.   Eight other countries allow judicial officers to participate in legislative activities in this manner (the Dominican Republic, Ecuador, El Salvador, Guatemala, Nicaragua, Panama, Peru, and Venezuela).   In Honduras this participation is even greater.   In the case of a bill that amends or repeals code law, if it does not originate in the supreme court, congress must hear the court's opinion before enacting the law.   Ecuador's national legislative commission, which will be discussed shortly, also may introduce bills.   State legislatures may propose laws to congress in Mexico.   And the Cuban constitution of 1940 provided for popular initiative, upon petition of 10,000 voters.

Major policy bills tend to originate with the executive, not simply because of presidential predominance in politics but because, as in most modern states, the executive is more directly aware of the need for new legislation and has the technical knowledge and aids to prepare it.   The president also has the political responsibility for action in the Latin American system of politics.   In this respect, the legislative process in Latin America is not unlike that of the United States and other democratic states.   What distinguishes the Latin American presidential bills from the legislation sponsored by the executive and introduced by a friendly congressman in the United States is that in Latin America they usually undergo little change as they are transformed into law.   Presidential initiative is usually exercised through the minister of *hacienda* for budget bills or through another minister of state for other matters.

Constitutional provisions or statutes in all of the countries grant the executive exclusive initiative in preparing and submitting budgetary proposals. Often the legislature is denied authority to increase budgetary totals without providing additional sources of funds. The president's authority to veto individual items in appropriation measures puts teeth into this restriction.[25] Beyond this, several countries grant the president exclusive rights in initiating other types of legislation. In Paraguay this right covers military bills; in Bolivia it embraces legislation concerning public employees. Uruguay's constitution includes a provision for sole initiative by the executive council for bills concerning the public debt, credit, creation of new public positions, increases in salaries and retirement benefits, and the granting or increasing of pensions or monetary compensation.

Bills introduced by the executive usually receive special precedence on the legislative agenda and in committee, by the rules of the chamber. Executive officers normally are entitled to appear on the floor of the legislature to advocate and defend departmental proposals, taking precedence over members during debate. Obviously, this privileged position under the rules of procedure further enhances the already great executive influence in lawmaking arising from the president's political power.

LEGISLATIVE COMMISSION IN ECUADOR. In recent years some countries have tried to achieve closer integration in lawmaking than is possible under the formal but often nonoperative separation of powers. In 1944 Ecuador took the novel step of setting up a legislative commission to prepare bills of major importance. This five-member commission consists of representatives of each of the legislative chambers, the executive branch, the judicial branch, and the dean of the law school of the Central University, *ex officio*. It prepares bills dealing with constitutional amendments and with budgetary, defense, and other specified matters. Its proposals are presented to a joint session of congress, which votes without

[25] For the influence of the chief executive in this realm, see Paul A. M. Philips, *Public Finance in Less Developed Economies* (The Hague: Nijhoff, 1957); Arizio de Viana, *Budget-Making in Brazil,* translated by Harvey Walker (Columbus: Ohio State University Press, 1947); John H. Adler, *et al, Public Finance and Economic Development in Guatemala* (Stanford, Cal.: Stanford University Press, 1952); Robert E. Scott, "Budget Making in Mexico"; Leo B. Lott, *op. cit.,* and *Ecuador, hacienda pública y política fiscal* (Washington: The Pan American Union, 1954).

referring them to committee. If approved by a two-thirds majority of the joint session the measures are sent to the president for his signature and promulgation.

It is noteworthy that this Ecuadorian experiment is being watched with keen interest by other Latin Americans, who think they see in it a more realistic approach to the lawmaking process than that followed under the present constitutional systems, one that more realistically reflects the positive role of the president in present-day Latin America.[26] Yet even if the Ecuadorian example proves successful in practice, it should not be expected to mark a trend away from political thinking based on the concept of separation of powers. Even in those countries where the president or the council of state already has quasi-legislative powers, the magic of the theoretical separation of powers as a means to limited government remains strong in the minds of Latin Americans. The balance of powers continues to be a Latin American objective. Yet if a better balance among the branches of government is to be achieved, it must come from real changes in the political environment, from an expanded understanding of and participation in the political process by the general citizenry, rather than from tinkering with the written constitutions.

CONGRESSIONAL COMMITTEES: ORGANIZATION. The structure of congressional committees is not dissimilar to that in other modern legislative bodies. A few congresses use nonspecialized committees to which work is distributed without regard to subject matter, but most legislatures now have standing, subject-matter committees. Sometimes the two systems are combined. The rules of congress in Mexico, for example, call for forty-seven permanent subject-matter committees in each chamber, but in practice there have sometimes been more than sixty. During one recent session the chamber of deputies had four committees on collective farm affairs and the senate three on defense matters. Typically, the jurisdiction of standing committees roughly parallels the division of government activity in executive departments, such as defense, budget, or education.

Committee size varies greatly. In Chile the twelve senate standing committees have five members each, and the thirteen chamber committees have thirteen members. In Brazil each of the ten standing senate committees consists of five members and the fourteen committees in the lower chamber of seventeen members. The Mexican system is one of many small committees. Except for a five-member budget committee, the usual committee

26 See Blanksten, *Ecuador, op. cit.*, pp. 112–116.

has three members and an alternate (*suplente*). Depending on the size and number of the committees, a member of congress may serve on one standing committee, as in Mexico, or on as many as six or seven, as in Brazil.

Standing committee assignments may be made by a prearranged vote of the chamber, or decided by a "committee on committees." Committee membership is usually proportional to party strength in each chamber, though opposition members sometimes refuse to participate because they do not wish to lend support to the administration. This happened in Argentina under Perón and in Brazil under Vargas. On rare occasions it has occurred in other countries. Conversely, under Mexico's system of many small committees, the small number of opposition deputies makes it impossible for them to sit on all committees.

FUNCTIONING OF COMMITTEES. As compared with legislative committees elsewhere, those of most Latin American countries play a relatively unimportant role in the lawmaking process. Because they lack staff and technical aids, their more able or energetic members may exercise disproportionate influence. Committees also suffer from lack of continuity in membership, either because of prohibition on immediate re-election or because a change in the presidency carries with it a higher turnover of legislators than it does, for example, in the United States.

Congressional committees often seem to be merely ratifying what has been decided outside the halls of congress. Public hearings are relatively infrequent, and witnesses from outside the executive branch are seldom heard. As a result, committee reports on pending legislation too often reveal lack of a serious review of proposals and little intention to challenge legislation sponsored by the president.

The function of congressional committees seems to be increasing in those countries in which the legislature plays an independent role. In Chile, Uruguay, and Costa Rica legislative committees are consistently important in the legislative process. In Brazil, Argentina, and Colombia, on the other hand, countries in which legislative committees have had great importance in the past, their effectiveness seems to have decreased in recent years. Mexico's standing committees have recently begun to hold out-of-session investigations in matters of their competence, somewhat in the manner of legislative commissions in several of the state governments of the United States. But the Mexican committees have been reluctant to intrude upon matters in which the executive has shown interest or expressed intent.

Rules for the standing committees vary widely. In Argentina, for example, with the exception of the budget, committees need not report out bills for consideration of the whole chamber. But in Mexico and Chile congressional committees must report out every bill assigned to them. In some legislatures the committees are permitted to make extensive revisions in the content of bills, in others they may not, particularly if the bill has been sponsored by the executive. In Ecuador, as noted previously, bills introduced by the legislative commission do not pass to committee, while in Peru a simple majority vote of the chamber may eliminate this committee review. In Argentina, committees state orally the reasons for changes they have made in a bill. In many other countries this is done in writing; in a few it is not done at all.

Once a bill has been approved by a majority of the standing committee, it passes to the chamber and is placed on the legislative calendar. As in the United States, bills are moved up on the calendar in accordance with their importance, by decision of the political leaders of the chamber.

CONGRESSIONAL DEBATE. Debate on the floor of congress, like votes in committees, generally follows party lines. Opposition members often attempt to hinder enactment of laws by employing obstructionist tactics, or even by remaining away from sessions in hopes of preventing a quorum. During Cuba's short-lived parliamentary experiment, the opposition regularly resorted to this latter tactic. When presidential supporters lost control of the congress they retaliated by doing the same thing.[27] Similar opposition tactics succeeded in Peru under President Bustamante during the late 1940's. Such efforts failed, however, when employed against Perón in Argentina.

In debate, the opposition may criticize proposed legislation harshly, but direct attacks generally are pointed at legislative colleagues or the responsible minister. The chief executive is rarely criticized in congressional debate. In part this is because of traditional respect for the office. But experience has also shown that despite constitutional guaranties of immunity accorded statements made in the legislature congressional affronts to the *dignidad* of the president may bring unfortunate consequences, whether or not the crime of *desacato* has been defined in law.

Unless the opposition carries its attacks to unreasonable extremes, however, it is generally permitted to express its views to the con-

[27] Stokes, *op. cit.,* pp. 356–359.

gress. When free debate is permitted, these expressions of opposition views—of opinions which do not coincide with those of the administration—have great value. Unfortunately, the opposition often goes beyond reasonable limits in debate. It would be contrary to Latin American political psychology if it failed to do so. The government party may then retaliate with tighter restrictions on debate, remove opposition members from the chamber, or even employ force against them.

VOTING ON BILLS. Voting procedures vary in details. But generally, after the constitutional requirement for one or more readings has been met, a bill is approved in each chamber by voice vote. The vote may be by roll call if requested, but some legislatures require that more than one member must make this request, sometimes in advance. A number of countries, including Argentina, Mexico, and several of the Central American and Carribbean states, have installed electric voting systems.

In the bicameral legislatures, disagreements between the two houses, expressed in differing versions of a bill, are settled in various ways. In Uruguay, Ecuador, and Venezuela, in such cases, the two chambers meet as a single body to vote on the bill. In Brazil, the standing committees which considered the bill in each house meet jointly to iron out the differences. In Colombia, an informal meeting of party leaders in the two chambers tries to accomplish the same purpose. In Argentina and Chile the house in which a bill originates may override the other chamber's amendments or additions by a two-thirds vote. In Mexico agreement must be reached by the two chambers, although by absolute majority vote the two houses may agree to send the president those parts of a bill on which they are not in disagreement. Most of the other bicameral legislatures use conference committees like those employed in the United States.

PREDOMINANCE OF ADMINISTRATION BILLS. In the light of the facts in the preceding discussion it is not surprising that a high proportion of major legislative business reaching the floor of congress originates with the executive. Where a bill cannot be traced directly to the president, it may have been inspired by the executive branch indirectly. Non-administration bills fall by the wayside for a variety of reasons. Obviously, those entailing expenditure of money will fail because of the strict control of the purse enjoyed by the president through his item veto. Some others fail to pass as a result of decisions made by the political leadership of the chamber when faced with the inevitable last-minute rush before adjournment.   Others, of course, fail because they lack merit.[28]

Furthermore, most of the bills sponsored by the president become law. During the three-year term of the Mexican congress, ending in 1952, the legislature enacted 138 measures. Of these, seventy-two were general laws, thirty-one granted permission to accept foreign medals or decorations, seven permitted Mexicans to work for foreign governments, and twenty-eight authorized pensions. Only seven of the 138 originated with members of congress; the remainder were introduced by executive officers. Few if any changes and no major amendments were made in these administration bills as they passed through congress. It should be noted, however, that three presidential bills were still pending when the session closed, indicating that the Mexican congress is not merely a rubber-stamp for the executive.[29] Fortunately, few Latin American legislatures today share the fate of that of Venezuela under President Juan Vicente Gómez, in which, as one member of congress stated, "Everyone knows that orders accompanied every bill not to change so much as a comma."[30]

THE PRESIDENTIAL VETO. After passage, a bill is sent to the president for signature and promulgation. The bill becomes law when he signs it and goes into effect when published in the government's official journal. As noted previously, the president has the power to veto legislation, constitutionally in nineteen countries and by custom in Peru. In most nations this power also includes the item veto, so that he may reject part of a bill to which he may object without losing those portions of it which he desires. Nor is the importance of the item veto limited to budget matters, because in most states the president may veto items in general as well as fiscal legislation. In practice, however, since the bills emanating from the halls of congress usually have been sponsored by the executive and have undergone little change in passage, the president seldom needs to resort to use of the veto.

It is even less common for a legislature to override a presidential veto, but by an interesting coincidence this occurred twice within a single month in 1957. During the first part of April the

[28] On presidential initiative and domination of legislative bills see, for example, William S. Stokes, *Honduras: An Area Study in Government* (Madison: University of Wisconsin Press, 1950), pp. 286–287; Blanksten, *Perón's Argentina*, p. 116; Blanksten, *Ecuador*, p. 101.   Uruguay, and possibly Chile and Costa Rica, are exceptions.

[29] This information on one session, gathered by the writer, is typical of most Mexican legislative sessions.

[30] Cited by Lott, "Executive Power in Venezuela," p. 437, quoting Ernesto Wolff, *Tratado de derecho venezolano* (Caracas, 1945), I, 316–317.

Brazilian congress rejected President Kubitschek's veto of a bill permitting congressmen and judges to import automobiles free of import duties.   Later the same month, the legislature of El Salvador passed a new tax bill for San Salvador over the veto of President Lemus. But such actions are scarcely typical enough to be called a new trend.   The Brazilian case demonstrates how, even in a financial crisis, legislators may act for personal benefit if the president is not strong enough politically to control them.   And the veto action in Salvador was reportedly instigated by the president himself, in order to avoid the responsibility for a potentially unpopular law without losing its benefits.

Problems and Trends

While numerous changes are under way in the congresses of Latin America, less significant over-all trends are apparent here than in some other constitutional and political organisms, due probably to the less dynamic role legislatures play in the political system.   Except for a few vestigial remains, the earlier trend to parliamentarianism seems to have subsided.   While the permanent committees of congress continue in those countries which have adopted them, no new nations have been added to the list recently. Nor does the unicameral legislature display any tendency to expand into additional countries.   The war-time trend toward greater activity of congressional committees has declined in recent years, but may revive again.   There are some indications of a tendency to provide congress and its committees with better information facilities, but hardly enough to justify speaking of a trend.   A few countries are following the example of Chile in establishing greater control over government expenditures through a tribunal or office of accounts, and congress increasingly has become the arbiter of controversial or indecisive presidential elections.   The reporting of congressional debates and of committee actions shows improvement.   But, in the final analysis, the general weakness of congresses is still one of the major shortcomings of Latin American government, one upon which the present rapid growth of government focuses increased attention.

The present role of the legislature in Latin America is not what the constitutions say it is.   In most countries congress does not participate in determining national policy in the independent manner and to the extent usually deemed necessary to the successful operation of democratic and responsible government.   Will, then, congress ever assume its legislative function as described in Latin America's constitutions?   Or, if the constitutions are changed to conform more nearly to the political habits and needs of the citizens, will the role of the legislature be appreciably stronger than at present? In either event, what can legislators do to prepare themselves to assume greater responsibility in politics?

It is impossible to answer these questions categorically, either for all of the countries in general or for any given state. Common cultural and historical backgrounds have produced certain similarities in political practices, but political progress must develop upon the experience of each nation and upon the social and economic changes affecting politics in each country. One thing is reasonably sure, however: any real change in the status of the legislature is closely related to the development of more responsible democratic government. There is no easy way to legislate an effective congress into existence. Tinkering with constitutional provisions has done little in the past to strengthen the role of congress, and premature attempts to establish a new role for the legislative branch cannot be expected to accomplish more in the future.

But the search for an easy solution to the problem of congressional weakness continues. Suggestions for parliamentary government were heard in Brazil during 1955, and constitutional amendments to strengthen the Argentine legislature at the expense of the executive were proposed in 1957. But one may predict that, unless the basic social, economic, and political conditions which lead to exaggerated presidentialism also change, these and other attempts to expand the functions of congress are doomed to fail, as so many others have.

This does not mean that there is no hope for effective legislative function in the foreseeable future. Far from it. The dynamics of social and economic change are bringing into being conditions under which responsible and constitutional government can develop. As democratic tendencies increase, the role of the legislature is likely to change also, although what form this change will take is not certain. The chances are that the legislative branch in most countries will remain part of a system of presidential government. Yet the real function of congress might become much more important and quite different from that now described by the constitutions.

Changes in the factors affecting political life in any particular country, when they become strong enough, may well bring a new relationship between executive and legislature. The president is now the center of the power structure in most nations, balancing a limited number of competing interests which bring pressure upon the government. But as the base of politically active citizens widens and the interests which must be served become more numerous and complex, the machinery for satisfying demands, machinery now manipulated by the president largely on a nonconstitutional basis, may prove insufficiently flexible and effective. The center of power may then pass to the legislative branch, in which the mechanics of policy-making and interest-satisfying are less personalized.

One cannot predict that changing social and economic conditions will inevitably promote democratic political tendencies or replace the present exaggerated presidentialism with a system relying upon a stronger legislature. It is indeed a question whether, in most countries, a reduction in executive power would really increase congressional responsibility to the general citizenry, since the presidency is on the whole a more popular institution. Certainly a power structure conforming to constitutional provisions would bring little, if any, more popular participation in the political process, because the people in most countries are not yet ready for it.

Chile is a case in point. The center of power has virtually been transferred from president to legislature, but the change has not brought stable and effective government. In Colombia, the transition to shared legislative–executive political power once seemed accomplished, but a reversion to presidential domination occurred in recent years, because the factions of the Liberal party dominating the congress could not compromise their differences sufficiently to make the system work. In Uruguay alone does the transition from presidential to legislative control appear to be providing a workable system of government.

Perhaps the experience of Mexico is even more to the point. There are indeed few countries in Latin America or elsewhere in which an equal degree of social change and economic progress has occurred in so short a period, or where the political base has been widened so rapidly. But the democratic tendencies accompanying all these changes have not transferred the policy-making functions or the ability to satisfy various interest groups from the president to the legislature, or even resulted in the legislature's attempting to share these functions. On the contrary, the Mexican president is today stronger than ever, for the official PRI party has given him auxiliary mechanisms to control the policy-making process. And this pattern may be duplicated in other states undergoing a similar rapid development, such as Bolivia, Venezuela, and Brazil.

This is not to say that the legislature will not rise to the occasion when conditions reach a proper stage in a given country. Many nations have already come a long way. Constitutional formalization has regularized the lawmaking process, at least outwardly. The facts for determining and directing the operation of government are at hand or quickly obtainable. The hard fact remains, however, that control does not usually rest today in the hands of congress.

Suggestions for Reading

Except for the short statements in Asher N. Christensen (ed.), *The Evolution of Latin American Government: A Book of Readings* (New York: Henry Holt & Co., Inc., 1951), and other textbooks, such as William W. Pierson and Federico G. Gil, *Governments of Latin America* (New York: McGraw-Hill Book Co., Inc., 1956), there is no general discussion of the Latin American congress in English. William S. Stokes, "Parliamentary Government in Latin America," *The American Political Science Review*, XXXIX (June 1945), 522–536, considers weaknesses of the legislative branch which led to a desire for parliamentarianism, and his "The Cuban Parliamentary System in Action, 1940–1947," *The Journal of Politics*, XI (May 1949), 335–364, pictures political action in Latin America's legislatures as it occurs. The latter article cites several useful works in Spanish by José Manuel Cortina and others on the problems of executive–legislative relations in Cuba.

Most national studies in Spanish are legal in character. Illustrative of such works are Carlos Estévez Gazmuri, *Derecho constitucional* (Santiago: Galcón, 1947); José Duarte, *A constituição brasileira de 1946: Exegese dos textos a luz dos trabalhos da Assembléia Constituinte*, 3 vols. (Rio de Janeiro: Imp. Nacional, 1948); and Gabino Fraga, *Derecho administrativo* (6th ed., México: Porrúa Hermanos, 1955).

Carlos A. Tagle, *Estado de derecho y equilibrio de poderes en la constitución argentina* (Santa Fe, Argentina: Univ. Nac. del Litoral, 1944), and Jorge Cabral Texo, *El régimen de los decretos: Leyes en derecho público argentino* (Buenos Aires: Librería Jurídica, 1949), offer Argentine views on two matters which concern the legislature. José María Oceguera Ochoa, *La presidencia de la cámara* (México: Univ. Nac. Aut. de México, 1945), discusses that office in Mexico. Few indeed are the countries where legislative activities are so meaningful as to produce a study as technical as Eduardo Rodríguez Piñeres, *Táctica parlamentaria* (Bogotá: Librería Colombiana, 1937).

Chapter 12

Law and Court Systems

Basis and Origins of Latin American Law

The objectives of law differ little from one legal system to another. All legal systems seek to maintain social harmony and public order, to protect both individuals and society against crimes, to uphold and defend the rights of individuals in their person, property, and moral well-being, and, in general, to regulate the physical, intellectual, moral, and religious progress of the nation as a whole. While these are the objectives of law, they are also objectives of any organized political society. In Latin America, however, the legal system is a factor of unusual social significance, either because of something in the civil-law system or something in Latin American political thought. One Argentine author has expressed this importance of law as follows: "The national organization which all statesmen concentrated on developing in Argentina was principally a juridical organization. The constitutional and legislative order implanted in 1853 was the one which has determined and shaped the development of our country in every other respect of its national life. Without law, the Republic could never have outgrown *personalismo* in its political administration nor insecurity in its private activities."[1]

All of the Latin American republics adhere to the civil-law system, one of the two great legal systems in modern civilization. The eighteen Spanish American nations derive their system from Spanish antecedents with some French influence, while Brazil's heritage is from Portugal, and that of Haiti from France. But all share the civil-law heritage.

[1] Ricardo Zorraquín Becú, *Marcelino Ugarte, 1822–1872* (Buenos Aires: Instituto de Historia de Derecho, 1954), p. 159.

COMMON LAW.   Custom and judicial precedent are the life-blood of any common-law jurisdiction. Anglo-Saxon law, known to us as common law, was based on custom, as developed through the courts. According to *Black's Law Dictionary,* common law is "a body of principles and rules of action, relating to the government and security of persons and property, which derive their authority solely from usages and customs of immemorial antiquity, or from the judgments and decrees of the courts, recognizing, affirming and enforcing such usages and customs; and in this sense, particularly the ancient unwritten law of England."

This definition of common law, as employed in the United States, has been somewhat modified by adding early acts of the British parliament to the "unwritten law" and by adopting the year 1776 as a limitation in time. In short, it includes British customary and unwritten law, plus acts of the British parliament which had been adopted prior to 1776, together with judicial interpretation in England prior to 1776 and, subsequent to that date, in the United States in cases involving interpretation of the British "common law."

Certain advantages of the common law over civil law have been pointed out. One eminent legal historian[2] has noted common law's great flexibility and its use in molding experience and traditional customs to actual practice, permitting an orderly march of continuous growth which keeps law in touch with life. The shortcomings of common law lie in its great dependence upon case law and judicial precedent, which makes the study and practice of law progressively more unwieldy as the body of precedent grows. The same legal historian, therefore, remarks, "Case law is gold in the mine—a few grains of precious metal to a ton of useless matter—while statute law is coin of the realm, ready for immediate use." Another author has written that in 1947 the student of common law faced the problem of considering "325,000 pages of United States statute law and a yearly production of 500 volumes of court decisions."[3] This writer later remarked that "our law is in grave danger of being crushed under the sheer weight of its two million reported cases and tons of statutes."[4]

CIVIL LAW.   The term "civil law" designates the body of jurisprudence derived from the principles of law compiled by the Emperor Justinian in the Corpus Juris Civilis. (This is, of course, an over-

[2] Sir William S. Holdsworth, *Some Lessons from Our Legal History* (New York: The Macmillan Co., 1928), p. 19.

[3] Arthur Vanderbilt in *New York University Law Review,* XXIV (1929), 22.

[4] Arthur Vanderbilt, "Law and Government in the Development of the American Way of Life," Address delivered on November 12, 1951 (University of Wisconsin, Madison).

simplified definition, but an adequate one for the present purpose.)
In a much broader sense, the term also applies to the national systems of law based on the Roman law, even when the individual
national systems have developed in quite distinct directions because
of local circumstances and conditions.

Two characteristics distinguish the civil from the common-law
system. In the first place, the civil law is a scientific, systematic
body of written law, carefully codified, where the doctrines of
stare decisis and judicial precedent have no important role. Second,
custom and usage are regarded as unimportant sources of law in
the civil system, whereas they constitute a fundamental basis of
the common law. Sometimes it happens that these relatively small
differences are overemphasized and the greater similarities and
common objectives of the two systems overlooked. This is unfortunate, for behind both systems lie great common principles of
law which dwarf the differences.

SPANISH, PORTUGUESE, AND FRENCH INFLUENCES. Many years
prior to the implantation of the legal systems of Spain and Portugal
in their overseas possessions, codes, or *fueros,* were developed in
the Iberian Peninsula whose influence in Latin American law persists even to the present time. Each of the various invaders of the
peninsula exercised some influence, so that we find strong Germanic, Arabic, and Roman traces in the legal institutions. The
sixth-century Visigothic Code, or Fuero Juzgo, represents Germanic
influence. Las Siete Partidas, the thirteenth-century code of King
Alfonso the Wise, is well known for the part it has played in the
law and court decisions of the states of Louisiana, California, and
Texas. The Laws of the Indies, best known in the later Recopilación (1681), were enacted specifically for the New World. In the
commercial field, the Consulate of the Sea provisions applied to
maritime trade and the Ordenanzas de Bilbao to land commerce.
These codes, among others, formed the legal background of present-
day law in Spanish America.

In Portugal, an early history shared with Spain also gave an
overcast of Germanic, Arabic, and Roman influences to the early
legislative compilations. The ordinances carefully compiled and
issued at various times were generally titled according to the name
of the monarch in whose reign they were issued. Subsequently
implanted in Brazil, they are still influential in modern Brazilian law.

The French influence in the Western Hemisphere, aside from that
in Quebec and Louisiana, is most noticeable in the laws of Haiti.
Even as a colony, Haiti was regulated by French customary law,
and additional royal decrees were directed specifically for use there.

The Napoleonic codes are the direct antecedent of the Haitian codes of today. But French influence has also been felt in the Spanish American republics, both directly and indirectly. Since at the dawn of Latin American independence in the 1800's Spain did not have modern codes in some private law fields suitable for adaptation, the new nations naturally turned to the new Napoleonic codes to supply the gaps. A number of the countries merely translated these codes into Spanish, with little thought as to the applicability of some of the provisions. The nations that did not codify until later in the century had the advantage of the Spanish codifications of the mid-century. Even in these cases, however, French influence in the New World was still felt, since the Spanish code-drafters also drew on the French codes for inspiration.

Modern Law in Latin America

CODIFICATION AND INCORPORATION. The written law which is compulsory in Latin America and in other civil-law jurisdictions may be enacted either by codification or by incorporation. Codification takes place when a particular branch of law has achieved the degree of completion and crystallization which permits it to be molded into a coherent single body of legislation. This is then enacted as a law, complete in itself. In general, a code is issued as a body of law "with unity of thought and of time," as differentiated from the loosely linked legislative compilations of early Spanish legal history.[5]

Incorporation, on the other hand, occurs when laws have been enacted individually or in isolated form over a period of time, as needed. It can be readily understood that certain fields do not lend themselves readily to codification for one reason or another. Contemporary examples include labor law, administrative law, and the law of taxation. Unreadiness for codification may result from the law being in a state of flux and lacking well-defined, permanent characteristics. Or it may result from insufficient experience and practice because of the comparative novelty of the field. In such cases, the legislation tends to be enacted by incorporation.

Interest in codification began in all of the Spanish American republics as soon as they had established their independence from Spain. Even though they entered upon their independent national life more or less simultaneously, and with similar legal and institutional backgrounds, they developed legal systems with distinct

[5] Felipe Sánchez Román, *Estudios de derecho civil* (Madrid: Rivadeneyra, 1910), I, 32.

national characteristics deriving from differences in their national histories and in national social and economic conditions. The variations in the codes were mostly in matters of detail, however, while the systems as a whole displayed those resemblances which might be expected in view of their common inspiration in the Napoleonic codes of the first decade of the nineteenth century and the Spanish codes of the latter half of the century.

BASIC DIVISIONS OF THE LAW. Latin American legal systems, whether Spanish, Portuguese, or French in origin, thus display much uniformity, both in form and in substance. Much of the law is usually embraced in four or five basic codes. A civil code, governing the rights of individuals, family and domestic matters, property and property rights, and contracts, is usually accompanied by a code of civil procedure. A criminal code, which defines crimes and punishments, is likewise accompanied by a procedural code regulating judicial enforcement of the substantive code provisions. A commercial code covers most matters connected with business and trade in general. The law on associations and corporations was formerly to be found in the civil code, but such provisions now appear in commercial codes. Commercial codes include laws relating to merchants, brokers, business bookkeeping, negotiable instruments, bankruptcy, and similar matters. Procedural law is usually divided into civil and criminal codes, but in a number of nations the several types of procedure are concentrated in a single body of procedural law.

Several nations have codified administrative law to some extent. Labor and tax codes are also found, but these are generally only an orderly compilation of individual laws amending the basic organic law on the subject. Other fields of law are generally uncodified.

The arrival of the machine age, with its accompanying expansion of trade, the growth of international contacts, and the development of new sources of wealth, has given rise to many legal problems, the solution of which has required changes in traditional principles of law. Among these new developments, for example, are trusts, security transactions such as chattel mortgages and conditional sales, and cooperative ownership of apartment and business buildings—all matters unforeseen by the legislators of decades ago when the basic codes were adopted. In order to render justice in these new situations, courts have had to adopt certain legal fictions, finding roundabout ways to arrive at a legal solution which yet would not do violence to the written law.

LEGAL EDUCATION. Differences between the civil- and common-law systems are reflected in differences in the education of the lawyer to practice his profession in the two separate jurisdictions. Under both systems, of course, education is based on certain universal principles of law. In the methods of instruction and in the emphases given to certain studies, however, great divergences may occur. The cause lies partly in the form of the law, that is, in the codified form of civil law as contrasted with the diffuseness of customary and judge-made common law. Another basis lies in the different vocational objectives of legal education in the United States and Latin America. Approximately three-quarters of the law graduates in the United States devote themselves to the practice of law, deriving their living from their professional fees. In most Latin American countries this proportion is smaller. The independent practitioner there has difficulty in making a living unless he supplements his practice with teaching, a government post, counselling in the business world, or some other employment. There are relatively few large law firms like those commonly found in the cities of the United States.

Lawyers, however, are never merely practitioners or jurists, in either common- or civil-law countries. They are community leaders, public servants, politicians, statesmen, diplomats, and legislators. The alliance of politics and law is even closer in Latin America than in the United States. Latin American law graduates exercise a preponderant influence in legislatures and in public administration. The science of government always relies heavily upon legal science. But the lack of development in political science in Latin America makes this dependence even greater.

Methods of legal instruction also reflect the differences in the two legal systems. The great dependence of the Anglo-American system on precedent and *stare decisis* has led to general adoption of the case method in the United States. Under this system the student digests numerous court decisions, learning by the inductive method the principles of law which are involved, noting both majority and minority rulings and variations from one jurisdiction to another.

The student of civil law, on the other hand, listens to lectures which are essentially expositions of codes and other fundamental laws. He also reads treatises of a doctrinal nature by national and foreign authorities. He begins his curriculum at a younger age and his course is longer than that of the common-law student, permitting, during the first years, some study of such general subjects as sociology, economics, and history, though not as much as a North American student usually has in his pre-legal college education. The civil-law student's curriculum also includes certain broader courses on legal philosophy, history of law, jurisprudence, international and comparative law, which the common-law student generally gets only as electives, frequently in postgraduate work. Some observers would contend that case study is a down-to-earth method which gives the graduate better preparation for practical problems of the practice of law, for it trains him to deal with facts and to argue a case from them with authority. A student of civil law, on the other hand, must spend some time after graduation learning to grapple with the practical problems of his profession. In some ways, perhaps, the greater breadth and more theoretical character of civil-law study make him more ready to undertake tasks of statesmanship and policy-making than is the common-law graduate. But the nature of his training also seems to contribute to an exaggerated reliance upon legal enactments which lack an essential basis in social realities—the kind of "legalism" and verbalism which plagues Latin American political life.

Certain contemporary trends in legal study suggest that the difference between the two methods may be diminishing. In some common-law jurisdictions, there is less concentration on case study, while in civil-law countries greater attention is being given to *jurisprudencia,* or judicial precedent, to be discussed later in this chapter. In both cases, the new trend appears as a supplement to the older method; that is, readings and doctrinal lectures supplement the case study, while illustrations by court decisions supplement the civil-law lectures.

Relation of the Judicial to Other Branches of Government

The province of the judicial power is primarily the administration of justice under law. In theory, it is independent and separate from the other branches under a tripartite system. The judicial power has seldom been as clearly circumscribed as the other two powers, however. At times it has been dominated by the legislative power and in other instances has been dependent upon the executive. In most modern democracies, however, it has finally attained a high degree of autonomy, even though the lines separating it from the legislative and executive powers are not always sharply drawn. Indeed, it has been difficult in practice to maintain the complete separation of powers, and we have learned that it is not always desirable. Modern legislatures exercise judicial functions, the executive has taken on certain judicial and legislative duties, while the judicial branch also legislates, after a fashion. The essential question, from the standpoint of the judiciary, is not whether a sharp theoretical division of powers is drawn. If it were, the Latin American constitutions would have solved the problem, for a theoretical division is always made on paper. The important question is not this theoretical one, but whether the courts enjoy the degree of autonomy essential to the proper administration of justice.

THE EXECUTIVE AND JUDICIAL POWERS. The executive branch in Latin American governments, as noted in an earlier chapter, is the strongest of the three classic powers of state, whether the government is dictatorial or constitutional. The Latin American executive is granted power to intervene in the field of justice in ways that vary from country to country. The executive generally participates in, if he does not actually make, judicial appointments. His power to initiate legislation includes that concerning the judiciary.

The constitutions and organic laws on the judiciary generally state clear injunctions against the intervention of other powers in judicial administration. Yet one kind of intervention, which has increased in modern times, seems to have circumvented these injunctions. It arises from programs of social legislation which tend to permit social interests to predominate over the rights of individuals as private citizens. This kind of intervention occurs particularly in respect to property rights, which today seem to be more closely linked with administrative law and less with private civil law than in the past. This innovation gives the executive the power to regulate the rights of the individual by administrative acts, sometimes depriving the individual, to some extent, of appeal to the regular courts. In such cases, the administration becomes both the prosecutor and the judge, and the opportunities for a miscarriage of justice are obvious. The establishment of administrative courts to meet the problems created by this intervention of the executive power in the judicial field will be discussed more fully later in this chapter.

Other judicial duties delegated to the executive by the constitutions include granting pardons and commuting sentences. The office of public or government attorney (*ministerio público, procuraduría pública*) also provides an important link between the judicial and executive branches. The man in this office generally represents the "people" in litigation and is vested with a mixture of administrative and disciplinary duties. The office is generally a part of the executive branch, although in some cases it is attached to the judiciary and to some extent it is often autonomous. The public attorney must be represented in the trial of every case in which the state or some political subdivision is a party or has substantial interest. He is a party in all criminal trials. In civil cases involving minors, married women, or incompetents, and in cases of divorce or expropriation or judicial attachment of property, he attends in the role of guardian and protector. In order to correct abusive practices, the government attorney is authorized in some countries to take disciplinary action against court officials. His authority may even extend to pointing out to the legislative power the need of impeaching a judge when some miscarriage of justice has been discovered.

THE LEGISLATURE AND THE JUDICIAL POWERS. Even in the most successful Latin American democracies, as noted in Chapter 11, the legislative branch has proved in practice to be the weakest of the three divisions of government, although in some countries it runs a close race with the judicial power for this dubious prize. The principal function of the legislative branch obviously is lawmaking. The unicameral and bicameral legislatures of Latin American republics are authorized by and function under their respective constitutions, which provide that laws enacted by these bodies shall be obligatory on all persons. Since the parliaments must often legislate in an abstract or generalized form, it is the function of the executive, again under the terms of the constitution, to regulate the statutes in order that they may be made truly effective. Many laws would fail of their objective completely if executive decrees did not put teeth into them. This regulatory power is one form of delegated legislative authority conferred upon the executive. And the judiciary gives equal authority to both the laws and the decrees.

The legislative branch can also influence the judiciary through enactment of legislation expanding or limiting the latter's powers, rights, or functions. It frequently plays a part in the selection or approval of candidates for the bench, and in a few countries it has the power of appointment. Under all of the constitutions, the legislative body is granted the power of impeachment and trial of high officials in all branches of the government for misfeasance or malfeasance in office—the extent of the power, the types of crime punishable, and the impeachment and trial procedures varying from country to country.

An important tie between the legislative and judicial powers is the power of judicial review, the authority to declare laws unconstitutional. This power varies so greatly in extent and scope among the republics that a full discussion of its legal aspects is impossible within the limited scope of this chapter. A few general characteristics may, however, be pointed out.

In the majority of the countries, a judicial decree of unconstitutionality applies only to the actual case in court, rather than to the law itself, as in the United States. Sometimes this limitation comes by specific court ruling, but generally it derives from the court's lack of authority to nullify the unconstitutional law or precept in question. In Argentina (in certain cases), Colombia, Cuba, Panama, and Venezuela the declaration of unconstitutionality has an effect on the law practically as broad as that given it in the United States. In Ecuador and Peru, the congress itself, rather than the courts, has the right to declare a statute unconstitutional.[6] These limitations on the power of judicial review arise from the separation of governmental powers and the interpretation given to the provision of law generally found in the civil codes to the effect that only a law may repeal another law. To mitigate the effect of a strict interpretation of this rule, some countries permit an advance scrutiny of proposed legislation by the highest court for the purpose of advising on its constitutionality. The best example of this practice is found in Colombia.

In spite of these limitations, however, the judicial power, acting within its own jurisdiction, has considerable influence in national policy-making. No stronger evidence need be offered than the fact that when a Latin American executive assumes dictatorial powers his first step is often to limit the powers of the court by forbidding the issuing of *habeas corpus* writs, or writs of *amparo*, or by prohibiting the hearing of cases involving the constitutionality or legality of the government's decrees or acts. He may even dismiss or cause the impeachment of justices. The despot and the lawmaker cannot coexist and implement their respective roles, nor can the despot and the interpreter and applier of the law coexist if the jurist is not to become a mere puppet.

Under normal conditions, the Latin American jurist, through his decisions, can influence the passage of necessary legislation or prevent the enforcement of illegal or unconstitutional laws. Under some constitutions he may be permitted to draft legislation or offer advice upon it for consideration of the legislature. It is rare to find a code commission without a judge in its membership. Through a series of decisions, he may demonstrate the desirability of changes in policy, or may point up the application of policies already in effect. A recent supreme court decision in Mexico, for example, upset precedent in effect over a century by recognizing the validity for certain purposes of a Church marriage. The enmity between Church and state which has existed in Mexico for so long has shown signs recently of lessening in intensity, and the court's decision may

[6] Art. 189, constitution of Ecuador, and Art. 26, constitution of Peru.

be a sign of its cooperation in implementing this trend. Through interpretation of treaty provisions, a court may sometimes influence foreign policy. Many court decisions on the rights of aliens, for instance, have had significant repercussions on the "Good Neighbor" policy.

Precedent and Jurisprudencia

PRECEDENT IN CIVIL AND COMMON LAW. Precedent has been defined as "the adjudged case or decision of a court of justice, considered as furnishing an example or authority for an identical case afterwards arising on a similar question of law." This policy of the courts to "stand by precedent and not to disturb a settled point" is known in common-law countries as *stare decisis*. Latin American law furnishes no exact equivalent. The nearest concept is that of *jurisprudencia*, which does not mean jurisprudence or science of law as it is generally understood in Anglo-America but rather "a series of uniform judgments or decisions which constitute a habit or custom on the same point of law."[7]

Precedent plays a relatively minor role in legal systems based on Roman and civil law, as contrasted with its great importance in Anglo-American law. The latter's adherence to a policy of *stare decisis* constitutes the greatest difference between the two systems of law. In British and American courts, the decision of the judge not only serves to settle the issue in litigation but also establishes a rule of law for future litigation. Civil-law jurisdictions, as a general rule, limit the judge to interpreting the law or settling the issue in the case before him in court. If a provision of civil law is clear and unmistakable in its written text, it must be strictly and literally applied, and this, of course, makes the court's task relatively simple.

ADVANTAGES AND DISADVANTAGES OF THE CIVIL- AND COMMON-LAW POSITIONS. Certain obvious advantages and disadvantages can be seen in both systems. A common-law judge may be limited in exercising his discretion when a binding precedent exists in the form of a decision of the supreme court or highest court in the land. On the other hand, he has recourse to a seemingly endless line of decisions in which judges have ruled in similar cases. Through them he can benefit by the wisdom and experience of many ages. The common-law judge has a wide discretion and is trusted to interpret equitably under varying circumstances. The law in common-law jurisdictions is not frozen into a code, and can be more easily

[7] *Black's Law Dictionary* (4th ed., St Paul: West Publishing Co., 1951).

adapted to social and economic changes. The judges in civil-law jurisdictions, on the other hand, are obliged to give a strict and literal interpretation of the law where the law is clear and unmistakable. This leaves little leeway for discretion, even though the judge's decision might well be inequitable and unduly harsh in one case and just in another.

The fact that the legislator does not always keep pace with changes in social and economic conditions poses another problem for the judiciary. According to the civil code provisions in force in every country, the written law may not be affected by "disuse, custom or practice to the contrary." Thus a further limitation is placed on the discretion of the judge in civil-law jurisdictions. He must await legislative action to repeal a law or to declare it no longer appropriate to be enforced. In common-law jurisdictions, a judge, for all practical purposes, may override a statute, or fail to apply it, when it has patently fallen into disuse, or when it has failed to reflect prevailing custom for a long period of time.

GROWTH OF JURISPRUDENCIA. One of the most eminent authorities on modern civil law[8] believes that the lack of respect accorded to precedent might well be considered a defect in civil-law systems. He is of the opinion that a solid and compulsory body of *jurisprudencia* (cumulative precedents) might give substantive law greater firmness and, at the same time, serve to round out and complement the written law. In any case, perhaps it would be of more practical use than the theoretical and philosophical comments of the authorities to which the judges now give so much weight.

Evidence of a Latin American tendency to attach greater importance to legal precedents may be seen in the "statement of reasons" included in the Mexican Law of Amparo.[9] In this statement one reads that "*jurisprudencia* should be compulsory but not static," that it should be altered to reflect progress in national life, and should serve as an expression of "fundamental exigencies of life and ideal ethics of justice." The tendency to follow precedents is particularly strong in constitutional and administrative law, perhaps because they are not based so strictly on civil-law concepts as are other fields of the law. We may note here that in some countries, notably Argentina and Brazil, cases of the United States Supreme Court have been cited as "persuasive" in these two fields, meaning that the courts may be guided by them, though they can-

[8] Óscar Rabasa, *El derecho angloamericano* (Mexico: Fondo de Cultura Económica, 1944).

[9] *Ley de amparo,* adopted 1936, and the subsequent Regulation (*reglamento*) of 1950.

not be bound by decisions of foreign courts. *Jurisprudencia* can be as binding on all courts of certain Latin American countries as precedent established by the United States Supreme Court can be on the lower courts. Although this does not actually repeal or alter a law in fact, it does bring pressure to bear on the legislative body to correct the defect, to fill some gap in the law, or otherwise act to harmonize the law with justice.

Article 95 of the new Argentine constitution of 1949, a charter recently repealed, stated a somewhat broader doctrine on *stare decisis* than the preceding constitution. Decisions rendered by the supreme court in interpretation of the provisions of the constitution and of certain enumerated codes and laws, when such cases reach it through the channel of extraordinary appeal or for review, will create precedent binding on all other courts and judges in the nation. Colombia, as early as 1893, established that three uniform decisions rendered by its supreme court, when sitting as a court of cassation, should create *jurisprudencia*, binding on all other courts. However, only in this limited field, does it recognize precedent. In Mexico, the Law of Amparo, mentioned above, provides that *jurisprudencia* is created by a series of five decisions of the supreme court, or some division thereof, with specified counting of votes, uninterrupted by a decision holding to the contrary. This is likewise limited to cases arising under constitutional provisions and federal laws, which are specified in the Law of Amparo.

The Suit of Amparo

GENERAL NATURE OF THE SUIT. In the course of the past century, Mexico has developed a judicial procedure known as *amparo*, which is in some respects uniquely Mexican. There is no true equivalent in Anglo-American law.

Literally, *amparo* means "protection." Under this writ an individual has a ready opportunity to request a redress of injustice by applying to the federal courts when some law or some act of a government official or judge has resulted in injury to his rights enumerated in the first twenty-nine articles of the Mexican constitution. Moreover, a state may sue the federal government in the same manner if its field of sovereignty, as defined in the constitution, is invaded. *Amparo* may also be used when a law of one of the states invades the sphere of federal authority.[10]

[10] Manuel Gual Vidal, former dean of the Faculty of Law of the University of Mexico, in an address before the American Bar Association, published in *Proceedings of the Section of International and Comparative Law, 1941*.

ORIGINS. While most authorities agree that the writ of *amparo* was inspired by the "supreme law of the land" clause in the United States Constitution,[11] some have traced its origin to France or Spain, or have found its source in strictly Mexican elements,[12] or in some combination of foreign and domestic factors.[13] Whatever its origin, it first attained definite outlines as a legal institution in the Constitution of 1857. Today, similar provisions are found in Articles 103 and 107 of the Constitution of 1917. These are implemented by a statute, the Law of Amparo, enacted in 1936. Substantial amendments in 1950, relating largely to its application in the relatively new fields of labor and social legislation, have made this historic writ an effective instrument in the hands of the federal judicial power for the protection of human rights.

THE SCOPE OF PROTECTION. The Mexican federal courts have never been authorized to protect or champion the constitution as "the supreme law of the land," as we understand it in the United States. They have jurisdiction over controversies between two states, however, or between the governmental powers within one state, involving the constitutionality of their acts. And through the *amparo* the judiciary indirectly passes upon the constitutionality of laws.

The power to make or repeal laws in Mexico has been assumed to be exclusively a legislative function. Thus, if a law violates a constitutional provision, the courts act only to protect an individual whose constitutional rights have been violated or infringed. Thus, the *amparo* does not protect the constitution as such, since the function of the court is in relation to the violation of an individual right only. The basic rights protected are the "individual" rights defined in the first twenty-nine articles of the constitution, but the supreme court has held that violations of other constitutional articles, causing injury to an individual's rights, may also be protected when they are related to the individual guaranties, through application of the general "due process" clause, found in Article 14.

The *amparo* suit thus gives the Mexican citizen broad protection in his constitutional rights insofar as the courts and judicial pro-

---

[11] Carlos Echánove Trujillo in *Revista de la facultad de derecho* (Mexico), January–June, 1951, p. 91.

[12] Ignacio Burgoa, *El juicio de amparo* (3d ed.; Mexico: Porrúa, 1950-51). Miguel Lanz Duret, *Derecho constitucional mexicano* (4th ed.; Mexico: Impr. L. D., 1947).

[13] Gual Vidal, see note 10.

cedure can do so. It does not, however, serve to protect the constitution against legislative or executive action and is not intended to do so.

ESSENTIAL FEATURE OF THE SUIT. Suits may be brought either in the lower federal courts (indirect *amparo*) or in the supreme court itself in special instances (direct *amparo*). *Amparo* resembles some North American legal writs, especially the *habeas corpus* and the injunction. It also contains elements of the Anglo-American writs of error and *certiorari*. In some ways it is a combination of all of these extraordinary remedies, protecting the individual's person, property, and rights. An *amparo* may be brought for failure to apply the proper rules of judicial procedure, resulting in injury to the party, or against final judgments which deprive a person of constitutionally guaranteed rights of defense. It may also be brought when the act of some authority molests an individual in his person, his private papers, or his property rights without proper warrant or legal justification; when a person is arrested or detained without warrant or held for more than three days without arraignment; when a person is denied bail without justifiable cause; when he is tried without being able to face his accuser or without being apprised of the subject matter of his accusation; when he is denied a hearing in his own defense; or in certain administrative matters such as unjust taxation, overcharging of fees, and denial of grants or concessions, where he believes it unjustified.

JURISPRUDENCIA IN AMPARO CASES. To the North American, a multiplicity of suits, one after another, involving the same legal point, appears to be an expensive and cumbersome way to persuade the legislature to repeal or modify a law. As a matter of fact, the congress generally cooperates in changing laws found to be faulty. However, a provision has been inserted in the Mexican constitution and repeated in the regulatory Law of Amparo giving *amparo* decisions a broader binding effect under certain circumstances. When five judgments have been rendered on a constitutional case, if no contrary decision has been made on the same question, this ruling becomes fixed *jurisprudencia,* or binding precedent, when so declared by the supreme court. This becomes, in effect, a tacit repeal of the unconstitutional legal precepts without any recourse to legislative action. The supreme court may, however alter its own *jurisprudencia* by a decision to the contrary. Five consequent decisions supporting this contrary view are then required to establish this opposite ruling as binding precedent.

Laws Governing Civil Rights

CONSTITUTIONAL GUARANTIES. In colonial Spanish America, Spain exercised a tight control over all aspects of life, particularly religious and political affairs. At the time of independence, therefore, the new nations had no tradition of religious freedom, freedom of speech, freedom of press, or freedom of assembly. However, since the days of Bolívar, Latin American nations have sought to guarantee the unobstructed enjoyment of the basic rights of man and to provide their citizens with the necessary legal means to protect and preserve them. This ambition is still far from realization in some ways, but progress is being made toward the desired objectives, both through the individual efforts of the Latin American nations and through their participation in international activities heading in the same direction.

Some of the obstacles to progress include the high degree of illiteracy, the poverty of the lower classes, poor communications, lack of experience in public and international affairs, and lack of financial resources for economic development. Such conditions invite authoritarian rule and the restriction of civil liberties.

Every constitution sets forth principles, inspired originally in the French and North American charters, which guarantee certain inalienable rights of the individual, including freedom of thought, worship, assembly, and freedom from unwarranted search and seizure, as well as the right to certain legal and judicial safeguards and defenses. Upon the basis of these constitutional provisions, statutory law has regulated political and civil rights, placing reasonable limitations necessary to ensure good morals, public peace, the rights of other persons, and the interests of society. The penal codes and special constitutional remedies provide for penalties for any violation or infringement of the above rights and privileges.

CURTAILMENT OF CIVIL RIGHTS. The freedoms granted in the constitutions may be wholly or partially curtailed by a special law of congress or by the executive, with or without the approval of the legislature or of a council of ministers. These "suspensions of individual guaranties" and "states of siege" are in general authorized for use in all types of emergency situations, as noted in earlier chapters. An executive decree generally details which freedoms are being curtailed and for how long. These usually include a curfew, restrictions on travel or congregation of persons in assemblies, curtailment of freedom of the press and of speech, either completely or by subjecting them to advance censorship.

Elections and electoral campaigns may be prohibited. Courts may be prohibited from issuing writs of *habeas corpus*, or from hearing certain cases involving crimes connected with the emergency. Searches and seizures may be made without warrants, and property may be expropriated without proper safeguards or advance payment while constitutional and legal guaranties are in abeyance. A suspension of guaranties or a state of siege may thus produce partial or even complete paralysis of normal activities for varying lengths of time. The guaranties are generally restored by a second decree, unless a definite date was set in the original decree, so that guaranties are resumed if the period is not extended.

FREEDOM OF RELIGION. Because of their Spanish and Portuguese background, Latin Americans are generally Catholic. Consequently, the early nineteenth-century constitutions made the Roman Catholic Apostolic Church the only church protected or supported by the state. Even when freedom of religion was provided for in these early charters, statutory restrictions often prohibited the worship by other religious sects in buildings which had the appearance of churches, or which bore legends publicizing their use as such. An early constitution of Colombia, for example, provided that all public education should be under the care of the Church. Compulsory religious education in the Catholic faith was required in several nations. Many civil matters, including marriage, divorce, and birth registration, were left to the ecclesiastical authorities, pursuant to concordats celebrated with the Holy See.

Today, in the majority of the nations, Church and state are separated to a large extent and more tolerance is granted to non-Catholics. Such separation is clearest in the constitutions of Mexico, Cuba, Uruguay, and Honduras. On the other hand, in spite of constitutional guaranties of religious freedom, a strong tie still exists between the Catholic Church and the state in Peru and Colombia. The influence of the Catholic Church in education is still strong in many nations, and clauses in immigration laws discriminate against Protestant missionaries and teachers, probably as a result of such influence. On the other hand, the penal codes of most countries provide penalties for violations against a person's right to profess his own religion or attend the church of his choice. He may not be forced to change his faith by duress or to attend worship in another church.

FREEDOM OF ASSEMBLY. Freedom of assembly and association have not been regulated by statute to any great extent. All constitutions, without exception, establish the right of people to assemble and to form associations, as long as these are peaceful, unarmed, and for a lawful purpose. Police restrictions often require notice and advance permission for assemblies to take place in the open air or in a public place. Meetings of labor groups are generally permissible, unless clearly contrary to the security of the nation or dangerous to morals or public peace. In many countries it is a penal offense for officials to prevent persons from exercising the privilege to assemble or associate.

FREEDOM OF SPEECH.   Freedom of expression, whatever the medium of expression, unrestricted by any kind of prior censorship, is authorized as a principle in every Latin American constitution, although the Paraguayan constitution limits the right to "matters of general interest." As in other countries of the world, exercise of this right is subject to penalties for libel and slander and to regulations as to obscenity. Denunciations of public officials usually do not subject the author or editor to liability for damages if these charges concern their acts in *official* capacity. Freedom of speech via radio and television is subject to regulations of the use of these communications, which in many countries are government controlled.

FREEDOM OF THE PRESS.   In most countries laws also regulate the press. These laws often forbid the closing of printing shops, radio stations, and similar institutions, the confiscation of presses, or interruption of work for violations. Other penalties, however, are provided in the form of fines and imprisonment. Brazilian law prohibits anonymity in publication.

Recent limitations on freedom of the press in Argentina and elsewhere in Latin America have attracted attention on the part of international press groups. In some countries, although the press is not controlled directly, it has been controlled indirectly by restrictions on paper or electric power. The importation of necessary machinery may be prohibited or labor disputes may be encouraged. Some Latin Americans have defended these measures. They say foreign newsmen are overcritical because they measure freedom of the press by their own yardstick. Such freedom, they claim, might bring political chaos. There are some signs, however, of a growing freedom of press. This new freedom has been stimulated to some extent by the insistence of the international press, as well as by the critical attitude of foreign governments when restrictive measures have been adopted.

DESACATO.   Closely connected with this subject of freedom of speech and of press is the old offense of *desacato*, which has taken on an added depth of meaning in recent years. Originally the term denoted disrespect or contempt of court. But in more recent years, at the hands of certain national governments under criticism, it has become a broad offense covering almost any disrespect for public functionaries. The outstanding recent example of a broad extension given to the offense is the 1949 decree in Argentina, fixing prison terms of from three months to three years for *desacato*. Under this decree, the offense could embrace criticisms aimed at anyone from the president down to minor officials, or even to their offices or functions, and need consist of no more than an allusion. The most disturbing provision was that which deprived the accused of his only defense: he was allowed no opportunity to prove the truth of his statement. Under such circumstances, any trial for *desacato* was a mockery, and it is not surprising that one of the first acts of the new administration after Perón's downfall was to repeal this 1949 decree.

Judicial Systems

COLONIAL BACKGROUND. No clearly defined judicial plan appeared in the Spanish colonies prior to the eighteenth century, but three types of courts developed as the need arose. The first group were specifically designated by the king for judicial purposes, and included the *audiencias, intendencias, corregimientos,* and ecclesiastical bodies. A second type, known as *jueces capitulares*, included city mayors (*alcaldes*), persons charged with certain special responsibilities for ordinary civil and criminal matters, and special *alcaldes* for cases involving water rights, Indian affairs, or ecclesiastical questions. The third type of court consisted of officials appointed locally by the *audiencias* to exercise jurisdiction over some specific kind of litigation, or over some special matter on a temporary basis. This third type thus included magistrates responsible for the estates of the deceased (relating only to Spaniards), magistrates for questions relating to public lands, or those appointed to investigate some special community. All three types of magistrates usually combined administrative duties with judicial powers. An *audiencia*, for example, was not only the highest court of appeal in a given area, but also the highest agency of local government. Appeals from the *audiencia* went to the Council of the Indies or to the king in Spain for final judgment.[14]

As the colonies grew in population and wealth, their institutions of government also took on more order. The number of authorities dispensing justice was reduced, and the quality of the judges improved. Whereas in the earlier years any person of good moral

---

[14] Alberto Bremauntz, *Por una justicia al servicio del pueblo* (Mexico: Casa de Michoacán, 1955), p. 43.

character was considered to be qualified for these positions, by the eighteenth century career men with legal training were more frequently appointed. A more centralized and simplified system slowly emerged, particularly as a result of the reforms introduced by the Bourbon kings in the eighteenth century. It was this reformed system which the Spanish American nations inherited as the basis for the development of their national legal systems.

PRESENT SYSTEMS. Despite the persistence of Iberian tradition, however, the organization of the judiciary does not differ widely from that under Anglo-American common law. The organs of justice are known as courts, tribunals, and judgeships, while the persons dispensing justice are called judges, magistrates, ministers, or justices, depending upon their rank or the titles used in the several nations. Constitutional provisions generally recite broad principles of justice, outline the hierarchy of courts, establish qualifications for office, at least for the highest court, and prescribe jurisdiction and competence. Organic laws on the judiciary implement these constitutional precepts. All Latin American nations have public or government attorneys, similar to prosecuting and government attorneys in the United States. Their functions and powers resemble those of the United States Attorney General or those of the various state attorneys, combined with certain functions of the department of justice.

UNITARY AND FEDERAL SYSTEMS. In the unitary nations, the judiciary consists of a single pyramid of courts headed by a supreme court, usually located in the capital city, which exercises national jurisdiction. Justice of the peace or mayor's courts are found in practically every fair-sized town. The larger towns have first instance courts or district courts, and the capital of a province or department has the highest type of local tribunal below the supreme court.

A dual system of courts, federal and provincial or state, has functioned with varying degrees of success in Argentina, Brazil, Mexico, and Venezuela. Venezuela vacillated between the unitary and federal systems until 1945, when the two sets of courts were merged into a single national system. Constitutional reforms adopted in Brazil in 1937 also tended toward greater centralization of the national judicial power, merging the federal and state courts at the intermediate levels, with the exception of a single federal tribunal of appeals. This system remained virtually unchanged when the constitution was revised in 1946. Even in Argentina, where the federal dual system of courts was most firmly established, constitutional changes in 1949 curtailed the jurisdiction of local courts in certain matters. Mexico thus remained the only true exponent of the dual system of courts for a time, although the overthrow of Perón in Argentina may lead to full restoration of the dual system there.

The names assigned to courts vary considerably from country to country, even though the jurisdiction and competence tend to be similar. The highest tribunal may be termed the supreme court, but is most commonly called the supreme court of justice, supreme court of justice of the nation, supreme tribunal, supreme federal tribunal, high federal court, or Cassation Tribunal. Lower courts carry such names as superior court, district court, appellate court, circuit court, *audiencia,* first and second instance court, municipal court, justice of the peace court, and mayor's court.

SUPREME COURTS. The number of justices forming the bench of the highest court in 1957 varied from three in Paraguay to thirty-one in Cuba, half of the courts having ten or less members, and half having more than ten. The size of the courts has been changed frequently in some countries, however, either by statute or by constitutional amendment. Such a change was made during the three-year period 1954–1956 in Colombia, Haiti, Nicaragua, and Panama.

Typically, the courts sit in several divisions to hear different classes of cases. The most common divisions are civil, criminal, and administrative, but other special divisions, such as labor, social guaranties, or military are found in some of the courts (see Table XVI). The supreme courts of Argentina, Brazil, Dominican Republic, Haiti, Honduras, Nicaragua, Panama, Paraguay, and Uruguay always sit as a unit. In those nations where the more common cases are handled in *salas* or divisional courts, the entire bench of the supreme court is called in plenary session only for the more important types of litigation. These include the review of basic questions of law to assure uniformity of ruling, questions involving the legality or constitutionality of laws in determined cases, review of the court's previous decisions, and administrative duties.

QUALIFICATIONS OF MAGISTRATES. Constitutional qualifications for members of the supreme courts vary little from country to country, except as concerns maximum and minimum ages and the required number of years of legal practice. The minimum age for appointment varies from thirty years in Argentina, the Dominican Republic, El Salvador, Haiti, Honduras, and Venezuela to forty in Cuba, Ecuador, Nicaragua, Peru, and Uruguay. El Salvador and Peru set the maximum age at seventy and seventy-five years, respectively, in matters of appointments, while Brazil requires

TABLE XVI. SUPREME COURTS*

Country	Official Name of Court	Divisions	Number of Judges	Selection of Judges	Term of Office
Argentina	Corte Suprema de Justicia	Sits *en banc*, no divisions	5	By president, confirmed by senate	Good behavior
Bolivia	Corte Suprema	Civil; criminal	10	By congress	10 years
Brazil	Supremo Tribunal Federal	Sits *en banc*	11	By president, confirmed by senate	Life
Chile	Corte Suprema	Generally *en banc*; on special occasions in divisions	13	By president; panel submitted by court	Good behavior
Colombia	Corte Suprema de Justicia	Civil; constitutional; criminal; labor; general	20	Senate and chamber each elects half	5 years
Costa Rica	Corte Suprema de Justicia	Two civil; criminal; cassation	17	By president, confirmed by congress	8 years
Cuba	Tribunal Supremo de Justicia	Civil; criminal; administrative; constitutional and labor guaranties	31	By president, confirmed by congress	Life
Dominican Republic	Suprema Corte de Justicia	Sits *en banc*	7	By senate	5 years
Ecuador	Corte Suprema	Civil; criminal; cassation	15	By congress	6 years
El Salvador	Corte Suprema	Civil; criminal; *amparos*	9	By president, confirmed by congress	3 years

Country	Court	Description	Number	Appointment	Term
Guatemala	Corte Suprema de Justicia	Sits *en banc*; special for military and cassation appeals	5	By congress	4 years
Haiti	Tribunal de Cassation	Sits *en banc*	12	By president	10 years
Honduras	Corte Suprema de Justicia	Sits *en banc*	5	By president, confirmed by congress	6 years
Mexico	Suprema Corte de Justicia de la Nación	Civil; criminal; administrative; labor	21	By president, confirmed by senate	Good behavior
Nicaragua	Corte Suprema de Justicia	Sits *en banc*	7	By congress	6 years
Panama	Corte Suprema de Justicia	Civil; criminal; administrative; general	9	By president, confirmed by congress	18 years
Paraguay	Corte Suprema (since 1940)	Sits *en banc*	3	By president, confirmed by council of state	5 years
Peru	Corte Suprema de Justicia	Civil; criminal	11	By congress	Good behavior
Uruguay	Suprema Corte de Justicia	Sits *en banc*	5	By congress	10 years
Venezuela	Corte Federal		5	By congress	5 years
	Corte de Casación		10		
	(1945-53 Corte Suprema de Justicia)	Criminal; civil; mercantile; and labor	(Total of 15)		

* Data based on constitutions and laws in effect in 1957.

retirement at the age of seventy. In Mexico, appointments are limited to persons under sixty-five, and seventy is the age for compulsory retirement. A 1955 decree in Costa Rica also made retirement obligatory for judicial employees at seventy years. Age limits for lower courts are less frequently set by constitutional provisions and are less stringent.

Candidates for the supreme courts are required to be lawyers by profession. The required number of years of legal practice varies, but the average is ten years. Peru, however, requires twenty years; Chile, Ecuador, and Panama, fifteen years; while Colombia requires only four, Mexico five, and Haiti seven years. In some countries candidates are also required to have held judicial posts in the lower courts. There is a growing tendency to require that judges in the lower courts also be trained in law. In Chile, for example, this requirement extends to the very lowest courts.

Candidates for the highest judicial offices are universally required to be of secular status and must enjoy full civil rights. Some countries require competitive examinations, others demand seniority in office in lower courts. Good conduct and reputation are frequently indicated as qualifications. Brazil's constitution requires candidates to be of "outstanding knowledge and spotless reputation," while those of Mexico and Nicaragua specify "irreproachable conduct and good reputation." Paraguay's law demands that aspirants must be "blameless in both public and private law." It is a common requirement that a candidate should not be related to other members of the court or to officials or legislators who must approve his appointment, that he have no criminal record, and that he possess good hearing and eyesight.

SELECTION OF JUDGES. Methods of appointment of justices to the supreme courts generally fall into one of two patterns. In some nations, the president appoints supreme court justices, with the consent of one or both houses of the legislature. This is the case in Argentina, Brazil, Mexico, Paraguay, Panama, Honduras, and Costa Rica. Congressional approval is not required in Chile or Haiti. In other nations, the legislature elects the judges, usually choosing from slates of candidates prepared by the executive. In Bolivia, Colombia, Uruguay, Guatemala, El Salvador, Nicaragua, Peru, and Venezuela, the legislature elects from panels proposed by the executive. In the Dominican Republic the senate elects, and in Colombia the senate and the chamber of deputies each elects half of the judges. In Peru election was traditionally from two lists (*terna doble*), one of magistrates and one of licensed attorneys, and the method is still employed for some appointments there. If a generalization may be ventured, it is that the participation of both executive and legislative branches in judicial appointments has been found the most satisfactory method. The use of competitive examinations, the practice of appointing career judges, and the use of slates or panels prepared by other agencies, even by the judicial branch itself, have in some countries contributed to reducing political pressure in appointments.

The *presidente,* or chief justice, is sometimes appointed, sometimes elected by his colleagues. He may be chosen in accordance with a system of rotation or may receive office by seniority. His term may be for one year, for a certain number of years, or for the duration of his tenure.

In most of the nations, equally qualified persons are chosen to act as alternates (*suplentes*) for the justices (*conjueces*). One may be elected for each incumbent, or a panel may be named from which one is to be chosen in case of the illness, death, or absence of any justice. The object is to have a competent judge ready to step in when a principal judge is disqualified for any reason. Other judicial officials, known as *fiscales,* are also appointed, usually in the same manner as the regular judges. The *fiscal* is an adviser to the court on technical matters. He gives opinions in all cases involving some public interest. Records of the investigations he conducts become a part of the official documentation of the case. In domestic relations cases his opinion may be required upon decrees of annulment or divorce.

Administrative arrangements, including provisions for vacations, discipline, and financial matters, are considered by the court sitting as a whole, some particular judge perhaps being delegated to see that these *acuerdos* are carried out. Administrative visits to lower courts are included among the duties of the justices of the supreme courts in some countries.

The manner of appointment to a lower court varies according to its rank within the judicial hierarchy of a country, as well as from one country to another. In some nations, the president makes or recommends judicial appointments on all levels. In other countries, the legislature elects them. In Honduras and Guatemala, for example, the supreme court itself makes the appointments to the lower ranks of the judiciary. In Mexico, and in other federal countries with a dual system of courts, the state or provincial governors may make appointments to courts within the state or province. The offices of municipal judge and justice of the peace were once considered honorary in the smallest towns, and in some instances service in such posts was considered a civic duty, compulsory unless excused on valid grounds. Today this gratuitous exercise of administration of justice has practically disappeared. The appointment of judges in all minor courts in some countries is made by the supreme court or, for each rank of courts, by the judges of the rank immediately higher. The judges on the lowest levels are often elected by the municipal government, or by the people in local elections.

TENURE IN OFFICE. The doctrine that a judge should enjoy permanent tenure, subject only to the requirements of good behavior and responsibility for incorrupt administration of justice, is essential to the autonomy of the courts. This principle is gaining ground only slowly in Latin America, since the effects of the Latin American history of political instability are not easily counteracted. However, even when political influences affect the highest court, because it is sensitive to changes in the structure of power, the lower courts often continue to exercise their duties with a great degree of continuity and independence.

The life tenure of supreme court justices in Argentina was undermined during the administration of President Perón by his abuse of the impeachment procedure, but Perón's successors have given assurance of tenure. Argentina, Chile, Cuba, Mexico, Peru, and Brazil provide for life tenure, or "good behavior" terms to judges. Mexico has vacillated between life tenure and the six-year term of the presidency and the senate. In the other republics (see Table XVI) the terms of offices vary from three to eighteen years, generally with the privilege of reappointment or re-election. A new trend appears in 1956 statutes in El Salvador and Guatemala which authorize a justice to hold office until the compulsory retirement age of seventy, provided he has been elected to and served three terms of three years each, or two terms of four years each, in succession.

The term *inmovilidad* is often used in connection with judicial tenure, but should not be taken literally in the sense of "non-removability," or as denoting life tenure. It merely means the right of the judge not to be removed from office, demoted, or transferred, (except possibly for promotion) without his consent, except by appropriate legal action. This applies only during the term of office, whatever that may be, and is limited, of course, by the requirement of good behavior in office. Removal may take place only after appropriate hearings, and generally through impeachment. In the lower courts, disciplinary measures short of removal are sometimes imposed. Such measures are generally decreed by the supreme court as head of the judiciary system and take the form of censure or warning. Some nations have strong laws on "responsibility" of public officials, setting up ethical codes and providing fines and prison terms for violation of the provisions. These provisions apply to judges as well as other officials. But politically appointed judges in the highest courts who abuse their power, neglect their duties, or become "unjustly" enriched often go unpunished because of their political influence or because the period for prescription of actions expires in one year or less.

In addition to these disciplinary functions the supreme courts often perform other administrative duties. Such duties include granting leaves and vacations, making promotions or transfers, regulating financial matters of the court system, publishing decisions and annual reports, compiling legal statistics, and maintaining files and records, including notarial registers.

In some nations the highest courts may act, upon request, as legal advisers to other branches of government. They may also assist in the drafting of legislation, particularly that relating to the courts and legal procedure. Moreover, as previously pointed out, individual justices often serve on national code commissions.

Special Courts

THE EXPANSION OF GOVERNMENT ACTIVITY. Since other chapters discuss the increased role of government in society, it will be noticed here only briefly. During recent decades, the executive branch has grown to such an extent, because of new legislation and new administrative agencies, that its relationship to the other two branches of government cannot be defined as clearly as before. The social revolution of the twentieth century has forced the nations to adopt new administrative agencies devoted to the general social welfare and to the protection of individuals and groups against certain social risks and grievances. These, in turn, have required special procedures and organs of justice in the various specialized fields.

Such legal agencies and procedures have arisen in connection with the laws relating to labor, social security, insurance, education, conservation of natural resources, and exchange controls, among others. They were established because the general courts lacked the specialized knowledge and personnel to handle the problems raised by the new laws, both those of implementation and of interpretation. It was also felt that speedier decisions and more flexibility were needed than the regular courts could provide.

In addition to these special courts in the administrative branch, which constitute the greatest intervention in the judicial field, special procedures and courts have also been established in other legal fields because they involve special groups, such as minors in juvenile courts or military personnel in martial courts. The juvenile courts, for purposes of this discussion, are "special," although usually they form part of the regular judiciary.

CONSTITUTIONAL ASPECTS. The Latin American courts have sometimes resorted to legal fictions to avoid the almost universal constitutional requirement that the judicial power shall be the exclusive dispenser of justice. But the increasingly complex jurisdiction of the modern state has seemed to necessitate some relaxing of this old prohibition against executive intrusion in the field of justice. Some nations have added new specialized organs to the judicial power, while others have created special autonomous agencies for the new functions or attached them to the executive branch. In either case, whether special procedures have been added in established courts of law or whether new extra-judicial organs have been created, the regular judiciary is still relied upon in many cases, generally in cases of appeals or for rulings of law.

The objection of lawyers to the special courts established outside the regular judiciary is that they are not easily subject to supervision or control by the judicial power. Moreover, when such special organs form part of the executive branch, thus mixing executive and judicial functions, the theoretical balance among the various powers of government is upset. Since in administrative litigation the "trial" stages of a case take place within the hierarchy of a government department or agency, it has been considered best in some countries to have appeals go to a tribunal which is part of the administration or one which is autonomous in character.

The use of special courts in administrative cases is defended on the grounds of the need for less formal and more prompt administration of justice, the value of using personnel expert in the particular matters involved, and the necessity of weighing the individual's rights against those of society in pursuance of definite policies of the administration. The extent to which special courts and procedures have been established in recent years seems to reflect a widely felt need of this kind in dealing with grievances arising under the new social legislation. Administrative justice also includes matters which do not constitute litigation and would not, therefore, be properly brought into a court of law, such as the granting or denial of concessions in mining and petroleum, the issuing of patents and trademarks, the use of waters, and questions relating to public lands. They also include certain problems in

taxation and finance—cases for which the government can agree
to compromises which are not permissible in a law court if the law
is strictly administered.

In bypassing the constitutional prohibition against establishment
of "exceptional" tribunals, Mexico, for example, has created a
tribunal fiscal and a system of labor courts. The constitutional
reasoning, according to many authorities, is that these are not
in fact "exceptional" tribunals, because they are authorized by law
to exist as *permanent* organs in the special fields. These authorities
interpret the constitutional prohibition as referring to *ad hoc* boards
or courts which might be set up temporarily.

TYPES OF SPECIAL COURTS. Special military courts are needed
wherever modern armed forces exist, in order to ensure prompt
and fair application of the special codes governing military service
in cases of violation of these laws, as well as in cases of offenses
against general laws by members of the armed services. Today
these courts are created and function under laws and with procedures which avoid the criticism against special jurisdictions, which
caused the abolition of military and ecclesiastical tribunals in the
nineteenth century.

Electoral courts represent another kind of special tribunal. These
courts exercise functions which are more administrative than judicial. Special procedures for the trial of juveniles, either in the regular courts or in special courts, also have become wide-spread. Since
1919, practically every country in Latin America has instituted at
least one juvenile court, generally in the capital city, or appointed
a special judge for the purpose. It is not clear whether in practice
juvenile problems are usually brought to the capital from other
parts of the country, or whether they are tried there by the regular
law courts, perhaps with the use of special procedure. Many
countries have children's codes dealing with delinquency, but also
including welfare, work provisions, and other matters.

Chile is one of the foremost leaders in the field of child welfare,
with two juvenile courts in Santiago and one in Valparaiso. Special
correctional institutions have been established, and welfare organizations cooperate in the preliminary investigations of cases and
in the execution of the courts' decisions. In Mexico, juvenile court
organization is on the state level. This is true also in Argentina.
Other countries are not as far advanced in the treatment of juvenile offenders, but usually a judge is specially assigned, if not specially trained, to hear this type of litigation. These courts usually
make some use of psychiatrists, nurses, correctional officers, and
social workers.

One of the fastest growing fields for special tribunals is that of labor. Labor courts are "administrative" courts, but in practice they extend beyond simple government intervention and control over conflicts between capital and labor by means of the department or agency concerned with labor matters, or through boards of arbitration. Labor cases require special handling because of the need for greater speed and unhampered solution of conflicts which would hamstring industry and commerce if permitted to drag their way through the regular courts of law. Specialized knowledge on the part of the judges is also needed—knowledge which not all judges on the law courts possess. The settlement of these cases calls for representation of both capital and labor, and greater use of measures of arbitration and conciliation rather than application of the law.

In some Latin American countries, the labor courts are free from control by either the administrative or the judicial branch of government. In others they form part of the administration. In this connection, it should be noted that conflicts between capital and labor are of various kinds, falling generally into two large divisions—legal and economic. In some countries purely legal conflicts, such as those involving the interpretation of some provision of law or of a contract, or the inequitable application of law, are submitted to law courts, while the economic cases dealing with wages and conditions of work or those disputes involving contract provisions are settled by conciliation or arbitration. Individual grievances often go to labor courts, while collective conflicts are within the jurisdiction of boards of arbitration.

A complete hierarchy of labor tribunals, from trial courts to a supreme court in this special field, are found in Brazil and Colombia. In Peru and Ecuador, the trial courts are special tribunals, but appeals go to the regular law courts. In Panama and other countries, labor courts have been set up at the lower levels, and provision has been made by constitution or law for a special higher court to hear appeals, although these provisions have not been implemented to date. Until these special higher courts are established, appeals will continue to be heard, as in the past, in the regular courts of law.

In the fields of government accounting and taxation, special courts have both administrative and judicial tasks. They form part of the system of administrative tribunals where such systems exist. In other countries they are maintained as single autonomous bodies, or are established as part of the general administrative structure of government.

Administrative Litigation

Administrative law covers all the acts and activities of the executive power, including activities of local or regional authorities, as well as those of the national or central governments. The recent expansion of economic and social activity of the state by increasing the scope of action of the administrative departments and agencies has sometimes subordinated the interest of the individual to that of society at large. This may cause injury or neglect of the individual's rights and privileges, however. To guard against this danger, the state finds it necessary to create special agencies to protect the individual against official acts or omission of acts. The simplest examples are conflicts in a government agency between employer and employee. But many other kinds of cases arise in relations of individuals with officials, or between various officials of government in such fields as taxation, mining, transportation, communications, public utilities and services, patents, trademarks and copyrights, and the expropriation or attachment of private property in the public interest.

CONTENTIOUS-ADMINISTRATIVE SUIT. The special procedure usually used in these administrative law cases, whether in a regular court of law or in special administrative tribunals, is the *recurso contencioso administrativo,* or contentious-administrative suit. Three general requirements of this suit are to be noted. (1) It excludes certain types of administrative acts from the special jurisdiction, as for example, when the government or its agents act as private persons, rather than as a public power, in the commercial or contract field. Such cases must come before the regular courts. (2) The complaint must be based on lawful acts, as differentiated from discretionary powers; that is, the act must be based on powers granted by law rather than discretionary powers under which the government agency or authority exercises its own judgment. (3) All other sources of remedy must be exhausted before recourse may be had to the courts.

The purely administrative appeal, the most common source of relief other than the contentious-administrative suit, is distinct from the legal action before an administrative court. An administrative appeal may be directed either to the agency or the official involved, requesting reconsideration of the matter, modification of some decision, or perhaps a reversal or revocation of some order. Or it may be made to an official superior to the one who has provoked the appeal, requesting reversal, confirmation, or modification of the subordinate official's act or omission of action.

Four important exceptions are made to the use of the contentious-administrative suit. It may not be used when the laws or procedures complained against are unconstitutional, since other legal remedies are provided in such cases. Nor may it be used in cases where administrative authority arises from legislative powers specifically delegated to the executive, unless the regulations have injured rights of the individual which might be considered strictly administrative. A third exception consists of administrative acts which are merely political in character, while a fourth embraces cases in which the government has acted in the capacity of a private person or corporate body. In this latter case, as previously mentioned, the government may be sued in the same courts and is subject to the same procedures as an individual. When the basis of the complaint against the administration is a disciplinary measure, such as those involved in enforcement of health measures, immigration restrictions, or dismissal of employees for insubordination, the administrative act may not be the basis of a suit in an administrative court. The only means of relief is an administrative appeal within the department or agency concerned, perhaps with a right of appeal to a court of law if there has been a denial of justice.

VARIOUS NATIONAL SYSTEMS. In Argentina, administrative litigation is heard in the law courts of the federal system, using the contentious-administrative procedure. Some of the Argentine provinces, however, have instituted special administrative courts on the local level. Colombia has modeled its system after that of France, establishing a number of administrative tribunals on the lower level for the trial stages. These are independent of both the executive and judicial powers. On the highest level, appeals go to the council of state, a body which also exercises administrative and advisory functions in connection with government. The Dominican Republic has not created special lower administrative courts, but uses the administrative agencies and the regular law courts for the initial stages. Appeals may be carried, however, to a special administrative court called the *tribunal superior administrativo*. Panama has provided by law for a *tribunal de lo contencioso administrativo* as the highest special administrative court. Appeals come to it from the departments for non-litigious cases and from the lower law courts in contested cases. Ecuador uses a similar system, appeals going to its council of state as the highest administrative organ.

The provision in Chile's Constitution of 1925 for an autonomous system of administrative courts had not been implemented thirty years later. Instead, Chile has a variety of special boards and courts, generally in connection with the basic organic law in some special field. These boards or courts exist in such fields as taxation, finance, customs, patents and trademarks, hunting and fishing, mining, health, communications and transportation, agricultural exports, compulsory insurance, and the assessment of real property. Their jurisdictions are generally confined to fines and light penalties, such as cancellation of a concession, expropriation of property, and similar measures.

Guatemala has a single administrative court with a bench of three judges, forming part of its regular judicial system. In Costa Rica, a special judge or judges are appointed in the regular law courts to take cognizance of cases involving contentious-administrative matters. These judges are known as *jueces de lo contencioso administrativo y civil de hacienda*. As their title indicates, they also have jurisdiction over tax and fiscal cases. They hear suits on behalf of or against the nation, its banks and institutions, suits involving claims, judicial sales, violation of tax laws, and similar matters, in both civil and criminal actions.

Uruguay's highest court of administrative justice is also called the *tribunal de lo contencioso administrativo*. Organized within the regular judiciary, and dual in capacity, the trial administrative courts are known as *juzgados de hacienda y de lo contencioso administrativo*. Administrative controversies are divided into three classes —fiscal litigation, suits involving public law, and ordinary administrative suits. *Juzgados de hacienda* are competent to hear the first of the three types, while the judges of contentious-administration hear the other two. Pursuant to the constitution of 1940, Paraguay's legislature transferred administrative litigation from the supreme court, where it had formerly been heard, to the *tribunal de cuentas*, which had already functioned for some years in the field of taxation.

Bolivia, Brazil, Cuba, Haiti, Honduras, Mexico, Nicaragua, Peru, El Salvador, and Venezuela do not yet have special administrative court systems, but use special procedures for administrative cases in their regular courts of law. Cuba, however, has devoted one of the four divisions of her supreme court to appeals in contentious-administrative matters.

Behind the development of special administrative courts lies the feeling that special procedures are necessary in order to achieve greater flexibility and more prompt administration than the regular procedures of law provide. This is a matter of public interest as well as concern for rights of the individuals concerned. An appeal within the department or agency involved is always used first, but this makes interpretation and application of somewhat uncertain consistency to say the least, since a multitude of officials and authorities are entrusted with the tasks, some of whom lack legal training or are incapable for other reasons of handling the appeals adequately. The administrative court must, therefore, have sufficient flexibility to be able to revoke, alter, or add to the administrative decisions, amend contractual conditions, apply equitable solutions, and employ other measures which the law would not permit in the regular courts.

Conclusions

The Latin American nations have greatly modified the systems of law and justice of colonial times, but present-day legal systems and institutions still have important roots in that legal heritage. The Latin American legislator has had to learn much from foreign experience, since the democratic system was unknown in Latin America at the time of independence. But the jurist has been able to build on the basis of the early Spanish and Portuguese principles of law and procedure. Today, both the judge and the advocate occupy positions of greater prestige and social standing than formerly. They are generally well-trained professionally, and the judges are frequently selected for their professional attainments. From their breadth of experience and actual application of law, they even make contributions to the drafting of improved legislation, often serving as members of code commissions.

Latin American law also exhibits a tendency to adapt common-law models, particularly in the field of commercial law. Conditional sales, chattel mortgages, and security transactions, all of which were alien to civil-law principles, are being initiated either directly or through some legal fiction. Trusts are also taking root in Latin American law. Such tendencies are not surprising, of course, in the light of the extent of inter-American trade and investment. A trend toward increased reliance on precedent appears in a growing tendency to rely upon established *jurisprudencia*.

An enlightened policy on civil and political rights grows slowly and painfully, as shaped internally in the various republics by improved economic conditions, better communications and transportation, more extended educational facilities, and greater stability in government. External influences apparently exert almost as potent an influence, particularly visible in the field of labor rights and women's rights—influences which stem from international organizations and conferences and their resulting treaties. The work of the International Labour Office and of the United Nations has contributed greatly to this field. Censure and criticism on the part of foreign governments and the international press have exerted some influence in extending freedom of speech and of press in Latin American countries.

Suggestions for Reading

Max Rheinstein has compared the two legal systems in "Common and Civil Law: An Elementary Comparison," in the *Revista jurídica de la universidad de Puerto Rico*, XXII (1952-53), 90–107, and Phanor J. Eder compares the laws of North and South America in *A Comparative Survey of Anglo-American and Latin American Law* (New York: New York University Press, 1950). See also *Latin American Legal Philosophy*, published by The Association of American Law Schools (Cambridge, Mass: Harvard University Press, 1948). For legal education see H. C. Horack, "Legal Education in the Latin American Republics," *Journal of Legal Education*, II (1950), 287–297, and other articles in the same journal. Francis Deak has treated the differences in the field of judicial precedent in "The Place of the 'Case' in the Common Law and the Civil Law," *Tulane Law Review*, VIII (1934), 337–357.

An outline of the Latin American judicial systems will be found in Helen Clagett, *Administration of Justice in Latin America* (New York: Oceana Publications, Inc., 1952). For individual countries, see Guillermo de Montagu's "Judicial Organization in Cuba," *Journal of American Judicature Society*, XXXII (1949), 166–170; Jorge Luna y Parra, "Summary of the Courts in the City of Mexico," *Journal of American Judicature Society*, XXVII (1943), 70–73; and Manuel Tagle Valdés, "Appointment of Judges in the Republic of Chile," *Law Notes*, L (1946), 5–7. A pamphlet by Anna Kalet Smith, "Juvenile Court Laws in Foreign Countries" (Washington, D.C.: Government Printing Office, 1949), issued by the U.S. Children's Bureau, gives a concise description of the special jurisdictions for juvenile offenders. For labor courts, see the publication by the International Labour Office entitled *Labour Courts in Latin America* (Geneva: International Labour Organization, 1949).

Two general works in Spanish deserve special mention. Alberto Bremauntz, *Por una justicia al servicio del pueblo* (Mexico: Casa de Michoacán, 1955), describes court organization, methods of judicial appointment, qualifications for judicial careers, and judicial salaries on the federal and local levels in Mexico. Ignacio Burgoa has written of the rights of man, as constitutionally protected, in *Las garantías individuales* (2d ed.; Mexico: Porrúa, 1954). See also his 2-volume study of the Mexican *amparo, El juicio de amparo* (3d ed.; Mexico: Porrúa, 1950-51).

Chapter 13

Municipal Government

Colonial Tradition

COLONIAL CITIES. Municipal life in America began with the transplanting of Hispanic institutions during the Conquest. None of the native peoples, not even those of the great empires of Mexico and Peru, had municipal institutions comparable to those of European origin.[1] The highly developed organizations of the Mayas, Aztecs, and Incas included true cities. That is to say, they had the material and human elements characteristic of city life—houses, inhabitants, and social relations. From the political or juridical point of view, however, the government of these agglomerations had nothing in common with European municipal institutions. Nor were such indigenous economic and political institutions as the *calpulli,* the *ayllu,* or the *cacicazgo* analogous.

By express order of the crown, Spaniards generally respected the customary law and the political institutions encountered in the native towns and cities, such as the *cacicazgo* (native chieftainship). In a royal *cedula* of August 6, 1555, later incorporated in the Recopilación of 1680 (*ley 4, t. I, libro 2*), Charles V ordered that "the laws and good customs which the Indians had of old for their good government and police, their uses and customs observed and respected since they became Christians, and which do not conflict with our sacred religion, together with those newly enacted and ordered, should be observed and executed . . ."

MUNICIPALITIES IN CONQUEST AND COLONIZATION. Municipalities, decadent in Spain under the centralizing policy of the Hapsburgs,

[1] See Alberto María Carreño, "La iniciación de la vida jurídica y municipal de la Nueva España," in *Revista del Instituto de Historia del Derecho* (Buenos Aires, 1951), No. 3, pp. 35 ff.; and T. Esquivel Obregón, *Apuntes para la historia del derecho en México* (México: Ed. Polis, 1938), II, 207 ff.

who crushed the power of the commoners (*comuneros*) in Villadar in 1520, flourished in Hispanic America for several reasons: the decentralization imposed in America,[2] the individualism and localism stimulated by distance, and the granting of privileges to American *cabildos* (town councils) which were denied at that time to the councils in Castile.[3] Thus the institution of the *corregidor* (royal governor) was rare in the Indies.

The conquest and colonization of America took on an essentially urban character in the sense that it was carried out by founding cities which were political, administrative, military, and cultural centers. Thus, the Laws of the Indies, as is well known, show great concern for everything relating to the founding of cities, the material basis of the municipal institution, and the manner of appointing its officials.

Municipal councils (*cabildos*), despite the criticisms they deserve for corruption and such abuses as the sale of some council offices, should be considered "popular" institutions which contributed, with other agencies, to making the absolutism of the Spanish monarchs less severe in America.[4] Under the absolutist and centralizing policy of the Bourbons in the eighteenth century, however, the *cabildos* declined. The most notable curtailment of their powers was made in the Royal Ordinance of Intendants of 1782.

MUNICIPALITIES IN THE COLONIZATION OF BRAZIL. In the Portuguese colonization of Brazil the municipality showed traits distinct from those of Spanish America. To avoid charges on the royal treasury, territorial grants called *capitanias* were made to *donatarios* (grantees) in 1534 with authority to colonize the new lands. These *donatarios* received broad powers from the crown, even those of civil and criminal jurisdiction. As Renato de Mendonça says, the owner of a captaincy was a real feudal lord, exercising in his dominion the prerogatives of a king. He named judges and administrative officials, collected tributes, held a monopoly of the nascent industries and the privilege of enslaving the Indians.[5] These grantees

---

[2] Ricardo Zorraquín Becú, "El sistema político indiano," in *Revista de la Facultad de Derecho de Buenos Aires*, IX, No. 39 (July–August, 1954), 747.

[3] José María Ots Capdequí, *Manual de historia del derecho español en las Indias y del derecho propiamente indiano* (Buenos Aires: Edit. Losada, 1945), pp. 368 ff.

[4] Juan Agustín García, *La ciudad indiana* (Buenos Aires: Ed. Angel Estrada y Cia., 1900); and Carlos Mouchet, "Las ideas sobre el municipio en el período hispanoindiano," in *Revista de la Facultad de Derecho y Ciencias Sociales* (Buenos Aires, 1955), No. 44. For a sharper criticism of the colonial cabildo, see Clarence H. Haring, *The Spanish Empire in America* (New York: Oxford University Press, 1947), Chap. ix.

[5] Renato de Mendonça, *Breve historia del Brasil* (Madrid: Instituto de Cultura Hispanica, 1950), p. 7.

founded the first towns and cities, establishing municipal councils (*câmaras*) under their authority, in accordance with the traditions of the kingdom of Portugal. Martim Affonso founded the first town, São Vicente, in the captaincy of that name, in 1531. Santos was established in 1536 and São Paulo in 1560.

The outstanding nineteenth-century Brazilian student of municipal development, Carneiro Maia, insisted that the Brazilian municipality was a product of Brazilian experience, not the creation of the state. "The territorial extent of our first municipalities," this author wrote, "was almost as vast as that of some provinces today. New towns which acquired a certain level of development within these territories, moved by the difficulty of seeking justice so far from the center of the jurisdiction, aspired to local independence and constituted themselves municipalities. Thus the phenomenon of administrative decentralization arose in the bosom of towns as a necessity of the circumstances. The social life of the municipality was imposed by public exigency; the hand of government merely confirmed it."[6] Thus municipalities were not always created by central authority. Sometimes the town freed itself by electing a town council which later acquired a certain legality, sometimes by the tacit recognition of the government, at other times by later actions confirming the action of the inhabitants.

The situation of the Brazilian municipalities changed with the change in the political status of the country when the grants made to the first governors reverted to the crown. In 1549 a general center of government for all the captaincies was established in Bahia. This action freed the municipal councils from the feudal supremacy of the former governors, restoring their full jurisdiction and tax powers.

Events of the first half of the seventeenth century brought changes in the municipal institution. In the north, Dutch conquerors replaced the Portuguese municipal councils with their own system of councils of *escabinos* under the presidency of an *esculteto*. In these councils the people of Pernambuco had equal representation, but the president was a Hollander. The *esculteto* combined the functions of an executive representative, a promoter of public affairs, and the public treasurer. This situation continued until the invader was finally dislodged by Portugal in 1655.

The southern municipalities fought with the Jesuits, who were supported by the governor of Rio de Janeiro and received support from the crown. The Jesuits intervened in the temporal affairs of

---

[6] João de Azevedo Carneiro Maia, *Estudos de administração local* (Rio de Janeiro, 1883), pp. 29, 33.

the towns. These cities of the south also had trouble with the military when the latter tried, as they did in Rio de Janeiro, to intervene in the affairs of the municipalities and of justice.

In general, the prestige of the municipalities increased. On February 1, 1642, the crown granted the inhabitants of Rio de Janeiro "the same honors, privileges, and liberties" as the Royal Charter of 1640 and later charters had conceded to the city of Oporto. Similar rights were granted later to Bahia, Pernambuco, Pará and Maranhão.

In the eighteenth century, municipal councils achieved even greater importance. In defending popular interests, they obtained from the metropolis the suspension or revocation of decrees counter to the welfare of the country. They engaged in conflict with governors and other royal officials and with the Jesuits, even supporting revolts against the authorities.

In the middle of the century, Manoel Guedes Aranha, prosecuting attorney of the municipal council of Maranhão, presented to the Portuguese court his famous memorial, the *Papel político,* in which he said: "If governors represent the royal person, republics (chambers and senates) represent the original governments of the world."

SPANISH COLONIAL CITIES. The municipal institution of the Spanish cities was the *cabildo,* a collegiate body consisting of ordinary *alcaldes* (magistrates) and *regidores* (councilmen) varying in number according to the importance of the city, though generally there were not more than six. Some were chosen annually, with the peculiar arrangement that the retiring officials should choose their successors. Other officials included the *alferez real* (standard bearer), the *fiel ejecutor* (supervisor of weights and measures), procurators, clerks, and the *alguacil* (constable).

The *cabildos* supervised most of the activities of the city, exercising much more extensive authority than those in present-day municipalities. They performed electoral, judicial, political, economic, military, and financial functions, as well as the ordinary tasks of government. Judicial functions were carried out by the *alcaldes,* who had jurisdiction in the first instance over civil and criminal cases, and by the *cabildos* in special cases. In purely community matters, the *cabildo* was concerned with food supply, public works, price regulation, and the distribution of water in inland towns. It also established the standards for rural work assignments.[7]

[7] Ots Capdequi, *op. cit.,* p. 368; Ricardo Zorraquín Becú, "Los cabildos argentinos," *Revista de la Facultad de Derecho y Ciencias Sociales* (Buenos Aires, 1956), XI, No. 47, 95 ff.; and Constantino Bayle, *Los cabildos seculares en la América española* (Madrid: Sapientia, 1952).

The *cabildos* had the authority both to meet in ordinary sessions and, in special circumstances, to convoke a *cabildo abierto* (open meeting). They drew up and adopted their own ordinances, subject to confirmation by higher authority, such as the king or viceroy. To meet their needs and expenses the *cabildos* had their own possessions, chiefly lands and Indians—the latter for public works and services—as well as the authority to impose taxes.

PORTUGUESE CITIES. The characteristic institution of the Portuguese city in America was the *câmara municipal* (municipal council). The presiding magistrate might be a royal appointee, trained in law, with the title *juez de fora*. More frequently he was a layman, elected in the same way as other members of the council and called *juez ordinario*. "The ordinary magistrates," writes one Brazilian, "were always two, exercising their functions during alternate months of the year for which they had been elected. In contrast to the magistrates *de fora* they served without pay, as did the other members of the council. These other members included three *vereadores* (overseers) and a *procurador* (prosecutor). Elections were popular, that is the people voted, or more accurately, qualified persons voted—*os hommes bonos*, according to the phraseology of the laws." The reference is to those persons on lists made especially for this purpose. This question of the right to vote, including the right of election to the council, sometimes became a source of discord and even a weapon among enemy factions: landowners and natives of the colony on one side and merchants and *peninsulares* (Portuguese) on the other.[8]

Conflicts with other authorities were frequent, either because the latter interfered in municipal affairs or because the councils exceeded their authority. In general, the councils were similar to the Spanish American *cabildos*, except that the latter, save for very rare exceptions and practical circumstances, were not popularly elected.

"The legislative power of the councils," writes one authority, "were practically unlimited. The *oidores* [judges] of the captaincy at one time stopped going to the city of São Paulo for three years."[9] Their freedom is explained by the distance between the towns and the seat of the central authorities in America or Portugal. The same thing happened as with the *ccbildos* of Spanish America, that within their respective territories they were "supreme legis-

---

[8] Caio Prado Junior, *Formação do Brasil contemporaneo. Colonia.* (São Paulo: Livraria Martins, Editora, 1942), pp. 312–313.

[9] Eulalia María Lahmeyer Lobo, *Administração colonial luso-espanhola nas Americas* (Rio de Janeiro: Companhia Brasileira de Artes Gráficas, 1952), p. 261.

lators."[10] In the distant backlands (*sertão*) municipal magistrates alone imposed some order on a turbulent population, often exceeding their authority. The broad powers of the municipal councils appeared also in their economic authority. They regulated industries and policed the trade in articles of prime necessity. As Carneiro Maia remarks, "although their powers were limited by the ordinances, they still followed [the examples of] the old councils, arrogating to themselves diverse powers, some conceded by the metropolis, others born of the governors' custom of convening them for matters of grave importance. For their part, they also convoked *juntas*, decided upon war, and upon cases of succession to vacant offices. They imposed tributes or rejected those they judged unsuitable, and they performed many other administrative functions beyond the sphere of their competence."[11] Royal orders of 1677 and 1693 tried, not too successfully, to limit the action of municipal councils to their proper purposes.

INDIGENOUS TOWNS. The Spaniards respected the customs and institutions of the Indian towns and grouped the dispersed Indians into exclusively Indian municipalities. These towns also had native municipal officers, such as *alcaldes* and *regidores,* whose number corresponded to the number of houses, in conformity with the Spanish model. *Alcaldes* and *regidores* were chosen annually by the inhabitants. Spaniards, mestizos, and mulattoes were forbidden to live in these Indian towns.[12]

Municipalities in the Independence Movements

HISPANIC AMERICA. At the beginning of the nineteenth century, many *cabildos* revived and took an active part in the revolutionary movements. *Cabildos abiertos* (open meetings) assumed a revolutionary form apparently not foreseen in the Laws of the Indies. The Spaniards themselves gave it this character at times, as happened when the *cabildo abierto,* meeting in Montevideo on August 16, 1809, because of the English invasion, rejected the vice-regal authority and formed a local governing *junta.* Thus they set an example, later to be damaging to them when the creoles in turn used the same system to replace the established authorities. The *audiencia* of Buenos Aires took cognizance of the fact, condemning the movement of Montevideo on the basis of existing law in a decision which read: "The procedure of the *cabildo* of Montevideo may bring the ruin of these provinces, the complete subversion of

[10] Ricardo Levene, *Historia del derecho argentino* (Buenos Aires, 1945), II, 307.
[11] Carneiro Maia, *op. cit.,* pp. 48–49.
[12] T. Esquivel Obregón, *op. cit.,* II, 276.

our government, the overthrow of our wise constitution, which would without doubt lead to a precipice." The Argentine historian-president Bartolomé Mitre saw in this action of the Buenos Aires *audiencia* "the revolution of independence presented by the interpreters of colonial law and the depositaries of the supreme judicial and political authority of America."[13]

The *cabildo* of Buenos Aires, in revolutionary spirit, twice removed viceroys—on August 14, 1806, and on May 22, 1810. The *cabildo* exceeded its authority in this intervention in politics, and this practice later brought about the ruin of the institution in some of the new nations. Early revolutionary *juntas* were later formed in the *cabildos* of such other cities as Caracas (April 19, 1810), Buenos Aires (May 25, 1810), and Bogotá (July 22, 1810). The revolution of 1810, which initiated the movement for independence, had its juridical basis in the rules of order (*fueros*) of the *cabildo* of Buenos Aires, and the nation's earliest constitutional provisions were thus dictated by that municipality.

PORTUGUESE AMERICA. The municipal *câmaras* of Brazil encouraged independence from the metropolis through their activity as decentralized organisms. Their activity differed from that of the Spanish American *cabildos*, however, because independent Brazil (1822) did not directly become a republic, but passed first through the stage of the empire (1822–1890). Some of the declarations of these bodies, such as that made by the *câmara* of Rio de Janeiro when the metropolis tried to continue governing the American provinces with appointed officials under the Regency after 1821, expressed not only rebellion against metropolitan decisions but also a spirit of localism which is equivalent to the municipal spirit.[14]

Municipalities Under the New Nations

SPANISH AMERICA. The *cabildo*, like other Spanish institutions in America, changed greatly after independence. However, in such nations as Cuba, which gained independence later, the *cabildo* was affected by Spanish ideas and legislation for a much longer time.

In Argentina, the *cabildos* passed through a crisis in 1820 and disappeared completely in 1837 throughout the country, provincial governors and legislatures taking over their functions. The continuity of institutions of Spanish origin, continued in other countries, was thus broken. After the end of the Rosas dictatorship, municipalities were re-established in Argentina under the Consti-

---

[13] Bartolomé Mitre, *Historia de Belgrano,* in *Obras Completas* (Buenos Aires, 1940), X, 250.

[14] Océlio de Medeiros, *O governo municipal no Brasil* (Rio de Janeiro, n.d.), p. 39.

tution of 1853, which guaranteed the municipal regime, though without defining its exact form.[15]

In Mexico, independent in 1821, municipalities retained their juridical character under Spanish rule until the centralist constitutions of 1836 and 1842. These constitutions did not favor the development of municipal life, but instituted *jefaturas políticas*, agencies of the departmental governments in the cities. Later, the economic functions of the municipalities were restricted and placed under more rigorous control by central agencies. This situation was improved only with the adoption of the Constitution of 1917 which created the free municipality (*municipio libre*).

The institutional vicissitudes of the Iberian peninsula had a decisive influence on community life in Cuba, independent only after 1898. The Spanish Constitution of 1812 gave a new direction to municipal life, freeing it in many respects from the former centralization under captains general. After 1823 a return was made to centralism because of the Spanish constitutions and the ordinances dictated for the islands, such as the Ordinances of Concha of 1859, which again placed the municipalities under the authority of the captains general. In 1877 an organic municipal law was promulgated in Spain, applicable also in Cuba. Although it conceived of the municipality as a mere legislative creation, it tended to give the Cuban commune greater independence of personality and more extensive functions in relation to the central government, by granting the *cabildo* powers of its own within the limits set by law.

After Cuban independence, the important municipal law of 1908, inspired by Dr. Carrera Justiz, was adopted. It sought to break with previous Spanish law, seeking the bases of the municipal institution in other sources. In spite of this measure, however, the basic principles of the reform were Spanish.[16] The Carrera law was changed by the constitution of 1940.

Another important influence during the second half of the nineteenth century was de Tocqueville's *Democracy in America*, which had a great effect upon municipal thought in Hispanic America. One of the most significant things about de Tocqueville's ideas was the great importance he saw in the municipality for the survival and progress of political liberty.[17]

[15] Carlos Mouchet, "Las ideas de Echeverría, de Alberdi y de los Constituyentes de 1853 sobre el régimen municipal," *Revista "La Ley"* (Buenos Aires), LXXXIII, September 6, 1956.

[16] Fernando Albi, *Derecho municipal comparado del mundo hispánico* (Madrid: Aguilar, 1955), p. 593.

[17] The wide circulation of the work of de Tocqueville was aided by various Spanish translations: in Paris in 1837 by A. Sánchez de Bustamante, in Madrid in

BRAZIL. The constitution of 1824, adopted after the founding of the empire (1822), included, among the administrative and financial arrangements for the provinces, the bases of a municipal regime inspired in some respects by the principles of Anglo-Saxon "self-government." It authorized municipal councils in all existing towns and cities, as well as in those to be created, granting them the authority of "economic and municipal government." These councils and the justices of the peace, popularly elected, represented an interesting experiment under hereditary constitutional monarchy. Under the constitution, a statute was to regulate the functions of the councils, fixing their police powers and their public expenditures.[18] The law of October 1, 1828, did this, conferring ample police authority upon the municipalities and strengthening their power to manage local affairs, not only in urban centers but also in the adjacent rural areas.

The additional act of August 12, 1834—an amendment to the constitution of 1824—while accentuating the federalist tendency of political organization in Brazil by granting appropriate legal personality to the provinces, represented a tendency toward centralization as it affected the municipalities. The legislative assemblies of the provinces were strengthened by giving them ample power to legislate on municipal matters.[19] During this period the municipalities languished under excessive provincial centralization.[20]

The federal republican constitution of 1891 recognized the autonomy of municipalities and established their legal authority more in accord with their functions. "The States will be organized in such form," Article 68 provided, "that the autonomy of municipalities will be assured in everything relating to their peculiar interests." On the basis of this norm the states enacted more liberal laws on municipal organization.

The constitution of 1934 retained the previous norm on municipal autonomy and perfected it by assuring (1) the election of the pre-

---

1854 by E. Chao, in Buenos Aires in 1864, published by Bartolomé Victory y Suárez. Bartolomé Mitre said "the *Democracy in America* of Tocqueville was the leading book of that generation." For the influence of de Tocqueville on Sarmiento see Carlos Mouchet, "Sarmiento y sus ideas sobre el municipio indiano y patrio," *Cuadernos del Instituto Interamericano de Historia Municipal e Institucional* (Havana), No. 8, April 1954. See also Carlos Mouchet, *Pasado y restauración del régimen municipal* (Buenos Aires: Ed. Perrot, 1952).

[18] Yves Orlando Tito de Oliveira, *A organização municipal depois da independencia do Brasil* (Bahia, Brazil: 1949), pp. 3 ff.

[19] During this epoch a crisis arose in the Argentine provinces when the creation of provincial legislatures brought the disappearance of the *cabildos* between 1820 and 1837.

[20] Medeiros, *op. cit.,* p. 53.

fect and the members of the municipal council, the former to be chosen by the latter, (2) its authority to approve taxes and to receive and disburse the revenues, and (3) the authority to organize appropriate public services (Art. 13).

The municipal regime was extended in the constitution of 1946 which, according to Yves Tito de Oliveira, is "a truly municipal constitution." We shall note that Brazil is greatly advanced in municipal matters when the question of municipal autonomy is discussed.

PRESENT SIGNIFICANCE OF THE MUNICIPAL TRADITION. In much of Latin America, Spanish municipal thought, modified by the liberal French ideas in the Spanish Constitution of 1812, in the instruction of 1813, and in the laws of 1845 and 1877, has been influential. This municipal tradition has helped to revive the tradition of the Hispanic American *cabildo*. Such was the case in Mexico, Venezuela, Costa Rica, Guatemala, Nicaragua, Honduras, El Salvador, the Dominican Republic, and Peru. In Cuba the Spanish influence was prolonged longer, until the adoption of the law of 1908 previously mentioned. Subsequently, Cuba developed its own philosophy of municipal autonomy, based on the idea of the municipality as a natural social institution, rather than on the Spanish idea of the municipality as the creation of the legislator.[21] The Cuban constitution of 1940 shows the influence of North American ideas of municipal government.

Argentina, Uruguay, Bolivia, and Paraguay—formerly constituting the vice-royalty of Río de la Plata—form a separate group which, while retaining the Hispanic American tradition, have emancipated themselves sufficiently to look toward the example of the Anglo-American countries in many respects.[22]

Brazil and Puerto Rico deserve a separate comment. In the first of these countries the survival of Portuguese influence has been relatively small, since during the past century, Brazil, like Argentina, has shown great admiration for North American institutions. A federal country of twenty states and a federal district, Brazil has constitutional bases in municipal matters which have given rise to rather uniform state legislation. In Puerto Rico—a freely associated state since 1952—North American influence has been decisive since 1898, although some norms and customs of the Spanish tradition

[21] Adriano G. Carmona Romay, *El gobierno municipal de las Antillas mayores españolas y la influencia que ha podido ejercer en su formación y desarrollo el de los Estados Unidos de América* (pamphlet; Havana, 1952).

[22] See Fernando Albi, *op. cit.*, pp. 600 ff. For a sketch of the sources of municipal government in Latin America, see Adriano G. Carmona Romay, *Programa de gobierno municipal* (Havana: Martí, 1950), pp. 45 ff.

survive, as in the popular title of *alcaldesa* given to the present woman mayor of the city of San Juan.

Municipal Organization

CONSTITUTIONAL BASES OF AUTONOMY.   The problem of municipal autonomy involves the very basis of the nature of the municipality and its place in the modern state.   The municipality cannot be considered merely a creation of the legislator, since it is a natural political entity with its own ends to fulfill.   Nor can we think of it as entirely autonomous within the state with which its action must be in harmony.

The "postulates" of American municipalism, stated in 1948 by the Argentine Alcides Greca and the Brazilian Yves Tito de Oliveira, adopt as the basis of effective municipal autonomy the principles, formulated in 1904 by the North American, D. F. Wilcox: freedom of the city inhabitants to form their own political-administrative organization; freedom of the city inhabitants to determine the authority and scope of local government, in harmony with the process of state government; and freedom to elect the officials of local government.[23]

Autonomist tendencies in city government reach their highest point in the home rule charter plan granted municipalities by state legislatures in the United States since 1875.   In Latin America the Brazilian state of Rio Grande do Sul (Art. 154, II) was one of the earliest to authorize home rule in a state constitution.   The organic law for the government of the city of Porto Alegre, enacted under this provision, authorized the municipality to organize itself.   This may be the only municipality in Latin America ruled by a charter adopted by its own inhabitants.   The system was also in effect temporarily in the Argentine province of Sante Fe, whose 1921 constitution, in effect from 1932 to 1935, established the system for cities of over 25,000 inhabitants.   Under this provision, the cities of Rosario and Sante Fe adopted their own charters.

Most American constitutions contain declarations and provisions governing the place of the municipality within the state, some of them concrete affirmations of autonomy.   Limits to the municipal autonomy which may be granted are usually fixed by the constitution.   But only when the constitution expressly fixes a pattern of municipal independence, enumerating its functions and thus placing it outside legislative regulation, may a municipality be said to have a definite position as a component of the state.

[23] Alcides Greca and Yves Tito de Oliveira, "Postulados do municipalismo americano," *Revista de Direito Municipal* (Bahia, Brazil), January–February 1941, p. 51.

The 1946 constitution of Brazil (Art. 28) expressly guarantees municipal autonomy in the election of the prefect and the members of the municipal council, in the administration of anything relating to its special interests, in the authorization and collection of taxes within its competence, in the appropriation of revenues, and in the organization of local public services. Although a federal republic, Brazil does not give the state constitutions complete freedom to establish the bases of local government. Moreover, the constitution gives the central government authority to intervene in the states to assure municipal autonomy (Art. 7). The essential thing is the grant of financial self-sufficiency to municipalities, without which that of political and administrative autonomy is relatively meaningless.

The case is different in Argentina, where the federal constitution (Art. 5) merely requires the states to guarantee the municipal regime, leaving to their judgment the question of municipal organization. This provision has led the supreme court to the theory that municipalities are mere delegations of provincial powers. The lack of broader provisions in the Argentine constitution has permitted a centralized municipal government in the federal capital and the capitals of the provinces, contrary to the dominant ideas of the constitution-makers of 1853.[24]

The 1940 Cuban constitution declares that "the municipality is autonomous" and "municipal government is invested with all the necessary powers to resolve freely the affairs of the local community" (Art. 212). It also authorizes municipal home rule (Art. 223). Other provisions guarantee the political and financial autonomy of the municipality against the intervention of other powers. These provisions are given statutory form in the Fundamental Law of 1952.[25] But the provision for home rule has not been carried out.

Existence of the so-called "free municipality" is assured in the Mexican federal constitution (Art. 115) by establishing certain fundamental bases. The municipality is the basis of the territorial division of each state, and its officials are freely elected by the people. It has freedom to administer its funds, which consist of taxes established by the legislatures and which are to be sufficient for municipal needs.

STRUCTURE OF MUNICIPAL GOVERNMENT. The form of municipal government, based on the system of the division of powers created

[24] See Carlos Mouchet, "Las ideas de Echeverría, de Alberdi y de los Constituyentes de 1853 sobre el régimen municipal."

[25] See the texts in Mariano Sánchez Roca, *Legislación municipal y provincial de Cuba* (3d ed., Havana, 1955), pp. 13 ff.

in the United States for the federal government, according to Fernando Albi, is "the most widespread in the Hispanic world, in spite of its evident decadence in the country of origin. In essence, it is an almost exact reproduction of the federal government of the United States, carried into the local sphere. It establishes a complete differentiation between the normative (legislative) functions and those of action. As a consequence, the two powers are parallel, with independent orbits and without the subordination of one to the other."[26] It is followed in Argentina, Brazil, Uruguay, Paraguay, Puerto Rico (except the capital), some Mexican states, Cuba, Costa Rica, the Dominican Republic, Ecuador, and Bolivia. Under this system two organisms act: a popularly elected deliberative assembly or council and an executive organ (*intendente, alcalde, síndico,* or *prefecto,* according to the country) which supervises municipal administration. It may be popularly elected or appointed. When the two organisms are of different origin, conflicts often occur between them.

The North American system of city commission and manager, aimed at a technical administration as independent as possible from politics, has had no success in Latin America, unfortunately. Only the city of San Juan, Puerto Rico, has accepted it, in its office of Administrator of the Capital. A provision to this effect is also found in the Cuban constitution of 1952, permitting municipalities to choose this system by referendum (Art. 200).

In many countries the inefficiency of municipal government has been sensed especially when excessive political interference decreases the technical efficiency of administration. The problem is one of reconciling democracy with efficiency. This realization has brought critical study of current systems to achieve greater technical efficiency and the stability of municipal institutions.

One of the factors most disturbing to municipal government is the lack of stability and of continuity in its authorities and officials. Eight municipal *intendentes* succeeded each other between 1947 and 1957 in Buenos Aires, each change bringing with it the removal of a large part of the higher ranking administrative and technical personnel. Such change is obviously excessive, even though it occurred largely during a period of autocracy in Argentine politics.

FINANCIAL POWERS. To be effective, local governmental autonomy requires a sphere of economic and financial power of its own. Without this the life of a municipality is weak, or it is made subject to other organisms of the state. Under the sociological and natural

---

[26] Fernando Albi, *op. cit.,* pp. 284 ff.

law concept of the municipality, if city inhabitants are obliged to pay the charges originating in their community life, the municipal government should also have the powers to establish imports and taxes within its jurisdiction, without the intervention of any other power.[27] But such ample autonomy exists nowhere in the laws now in effect in Latin America.

The financial bases of the municipal regime are found in the national constitutions (as in Brazil), in national statutes, or in provincial constitutions or laws, according to the organization of the state. Added to these, generally, are forms of financial control exercised by superior bodies in the institutional hierarchy. The guaranty of effective financial autonomy lies in the fact that its fundamental bases, even in federal states, are found in the constitution of the central government.

In general the municipality cannot establish taxes other than those fixed by the law limiting municipal tax authority. But we find in Latin American legislation a variety of systems, ranging from the general listing of taxes, to permit a certain elasticity in establishing rates, to the strict enumeration of all taxes and rates.

In Brazil the financial bases of the municipal regime are found, as mentioned earlier, in the federal constitution. This assures the municipalities more effective autonomy, even though their financial policy may not invade the state or national sphere.

Municipal income is derived from various sources. Taxes on real estate, rates for public services, and levies for improvements figure in the table of receipts of almost all American cities. In some countries, municipal taxes are also levied on capital, consumption, and commercial activities. Some cities also share in provincial or national taxes. Municipal financial resources are extended by the use of credit and by the development of public resources through concession or lease, by conducting certain public services, and in some cases by industrial activities.

The problem of financial autonomy merited a long discussion in the First Congress of Ibero-American Municipalities, held in Madrid in 1955. It also figured in the agenda of the Sixth Meeting of the Inter-American Municipal Congress in Panama in August, 1956.

GOVERNMENT IN NATIONAL CAPITALS. The relations and tensions between central governments and municipal authorities present a special problem in those cities which are the seat of a national government, particularly that of a nation organized under the federal regime. This has resulted in the establishment of distinctive

[27] Adriano G. Carmona Romay, *La autonomía financiera municipal, a la luz de la escuela sociológica del municipio* (Madrid, 1955).

regimes for capital cities. Typical American examples are Washington, D.C., and Buenos Aires (since 1941).

An episode which occurred in Buenos Aires in 1889 illustrates the nature of the conflicts which may arise in capital cities. In that year the municipal government of that city refused President Domingo F. Sarmiento permission to review the military parade on the national holiday of May 25 from the balcony of the municipal building. The refusal prompted Sarmiento to ask whether the municipality of Buenos Aires wished to emulate the Paris Commune of 1871.[28]

Buenos Aires, with various changes, had a popular municipal government, at least in its legislative branch, until 1941, when the national executive dissolved the elective deliberating council. Because it had no express provision for the government of this city but gave the president the local headship (jefatura local) of the capital, Article 86 of the constitution had given rise to contradictory theories. Those who denied the constitutional possibility of an autonomous deliberating organ of popular origin, and who maintained that the organic municipal law had invaded the powers of the president, were thinking of the regime in Washington, D.C.[29] The centralist tendency became more marked after 1949, the executive constantly absorbing additional functions of the municipality. After the revolution of September 17, 1955, and the abrogation of the constitutional reform of 1949, the legal situation remained much the same, with perhaps even greater powers in the hands of the municipal intendant, the representative of the president. But the political parties which took part in the revolution and the provisional government itself look forward to giving back to the city of Buenos Aires a municipal regime with powers emanating directly from the people. The decree-law 15.374 of July 23, 1956, re-establishes in full force the organic municipal law of the year 1882 and implies the re-establishment, at least potentially, of the deliberating council.

The Federal District of Mexico also has a very special institutional situation. The Mexican Constitution of 1917, as amended in 1948, places the government of the Federal District under the charge of the president of the republic, who names the governor of the District (Art. 89, II). Municipal organization based on popular election has been suppressed since 1928. The Department

[28] Carlos Mouchet, "Sarmiento y sus ideas sobre el municipio indiano y patrio," *Cuadernos del Instituto Interamericano de Historia Municipal e Institucional* (Havana), No. 8, April 1954.

[29] Máximo I. Gómez Forgues, "El régimen municipal en la Capital Federal," *Revista de la Facultad de Derecho y Ciencias Sociales* (Buenos Aires, 1949), pp. 135 ff.

of the Federal District includes the city of México and various neighboring towns. It is governed by the chief of the department, aided by a consultative council (Organic Law of 1941, Arts. 5 and 6). Its organization, as established in the law, constitutes a centralized administrative system, since the powers of command, of police, and of control are not found in the hands of an organ separated from the central administration, but are assigned, rather, to the chief of the federal administration, that is to the president of the republic, the supreme authority in the Department.[30]

Caracas, the capital of Venezuela, a nation organized on the federal plan, has a popularly elected municipal council and a governor of the Federal District appointed by the president of the republic. Article 18 of the constitution of 1953 provides that "a municipal council, autonomous in respect to its fiscal, economic, and administrative regime, will exercise the municipal authority in each district of the states, in the Federal District, and in the federal territories, without other restrictions than those established by this Constitution." It adds that "the organic law of the Federal District may establish a special regime for its municipal authority, to be in accord with the dispositions of this Constitution."

In Brazil, the remaining federal country of Latin America, the Federal District is under a mixed system of municipal government: a prefect named by the president of the republic, and a legislative organ of popular origin (constitution of 1946, Art. 26).

Some centralized nations exhibit a tendency to place their capital cities under a distinct system, making them more subject to central control than other cities. Tegucigalpa, Honduras, is governed by a commission appointed by the executive. In Managua (Federal District) the president of Nicaragua is the local authority, through a minister. The District of Santo Domingo in the Dominican Republic has an administrative council appointed directly by the president.

La Habana (Havana) maintains its autonomy and the system of democratic election of its officials. The Cuban constitution of 1952 authorizes the creation by law of a metropolitan district, federating the capital with the surrounding towns in such number as the law may determine. The federated municipalities, it provides, shall have direct representation in the metropolitan district, retaining their democratic and popular organization (Art. 207).

San Juan, Puerto Rico, influenced by the United States, has a commission–manager system, which is an exception even in the

---

[30] Gabino Fraga, *Derecho administrativo* (3d ed.; Mexico: Porrúa, 1944), pp. 466–474.

municipal system of this "freely associated" state. The municipal commission is of mixed origin: the majority chosen by direct election and a minority by gubernatorial appointment. The commission, in turn, chooses the administrator of the city.

Advocates of these centralizing tendencies, opposed to the elective municipal system, invoke various reasons in support of this policy: that the capital belongs to the whole nation and should, therefore, be governed exclusively by its central authorities; that strife which might affect the power and security of the national authority in the capital should be avoided; that the services rendered in the capital benefit all the inhabitants of the country (political and administrative organs, educational institutions, and hospital centers).

Problems of Municipal Administration

EXPANSION OF PUBLIC SERVICES. Furnishing public services is a characteristic function of municipalities and one of the essential purposes of community organization. Hence, in the theory inspired by the doctrines of Duguit, Jeze, and other writers, the municipality is considered as nothing more than a conjunction or system of public services.

The constitution of Brazil prudently includes among the guaranties of municipal autonomy "the organization of local public services" (Art. 28). The constitutions of Cuba (Art. 188), Venezuela (Art. 21), Bolivia (Art. 155), and others also grant to municipalities the appropriate powers to establish local public services.

In this connection various problems arise. What public services are within the competence of the municipalities; that is, what is a local public service? What private activities should be regulated as public services? And, finally, what is the form of action: (a) by direct administration (municipalization), (b) by concession, (c) by a mixed economy, or (d) by lease?

The present tendency in Latin America—coinciding incidentally with developments in Europe—is not to limit public services to what was formerly considered their specific realm, such things as hygiene and health, public lighting, urbanism, morality, and food supply. Their scope is now being extended, in accordance with the modern concept of the state, to matters such as urban transportation, construction of housing, and especially into the fields of public welfare and cultural life. There are also areas of concurrent authority and activity with the state, such as sanitation, culture, and social security.

The sphere of municipal authority in these matters is broadened or narrowed in accordance with the authoritarian or decentralizing tendencies prevailing in a country. A typical case is that of the city of Buenos Aires. By virtue of a policy initiated some fifteen years ago, such services as urban transport, operation of slaughterhouses, the control of cinemas, and the collection of taxes were absorbed by the national government. After the revolution of September 16, 1955, overthrew the Perón regime, there was to be noted the beginning of a policy of restoring these services and functions to the municipality, and even of adding other services considered municipal in nature (some hospital services). In Buenos Aires the sewer service and the water supply are, however, furnished by an agency dependent on the national government. Fire-fighting services in the city also depend on the national government.

Municipalization has increased because of politico-social considerations derived from the growth and greater complexity of urban life.[31] In general, Latin American municipal laws authorize the municipalization of those public services which satisfy basic necessities or urgent needs of the people. Urban public services do not always have an economic or industrial character; this is true of such services as transportation, operation of slaughterhouses, and electrical or water supply. They also meet new duties of the municipality to the general public (public welfare and cultural services). Many countries of Latin America (but not Argentina) retain the tradition of the elementary school run by the city.

URBAN DEVELOPMENT. Throughout Latin America, the simple provisions relating to urban development contained in the legislation of the late nineteenth century, limited to such things as the opening of streets, control of building, and drainage works, are being supplanted by much broader provisions for the organic growth of cities in accordance with previous plans and studies. These are the beginnings of a policy, inspired by North American and European examples, to consider city planning in relation to the plans of the region in which the city is located, or even with the integral planning of the country.[32] An outstanding example of this tendency may be seen in the group of projects in Brazil called *operação municipio.*[33]

[31] Rafael Bielsa, *Principios de régimen municipio* (Buenos Aires, 1940), pp. 345 ff.

[32] Fernando Albi, *op. cit.,* pp. 203 ff. and 267 ff.; and José María Pastor, *Urbanismo con planeamiento* (Buenos Aires, 1946), pp. 110 ff.

[33] Francelino de Araujo Gómez, *Operação municipio. Fundamentos do plano nacional de obras e servicios municipais* (Rio de Janeiro: Inst. Internacional de Ciencias Administrativas, secão brasileira, 1955); Francisco Burkinski, *A crise brasileira e a operação municipio* (Rio de Janeiro: Inst. Int. de Ciencias Administrativas, secão brasileira, 1955); Araujo Cavalcanti, "Sentido e importancia de la

Such provisions for metropolitan regional planning are necessary, for while not all America has experienced the North American phenomenon of the replacement of rural by urban growth, the tendency is in that direction, as may be seen in the very rapid development of such large cities as Buenos Aires.[34] In general, Latin American cities have been growing in a disorderly manner, and even large cities have lacked government by skilled technicians during many periods.

Another great problem confronting the rapidly growing cities is that of the *arrabales,* districts of improvised and miserable housing, which grow up outside all city planning or authorization. The *favellas* of Rio de Janeiro, *Miseria* and similar communities in Buenos Aires, and districts like *el fanguito* of San Juan, Puerto Rico, are a few examples of what is happening throughout Latin America.

Some countries have enacted laws or ordinances which do not impose truly regulatory plans and which also overlook the necessary coordination of urban development with that of zones adjoining urban areas. In Chile, a law and general ordinance on construction and urbanization was enacted in 1925. Authorized by the decree-law 9434-1944, establishing restrictions on property rights, the city of Buenos Aires adopted a building code in effect since 1944, important in relation to zoning, approval of building, and land use. But it fell short of a truly regulatory plan. The Cuban constitution of 1952 requires cities to adopt "a plan for the growth and beautification of cities" (Art. 190). In 1941, Peru enacted a national regulation of urbanization. The most complete and interesting experiment is that of the Puerto Rican commission of planning, urbanization, and zoning. It is not limited to strictly municipal matters, but proposes as its goal the orderly development of the activities of the whole island (Art. 3 of the Planning Law of 1942).[35]

While in most cases the promotion of regulatory plans, building codes, and laws of urbanization is a responsibilty of the municipalities, in other cases this function is entrusted to decentralized or extra-municipal local agencies, or even to state or national organs. The planning agencies of the Federal District of Mexico and the

operación Rio de Janeiro," *Revista Municipal Interamericana* (Havana), January–June 1956; Océlio de Medeiros, *Problemas fundamentais dos municipios brasileiros* (Rio de Janeiro: Departamento Administrativo de Serviço Público, 1956).

[34] See the study by A. Morales Carrión, *Las relaciones humanas entre el municipio y la ciudadanía,* presented at the Fifth Meeting of the Inter-American Municipal Congress, Puerto Rico, 1954. Published by the government.

[35] See Santiago Iglesias (hijo), "Organización, funciones y objetivos de la Junta de Planificación de Puerto Rico," *Cuadernos del Instituto Interamericano de Historia Municipal e Institucional* (Havana), No. 2, April 1952.

departmental *juntas* of public works of Bolivia belong in the first group. Of the second type are the Peruvian national urban council, the central commission of planning and urbanization of the State of Mexico, the planning commission of Puerto Rico, and the national planning commission of Cuba (established in 1955).

Provisions for regulatory plans appear in the municipal law of Ecuador (Art. 41), the Organic Law of the Federal District of Rio de Janeiro (Art. 40), and the Urbanization Law of the Dominican Republic (Art. 1). And this matter has merited special attention in the Inter-American Municipal Congresses. The Fourth Inter-American Congress on Municipal History (Buenos Aires, 1949) recommended that cities undertake the study and formulation of regulatory plans, not only because of the need of anticipating this development, but also for historical and social reasons. It urged that these plans should not be limited to the borders of the community, but should extend to the surrounding region, with national coordination (Resolution XXI). The Fourth Meeting of the Inter-American Municipal Congress (Montevideo, 1953) adopted diverse resolutions and recommendations on municipal planning, including "the complementary structures of city and countryside," and their coordination with regional and national regimes. In respect to the coordination of planning, it recommended the establishment in each country of a "planning organ made up of municipal, regional, and national representatives, endowed with powers compatible with those of the member institutions" (Theme IV).

These expressions of desire in inter-American meetings make it clear that planning—whose irresistible future advance may be forecast because of its obvious necessity—cannot remain limited to the perimeter of each municipality. This planning tendency may also influence adversely the movement toward greater municipal autonomy, since cities must base a good part of their action on regional and national regulatory plans drawn up by superorganisms of planning. This danger may be averted by adequate precautions which allow coordinated action without restricting municipal autonomy.

MUNICIPAL CIVIL SERVICE. The spoils system, which ceased in the United States at the end of the past century, "is still the standard which obtains in most of the Hispanic countries of the American continent," writes one author,[36] and with much justification. It is easy to point out the disastrous effects of this system on the efficiency of work of municipal administration, an eminently technical matter which requires both specialized skill and a stable

[36] Fernando Albi, *op. cit.*, p. 325.

bureaucracy. With rare exceptions, however, the political rather than the professional system for appointing and removing city officials is practiced in the Latin American countries.

The untrained officials who assume political or governmental positions in municipalities need to have at their disposal technicians acquainted with the complex problems of urban communities. Instead, they frequently appoint loyal but untrained followers who turn out to be sorry advisers or officials. To remove competent career officers the fallacious argument of "confidence" is invoked, when the real need is for the functionary with qualifications which merit the confidence of the administration and not for some transient politician. All these weaknesses are betrayed in lamentable changes in plans of work, in constant reorganizations of administrative structures, and above all in the alienation and inefficiency of functionaries.

The European and North American tendencies to regulate the agents and officials of municipal government by a statute which provides for selection on a scientific basis and assures tenure and promotion in office is beginning very slowly and precariously in Latin America. In the constitutions, laws, and ordinances of some nations we find standards for selection and guaranties for municipal administrative personnel, but the practice does not always conform to the legal provisions.[37] Still, the standards contained in the constitutions of Cuba and Brazil have great significance. Article 105 of the fundamental law of Cuba of 1952 provides: "Functionaries, employees, and civil public workers of all agencies of the state, the province, the municipality, and all autonomous entities or corporations are exclusively servants of the general interests of the Republic, and their irremovability is guaranteed by this constitution, except those who exercise public charges of confidence."

The constitution of Brazil also contains the principle of tenure for public officials and regulates cases of removal (Arts. 184–190). Provisions on the point also figure in a few other constitutions, those of Guatemala, Panama, El Salvador, and Nicaragua. The constitution of Panama (Art. 421) provides that the appointment and removal of officials and employees are not within "the absolute and discretionary power of any of the organs of public authority." There are laws on the status of administrative personnel in Colom-

---

[37] This contradiction between legality and practice is made clear in a study by Torres Braschi, *Las relaciones humanas entre el gobierno municipal y su personal*, presented to the Fifth Meeting of the Inter-American Municipal Congress, San Juan, Puerto Rico, 1954. Published by the government.

bia (1938), Chile (1946), and Peru (1950). Thus it might be said that there is a certain tendency, weak though it may be, toward stability and efficiency. Many municipalities establish tenure and career service on a local scale, but this is often violated by practices and exceptions which open the doors to exclusively political motives.

LOCAL COURTS AND POLICE ADMINISTRATION. Little remains of the Spanish tradition which entrusted to the municipality the administration of justice in the first instance in many matters. This is now considered a function within the jurisdiction of the national state or the provinces. Only in a few Mexican and Venezuelan states are the petty magistrates named by municipal organizations. In Colombia municipal judges are elected for two-year periods by the superior tribunals of the respective districts (constitution of 1886, modified in 1945, Art. 158).[38] Municipalities still have charge of punishing infractions of their ordinances, whether through regular administrative officials or through administrative judges, such as those called *jueces de faltas* in the city of Buenos Aires, which are not part of the judicial authority.

As for the security police, in contrast with the practice in the United States and in many European cities, municipalities are generally excluded from their control.

Municipal Democracy

The agencies of municipal government are chosen by popular suffrage in almost all places in America. This is one of the bases of American municipalism. Exceptions to the principle occur, however, especially in the designation of unipersonal executives, as we have noted in some cases, by the central government, or by the municipal deliberative body.

Suffrage in Latin American city government often has special characteristics. For example, passive and active suffrage is generally extended to foreigners, a practice which is not found in Europe.

Democratic progress toward universal suffrage tends to reduce discrimination in the exercise of this right. In 1873, the Argentine Juan Manuel Estrada maintained that the right of suffrage could not continue to be limited to tax-paying residents and nationals. "Directly or indirectly," he asserted, "all contribute to the public revenues. Moreover the municipal interests, education, beautification, security, and hygiene affect equally and without distinction all those who have a life to defend, children to educate—in a word

[38] Fernando Albi, *op. cit.*, pp. 143 ff.

all, since the community is the common family and the municipality is the *patria pequeña* to which loyalties and hopes link us."[39]

In municipal elections, most Latin American countries follow, with some variations, the system of proportional representation. Others, to a lesser extent, follow the system of limited vote, or combine both systems. Proportional representation permits participation in city elections not only by the major parties active on the national or provincial scene, but also by civic groups formed especially to advocate certain local programs. As one authority puts it, "Systems of election by simple majority, or by majority and minority, are not just, nor judicious, nor desirable in the municipal sphere."[40] Such systems do not permit the differentiated defense of the distinct nuclei of interest which make up municipal life.

Moreover, in the municipality certain forms of direct democracy function which would be inapplicable in larger political systems, such as the referendum, the right of initiative in legislation, and the recall for the removal of officials.

New Trends in City Government

Present trends in municipal government and administration are being defined in the Inter-American Municipal Congresses and in the writing of specialists on the subject, all of which are slowly influencing municipal law and policy.[41]

Although political realities in some countries with authoritarian governments favor increased centralism, the predominant trends in present-day thought are oriented decidedly toward greater and more effective autonomy in city organization. Equally manifest is the concern for encouraging administrative and technical efficiency, without sacrificing the democratic basis of municipal organization for the purpose. The idea of city planning is also penetrating in the new conceptions of municipal activity. Although ideological and legislative influences from Spain, Portugal, and, in some respects, France persist, the influence of North American ideas and methods of municipal organization are felt more and more. Opinion is practically unanimous on the necessity of giving constitutional category to the fundamental principles of municipal organization and the essential bases of democratic political and financial autonomy, in

[39] Juan Manuel Estrada, *La política liberal bajo la tiranía de Rosas* (Buenos Aires: Imprenta Americana, 1873), p. 301.

[40] Rafael Bielsa, *op. cit.*, p. 54.

[41] Especially the Fourth Inter-American Congress on Municipal History, Buenos Aires, 1949, and the Fourth Meeting of the Inter-American Municipal Congress, Montevideo, 1953.

order to free municipal authorities and powers from legislative changes.

While the need is recognized for rationalizing and planning municipal activity, particularly in its aspects of finance and urban development, the necessity of coordinating these plans with those of the provinces and the nation is emphasized equally. Thus, in the Fourth Meeting of the Inter-American Municipal Congress (Montevideo, 1953) it was resolved that the planning of localities, regions, and cities should be strengthened and affirmed "in a coordinated relationship between community governments and the national authority, through inter-administrative accords and agreements." It was also recommended especially that the municipality coordinate with the state its regional bases and plans relating to social welfare, health, education, and culture. It was further resolved "that the right should be recognized for municipalities, in all financial matters, to maintain themselves with their own resources, including the making of loans, without other limitations than those the constitutions expressly establish and within the spirit of coordination and cooperation with the national or regional government."

The First Ibero-American Congress of Municipalities (Madrid, 1955) declared that "the fundamental scope of municipal authority must be recognized by the state in its basic laws, since the development and operation of their fiscal systems is completely within the municipal sphere." Also to be recognized is "the greater ability and initiative of cities in administering and exploiting rationally and economically all kinds of property and maintaining public enterprises to satisfy collective interests."

The renaissance of the municipal spirit usually appears after the passing of dictatorial or strong political regimes. In Argentina there may be seen, not only in the federal capital but also in the provinces, a general movement of opinion in support of the need for strengthening municipal life as one of the essential bases for the civic and institutional restoration of the country. Without awaiting the advent of a normal constitutional regime, the provisional government is giving back to the cities the functions and authority of which they had been deprived.

Brazil is preparing a vast plan for revitalizing municipalities, called municipal action (*operação municipio*). It is a movement bringing together politicians, technicians, and municipal associations to carry out a group of proposals and concrete plans, not only for the socio-economic development of the cities but, through them, of the state as well. The *operação municipio* consists of a series of regional plans, such as that for the Brazilian state of Rio de Janeiro.

The proponents of this movement claim that these plans express a new-style municipalism. "Municipal Action," declares one of these proponents, "represents an organic and technical municipalism which pays tribute to the emancipation of the municipality and at the same time opposes any sacrifice whatsoever of the powers, prerogatives, and resources of the union." He adds that "one of the greatest services Municipal Action has rendered to the country is that of eliminating the kind of primitive urbanism, saturated with the desire for revindication, which tries to strengthen the cities at the expense of the Union and the States. Municipal Action restores the integrity of the federal system. All problems are resolved in the light of scientific criteria, by developing and perfecting the complex system of inter-administrative relations and inter-governmental cooperation. Principles and technics of planning are implanted."[42]

Finally, it may be said that Latin America has a consciousness of the need for assuring and developing municipal institutions as factors of civic progress and collective well-being. These must rest upon bases which respond to democratic needs as well as the efficient performance of the technical labor which the inhabitants expect of their cities.

Suggestions for Reading

George I. Blanksten lists no English-language work on Latin American municipal government in his "Bibliography on Latin American Politics and Government," *Inter-American Review of Bibliography*, IV (1954), No. 3, 191–214. Clarence Haring treated colonial municipal government in *Spanish Empire in America* (New York: Oxford University Press, 1947). Leo S. Rowe, *The Federal System of the Argentine Republic* (Washington: Carnegie Institution, 1921), Graham H. Stuart, *Government System of Peru* (Washington: Carnegie Institution, 1925), and William M. Gibson, *The Constitutions of Colombia* (Durham, N.C.: Duke University Press, 1948), provide useful discussions for those nations. Chapters on municipal government are found in two textbooks called *Governments of Latin America*, one by Miguel Jorrín (Princeton, N. J.: D. Van Nostrand Co., Inc., 1953); and one by William W. Pierson and Federico G. Gil (New York: McGraw-Hill Book Co., Inc., 1957).

The Spanish-reader may consult Alcides Greca, *Derecho y ciencia de la administración municipal* (Santa Fe, Argentina: Imp. de la Universidad, 1943), José María Sáenz Valiente, *Bajo la campana del cabildo* (Buenos Aires: Guillermo Kraft, 1952), Julio R. Alemparte, *El cabildo en el Chile colonial* (Santiago: Universidad de Chile, 1940), and Fernando Albi, *Derecho municipal comparado del mundo hispánico* (Madrid: Aguilar, 1955). The Portuguese-reader will find municipal government in Brazil treated in Océlio de Medeiros, *Problemas fundamentais dos municipios brasileiros* (Rio de Janeiro: Serviço de Documentação, 1956), and Francelino de Araujo Gomes, *Operação municipio. Fundamentos do plano nacional de obras e serviços públicos* (Rio de Janeiro, 1955).

[42]Araujo Calvacanti, *op. cit.*

Chapter 14

Organization and Conduct
of International Relations

Latin America and Contemporary World Politics

The need for an orderly world community in which American regionalism can preserve its separate identity underscores the present Latin American view of international relations. This preoccupation with both regional and universal concepts appeared as early as 1826 when Bolívar envisaged a continental federation as the first step toward the creation of a world community of nations. A basic adherence to international law has marked the foreign policies of Latin American states ever since. Debilitating domestic conflicts and the intervention of outside powers often precluded extensive multilateral efforts at international law and organization during the nineteenth century, yet the Latin Americans held seven international conferences between 1847 and 1888. And, at the turn of the century, when the United States directed its attention southward, the Latin Americans joined their northern neighbor in constructing a hemispheric organization based on the principles of sovereign equality, nonintervention, the imposition of sanctions on aggressors, and the pacific settlement of disputes.

After World War I, distrust of "Yankee" imperialism swung the Latin Americans away from regionalism and toward the universalism promised by membership in the League of Nations. By the time Latin Americans had become disenchanted with the League, the United States had swung full circle and pledged itself to the policy of the Good Neighbor. In contrast with the vacillating relationships of previous decades, the solid achievements of the inter-

American community after 1933 gave substance to the claim of the distinguished Panamanian jurist and statesman Ricardo J. Alfaro that "in the field of international organization and cooperation Europe had nothing to teach America, whilst the Old World had something to learn from the New." Membership in the United Nations once again expressed the Latin American predilection for universalism, but this time it did not mean giving up their own regional system.

Only during the present century have Latin American states become active and autonomous participants in international affairs. For four centuries their role was largely that of a pawn in the great power rivalries. In fact the whole New World was "the first great battleground whereon European nations fought for the privilege of gathering in resources and of civilizing, Christianizing, exploiting, and sometimes even exterminating the native peoples."[1] This power rivalry was ended by political independence in some respects, but in other respects it even intensified. For while the growth of the United States introduced an important new element into the power balance in the Western Hemisphere, Latin America continued during the nineteenth century to invite use or seizure by powerful states for their own ends. Two world wars, the Great Depression, the Good Neighbor policy, and the "cold war" paved the way for the new international role that the Latin American states enjoy. Today they constitute the largest voting bloc within the United Nations and possess, together with the United States, the oldest and most successful regional organization in the world. Their statesmen have distinguished themselves in many ways in international diplomatic circles. They have the raw materials essential to modern military organization and are beginning to develop the necessary industrial strength.

It may well be a question, however, whether this influence can continue to grow in the future. If it is true that the center of world power is shifting from West to East, all the nations of the West, including those of Latin America, may have to adapt themselves to a world whose destiny they no longer control. Some students of geopolitics insist that because Latin America lacks a favorable position in relation to the world's principal communication and transportation lines, only outstanding development in technology, the productive arts, and industrial output will enable her to improve her power position during the decades to come. While it is possible to speculate on the importance of an area which some

---

[1] J. Fred Rippy, *Latin America in World Politics* (3rd ed.; New York: Appleton-Century-Crofts, Inc., 1938), pp. 1–2.

optimistic predictions would give a population of four to five hundred millions in the near future, the fact is that today the region as a whole brings to the diplomatic table less real bargaining power than does the Soviet Union, or even some Asiatic nations in stages of progress similar to its own. One major reason is its lack of political union. But even considered as a unit, Latin America has fewer inhabitants than the Soviet Union, and the largest nation, Brazil, possesses less than one-sixth the population of either China or India.

To be sure, these crude power differentials are merely one measure of international stature, to be considered along with national ideologies, national character, and public opinion. The organization of the foreign ministries and the caliber of the diplomatic corps are further variables in the formulation and administration of foreign policy, and these institutional controls on policy-makers may significantly determine policy formulation. Before we examine these agencies responsible for foreign relations, however, our attention must turn to the actual substance of foreign policies. This analysis will involve the contacts of Latin American states with each other; their relations with other nations in the Western Hemisphere, especially the United States; their relations with nations outside the hemisphere; the evolution and present organization of the inter-American system; and the role of Latin American states in world organizations.

Inter-Latin American Relations

It is a popular misconception regarding the foreign affairs of the Latin American republics that their relations with one another are always cordial and friendly. This is far from the truth, despite the many cultural bonds which unite them. Every nation at some time, some of them frequently, has shown antipathy toward a sister republic. Argentines, for example, are annoyed by the unwillingness of the other republics to regard seriously her aspiration to Latin American leadership. They criticize the citizens of their largest neighbor, stereotyping Brazilians as "monkeys" and "chatterboxes." Brazilians in turn call Argentines "wooden heads," exaggerating their stubbornness. Some states have nursed grudges toward another state for many decades—for example, Haiti and the Dominican Republic, or Costa Rica and Nicaragua. Chile resents Argentina's unwillingness to grant territory at the southern tip of the continent for an Atlantic outlet, and these two countries also have conflicting claims in Antarctica. Mexico and Guatemala contest each other's rights, as well as those of Great Britain, to

British Honduras. Ecuadorians regard Peruvians as bullies. Bolivia, Colombia, and Peru seek concessions of territory from Brazil in their ambitions for easier access to the Amazon. In addition, Bolivia resents her loss of a Pacific frontage in the "War of the Pacific," and also wants access to the River Plate system.

INTER-LATIN AMERICAN WARS. Relative geographical isolation seemingly would have permitted the Latin American states to indulge in disputes more regularly than most small nations elsewhere in the world. It is surprising, therefore, that during more than 125 years of national independence no more than five conflicts brought extensive international warfare, and in no instance did the struggle involve more than four countries. In the first of these conflicts, Argentina and Brazil fought intermittently during the period 1825–1828 over territorial claims. The conflict resulted in the creation of Uruguay as a buffer state between the two powers. From 1837 to 1839 Chile fought against Peru and Bolivia to thwart their attempts to confederate and thereby upset the power politics of the southern Pacific region. In 1865, Argentina, Brazil, and Uruguay united against Paraguay to stop the imperialistic ambitions of the Paraguayan dictator, Francisco Solano López. This five-year war was very costly in the number of Paraguayan lives lost. Again from 1879 to 1883, Chile engaged Peru and Bolivia in warfare, this time a dispute over rich nitrate deposits. This "War of the Pacific" ended in the Peruvian loss of Tarapacá and Arica to Chile. Bolivia paid an even heavier price, losing its Pacific coastline. Finally, from 1933 to 1938, the long-drawn-out Chaco War between Bolivia and Paraguay gave the latter the lion's share of the Chaco region.

IDEOLOGICAL CONFLICTS: POLITICAL REFUGEES. Thus, inter-Latin American conflicts have usually arisen from boundary disputes, but occasionally they have involved ideological issues. When liberal and reactionary regimes exist in neighboring nations, friction has frequently resulted. In the feud between the Somoza family in Nicaragua and José Figueres in Costa Rica the personal antagonisms represent deeper social issues. Acción Democrática in Venezuela, the *apristas* of Peru, the *auténticos* in Cuba, political groups opposed to Somoza in Nicaragua, and those opposed to Trujillo in the Dominican Republic have frequently found it expedient to seek refuge in countries under more liberal administrations. During the Perón era, Bolivian *falangistas* sought political asylum in Argentina when they met with difficulty at home. The activities of such refugees frequently create international tension. Argentine Socialist and Radical party members chose Uruguay as their base of operation against Perón. Trujillo has accused other governments in the Caribbean region, particularly those of Costa Rica and Guatemala, of designing and financing plots to overthrow his regime. Guatemalans plotting the overthrow of the Arbenz Guzmán government in 1954 unquestionably obtained assistance from neighboring countries. In 1957 it was revealed that Cuban exiles in Mexico were conspiring to overturn the Batista regime.

TOURISM. Political refugees, happily, constitute only a fraction of the number of citizens traveling from one country to another. Increase in tourist and other travel is a notable characteristic of twentieth-century inter-American relations. Consular officials of some nations probably consume as much time in the issuance of tourist visas as in all commercial affairs combined. The two-way traffic between Argentina and Uruguay and between Uruguay and Brazil is particularly notable. Many Mexicans travel to Central America and Cuba, while thousands of Guatemalans enter Mexico yearly. This increase in tourism presents the appealing prospect of promoting cultural appreciation, good will, and international understanding.

INTER-LATIN AMERICAN COMMERCE. In the past, the orientation of commercial relations of the twenty republics toward markets in Europe and the United States has encouraged the production for export of a single crop or the mining of a particular metal. Such dependence upon a single product for export has sometimes led to friction among countries exporting the same commodity, as in the case of the large coffee-growing nations of Brazil, Colombia, Costa Rica, Guatemala, El Salvador, and Nicaragua. In this case, the friction has been lessened by a marketing board set up to watch over the mutual interests of the growers concerned. But on the whole, these competitive economies present barriers to the development of significant trade among the Latin American countries. There are notable exceptions. Argentina, which exports more wheat, corn, and hides than any other country in the world, and Venezuela, a large exporter of oil and iron ore, have both increased their trade with other Latin American nations. And Mexico is apparently outstripping both in the diversification and balance of its economy. Inter-Latin American trade grew from some 6 per cent of total Latin American foreign trade before World War I to at least 10 per cent in the years following World War II, and it is steadily increasing, as noted in Chapter 3. Such an increase in the relative volume of trade among the nations of the area has important implications for their political relations with each other, even though the foreign trade of the area is still dominated by

European and North American markets for exports. The Organization of Central American States furnishes an example of the effect of these increased economic ties, as we shall see later.

Latin America and the United States

INFLUENCE OF THE UNITED STATES. Peace in the Western Hemisphere owes much to the fact that one of the twenty-two American states (twenty Latin American, the United States, and Canada) possesses overpowering wealth and strength. Unlike Europe and Asia, this hemisphere has escaped the kind of balance of power in which powerful political rivals of about equal strength are competing. World leadership in technology and industrial output, in surplus goods and capital available for foreign investment, places the United States on an unchallenged plane in hemispheric economic relations. In the political and strategic realms, the United States has clearly overshadowed its sister republics in the twentieth century. And if peaceful means fail to protect its interests, large mobile military forces stand prepared to move quickly as a last, but effective resort. This disproportion in the strength of the United States and the other American nations placed a severe strain on inter-American relations in earlier years. But since 1930 a more benevolent attitude has emerged from a growing awareness on the part of both Anglo- and Latin America of their importance to each other; both sides have come to recognize the mutuality of commercial, strategic, and political interests that bind them.

THE MONROE DOCTRINE. The relatively cordial relations existing today between the United States and the Latin American states developed slowly and painfully. During trials and tribulations, advances and retreats, basic United States policy has centered on the Monroe Doctrine, which expressed a policy based on the principle of national self-determination in America.[2] The United States assumed a friendly interest in Latin American independence and in 1822 was the first government to accord diplomatic recognition to the new republics. Yet independence had not eliminated the threat of European intervention in America. Relying also on the essential freedom of the United States' position, which arose partly from British sea power, President Monroe pronounced his

[2] The standard work on the Monroe Doctrine is a three-volume study by Dexter Perkins, but his *Hands Off: A History of the Monroe Doctrine* (Boston: Little, Brown & Co., 1941) is more readily useful to the general student; also, see Samuel F. Bemis, *The Latin American Policy of the United States* (New York: Harcourt, Brace & Co., Inc., 1943), and Graham H. Stuart, *Latin America and the United States* (5th ed.; New York: Appleton-Century-Crofts, Inc., 1955).

now famous Doctrine in a message to Congress on December 2, 1823. He first laid down the principle that "the American continents, by the free and independent condition which they have assumed and maintain, are henceforth not to be considered as subject for future colonization by any European power." Next he declared that the political system of the powers allied in the Holy Alliance was dangerous to the new Latin American republics and the United States alike.

. . . we should consider any attempt on their [the European powers] part to extend their political system to any portion of this hemisphere as dangerous to our peace and safety. With the existing colonies and dependencies of any European power we have not interfered and shall not interfere. But with the Governments who have declared their independence and maintained it, and whose independence we have, on great consideration and on just principles, acknowledged, we could not view any interposition for the purpose of oppressing them, or controlling in any other manner their destiny, by any European power in any other light than as the manifestation of an unfriendly disposition towards the United States. . . .

Although the Doctrine thus asserted the solidarity of the United States with the Latin American nations, and although those revolutionary leaders of Latin America who took notice of it received it approvingly, it was a national policy stated in terms of national interest. Only with the passing of a century did this germ of the later inter-Americanism achieve the multilateral character which some Latin American statesmen wished to see in it from the beginning. Moreover, the application of the policy was obviously dependent upon the strength of the British Navy. These two aspects of the Doctrine led many Latin Americans to look upon it as a mere cloak for British nineteenth-century ambitions in the River Plate region and in Central America, and for the annexation of Texas and California by the United States. Public opinion in the United States, on the other hand, came to see in the Doctrine an increasingly important basis of national foreign policy, because of this very identification with national expansion and "manifest destiny."

Successive interpretations of the Doctrine paralleled the growth of the United States. Even while absorbed in the Civil War, the United States protested Spain's reannexation of Santo Domingo, her seizure of the Chincha Islands off the coast of Peru, and the French occupation of Mexico on behalf of the Emperor Maximilian. In 1881 Secretary of State James G. Blaine warned the European powers that the United States would oppose control by any European nation of a canal across the Central American isthmus. In

1895, Secretary of State Richard Olney invoked the Doctrine even more emphatically in a boundary dispute between Great Britain and Venezuela, declaring that the United States was virtually sovereign upon this continent and that "its fiat was law upon the subjects to which it confined its interposition." This "doctrine of paramount interest," as it is known, made the United States the sole judge of what constituted "American affairs." During the three decades which followed, the United States intervened frequently in Latin American affairs, as we shall see.

THE ROOSEVELT COROLLARY AND INTERVENTION. President Theodore Roosevelt gave an enlarged interpretation to the Monroe Doctrine in several instances, beginning with the Venezuelan Claims Controversy of 1903. In 1904, an arbitration panel of The Hague Court ruled that, because Great Britain, Germany, and Italy had engaged in military operations against Venezuela to force her to pay the claims of their citizens residing in Venezuela, these claims should enjoy priority over claims pending from other resident aliens. This reassertion of the traditional rule of international law authorizing use of armed force as a means of collecting debts seemingly opened the Americas to European armed intervention and led President Roosevelt, in 1904, to assert the principle with which his name is connected: that it might be necessary for the United States to enforce international law in American countries that were chronic wrongdoers in order to prevent European intervention.

Whether danger of intervention by European powers was imminent or not, after the Spanish-American War the Monroe Doctrine was frequently invoked to justify United States intervention. Described by its critics as the policy of the "Big Stick," or "Dollar Diplomacy," such unilateral action reflected diverse political, economic, military, strategic, and even religious interests. "Imperialistic interventionism" led the United States, during the first three decades of the twentieth century, to engage in six major interventions in Central America and the Caribbean. This "experiment in colonialism" is now considered an aberration in the true course of United States policy, and no one seriously defends it today. Yet it should be pointed out that it was not motivated merely by expansionism, but had a sounder basis in the American desire to strengthen and enforce the rule of international law.[3]

[3] A good general summary is Julius W. Pratt, *American Colonial Experiment* (Englewood Cliffs, N.J.: Prentice-Hall, Inc., 1950). On American intervention in Panama, see Bemis, *op. cit.* On interventions in the Caribbean, see Wilfrid H. Calcott, *The Caribbean Policy of the United States* (Baltimore: Johns Hopkins Press, 1942), Dana G. Munro, *The United States and the Caribbean* (Boston: World Peace Foundation, 1934), and Dexter Perkins, *The United States and the Caribbean*

The first experiment in intervention concerned the Isthmus of Panama. Intent upon United States control of any interoceanic canal, President Theodore Roosevelt negotiated the Hay-Pauncefote Treaty of 1902, under which Great Britain conceded its previous right to share in the control of an isthmian canal. The next step was to acquire the permission of Colombia, and to this end the Hay-Herrán Convention of 1903 was negotiated, giving the United States exclusive rights to construct, operate, and control a canal through Panama. When the Colombian senate rejected the proposed treaty by a unanimous vote, the Frenchman Philippe Bunau-Varilla, who had just negotiated the sale of the French New Panama Canal Company to the United States, cunningly instigated and carried through a revolt in Panama. Bunau-Varilla had anticipated that Roosevelt, relying on the 1846 treaty with Colombia, would not permit Colombian military action to crush the secession. The United States acted as expected, and an independent Panama granted even more generous privileges for the construction of the canal than those sought in vain from Colombia.

The chronic financial difficulties which beset the Dominican Republic in 1905 brought United States intervention. Provisions constituting a protectorate had been written into treaties with Cuba and Panama, and Roosevelt had come to think of this arrangement as the only way to assure stability in some of the Latin American nations. The United States assumed control of the Dominican Republic's customs and foreign debt payment in an interposition that continued until 1940, and included eight years of military occupation (November, 1916, to September, 1924).

The Mexican Revolution brought a different kind of "intervention." In 1914 American armed forces shelled and seized the city of Veracruz, and in 1916 General John Pershing invaded Mexico in pursuit of Francisco Villa, under the provisions of a border treaty but without the permission of the Mexican government. In a more subtle form of intervention in Mexico, during the anarchic civil war which followed the assassination of President Madero, and again during the Obregón administration, the United States withheld recognition of the established governments.

United States Marines landed in Haiti in 1915 and remained there until 1934. Under the provisions of the Cuban treaty (the Platt Amendment), not abrogated until 1934, United States forces

(Cambridge: Harvard University Press, 1947). On American interventions in Mexico, see Howard F. Cline, *The United States and Mexico* (Cambridge: Harvard University Press, 1953). The outstanding book of literary Yankeephobia is Manuel Ugarte, *El destino de un continente*, first published in France in 1923.

intervened several times to maintain order in that nation. Detachments of United States Marines were sent to Nicaragua in 1912, and some remained until 1933.

Regarded as mere hunger for new bases, new markets, and an unchallenged place in the sun at the expense of Latin American friendship, dignity, and sovereignty, the policy based on the Roosevelt Corollary elicted passioned appeals from Latin Americans for its replacement by a policy based on nonintervention. The concept of nonintervention is almost as old as the literature of international law. In America it stems from the Argentine jurist, Carlos Calvo. In 1868, Calvo asserted that the decisions of a nation's courts are beyond appeal in instances where the rights of foreign nationals are involved.[4] The doctrine derives its name, however, from Luis Drago, Argentine foreign minister, who proposed in 1902 that "the public debt [of an American state] cannot occasion armed intervention nor even the actual occupation of the territory of American nations." Roosevelt was favorably impressed, and at The Hague Conference of 1907 the United States signed a convention embodying the Drago thesis, qualified, however, by the requirement of arbitration. The reluctance of European powers to give up the traditional right of intervention nullified the effect of this move, however, and United States intervention continued for two more decades, until the Montevideo Conference of 1933 produced a solemn inter-American agreement on nonintervention.

GOOD NEIGHBOR AND GOOD PARTNER POLICIES. By the late 1920's, reappraisal of the Monroe Doctrine and the Roosevelt Corollary was long overdue. Some constructive steps to improve relations had been taken by the United States during earlier years of the decade, such as support of a Central American Tribunal, the Gondra Treaty of 1923 for the pacific settlement of inter-American disputes, and the mission of Dwight W. Morrow in Mexico.[5] Sentiment against intervention became so strong during the last days of the Coolidge administration that Secretary of State Kellogg asked J. Reuben Clark to undertake a re-examination of the Monroe Doctrine. This was done, and in the early days of the Hoover administration the resulting Clark Memorandum was dispatched to all

---

[4] Calvo's name is associated today with the so-called Calvo Clause inserted by Latin American governments in contractual agreements with foreign nationals. This clause generally stipulates that "in case of any doubts or disputes arising out of the contract, the foreign party to the instrument agrees that they shall be settled by the courts of the country, and forswears the right to appeal to his own government for the defense of his rights." Bemis, op. cit., p. 230.

[5] On Morrow's mission, see Harold Nicholson, Dwight Morrow (New York: Harcourt, Brace, Inc., 1935), especially chapters xv, xvi.

Latin American governments as a quasi-official statement of principles to guide future United States policy. Clark described the Doctrine as an "effective guaranty of their [Latin American] freedom, independence, and territorial integrity against the imperialistic designs of Europe." In view of the fact that "the Doctrine states a case of United States vs. Europe, not of United States vs. Latin America," he concluded that "it is not believed that this [the Roosevelt] corollary is justified by the terms of the Monroe Doctrine, however much it may be justified by the application of the doctrine of self-preservation."[6]   Publication of the Clark Memorandum helped to reduce inter-American tension. It was not an official and unqualified rejection of intervention. Yet, in general, it may be said that by June, 1930, "the Roosevelt Corollary had been definitely and specifically repudiated."[7]

By making public the Clark Memorandum, President Hoover repudiated the Roosevelt Corollary and inaugurated the "good neighbor" policy which, with minor interruptions, has since guided United States relations with Latin America. He made a good will tour of Latin America before assuming the presidency, encouraged the pacific settlement of the Tacna-Arica controversy, withdrew the American Marines from Nicaragua, provided for the termination of the military occupation of Haiti, and refused in general to use nonrecognition as an instrument of political pressure. By the end of his term he had liquidated the American experiment in imperialism.

This new Latin American policy was officially labeled the Good Neighbor Policy and further developed in President Franklin D. Roosevelt's first inaugural address, in which he pledged the United States "to the policy of the good neighbor—the neighbor who respects himself, and, because he does so, respects the rights of others—the neighbor who respects his obligations and respects the sanctity of agreements in and with a world of neighbors." A few of the more noteworthy accomplishments of the Roosevelt administration include the termination of military occupation, abrogation of the Platt Amendment, the reduction of tariff barriers and encouragement of trade through Secretary of State Cordell Hull's reciprocal trade agreements, the promotion of cultural exchange, and the extension of health and educational assistance. Nonintervention was repudiated by treaty agreement, and the principle was unfalteringly observed, even in the dramatic case of

[6] J. Reuben Clark, *Memorandum on the Monroe Doctrine* (Washington, D.C.: Government Printing Office, 1930), p. xxiii.

[7] Perkins, *op. cit.*, p. 344.

Mexican expropriation of foreign oil company properties in 1938. The Good Neighbor Policy made for closer relations of the two Americas during World War II, although Argentina dragged her feet. One of the outcomes of this solidarity was the strengthening and developing of the inter-American regional organization.

Since World War II, the responsibilities of the United States as a world power have brought a shift in the emphasis of national foreign policy from hemispheric affairs to those of other areas. Because of this change, the United States has not fulfilled Latin American expectations for large-scale financial assistance. Yet the ties between the two Americas have not perceptibly lessened. Latin American nations, with minor exceptions, have maintained cordial relations with the United States during the years since the war. After the blundering interference by Ambassador Spruille Braden in the Argentine elections of 1946, President Truman restored more friendly feelings by visiting Mexico on March 3, 1947, by attending the Rio de Janeiro Conference of 1947 which drew up the Treaty of Reciprocal Assistance, by initiating the "Point Four" program to provide technical assistance to countries in Latin America as elsewhere, and by strengthening inter-American peace and security machinery in the Washington Conference of American Foreign Ministers (1951).

President Eisenhower renamed the policy of mutual understanding the "Good Partner Policy."[8] Shortly after his inauguration he dispatched his brother, Dr. Milton Eisenhower, on a good will and fact-finding mission to explore ways of helping Latin American economic development. To encourage closer understanding with Canada and Mexico, the President met personally with the heads of state of these two countries at White Sulphur Springs, West Virginia, in 1955. He also sponsored a unique meeting of presidents of the American republics at Panama City in June, 1956. On the debit side of the ledger is the controversy over the alleged United States support of Castillo Armas in overthrowing the Communist-supported Arbenz Guzmán regime in Guatemala in 1954, a seeming violation of the principle of nonintervention.[9]

Both the Truman and Eisenhower administrations relied on encouraging private investment abroad, despite the Latin American preference for government-to-government grants and loans. This basic disagreement has made it more difficult in postwar years to

[8] For an opposing view, see Simon G. Hanson, "The Good-Partner Policy," *Inter-American Economic Affairs*, X (Autumn 1956), 45–96.

[9] For American participation, see Philip B. Taylor, Jr., "The Guatemalan Affair: A Critique of United States Foreign Policy," *The American Political Science Review*, L (September 1956), 787–806.

achieve multilateral inter-American economic policy through the Organization of American States. Notwithstanding this difficulty, private investment of American capital in Latin America had increased to nearly nine billion dollars by mid-1956, with anticipated total profits for 1956 expected to reach one billion dollars. By 1957, trade between Latin America and the United States had reached an unprecedented peak of approximately four billion dollars in each direction. Meanwhile, the United States government was also extending considerable assistance under the Point Four program and various bilateral military agreements. Private investment sources, encouraged by these friendly politico-economic relations, announced in 1957 plans to combine with the Export–Import Bank in financing atomic power reactors in Brazil, Cuba, and Mexico.[10]

Latin American Relations with Europe

The influence of European institutions, customs, politics, and ideas on Latin American civilization has not, in general, brought close political ties with Europe. Hence, since independence, the Latin American nations have remained virtually aloof from the power struggles of Europe, except for the two major wars in the twentieth century and the European political questions which entered into the deliberations of the League of Nations and those which today affect the United Nations. The participation of Latin American states in such international organizations as the League of Nations and the United Nations will be discussed later. But at this point, before examining the relations with individual European nations, it seems appropriate to comment briefly on the role Latin America played in the two world wars.

WORLD WARS I AND II. Unanimity of action was clearly lacking in the relations of the twenty republics to World War I. Eight nations eventually declared war against Germany and her allies: Brazil, Cuba, Costa Rica, Guatemala, Haiti, Honduras, Nicaragua, and Panama. Five severed relations with Germany: Peru, Bolivia, Uruguay, Ecuador, and the Dominican Republic. Seven remained neutral: Argentina, Chile, Colombia, Mexico, El Salvador, Venezuela, and Paraguay. The military contribution of Latin America was exceedingly modest, only Brazil and Cuba becoming active belligerents, but the assistance given the United States and her allies in essential raw materials was much greater.[11]

During World War II, every Latin American nation declared

---

[10] Statistics and other data from The New York Times, January 4, 1957.

[11] Percy A. Martin, Latin America and the War (Baltimore: World Peace Foundation, 1925), pp. 1–2.

war against the Axis powers, although the declarations of Chile and Argentina, the latter under great pressure from the other American nations, were made when the defeat of Germany was clearly imminent. Pro-German and pro-Italian sympathies ran high in some parts, and particularly in such communities of large German population as the town of Blumenthau in Brazil. Brazil was an active belligerent. She sent an expeditionary contingent into the Italian campaign, made available the Allied air base at Natal, and took an active part in the campaign against submarines. Mexico, the other active belligerent, lost two ships early in the war. This loss helped to unite that nation against the Axis powers, despite the fact that pro-Fascist sentiment was strong during the early war years and never completely disappeared. As in World War I, the greatest Latin American contribution was the material assistance rendered the United States and her allies.

RELATIONS WITH SPAIN. Of all European states, Spain unquestionably left the greatest mark on Spanish American life. In politics, in religion, and in language Spanish influence is still very strong today. Yet Spain no longer enjoys a strong political position. Estrangement of Spain from her American colonies began before the wars of independence and continued in general until the closing days of the nineteenth century. During this time Spain reluctantly accepted the new independent status of her former colonies. She intervened with military forces in Mexico (1829), in the Dominican Republic (1861–1865), and in the Chincha Islands off the Peruvian coast (1864). She preserved her rule over Cuba and Puerto Rico, extended diplomatic recognition belatedly—in the case of Uruguay and Honduras not until 1882 and 1894, respectively—and pursued essentially eighteenth-century mercantilist polices in her trade relations. Such conduct strengthened Latin American memories of the unpleasant aspects of Spanish colonialism and worked against the creation of more friendly attitudes based on Spain's cultural contributions to Spanish American development.

Improvement of relations thus depended more on Spain's own conduct than on that of Latin America. Ironically, it was the final downfall of the Spanish Empire in 1898 which, by stimulating Spain's intelligentsia to analyze the reasons for Spanish failure, produced the basis for a new approach to Spanish-American relations. The most influential of these intellectuals, the so-called "Generation of 1898," urged that improved relations depended on strengthening the common bonds of Spanish culture. This doctrine of *Hispanidad* or Pan-Hispanism produced in Latin America favorable reinterpretations of Spain's contributions to the New World. Unable to play a great role in world power politics, Spain adopted *Hispanidad* as a cardinal objective of Spanish American policy, thereby lifting its official relations to a higher plane, at least until Franco gave *Hispanidad* a narrowly partisan and fascist-like content. Franco's *falangismo*[12] offended many Latin Americans, particularly in those nations that had permitted the immigration of large numbers of refugees from the Spanish Civil War. Recognition of Franco's regime also constituted a thorny diplomatic problem for several Latin American nations, because of the Spanish dictator's affinities for Hitler and Mussolini. Spain was admitted to the United Nations in December, 1955, and, although it has since collaborated on several issues with Hispanic American states in the UN,[13] the more liberal-oriented governments in Latin America still decry Franco's domestic politics. Mexico, through loyalty to the Spanish Republican cause, persists in withholding diplomatic recognition.

RELATIONS WITH PORTUGAL. Relations between Brazil and Portugal never suffered from the debilitating tensions which troubled the relations between Spain and Spanish America. There were several reasons for this difference. First of all, even before independence, Brazil overshadowed the mother country in wealth, population, and territory. Second, Portugal accepted the Brazilian independence promptly, through British good offices, thus avoiding the scars usually resulting from political or armed conflict. Third, Brazil permitted a member of the Portuguese royal family to steer its destinies during the first sixty-five years of national independence. Fourth, by the time the Brazilian Empire finally became a republic (1889) cordial relations with Brazil had become so vital to Portugal's economic and political survival that she gave little thought to risking opposition. What was to be gained? Then, as today, Brazil enjoyed unqualified leadership of the Portuguese-speaking world. Portugal's relations with other nations of Latin America are similarly cordial, although her trade with them is small.

RELATIONS WITH GREAT BRITAIN. British policy was adapted to the aspiration of Latin America during the independence movements. Great Britain pursued successively policies of mediation between Spain and Latin America (1810–1820), of preparation for recognition (1820–1824), of recognition of Mexico, Colombia, and Argentina (1825), and of reconciliation of Spain and her former colonies

---

[12] See Chapter 8.
[13] "Issues Before the Eleventh General Assembly," *International Conciliation*, No. 510 (November 1956), especially pp. 130–135.

(1825–1836).[14] While the twentieth century has been the century of predominant United States influence in Latin America, the nineteenth century belonged to Great Britain, which exercised the roles of international policeman, the world's banker, and leader in world trade. Her naval, financial, and commercial supremacy gave Great Britain considerable influence over Latin American development. British military strength was applied in various ways. During the last phases of the independence movements, reconquest by Spain was prevented more by the timely disposition of the British fleet than by local military forces in the New World. In the middle years of the century the British intervened frequently to defend their own interests, occupying the Falkland Islands claimed by Argentina, extending the southern boundary of British Honduras, joining with other European powers in the occupation of the port of Veracruz, and blockading the Venezuelan coast. To enhance their naval position, the British also sought to develop an isthmian canal under their control, an objective not abandoned until the Hay-Pauncefote Treaty of 1902. In assessing the over-all use of British military power in Latin America it seems appropriate to state that seldom has a nation possessing such preponderant power exercised greater restraint and benevolence.

As investment banker and commercial trader, Great Britain enjoyed a favored status from the outset of Latin American independence. Except for French capitalists, British investors met few competitors in Latin America during the first half of the nineteenth century. By 1913 Great Britain had invested approximately five billion dollars in Latin America. Her investors generally preferred Argentina to other Latin American countries, particularly because of the British demand for wheat and beef and because of the Argentine market for English manufactured goods. But they also made substantial investments in Chilean nitrate mining and in various mining enterprises in Colombia, Mexico, and Venezuela, as well as in railroads and various agricultural activities. Both world wars seriously damaged Britain's Latin American trade. Although her trade recovered considerably after World War I, it experienced another decline in the late 1930's and since World War II has fallen off still more.

Several territorial issues today becloud the otherwise amicable relations between Latin American nations and Great Britain. Argentina seeks jurisdiction over the Falkland Islands, while Guatemala and Mexico maintain separate claims to British Honduras (Belize).

[14] C. K. Webster, *Britain and the Independence of Latin America, 1812–1830* (London: Oxford University Press, 1938), I, 12.

There are political problems as well. Independence parties demand Great Britain's withdrawal from British Guiana and from the non-self-governing territories under its authority in the Caribbean, although this agitation may subside as the federation of Jamaica, Trinidad, Tobago, and other British islands becomes a political fact.

RELATIONS WITH GERMANY. Before World War I, German activity in Latin America was largely confined to promoting German commerce, investments, and emigration. German military chiefs would have liked naval bases in the Caribbean and Central America, but the United States successfully opposed moves in this direction, with British support. Within their limited sphere of activity, however, the Germans achieved real success. By 1913 German trade was some 470 million dollars a year, German investments totalled around two billion dollars and German settlers numbered some 600,000 to 700,000.[15] German educators were guiding certain aspects of Chile's educational system, and German military officers were training the soldiers of several South American states. Although German immigrants preferred to settle in Argentina, Brazil, and Chile, substantial numbers took up residence in Guatemala, Mexico, and Venezuela. They generally wished to remain in compact racial groups, often maintaining their own language and culture in spite of the aggressive nationalism of the countries in which they settled. The story has often been told of a Spanish-speaking shopkeeper, elected mayor of a small town in southern Chile, who discovered that the town records were written in German.

Germany was cut off from its markets during World War I, but recaptured its trade position during the 1920's and especially in the 1930's, only to lose it again during World War II. German prestige suffered everywhere in Latin America because of the Hitler dictatorship and Nazi propaganda methods, yet remained high in some places despite the regime in Germany. Since World War II German firms have again made successful bids for Latin American markets, but in 1957 German trade was still far from prewar 1939 levels. The Germans had not yet begun to make large-scale investments, although the Friedrich Krupp Industries had announced their intention to invest in a new steel mill in Mexico.

RELATIONS WITH FRANCE. The Latin American states' political relations with France have usually been cordial, reflecting deep respect for French culture. The French interventions in Mexico on behalf of Maximilian and in the River Plate area to force collection of debts caused hostility, and fervent anticolonialists sometimes

---

[15] Rippy, *op. cit.*, p. 143.

raise their voices against the French imperium over Inini (French Guiana) and various Caribbean islands. Bitter memories of French colonial abuses severely strained French–Haitian relations for many years. But French remains the official language, and French culture dominates the island republic. Everywhere in Latin America French philosophers, from Rousseau and Comte to Bergson and Sartre, have enjoyed great prestige. French art, French customs, and the French language and literature have stood for the highest cultural standards in Latin America. Many Latin Americans probably still consider Paris their cultural capital, although since World War II wealthy parents seem to prefer to send their children to the United States for higher education, while the study of French has yielded to English in the schools. Trade with France is much less than that with the United States and Britain. Moreover, many French markets built up in Latin America during the immediate post-World War II years are now falling into the hands of German firms.

RELATIONS WITH ITALY. Italian influence enters Latin America most profoundly through its millions of citizens of Italian ancestry. Unlike the German and Japanese immigrant, the Italian has been assimilated rapidly into his adopted nation. Italian descendants may account for as many as six million Argentines. One writer has wryly described Argentina as "an American nation financed with British capital, and peopled with Italians who speak bad Spanish."[16] Italians also constitute substantial minorities in Uruguay and Brazil. Noteworthy incidents in the political relations between Italy and the Latin American states have been limited to Italy's action in forcing collection of debts from Venezuela at the beginning of the century and to the diplomatic ruptures occasioned by World War II. Italian trade with Latin America about equals that of France.

RELATIONS WITH THE VATICAN. The numerous diplomatic agents of the Vatican accredited to Latin American governments, as well as the substantial number of diplomats representing Latin American states before the Holy See, are a measure of the extensive diplomatic intercourse between the Pope and governments south of the Rio Grande. The older Vatican tendency toward nineteenth-century nationalism is witnessing a modification in line with the current emphasis on the liberal social program based on the Encyclical *Rerum Novarum*. In the post-World War II period few tensions have marred the generally cordial relations. The Mexican govern-

[16] Austin F. Macdonald, *Latin American Politics and Government* (2d ed.; New York: The Thomas Crowell Co., 1954), pp. 25–26.

ment and the Vatican have a long-standing difference of opinion over Mexico's legislation curbing Church activities. In the closing years of the Perón administration in Argentina, diplomatic agents of the Pope reportedly interfered so openly in Argentine affairs that their continued presence was embarrassing to Perón, and contributed to his rupture with the Church. But the Mexican question is dormant, and the Argentine problem subsided with Perón's overthrow.

RELATIONS WITH OTHER EUROPEAN AND ASIATIC POWERS. The ties that bind Latin American states to other nations in Europe and Asia are predominantly economic. To the degree that these other nations share common political aspirations with Latin America, these bonds may become political or psychological. The Netherlands, Switzerland, and Belgium both import from and export to Latin America. In recent years India has made sizable purchases in Argentina. Japanese influence is felt principally through commerce and colonization, the largest Japanese colonies being in Brazil and Peru. Latin America has been anti-Communist traditionally, and official relations with Soviet Russia have frequently been strained, centering on the issue of recognition. Only Argentina, Mexico, and Uruguay at present maintain diplomatic relations.[17] Finally, as in the case of the British and French colonies, cries are sometimes heard in Latin America for the independence of Dutch colonial possessions in the Caribbean region. Since Aruba, Curaçao, and Surinam joined in a quasi-autonomous federation, these complaints have become less frequent.

Origins of the Inter-American System

LATIN AMERICA AND INTERNATIONAL LAW. The fact that international agreements and resolutions of international conferences often fall short of their objective makes more noteworthy the achievements of the Latin American states in the fields of international law and organization. The international community has received valuable lessons in collaboration from the successful experiences of these twenty republics—successes which can be attributed partly to the geographical isolation of Latin America from the main stream of world politics, partly to the mature attitude toward international affairs assumed by the United States in the twentieth century, and partly to the fact that Latin American diplomats and jurists, since the days when Andrés Bello laid the basis of Chilean foreign policy in the early nineteenth century, have had a high sense of the im-

[17] On communism, see Chapter 8.

portance of international law as the basis of foreign policy. The threat of domination by foreign interests during years marked by debilitating domestic tensions early led the Latin Americans to search for international legal norms to redress their national grievances and prevent future injustices. No formulas were left unexplored, few methods untested. Settlement of international controversies by pacific methods, including arbitration and adjudication, good offices and mediation, inquiry and conciliation, has been a cardinal point in the policy of all Latin American nations. Codification of international law was undertaken and is still a major obligation of the Organization of American States. Systems of collective security and various regional arrangements were advanced to thwart would-be aggressors. Despite the mid-twentieth century disillusionment, and despite the development of intense nationalism, Latin American foreign policies still find a fundamental basis in international law and organization.

LATIN AMERICAN PHASE. The first nineteenth-century attempt by Latin American states to agree on matters of international organization and international law grew out of a proposal by the Liberator Simón Bolívar. Bolívar envisaged the creation of a Latin American confederation to protect against attack from Europe and to preserve the peace in the Western Hemisphere. For this purpose he invited all of the Spanish American nations to send representatives to a congress at Panama in 1826. Four of the Spanish American nations—Colombia (at that time composed of the present states of Venezuela, Ecuador, Panama, and Colombia), Mexico, Peru, and Central America (then comprising the present states of Costa Rica, El Salvador, Guatemala, Honduras, and Nicaragua)—sent representatives to this famous Congress, which drew up a Treaty of Perpetual Union, League, and Confederation. The treaty pledged their governments to the collective self-defense of all signatory nations and provided for the establishment of a permanent General Assembly of Ministers Plenipotentiary, which was to serve as a supreme council in the event of conflicts involving member states. Bolívar's great dream of hemispheric organization failed to become a reality because only Colombia among the four signatories ratified the treaty.

The Congress of Panama was succeeded by seven other conferences of Latin American states in the nineteenth century. The first three of these assemblies attempted, with little success, to establish defensive alliances. The American Congress, held at Lima, Peru, from December 11, 1847, to March 1, 1848, was attended by representatives of Bolivia, New Granada, Chile, Ecuador, and Peru.

When the three states last mentioned next met, in Santiago, Chile, at the so-called Continental Congress of September 15, 1856, they signed a defensive alliance, the "Continental Treaty." The third conference, meeting from November 14, 1864, to March 3, 1865, is today remembered as the Second American Congress of Lima. The seven states represented, Bolivia, Chile, Colombia, Ecuador, Guatemala, Peru, and Venezuela, moved away from Bolívar's idea of *confederation* in favor of the less formal concept of a *family of nations*. Despite the meager representation at these early international meetings and the fact that the various treaties signed did not become effective, these conferences made important contributions to the development of inter-Americanism. Later inter-American cooperation owes to them such basic principles as equality of states, political independence, nonintervention, application of sanctions, renunciation of war, and the peaceful settlement of disputes.

Contribution to future inter-American organization also emerged from four more specialized international congresses held during the 1870's and 1880's. The American Congress of Jurists, convened at Lima (December 9, 1877, to March 27, 1879), and the International South American Law Congress, held at Montevideo (August 25, 1888, to February 18, 1889), drew up treaties that advanced the cause of uniformity in private international law. The Sanitary Congress of Rio de Janeiro (November 1 to 25, 1887) and the American Sanitary Congress of Lima (January 2 to March 12, 1888) reached agreements on means for combating and controlling yellow fever and cholera. Although these eight conferences were planned and attended exclusively by Latin Americans, it will be readily seen that in going beyond strictly Latin American concerns they were the institutional forerunners of the modern Pan American movement.

THE INTER-AMERICAN SYSTEM TO 1933. In the late nineteenth century, these exclusively Latin American schemes for hemispheric organization gave way to joint United States–Latin American efforts. Cooperation between the two Americas had been slow in developing, partly because of the preoccupation of the United States with domestic affairs. But at the turn of the century several new factors had begun to change this situation. Important among these changes was the growing need of the United States for overseas markets and for new investment opportunities. Both Americas also became sensitive to the potentiality of a new imperialism from outside the hemisphere. But while the Latin Americans were interested in gaining new markets through closer cooperation with the United States, they also feared uninvited "Yankee" imperialism. Thus, they tended to turn to international organization, both regional and universal, for safeguards.

The first institutions created by the American republics for advancing their mutual interests were an Inter-American Conference, formally styled the International Conference of American States, and an administrative secretariat, soon named the Pan American Union. These organs were supplemented by numerous specialized organizations, various conferences on technical matters, and several emergency meetings of foreign ministers. Sixty-one years after Secretary of State Blaine initiated the first Inter-American Conference at Washington, on October 3, 1889, "under the inspiration of Bolívar's dominating thought and vision," a total of ten such conferences had been convened. Four of these were held prior to World War I. All four confined their labors primarily to formulating rules for improving commercial relations (patents, trademarks, custom regulations, etc.), to promoting cultural exchanges, and to the peaceful settlement of international disputes.

Only the Dominican Republic, out of a total of nineteen American republics then in existence, was not represented at the first Inter-American Conference. Universality or near-universality also marked the subsequent conferences. All nineteen states were represented at the second meeting, at Mexico City (October 22, 1901, to January 22, 1902). Haiti and Venezuela failed to send delegates to the third meeting at Rio de Janeiro (July 21 to August 26, 1906), but two new arrivals to the inter-American community, Cuba and Panama, were represented. Only Bolivia was absent from the fourth conference at Buenos Aires (July 12 to August 30, 1920). Compared with the program of modern international organizations, Inter-Americanism before World War I was very limited in scope, yet this should not obscure its importance as an effective growth of internationalism in an age which provided no alternative in a more universal international association.[18]

After World War I, American regionalism was both a supplement and an alternative to the League of Nations. Like the League, moreover, the regional system dragged its feet on the basic issue of mutual security, although it made progress in other matters of international cooperation. The Inter-American Conference continued to be its focus. The Fifth Inter-American Conference at

[18] On the ebb and flow of inter-Americanism, see Arthur P. Whitaker, *The Western Hemisphere Idea: Its Rise and Decline* (Ithaca, N.Y.: Cornell University Press, 1954), and his earlier "Development of American Regionalism," *International Conciliation*, No. 469 (March 1951), p. 126. A useful collection of documents is Robert N. Burr and Roland D. Hussey, *Documents on Inter-American Cooperation* (Philadelphia, University of Pennsylvania Press, 1955).

Santiago (March 25 to May 3, 1923) produced the Gondra Treaty, which attempted to prevent armed conflicts by providing for commissions of inquiry to investigate disputes.[19] At the Sixth Inter-American Conference, meeting in Havana (January 16 to December 20, 1928), the Latin Americans failed in their primary aim of getting the United States to join in renouncing the right of intervention. Yet they adopted the Bustamante Code, a noteworthy step forward in the codification of private international law. The next assembly, a special conference on conciliation and arbitration that met in Washington (December 10 to January 5, 1929), drew up several conventions designed to promote the settlement of international disputes by peaceful means. Finally, a series of technical and scientific conferences studied such broad facets of hemispheric relations as highways, teachers and education, the rights of women, architecture, postal rates, aviation, sanitation, agriculture, coffee, and public health.

Strengthening the Inter-American System

The Good Neighbor Policy generated sufficient spirit of cooperation and enough mutual respect to make possible the beginnings of a hemispheric security system by the late 1930's. The way toward this system was paved at the Seventh Inter-American Conference, held at Montevideo (December 3–26, 1933). Under a treaty drawn up at this conference, the United States accepted the principle of nonintervention, pledging itself to abandon the "Big Stick" tactics of bygone decades.[20] An important step toward a collective security system was taken by the American republics at the Conference for the Maintenance of Peace, Buenos Aires (December 1–23, 1936). A treaty was drawn up in which the nations agreed to regard a threat to the security of any American republic as a threat to all, and to consult together on procedures for meeting such a threat.

SPECIAL MEETINGS OF FOREIGN MINISTERS. Despite the failure of nations to ratify the Buenos Aires treaty, the Eighth Inter-American Conference in Lima (December 9–27, 1938) agreed by resolution on the consultative machinery to come into play whenever a threat to inter-American security arose. The consultation procedure adopted

[19] For the significance and meaning of the Gondra Treaty, see Charles G. Fenwick, *The Inter-American Regional System* (New York: The Declan X. McMullen Co., Inc., 1949), pp. 38–39.

[20] Secretary Hull insisted, however, on some reservations to the renunciation of intervention, such as specific treaty obligations then in force.

was the Meeting of American Ministers of Foreign Affairs, to be convoked at the request of any member government.

As war clouds gathered over Europe and Asia in the late 1930's, this new organ of consultation became an increasingly important forum of New World deliberation. To meet successive crises during World War II, three of these Meetings of Foreign Ministers were held. Immediately after the outbreak of war in Europe, the high-ranking spokesmen on foreign affairs, meeting at Panama (September 23 to October 3, 1939), asserted their adherence to the principle of neutrality and adopted measures to protect the Western Hemisphere against belligerent activities. Following the fall of France, they convened at Havana (July 21–30, 1940) to provide for the provisional administration of European colonies and possessions in the Americas. And again, meeting at Rio de Janeiro (January 15–28, 1942) after the attack on Pearl Harbor, they recommended that all American nations break diplomatic relations with Japan, Germany, and Italy.

These meetings also created new boards and agencies for political, economic, and military cooperation among the American republics.[21] Some of these organs, such as the Neutrality Committee, the Committee on the Administration of European Colonies and Possessions in the Americas, and the Emergency Advisory Committee on Political Defense, being no longer useful no longer exist. But others, such as the Inter-American Defense Board and the Inter-American Juridicial Committee, continue as organs of the regional system. An Economic and Financial Advisory Committee evolved into the Social and Economic Council of the present organization.

The Foreign Ministers have met only once since World War II. The occasion for this conference was the Korean War, which gave rise to the feeling of a need for hemispheric cooperation against "the aggressive policy of international communism." Meeting in Washington (March 26 to April 7, 1951), the foreign ministers recommended measures for military, economic, and political defense against Communist infiltration.[22]

[21] For the accomplishments of the Meetings of Foreign Ministers, the student is referred to three publications: *Report on the Meeting of the Ministers of Foreign Affairs of the American Republics, Panama, 1939; Report on the Meeting . . . , 1940;* and *Report on the Meeting . . . , Rio de Janeiro, 1942* (Washington, D.C.: Pan American Union).

[22] An extensive treatment of the meeting, including the text of the "Declaration of Washington," may be found in *Fourth Meeting of Consultation of Ministers of Foreign Affairs of American States, Washington, D.C., March 26–April 7, 1951* (Washington: Department of State Publication 4928, International Organization and Conference Series II, American Republics 10, 1953).

TREATY OF RECIPROCAL ASSISTANCE. As World War II neared its end, the question naturally arose of continuing and strengthening the collective security arrangements of the inter-American regional system, as developed in the Meetings of Foreign Ministers. Assembling in Mexico City (February 21 to March 8, 1954) on the eve of the United Nations Conference at San Francisco in 1945, and spurred by the questions which would be raised there, the Inter-American Conference on Problems of War and Peace clarified and extended the system of regional security set up by the conferences of the 1930's, declaring that aggression from within as well as from without the hemisphere was subject to the collective action of the American republics. This "Act of Chapultepec" was merely a temporary wartime alliance, but the delegates at Mexico agreed that a hemispheric defense treaty should be adopted forthwith. Actually, more than two years elapsed before the system of inter-American security was given permanent form in the Treaty of Reciprocal Assistance drawn up at the Inter-American Conference for the Maintenance of Continental Peace and Security at Rio de Janeiro (August 15 to September 2, 1947) and subsequently ratified by all the American republics.[23] Today, the "Rio Treaty" constitutes the principal contractual agreement on continental solidarity. The heart of the agreement is Article 3:

The High Contracting Parties agree that an armed attack by any State against an American State shall be considered as an attack against all American States and, consequently, each one of the said Contracting Parties undertakes to assist in meeting the attack in the exercise of the inherent right of individual or collective self-defense recognized by Article 51 of the Charter of the United Nations.

Two provisions of this treaty merit special attention: the delineation of the area to be defended and the rule of voting to be employed in the consultation. The treaty limits the application of Article 3 to a region marked by two lines running irregularly from the North to the South Poles, one through the Atlantic and the other through the Pacific. Should an attack occur outside this region, the American republics are obligated merely to consult each other concerning the measures to be taken. The Rio Treaty thereby varies the obligation of collective security with respect to the location of the attack. Second, determination of what con-

---

[23] For a report on the Conference and the text of the Rio Treaty, see *Report of the United States Delegation on the Inter-American Conference for the Maintenance of Continental Peace and Security, August 15–September 2, 1947* (Washington: Department of State Publication 3016, International Organization and Conference Series II, American Republics 2, 1948).

stitutes an act of aggression and of what measures to adopt in order to meet such danger is to be by a two-thirds vote which binds every American republic, save that no nation may be compelled to contribute armed forces without its consent. This provision was a decided improvement over the veto system in the United Nations Security Council, in that the Rio Treaty permits a two-thirds majority to go forward unencumbered by veto action but at no time obligates either a majority or a minority member to participate in the measures adopted if they involve armed force.

BOGOTA CONFERENCE. Bolívar's aspirations for a closely knit hemispheric organization were dramatically fulfilled in Bogotá, the capital of Colombia, when the Ninth International Conference of American States (March 31 to May 2, 1948) drew up a constitution for the inter-American regional system. The responsibility of constitution-making had devolved on the delegations to Bogotá by virtue of a resolution adopted at the Chapultepec Conference of 1945, providing for the formalization of the inter-American structure. The numerous instrumentalities and agencies which had evolved since the first International Conference were now brought together under a new and permanent juridical structure, or charter. This charter gave the inter-American system a new name, the Organization of American States (OAS) and greatly strengthened its administrative machinery. The conference incorporated into the new charter the fundamental principles of pacific settlement of disputes, just as it incorporated the general provisions of the Rio Treaty concerning collective security. But it also adopted a separate American Treaty on Pacific Settlement.

Commonly known as the "Pact of Bogotá," this treaty was a major contribution to regional cooperation. It established appropriate procedures for the peaceful settlement of disputes, ranging from the employment of good offices and mediation to adjudication by the World Court. But the Ninth Conference did not stop here. It also produced the Economic Agreement of Bogotá, an Inter-American Charter of Social Guarantees, and a Declaration of the Rights and Duties of Man, in addition to reaching agreement on various other subjects.[24]

[24] For a concise account of the Bogotá Conference, see William Sanders, "The Organization of American States: Summary of the Conclusions of the Ninth International Conference of American States, Bogotá, Colombia, March 20–May 2, 1948," *International Conciliation*, No. 442 (June 1948). The original Spanish, English, French, and Portuguese versions of the Rio Treaty, the Charter of the OAS, and the Pact of Bogotá are conveniently included in the *Inter-American Juridical Yearbook, 1948* (Washington, D.C.: Pan American Union, 1949), pp. 259–388.

LATER CONFERENCES. Before setting forth the major organizational lines of the OAS as laid down at Bogotá, brief mention should be made of the accomplishments of conferences held since 1948 to complete the story of the evolution of the inter-American system. Since the Bogotá Conference, the problem of inter-American security has centered on the issue of international communism. Some Latin Americans feel that too much of the impetus in this direction has come from the United States. Measures to combat this threat to the safety and welfare of the hemisphere were adopted at the Fourth Meeting of Foreign Ministers, as noted earlier, and again at the Tenth Inter-American Conference (Caracas, March 1–28, 1954). Though both meetings served as sounding boards for cold war propaganda, the "Declaration of Washington" managed to reactivate the Inter-American Defense Board, first set up in 1942, and lift it to the status of a permanent hemispheric military organ,[25] while the "Caracas Declaration" specifically provided that an emergency meeting of consultation should be convoked if the government of any American republic fell under the domination or control of international communism.[26]

Economic relations have also held a foremost place on recent inter-American agenda, with the United States and the Latin American nations assuming opposing positions on several issues. Both at Caracas and at a special meeting of Ministers of Finance and Economy (Rio de Janeiro, December, 1954) Washington policymakers found themselves unable to accept Latin American demands for large-scale financial assistance from the United States. While the Department of State favored private investment over public loans or grants, most Latin American states preferred large-scale grants on a government-to-government basis or through an international fund. This controversy is not one which will be settled quickly, and will doubtless reappear in many future conferences.

Finally, specialized (technical) conferences held since 1948 in formal association with the OAS have included, among others, the Inter-American Conferences of Agriculture, Public Health, Travel, Statistics, and Copyright Experts; the Highway and Sanitary Con-

[25] The significance of the politico-military implications of this shift is discussed in Whitaker, "Development of American Regionalism," op. cit., pp. 140–141, 148–149.

[26] For an account of the Caracas Conference and for the text of the "Caracas Declaration," see Tenth Inter-American Conference of American States, Caracas, Venezuela, March 1–28, 1954 (Washington, D.C.: Pan American Union, 1955) and Tenth Inter-American Conference: Final Act (Washington, D.C.: Pan American Union, 1954).

ferences; and the Assemblies and Consultations of the Pan American Institute of Geography and History.[27]

The Organization of American States

The Ninth Inter-American Conference produced, as previously observed, the first constitution of the inter-American system. This charter, the Pact of Bogotá, and the Rio Treaty today govern the affairs of the hemispheric organization. The charter gave the inter-American system a new name, the Organization of American States, and clearly defined its purposes, powers, and procedures. Its new name indicates that the inter-American system is a voluntary association of independent, sovereign states of the Western Hemisphere. Replacing the former phrase "American Republics" with that of "American States," the present member nations opened the door of admission to Canada and to any new states that might subsequently arise in the hemisphere. The charter asserts that the fundamental purposes of the OAS are to maintain peace and to promote human welfare, and that underlying these purposes are certain basic principles reaffirmed by the American states from the experience of their hemispheric relations. Briefly summarized, these standards are: (1) international law and order shall govern the relations between states, particularly the principle of the absolute juridical equality of all member states; (2) an act of aggression against any American state is an act of aggression against every American state; (3) controversies arising between two or more American states shall be settled by peaceful procedures; and (4) lasting peace and the well-being of the American peoples are based on political democracy, social justice, economic welfare, and respect for the cultural values of the respective American nations.[28]

These principles are to be applied and these purposes accomplished through a structure of six organs. Three of these organs, the Inter-American Conference, the Meeting of Consultation of Ministers of Foreign Affairs, and the Specialized Conferences, are assemblies of representatives meeting periodically. The other three, the Council of the OAS, the Pan American Union, and the Specialized Organizations, are constituted as permanent organs (see chart: Organization of American States, pp. 422–423).

THE INTER-AMERICAN CONFERENCE. The supreme organ of the inter-American system is the Inter-American Conference. The

[27] A complete list of the specialized conferences held since the Bogotá Conference, through June, 1955, may be found in Margaret Liser, *Organization of American States* (4th ed.; Washington, D.C.: Pan American Union, 1955), pp. 36–37.
[28] *Ibid.*, pp. 10–12.

Conference "decides the general action and policy of the Organization and determines the structure and functions of its Organs," and in addition possesses "the authority to consider any matter relating to friendly relations among the American States." Normally convened every five years, the Conference may also meet in special circumstances with the approval of two-thirds of the member governments. All members have the right to be represented at the Conference, each state enjoying the right to one vote.

THE MEETING OF FOREIGN MINISTERS. The Meeting of Consultation of Ministers of Foreign Affairs is an emergency assembly reserved exclusively for matters of great urgency. The Meeting of Consultation originated in the procedure of emergency consultation set down at Lima in 1938 and had previously convened on four occasions, as noted. The Meeting of Consultation also performs special functions assigned it by the Rio Treaty in cases of armed attack and threats to the peace. To advise the Foreign Ministers on military affairs, an Advisory Defense Committee was established, composed of the "highest military authorities" of the member states. The Committee is assisted by the permanent military organ of the OAS, the Inter-American Defense Board. As in the case of the Conference, every member state has the right to be represented and to cast one vote.

SPECIALIZED CONFERENCES. The Specialized Conferences are intergovernmental conferences or congresses which deal with special technical aspects of inter-American cooperation. They are convened either by the Conference, the Meeting of Foreign Ministers, the Council of the OAS, or automatically by the provisions of certain inter-American agreements. Since the early days of the regional system more than one hundred such Specialized Conferences (called Technical Conferences until 1948) have been held in such broad areas of interest as cartography and geography, culture and education, public welfare, commerce and industry, and law.

THE COUNCIL. Though inferior to the Conference and the Meeting of Foreign Ministers, the Council of the OAS is the only political supervisory organ of the whole inter-American system to enjoy permanent, day-by-day existence. In transforming the old Governing Board of the Pan American Union into the Council of the Organization, the Bogotá charter gave it political functions not previously possessed and in other ways enlarged its responsibilities and sphere of action. The political duties of the Council are assigned to it in relation to the Rio Treaty, under which "the

ORGANIZATION OF

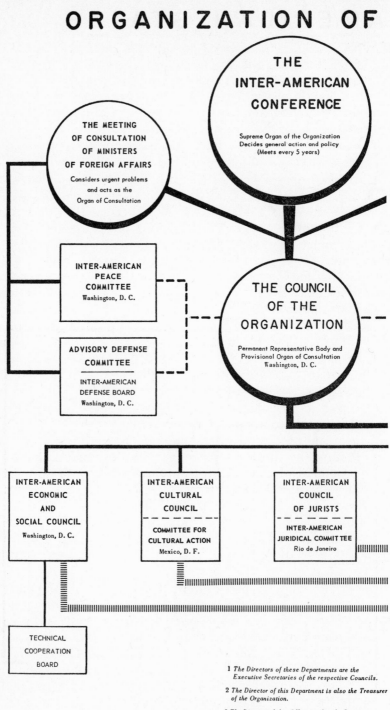

THE INTER-AMERICAN CONFERENCE

Supreme Organ of the Organization
Decides general action and policy
(Meets every 5 years)

THE MEETING OF CONSULTATION OF MINISTERS OF FOREIGN AFFAIRS

Considers urgent problems
and acts as the
Organ of Consultation

INTER-AMERICAN PEACE COMMITTEE
Washington, D. C.

ADVISORY DEFENSE COMMITTEE

INTER-AMERICAN
DEFENSE BOARD
Washington, D. C.

THE COUNCIL OF THE ORGANIZATION

Permanent Representative Body and
Provisional Organ of Consultation
Washington, D. C.

INTER-AMERICAN ECONOMIC AND SOCIAL COUNCIL
Washington, D. C.

INTER-AMERICAN CULTURAL COUNCIL

COMMITTEE FOR
CULTURAL ACTION
Mexico, D. F.

INTER-AMERICAN COUNCIL OF JURISTS

INTER-AMERICAN
JURIDICAL COMMITTEE
Rio de Janeiro

TECHNICAL
COOPERATION
BOARD

1 *The Directors of these Departments are the Executive Secretaries of the respective Councils.*

2 *The Director of this Department is also the Treasurer of the Organization.*

3 *The Director of this Office is also the Secretary General of the Inter American Statistical Institute.*

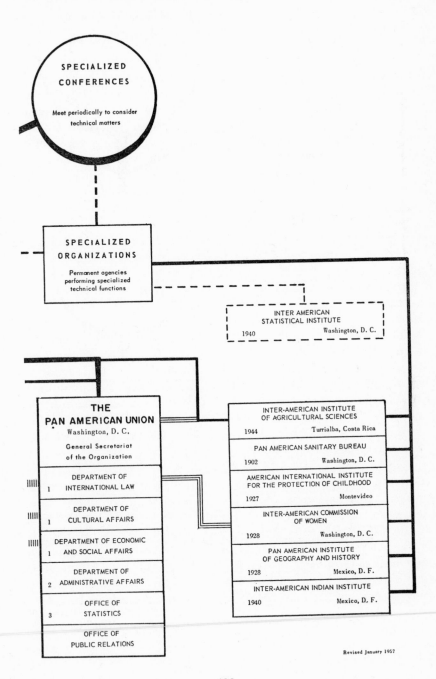

Council is to act provisionally as the organ of consultation under all the circumstances envisaged in the Rio Treaty,"[29] and in relation to tasks assigned it by either of its superior organs, the Inter-American Conference or a Meeting of Foreign Ministers. The Council thus became the central political organ of the OAS as well as its major supervisory and coordinating organ. In performing the latter function, the Council supervises the management of three subsidiary organs, an Economic and Social Council, a Council of Jurists, and a Cultural Council, and of the two other permanently established OAS organs, the Pan American Union and the Specialized Organizations. Composed of one representative (ambassador) of each member state, and operating on the principle of one vote per member state, the OAS Council conducts the bulk of its business by majority decision, settling affairs of more critical importance by a two-thirds vote. The permanent seat of the Council is in Washington.

THE PAN AMERICAN UNION. The Pan American Union (PAU) is the central and permanent organ of the OAS, and its General Secretariat. Its primary mission is to promote, by means of its technical and information divisions and under the supervision of the Council, the economic, social, juridical, and cultural relations among all OAS members. The PAU is headed by a Secretary General and Assistant Secretary General, both elected by the Council for ten-year terms. Since the founding of the OAS in 1948, the post of Secretary General has been held successively by Alberto Lleras Camargo of Colombia, who resigned in 1954, Carlos Dávila of Chile, who died two years after assuming office, and José A. Mora of Uruguay, appointed in 1956. Dr. William Manger of the United States had been the sole Assistant Secretary General, until replaced by William Sanders in 1957.

THE SPECIALIZED ORGANIZATIONS. A Specialized Organization is an inter-governmental agency, established by multilateral treaty to deal with certain technical matters of common interest to the American states. It must be registered as such by the Council of the OAS after duly defining the agency's relationship with the OAS. To date, the Council has bestowed the designation of Specialized Organization on six agencies: the Pan American Sanitary Organization (Washington), the Pan American Institute of Geography and History (Mexico City), the American International

---

[29] Quoted in Whitaker, "Development of American Regionalism," *op. cit.*, p. 143, from *Report of the United States Delegation on the Ninth International Conference of American States* (Washington: Department of State Publication 3263, International Organization and Conference Series II, American Republics 3, 1948), p. 22.

Institute for the Protection of Childhood (Montevideo), the Inter-American Commission of Women (Washington), the Inter-American Indian Institute (Mexico City), and the Inter-American Institute of Agricultural Sciences (Turrialba, Costa Rica).

OTHER AGENCIES. To complete the description of OAS machinery, attention should be given several agencies which fit no neat classification but nonetheless have formal ties with the OAS. Of this character there are the official agencies—the Inter-American Peace Committee, which works closely with the Council to settle disputes arising between OAS members; the Inter-American Radio Office; and the Permanent Inter-American Committee on Social Security. There are also semi-official organizations, such as the Inter-American Statistical Institute, the Pan American Railway Congress Association, and the Pan American Coffee Bureau.

Finally, there is the Organization of Central American States (OCAS), which functions as a regional agency within the OAS framework. Created in 1951, OCAS is the product of a long series of attempts, dating back to 1823, toward closer union of the five nations of Central America (Costa Rica, El Salvador, Guatemala, Honduras, and Nicaragua). The five organs of this subregional organization—the meetings of heads of state, of foreign ministers, and of other cabinet members; a general secretariat; and an economic council—are guided by certain objectives set forth in its charter. The member states pledge themselves to "mutually consult on the means to consolidate and preserve the fraternal coexistence of their region of the continent, prevent disagreements and ensure the peaceful solution of conflicts which might occur among them, seek collective answers to their common problems, and promote their economic, social and cultural development, through co-operative and solidary action."[30] In line with these principles, the OCAS has already approved measures for the creation of free trade zones, a regional industrial system, and for the free and unlimited passage of tourist automobiles across borders.

Latin America and the League of Nations

Idealistic, universally oriented, and straightforward in pledging weaker states protection from the arbitrary intervention of strong nations, the Covenant of the League of Nations appealed forcefully to Latin Americans. Latin American statesmen accepted

[30] Luis Quintanilla, "Controls and Foreign Policies in Latin American Countries," in Philip W. Buck and Martin Travis, Jr. (eds.), Control of Foreign Relations in Modern Nations (New York: W. W. Norton & Co., Inc., 1957), p. 219.

enthusiastically the basic law of the League of Nations, except for Article 21 recognizing the Monroe Doctrine as an instrument for the maintenance of peace in the New World.   They viewed the League as a promising counterweight to the United States, and their fear of the "colossus of the North" increased when the United States Senate failed to ratify the Covenant.   Ten of the Latin American nations became charter members of the League and all eventually joined.   Many Latin Americans held high posts in the Assembly and Council of the League, as well as in the Permanent Court of International Justice.   No group of states outside Europe showed more concern for the success of the League, at least not until the prestige of the world organization had dropped sharply because of its failure to halt military aggression during the 1930's.   But by the time this general disillusionment set in, Latin American states were drifting away from the League, shifting their interest from the world organization to an effective regional system in concert with the United States.[31]

Direct intervention of the League in inter-Latin American military conflicts occurred on two occasions.   Efforts of the League to settle the disputes were disappointing in the first instance, the Chaco War, but they were highly successful in adjudicating the later Leticia dispute.   In the Chaco dispute, fighting broke out between Paraguay and Bolivia in 1928.   In 1932 Paraguay appealed to the League and, after a truce had failed, Bolivia took similar action.   As a result of a munitions embargo imposed on both sides by the Assembly of the League, Paraguay withdrew from the world organization.   The difficulties of the League in trying to mediate the dispute were enhanced by the resentment of the United States toward "outside" interference in hemispheric affairs and by the political fumbling between the inter-American system and the League.   The United States and certain other American nations succeeded in bringing about a settlement between Bolivia and Paraguay in 1936, but neither the League nor the inter-American system could take credit for halting hostilities.

In the Leticia dispute of 1932–1934, the United States, in contrast to its conduct in the Chaco dispute, gave diplomatic support to League efforts to effect a settlement.   In 1932, after failing to dislodge Peruvian troops that had seized its upper Amazon settlement of Leticia, Colombia appealed to the League Council.   The League ordered a cease-fire, requested Peru to withdraw, and sent

[31] For Latin American participation in the League, see Warren H. Kelchner, *Latin American Relations with the League of Nations* (Boston: World Peace Foundation, 1930); also see Rippy, *op. cit.*, pp. 267–275.

a commission to administer the Leticia territory until its return to Colombia. By 1934 Peru and Colombia had signed a protocol settling the dispute.

Latin America and the United Nations

PREPARATION FOR POSTWAR ORGANIZATION. Several months before the United Nations Conference convened at San Francisco in 1945, the Latin Americans, meeting in Mexico City, had agreed upon the functions and scope of activities which the new organization should possess. This Latin American consensus had emerged from their experiences in international politics, their participation in the League, and above all from the preparations for postwar organization of the inter-American system. Their agreement was premised on their desire to keep the inter-American regional system intact and to protect small states against the intervention by the great powers. As early as 1942 the Rio de Janeiro Meeting of Foreign Ministers had instructed the Inter-American Juridical Committee to prepare recommendations on postwar world organization. The Committee drew up fourteen specific recommendations that stressed universalism, international law, "priority of the moral law," economic and social interdependence, pacific settlement of disputes, collective security, abandonment of the balance of power system, limitation of armaments, and the elimination of all forms of imperialism.[32] Latin Americans had participated in the wartime conferences which established the United Nations Relief and Rehabilitation Administration (1943), the Food and Agriculture Organization (1943), the International Monetary Fund and International Bank for Reconstruction and Development (1944), as well as in the conferences on the International Civil Aviation Organization (1944) and the International Labor Organization (1944).

These activities clearly indicate the Latin American desire to be "on the inside" of such organizations at the end of the war, hence it is easy to understand their feeling of being left out when they were not invited to the Dumbarton Oaks discussions and were not even consulted by the United States Department of State before the meeting convened. The fact that they were not being consulted caused many Latin Americans to fear that the United States was overemphasizing globalism at the expense of inter-American regionalism. Their representatives held meetings of protest while the Dumbarton Oaks discussions were under way

[32] For the fourteen recommendations, see John A. Houston, *Latin America in the United Nations* (New York: Carnegie Endowment for International Peace, 1956), pp. 10–13.

and later presented a highly critical report of the Dumbarton Oaks Proposals prepared by an *ad hoc* coordinating committee.

Partly because of the treatment accorded them at Dumbarton Oaks, the Latin Americans pressed next for an inter-American meeting to re-examine the whole problem of postwar international organization and to formulate measures necessary for strengthening their regional system and ensuring its permanence. As a result, the Inter-American Conference on Problems of War and Peace (the Chapultepec Conference) met at Mexico City in February and March, 1945. Resolutions adopted by this Conference called for several modifications of the Dumbarton Oaks Proposals, recommending a clarification of the principles and purposes of the world organization, an amplification of the powers of the General Assembly, an enlargement of the jurisdiction and competence of the "International Court," the creation of an international agency responsible for "promoting intellectual and moral cooperation," the formal recognition of the inter-American system, and adequate representation of Latin America on the Security Council. The Conference adopted other measures to strengthen the hemispheric regional system, particularly the "Act of Chapultepec," which, as we have seen, foreshadowed the "Rio Treaty," and an agreement which led to the adoption at Bogotá of the OAS Charter and the Pact of Bogotá. Finally, in agreeing to restore the Argentine government to inter-American counsels and support its admission to the approaching United Nations Conference, the Chapultepec Conference closed inter-American ranks and readied the regional system for concerted action at San Francisco.

THE SAN FRANCISCO CONFERENCE. But their solidarity, even though they constituted two-fifths of the nations present, was insufficient to accomplish all the Latin Americans desired at San Francisco. As the Conference proceeded the Latin Americans developed two major, though somewhat contradictory, objectives. They sought "to strengthen their relative position with the United Nations," and they hoped "to secure their regional system from too much interference by the world organization."[33] On the first count they clashed with the great powers in their attempt to secure representation on the Security Council, recognition of the *juridical* equality of states in the UN Charter, and several other limitations on the extensive powers granted to the "Big Five" nations. Although the Latin Americans failed to secure these demands because of the united opposition of the great powers,

[33] *Ibid.*, p. 27.

they successfully backed the fight of the smaller nations to secure for the General Assembly the right to discuss any question not on the Security Council agenda. On the other hand, their failure to obtain assurances that their regional interests would be properly served within the United Nations swung them more and more to rely on the inter-American regional system. This shift in the direction of Latin American efforts at San Francisco was primarily responsible for introducing Article 51 into the UN Charter, authorizing individual or collective defense against aggression, pending action by the Security Council. By securing this provision in the charter the Latin Americans had won an important victory, not only for their own regional system, but, as subsequent world events were to prove, for NATO, SEATO, the Baghdad Pact, indeed, for the entire Western world.

THE LATIN AMERICAN BLOC. In the years since 1945, the voting record of Latin Americans in the United Nations has been consistent enough on major issues to validate the contention that these twenty republics constitute the most important single bloc of votes in the General Assembly. In fact, the percentage of solidarity of the Latin American voting bloc dropped below 50 on only one occasion. They have agreed, for example, on virtually all issues related to the cold war, the aspiration of dependent peoples for self-government, and financial assistance to underdeveloped areas. Of these three basic problems confronting the United Nations, the Latin Americans generally have stood shoulder to shoulder with the United States on the first of them, but aligned themselves against their northern neighbor on proposed solutions for the other two. The evidence seems to indicate that the Latin Americans almost instinctively oppose measures which can be said to be tinged with "colonialism," while the United States often follows a policy more calculated to preserve its alliance with other powers. Hence, despite the antipathy of Latin Americans for communism, despite their intimate relationship with the United States in the inter-American system, the Latin Americans have aligned themselves with the Soviet bloc on several colonial issues.[34]

The splitting of the Latin American vote, a phenomenon by no means uncommon, would probably occur more frequently were it not for the coordinating efforts of the informal Latin

[34] For an excellent account of Latin American views on colonialism, see Arthur P. Whitaker, "Anticolonialism in Latin America," *Orbus*, I (April 1957), 51–76. Identity of the Latin American and Afro-Arab-Asian nations is a major thesis of the recent work of Vera Micheles Dean, *The Nature of the Non-Western World* (New York: The New American Library, 1957); see especially Chapter 9, "Latin America: Where Westernism Stopped."

American "group" in the United Nations. At the first session of the General Assembly held in 1945, the Latin Americans, aware of their collective voting strength, met together informally to plan for the election of as many Latin Americans as possible to top positions. Their initial successes led to subsequent meetings and to an extension of their activities to include discussion of all important issues. Meetings are called by the president of the group, in recent years the Latin American Vice-President of the General Assembly, except when a Latin American is President of the Assembly; by one or more members; or, on occasion, by the United States representative, a frequent guest of the group.[35] Acutely aware of the diminution in their relative voting strength by virtue of the admission of new members,[36] Latin Americans will probably rely more and more on their "group" in the future in seeking the support of other blocs.

The coordinated action of this group, coupled with the UN principle of distributing posts geographically, has permitted every Latin American state to name representatives to high positions in the world organization. Among the Latin American members of major committees at the San Francisco Conference were such statesmen as Ezequiel Padilla and Manuel Tello of Mexico, Camilo Ponce Enríquez of Ecuador, Héctor David Castro of El Salvador, and Alberto Lleras Camargo of Colombia. On four occasions a Latin American became President of the General Assembly: Oswaldo Aranha of Brazil (twice), José Arce of Argentina, and Luis Padilla Nervo of Mexico. Since the first session Latin Americans have occupied two of the six nonpermanent seats in the Security Council and three or more of the eighteen seats in the Economic and Social Council. In addition to their active role in the UN itself, the Latin Americans placed four jurists on the first panel of the International Court of Justice and have managed to retain this number of judgeships ever since. Finally, Latin American states are members of such Specialized Agencies affiliated with the UN as UNESCO, the International Monetary Fund and International Bank, ILO, WHO, and the FAO. Through these organizations world-wide fame has more than once come to an individual Latin American, as when Jaime Torres Bodet of Mexico was chosen to serve as Director General of UNESCO.

[35] Houston, op. cit., pp. 6–7.
[36] While the membership of Latin American states remained constant at twenty, total UN membership increased from fifty-one in 1945 to eighty-one in 1957.

Foreign Ministries

The presidential system of government permits the Latin American chief executive virtually complete control of foreign relations. The appointment of ambassadors, ministers, and foreign secretaries, the initiation and alteration of foreign policies, and the promulgation of treaties and other international contracts are within the province of presidential discretion. Public opinion and pressure groups may from time to time exert an influence on policy formation through elections or otherwise, but their day-to-day impact is obviously small in nations in which literacy is low and transportation and communication media undeveloped. Parliamentary controls on foreign policy are restricted in many nations, even in those countries whose constitutions provide for legislative approval of treaties, appointments, declarations of war, and similar measures initiated by the chief executive. Despite this weakness of formal political controls, the president is far from a free agent in foreign policy. Historical precedents are strong. Traditional policy and treaty obligations may not be ignored without endangering a nation's security and its standing in the international community, or running the risk of revolution at home.

Foreign ministry organization within the twenty republics follows a fairly uniform pattern. It is headed by a minister or secretary of cabinet rank, directly responsible to the president and, in a few countries, answerable for his acts to the legislature as well. The foreign minister is generally assisted by a top level advisory council, a deputy foreign secretary, and a chief of administration (*oficial mayor*). These officials hold the top rungs in a bureaucratic hierarchy that normally includes divisions for political (or diplomatic) affairs, economic affairs, a foreign service, consular and commercial affairs, international boundaries, international organization, administrative services, protocol matters, documents and archives, and juridical or counselor affairs. Coordination of policy with such other executive departments as ministries of finance and the armed forces usually depends upon the president.

Every Latin American nation has a foreign service, subject in some degree to regulations in an organic law. To enter the foreign service of his country, an applicant normally must be a citizen in good health and of sound character, have a university education, and demonstrate competence on a written examination. The diplomatic career has been attractive enough to enlist some of Latin America's most promising young men, but low salary scales, mediocre living allowances, and inadequate retirement benefits keep out many professional men and business executives. Low salary scales help to explain the high percentage of noncareer diplomats among chiefs of missions abroad, although political considerations also enter into these appointments. Most Latin American nations have set up a Foreign Service Institute for training their diplomats in leadership, discipline, languages, and protocol, but the training they provide often leaves much to be desired. Despite these limitations, however, Latin American diplomats demonstrate a high level of competence in practice, as evidenced by their enviable record of participation in international organizations.

Conclusions

No crystal ball is necessary to ascertain some of the more obvious features of foreign policy to be seen by projecting the present trends in Latin American development on future international policy. Putting aside the possibility of a third world war, the following trends and features appear. Regionalism and universalism are likely to remain policy objectives, since both the Organization of American States and the United Nations express the Latin American desire for a world order based on the principles of the juridical equality of states, collective security, limitation of armaments, nonintervention, the application of sanctions on aggressors, and the peaceful settlement of international disputes. As inter-Latin American trade grows, the lowering of customs barriers and the development of supra-national industrial systems will receive more serious attention from the Latin Americans themselves. Suggestions of such integration already appear in recommendations by the United Nations Economic Commission for reducing and eliminating trade barriers. In this respect the current success of the Organization of Central American States will have a psychological effect on all Latin America. Economic issues will also continue to loom large in inter-American relations. While the United States will presumably continue to favor private capital investment, Latin Americans will prefer large-scale financial assistance through international loans or grants. This issue, more than any other, promises to test the ties of inter-Americanism. Whether the billions of dollars invested in Latin America by private foreign capital since the end of World War II will encourage billions more, both foreign and domestic, thus providing a sufficiently broad tax base to enable governments to provide those essential social and economic services which make no appeal to profit-seekers, remains to be seen. In the meantime, the twenty republics continue to exert pressure on the United States government for large-scale financial assistance, preferably through some new lending agency of an international character.

Another trend of importance is that growing popular participation in Latin American government is slowly giving public opinion and pressure groups a greater influence over foreign policy. A broadening of educational systems, both numerically and qualitatively, contributes to this end while also improving the professional caliber of foreign service personnel.

And finally, from the standpoint of the United States and Europe, it is important to note that the days of treating Latin American states as pawns in the game of international politics have ended. Latin America today participates in world affairs as an independent player. On the issues of the cold war the Latin American nations side with the United States only when their own vital interests clash with those of communism. On such other issues as colonialism and economic development they join with nations of similar outlook and economic status, regardless of the position assumed by the United States.

Suggestions for Reading

Useful one-volume historical interpretations of the Latin American policy of the United States include Samuel F. Bemis, *The Latin-American Policy of the United States* (New York: Harcourt, Brace & Co., Inc., 1943), Dexter Perkins, *A History of the Monroe Doctrine* (Boston: Little, Brown & Co., 1955), and Graham H. Stuart, *Latin America and the United States* (5th ed.; New York: Appleton-Century-Crofts, Inc., 1955). Among numerous works treating the relations of the United States with single nations or groups of nations, special mention should be made of the series published by the Harvard University Press: Howard F. Cline, *The United States and Mexico* (1953); Dexter Perkins, *The United States and the Caribbean* (1947), and Arthur P. Whitaker, *The United States and South America: The Northern Republics* (1948) and *The United States and Argentina* (1954). On inter-Latin American relations, including the organization of the respective ministries of foreign affairs, see Luis Quintanilla, "Basic Tenets of Latin American International Policy" and "Controls and Foreign Policies in Latin American Countries," in Philip W. Buck and Martin Travis, Jr. (eds.), *Control of Foreign Relations in Modern Nations* (New York: W. W. Norton & Co., Inc., 1957).

On Latin American relations with Europe, including World War I and the postwar League of Nations era, the reader is referred to Venancio Balbueno Galeano, *L'Amérique Latine: Les États-Unis et la Société des Nations* (Thesis, University of of Paris, 1927), Gaston Gaillard, *L'Amérique Latine et l'Europe Occidentale* (Paris: Berger-Levrault, 1918), Warren H. Kelchner, *Latin American Relations with the League of Nations* (Boston: World Peace Foundation, 1939), Percy A. Martin, *Latin America and the War* (Boston: World Peace Foundation, 1930), J. Fred Rippy, *Latin America in World Politics* (3d ed.; New York: Appleton-Century-Crofts, Inc., 1938), and *A Study of Trade between Latin America and Europe* (Geneva: The United Nations, Department of Economic Affairs, 1953). For Latin America and the United Nations, see Manuel Canyes, *The Organization of Amer-*

ican States and the United Nations (3d ed.; Washington, D.C.: Pan American Union, 1955), and John A. Houston, *Latin America in the United Nations* (New York: Carnegie Endowment for International Peace, 1956).

Documents relating to inter-American organization are conveniently arranged in *The International Conferences of American States, 1888–1928* (1931), and its companion volume, *First Supplement, 1933–1940* (1940) (New York: Carnegie Endowment for International Peace). These documents are also readily available in Robert N. Burr and Roland D. Hussey, *Documents on Inter-American Cooperation* (Philadelphia: University of Pennsylvania Press, 1955). For current documentary material, the reader is referred to the volumes of the Pan American Union, the *Annals of the Organization of American States* and the *Inter-American Juridical Yearbook*. Finally, among the more recent interpretative works on American regionalism are Laurence Duggan, *The Americas: The Search for Hemispheric Security* (New York: Henry Holt & Co., 1949); Charles G. Fenwick, *The Inter-American Regional System* (New York: The Declan X. McMullen Co., Inc., 1949), John Humphrey, *The Inter-American System: A Canadian View* (Toronto: The Macmillan Co., 1942), Arthur P. Whitaker, *The Western Hemisphere Idea: Its Rise and Decline* (Ithaca, N.Y.: Cornell University Press, 1954), and Whitaker, "Development of American Regionalism," *International Conciliation*, No. 469 (March 1951).

III

EXPANSION OF GOVERNMENT

Chapter **15**

Government and
the Economic Order

Increased reliance on the state as the instrument for accelerating the attainment of the good society has brought an increase in government participation in economic life in the modern world. In general terms, the objective of such state activity is economic development. For this purpose, governments have introduced new institutions or modernized old ones to achieve such varied goals as increased farm production, improved systems of transport, greater supplies of electric power, accelerated industrialization, a broadened base for vocational and technical education, and increased efficiency of public administration. It is against this general background that this chapter discusses the nature of the main economic problems in Latin America, government policies adopted to deal with them, and the agencies of government that operate in the economic field.

The Economic Setting

PRESSURE FOR ECONOMIC DEVELOPMENT. The scope and functions of government in contemporary Latin America are being shaped in large degree by the pressing desire to accelerate economic development. In the past, each country characteristically produced one, or at most a few, staple export products: cereals and meat (Argentina), coffee (El Salvador, Colombia, and Brazil), sugar (Cuba and the Dominican Republic), cotton, sugar, and non-ferrous metals (Peru), copper and nitrates (Chile), oil (Venezuela), and bananas (Ecuador and Honduras). These few export products in which local producers enjoy the greatest comparative advantage have traditionally been exchanged for a wide variety of imported manufactures. Most Latin Americans realize that such traditional exports are at present a source of economic strength, but they fail to see opportunities for spectacular growth along such lines, except, perhaps, in oil. Rather, local production of many manufactures, particularly the simpler varieties, is deemed by many to be the best road to substantial economic growth. And this attitude is not without statistical support. It seems to be borne out by the fact that the value of annual production per industrial worker in nearly every country of the world is greater than the production per farm worker. What is not so well known, however, is that capital requirements per industrial worker are usually much greater than those per farm worker and that capital —which depends on savings—remains among the scarcest of resources.

THE PROBLEM OF DEVELOPMENT. Although it is an oversimplification, we may define economic development for the purpose of this discussion as consisting largely of broadening the production base by introducing new (principally industrial) products, new methods of production (especially in farming), and improved systems of storing, transporting, and marketing commodities. The general aim is to increase the output per worker. Many Latin American countries have made significant progress in their economic development in this sense during recent decades.

How is this economic growth being achieved? In part, it is occurring on a piecemeal basis—reflecting the individual efforts of producers in both industry and agriculture. Thus, men with initiative and modest capital have set out to produce the simplest forms of the type of products usually imported; coarse textiles are an example. Or farmers have expanded their operations. Some enterprising farmers have introduced new strains of plants and new breeds of animals to increase output per acre. In the process they have provided a kind of apprentice training to farm hands, some of whom later branch out into production for themselves, thus spreading superior production methods to other parts of the farm sector. Such innovating tendencies inevitably spread over ever-widening areas. These changes in turn beget other transformations, because expanding real incomes among rural people provide growing markets for producers in the cities, where most industry is located. As markets grow, "assembly-line" production becomes more and more feasible in the industrial areas. Industrial growth, in turn, increases the market for the output of the nation's farms.

Such mutually reinforcing tendencies constitute the essence of true economic development.

THE ROLE OF GOVERNMENT. Government policy, in various ways, catalyzes and channels the dynamic elements which further growth. In agriculture, Latin American governments have begun to make use of extension services to bring knowledge of superior production techniques to farmers. The government has established drying plants for reducing the moisture content of corn and rice —staples of the diet in many countries—to assure that crops which formerly were exposed to tropical dampness became available in full for human and animal feeding. Governments have introduced low-cost farm credit, relieving many farmers of dependence on the usurious merchant–lender. Thus, as a result, the farmer can reserve more of his output for family consumption and can use this additional extra income for such purposes as increasing soil fertility, improving drainage, or constructing simple storage facilities. Few government measures to aid agriculture are spectacular. But these less dramatic forms of aid are important because of their cumulative impact on the important rural sector of the Latin American economy.

Not all government actions in agriculture are of this small-scale variety, however. Government irrigation projects, which can transform an entire region, usually are large-scale operations, involving changes of impressive scope. They often include land reclamation and the opening up of new regions to farm production, increased opportunities for land ownership, and new and practical educational facilities for former tenants who may be allowed to farm reclaimed land on condition that they cooperate with the government's agricultural technicians in the use of low-cost methods of production. Better rural housing is encouraged, rural schooling for farm children is improved, and production and marketing cooperatives are sometimes organized.

Though government activity in agriculture has great social importance in view of the size of the rural population[1] and the relatively low levels of farm productivity and real income, the industrial sphere is usually of more concern to governments. The public also gives stronger support to industrial development than to most other forms of new economic activity. The people cheer

[1] For Latin America as a whole, 52 per cent of the economically active population is in agriculture. The range is from 20 per cent in Uruguay to 83 per cent in Haiti. In contrast, only 18 per cent of the workers are in industry, on the average. See United Nations, *Progress Report on the Manpower Survey in Latin America* (New York, 1955), p. 34.

the advent of local industries producing articles formerly obtained only by import, unless they have been established extravagantly. They see the increased opportunities for local employment, the greater productivity of labor, and new domestic outlets for local raw materials. In a word, they feel a sense of greater national economic "independence." Yet such favorable results are usually obtained only when priority is given to new industries that are well suited to the local economy.

But this expanded production, whether agricultural or industrial, attains its maximum social usefulness only when the products are efficiently moved to centers of consumption or export. Hence, storage and transport are other spheres in which intelligent government policy can spur economic development. Storage facilities appropriate to the main crops, farm-to-market roads, trunk highways, modernized river transport systems, and improved port facilities all make their demands on available resources.

We cannot conclude this brief discussion of the economic setting in which governments must operate to speed economic development without a further comment on the problem of savings. Real improvements in agriculture, industry, and transport absorb large quantities of physical resources and technical skills. Such resources are not easy to come by. The people can choose to have more consumer goods and save less of their income. But if they do so, insufficient national resources will be released for the vital tasks of building up the agricultural, industrial, and transportation plants. Farmers do not knowingly fail to provide for their requirements of seed corn, but the public in general may fail to do the social equivalent by failing to save adequately if government policy fails to promote saving and investment by a large part of the citizenry.

Government and Industry

NATURE OF GOVERNMENT PARTICIPATION. If one contrasts Latin America and, say, the United States with respect to government participation in economic life, he is struck with the fact that governments in Latin America typically are substantial direct participants in types of economic activity which are in private hands in North America. Many Latin American governments engage in the production of steel, operate ocean shipping companies, own and operate facilities for refining sugar, produce chemicals, run railways, operate telephone systems, and generate electric power. Some governments operate commercial banks, integrated oil industries, airlines, hotels, milk pasturization plants, powdered milk factories, and grain storage facilities.

TABLE XVII. PRIVATE AND PUBLIC INVESTMENT IN LATIN AMERICA, 1950–1956

Year	Investments in Billions of Dollars (in terms of 1950 prices)		Public Investment as Percentage of Private Investment
	Private	Public	
1950	4.6	1.9	41%
1951	5.4	1.9	35
1952	5.7	1.8	32
1953	5.7	1.8	32
1954	6.0	2.0	33
1955	6.4	2.0	31
1956*	6.9	2.0	29

SOURCE: United Nations, *Economic Survey of Latin America, 1956* (New York, 1957), p. xxiv, table 6.
    * Estimated.

If the contrast is marked when it is made in terms of types of business operations in which governments north and south of the Rio Grande are engaged, it becomes even more striking when the size of the government-run business sector is compared with that of the private business sector. Such a comparison shows that goods and services produced in government-owned plants in Latin America usually bulk large in relation to the output produced in the private nonagricultural economy. Though direct statistical evidence is lacking, interesting indirect evidence appears in the data on investment. Thus, as Table XVII shows, new public investment in Latin America in any given year usually averages about a third of the new private investment. In marked contrast, federal government gross civilian investment in the United States in 1956 amounted to about 2 per cent of gross private domestic investment.

Why does the business activity of Latin American governments include more than merely operating postal systems and running military arsenals? For one thing, government has engaged in some operations because private capital has not shown much interest. Private investors were able to earn a greater return elsewhere, especially in commerce and in export production. Second, the scarcity of domestic private capital and the strong attractions of investment in export production and in commerce have made foreign private investment the only large-scale alternative to government ownership in many cases. But the people, and particularly the military, have not wished to see foreign capital and management in such sensitive operations as, for example, communications systems. This concern for national security largely explains why so many Latin American governments provide telephone service. Third, governments have found the state monopolies a useful supplementary source of public revenue. Government operation of distilleries illustrates the advantages of this policy. Fourth, public opinion in several countries has been influenced by strong emotional considerations to oppose private, and especially foreign, exploitation of petroleum resources. Government oil monopolies thus exist in the largest countries—Argentina, Brazil, and Mexico. Fifth, in order to speed up the tempo of resource development or to assist farmers, governments have pushed ahead with their own plants rather than waiting for the slower development by private domestic or foreign capital. Some national steel companies and government-owned sugar mills, for example, may be accounted for in this way. Finally, governments have nationalized some foreign-owned but long publicly regulated businesses, chiefly when such businesses no longer yielded attractive financial returns to their foreign owners in the face of prevailing regulatory norms. State ownership of railway systems in several countries owes its origin to this factor.

It is sometimes difficult to characterize or to measure the economic impact of government participation in industry. For example, the extent of employment in government-run industrial operations is not known in detail. It is believed, however, that it amounts to well over 10 per cent of all industrial employment in a number of Latin American countries.

PROBLEM OF MANAGEMENT. The management problem is an impressive one in these government-controlled enterprises, especially those which represent complex industrial undertakings. The autonomous institute is perhaps the most common institutional form used to meet the problem. The institute usually assures appropriate influence on the part of the administration in office, while providing (in some but not in all cases) a measure of continuity and security for management. The joint-stock company is customarily used, however, when there is private participation in the enterprise. The National Steel Company of Brazil (Volta Redonda), in which private capital participates on a minority basis, is so organized, as is the Pacific Steel Company of Chile (Huachipato), in which the government's share of the capital, though originally a majority, is now somewhat less than half.

But not all joint-stock companies necessarily involve private participation. Pemex, Mexico's integrated oil monopoly, is organized as a joint-stock company, but all the stock is held by the government. The wholly government-owned Banco de la Nación, Argentina's largest commercial bank, also has the structure of a joint-stock company.

Government and Agriculture

Except for the operation of an occasional "agricultural colony" or integrated farm community, Latin American governments participate only indirectly in farm production. The agricultural colony is little more than a good-sized village with its farm hinterland, carved out of a jungle or undeveloped area. Its purpose is to open up a hitherto inaccessible region to farming on a modern basis. Since the initial cost of a feasible operation of this type is high, a specialized government entity has been found useful to effect this pioneering activity. In some cases farmers in these "colonies" rent from the government, and in others they are purchasers who pay for the land on long-term instalments. The alternative is for the government merely to build roads, taking the risk that the countryside may be occupied by squatters practicing small-scale rudimentary agriculture.

In most cases, however, government activity in farming seeks to influence the pattern of production and farm life rather than to acquire and operate property. This "indirect participation," at least in the institutional form, is not very different from the now traditional relationship of government to agriculture in the United States. Specifically, most Latin American governments play an educational role mainly in the operation of extension services (a relatively new field), grant low-cost credit to certain categories of agriculturists, operate experiment stations, (occasionally) promote farm cooperatives, and (also occasionally) engage in price-support operations covering a limited range of farm products. Apart from the credit operations, most of these activities are conducted by the ministry of agriculture, though in a few instances a government-owned agricultural credit bank also carries out limited price support activities.

Government's Role in Economic Stabilization

THE PROBLEM OF GROWTH AND STABILITY. Throughout the noncommunist world, modern government has come to attach considerable, if not overriding, importance to the conditions that make for economic growth with stability. Expansion for a year or two, followed by a violent decline in economic activity and another burst of expansion subsequently, is a sequence that is no longer tolerable. Growth with stability is to be encouraged by government, but only by activities that do not unduly restrict the initiative and enterprise of individual capitalists.

Two major policy devices are used for stabilization purposes.

These are fiscal policy, which has to do with the government's tax and expenditure policies, and monetary policy, which is concerned with the cost and availability of bank credit. If the economy is lagging and a "shot in the arm" seems desirable, the government may adjust its fiscal policy to achieve a surplus of expenditures over tax receipts, or it may loosen bank credit by expanding the banking system's reserves and hence its capacity to lend to businessmen. If inflation threatens, the government may act in an opposite manner. It may expand its tax receipts in relation to its expenditures, either by curtailing government outlays or by increasing taxes (or both). Usually it would simultaneously follow a restrictive monetary policy by reducing the banking system's power to lend.

Only countries with fairly well-developed financial institutions and with commercial banks that do not themselves hold heavy cash reserves of their own are able to carry out strong monetary policies. But few Latin American countries yet possess such institutions. Hence, the governments' role in economic stabilization is largely confined to the field of fiscal policy.

STABILIZING AN EXPORT ECONOMY. International trade introduces another complication. Latin America, as previously mentioned, depends heavily on imports for its well-being, and pays for them with its exports. It is characteristic of the typical Latin American economy that import demand is fairly stable or rises steadily (to meet requirements for consumption, and machinery and equipment needs for growth), while the value of exports is subject to considerable annual fluctuation, either because of the impact of weather on the volume of exportable crops or because of ups and downs in world market prices. Imports show less price fluctuation than exports because they consist mainly of manufactured goods, the supply of which can be expanded by United States or European factories when foreign demand is strong and reduced when demand declines. Exports, on the other hand, fluctuate greatly, according to the world market.

A marked rise in the value of Latin American exports has two main effects. Increased export, representing a considerable fraction of the national product, greatly expands the national income. People therefore have increased spending power and usually spend more on imported products, as well as on those of local origin. When the value of exports declines, however, the country cannot readily retrench on imports. In theory, a nation might pay for undiminished imports from its own export earnings if it managed to build up sizable foreign exchange reserves, dipping into such reserves in lean export years.   But most Latin American countries have not been able to accumulate such reserves (or have not wished to make the sacrifices necessary to acquire them), seemingly prizing current imports more highly than larger exchange reserves.   In theory also, the Latin Americans might continue to enjoy a steady volume of imports if they were able to borrow abroad in lean export years. But they cannot rely on such borrowing, either because they may have become "loaned up" in the preceding good years or because lenders abroad are uncertain of the extent and duration of the lean export period.

Clearly, fluctuating exports create a serious problem for economic stabilization.   The gist of the problem is that economic expansion and contraction occur autonomously, in response to the behavior of exports.   The problem is further complicated by the fact that while imports are markedly responsive to upward movements in exports, they are only mildly sensitive to decreases.

What can fiscal policy do to offset undue contraction in an export economy?   In lean periods, government expenditures may have to be increased, taxes may be reduced[2] by a monetary magnitude approximately equal to the reduction in the value of exports, or both.   But the external factors that work to reduce Latin American exports also affect the exports of underdeveloped areas outside the hemisphere.   Hence, if Latin America is not to see its export position weakened in relation to that of competing export areas, comparable fiscal policies would have to be introduced elsewhere. Such coordinated international action, though not impossible, has yet to be adopted with respect to any considerable group of commodities.

Nevertheless, most Latin American governments have used independent national public expenditure programs to moderate fluctuations in income and employment levels in periods of declining exports.   They have done so by financing deficits and by increasing the note circulation, usually with the result that the increased money supply has brought inflationary price movements.   It may be remarked in passing that the inflationary effects show that such deficit financing has generally exceeded the amounts required for maintaining relatively stable national income and employment.

[2] In many cases, tax revenue would decline automatically as the yield of export taxes fell.   Scope for such a decline is indicated in the following data, which show export taxes as a percentage of central government ordinary revenue for selected countries: Chile, 33 per cent; Colombia, 8 per cent; Costa Rica, 14 per cent; El Salvador, 27 per cent; Guatemala, 19 per cent; Mexico, 14 per cent; and Peru, 9 per cent.   These figures are cited in United Nations, *Economic Survey of Latin America, 1955* (New York, 1956), p. 133.

In some cases an increase in exports offers greater opportunity for independent national action for purposes of economic stabilization. The fluctuations caused by the increase may be controlled if the country is able to impose special (temporary) export taxes without seriously affecting its international competitive export position. Some of the coffee countries in Latin America were able to do this successfully a few years ago, and Mexico took similar action in the case of cotton over several seasons. The effect of such policies is to increase tax income relative to government expenditures. Available purchasing power, which would otherwise be associated with expanded exports, is siphoned off; some has been used to build up foreign exchange reserves. The necessary conditions to permit this increase in export taxes, it must be noted, are not commonly realized when competition in the world market is keen.

If tax adjustments are to be counted on to help with economic stabilization, a key requirement is that it must be technically and politically feasible to alter taxes with some degree of flexibility. Most Latin American taxes, as will be explained below, are derived from custom duties and consumption taxes. The former are difficult to reduce without upsetting protected local industry, and the government does not desire to raise them for purposes of economic stabilization because, once increased, they are difficult to lower without again more or less painfully affecting protected industry.

Consumption taxes, too, though seemingly more flexible, are not adjustable (upward or downward) without difficulties. Tax reductions are likely to be viewed as permanent rather than as one phase of a flexible fiscal program. Increases of consumption taxes are bound to be unpopular. They are almost sure to be opposed, either on grounds that the objectives themselves are questionable or that they are attainable by other means, for example, by the income tax. But the income tax is not firmly enough established in many Latin American countries to serve the purpose. A particular weakness in its operation stems from the fact that the principle of self-assessment is not widely accepted in practice. Hence, resort to enforced income taxation, or the increase of rates when income taxes already exist, induces people to transfer funds to foreign centers (the problem of the "flight of capital"). Such transfers retard growth. They deprive the countries of capital needed for their development; they tend to weaken currencies, perhaps at a time when they are beginning to reflect strength as the result of previous politically courageous policy actions; and the weakening of currencies in turn impairs incentives to save, thus reducing domestic resources available for investment and the national economic build-up.

The upshot is that the job of economic stabilization under Latin American conditions is a trying one. In skilled hands, however, fiscal policy can make a positive contribution to economic stability. It will be more successful (1) the larger the foreign exchange reserves held by the countries (or the greater their ability to engage in foreign borrowing), (2) the more amenable the leading export industries are to temporary export taxation, and (3) the greater the relative importance of the income tax in the local tax system (and the greater the citizens' compliance with tax laws).

The Tax System

THE TAX STRUCTURE. A good clue to the revenue system is provided by information on the tax structure. Typically, income taxes contribute a relatively small part of total tax revenues. This is one of the most important features of the Latin American tax structure. In fact, income taxes, personal and corporate, which account for nearly two-thirds of federal revenues in the United States, average roughly one quarter of the total in Latin America. Except in a few cases, such taxes are less important as revenue sources than are import duties, and are only a little larger on the average than consumption taxes.

TABLE XVIII. Tax Revenues from Leading Sources Expressed as Per Cent of Total, for Selected Countries, 1953

Country	Income Taxes	Import Duties	Consumption Taxes	Other Taxes Direct	Other Taxes Indirect
Argentina	37.9	2.3	20.3	7.5	32.0
Brazil	20.4	11.3	44.7	4.8	18.7
Chile	35.4	13.8	12.7	21.2*	16.9
Colombia	31.2	23.9	25.1	14.4	5.4
Costa Rica	15.5	52.6	16.5	11.9	3.1
El Salvador	7.8	38.8	16.2	31.0*	6.2
Guatemala	6.3	36.5	23.8	20.6*	11.1
Honduras	21.4	52.4	9.5	2.4	14.3
Nicaragua	5.0	63.4	19.8	7.5	3.7
Venezuela	48.7	24.8	12.3	9.2	5.0

SOURCE: United Nations, *Economic Survey of Latin America, 1955* (New York, 1956), p. 138. Note: This source includes tabular data for Ecuador, Mexico, and Peru; these have not been used because the figures are internally inconsistent.

* Largely export taxes.

A cross-section tax picture may be obtained from Table XVIII, which shows how taxes are distributed among income taxes, import duties, consumption taxes, and other direct and indirect taxes. Only Venezuela approximates the United States as far as the relative importance of the income tax is concerned, but even this case must be qualified by recognizing that a large part of the tax is derived not from broadly-based domestic income but from extremely profitable oil exports. In other cases, the income tax contributes from as low as 5 per cent to as high as 38 per cent of revenues. For half of the cases shown, both import duties and consumption taxes are relatively more important than the income tax. "Other direct taxes" comprise those on inheritances, exports, property, and capital; "other indirect taxes" include sales, production, and turnover taxes.

One further observation: Import duties, it will be noted, are only a small part of total revenue in Argentina. This does not mean that imports are lightly taxed; actually, they are burdened with revenue-raising foreign exchange rates[3] that function as concealed taxes on a wide range of goods.

THE EFFECTS OF TAXES. Latin America has a relatively regressive tax system. That is, most of the taxes bear proportionately more heavily on people with low incomes than on those with high incomes. For example, taxes on ordinary foods are high, while those on expensive jewelry are not. As a rule, indirect taxes are regressive. There are important cases in Latin America, however, in which indirect taxes may be progressive. For instance, many countries in the area tax automobiles, often heavily. Since the ownership of cars is concentrated among the well-to-do in most Latin American countries, such taxes are progressive.

Regressive taxes are not highly regarded when the main criterion is equity in taxation. On the basis of this test, Latin American taxes leave much to be desired. But equality of shares in national income is only one possible criterion. Equality of economic opportunity for the people over the medium and long term is another, especially in the case of countries that find themselves in an early stage of economic growth. By this test, Latin America's tax system on balance helps to expand national savings and thus facilitates a higher level of capital formation. Regressive taxes favor people with a high savings potential, and savings rather than consumption are the main factor limiting expansion of the economy's productive plant in an underdeveloped country.

The Nature and Impact of Public Expenditures

Government expenditure in Latin America represents a substantial share of total national expenditure. Even where public expenditure is relatively low, in Honduras for example, it amounts to a

---

[3] So-called multiple exchange rates.

tenth of the national income. In most of the larger countries it approximates a fifth of the national income.[4]

There are three major categories of central government outlays: current expenditure, investment, and transfer payments. For Latin America as a whole, these have been running in the 1950's at about 50, 30, and 20 per cent, respectively, of total central government expenditures.

Current expenditures may be broken down into outlays for general administration (salaries and regular purchases for the account of the legislative, judicial, and executive departments of government apart from the military establishment), national defense, education, and health. These four divisions of current expenditure for Latin America as a whole have recently comprised the following approximate percentages of total current expenditures: general administration, 50 per cent; national defense, 22 per cent; education, 18 per cent; and health, 10 per cent.

Investment outlays, such as those made in connection with an irrigation project, are treated separately in order to isolate expenditures that contribute primarily to augmenting productive assets. Increasingly, governments in Latin America are endeavoring to devote a larger share of their resources to investment. Real public investment, especially that which is complementary to private investment, is probably the principal means by which governments contribute to economic development.

Transfer payments are the final category of government expenditures. Their distinguishing feature is that they represent, not final consumption by units of the central government, but transfers of purchasing power to local governments and other sectors of the national community. They include social security transfers, grants-in-aid to local governments, and payments on the public debt. Variability within Latin America is greater in the field of transfer payments than in current expenditures or in investments. Thus, transfer payments in recent years have been less than 5 per cent of total government expenditures in the case of Honduras, Nicaragua, Guatemala, and El Salvador; in contrast, they have made up a third of the total in Argentina and over a quarter in Brazil.

The effects of public expenditures are numerous and important. Perhaps the most important economic effects are those upon price levels, foreign exchange, and the position of the currency. In most cases, at least since the war, public expenditures have been in excess of the resources made available by the people in the form of taxes

---

[4] These facts are drawn mainly from United Nations, *Economic Survey of Latin America, 1955* (New York, 1956), pp. 113–130.

and voluntarily released as savings. Inflation has been the result in a majority of the countries. Governments wise enough to know when to spend and to what degree, and strong enough to carry out policies based on economic realities, could vary their expenditure policies to achieve employment, investment, and other objectives. But most governments, including those in Latin America, have not yet attained the required maturity. For them, the traditional rule probably is still the one to follow: they should seek an annually balanced budget, which is the safest prescription for achieving the important objective of internal financial stability.

Government and Economic Growth

As has already been indicated, the main focus of government economic policy is economic growth. In general terms, the aim of a policy of economic growth is to accelerate improvement in the material well-being of the people. In more specific terms, the objectives include the desire to minimize the economic and social impact of unstable exports, the improvement of productivity in the big agricultural sector of the economy, the expansion of opportunities for processing local raw materials into semi-finished and finished products, the desire to upgrade the nation's human resources, mainly by increasing the number and variety of economic activities calling for people with skills and professional training, the attainment of greater military self-sufficiency by way of more diversified industrial production, and the enhancement of national prestige through the production of complex products usually identified with advanced industrial nations.

Each of the specific objectives usually plays a role in the growth process. Diversification of the economy in itself reduces the relative importance of production for export, so that fluctuations in the latter generate smaller fluctuations in over-all economic activity once a country has achieved a measure of economic development. When a nation is able to increase the extent to which it may efficiently process local raw materials, it increases the economic yield of raw materials and the productivity of labor. The increased variety of economic activities, in turn, enlarges the range of skills for which above-average rates of remuneration are offered. This situation increases interest in technical education on the part of the youth, as well as the willingness of parents to make the necessary sacrifices for their children's education. Improved agricultural productivity is still another important goal of government development policy. Higher output per farm worker not only makes a direct contribution to the well-being of people on the land; it also expands the real purchasing power of the economy's largest sector, enlarges the national market, and increases opportunities for industrialization. In short, forward movement along the entire economic front can be made to work in such a way that each advance positively stimulates other advances in a cumulative fashion.

Coordinating the Economy

NATIONAL ECONOMIC COUNCILS. The pace of economic development and the technical complexity of government operations in the economic sphere are such that traditional cabinet management no longer suffices. In this respect Latin America's experience has been no different from that elsewhere. Many of the countries have placed a well-trained economic advisory staff in the office of the president. This top-level advisory body is known by various names. In Brazil it is the Economic Development Council, in Argentina it is the National Economic Council, and in Venezuela the Office of Special Studies. It consists of economists and other technicians, including specialists in public administration. One of its jobs is to take a government-wide look at the task to be done and to relate this job to the available resources. In nearly every country, the size of the job greatly exceeds the resources at the disposal of the government. Hence, it is necessary to assign priorities to the various projects in order to assure that the most important are given first claim to resources.

Another job of the economic council is to evaluate existing economic policies and to recommend new measures or the revision of old ones. Problems on which the president may request the council's advice include controlling inflation, deciding whether to grant new or increased tariff protection for this or that industry (realizing that each such grant gives an upward push to prices), the adoption of policies to guide the scheduling of public utility rates (especially of foreign-owned public utilities), and the formulation of wage policies.

Experience with these economic councils has been favorable on the whole. In countries where they have been established the president no longer depends solely on his ministers for technical advice. Confronted with an expert group at the president's elbow, the ministries and autonomous agencies have found in most cases that they must keep on their toes if they are to function as a team in the manner that will satisfy an exacting president. In particular, the ministers and heads of independent agencies realize that they form a part of an interdependent operation. This has meant an increase in inter-ministerial and inter-agency contacts, at intermediate as well as at higher levels of each agency. The effect has been to accelerate decision-making, to improve the technical quality and consistency of government actions, and indirectly to give a fillip to economic activity and longer-range planning in the big private sector of the economy.

THE DEVELOPMENT CORPORATION. The *fomento,* or development corporation, though only one of several instrumentalities through which governments foster economic growth, is important as a Latin American innovation in government. This specialized government agency conducts practical studies of the means for speeding economic growth in areas within its jurisdiction, setting forth priorities for its development investment; makes loans for promising ventures; and sometimes operates agricultural and industrial establishments.

About half of the Latin American republics have a *fomento* corporation or its equivalent. The oldest of these is the Chilean Development Corporation, which began in 1939 as an agency to carry out reconstruction work following a severe earthquake. Bolivia and Venezuela also have agencies known as development corporations. Colombia, Ecuador, Guatemala, and El Salvador have development institutes, which are essentially the same as development corporations. In still other cases, such as Mexico's Nacional Financiera and Brazil's Banco de Desenvolvimiento Econômico, the development institution is mainly an agency for financing industrial and other projects designed to speed national economic development. Countries in this latter group also have other specialized development agencies. Mexico, for example, has a Mineral Development Commission which assists small mining enterprises.

The objective of the development corporation is the soundest possible growth of the economy as a whole. This objective is generally sought along two lines: an increased volume of investment, and improvement in the composition of this investment. Specifically, the development corporation endeavors to broaden the development of natural resources, expand output, achieve lower production costs, and improve the nation's foreign trade position. It works both through projects of its own and by promoting private enterprises. In general, the development corporation establishes its own production facilities only when private capital, domestic or foreign, is not prepared to act.

The financial resources of the development corporation come from various sources. Some, usually a major part, are provided in the regular budget of the national government. Earnings from ventures in which the corporation is engaged also contribute to available resources. In a few instances, savings of the people are tapped by the sale of securities. In some cases, foreign public capital is also obtained. Most of this foreign public capital thus far has come in the form of loans from the Export–Import Bank in Washington.

Operations of the development corporations vary somewhat from country to country, but the pattern is much the same in all countries. In all cases, the corporation lends funds to firms in various lines of business, usually in accordance with a general national investment program. Either the corporation will lend to private parties, or, if private capital is not anxious to participate in a certain venture, it will invest the corporation's funds. It may, for example, invest in silos and warehouses, or in programs for improving the quality of livestock. Electric power production has been another significant field of activity. Important, but not typical, operations have also been conducted in mining (coal and petroleum), steel, locomotives, cement, chemicals, and forest products. In a few instances, development corporations have also acted to support the prices of farm commodities.

Typically, the development corporation is managed by a board of directors and a president, most of whom are appointed by the nation's chief executive. Though the development corporation is nominally autonomous, it is usually in effect an agency of the executive branch of the government.

THE MINISTRY OF NATIONAL ECONOMY. The regular government ministry most concerned with the work of the development corporation is that of national economy. The interests of this ministry correspond roughly to those of the United States Department of Commerce. It finds the development corporation useful in many ways for carrying out the ministry's basic task of encouraging domestic and foreign trade and industry. The ministry seeks to promote new businesses, hence its interest in the development corporation. The ministry encourages the adoption of modern methods of protection; it is interested, therefore, in pioneering ventures financed or carried out by the development corporation. Since the ministry also conducts various economic studies of its own, it is frequently in a position to offer suggestions to the development corporation or to make an independent evaluation of studies and recommendations prepared within the development corporation.

But the ministry, as an "old-line" government agency, performs many functions other than those relating to the work of the development corporation. Typically, it regulates public untilities, issues export licenses, receives appeals from domestic firms for tariff adjustments, encourages tourist trade, regulates the issuance of trade-marks, operates or works closely with the central statistical office, and recommends temporary tax exemption for promising new industries.

Because the work of the ministry touches upon so many phases of the national economy, it participates in numerous inter-agency activities within the government. If the government has an autonomous electricity agency, for example, the ministry must work with it on all questions that directly or indirectly affect ministry functions in, say, the sphere of electricity rate regulation. The ministry's activities in promoting new industries by granting tax relief requires that it work closely with the ministry of finance. By this cooperation with other agencies, especially when the country does not have a national economic council, the ministry helps coordinate economic policies as these are formulated and implemented in other ministries or in the different autonomous agencies. The effectiveness of such coordinating efforts depends in part, of course, on the way the ministry itself is managed and the quality and cooperative spirit of its personnel. It also depends partly on the composition of the president's cabinet. In countries where a president's economic council exists, it depends as well on the experience and judgment of that body.

THE MINISTRY OF AGRICULTURE. Because over half the population of Latin America makes its living from the land, and because farm incomes are typically well below the national average, no little economic importance is attached to the work of the ministry of agriculture. Hence, in most countries, this ministry is a key agency in national efforts to accelerate economic development. But this interest in agricultural development is a rather belated one. Until recently, most countries, even though they had established ministries or subministries, were content to let agriculture develop (or stagnate) without much attention from government. Now most ministries of agriculture have expanded their activity. They are conducting studies on how to improve land use, carrying out extension programs, modernizing and expanding experiment stations, providing low-cost farm credit, improving their technical services, conducting programs for the eradication of plant and animal diseases, and collecting basic production and market statistics.

The challenge facing most ministries of agriculture today is not so much what needs to be done to aid farmers as how to carry out the indicated measures for improvement, how to increase the number and quality of the personnel available to do the work, and how to determine the share of the nation's total development resources to be placed at the disposal of agencies serving the farm economy. Experience has shown that it is necessary to adopt new approaches to the farmer, placing the emphasis upon the services that the ministry is prepared to offer for the farmer's benefit. It has also shown that more trained and devoted personnel are needed to cover the farm sector adequately, especially in the field of agricultural extension, and that a larger share of total public investment should be used for essential capital projects in rural areas, such as farm-to-market roads, storage facilities, and irrigation projects.

Furthermore, the ministry of agriculture finds that it must be increasingly active in the development of basic plans at the inter-ministerial level. For there are agricultural aspects to government operations seemingly quite independent. For example, the road-building and road-maintenance work of the ministry of public works interests agriculture, as does the formulation of national credit policies by the central bank and the ministry of finance. Much the same may be said about the negotiation of trade agreements by the ministry of foreign relations. The ministry of agriculture participates in such discussions within the government and must be prepared to defend the best interest of the nation's farmers as well as that of a strong over-all economy. To do its job, it must carry out a variety of empirical studies, maintain an experienced and versatile executive staff, and coordinate suitably the manifold activities of the ministry.

The ministry must also see that the policies and operations of autonomous agencies serving agriculture make a coordinated whole. Farm credit institutions in particular must work in cooperation with the ministry. If there is also an agency to accelerate the settlement of new lands (agricultural colonization), this too must come within the purview of the ministry. The task of coordination is more complicated in some countries which have not one but two official farm credit institutions, one to serve the small farmers, frequently those on land held under restricted rights of transfer, and another to serve all other farmers. Mexico, for example, has a National Bank of Ejido Credit and an Agricultural and Livestock Bank. The former makes loans and gives technical assistance on a specialized basis to small *ejidatarios*. The latter makes loans to medium- and large-scale farmers. In these relations with credit institutions the importance of the ministry's role of coordination is clearly apparent. Loan operations must fit into agreed short- and long-range programs for agriculture, while the technical assistance work of the credit institutions must also be made to complement related efforts of the ministry.

Organizational and Administrative Problems

Though most Latin American governments have made significant contributions toward the acceleration of economic growth, especially since World War II, much remains to be done. Governmental organization and public administration particularly require attention. If the momentum of the governments' economic efforts is to be maintained, it is important that problems in these fields be tackled successfully within a relatively short span of time. It is important to keep in mind the fact that central government is the biggest business in operation in Latin America; and its growing participation in national economic life requires sound organization and efficient machinery of administration. While problems of public administration will be discussed more generally in Chapter 17, it should be noted here that if government is to achieve its economic objectives effectively, it must be neither top-heavy nor disjointed. Teamwork must be the rule rather than the exception, key positions must be filled by individuals of capacity and integrity, systems of adequate reward with job security must prevail, and government must not be regarded as a haven for unproductive workers.

AREAS FOR IMPROVEMENT. Strengthening the executive office of the president in its economic activities is a key requirement. Those countries which do not now have a national economic council or its equivalent in the president's office would do well to establish such an agency. The nations which have one must see that it is staffed only with devoted and competent men. Such a council is ideally located to make continuing analyses of the economy as a whole, as well as to study the diverse measures government is taking, the official action still required, and the extent to which the various ministries and agencies are pulling together. The information systematically gathered and analyzed by such a council, and its policy recommendations, are indispensable both to the executive and to the legislative branch of government.

Strengthening of the civil service is another requirement for success here. Able individuals must be attracted to serve in the economic agencies of government in greater numbers than has been the case to date in most countries. To accomplish this, local universities will have to offer more work in economics, statistics, and public administration. Government salaries will have to be adjusted and suitable guaranties of tenure provided so that individuals will find attractive full-time careers in specialized areas of government. Wholesale turnover of personnel, which occurs in some countries with each change of administration (or even, in individual ministries, with every change of minister), must be made a thing of the past if government is to play its enlarged role in economic development and is to achieve the results which are so generally desired.

The streamlining of ministries and agencies, giving officials in regional offices a larger role in policy formation, is necessary to assure that actions properly reflecting varying local conditions will also improve the effectiveness of government economic policies. Periodic review of key ministry operations by the national economic council, and the interchange of information and ideas between council and industry officials, are perhaps the best means of streamlining operations, upgrading superior personnel, and assuring that all relevant aspects of policy issues are duly considered.

Organizational and administrative measures to expand the scope and increase the quality of official statistical reporting of economic phenomena, especially basic census data, rank high among the requirements for improving the government's role in economic life. The present lack of authoritative data continually blocks effective, prompt action by ministries that are otherwise willing and able to push ahead more vigorously to spur economic growth. In many cases, wrong steps are taken or good actions carried out with undue delay, solely because the facts that are grist for the policy mill are not known or become available long after action has had to be taken.

Finally, the process of annual budget-making, and all the intragovernmental planning that it involves, must also be given the truly pivotal position befitting so important an operation. This means that the separate ministry and agency claims on limited government resources must be convincingly documented and their cases persuasively made before the executive incorporates them into the budget. It also means that the national economic council, or some other appropriate body, should check previous ministry commitments against the recent record, using the results both to point up weaknesses in earlier budgetary procedures and standards and to evaluate current budgetary requests.

Latin American governments thus have much to do before they can claim to be making their maximum contribution to national economic well-being. But the governments have made a good start in most cases. Improvements in organization and administration, coupled with the adoption of appropriate national economic policies, should hasten the day when Latin America will have the kind of economy which nature, modern technology, and the resourcefulness of the people can bring within her grasp.

Suggestions for Reading

John H. Adler, *Public Finance and Economic Development in Guatemala* (Stanford: Stanford University Press, 1952), is useful in highlighting the economic side of development problems. William Ebenstein, "Public Administration in Mexico," *Public Administration Review*, Spring, 1945, shows an important country's experience and thought on the subject. Herman Finer, *The Chilean Development Corporation* (Montreal: International Labor Office, 1947), covers the early history of the institution. Alexandre Kafka, "Brazil," in B. H. Beckwith (ed.), *Banking Systems* (New York: Columbia University Press, 1954), provides insights from the financial side. "Monetary Policies in Latin America," in the Federal Reserve Bank of New York *Monthly Review*, April, 1956, is a useful survey. The International Bank for Reconstruction and Development's *Development Corporations and Related Institutions in Selected Countries* (Washington, 1951) gives an excellent summary of development institutions. Virgil Salera, "Approaches to Economic Development," *Inter-American Economic Affairs*, Spring, 1955, and "On Anti-Venezuelan Economic Biases," *Inter-American Economic Affairs*, Summer, 1957, point up some economic-political issues. T. W. Schultz, *The Economic Test in Latin America*, Bulletin 35, New York School of Industrial and Labor Relations (Ithaca, 1956), contains three significant lectures on the subject, and United Nations, *Development Corporations and Development Financing in Latin America* (New York, United Nations, 1952), is a useful summary. United Nations, *Economic Survey of Latin America* (New York, 1957), provides an authoritative annual survey. Four U.S. Department of Commerce publications, *Investment in Colombia* (1953), *Investment in Mexico* (1955), *Investment in Paraguay* (1955), and *Investment in Venezuela* (1954), contain considerable basic economic information on the countries covered.

Chapter 16

Government and
the Social Order

Governments in Latin America are taking an increasing interest in the social problems of their fast-growing populations today. The problems now being faced are not really new, but they are more extensive than in the past. Yet certain factors, as pointed out in earlier chapters, intensify these problems as well as accentuate current governmental efforts to deal with them. The growth of political consciousness among the Latin American masses causes power groups to realize that their survival requires constructive social action. At the same time, better communication with other peoples of the world brings an increasing realization among Latin American adults that poverty, disease, and ignorance need not be a permanent heritage for their children.

Government programs to accelerate economic development, described in Chapter 15, have inevitably stimulated the desire of both the people and the governments of Latin America to see general economic progress translated into better living and working conditions for the people who are such an important part of this new economic development. This process and the growth of new industries have, of course, created new problems, while intensifying some already existing. As pointed out, political stability is essential to the planning and execution of sound economic programs. And, in their turn, effective social welfare programs are today becoming increasingly necessary to maintain political stability.

The efficiency of general public administration, to be discussed in Chapter 17, affects the efforts of Latin American governments to deal with social problems because of the close connections between the way governments plan and carry out public programs, the way they select and train the staff for carrying them out, and the effectiveness of these programs in meeting social needs. Technical assistance in social affairs, whether national or international, must also operate within the limitations of the administrative ability of each country. Moreover, such help must conform to the cultural patterns of national life and to the economic capacity of the country to sustain social programs.

Background Factors

DEPENDENCE ON GOVERNMENT. As we have seen in earlier chapters, relations between government and the people in Latin America differ historically from these relationships in the United States. The people of the United States have a background of pioneer effort and mutual help in the solution of community problems. This latter trait was also found among the indigenous populations of Latin America and has persisted in certain areas in spite of opposition by the European conquerors. But as the Indian peoples of Latin America have been integrated into the general population, they have largely lost this heritage of joint action. Thus, in most of Latin America today one finds great dependence on governmental action. This dependence finds its response in the increasing part which government plays in meeting the social needs of its people.

POLITICAL AND CONSTITUTIONAL BASIS. The centralization of government in Latin America, noted in previous chapters, is also manifest in governmental action in the social field. Municipalities have little independence of action and their efforts to solve social problems, while praiseworthy, generally do not form part of any coordinated plan and often are unrelated to other efforts, public or private, on a national scale. Since states, departments, or provinces are generally dominated by the central government, this chapter will be concerned chiefly with the actions of the central governments.

All Latin American countries have established ministries responsible for activities in the social fields. These ministries have such titles as Public Health and Welfare or Labor and Welfare. Many of the programs are in fact carried out by autonomous or semi-autonomous institutions which have ties to either the health or the labor ministry. The amount of control and coordination between the ministries and the autonomous institutions differs greatly from country to country, and in many situations lack of coordination prevails. The result sometimes is competition, dupli-

cation, or overlapping in the work of the ministry and the autonomous agencies supposedly under its wing.

The social welfare obligations of government are frequently
defined in detailed constitutional guaranties. These constitutional
provisions, however, are usually a goal which governments hope
to achieve rather than an accurate statement of existing government responsibilities for the welfare of its citizens.

RURAL MIGRATION TO CITIES. Some nations, like Argentina,
are highly urbanized, but in many of the countries, as in other
less-developed areas of the world, most of the people still live
in the rural areas. The percentage of rural population varies, of
course, from country to country, but a little over half of the
economically active population in the entire Latin American area
is employed in agriculture.

Governmental social programs are confined mainly to the cities,
however, and their lesser application to rural areas encourages
rural migration to the cities, where growing industries offer hope
of a better way of life for the worker and his family. Many times
this hope is an empty one, because government has not yet succeeded in its efforts to improve the living and working conditions of
the city inhabitants. Hence rural migration often complicates the
already serious urban social problems. It also has economic
effects, reducing food production and forcing governments to use
scarce foreign exchange to buy food for their growing urban
populations. Such temporary dislocations have accompanied economic development in other parts of the world, of course, and will
be resolved as the national economies are diversified and as improved production methods in agriculture permit greater output by
fewer workers.

POPULATION TRENDS. Population developments in Latin
America have a definite bearing on the social policies of the
governments. As pointed out in Chapter 2, modern medicine and
new public health methods have brought striking decreases in
infant mortality and increases in life expectancy in Latin America.
Since the reproduction rates of the population are based to a
great extent on long-standing customs, habits, and beliefs, and,
therefore, do not change so rapidly, the population of Latin
America is increasing at a rate which exceeds that of most of the
areas in the world.

Another aspect of this rapid increase is the general youthfulness
of the population. This may be considered a favorable factor
for nations trying to accomplish in decades what has taken centuries in other regions. But it means that the leaders of gov-

ernment in many countries are also relatively young. This fact is noteworthy, since youthful leaders have a disposition to accept change and progress and a natural impatience with long-range programs which are not likely to produce spectacular visible results in short periods. The short-lived existence of many political regimes also reinforces their tendency to concentrate on limited projects and programs expected to win immediate political acceptance among the population. Hence, such considerations prejudice some very solid, long-term efforts and complicate the task of those political leaders who are aware of the difficulties involved and the time required to achieve more basic improvements.

Many of these youthful officials have had training in other countries and are disposed to adapt the methods learned there to their countries' needs. They also understand and welcome the help of consultants in the various technical assistance programs in solving problems, in the social field as well as in other technical areas. Many of them have learned the importance of gaining the understanding and cooperation of groups affected by proposed changes and try conscientiously to gain their support for these new programs. North Americans are apt to take for granted this elementary approach to social welfare administration, but it is one most Latin American administrators have had to learn through painful experience. Any North American student of what government in Latin America is trying to accomplish in the way of social progress must take all these factors into account in order to see the problems in perspective.

ETHNIC PROBLEMS. The large Indian population of several Latin American countries (Mexico, Guatemala, Ecuador, Peru, and Bolivia) also affects what governments in those regions are doing to improve the social conditions. The fact that most of these millions of persons exist on a subsistence basis, making little contribution to the general social and economic life of the country, presents a challenge to governments already overburdened with other social problems. Yet this indigenous population needs the benefit of social programs even more than many others. Unfortunately, many special problems are involved in trying to include them as beneficiaries of governmental efforts. They have their own cultures and traditions going back thousands of years, their own languages which they jealously preserve as remnants of their past glory. With this group even more than with any others, it is necessary to understand why they are as they are and to realize that changes in their living standards and working conditions must be introduced gradually and be consistent with their mores.

Despite these difficulties, however, most governments in Latin America are trying to integrate these ethnic groups into the general population so that they may make their contribution to national cultural, economic, and social activity. Governments have learned that they cannot solve the problems of Indian life on a piecemeal basis, but must bring to this large and important body of the population the benefit of all the principal social services, in an integrated program including health, education, handicraft and agricultural improvements, and housing. Only in this way can they hope to accomplish the herculean task of overcoming the result of centuries of drift.

To summarize, several distinctive background factors influence what governments are doing to improve the social order in Latin America. These factors include the history of political institutions, the high degree of centralization in government, the predominance of a rural population, and the tendency of many rural people to migrate to urban areas because of the lure of industry and because measures to improve the lot of the peasants have been very limited in scope. Other factors include the rapid increase of population because of a decreased death rate, the resulting youthfulness of the population, and problems involved in the technical assistance programs conducted by international organizations and the United States. Finally, the fact that large indigenous groups live at the margin of national life complicates attempts to integrate all citizens into the social, cultural, political, and economic life of the countries.

The Scope of Government Activities

ROLE OF ORGANIZED LABOR. The influence of government is direct and substantial in the labor field. The important role of government has its origin in the guaranties to workers contained in constitutional provisions and legislation in almost every country. As noted in Chapter 7, both the workers and management look to government to establish and enforce the provisions of law relating to holidays, working hours (including the special regulations for women and children and night employment), the right to discharge workers with or without cause, and minimum wages. Inspectors from labor ministries visit commercial and industrial establishments to ascertain whether the physical working conditions meet legal requirements and whether the required accident prevention and industrial safety programs are in force.

The important role which organized labor plays in everyday politics has been discussed in Chapter 7, and Chapter 12 discusses the machinery for the settlement of labor disputes, including both labor courts and administrative tribunals similar to the National Labor Relations Board in the United States.

The close ties which bind organized labor to the government in power oblige governments to defend the rights of those on whom they depend for important political support; sometimes this results in very advanced legislation which cannot be enforced. In many countries, unions must be registered with the labor ministries in order to exist and defend the rights of their members. This constitutes a powerful weapon in the hands of the authorities for controlling the labor movement. Increasingly, however, unions are asserting their independence, realizing that ties to a particular government may hamper their actions and even their existence. And the fears of labor are real. Political changes in Latin America have wiped out entire labor movements. Even today we still find restrictive legislation in most countries regarding the right to organize workers employed in agriculture, the right to strike, and the right to organize nation-wide confederations or to establish ties with international labor bodies.

The effectiveness of labor unions is also hampered by the provision in some countries that their officials must be full-time employees in industry. Therefore, their union activities must take place after working hours and they are deprived of the opportunity to consult with government labor officials. However, such restrictions are likely to be short-lived in most nations. With increasing social and political maturity, there is bound to be a recognition of labor's place in society and its contribution to the economy, transcending the momentary fortunes of any particular political creed.

The mere passage of advanced legislation does not achieve in Latin America the mutual respect for each other's position that labor and management in other parts of the world have developed. The path to technical progress in industry can often be shortened and smoothed by borrowing from advanced countries, but borrowing is not so simple in the field of labor–management relations. Recognition of the importance of human relations in industry is a prerequisite and comes through slow and solid progress, mainly in the educational sphere. A worker education movement has begun, chiefly under government auspices but with the growing cooperation of labor unions. It is designed to help workers understand their rights and obligations, not only as workers and members of unions, but also as members of the communities in which they live. One result is that labor is now taking a more sympathetic interest in efforts to raise productivity. If this movement adheres to technical lines, avoiding politics, it gives promise of making a valuable contribution to industrial relations as well as to the effectiveness of government.

RECRUITMENT OF MANPOWER. Closely related to government activities in the labor field are its efforts to provide a supply of trained manpower for the growing commercial and industrial enterprises of Latin America. One of the usual functions of government in the manpower field is the operation of employment or placement offices to bring together men in need of employment and employers offering job opportunities. Increasing industrialization, coupled with chronic underemployment and "hidden" unemployment in many countries, provides a strong justification for the expansion of this government activity. However, only a few countries have well-developed employment services, though the number is constantly increasing.

Most countries find themselves with insufficient trained personnel in many fields of activity. Governments have attempted to remedy this deficiency by encouraging immigration, mainly from certain overpopulated countries of Europe. Some governments are attempting to attract immigrants by providing them with land and even with homes and farm implements. A few Latin American governments have established special offices in certain European countries to recruit immigrants suited to their special needs. Agreements including long-term loans and other facilities have been signed with European organizations interested in promoting emigration.

Emigration from Europe could have significant favorable consequences for many Latin American countries. Some of the most advanced countries, such as Argentina, Brazil, Chile, and Uruguay, are those which have had a large influx of European immigrants. On the other hand, these programs are often undertaken without the proper evaluation of manpower needs. Moreover, the policies of some governments in encouraging immigration still show numerous gaps, as in the lack of measures for the reception, placement, and assimilation of immigrants. Such measures are necessary to overcome the natural prejudices of native-born citizens who have little concern for the long-run value of immigration to their countries and resent the competition of more skilled foreign technicians who can command higher salaries than their own.

Coupled with a fear of a large influx of foreigners is the realization in some nations that the policies which attract European immigrants to settle new lands can be applied to improve the productivity of their present manpower. The same inducements of land, housing, and loans will encourage native citizens to colonize sparsely settled regions or to improve agricultural production on large, poorly cultivated landholdings.

VOCATIONAL TRAINING. Vocational or technical training constitutes another important program designed to increase the supply of trained manpower for economic development. Through their labor and education ministries, governments are opening schools, both part-time and full-time, to train workers in the new skills needed by industry. Some examples which can be cited are the programs of Senai in Brazil, the Universidad Tecnológica in Argentina, the Chilean State Technical University, and the technological schools in Mexico.

Industry itself is taking an increasing interest in technical training, looking upon the matter, not as an obligation, but rather an opportunity to obtain trained workers. An industrialist investing in costly foreign equipment realizes he must train people in its use. In fact, contracts for the purchase of equipment usually include a clause requiring the manufacturer to train local personnel in its use and maintenance. Such training increases in importance as the educational base broadens and as management realizes that the traditional education provided when a small percentage of the children attended school no longer meets the needs of larger numbers of children preparing to earn a living with their hands.

The development of vocational education in Latin America is hindered by the traditional social prejudice against those who earn their livelihood through manual labor. This important but intangible obstacle on the road to economic progress in Latin America will disappear only with time. It is an example of how dominant economic patterns and the attitudes of the economic and social elite promote or retard progress. It also shows how important it is to keep in mind the impact of custom when planning development programs, even though it may be desirable to change the customs gradually.

PROBLEM OF INDIAN WORKERS. The most effective use of manpower in Latin America is also impeded by a legacy of policies affecting the Indian populations. Many governments are now dealing with the problem, establishing special schools and programs to develop the productive capacity of their indigenous groups. Within the framework of the Organization of American States, the governments have created the Inter-American Indian Institute, with headquarters in Mexico City, as an official center for studies of indigenous populations. The United Nations and its specialized organizations are working with the governments of Bolivia, Ecuador, and Peru to raise the standard of living of their Indian populations and integrate them into their economies.

Significant results may be expected, since native communities frequently show great interest in schools and need but little encouragement to develop their natural artistry and native skills in small handicraft industries, to take one example. Problems of the Indian groups and their exceptional situation arise in connection with almost all the official programs mentioned elsewhere in this chapter. But the chronic underutilization of the Indian population in the total economy is the most serious aspect of all these problems. At the same time, there is an awakening realization of the value of maintaining many of the indigenous cultures and customs because of their historic value and their consequent importance in developing a feeling of national pride to unite all sectors of the national population. Hence, the real problem of the Indian is how to progress without sacrificing important cultural values and traditions.

The Negro population of such countries as Brazil and Cuba is considerable, and Haiti is an all-Negro republic; but the Negroes, unlike the Indians, are not separated culturally from the rest of the country and do not represent a problem in the labor force.

The Basic Programs

HEALTH SERVICES. Governments in Latin America provide a wide range of health services to their people. The range of services is what might normally be expected. But because of political centralization and the relative lack of effective units of government at local levels, the source of these services is often much different from that to which the student in the United States is accustomed. Moreover, public health in many Latin American countries has received great impetus from the cooperative programs in the health field carried out jointly, through the Institute of Inter-American Affairs, by the United States and the national ministry of health in cooperating countries.

Thus, international technical assistance programs have aided the construction and operation of health centers for children and expectant mothers. The United Nations International Children's Fund (UNICEF) program has stimulated such health programs by providing medical equipment and powdered milk. These child health centers are a good example of how international aid and good will can catalyze latent local interest, for many of them have come into existence not alone by central government action, but aided also by local donations of land, buildings, materials, and money.

Because of the relatively low average income in many of the Latin American countries, and especially the low income of the small but emerging middle class, governments in Latin America participate to a great extent in planning and carrying out direct medical services for the people. Clinics and hospitals are built and operated by government. Attendant physicians receive monthly salaries based on the number of hours they work in these official assignments. Large portions of the population use these government services which they have come to regard as an essential public function. In many countries, however, contributory social insurance systems covering the risks of illness and maternity are taking over part of the task. Such systems provide a valuable means of improving the level of medical services as wage-earners and their families become aware of and demand better health care than can be expected from the free government clinics.

In many cases governments have maintained the appearance of earlier philanthropic organizations, *instituciones de beneficencia,* by simply taking over the support of their clinics and hospitals. The Catholic Church has played and continues to play an important role in the provision of much-needed medical care to the general population, nearly all of which is Catholic. Numerous medical institutions owe their origins to the Church, and many of the important technical and general nursing and maintenance services in them are performed by members of the religious orders.

In contrast with the situation a few decades ago, most Latin American governments today take an active interest in promoting public health. They are doing much to provide modern water, drainage, and sewage-disposal systems. In many places, however, unsatisfactory conditions still exist. The World Health Organization and the Pan American Sanitary Organization have contributed technicians to help in campaigns against such debilitating diseases as malaria, yaws, hookworm, and sleeping sickness. Measures now being taken by the governments include nutrition education to improve the diet of the people, a school lunch program, and the establishment of clinics concentrating on this aspect of preventive medicine.

Industrial hygiene and integrated rehabilitation services are also developing. These, like the other parts of a complete health program, have special importance for economic development. The rapid increase in industrial plants has highlighted the existence of unsafe and unhealthy working conditions. Industrial growth and the consequent need for trained, healthy workers have impressed on management as never before the economic, as well as human, loss represented by idle, sick, or injured workers whose services need not be lost permanently. As a result, health ministries increasingly include industrial hygiene services in their activities. Beginnings are also being made in the establishment of physical and vocational rehabilitation centers in some countries.

EDUCATION. Latin American governments are devoting an increasing proportion of their budgets to education. Mexico set the example in the early days of her Revolution by insisting that the national educational budget exceed military expenditures. Some idea of the percentage of national budgets being devoted to education is seen from the figures in Table XIX.

TABLE XIX. NATIONAL EXPENDITURES ON EDUCATION, 1954

Country	Per Cent Spent for Education*
Argentina	16
Brazil	8
Chile	22
Colombia	16
Costa Rica	34
Ecuador	16
El Salvador	22
Guatemala	26
Honduras	16
Nicaragua	18
Venezuela	11

SOURCE: United Nations, *Economic Survey of Latin America, 1955* (New York, 1956).
* Some capital expenditures included.

This growing emphasis on education springs, of course, from the realization that national development and education must proceed hand in hand, and that rapid development cannot be expected if a high rate of illiteracy prevails.

Similarly, school enrollment has been steadily increasing, rising in Venezuela from 27.8 per cent in 1936 to 51.3 per cent in 1950.[1] In the case of Chile, the percentage of children of school age registered has increased from 21.4 per cent in 1901 to 42.3 per cent in

[1] These figures are from a paper presented by the Central Directing Council of the Venezuelan School Teachers Federation to the XVI National Teachers Convention, San Felipe, Venezuela, August 1955.

1950.[2] Colombia had 64.5 students registered for each thousand inhabitants in 1935 and 90.9 per thousand in 1954.[3]

Not only has there been an expansion of programs devoted to children of school age, but adult education programs are being developed in an effort to remedy educational deficiencies among older people. Education is considered a function of the government in all countries, even though much of the instruction continues to be given in religious schools. In contrast to the United States, where school supervision is local, national governments supervise education; and this supervision over curricula and related matters is both extensive and detailed.

Despite heroic efforts, school attendance is still low in many countries, especially in rural areas where children are needed to help the family eke out an existence. Because of the rapid increase of the school-age population there is a shortage of teachers and schools in most countries. Governments tend to emphasize technical or vocational education, as already mentioned, and sponsor campaigns to promote literacy and basic education. These programs attempt to raise the educational level of adults by teaching them to read and write and then helping them maintain their newly won ability by providing simple reading material designed to be useful in their daily life. In brief, the general tendency is to make education the possession of all rather than of a few privileged persons as in the past; hence, increased emphasis is given to the relation between education and life rather than to more traditional educational content.

There is a gradual tendency to de-emphasize the professional training in law and medicine which was previously the goal of those able to continue their education. New normal schools, schools of nursing, schools of social work, and others of this type are coming into existence as Latin American society accepts these other fields as proper occupations for the growing middle class.

Government control of education extends even to the university level, though many of the universities traditionally enjoy autonomy despite their economic dependence on the government budget. A few privately supported universities are making their appearance in Latin America, such as the Instituto Tecnológico

[2] "La educación primaria y la economía en Chile," Document FCE/9, prepared for the Unesco Regional Conference on Free and Compulsory Education in Latin America, Lima, Peru (April 23–May 5, 1956), p. 53.

[3] "Informe nacional sobre la educación obligatoria sometido por la Comisión Nacional de la Unesco en Colombia," Document FCE/8, prepared for the UNESCO Regional Conference on Free and Compulsory Education in Latin America, Lima, Peru (April 23–May 5, 1956), p. 8.

de Monterrey, Mexico, and the new University of the Andes in Colombia. Catholic universities have existed for a number of years in some countries. The distinguished Colombian statesman and former Secretary General of the Organization of American States, Alberto Lleras Camargo, believes that the private university represents one of the real hopes for the future of Latin America.

Many governments in Latin America have received help from outside sources for the development of educational programs. The United Nations Educational, Scientific, and Cultural Organization (UNESCO) has sent foreign experts to help ministries of education organize and carry out their programs. The technical cooperation program of the Organization of American States has established a center in Venezuela to train teachers in rural normal schools to meet the great need for teachers in rural education.

Summer courses are now being used to broaden the training of the teachers and to make up for deficiencies in their preparation. American educational consultants are employed, and scholarships furnished by the United States technical assistance program provide advanced training for teachers. Financial help has also been received for new school buildings and equipment.

The scope of official educational activities extends to programs designed to further popular appreciation of the arts, music, the theater, and literature. It is no longer rare to see free open-air concerts sponsored by ministries of education so that all citizens may come to know and appreciate good music. Young painters and sculptors are given an opportunity to obtain training, and their works are shown at government-sponsored exhibitions. Museums are being developed and popularized. Some Latin American governments subsidize theater and dance companies to assure performances at moderate prices within reach of their citizens. Popular, low-cost editions of literary works are published under government subsidy or sponsorship. Such activities by government may seem strange to the North American who takes for granted the ready availability of these cultural media and his ability to take advantage of them. But in those countries where public-spirited citizens and organizations have not made a special effort to bring the benefits of general culture to their fellows, government has felt an obligation to step in and meet the need.

WELFARE AND SOCIAL SERVICES. In its welfare programs and social services government touches upon the daily lives of its citizens. In the past, private and church-sponsored organizations have led the way in philanthropy, and in many countries these organizations continue to operate. But since Latin American needs in this realm are overwhelming, governments have increasingly taken over the burden of financing. Thus, in recent years, new welfare agencies have usually been organized and managed by ministries of welfare.

The needs are so great, however, and the resources and personnel, both private and official, so limited, that services lag far behind the needs. However, there is growing recognition that the function of government should be to set standards for the services and the staffing of agencies and secure adherence to these standards by giving supervision and technical advice to the agencies providing the welfare services, whether their funds come from public or private sources or a combination of these. The alternative is to risk becoming involved in the details of day-to-day operation of programs which may cause governments to neglect the more important and far-reaching functions of planning, coordination, and evaluation on an over-all basis.

A sound welfare policy encourages the development of individual ability to cope with problems, strengthening the family unit and the parental sense of responsibility for the care and support of children. Seventy schools of social work under government and church auspicies are training social workers imbued with these principles. But since the profession of social work is still in its infancy in many countries, needs for social services still outstrip the supply of trained workers. It is felt that social work should be directed to deal with the problems of groups and communities as well as with individual problems, and that social workers should continue to be included in the teams of doctors, nurses, teachers, and other specialists sent into communities to improve the living standards.

The problem of dependent children is especially acute. Such dependency occurs frequently in broken families, since the mother often must enter the labor force to earn a living. Day-care nurseries operated by governmental and private organizations frequently care for the children of such mothers, but often children must be placed permanently in institutions. It is seldom possible to give children foster homes as is so often done in the United States. Although placing children in institutions is not the most desirable solution to the problem of dependency, it is common in Latin America and probably will continue to be so until the general economic situation of the population improves. This is another example of the close interrelation between economic and social problems.

One of the distinctive characteristics of welfare programs in Latin America is the almost complete absence of public assistance programs. In many countries, families economically dependent because of old age, blindness, or other disabilities are usually given sums of money periodically to enable them to purchase necessities. Such a practice is based on the assumption that families either have the ability to spend these funds or should be trained to do so. Extensive programs of this kind are still not possible in the majority of Latin American countries because of the low level of general education and the limited government funds available for welfare purposes. Hence, assistance in kind and work opportunities are used to help needy families. As effective employment services are established, another approach to the problems of economic dependency becomes available. But such employment services are not yet a reality in most countries.

Another growing welfare activity in Latin America is that of providing recreational opportunities for the general population. This activity springs from a realization that urban living conditions make necessary parks where families can enjoy healthy outdoor recreation. Throughout Latin America parks and recreational areas for family weekends and holidays are multiplying. And governments in Latin America also promote athletic competition; almost all countries have magnificent stadiums in which to hold athletic contests, both national and international.

HOUSING AND PLANNING. One of the most serious problems in most of the countries is the need for better housing, both urban and rural, and more community planning. Low incomes and rapid population growth in Latin America have contributed to the increased magnitude of the job to be done. Here again government efforts are the only significant ones. The usual instrument used is the autonomous housing and planning agency, financed by public funds or by loans from public social insurance institutions. Some countries have left this function to the social insurance agencies, since agencies' funds are involved. But the general tendency is away from this practice and toward the use of special housing authorities. Social insurance officials are realizing that subsidized housing may be necessary because the return they must get on their money may not be compatible with the low economic status of those most urgently in need of improved housing.

Latin American governments struggling to remain in power have learned that substantial investment in housing is not only socially wise and economically productive, but politically advisable as well. Better housing means healthier workers. Moreover, workers properly housed have a greater incentive to produce.

They have acquired a good reason for changing their patterns of consumption and saving and no longer have the feeling of hopelessness that characterizes the man who sees no possibility of acquiring decent housing for his family. Lowering the cost of housing will be achieved mainly by improving construction methods. Hence, the Organization of American States sponsors a special center to study means of utilizing local materials in home construction and other methods of lowering building costs. Another approach to this problem has been to encourage individuals to construct their own houses on a self-help basis, with the aid of others, in their spare time or during periods of seasonal unemployment. In such cases, governments provide technical advice, building plans, and help in obtaining necessary materials at reasonable cost.

Many of the cities of Latin America were founded several centuries ago to serve essentially agrarian societies. Today, when they must accommodate an ever-growing population moving in from the rural areas, they face serious problems of community planning. These include the moving of modern traffic through old, picturesque, but narrow streets, and providing such essentials as water, sewage disposal, lighting, garbage removal, and police and fire protection. These problems are further complicated by the expansion of cities to suburban areas. Many large cities have adopted master plans to regulate and plan their growth, and an increasing number of planning agencies reflects government efforts to deal with various aspects of civic growth.

SOCIAL INSURANCE. Although it is not generally known, several Latin American nations established social insurance prior to its adoption in the United States. All the Latin American countries except Honduras had social insurance programs by 1957. Most of these programs are administered through autonomous institutions managed by boards representing employers, workers, and government, a practice growing out of a general distrust of the administrative and fiscal practices of the regular government agencies. Unfortunately, however, the autonomous organizations have not provided any magical solution to the problem. Government representation is based on the premise that it should have a voice in administration commensurate with its share of the cost. But in actual operation, governments, by one means or another, exercise a controlling voice in the management, even though they have frequently failed to meet their legal financial obligations in support of the programs.

Latin American social insurance emphasizes protection against the costs of illness and maternity, in contrast to programs in the United States where old-age, survivors, and unemployment insurance features predominate. This difference is due to the extremely serious health needs in Latin America and the absence of adequate services to meet these needs through publicly supported programs. Social insurance coverage is usually limited to commercial and industrial workers in the principal urban areas, partly because of administrative difficulties in providing medical services, as well as cash benefits, in isolated rural areas, and partly because of rural social and economic conditions which have been noted in various connections earlier in this book.

Basic social insurance legislation was usually patterned on the systems of European countries which had more highly developed economies and administrative systems. Some of the most serious Latin American problems arise from the fact that their economic and administrative abilities have not yet developed sufficiently.

Despite the fact that most of the Latin American systems of social insurance have existed for some decades, they still apply only to limited areas and to restricted groups of the population. Very few of the systems, for example, have proceeded according to any orderly plan in providing protection for the majority of wage-earners against the risks of old age, disability, death, illness, and unemployment. In many countries, maternity benefits in the form of cash and medical services are provided to working women; in a few countries medical services only are given to the wives of wage-earners. Other groups still lacking protection, such as the numerous domestics, farm workers, and the self-employed, have scarcely been considered. Costs of administration mount rapidly and contributions take an increasing percentage of pay-rolls, while production in the industries affected does not usually increase enough to make up for the increases in cost.

Social insurance has great economic importance in Latin America because the reserves of many of the systems constitute the greatest source of national savings. They are naturally looked upon by politicians as sources for financing desirable, but relatively unproductive, public projects. They can also be used to finance sound programs of economic development which, in turn, will provide increased employment opportunities in new industries. Sound investment of the reserves, however, requires better planning and coordination at the highest governmental levels than has been the rule to date.

Trends and Problems

This chapter has dealt with the development of government activity in much-needed social programs. We have seen what government is trying to do, how policies are applied, and the kinds of agencies used by governments to carry out these policies. All of the nations show a sincere desire to provide better living and working conditions for their people. They have received substantial assistance in their efforts in this direction from international organizations and from the bilateral technical assistance programs of the United States.

There has been an increasing recognition by governments of the existence of social problems and the need to do something about them. Governments realize that social programs are an indispensable part of the general development of a country and can definitely contribute to the economy. More funds are being devoted to these programs, and these are coming mainly from the central government, which has correspondingly increased its control over the activities to which it contributes.

Social needs are deep-seated and not easily remedied, but governments have generally responded with all the resources at their disposal. Where programs are deficient, the explanation often lies in fundamental economic and administrative difficulties. What the various governments are doing to solve these latter problems is discussed in Chapters 15 and 17. Social, economic, and administrative development are inextricably linked together, and progress in one area depends upon advancement in the others.

Suggestions for Reading

The reports prepared by the International Bank for Reconstruction and Development before granting loans are a valuable source of information on the growing role of government in the social order, as well as on the basic relationship between social programs and the economy. See *The Economic Development of Guatemala* (Washington: The International Bank, 1951), *Report on Cuba* (Washington: The International Bank, 1951), and *The Economic Development of Nicaragua* (Baltimore: Johns Hopkins University Press, 1953).

The United Nations has prepared similar studies. See, especially, its *Report of the UN Mission of Technical Assistance to Bolivia* (New York, 1951), a report considered an outstanding example of its kind. The United Nations, *Preliminary Report on the World's Social Situation* (New York, 1952), discusses population and population trends, health conditions, housing, education, conditions of work and employment, and special circumstances affecting standards of living.

The Organization of American States has prepared publications on some of the social problems of Latin America. See, especially, *Problems of Housing of Social Interest* (Washington: Pan American Union, 1954), and *Development of the Cooperative Movement in America* (Washington: Pan American Union, 1954). Asher N. Christensen (ed.), *The Evolution of Latin American Government* (New York: Henry Holt & Co., 1951), contains several useful selections for reading on this subject.

Chapter 17

Public Administration
and Civil Service

Previous chapters in this volume have touched upon organization and administrative problems in various fields of government activity. This chapter will discuss some general characteristics of Latin American administrative systems and the civil services that staff them. Clerks, files, procedures, and paper clips are not in themselves particularly exciting subjects, and public administration in terms of minutiae has little interest for the layman or the general student of government. On the other hand, if one considers the whole complex of laws, regulations, organizations, people, and workways that make up an administrative system, or bureaucracy, the subject has rich significance for an understanding of political process.[1] In this chapter we will discuss public administration in the latter, broad sense, relating it to the past, present, and future of government in Latin America.

The Administrative Inheritance

The administrative systems of the Latin American republics reflect their cultural heritage and are imbued with their political experience. Thus it is important to begin with a look at some of the historical roots and traditional characteristics of public administration in the region.

[1] Used in one sense, "bureaucracy" has negative connotations of red tape, inefficiency, and uncivil civil servants. However, in the usage of most social scientists, bureaucracy refers to any administrative system or body of government officials and employees, and a "bureaucrat" is an individual official or employee. No value judgments are implied. The latter usage is followed in this chapter.

Present-day Latin American administrative systems combine several aspects of Old and New World institutional development. In large part, of course, they are derived directly from Latin American constitutions. After achieving independence, the new nations broke with the monarchical past and adopted republican constitutions providing for the separation of powers. Because of this decision, Latin America has executive branches theoretically coordinate with the legislative and judicial powers, although the executive has usually been dominant. At any rate, the lines of administrative authority run only to a chief executive, not to a congress or parliament. Within the separation of powers framework, Latin America developed administrative systems that partly reflect the Hispanic and colonial heritage and are in part patterned after the orderly administrative structures installed in France as Napoleonic reforms and later much admired and spread around the world in the nineteenth century. The basic systems have, of course, been continuously modified by local experience and by further influence from Europe and the United States.

There have been occasional Latin American experiments with federalism. Argentina, Brazil, Mexico, and Venezuela are well-committed to this system, but the other countries have retained the unitary concept, with all constitutional powers residing in the central government. The four federal nations are divided into states which, particularly in Brazil, have substantial powers and functions of their own; many of the things said in this chapter about national administration would apply to these units as well. The other sixteen republics are divided into departments or provinces which, despite many historic associations and boundaries, are essentially only administrative and election districts of the central governments. Provinces are divided and sub-divided through several layers of symmetrical hierarchy down to the smallest municipalities and rural districts.[2] While there may be elected assemblies or councils at various levels, their powers are tightly circumscribed; power flows down in the hierarchy, not up. Provincial governors ordinarily are appointed by the president and, like the French prefects, serve as representatives of national authority and coordinators of the provincial agents of the central government. The capstone of each system is a national ministry of interior, or *gobernación*, which has great authority over all activities outside

[2] For example, Paraguay is divided into sixteen departments, governed by delegates appointed by the president. The departments are divided into municipalities and rural districts called *partidos;* the latter are in turn divided into village-sized units called *compañías*. George Pendle, *Paraguay: A Riverside Nation* (London: Royal Institute of International Affairs, 1954), pp. 51–52.

the capital, including usually such strategic elements of control as local finance and the police.

The Administrative Hierarchy

The national administrative systems of Latin America are remarkably similar in basic structure. Each, of course, has its unique characteristics, but all retain concepts and terminology from the Napoleonic era. The principal administrative units are from eight to twelve ministries, whose heads are appointed by the president and collectively make up a cabinet or council of ministers. Cabinets play various roles, according to national traditions and political circumstances, but as a general rule they are not strong institutions, either politically or administratively. In spite of the common requirement that presidential decrees and certain other classes of papers be signed by the whole cabinet, there is very little collective responsibility in the sense that it exists in the British government, for example. As in the United States, Latin American presidents dominate their cabinets and deal directly with individual members on most matters within their respective ministries; the cabinet itself is a convenient but not mandatory device for advice and coordination.[3]

Ministries are divided and subdivided in hierarchical fashion. Beneath the minister there may be a vice-minister who acts as a general deputy. At the next level down, corresponding to the bureaus in the United States scheme, there are a handful of general directorates, headed by director-generals. Next come the directorates (*direcciones*), each with its own director. Directorates are divided into *oficinas,* or *servicios,* or *administraciones,* and these further subdivided into *secciones.* Each subordinate unit has its own *director* or *jefe.* On the lower levels the terminology varies a good deal from country to country, and even from ministry to ministry within a given country.

Titles and functions are assigned to ministries in a quite common pattern. The leading ministries are likely to be government, foreign affairs, defense, and finance. The importance of *gobernación* as the controller of the structure of provincial and local government

[3] Uruguay, with its collegiate-type chief executive, the National Council of Government, is of course the chief exception. In theory, the distinction is clear between the duties of the members of the council, who are collectively responsible for the whole executive branch, and the duties of the ministers, who are chief administrators of their respective agencies and report individually to the whole council. It will be interesting to see whether collective responsibility of the council can be maintained against a probably inevitable tendency for its members to divide up the ministries among themselves for purposes of general supervision.

has already been mentioned. The eminence of foreign affairs has sometimes rested more upon tradition than upon real power, but the increasing complexity of international relations in recent years has given the foreign offices new importance. The minister of defense is usually chosen for his ability to control or to placate the ultimate sources of power; if he is successful in either method, the status of his ministry is enhanced and he becomes a likely presidential successor. When political situations are reasonably stable, the minister of finance is a powerful figure. His duties normally include collection of customs and taxes, custody of public funds, management of the public debt, and (depending upon the government's relation to the central bank) some degree of responsibility for the monetary system. The ministry of finance (*hacienda*) also usually has the budget and other control functions which give it a certain supremacy in administrative matters. In this respect it resembles the French Ministry of Finance or the British Treasury more than the Treasury Department of the United States. Other traditional government functions are parcelled out among ministries of justice, education, culture, labor, economy (commerce and economic development), welfare, agriculture, public works, and so forth.

INDEPENDENT AGENCIES. In virtually all Latin American countries, the original simple structure of ministries has, in the course of time, been surrounded—sometimes almost covered over—by an intricate embroidery of "independent" administrative agencies. A few of the independent agencies, such as the national universities, or the constitutionally established tribunals of accounts, are as old as the ministries themselves. Most of them, however, have grown up in more recent times, with the advent of the ambitious economic and social programs described in previous chapters. The operation of lending agencies, public utilities, nationalized industries, social insurance, and a host of other enterprises seems to call for more dynamic administration than is likely to be found within the tradition-bound ministries. In the hope of achieving flexibility and taking these functions out of politics, they are set up as independent agencies, with varying amounts of insulation from day-to-day presidential or ministerial control. This autonomy sometimes does result in administration of a quality noticeably above the national average, but not invariably so. In any cases, continuous proliferation of agencies creates a difficult problem of coordinating the autonomous enterprises with the ministries and with each other.[4]

[4] A recent tabulation of the *principal* executive agencies in Uruguay showed the following: 9 ministries; 13 decentralized services (including pension agencies, the national broadcasting service, postal savings, low-cost housing, and sanitary works);

The autonomy of these agencies is, of course, only relative. Their heads are normally chosen by the president, sometimes serving completely at his pleasure. In other cases, particularly in the agencies headed by boards rather than single executives, the heads serve for specific terms, sometimes longer than the presidential term, and are not easily removed. Regardless of their independence, however, autonomous agencies do not often defy a president. Occasionally, independent agencies are loosely attached to particular ministries for reporting purposes, or have ministers serving *ex officio* on their boards of directors.

CENTRAL STAFF AGENCIES. Despite the coordination problems created by the centrifugal tendencies just discussed, Latin American governments have been slow to evolve central staff, service, or coordinating agencies above the ministerial level. In view of the power of most Latin American presidents, it would seem natural for them to push the development of executive offices, cabinet secretariats, central budget and personnel offices, and other institutional devices that normally are found useful for achieving policy and managerial control. Indeed, certain beginnings along this line have been made. Since 1938 Brazil has had a Departamento Administrativo do Servico Público (DASP), a presidential agency with central budget, personnel, and other administrative control functions. Argentina has a Secretariat of Technical Affairs, and Venezuela an Office of Special Studies, both attached to the presidency. And Mexico's Secretaría de Bienes Nacionales y Inspección Administrativa has some analogous functions.

In the years since World War II, other presidential-level agencies, particularly in the field of economic policy coordination, have appeared. The prospects are for further growth of this administrative apparatus, which indirectly strengthens the political aspects of the presidency. Nevertheless, faulty coordination as a result of scattering related functions among many agencies, without providing adequate integrating machinery at the top, is still a major problem. Ministries jealously guard their prerogatives, and most presidents seem to prefer to deal directly with ministers on both major and minor matters rather than to institutionalize power at the executive office level. The characteristic coordinating device is still the com-

---

1 autonomous service without defined relationship (the national meat-packing plant); 1 provisional service (a child welfare agency); 10 autonomous entities or government corporations (banks, public utilities, the national university, and several miscellaneous enterprises); 3 independent constitutional organizations (an electoral court, the tribunal of accounts, and a court of administrative claims). John O. Hall, *Public Administration in Uruguay* (Montevideo: U. S. Institute of Inter-American Affairs, 1954), pp. 79–81.

mittee of ministers, with attendant opportunities for delay and the obscuring of responsibility.

The Civil Service

It may be admitted at the outset that Latin American civil services in the past have not been notable for stability, efficiency, incorruptibility, and other bureaucratic virtues. This judgment is subject, of course, to the usual reservations about generalizations concerning twenty countries and is made with full recognition that some agencies in some countries are effective operations by any standards. If public administration in Latin America could be compared with state government administration in some parts of the United States—a more appropriate yardstick than the federal government—the differences might not be great. Also, important changes are presently taking place in Latin America; these will be discussed later in this chapter. At this point, however, evaluation is less important than some understanding of the social and political forces that have shaped the civil services of Latin America.

WEAKNESSES IN THE BUREAUCRACY. Reflecting the weakness of the middle class in most Latin American countries, the bureaucracies tend to be rather tightly stratified along traditional class lines and to be deficient in the scientific, technical, and middle management skills. Heavy responsibility for leadership of the great mass of manual and lower clerical workers falls upon the relatively small group who have had access to higher education—education in a system which stresses study of the humanities and the practice of such traditional professions as law and medicine more than such modern vocation-oriented fields as science, engineering, and business management. Those with the necessary qualifications, frequently including the right political and family connections, enter the public service at or near the top; there are only limited opportunities for advancement for all others. The elite group, which receives great deference, is often hard-working, sophisticated, and politically skillful. Unfortunately it is also likely to be politically transient and limited in technical skill.

The most important factor in determining the nature of Latin American civil services is, of course, the heritage of political instability. In an environment where presidents are frequently replaced by violence or other nonconstitutional means, where party responsibility is a little-known concept, and where ministerial changes are frequent, a stable bureaucracy is unlikely to develop. In most countries the quality of administration is directly related to the recent political history. The usual situation is one in which each politician and administrator must use the organization at his disposal to protect and advance his personal cause. The primary values respected in such a situation are loyalty and responsiveness to the chief of the moment. With every change of leadership there is likely to be a major turnover and shuffling of personnel, all up and down the hierarchy. Some individuals may survive through political adroitness or the ability to make themselves absolutely indispensable, but the development of a stable corps of responsible administrators, whose loyalties transcend the government of the day and are attached to some broader concept of the state and the public interest, is very difficult.

CIVIL SERVICE REFORM. Latin America has always had its share of civil service reformers, but progress toward merit systems in the sense that they are known in the United States and in Europe is slow. One of the obstacles here is a tradition of decentralized personnel management, with each ministry responsible for hiring its own staff and establishing its own rates of pay and conditions of work. The actual facts sometimes do not fit the theory, since many presidents keep informal but effective control of appointments and promotions. But because of the reluctance of presidents to loosen the controls and the natural hostility of ministers to any further diminution of their authority, reformers have found it difficult to introduce the bipartisan or politically neutral civil service commissions which have been the spearheads of reform in the United States. Central personnel agencies of any kind are fairly recent innovations, and where they exist, as in Brazil and Costa Rica, they are closely tied to the presidency.

Some civil service reforms have had paradoxical results. A typical approach in the past has been to shield government employees by laws prohibiting arbitrary dismissals and establishing elaborate procedural safeguards for the individual. Some of these laws have been found completely unenforceable. Others have had the effect of conferring upon civil servants such substantial legal rights in their jobs that it is difficult to get rid of anybody for any reason. On the whole, these laws are more often observed in the letter than in the spirit. Protections against dismissal are not complemented with effective schemes of entrance and promotion by examination or other demonstration of merit. Patronage still dominates. Thus there are more ways into a bureaucracy than out of it. When a regime changes, if old employees cannot be fired, they are simply moved over to make room for more. Ministries become overstaffed, undisciplined, and difficult to organize along rational lines.

At this point, some governments find themselves in dilemmas

from which they cannot escape. Everyone agrees that they are greatly overstaffed, but legal obstacles, plus the human and economic consequences of turning thousands of ex-bureaucrats into an economy in which other employment opportunities are limited, prevent effective action. Since the payroll is a major drain on government financial resources, salaries are low, usually lagging behind a rising cost of living. The best employees, who can find other jobs, drift away. Those who remain are increasingly susceptible to corruption of various kinds, ranging from major graft at upper levels to the modest tip, or *mordida,* often required of the citizen if his papers are not to be lost sight of at lower levels. Civil servants often have to supplement their government salaries by taking on outside jobs. In governments where this has gone on for some time, it is generally understood that most employees do not work more than a half day; those with political pull appear only on pay day. Even conscientious ministers, who would like to install some sort of merit system, find no way of breaking the cycle. With salaries low and career prospects poor, the best people cannot be attracted to government service; to raise salaries and extend real job security would, in the short run at least, cost more than the government could afford and further solidify the vested interests of the unworthy. This unfortunate condition probably afflicts, to a greater or lesser degree, over half of the Latin American civil services.[5]

The Administrative Environment

To complete this picture, three additional characteristics of the traditional Latin American administrative environment, all closely related to the cultural environment, should be mentioned.

CENTRALIZATION. There has been a persistent tendency to centralization of power, within any given administrative agency and within any administrative system as a whole. Reluctance to delegate authority is probably a universal characteristic of administrators, but the tendency is accentuated in Latin America. There are many reasons. One is the unitary system of government which gives central ministries, particularly ministries of interior, a right and, in a sense, a duty to keep a close check on affairs throughout the country. In some countries it is impossible to build a bridge, hire a school teacher, or grant an innocuous permit in the remotest province without sending the necessary papers to the capital for approval.

[5] Public Administration Clearing House, *Public Administration in Latin America* (Washington: Pan American Union, 1955), pp. 36–39.

The political environment in Latin America also contributes to centralism. Presidents and ministers, insecure in office and sometimes governing by force, tend to keep as much decision-making authority in their own hands as possible. In an unsettled political atmosphere, lower officials are often uncertain what the policy is and are reluctant to take the responsibility of making important decisions; everything is referred upward. Social class patterns and the habits of deference which are still strong in some countries tend to encourage lower officials to seek specific permission before acting. Shortage of personnel with education and training adequate to the needs of modern government also has centralizing effects. Higher officials who are well aware of the costs of delay and of stifling initiative are reluctant to delegate authority to subordinates of uncertain quality. The men at the upper levels of Latin American government often work incredibly hard to handle the flood of papers and the visitors who will not be satisfied until the minister himself hears their cases, but the channels of decision-making become clogged nevertheless, and red tape and delay are endemic.

LEGALISM. Another important characteristic of Latin American public administration is a tendency to legalism. Statutes and decrees specify administrative purposes, organization, and procedures in fine detail. There is great emphasis in day-to-day administration upon formal compliance with standards of correct procedure. Administrative law—the rights and obligations of public officials and citizens in their dealings with each other—is a highly developed subject, whose study has traditionally been considered the proper training for the future official. By and large, administrative lawyers still dominate the civil services and set the tone of most studies of the administrative process. It has sometimes seemed to outside observers that Latin American administrators were bogged down in red tape and preoccupied with petty correctness rather than being concerned about the ultimate purposes of the law or the immediate consequence of their acts.

All this is quite understandable in the cultural context. Legalism is rooted deep in the history of governmental systems based on Roman law. It has probably been accentuated in Latin America by a century of striving for legality and order against the counterforces of instability and violence. The concepts of administrative law have at times provided valuable protection to individual rights against arbitrary state action. Formal norms of administrative procedure are especially important in systems in which much of the law is made by executive decree rather than by legislative enactment. Furthermore, the tendency to provide detailed regulations and instructions from the top can be at least partly explained by the perennial shortage of properly trained personnel at lower levels.

Legalism itself has a fascinating duality about it, because the more complex the statutes and decrees become, the more likely is it that they will be ignored, cut short, or circumvented. As a practical matter, administrators in Latin America are often ingenious in finding ways, despite the regulations, to get things done. Behind every formal system there is an intricate set of informal methods and understandings by which day-to-day administration is actually carried out.[6] These informal systems are seldom penetrated by the outsider. Latin Americans often feel that it is improper to describe them or even to admit that they exist. Most studies of governmental processes made in Latin America have a strong legal flavor, and there is a great scarcity of literature describing public administration in a realistic way.

ADMINISTRATIVE LEADERSHIP. A third point, which cannot be summarized in a word like centralization or legalism but is essential to an understanding of Latin American administration, concerns the atmosphere—the system of pressures, supports, and restraints—in which officials at upper levels operate. Perhaps the best way to illustrate the point is again to contrast Latin America with the United States. The administrator in almost any field of United States governmental activity, whether it be agriculture, labor, welfare, or any other, works at the center of a highly developed network of interest groups. Economic pressure groups, professional societies, and active citizens' groups of all kinds push and pull on him. They tell him what they want him to do and what he must not do; they give him technical advice and set professional standards of achievement; they furnish a supply of well-qualified recruits for government service at all levels of responsibility; and in the national policy-making arena they speak for the particular sector of activity they and the administrator are concerned with.

In Latin America, particularly in the less economically and technically advanced countries, the administrator finds himself in a considerably different situation. He works within the well-articulated system of administrative law; he also is likely to be subject to pressure from highly volatile personal and partisan political forces; but beyond this, he is more or less on his own. The interests are not likely to be organized, particularly those whose base is other

---

[6] "For nearly every rule a means of violation is known and employed. . . . 'When the rule is impractical the violation is justified.' It was thus expressed by an official of the government. Few employees are disciplined for this, as the situation is tacitly understood." Hall, *op. cit.*, p. 14.

than economic. Except for the lawyers, the professional men are few in number and relatively unspecialized in training and activity. The universities tend to stand apart from public affairs. The administrator himself may be the principal national authority on the subject he deals with, and he must bear a heavy responsibility for generating policy ideas, testing their possibility, and advocating their adoption. There is elbow-room for leadership; a brilliant young man may be a minister while still in his early thirties. If he is a strong man, in terms of personality or political standing, he is likely to have his way. If he makes mistakes, or is technically incompetent, there may be no one with sufficient standing to point out his errors or to take his place. But if he is weak, or unlucky, he may not have anyone to look out for him; he may be overridden by purely political forces, required to compromise the technical integrity of his program, or forced out and replaced by a complete incompetent. In short, administrative situations tend to be unstructured, with consequent instability of policy and personnel.

Pressures for Administrative Reform

It would be inaccurate and unfair to dwell too long upon the past or upon partly irrelevant comparisons with public administration in other regions. Despite shortages of trained personnel and the hazards of an uncertain political climate, many administrative agencies in Latin America operate efficiently, with vigorous leadership, competent and reasonably stable personnel, and up-to-date administrative methods. Furthermore—and this is the thesis of the remainder of this chapter—at the present time many of the administrative patterns of the past are rapidly giving way to new attitudes, methods, and organizational forms. It is difficult to say how far these changes will go, but it is certain that they are closely bound up with fundamental changes in the economies and societies of the region and are therefore more than superficial movements. Certainly the course of these administrative movements will have a strong bearing upon the aspirations of Latin America for rising standards of living and more effective democracy.

NECESSITIES OF ECONOMIC DEVELOPMENT. Most of the economic and social trends discussed in previous chapters come together in a drive for economic development, a goal to which increasingly articulate masses urge their governments and to which virtually every politician must now give at least lip service. This movement provides the main motivation for the significant administrative changes now taking place in Latin America.

Administration would be important even if Latin America were placing its entire reliance on private initiative. Private enterprise flourishes best under governments that can set the rules of the economic game in a rational way and enforce them evenly and effectively. But most of Latin America is overwhelmingly committed to economic development stimulated and guided by government, with public enterprise carrying out many of the specific missions. In such a system it is all the more important that government agencies be organized and staffed to make rational decisions, mobilize governmental resources effectively, and execute public policy with reasonable consistency.[7]

The critical role of public administration in economic development was emphasized by a United Nations mission which studied Bolivia at the invitation of its government in 1950. After surveying the country's resources and noting a sharp contrast between the Bolivians' potential wealth and the unsatisfactory state of their economy, the mission concluded—and flatly said in the opening pages of its report—that "governmental and administrative instability" was the root of the difficulty.[8] Then followed an analysis of Bolivia's administrative weaknesses and a number of specific suggestions for improvement. Throughout the entire report, economic analysis and recommendations were closely related to administrative problems and proposals for governmental reform. The report was accepted by the government of the day and in large part implemented by the Paz Estenssoro government which followed. The United Nations Bolivian report is now a landmark. Government circles throughout Latin America have now become convinced of its doctrine that "the success of any programme of national economic development will depend in great measure upon the degree to which the governmental organization can be expected to operate efficiently in this field."[9]

ROLE OF PUBLIC OPINION. Within the general framework of economic development interest, pressures for reform come, directly and indirectly, from a variety of sources. Occasionally administrative reform is a prominent topic of public discussion, although this is usually limited to short periods surrounding the displacement of especially ineffective or corrupt regimes. More often, public agitation and pressure affect administration in an indirect way by calling for fulfillment of promises for better roads, more schools, and so

[7] Frederick W. Riggs, "Public Administration: A Neglected Factor in Economic Development," *Annals of the American Academy of Political and Social Science,* CCCV (May 1956), 70–80.

[8] United Nations, Technical Assistance Administration, *Report of the United Nations Mission of Technical Assistance to Bolivia* (New York, 1951), pp. 2–4.

[9] *Ibid.*, p. 5.

forth. Delivery on these political promises frequently requires substantial reorganizations and the introduction of new staff and methods into agencies bound up in archaic procedures or shot through with patronage.

The growing effectiveness of citizen demands probably reflects the fact that a middle class is increasing in social importance. Industrialization and business growth have quite direct effects upon administration, for modern businessmen demand a stable environment of public policy, efficient public services, and impartial treatment in regulatory, licensing, and tax collection relationships.

EFFECT OF INTERNATIONAL INTERCHANGE. International influences supplement local pressures for administrative improvement. Latin American governments participate in many technical activities of the United Nations and the Organization of American States which expose the activities of all to outside view and tend to raise standards of performance. The importance of good administration is emphasized by the studies and other activities of the highly respected United Nations Economic Commission for Latin America. Agencies like the United States International Cooperation Administration and the International Bank of Reconstruction and Development, which offer technical assistance, economic aid, and loans, play an important role.[10] In addition to offering technical assistance in public administration itself, these agencies set high standards for the projects in which they participate and often require specific agreement on administrative measures to guarantee success of the projects before committing themselves to giving assistance.

Forces such as those just cited, mostly revolving around the theme of economic development, are changing the administrative atmosphere in Latin America. Many political leaders now seem convinced of the necessity of change and are willing to face some of the unpleasant consequences of reform.

TECHNICAL COOPERATION PROGRAMS. One of the most dramatic evidences of administrative ferment in Latin America is the rapid growth of programs of international technical cooperation in public administration. When the United Nations and the United States Point Four programs of technical cooperation were begun, there was considerable doubt about the inclusion of public administration as a field of activity. It was said that Latin American governments would talk but not do anything about administrative improvements, and that public administration was such a sensitive matter, so close to the heart of national sovereignty, that governments would not

[10] See references to International Bank reports in the Suggestions for Reading at the end of this chapter.

permit foreigners (particularly officials in the direct employment of the United States Government) to make studies and give advice in this field. Public administration programs were nevertheless begun in 1950, and quickly established a place for themselves. They are growing larger each year, and all Latin American governments now participate in them, although the enthusiasm and degree of involvement vary from country to country.

In 1956, for example, about fifty Point Four technicians were in Latin America, carrying on teaching and administrative improvement projects and advising governments on administrative matters. About a third of the technicians were general administrative advisers. The remainder were experts in such diverse fields as organization and methods analysis, personnel administration, budgeting, accounting, tax administration, customs and tariff administration, supply, records management, local government, police administration, statistics, and the management of postal services. During the same year, 218 Latin American government officials were brought to the United States for periods of specialized administrative training lasting several months.[11] The United Nations offers a similar but slightly smaller program of expert advice, fellowships for training abroad, and assistance in establishment of public administration training facilities.[12]

In both the United States and the United Nations programs, on-the-spot advice, local training, and fellowships for training abroad are used as methods for coordinated attacks on outstanding problems. All technical cooperation projects are carried on at the specific request of the government concerned. Unlike Point Four, the United Nations program draws its experts from all over the world, so that several Latin American countries have contributed as well as received.

INSTRUCTION IN PUBLIC ADMINISTRATION. Latin American universities have always offered courses in administrative law, and in the twentieth century there has been a rapid growth of curricula in business administration. But until recent years there were practically no facilities in the region for training in public administration. A program launched in the 1940's at the National University of Mexico had only limited success. In 1952, a School of Public Administration was begun in Brazil with the

[11] U. S. International Cooperation Administration, "Technical Cooperation in Public Administration Newsletter" (Washington), No. 9, January, 1957.

[12] For current information, see the *International Review of Administrative Sciences*, published by the International Institute of Administrative Sciences, Brussels, Belgium. *Progress in Public Administration*, published by the Institute from 1953 to 1956, is an excellent source for prior years.

assistance of the United Nations. This institution has become a major training center for senior and intermediate level civil servants and students of university age. Although most of the students are Brazilians, enrollment is open and there are scholarships available to students from other countries in the region.[13] In 1953 an Advanced School of Public Administration was founded in San José, Costa Rica, also with United Nations assistance, supported and used jointly by the five governments of the Central American region. Each year this school gives high-level training in general administration to a selected group of senior civil servants, plus courses for specialists in subject-matter fields like public health, education, and local government.[14] Public administration training is now also given at universities or other local institutions in Argentina, Bolivia, Chile, El Salvador, and Panama.

Areas of Administrative Reform

ADMINISTRATIVE REORGANIZATION. Several countries have had rather systematic government-wide administrative improvement or reform programs. For example, in the early 1950's El Salvador, completely on its own initiative, called in a private consulting firm for a general administrative survey, which was followed by intensive studies of several key ministries. Over a period of several years reorganizations were brought about, modern systems installed, and staff trained in their use. El Salvador is now one of the best administered of the Latin American countries.

To take another case, Argentina, in the closing years of the Perón regime, raised administrative improvement to the level of a major state objective. A Directorate of Rationalization, headed by one of the country's pioneer professors of public administration, was established in the central Secretariat of Technical Affairs, and counterpart rationalization offices were established in most of the

13 In 1955 there were 270 Brazilians and 42 from other Latin American countries in the advanced course and 135 Brazilians in basic and intermediate courses. United Nations, Economic and Social Council, *Annual Report of the Technical Assistance Board to the Technical Assistance Committee* (New York, 1956), p. 203.

14 "In 1955 academic activities were divided into a general course, which lasted from March until July, attended by twenty-five students recruited among higher administrators in the five Central American Governments, and a special course in customs administration, from September to December, with an enrolment of twenty-four students from the five countries. In addition to its academic activities the School continued its policy of spreading and promoting the knowledge and teaching of public administration in the area, one result of which was the establishment of national training centres in Costa Rica and El Salvador. The School also assisted in publishing texts and translations, in providing expert advice to the Governments of Costa Rica and Nicaragua and in organizing professional associations." *Ibid.*, p. 284.

ministries. With the central directorate calling the signals, a national program of internal administrative improvement and training was launched. It now seems likely that the rationalization movement, less certain original overtones of *peronista* indoctrination, will continue. Still other countries are adopting more gradual approaches to administrative reorganization, either by overhauling single ministries at opportune moments or by establishing offices to take local leadership in improvement.

PUBLIC FINANCE. The current stress on economic development leads naturally to a great deal of activity in improving administration of agencies dealing with economic planning, public finance, and fiscal administration. At the level of grand economic strategy, as noted in Chapter 15, national economic councils or their equivalents have been founded, or overhauled after periods of obsolescence, in several countries, such as Mexico, Colombia, Ecuador, and Brazil. Any government likes to increase revenues, and economic development projects increase the urgency of improving the collection of customs and taxes—an area of notoriously loose administration in the past. Such projects are under way in a number of countries.

While there has been a good deal of activity, Latin America still has a long way to go in the critical field of budget administration, also. The concept of the budget as an annual work program of government and a device for managerial and fiscal control, while usually accepted in theory, is not well implemented. Budget offices tend to be small and unable to exercise effective control of ministry expenditures. Multiple budgetary categories, specific revenues legislatively earmarked for specific purposes, and various other practices accumulated during years of financial improvising tend to blur the economic impact of government spending and frustrate executive control. With technical aid from the United Nations and other sources, these problems are being attacked with some success in such areas as Central America, where there is a surprising amount of international technical interchange, and in Bolivia, which is traditionally one of the most backward countries in budgeting.

PERSONNEL ADMINISTRATION. Concerning personnel administration, a survey made by the Public Administration Clearing House in 1955 found that: "A third of the governments are well on their way toward modern systems. Another third know the ritual and have the forms but little of the reality, except perhaps in terms of security and tenure. The final third of the governments have not yet chosen to start down the road toward a career system."[15]

---

[15] Public Administration Clearing House, *op. cit.*, p. 36.

Two points might be noted about recent developments in personnel administration. First, Latin American governments seem to be adopting, gradually, the United States' original doctrine that civil service reform cannot be left to the operating agencies but requires the leadership of a central personnel agency. Brazil pioneered in this respect with DASP in the 1930's. In the 1950's, Costa Rica and Panama have passed general merit system laws and established central personnel agencies. Several additional general merit systems seem to be in prospect.

A second important trend, however, is away from the earlier tendency to try to reform civil services in one blow by exhortatory legislation, and toward reliance upon a gradual and probably more realistic approach. There is now more emphasis upon creating the conditions under which genuine merit systems are possible, through employee training, more realistic salaries, equal pay for equal work, and recruiting and examination schemes suited to the jobs being filled. The attack tends to be upon one agency or one problem at a time, as conditions are opportune and trained personnel are available. There is undeniable movement down the merit and career road, but still an enormous distance to go before Latin America will have civil services equal to the policy commitments of its governments.

The Future of Bureaucracy

In the past ten years, public administration as a concept and as a profession has developed rapidly in Latin America. The political climate seems to be changing. Literacy, urbanization, industrialization, and wider political participation stimulate demands that can hardly be ignored. Leaders ranging from philosopher-presidents like Alberto Lleras of Colombia to buccaneers like the late Anastasio Somoza of Nicaragua have said that old methods no longer suffice. International economic and social programs, including UN and OAS specialized agencies, technical cooperation, economic aid, and even development loans, are focusing more sharply upon the job of assisting the less fortunate countries to develop institutions, both public and private, capable of dealing with new and complex social tasks. In Latin America there is a growing body of men who think of themselves as professional public administrators. Today there are schools; tomorrow there will be a professional literature, indigenous intellectually as well as geographically. Already professional societies have appeared in Mexico, Brazil, Panama, and elsewhere in Central America.

It is impossible to predict with any certainty how far these reforms will go. Obviously, Latin American bureaucracies will not be reconstructed overnight according to the efficiency experts' models. Change will proceed unevenly, and there will be reversions to the old ways from time to time. Possibly what now seems a major movement will turn out in the long run to have been only a superficial wave of reform that really changed nothing. However, it seems more likely that Latin America is entering a period in which governmental performance will reach higher levels of competence.

Considering the forces at work in the world today and the institutional habits of Latin America, it is quite possible that the bureaucrats—not only the specialists in administrative techniques, but public servants generally—will emerge in the near future as a key leadership group, joining or partially displacing such influential groups as the large landowners, the lawyers, the politicos, and the military men. It must be remembered that Latin America lacks trained manpower, the public is not well organized, political parties and legislatures are weak, and there is a tendency to look to government for leadership in many things. A large portion of the next generation of leaders may emerge from the group of able young men now rising rapidly in the bureaucracies. This is not to suggest that civil servants as such are likely to seize power; it is more likely that individual political leaders will start their careers in, and gradually rise out of, the upper bureaucracy. However, societies will become increasingly dependent upon their public services, and to the extent that the bureaucracies as identifiable groups have political interests and opinions they will have to be taken into account. Bureaucracies will shape, as well as be shaped by, the political future.

What this evolution implies for democracy is not entirely clear. Some of the new Latin American administrative writings contain overtones of technocracy, of a striving for rules and efficiency for their own sake, which are a little disturbing although it is still possible to dismiss them as probably temporary excesses of enthusiasm for a newly discovered field. Nevertheless, it is well to remember that advanced administrative techniques can be employed by any kind of political movement. In fact, at the present time the Latin American dictatorships seem to be slightly ahead of the more liberal regimes in sheer efficiency, probably because of the passing stability they offer. A fully streamlined, modern bureaucracy at the disposal of a totalitarian movement from either the right or left could be exceedingly dangerous.

On the whole, however, the implications for democracy seem to be favorable. Most of the men who are on the rise in the new bureaucracies seem to be motivated by a liberal conception of the public interest. Technical cooperation and other forms of international exchange, although scrupulously neutral politically in the narrow sense, obviously have liberal democratic working assumptions and will probably have a lasting influence on the new generation of public servants. Modernization of administrative systems should lead to more stability of policy, decisions made with decent respect to the economic and social facts, and wider sharing of power within each governmental system. Better administration also should lead to more productive economies, rising standards of living, increased literacy, and a more alert citizenry. Administrative progress cannot guarantee democracy, but it can enhance its prospects.

Suggestions for Reading

Most of the standard works on Latin American government, either general surveys or studies of individual countries, contain some material on public administration, although on the whole this aspect of government has not been examined thoroughly by United States students. We will cite here only the more specialized literature. The most recent general treatment in English is *Public Administration in Latin America: Opportunities for Progress Through Technical Cooperation*, a report prepared for the Inter-American Economic and Social Council by the Public Administration Clearing House (Washington: Pan American Union, 1955). There do not seem to be any general analytical or descriptive surveys in Spanish. Most of the public administration textbooks used in Latin America are translations of United States and European texts. The leading text originally written in Spanish is by a Puerto Rican, Pedro Muñoz Amato, *Introducción a la administración pública* (Mexico: Fondo de Cultura Económica, 1954).

Reports of international missions, although selective and tending to be critical, are among the best sources on individual countries. See United Nations, Technical Assistance Administration, *Report of the United Nations Mission of Technical Assistance to Bolivia* (New York, 1951); also several reports by missions of the International Bank for Reconstruction and Development (all published in Baltimore by the Johns Hopkins Press): *The Basis of a Development Program for Colombia* (1950), *Report on Cuba* (1951), *The Economic Development of Guatemala* (1951), and *The Economic Development of Nicaragua* (1953). Although their circulation is limited, occasional reports of Point Four public administration experts are useful; the most comprehensive is John O. Hall, *Public Administration in Uruguay* (Montevideo: Institute of Inter-American Affairs, 1954). One of the pioneer efforts by Latin American scholars is Lucio Mendieta y Nuñez, *La administración pública en México* (Mexico: Imprenta Universitaria, 1942). The Brazilian literature is quite advanced technically, and in recent years has become voluminous; the best entry is through the periodical of the Departmento Administrative do Serviço Público (Rio de Janeiro), *Revista do Serviço Público*, monthly since 1937. For current developments in Central America, see ESAPAC, Escuela Superior de Administración Pública en América Central (San José, Costa Rica), an occasional bulletin; current activities elsewhere in Latin America and around the world are summarized in *International Review of Administrative Sciences* (Brussels, Belgium: International Institute of Administrative Sciences); especially detailed material is available in the twenty issues of *Progress in Public Administration* published 1953–1956 by the same organization. For additional references, see Columbus Memorial Library, *Bibliography on Public Administration in Latin America* (Washington, D.C.: Pan American Union, 1954).

Chapter **18**

Trends and Prospects

Political institutions and the forms of political life and activity rarely stand still. They change, not only in accordance with modifications in their cultural context and in the level of political dynamics, but also under the pressure of the various "interests" and power groups which seek to dominate the political process. In such dynamic societies as those of contemporary Latin America, these changes are particularly apparent. In each of the preceding chapters, certain trends or tendencies, some with great and others with less momentum, have been pointed out. It is the purpose of the present chapter to re-examine these trends to see if they reveal new directions of a more general character which are important for the successful development of democratic government.

Dynamics of Politics and Political Power

One of the facts emerging most clearly from this book is that the various nations display different characteristics in their social and cultural development. It is also obvious that all are changing, while Latin America as a whole stands out in the twentieth century as one of the world's areas of most rapid population growth and social and economic development. Well endowed with the resources to support a much larger population than its present one hundred and seventy millions, it has the potentiality to become one of the world's great centers of economic and political power.

THE SOCIAL REVOLUTION. This rapid population and economic growth is accompanied by marked changes in social stratification, the breaking down of old class lines and of class divisions in general, which constitute a social revolution of far-reaching implications. In this connection, we have seen that rapid urbanization has been a notable influence. Those nations having large Indian populations are experiencing a process of ethnic assimilation which promises the early disappearance of the Indian as a distinct ethnocultural entity in many countries where for centuries he has been a major social phenomenon. For the Negroes the process is somewhat different, because Negroes, after emancipation, generally constituted a landless proletariat (with an important exception in Haiti), whereas Indians remained close to the land of their ancestors. But the end result in the twentieth century tends to be the same—ethnic assimilation to the national and New World cultural pattern. In Chile, Uruguay, Argentina, and to a considerable extent in Brazil and Cuba, the assimilation of large-scale European immigration has been the major twentieth-century demographic source of new dynamic qualities in social and political life. When all of these social and cultural changes in all the nations of the area are examined together, new "interests" are seen to be constantly rising from them to challenge the control of the state by older interests and groups, bringing changes in the social and political structure which can only be described as revolutionary.

THE CHANGING ROLE OF THE STATE. Political movements at midcentury continue to develop within the forms which appeared in the Mexican Revolution and in the *batllista* movement in Uruguay. These contemporary movements are vigorous and aggressive, as might be expected from the dynamic forces at work in society. *Peronismo, aprismo, arevalismo,* and the movements headed by Figueres in Costa Rica, Betancourt in Venezuela, Paz Estenssoro in Bolivia, and Vargas in Brazil have had distinct national characteristics, differing from each other in many ways. But they all express the demand for labor, social, and agrarian reform, to be achieved largely by state intervention in economic life to speed up industrial development and social welfare. This increased state intervention sometimes arises out of mere necessity. But a tendency toward state socialism is reflected in, and to some extent is based upon, trends in social and political thought. A great debate over social theory, including a search for a philosophy of history, is under way. In general it evinces a reaction against the deterministic and so-called "materialistic" and "positivist" sociology of the nineteenth century and emphasizes philosophical idealism and social voluntarism.

Since the state is part of society, its form and activity are greatly influenced by other aspects of culture. But the political institution also has the function of ruling, and with that function the capacity to dominate society. A certain independence of the state grows out of the freedom residing in the general will of a society. Revolutions of the twentieth century, viewed as conflicts for the possession of this structure of power, reveal less of the personalism of preceding periods and appear more frequently as conflicts of "interests" in society. In these conflicts minorities are often striving for protection or to impose policies for their own benefit. Occasionally, however, new power groups are formed by more fundamental and popular movements demanding agrarian and labor reform. It is these reform movements which are genuinely revolutionary. As yet no substantial alteration seems imminent in the pattern of changing government by revolution. Thus instability in the relationship of the state to society, that is, in the responsiveness of government to and its responsibility toward the social order, remains a striking characteristic of political life in the area. If the record of Mexico is a valid guide, however, progress of the general social revolution in other countries may be expected to bring a decrease in the number of revolutionary *coups d'état*.

THE ARMY AND POLITICS. It is an apparent contradiction of the previous assertions to state that since 1930 the army has tended to reduce the importance of middle-class civilian political parties as the determining factor in political life. Yet this is the case, although it may be merely a temporary trend, reflecting the violence and tempo of social change. In fact, army reforms, including the modernization and establishment of military schools and schools for soldiers' children, together with the army's increased dependence on more complicated arms and equipment, are changing the character of the armed forces. Expanding military budgets and additional duties assigned to the armed forces, such as supervising elections, censuses, and literacy programs, work to increase the army's political importance. There is growing resistance to militarism, not only among the old middle-class civilian political parties, but also on the part of labor unions and labor parties. In some cases, such as in Argentina, the army has joined forces with labor groups to encourage the industrialization needed to produce modern armaments. The partnership of army and labor is an old one in Mexico, but seems to be giving way to a system dominated by civilian politicians. In recent years, on the whole, the army has again tended to resume its professional role as guardian of order and neutral arbiter among parties, as in Argentina and Brazil in 1955 and Ecuador in 1956.

LABOR AND POLITICS. Organized labor is the most important new force which has altered the power structure and changed patterns of political behavior during the past quarter-century. The political influence of the labor movement and of labor leaders is growing rapidly. The character of the labor movements and of labor legislation have tended to tie unions closely to the ministry of labor, so that they customarily take their problems to the government for solution. Government influence on labor parties is a consequence.

Some of the new labor parties, such as those in Argentina and El Salvador, began with the cooperation of army officers who failed to find adequate outlet for their political activity within the army. Whether tied to the army or to the civilian government, labor parties have urged industrial development and the improvement of the economic and social position of urban workers. Rarely, except in Mexico, Guatemala, and Bolivia, have their efforts been coupled with effective agrarian reform.

The weaknesses and dangers of this political labor movement are its lack of solid autonomous labor unions and its dependence upon army leaders or political leaders closely associated with them. Such weaknesses open the way to penetration by Communist labor leaders, as in Guatemala. In countries where the social revolution is more advanced, the trend is for the unions to subordinate political to economic functions.

POLITICAL PARTIES. As the twentieth century opened, civilian political parties based upon the increasing political consciousness and economic prosperity of urban middle classes seemed to be making rapid strides. As we have seen, the second quarter of the century, dominated by the effects of two world wars, witnessed a reversal of this trend. Reaction to the rapid spread of urbanization, growth of the labor movement, and national pressures for industrialization brought the renewal of more active political intervention by the army, often in alliance with the older conservative forces of society. The Institutional Revolutionary party of Mexico has set a pattern of government successfully dominated by one big party which unites army leaders, bureaucrats, and labor leaders. At the same time *aprista*-type parties, expressing labor and agrarian discontent, mushroomed in many countries. They were supported sometimes by discontented military groups. On the whole, however, despite the resultant political instability manifest in numerous revolutions since World War II, civilian parties seem to show moderate increase in strength and organization. Their increasingly popular character holds out promise that they may play a more effective role in political life in the future, provided the violence, the fears, suspicion, and uncertainties which traditionally accompany the capture of the power structure by new elements and groups can be sufficiently allayed to permit freer operation of the party system. Further, one of the notable changes of the 1940's and 1950's has been the reform of electoral systems to provide better guaranties for free, secret suffrage and to solve electoral disputes through special courts. Multi-party systems in an increasing number of countries frequently result in elections in which no candidate has the required absolute majority. The effect is to make the congress more of a political arbiter, focusing attention upon the importance of increasing its effectiveness through better staffing and organization as well as through the increased independence from executive domination.

The Power Structure and Political Institutions

THE CHANGING POWER STRUCTURE. A century and a half has elapsed since the nations of Latin America emerged from the status of colonies. The political institutions they inherited were those of the Spanish and Portuguese imperial structure of political absolutism, and were based in part upon the conquest of America. In the twentieth century, political institutions have taken on greater definition and have also increased both in strength and in magnitude. Although the class structure is undergoing rapid change, a ruling class may still be seen in most countries. This class, which is small in some nations and broader in others, owes its continued influence partly to factors of tradition, especially in rural areas, and partly to the recruiting of new leaders provided from the classes below by the constant social ferment. Almost everywhere, today, the position of this class is under fire, and it is being forced to give ground. The revolutionary movements of the second quarter of the present century have shown, moreover, that it can no longer depend upon the loyalty of the army, as in the past. And in most countries the power structure rests to some degree upon the army. Occasionally a government appears to be based on naked military power, a device by which older social interests prevent the entrance of new forces into the power structure. Even when such a military power structure is used by leaders of seemingly popular movements to carry out revolutionary programs of reform, it lacks real responsibility to the society of which it is a part and often tends to come under the control of a dictatorial power group not genuinely representative of the wishes or the best interests of the nation. Constitutional forms then often become merely a means of concealing arbitrary actions behind a façade of legitimacy.

Middle-class civilian liberalism is weak, perhaps weaker in some ways than a quarter century ago, although it still tends to dominate the bureaucracies. Often disdainful of "personalist" politics, it sometimes boycotts the political process as the Argentine Radical party did in the early years of this century. It is not from the old parties, therefore, but from the new labor parties that the most profound change in the twentieth-century power structure has come, at least in those countries which have felt the impact of the political labor movement.

Written constitutions still contain too many provisions representing hopes and objectives, in the form of constitutional norms, rather than realities of the political structure. Lapses from constitutionality, if we omit actions which merely "provide a façade," are still much too frequent in the twentieth century. On the whole, however, the trend is toward greater realism in constitutional provisions. Constitutions of the twentieth century show serious and well-considered efforts to incorporate in basic law the results of a century-and-a-half struggle to achieve constitutional government, while resolving Latin America's profound economic and social problems. But the divergence between written constitutions and political practice is still wide.

INCREASED POWER OF THE PRESIDENCY. The strong presidency prevails. The fact is not only that the presidency is strong, but that it is growing stronger. The most notable exception, as has been seen, is the nine-man executive commission in Uruguay. Yet the relative strength of the Uruguayan executive power does not seem to have diminished sensibly, despite the frequent charges of executive weakness heard in that country. Cuba, Peru, Chile, and certain other countries to a lesser degree, reveal persistent tendencies to subject the executive to parliamentary or congressional control, but these efforts have been ineffective, except in Chile from 1891 to 1925. In general, the power of the presidency continues to grow through increase in the social and economic functions of government, growth of the bureaucracy, the strengthening of popular political parties, and the spread of the practice of direct popular election. Despite a popular impression to the contrary, the principle of no re-election of presidents has established itself firmly in Latin American political mores, at least in most countries.

ROLE OF THE LEGISLATURES. It does not seem likely that Latin American legislatures in many countries will soon become equal in political power to the executive. Certainly they have not profited to the same extent as the presidency from the new forces released by social revolution. Yet from a long-range view it is possible to see a tendency for legislatures to assume a somewhat more significant role in government. The need for them to do so is great. Congressional committees have increased in importance in Mexico, Chile, and Argentina (before and since Perón). Chile's example of an accounting office directly responsible to congress, which is influencing similar developments elsewhere, increases congressional control of expenditures. Much remains to be done, however, to provide legislative bodies with the adequate information and trained staff essential to effective operation, although beginnings may be seen in the congressional libraries in Chile and Argentina. Too frequently,in Chile for example, congresses have seemed to be the strongholds of vested interests while the presidency, more representative of new popular elements in political life, has led movements for social change. The growth of political parties may already be tending to strengthen the political position of congresses more than has become apparent on the surface of political life. But no major change seems to be occurring in the structure of congresses; the unicameral legislature is not spreading beyond the limited number of countries which have employed it for some time, chiefly in Central America; nor has the idea of corporative representation spread beyond Ecuador.

THE LEGAL AND COURT SYSTEMS. . . With the passing of the years, Latin American legal systems have tended toward greater autonomy. Traditional European influences tend to give way before American experience, especially in such relatively new fields as administrative, constitutional, and labor law. As the courts have grown in prestige and autonomy, they have adopted the practice of citing and following precedents, without, however, altering the basic concepts of the civil law system. Other influences of Anglo-American jurispudence appear in commercial law and in the practice of judicial review by supreme courts. A significant development in judicial review is the unique *amparo* suit in Mexico. Administrative law and administrative courts tend to take on greater importance with the expansion of the social and economic functions of government. The most striking trend in the field of special courts, however, is the extensive development of electoral and labor courts.

MUNICIPAL GOVERNMENT. The contemporary movement to reform and strengthen municipal government derives in part from the new emphasis given to municipal government by the Mexican Revolution, but in a larger measure from the rapid urbanization. Some of the best expressions of the movement are found in the Inter-American Municipal Congresses. A strong municipal tradition of Hispanic origin, partially lost sight of in the past century, has been strengthened by North American and European influences. The general trend is toward increased municipal autonomy, although in many countries local government is still strictly controlled by central authority. New constitutions often include guaranties of municipal financial and political autonomy, even in the federal states. The presidential type of government, with an elected or appointed executive and an elected council, predominates. The commission–manager plan, though adopted in San Juan, Puerto Rico, has not made headway elsewhere. Nor has the principle of home-rule charters spread beyond Cuba and one of the states of Brazil. Planning for urban development has become a major function of many municipal governments, an outstanding example being the *operacão municipio* of Brazil. The spoils system still predominates in municipal civil service, although the need for extending the merit system is increasingly realized.

INTERNATIONAL RELATIONS. Like the United States, the nations of Latin America began their national existence with a world view which attached signal importance to the development of international law as an object of national policy. At the same time, preoccupation with the problems of small, struggling nations led to the adoption of policies of neutrality which yielded but slowly to concepts of international solidarity in the twentieth century, at least until two world wars projected the New World nations into positions of greater international responsibility. The common origin of the numerous Spanish American states has tended to give a certain uniformity to their external policies as well as providing the basis for their successful association in the regional Organization of American States. In recent years their external policies have usually reflected the strong economic nationalism of domestic movements of social and economic change. Thus it has been easier to achieve Inter-American multilateral agreements in the political field than in economics, where bilateral arrangements continue to predominate. On the structural side, however, most of the governments have recognized the increased importance of international organization, both through active participation in these organizations and by developing offices within their ministries of foreign affairs for handling the affairs of international bodies.

Expansion of Government

No other aspect of Latin American government is so striking as its recent rapid growth at all levels—local, national, and international. Much of the cause lies in demographic factors, including the predominance of youthful groups in the population, a high rate of population increase, extensive immigration, large-scale movement to the cities, and the ethnic changes attendant upon the assimiliation of Indian and Negro groups. But a psychological cause is also to be noted. The twentieh-century trend toward industrialization and the spread of general education have given rise to a general feeling of impatience with slow economic development. This popular sense of urgency has created fluid and dynamic political situations, as we have seen, out of which new power groups arise to challenge political control, demanding more extensive programs of state action.

CHANGES IN PUBLIC ADMINISTRATION. Since 1930 bureaucracies have steadily grown as national budgets have increased, new agencies of government have been created to administer the expanding social welfare programs, and such new organs as the *fomento* corporation have begun to plan and help finance agriculture and industrial development.

Public administration is ceasing to be an occupation for the leisure hours of men of wealth and social position, and while the spoils system still predominates, government jobs are no longer simply the compensation for the conquest of political power. As government tends to become a major employer of the national labor force, attention is focused upon the more efficient organization of the public service. The emphasis tends toward "moralizing" the public service, as the process has been described by President Ruiz Cortines of Mexico, or toward laws improving the economic position of the civil servant and protecting him against summary dismissal as in Uruguay. Notable developments in this field include more numerous adoptions of comprehensive laws regulating the civil service, the establishment of university programs for training in public administration, and the development of in-service training programs within government. Technical competence is all too frequently lacking in such fields as statistics, economics, personnel, and budgetary administration, in which training is requisite for efficient public service. Moreover, many of the excellent laws regulating the civil service lack effective implementation to assure the security of position essential to responsible public service. Finally, public officials are generally underpaid, a situation which reflects in part the persistence of an inherited pattern of class stratification and a rapidly disappearing rural pattern of society in which government employees occupy an inferior social position. Improvement in salaries will not in itself eliminate the petty graft which is ingrained in the bureaucracies. What is needed is a more highly developed sense of professional ethics. But improved conditions of employment are an important pre-condition.

ADMINISTRATION AND POLICY OBJECTIVES. Obviously, the problem of developing and maintaining an efficient civil service is intimately connected with all other aspects of government. Improvement in public administration depends, in a fundamental sense, upon improvement in the conditions of effective democratic government. The militarism, personalism, and nepotism which have characterized government in the past will not quickly disappear. Most revolutions occur in the months immediately preceding presidential elections and the social, economic, and political changes of the twentieth century will continue to invite freqent resort to violence or the threat of violence in connection with the transfer of political power in many countries. But it is being increasingly recognized that improvement in the level of technical performance in the public service can in itself contribute to the development of a more responsible and stable political institution. It would be hard to name one Latin American president who has not by his actions and policies recognized this fact in recent years. In fact, as noted in the discussion of the presidency, the success or failure of a president is increasingly measured by his ability to use the complicated administrative machine over which he presides to solve national problems as they arise.

NATIONAL SOCIAL AND ECONOMIC POLICIES. Policy is inseparable from administration. It is a political truism that efficient administration requires the understanding of clearly defined policy which has been accepted as reasonable, practical, and socially responsible. The corollary of this principle is that policy grows in definition and clarity through responsible administration. The Latin American nations are passing through an era in which revolutionary changes are taking place in national policy, in line with the political and social movements discussed in this book. No nation has yet needed to adopt a policy of full employment, since the problem is chiefly one of underemployment of workers whose productivity could be increased under further industrialization, or by increased efficiency in agriculture. Most, however, have committed themselves to policies aimed at increasing the opportunities for industrial employment, at least to the extent of furnishing public capital for agricultural improvement and for building irrigation systems, railroads, highways, and other public works. Many nations have adopted measures to further the growth of the national credit and capital structure, making use of public financial institutions for this purpose, as well as encouraging the growth of savings and private credit systems.

All, in varying degrees, are trying to provide universal free elementary education and are beginning to offer technical training and higher education to a larger proportion of their youth. All have made the improvement of public health a major national policy, although only Uruguay has adopted a broad national program of socialized medicine. Many encourage the development of producer and consumer co-operatives. National policy generally accepts the organization of workers into labor unions, tries to improve wage levels and conditions of work, favors social security insurance, tolerates the efforts of church groups to "Christianize" labor unions and wean them away from anti-clerical and socialist traditions, and provides legal regulation of industrial disputes, in many cases establishing official machinery for their settlement. In general, this labor policy must be seen as a policy of erasing class lines, at least in respect to urban society, by improving the social and economic position of urban workers.

The improvement of agricultural production and the provision of public credit and other benefits for this purpose constitute another generally accepted policy objective. The legislation of most nations shows some degree of commitment to policies of land reform, aimed at liquidating inherited patterns of monopoly by a landowning class, at least to the extent of measures to assist farm workers in acquiring land. Yet the countries, such as Mexico, Guatemala, and Bolivia, which have a clear national policy of transforming their landless peasants and agricultural laborers into landowners are still a minority.

It would be a mistake to assume, at least for most countries, that such new and revolutionary tendencies go unquestioned. Strong interests challenge one or more of these social objectives in every country, and the violence of theoretical disagreements is often reflected in the violence of political life, as well as in bureaucratic inefficiency and political corruption. Not only the efficiency of the public service, but the very stability of political institutions and the orderly functioning of the political process often hinge upon the day-to-day policy decisions made by political leaders almost as much as upon the dramatic policy clashes involved in national elections. Wise political leaders learn that efficient and honest administration is becoming good politics, since inefficiency and corruption in the administration of national economic and social welfare programs tends to undermine the support of the urban working class upon which they depend more and more for their political power.

The Prospect for Democratic Government

Nothing is more characteristic of the political psychology of the twentieth century than the principle that good government must also be democratic government. The nearly universal adoption of democratic constitutions by the new nations which have arisen in Europe, Asia, and Africa following the two world wars calls for reconsideration of the ingrained Anglo-American view that certain peoples are unsuited, whether by tradition or by nature, for successful democratic government. It is no longer possible to believe that the democratic, or as we have usually preferred to say, the republican form of government can succeed only within the North American–European constitutional system and the Protestant-Christian tradition. The nations of the whole Latin American area are making rapid progress, some of them notably so, in reducing the poverty, illiteracy, and social insecurity which have been the principal obstacles to greater democratic achievement in the past. One can only believe that time and the confidence which comes from the successful political management of ever larger national affairs will modify the Latin American political tradition of "behavior marked by intemperance, intransigence, flamboyance, and the worship of the strong man" pointed out by an anonymous writer in *Foreign Affairs* as the greatest impediment to democracy.[1] Many of the new republics in the other so-called "backward areas" of the world already see in the political experience and success of the Latin American republics much to emulate, as well as dangers to avoid.

THE IMPORTANCE OF INTER-AMERICAN ORGANIZATION. The smallness and consequent political weakness of many of these states are great obstacles to their political success, and the importance of Latin American union for the political stability of these weaker states has been pointed out by political leaders.[2] But the old dream of a political union of Spanish America, if not of Latin America as a whole, seems even further from realization than during the nineteenth century, because of the growth of nationalistic rivalries. Yet by giving important political functions to the Organization of American States, by establishing the Organization

---

[1] Y, "On a Certain Impatience with Latin America," *Foreign Affairs,* XXVIII (July 1950), 565–579.

[2] For example, President José Figueres of Costa Rica and former president Rómulo Betancourt of Venezuela.

of Central American States, and by their active participation in other international organizations, the Latin American nations have taken steps in the direction of political solidarity, the full significance of which is not always recognized. The Rio de Janeiro Treaty of Reciprocal Assistance (1947) and the Bogotá Pact (1948) have within them great potentialities for more effective international collaboration, in political as well as economic and cultural affairs, if Latin American statesmanship rises to the occasion. As the nations see the possibility of joining in the pursuit of more and more common international objectives, the strength which arises from closer political union may also be expected to contribute to stabilize their political institutions and behavior.

DEMOCRATIC ADVANCES. To the political challenge presented by international communism, Latin America has already given at least as clear an answer as that of any other large area of the world. It seems unlikely, therefore, that the Latin American social revolution of the twentieth century will be captured by Russian Communism's political ideology or by the structure of a dictatorship based upon a proletarian party. Preceding chapters have shown the extent to which the patterns established in Mexico and Uruguay in the second and third decades of this century have already been followed in other countries. The Latin American social revolution is not unrelated to more universal changes, but it has its own roots.

Because of their common cultural and historical background, the republics seem to gain confidence from each other's successes and to learn from each other's failures. This may be seen in such important political achievement as the principle of non-re-election of presidents, which is today so generally accepted that the occasional examples of *continuismo,* although they attract great attention, are accurately described as exceptions which prove the rule. Prohibition of presidential re-election is not a complete solution of the problem of peaceful, constitutional transfer of control of the state from one power group to another. Nor does it, by itself, provide insurance against the abuse of the powers of the presidency. Uruguay seems to have achieved success in this critical problem of the transfer of political power by means of her collegiate executive, but no other nation seems to have been attracted to the system. Serious attention to electoral reform holds out greater hope, but much remains to be done to make these laws effective enough to inspire general public confidence. Yet within the context of Latin American political experience, these are achievements of major importance.

DEMOCRATIC FAILINGS. The ability to share the fruits of political experience may also be seen in the growing freedom of the press and of political discussion, in the notable improvement in the management of free democratic elections, even in some of the less advanced nations, and in the re-emergence of responsible and efficient local government. Nor is there a lack of skilled political intelligence. Public confidence in the management of the political process still fails too frequently at certain critical points, however. Such defaults may once have been adequately attributed to "peculiarities" of Latin American institutions and mores. Today, the critical observer is more likely to characterize them as failures of responsible statesmanship. It is upon such moments of default that opportunistic and demagogic political leaders thrive, however. Congresses default on their responsibility for conducting forthright debate on issues of national importance and for attempting to find solutions to basic policy questions. Presidents fail to use the great power in their hands to see that freedom of political discussion is protected, to ensure freedom to seek political office, and to guarantee freedom of suffrage in elections. They fail to see to it that written constitutional provisions actually govern the operation of the political process. Or they neglect that even more fundamental task of creating and directing a public opinion to support courses of action necessary for the solution of national problems and to accept the outcome of the process. Leaders of the armed forces fail in their fundamental obligation to support constitutional process. The rank and file of citizens all too frequently fail to understand the responsibilities of citizenship.

THE NEED FOR POLITICAL STUDIES BY LATIN AMERICANS. The conduct of democratic government obviously presents psychological and moral problems affecting many aspects of culture and social structure for which there is no simple solution. It is probably true that present-day social, cultural, and economic trends are bringing a stronger and better Latin American society. But since this study has been concerned primarily with political institutions and behavior, the question to be asked at this point is what political measures and principles may statesmen adopt to ensure that the governments engaged in improving the general welfare are "governments deriving their just powers from the consent of the governed"? For the lesson which Abraham Lincoln's Gettysburg Address led the people of the United States to see in their bloody Civil War is not parochial, but universal. The question, said Lincoln, is "whether this nation or *any nation so conceived and so dedicated can long endure.*" From Latin America such voices as those of Benito Juárez, Domingo F. Sarmiento, Eloy Alfaro, José Martí, Eugenio Hostos, Ruy Barbosa, and Francisco Madero have reiterated the proposition that popular government not only *can* but *will* endure to solve the most perplexing problems of social and economic change in their countries.

To inquire into the truth of this proposition as applied to their own experience is the challenge presented today to Latin American students of government and public affairs. They can do much more than they have done to analyze Latin American political experience and to describe the realities and needs of their political life. Frank Tannenbaum pointed out some of these needs a number of years ago in his *Peace by Revolution.*[3] More recently José A. Mora of Uruguay has urged the establishment of an official inter-American institute to carry on such studies,[4] while Luis Quintanilla of Mexico urges the formation of voluntary, private agencies for the purpose.[5] For nearly two decades the *Handbook of Latin American Studies*[6] has provided an annual inventory of the most important writings on Latin American government. Unfortunately, too few of the more important studies noted in this latter work are written by Latin Americans. Perhaps this is because Latin American scholars have often felt that they did not have the resources or lacked the freedom to carry on such inquiries. Perhaps it is because they have felt their studies might be misinterpreted as adventures in politics.

In many countries today the climate of public opinion and official attitudes make such studies possible, so that inability to gain access to suitable data, lack of the requisite leisure and financial resources, and inadequate training in political science have come to be the major obstacles. Changed conditions may soon remove these bars, and Latin American scholars may then be expected to reap the rewards certain to come from the more thorough study of their rich and varied political experience. And they will thus make an important contribution to the civic education essential at all levels and through all media of communication for the successful operation of democratic government. Their studies should also be of benefit to the millions in Asia and Africa who are struggling today to achieve self-government.

Many books on constitutional and political topics have come from the pens of Latin Americans since independence, but scien-

[3] New York: Alfred A. Knopf, Inc., 1934.
[4] In a lecture published by The American University, Washington, D.C., 1949.
[5] *Democracy and Pan Americanism* (Boston: Boston University Press, 1952).
[6] Prepared by the Hispanic Foundation of the Library of Congress and published by the University of Florida Press.

tific political studies such as those suggested above have been few. Yet serious political studies are essential for strengthening democratic government. They are needed both for the guidance of political leaders and for that enlightenment of the electorate upon which the success of the democratic process ultimately rests. Certain themes, among many which call for such study, are obvious and urgent. Some of these include the organization and financing of political parties, their electoral activity, and the working of the electoral process, both in urban and in rural areas. Studies of revolutions, labor in politics, militarism, political leadership, legislation, and administration, are also needed. Comparative studies should be undertaken of means employed in various countries to improve the efficiency and honesty of bureaucracies and to strengthen legislatures in relation to the presidency.

Certain countries have made important progress in the improvement of democratic municipal government since the days when the Mexican Revolution highlighted this need, but other nations need to have the lessons of this experience brought home to them. Rural local government and the operation of the democratic electoral process in rural areas call for special study. They are dark spots in the government of most of these countries, even where land reform and rural education are being stressed.

The North American student may be permitted to observe that Latin American experience demonstrates that presidents can govern constitutionally, that legislatures can be responsible forums for the discussion and resolution of national issues, and that elections can be demonstrably free and can be accepted by the nation as a legitimate expression of the general will. He may see that courts can be free in the exercise of their constitutional function of dispensing equal justice to all, that freedom of the press, academic freedom, and freedom of political discussion are possible, and that political power can be transferred from one party or group to another without violence. He may note that the most basic social and economic issues can be resolved by constitutional means, that armies can be the servants and not the masters of states, and that observance of these democratic principles can create that public confidence in constitutional government which is the only certain guaranty against demagogic appeals to violence. But it must be the work of Latin American statesmen and scholars to see how such principles can be applied within the context of national life and to devise and apply the measures which make them practicable.

Author Index

Subject Index

Date Due

OCT 20 '60			
APR 1 5 '69			
	PRINTED	IN U. S. A.	